RICHARD HOLMES is one of Britain's most successful historians and television presenters. He is the author of the bestselling *Redcoat* and *Wellington: The Iron Duke*. He has written and presented nine series for the BBC including *Battlefields*, *War Walks* and *The Western Front*. His dozen other books include *Firing Line*, and he is general editor of the definitive *Oxford Companion to Military History*. He has taught military history for many years, and is now Professor of Military and Security Studies at Cranfield University and the Royal Military College of Science. He lives in Hampshire.

For automatic updates on Richard Holmes visit harperperennial.co.uk and register for AuthorTracker.

From the reviews of *Tommy*:

'Indispensable for anyone who wants to understand what the life of a soldier on the Western Front was really like . . . Authoritative . . . Among the many virtues of his book, Holmes deploys a wonderful range of unfamiliar sources and voices. He captures the smell of the trenches, a mingling of "burnt and poisoned mud, and the stink of corrupting human flesh" . . . Holmes's book is full of good sense, yet never skimps the reality of the horrors'
MAX HASTINGS, *Daily Mail*

'What sets Richard Holmes apart is the sheer quality of his writing and his empathy with his subjects . . . Holmes's compassion for the men who endured and died movingly underpins the book . . . Powerful reading. *Tommy* will stand as a classic of First World War history'
Independent

'Compelling . . . This is excellent popular history: scholarly, highly readable and utterly absorbing'
Daily Telegraph

'*Tommy* is Richard Holmes at his impressive best'
BERNARD CORNWELL, *Evening Standard*

'Tommy tells it as it really was . . . Every page of this is worth reading'
Time Out

TOMMY

THE BRITISH SOLDIER ON
THE WESTERN FRONT
1914–1918

RICHARD HOLMES

HARPER PERENNIAL

Harper Perennial
An imprint of HarperCollins*Publishers*
77–85 Fulham Palace Road
Hammersmith
London w6 8jb

www.harperperennial.co.uk

This edition published by Harper Perennial 2005
1 3 5 7 9 8 6 4 2

First published by HarperCollins*Publishers* 2004

A catalogue record for this book
is available from the British Library

ISBN 0-00-713752-4

Set in Baskerville by
Rowland Phototypesetting Ltd, Bury St Edmunds, Suffolk

Printed and bound in Great Britain by
Clays Ltd, St Ives plc

For Lizzie, with love and admiration

CONTENTS

LIST OF ILLUSTRATIONS

to Battle of Pilckem Ridge, Durham Light Infantry being taken forward *(Imperial War Museum Q2641)*

Page 8: *Top:* English troops depart Rouen for the front, 1914 *(Robert Hunt Library)* **Middle:** Men of a midland regiment, entraining after a spell in the trenches *(Robert Hunt Library)* **Bottom:** Aerial photograph of the Western Front in the Auchy sector showing grecian key outline of trenches *(Imperial War Museum Q65490)*

SECTION 2

Page 1: *Top:* Shell bursting amongst the barbed wire entanglements on the battlefield at Beaumont Hamel, December 1916 *(Imperial War Museum Q1688)* **Middle:** German barbed wire entanglement *(Robert Hunt Library)* **Bottom:** Men of the 15th Royal Welch Fusiliers filling sandbags *(Imperial War Museum Q8372)*

Page 2: *Top:* A front line trench showing duck-boards *(Imperial War Museum Q17410)* **Middle:** Taking timber up for trench support *(Imperial War Museum Q5092)* **Bottom:** Fixing scaling ladders in trenches *(Imperial War Museum Q6229)*

Page 3: *Top:* Cavalry crossing a bridge over a communication trench *(Imperial War Museum Q6183)* **Middle:** Men of the border regiment resting in a front line trench *(Imperial War Museum Q872)* **Bottom:** Barbed wire gate, let down to form a block against raiders *(Imperial War Museum Q6020)*

Page 4: *Top:* Lancashire Fusiliers in a flooded communication trench *(Imperial War Museum Q4662)* **Middle:** Company Sergeant Major checking rockets in a trench *(Imperial War Museum Q10616)* **Bottom:** British Officer at the entrance to a dugout *(Imperial War Museum Q53502)*

Page 5: *Top:* The C.O. and officers of the 12th Royal Irish Rifles wading through the mud of a fallen-in communication trench *(Imperial War Museum Q10682)* **Middle:** Funnel communication trench leading to the firing line with signpost visible *(Imperial War Museum Q17327)* **Bottom:** Lancashire Fusilier in a trench looking through a box periscope, 1917. *(Imperial War Museum Q4654)*

Page 6: *Top:* Officers of the 12th East Yorkshires washing and shaving in their dug-out *(Imperial War Museum Q10623)* **Middle:** Worcestershires in the trenches at Ovilliers. Sentry looking out through a loophole *(Imperial War Museum Q4100)* **Bottom:** A ration party with food containers going up to the trenches, Arras, March, 1917 6th Queen's (Royal West Surrey) Regiment *(Imperial War Museum Q4839)*

Hawthorn Ridge redoubt *(Imperial War Museum)* **3rd down:** Battle of Albert. Laying a charge in a mine chamber *(Robert Hunt Library)* **Bottom:** British cavalry awaiting orders to move forward during operations in the Arras region, 1917 *(Robert Hunt Library)*

Page 8: *Top:* Battle of Arras, April 1917. A 9.2 inch howitzer in action *(Imperial War Museum Q5221)* **Middle:** Battle of Posieres Ridge. An 18-pounder battery *(Imperial War Museum Q4065)* **Bottom:** The Flanders Offensive. Hauling an 18-pounder gun out of the mud *(Imperial War Museum Q6236)*

SECTION 4

Page 1: An Ordnance School diagram showing how a shrapnel shell worked. *(Ordnance School)*

Page 2: *Top:* Preparation for Battles of Arras, Artillery Observation Post 1917. 12th Division artillery officers observing fire and RE field telephonists passing back results *(Imperial War Museum Q5095)* **Right:** British 3-inch Stokes mortar *(Robert Hunt Library)* **Bottom:** Soldier cleaning Mills bombs *(Imperial War Museum Q4115)*

Page 3: *Top:* A Vickers machine gun is mounted for anti-aircraft firing *(Imperial War Museum Q8430)* **Middle:** A Lewis gun post *(Imperial War Museum Q10902)* **Bottom:** Trench map sheet of the Somme including High Wood, 57c SW3, 31st July 1916, Longueval *(Imperial War Museum)*

Page 4: *Top:* A YMCA stall just behind the lines *(Robert Hunt Library)* **2nd down:** Fusing Stoke mortar shells and playing cards *(Robert Hunt Library)* **3rd down:** British and German officers in No Man's Land during the unofficial Christmas truce, 1914 *(Robert Hunt Library)* **Bottom:** A British firing squad aiming at a German spy *(© Bettmann/CORBIS)*

Page 5: *Top:* Soldiers' baths near Fricourt, with canvas troughs *(Imperial War Museum Q4110)* **2nd down:** Attending to the wounded at an advance dressing station *(Imperial War Museum E(AUS)715)* **3rd down:** Chaplain writing letters for wounded at a dressing station *(Imperial War Museum Q9518)* **Bottom:** Padre conducting a burial service in a trench *(Imperial War Museum Q11434)*

Page 6: *Top:* A Chaplain conducting Church parade from the nacelle of an FE 2B night bomber *(Imperial War Museum Q12108)* **Middle:** German prisoners arriving at the 'cage', Dernancourt *(Imperial War Museum Q1236)* **Bottom:** German prisoners captured during the fighting near Fricourt *(Imperial War Museum Q1229)*

Page 7: *Top:* British and French soldiers playing cards outside an estaminet *(Robert Hunt Library)* **Middle:** General Plumer decorating a woman ambulance driver for bravery *(Imperial War Museum Q6788)* **Bottom:** HM the King presenting the VC to the Rev. TB Hardy, Army Chaplain at the Fronen-le-Grand. *(Imperial War Museum Q11128)*

Page 8: Top: British troops arriving on leave at a London terminus *(Imperial War Museum Q30505)* **Middle:** British troops arriving on leave at a London terminus *(Imperial War Museum Q30518)* **Bottom:** Troops landing at Boulogne from the leave boat, 1918 *(Imperial War Museum Q6478)*

PROLOGUE: TOMMY ATKINS

In 1815 a War Office publication showing how the *Soldier's Pocket Book* should be filled out gave as its example one Private Thomas Atkins, No. 6 Troop, 6th Dragoons. Atkins became a sergeant in the 1837 version, and was now able to sign his name rather than merely make his mark.

By the 1880s the expression 'Tommy Atkins' was in wide use to describe the prototypical British soldier, and Kipling's poem *Tommy* summed up the nation's ambivalence about her defenders.

> . . . Then it's Tommy this, an' Tommy that
> an' 'Tommy, 'ows's your soul?'
> But it's 'Thin red line of 'eroes'
> when the drums begin to roll . . .

> . . . For it's Tommy this 'an Tommy that,
> an' 'Chuck him out, the brute!'
> But it's 'Saviour of 'is country'
> When the guns begin to shoot;
> An' it's Tommy this, an' Tommy that,
> an' anything you please;
> An' Tommy ain't a bloomin' fool –
> you bet that Tommy sees!

During the First World War the nickname was widespread, with derivatives like Tommy cooker, for a small trench stove, talking 'Tommy', to describe other rank repartee, or even 'Tommyness', to define certain attitudes and behaviour. When British and German soldiers yelled greetings or insults across No Man's Land it was always 'Fritz' and 'Tommy'.

A corporal writing in 1914 caught the man in all his lights and shades: 'Sometimes Tommy is not a pleasant fellow, and I hated him that afternoon. One dead German had his pockets full of chocolate.

They scrambled over him, pulling him about, until it was all divided.' An engineer officer saw a large Frenchwoman fall into a canal, to be tugged to the bank by 'two tommies' who, in their eagerness to help, pulled her dress up over her head, demonstrating that knickers were not then universal in rural France. The expression was, of course, prohibited. A divisional commanders' conference in October 1915 affirmed that: 'The use of the word "Tommy" to be absolutely barred. The term is never permitted in a good regiment.'

The order had as much effect as so many others, and the nickname persisted, sometimes as Tommy, sometimes as Atkins, and once, memorably, as 'Mr Atkins, gentleman', used by an officer who saw soldiers helping refugees with gentleness and generosity. Nicknames are not always popular with their recipients, and such was the case with Tommy. Many soldiers felt patronised by it, and its English implication grated on Scots, Irishmen and Welshmen. But Sergeant Charles Arnold, himself a quintessential Tommy, declared that:

> Tommy Atkins – full private – is, when all is said and done, the one who won the war. He won it by sheer dogged pluck ... When is something going to be done for the man who isn't a general or a guardsman or an Anzac, nor even a London Scot but just a clodhopper from Suffolk, or Devon, or Durham – the man who obeyed orders and stuck it out? Of this man little was heard, possibly because he had a habit of going into places a thousand strong and coming out a remnant of a hundred and fifty or so. Dead men tell no tales of their own glory.

INTRODUCTION

Contemporaries instinctively called it Great: *La Grande Guerre*, *Weltkrieg*, and we can easily see why. Of course it was not the largest single event of world history: that ghastly honour must go to the Second World War, which in terms of human suffering and material destruction was infinitely worse for the world as a whole. But for Britain alone the First World War caused more casualties, which partly accounts for the fact that it is remembered in a particular way here. Many who lived through both conflicts agreed with Harold Macmillan and J. B. Priestley that the First World War was a more significant watershed than the Second. Barbara Tuchman may have been the first to use the analogy of 1914–18 as an iron gate separating the present from the past, and it has proved to be an enduring and powerful image ever since.

So there it lies, overgrown, like the trenches that still lace the landscape of Northern France, but somehow dug deep into our consciousness. And it usually enters our minds not as history, but as literature. One of the problems with trying to write about the First World War is that most people have already read Wilfred Owen and Siegfried Sassoon, Pat Barker and Sebastian Faulks before you get to them. I am certainly not the first historian to complain that it was far too literary a war. Cyril Falls began the process even before the Second World War; Correlli Barnett continued the movement thirty years ago and only last year, Brian Bond's important book *The Unquiet Western Front* fired yet another well-aimed burst into an enemy who shows little sign of falling, but lurches on, stick grenades in hand, intent on doing yet more mischief to our understanding. Professor Bond suggests that 'the "real" historical war abruptly ceased to exist in November 1918'.[1] What followed was the resurrection and reworking of the war largely in terms of novels, memoirs and war literature in general. Indeed, Paul Fussell, in his influential book *The Great*

War and Modern Memory, maintained that the war was uniquely awful and as such lay 'outside history', explicable primarily through its literature.

This process has not simply affected the way we think of history: it strikes a resonance through the present and on into the future. Omer Bartov described what he termed 'the invention of memory' when he considered the effect of war literature in both France and Germany. 'Experience of loss and trauma extends beyond personal recollection,' he argued, 'and comes to encompass both individual and collective expectations of the future.'[2] It seems to me that Bartov has identified a key element of the process. By studying the war as literature we do not simply colour our view of the past and make it all but impossible to teach the war as history. We go on to tint our picture of the present and our image of the future too. When Second World War soldiers wanted to describe something going particularly badly they spoke of 'The biggest balls-up since the Somme.' For years it was impossible to attend a military presentation without a clip of *Blackadder Goes Forth* discussing the strategic imperative of inching Field Marshal Haig's drinks cabinet closer to Berlin, and in the first Gulf War British camps in the desert were named after Captain Blackadder and his cronies.

No sooner had its last shot echoed away than some participants recognised that the war they knew was being hijacked. Charles Carrington, who won his Military Cross as an infantry officer at Passchendaele, complained:

> It appeared that dirt about the war was in demand ... Every battle a defeat, every officer a nincompoop, every soldier a coward.[3]

Cyril Falls, a veteran turned Oxford don, saw how:

> Every sector became a bad one, every working party is shot to pieces; if a man is killed or wounded his entrails always protrude from his body; no one ever seems to have a rest ... Attacks succeed one another with lightning rapidity. The soldier is represented as a depressed and mournful spectre helplessly wandering about until death brought his miseries to an end.[4]

In practice it was not that simple, for many of the men writing in the 1920s and 1930s – Robert Graves and R. C. Sherriff amongst them – were actually ambiguous about the war, and actively resented being termed 'anti-war authors'.

Ambiguity became less marked as the war receded. Oddly enough, this happened at precisely that moment when, had the war been considered primarily as history, the appearance of a wide range of new sources, not least the first of the official histories, might have been expected to have broadened understanding. Erich Maria Remarque's *All Quiet on the Western Front*, first published in 1929 and made into a film the following year, was an important milestone. Remarque's own experience of the war was very limited. He never actually fought in the trenches, was slightly wounded by shrapnel, and after the war was censured for posing as a decorated officer. The undaunted Charles Carrington was infinitely more experienced, and was indeed what Remarque pretended to be. But *All Quiet* struck a powerful chord with many veterans looking back at the war from the deep disillusionment of the late 1920s, and in a sense more accurately reflects the state of its author and his friends in 1929 than the condition of the German army twelve years before.

Alongside the evolution of a literary cult which, by and large, came to see the war as waste built on futility and compounded by human error, there grew up a historical genre which was scarcely less influential. During the war there had been two major schools of strategic policy in Britain. One, the Easterners, took their tone from a letter written by Lord Kitchener to Sir John French, British commander in chief on the Western Front, at the very beginning of 1915. Kitchener suggested that the German lines in France might well be 'a fortress which cannot be taken by assault', and suggested that there might be merit in looking elsewhere. Gallipoli and Salonika were both offspring of this logic. The other, the Westerners, would have agreed with Sir Douglas Haig, who took over as commander in chief in late 1915, that the war could only be won by beating the German army in the field. And as Haig announced in his final dispatch, this could only be accomplished by 'one great continuous engagement'.

What happened in the 1920s and 1930s is that the Easterners, who had shown little sign of winning the war, certainly won the historical argument. Churchill's *The World Crisis* lambasted offensives on the Western Front which were, he declared, 'as hopeless as they were disastrous'. Churchill had served as a cavalry officer, charging at Omdurman in 1898, and had been a battalion commander on the Western Front in early 1916. I can forgive him much on those counts alone: whatever he lacked it was not physical courage. But what of Lloyd George, whose mid-1930s *Memoirs* announced the bankrupcy of 'narrow, selfish and unimaginative strategy and . . . [the] ghastly butchery of a succession of vain and insane offensives'? He accused generals not simply of professional incompetence and ignorance of the real conditions, but of personal cowardice. These accusations gloss over the fact that, as prime minister, Lloyd George had a direct personal responsibility for the very strategy he criticised. And Lloyd George was not right to carp about the cowardice of First World War generals. About fifty-eight were killed, or died of wounds received. Three divisional commanders were killed at Loos in September 1915, more British divisional commanders than were killed by enemy fire in the whole of the Second World War.[5]

There was a more reputable combatant in the wings. Captain Basil Liddell Hart, whose evergreen rank veiled about six weeks' service at the front followed by a longer stint in the Army Educational Corps, argued that Britain's commitment to the Western Front clearly violated his own, oft reinvented, strategy of indirect approach and clear-sighted description of the British way in warfare. Britain should have avoided that lethal concentration of troops and gone somewhere else. He thought that Gallipoli had been promising, and T. E. Lawrence had done really well in the desert. He could produce no evidence that the destruction of railways in the Hejaz made the teacups rattle in Berlin, but no matter. What had really brought Germany down, he argued, was naval blockade and internal collapse. I must not trivialise Liddell Hart, for he remains a commentator of rare insight, was helpful to students and, even late in life, was capable of surprising generosity to Haig. But he is the archpriest of the argument that there must have been a better way: his liturgy, after all these years, still has the power to inspire.

The historical debate – not really the right word, for there was never much debate about it – was rejuvenated in the 1960s. Events such as the Cuban missile crisis, the Aldermaston marches, the Vietnam War and the burgeoning of an independent youth culture encouraged an iconoclasm, in which the generals of the First World War received unprecedented critical attention. Despite the reduction in the release period of public records from fifty to thirty years, meaning that most documents on the war became available in 1968, there was no immediate rush to reinterpret the war based on this evidence. Indeed, perhaps the most influential book ever written on the war, A. J. P. Taylor's *The First World War: An Illustrated History*, was little more than a triumphant flambéeing (with the blowtorch lit by Liddell Hart) of the leftovers of the historiography of the 1930s.

On re-reading Taylor's book I am stunned by its brilliant, incisive juxtaposition of *bons mots*, real insights and excruciating errors. 'Failure [at Third Ypres in 1917] was obvious by the end of the first day to everyone except Haig and his immediate circle,' it declares. Obvious, that is, to everyone except the German high command, which grew gloomier as the battle wore on, and thousands of British participants, whose letters and diaries often testify to a confidence not shared by those writing in the foreknowledge of failure. Even the Australian Official History speaks approvingly of 2nd Army's attacks up the Menin Road in September, almost two months after everyone was meant to have lost confidence in the battle.

Leon Wolf's *In Flanders Fields*, whose publication actually predated that of A. J. P. Taylor's book, was in many respects a more reliable work. A study of the 1917 campaign around Ypres, it is well written, and makes good use of memoirs and interwar histories. But it too confirmed the primacy of a school of historiography which seemed more interested in expounding *a priori* assumptions than looking at the facts. It contains no real sense of the campaign's strategic purpose, nor is there any feel at all for the British army's vast improvements in tactical method. And lastly, Alan Clark's *The Donkeys*, for all its verve and amusing narrative, added a streak of pure deception to writings on the First World War. Its title is based on the 'Lions led by Donkeys' conversation that apparently took place between Hindenburg and Ludendorff. Sadly for historical accuracy, there is no evidence whatever for this: none. Not a jot or scintilla. The real problem is that such histories have sold well and continue to do so. They reinforce historical myth by delivering to the reader exactly what they expect to read.

But help is at hand. The scrabble of feet on duckboards announces the arrival of supports. First there was John Terraine's *Douglas Haig: The Educated Soldier*, published in 1963, and really a brave and remarkably impartial piece for its day. Terraine held his ground alone for some time, assailed by pastiches like *Oh What a Lovely War*, but by the mid-1970s revisionism with some real scholarly weight behind it crashed into the argument. Historians such as Tim Travers, Robin Prior and Trevor Wilson worked with the newly-released official documents to look at the British high command, Peter Simpkins examined the New Armies, Paddy Griffith charted the improvement of British tactics, and John Bourne, of the admirable Centre for First World War Studies at Birmingham University, initiated a mass of work on the background of British generals. It is a cruel reflection on book-buying that some of the most important work was not the most widely read: J. G. Fuller's *Troop Morale and Popular Culture* and Gary Sheffield's *Leadership in the Trenches* have never enjoyed quite the sales of Alan Clark's *The Donkeys*.

I do not applaud the appearance of these works just because some of them are revisionist – as it happens I find myself in the uncomfortable No Man's Land of historiography, collecting salvoes from both extremes – but because they are serious and scholarly in a way that an awful lot of earlier work simply was not. The war had already attracted too many historians who were determined to bend its events to fit their own analytical framework, jamming their pastry-cutters onto the evidence, and either discarding anything that lay outside their intriguing shape, or rolling it extra thin if there was not quite enough. Last year's publication of the first volume of Hew Strachan's magisterial *First World War* does, in a way, mark a turning point in the whole process: here we have scholarship blended with emotion, and a successful attempt to look at the conflict as a world war, not just as the Western Front with attached sideshows.

However, there is still a trend for many of the war's historians to be overly preoccupied with the big political, strategic and operational issues. Was the war avoidable? Had Britain any other course of action in 1914? Were British generals actually geniuses rather than donkeys? Was the Treaty of Versailles too hard or too soft? How well understood was the post-Somme doctrine for divisions in the attack? In the process they often lose sight of the men who actually fought the war. True, combatants get anthologised, and we have lots of examples – some of them actually very good – of the historian as copytypist. And there is an ever-widening use of oral history, so that the words of this fast-disappearing generation can reach out to help us understand what this war was really like.

Or can they? I make this point as gently as I can, for it is no mere conventional politeness to say how much I admire the men who fought on the Western Front. But the interviewing of veterans in the 1970s and beyond concentrated, as it had to, on those who had survived. Like accounts written long after the events they describe, interviews with survivors inevitably reflect the past through the prism of the present. Although A. J. P. Taylor was unduly harsh to write them off as 'old men drooling over their lost youth', they do require at least some degree of caution. Sometimes survivors played their roles too well: they became Veterans, General Issue, neatly packed with what we wanted to hear, exploding at the touch of a tape-recorder button or the snap of a TV documentarist's clapper-board. Up to my neck in muck and bullets; rats as big as footballs; the sergeant major was a right bastard; all my mates were killed. And sometimes, just sometimes, they tell us this because they have heard it themselves.

So we should be extra cautious about how we use and interpret oral history and other non-contemporary evidence. It is often far too late-recorded oral history: occasionally forgotten voices tell us about imaginary incidents. Much better to go back to what people thought at the time. And in the case of the First World War there is really no excuse for not doing so. Both the Department of Documents at the Imperial War Museum and the Liddle Collection in the Brotherton Library at the University of Leeds are bursting with letters, diaries and an assortment of ephemera. And when I say bursting, I mean just that: new material is arriving faster than a single diligent historian can keep up with. However gloomy I get about being an historian, I am always excited by opening one of those big brown archive boxes, and tipping out letters on YMCA notepaper from the infantry base depots at Etaples, a leather-bound Jermyn Street diary, or a field message book with its flimsy, carboned paper and waterproofed cover. There is something unutterably poignant about a diary entry written by somebody who didn't know whether he would be alive to eat his supper that day. I am not suggesting that we ought not to read Sassoon and Graves, Campbell and Carrington, all published after the war, but the closer we get to events the better our chance of finding out how people really felt.

The army of 1918, warts and all, represented the greatest collective endeavour of the whole of British history: over 4 million men went to France and nearly three quarters of a million stayed there forever. As the war went on they drifted apart from the land that had raised them, and lived in a world with its own rules, values, beliefs and language. They celebrated the armistice in silence, not with wild rejoicing. And then they went back to pick up their lives. For most of them the war was not, *pace* Paul Fussell, a break, a sundering. It was, as Private David Jones termed it, in parenthesis, bracketed into a busy life.[6] It soon became evident that they had won the war but lost the peace, and the corrosive effect of this sense of collective betrayal can hardly be over-emphasised. The positive diaries become bitter memoirs as Military Crosses and Military Medals went to the pawnshop. And so *we* remember the war not as we might, through the eyes of 1918, as a remarkable victory so very dearly won, but through the eyes of 1928 as a sham which had wasted men's lives and squandered their courage.

A brief word about terminology. When describing battalions in the British army I have followed the example of the Official Historian, Sir James Edmonds, and generally render 2nd Battalion The Queen's Regiment as 2/Queen's, and 2nd/7th Battalion The London Regiment as 2/7th London. Terms generally abbreviated, such as RFA for Royal Field Artillery or RMO for Regimental Medical Officer, are spelt out in full when they first appear, and a brief glossary at the end of the book should mitigate confusion. When an individual is identified by rank in the text, the rank given is that he held at the time of his mention: Harry Ogle, for instance, is variously private, corporal and captain.

Money features in these pages from time to time, usually mentioned because of its scarcity. It was reckoned in pounds, shillings and pence, with twelve pence (d) to the shilling and twenty shillings to the pound. A guinea, more common in Jermyn Street than the Gorbals, was twenty-one shillings. Prices rose in Britain throughout the war, with an almost regular ascent of 27 percent from its outbreak to January 1918. Food prices rose rather more swiftly, with a rise of around 133 percent from 1914 to 1920. Bread that sold for 4d a loaf in 1914 was 11½d at the end of 1917, and the price of a quart of milk over the same period rose from an average of 3½d to 7½d. A working man's overcoat, 27s 4d in 1914, was 46s 8d in 1918, and a good shirt rose in price from 4s 6d to 8s 2½d. A woman's hat, 8s in 1914, was 15s 11d four years later, and a corset, still an essential item of female dress, rose from 4s to 13s 8d.

There were sharp regional variations in working-class income: a bricklayer in Glasgow earned 10d an hour in 1914 and a cracking 22d in 1918, while his colleague in London drew 43s 9d a week at the start of the war and 88s at its end. Farm labourers, earning a broad average of 19s a week in 1907, took home 31s 9d in 1918. George Ashurst pocketed 12s 6d a week as a clerk in a Lancashire colliery. In 1914 J. B. Priestley, a clerk with literary ambitions, received 4s for a long day's work: his whisky was 3s 6d a bottle and his pipe tobacco 3½d an ounce. William Shotter, who lived in Wimbledon, got 6 shillings a week as a trained draughtsman and then 17s 6d for a seven-day week as a milk roundsman. A tailor-made suit cost him 17 shillings and a 'big dinner, roast beef, potatoes, pudding' was sixpence. A middle-class professional man could expect around £500 a year, and Sir George Sitwell, a well-to-do baronet, thought that £530 a year was quite enough to keep young Osbert in the cavalry, with horses, servant and groom. There was certainly serious money about: Sir John French, never a safe pair of hands where cash was concerned, had borrowed £2,000 off Douglas Haig, then his brigade major, in 1899.

A Lancashire mill worker might pay 6s a week for accommodation and, at the other social extreme, a sizeable family house in London could be rented for £100 a year. Even Sir George Sitwell only had to pay 12 guineas a week for a decent London house. Osbert, recovering from mumps at Scarborough, thought 4s 9d a day far too much for board and lodging. Many families lived in rented property: the national obsession with house purchase was still to come. But for those who wanted to buy, an attractive house in the Home Counties might cost £550, although a prospective purchaser noted that a water rate of £8 a year was 'not very satisfactory'.

Army officers had to buy their own uniforms. I. G. Andrew, commissioned from the ranks into the Cameronians in 1916, was delighted to get a uniform grant of £50 and to find himself on 7s 6d a day. The Bond Street outfitters Pope and Bradley ('By Royal Appointment to HM the King of Spain') charged from £3 13s 6d for a service dress jacket and £2 12s 6d for Bedford cord breeches (buckskin strapped). A waterproof trench coat cost £5 15s 6d, though there was a running debate as to whether a Burberry was a better bet than a stout oiled cotton coat. Maxims of London compromised, advertising a coat interlined with oiled silk for just £4 10s. A British warm, a square-cut knee-length coat with leather buttons, could be had for three or four pounds.

It was understood that most pre-war regular officers would not be able to live on their pay: an infantry officer in an unfashionable regiment might rub along on a private income of £160 a year. In 1909 a territorial infantry subaltern, training part-time, pocketed 5s 3d a day and the lieutenant colonel commanding his battalion 18s, both rather less than their regular equivalents. In 1918 a gunner lieutenant received 10s 6d a day, and 'with field allowances, etc, as long as I'm out here, I'll be getting nearly £250 a year'.[7] Officers habitually carried cheque books into battle so that they could pay for home comforts if they were captured: often a cheque drawn on Cox & Kings, in Germany, would find its way back via Switzerland, providing families with welcome news.

Soldiers' pay was low, with an infantry private beginning on 1 shilling a day and a Royal Horse Artillery Warrant Officer picking up 6 shillings. A complex system of additions, via proficiency pay and suchlike, and deductions for things like 'barrack damages' complicated army pay, and Gunner Bill Sugden ruefully told his fiancée that at the end of the process 'you end up with nothing at all'. He was fortunate because his employer, the decent Walter Heppenstall, topped up his army pay by sending his mother 5s a week. *King's Regulations* established fines for drunkenness at 2s 6d for the first offence and 5 shillings for the second, rising to a punitive 10 shillings if the offence had been committed within three months of a previous lapse.

On the continent men were paid in local currency, and although exchange rates varied, a franc was worth 10d in mid 1916, and there were twenty-five to the pound at the end of the war. Transactions were complicated by the fact that while *Banque de France* notes were good throughout the country, small-denomination notes issued locally were met with a curt *pas bon ici* outside their area of origin. In 1917 a Christmas turkey, at 3s 2d a pound, cost 30 shillings, arguably better value than an up-market Parisienne lady of the night who charged a subaltern £8 for the pleasure of her company, leaving him to muse on the cost of living – and the cheapness of death.

The Western Front: The British Sector

N

W E

S

English Channel

Dover

• Ostende

Nieuport

• Dixmude

Dunkirk

• Roulers

Calais

Yser

Poperinge • • Ypres

Messines

Balleul • • Messines

St. Omer • • Armentières

Hazebrouck •

Boulogne • *Lys* • **Lille**

Aire • Aubers

• Neuve-Chapelle

Bethune • • la Bassée

la Bassée Canal

Etaples • • Loos

Montreuil • • Lens

Canche • Vimy • Douai

Scarpe

Arras • • Monchy-le-Preux

Authie

Croisilles • • Bullecourt • Cambrai

St. Valery Doullens • • Bapaume

Abbeville • *Ancre*

Somme • Albert

Blangy • Querrieu • Corbie • Péronne

Amiens • le Hamel

Villers- • Harbonnières St. Quentin •

Bretonneux *Somme*

Avre

0   10   20   30 miles

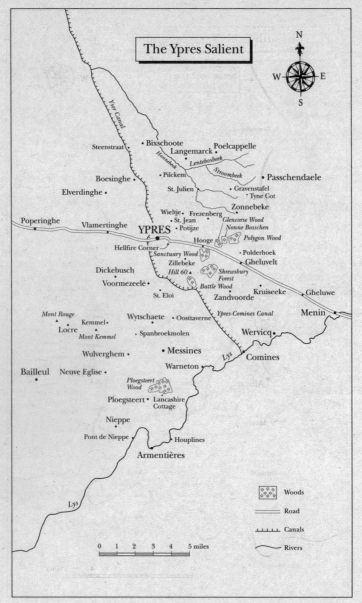

The Ypres Salient

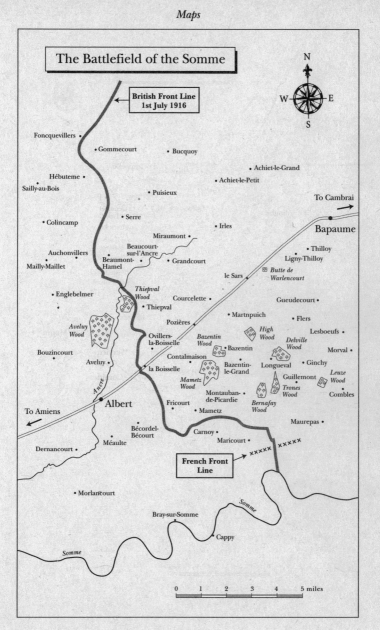

I

THE OLD FRONT LINE

ZERO HOUR

E ven his white cotton long johns, the last resort of comfort and
dignity, are soaked by the mud he has been lying in for the
past half hour. Although it is a fine night with bright moonlight,
there is little promise of spring this morning of 2 April 1917, and
the winter, the worst anyone can remember, still grips the front line
as it snakes down from Arras towards Bapaume like a slimy and
malevolent old serpent. The cold has its merits, for it makes lice less
lively: there is scarcely a man within three miles of the front who is
not aware of lice busy at his armpits and crotch. Corporal Thomas
Atkins is lying towards the right-hand end of a line of eighteen
similar figures, nine of them in his own section, on the western edge
of a long spur with the village of Croisilles, houses roofless and walls
gaping, but, unlike so many villages further west, still just recognisable as the little agricultural community it once was, on its far side.
They are in No Man's Land, with the rusting zigzags of the German
wire out of sight in front of them. Behind them is another similar
line: this little block of one officer and forty men constitutes No. 1
Platoon, A Company, 2nd Battalion The Queen's Royal West Surrey
Regiment.

To its left is No. 2 Platoon, looking much the same but, (for this
is 'Dozy Two', the despair of the company sergeant major and a
risk to all decent men) sounding noisier as Lieutenant Wills, its

long-suffering commander, adjusts something that sounds, across the chilly night, like a sack of scrap metal. It can only be Private Desmond, the company idiot, who has unfortunately not been left back with the transport where he can do no harm to himself or others. There are worse places to be on this long morning, thinks Thomas Atkins, and with No. 2 Platoon is one of them.

Atkins is twenty-five and unmarried, and was a butcher's rounds-man in Peckham before he enlisted in late October 1914. He joined the army because everybody else was doing it, and he did not want to miss the excitement. And he chose the Queen's because Jack Chamberlain, a roundsman with the same firm, had an uncle in the regiment, and told Thomas that its cap badge, the Paschal lamb, was the finest in the army. That was enough for a single train ticket to Guildford, and a long walk up the hill to Stoughton barracks, where a sergeant thought that there might just be two vacancies. Getting into the army was easier than getting to France, and it took three months of basic training – shooting on Ash Ranges and route marches along the Hog's Back to Farnham – and another three of hanging about the depot before his name appeared on a typewritten list fluttering outside the orderly room. His draft, two officers and fifty-eight men, marched to Guildford station and went by train to Southampton. An overnight crossing in a cattle boat took them to Le Havre, whence they were shuffled by railway to an infantry base depot at Etaples, and then posted to the 2nd Battalion, out of the line near Poperinghe, behind Ypres.

Having a chum in the same draft helped, and he recognised some NCOs from Stoughton. There were more decent blokes than bad bastards: any section had three or four good men, as many average, and one or two walking disasters, usually weeded out and sent off to the trench mortars in one of their periodic appeals for men. Officers were recognisably different in style and substance, and there were still enough pre-war regulars to give the battalion an old army feel of Blanco and brickdust.

The pattern of battalion life, with rotation between the front line, reserve trenches and rest billets (usually with more work than rest), came easily to Atkins. There was no sense in fighting what you couldn't change. Food was regular, if predictable, and there was not much to spend your pay on but omelette and chips, accompanied by thin French beer or sharp white wine. Two shillings a week went home to his mother. The rest, increasing from a private's miserable 1 shilling a day to a corporal's more respectable 1s 3d in July 1916, as Somme casualties created vacancies, went straight into his belly. He was shocked the first time he was shelled, and profoundly surprised the first time he was sniped at: rifle fire was so much more personal, and it seemed odd that a German he had never met should try to kill him.

By this April of 1917 he has become familiar with death and wounds, with enough of his friends dead to be aware of his own mortality but not so many lost as to make him obsessed by the risks he must run. He knows his job, thinks himself good at it, and believes that his superiors think so too. The only drawback to the promotion that cannot be far away is that it will make it harder for him to see his mate, Corporal Jack Chamberlain.

Further back down the gentle slope, towards the barbed wire in front of the British front-line trench, are Nos 3 and 4 Platoons, the remainder of A Company. Shiny A is the battalion's right-forward company. It is to attack at zero hour, 5.15 that morning, with B Company on its left and C and D Companies behind. The two rear companies, in the British front line and the communication trenches just behind it, will advance in section worms, little columns which will make them easier to control as they move forward, passing through the first wave of attacking companies to consolidate the captured ground.

The layout of the morning's plan is quite clear in Atkins's mind. Five minutes before the attack British field artillery will shell the German front line, while heavier guns will reach out more deeply in an effort to prevent the German artillery from responding effectively to the SOS rockets which their infantry will be sure to send up. As the advance begins the artillery will fire a creeping barrage, moving 100 yards every three minutes. Atkins knows that he and his men must 'lean on the barrage', leaving no more than 50 yards between the shell bursts and their advancing line. The trick is to arrive on the German front line, where the railway embankment runs across the front of the village, before its garrisons have emerged from their dugouts. Anyone who remembers the opening stages of the battle of the Somme the previous summer knows that it is better to risk losing men from the occasional shell that bursts short than to allow the barrage to spit and crack its way across the landscape too far ahead of the infantry, giving the Germans time to emerge to man their surviving positions and tuck machine guns into fresh shell holes.

The battalion is to take the German front-line trench and the embankment behind it, and then form a defensive flank facing north-east while the other three battalions in the brigade gain more ground. Brigadier General Hanway Cumming, the brigade commander, in a dugout a mile and a half further back, would tell us that the 21st Division on the left and the 4th Australian Division on the right will also be attacking as part of a larger plan conceived by 3rd Army. But this is not a matter for Atkins. He has seen the divisional commander on two occasions, but could not tell us that he is called Major General Herbert Watts and will soon have his reputation for being a very competent operator recognised by a knighthood. Getting to the railway embankment with skin intact will be quite enough for Atkins this morning, and the divisional plan is veiled from him in the mists of higher strategy. His men are to take the German front-line trench, and then work their way along it to the right until they meet the 22nd Manchesters, their right-hand neighbours. The company commander, with his unhappy facility for making the simple complicated (he was a lawyer in another life, which may explain it), calls it 'effecting a junction'.

An artillery forward observation officer and his two signallers will move up with the company, the signallers unrolling cable as they go to maintain telephone communication with the guns. Goodness knows how long it will last, for unburied cable is easily cut by shellfire or by the iron-rimmed wheels of wagons. The gunner subaltern, warned by his commander that his job is to stay alive as long as he can to keep in contact with the guns, is not at his best. Like most officers in this part of the field he is dressed as a private soldier, and Private Desmond, perhaps entirely innocently, has already asked him: 'Spare a fag, cocker?' Although Desmond was put in the picture by an outraged signaller, it was not a good start for any gunner's day.

Corporal Atkins's little band of nine is much the same as any other British section in France this chilly morning. Although this is in theory a regular battalion, there is actually only one regular in the section. Private Sammy Jacques, with his rheumy eye, droopy moustache and South African War medal ribbons, resolutely does no more and no less than his duty, honouring the oath he took, half a lifetime ago, to 'defend Her Majesty, her heirs and successors, in person, crown and dignity, against all enemies'. Although Atkins is nearly half his age, Jacques always properly calls him 'Corp', and never trades on his long service – except to lace his language with the impenetrable patois of the old India hand for whom a rifle is always a *bundook*, a girl a *bint* and a bed a *charpoy*. He is no problem out of the line, for he drinks to get drunk, and goes straight from upright and thirsty to horizontal and silent: no unseemly shouting, brawling or resisting the guard.

Atkins's second-in-command, rejoicing in the rank of temporary, unpaid lance corporal, is Henry Adnam, a solicitor's articled clerk and public school man who volunteered in late 1915, not long before conscription came into force. Had he joined a year before he might have got straight in with a commission, but those easy days have gone, and if he wants one now he will have to prove himself on mornings like this, and seems in a fair way to be doing so. There are four long-standing members of the section, Abraham, Bertorelli, Jarvis and Wolverton, all also from south London, a reflection of the regiment's pre-war recruiting base. They are known quantities and men of proven value – Jake, Bertie, Jackie and the Wolf amongst themselves, and to Atkins too, when the presence of an officer does not impose formality. Their preference for holding rations and food parcels in common is tinged with disregard of the property rights of those outside the charmed circle. If the company finds itself diffy (that is, deficient) of any of its stores when they are next checked by the regimental quartermaster sergeant, the Wolf will be let out to prowl and the missing items will be 'found', perhaps with file marks where serial numbers used to be.

The remaining three members of the section, Arlington, Kersley and Pryce-Owen, are recent arrivals, young 1916 conscripts drafted in through Etaples to replace men killed or wounded in the steady low-level attrition of a winter's line-holding. Arlington is from Middlesbrough, Kersley from Shaftesbury and Pryce-Owen from North Wales. Nowadays men are sent forward from the base without much regard for cap badge or local origin: these three became Queensmen at Etaples, and, as Jacques puts it, do not know 'Braganza' (the regimental march) from a Number One burner. It is too early to know what to make of them. The three are inclined to chum up, and this morning they lie side by side. Disregarding the allotted spacing of three yards between men, Kersley has wriggled across to Pryce-Owen, whose first battle this will be, and the tips of their boots are touching.

Only Atkins, Wolverton and Pryce-Owen have wristwatches: Wolverton's belonged to a previous platoon commander who mislaid it somewhere between the front-line trench where he was sniped and the regimental aid post only 250 yards behind. The worst thing about being watchless on a morning like this is not knowing how close the battle is: for many soldiers it is like standing on the scaffold with no idea of when the trap will be sprung. Even the fortunate few find their watches little help, for their hands seem to be sticking: this is the longest 5 o'clock in the history of the world.

All wear khaki tunic and trousers, with long puttees wound from ankle to calf. The comfortable service caps of the past have been replaced by battle bowlers, the broad-brimmed steel helmet, screened against shine by stretched hessian. The men have khaki webbing – a broad waistbelt, with water bottle on the right, entrenching tool and bayonet scabbard on the left, and braces which support ammunition pouches at the front and a haversack (containing 'the unexpired portion of the day's rations', a notionally waterproof 'gas cape' and a spare pair of socks) in the centre of the back. Large packs, now almost never carried at times like this, have been left with the transport in a village three miles back. It may be days before they are seen again, and there is always the danger that somebody else will have seen to them first. Four of Atkins's men are bombers, whose rifles will be slung from their left shoulders during the battle, and who will throw hand grenades, the popular and (generally) reliable Mills bomb, carried in the pouches of a webbing waistcoat. Four are bayonet men, who will work in concert with the bombers, dashing around the Grecian key traverses of German trenches as soon as the grenades explode, and then holding their ground while the bombers come up to repeat the process.

For the advance all, save the bombers, will carry their Short Magazine Lee-Enfield rifles with long sword-bayonets fixed, at the high port, obliquely across the chest. The section immediately behind comprises Lewis-gunners, their fat-barrelled machine guns with drum magazines on top. Corporal Chamberlain of No. 2 Section is kneeling over a Lewis gun whose 'No. 1', who carries and fires the weapon, is having trouble with the magazine. A dry snap tells us that Chamberlain has clipped it with the heel of his hand and it is now securely seated. His is that sort of hand.

Second Lieutenant Baker, the platoon commander, ghosts gently past Corporal Atkins's section with a glance and a grin. He wears the same uniform as his men and carries rifle and bayonet. Only a bronze star on each shoulder shows that he is an officer, and the ribbon of the Distinguished Conduct Medal (which he won as a corporal at the first battle of Ypres in November 1914) reveals that he is no stranger to this sort of morning. The company commander, Captain Roseveare, stands alongside Company Sergeant Major O'Hara 100 yards back, squarely in the middle of his company. Roseveare is taking occasional glances at his watch (his, too, seems stuck fast) and looking across to his left where his colleague, the commander of B Company, is just visible against the first hint of dawn's light.

They will never be quite sure what caused it, though first guesses are right, and it was in fact the repositioning of Private Desmond that alerted a German sentry. There is just enough light for his NCO to make out shapes beyond the wire, and a signal rocket shoots up from the German front line, and bursts into a spectacular golden shower. This is an urgent appeal for fire on what the British call the SOS, on which guns are laid when not otherwise engaged: in this case it is the valley west of the spur, where attackers might reasonably be expected to form up. And, sure enough, the call is promptly answered. The shells arrive before the sound of the 77-mm field guns that fired them, and a barrage of tightly-packed explosions, with six guns firing ten rounds a minute, falls in the bottom of the little valley. It is as well that the Germans are firing blind. An hour before they would have caught the battalion moving up, but now the valley floor is empty. Indeed, the barrage is so regular and methodical that the rear companies of the Manchesters, moving up towards the right, are able to advance to their forming up place by avoiding it as if it was a physical obstacle.

The German guns are still firing when there is a single dull thump somewhere behind the battalion, like dad slamming the front door after an evening on the town, thinks Atkins. It is a single 18-pounder of 7th Division's artillery, seconds ahead of the barrage programme. Almost immediately the other field guns join in, twelve six-gun batteries of 18-pounders and a single battery of 4.5-inch howitzers. Bigger, heavier guns further back add their lethal contribution: four 60-pounders, and two mighty 9.2-inch guns of a siege battery, Royal Garrison Artillery, named Charlie Chaplin and Vesta Tilley by popular vote of their gunners. The shells sound like trains rushing overhead: for the infantry the sensation is like nothing so much as standing under a railway bridge on a busy line, with the shells sounding 'like an iron shod tyre going round a gritty corner of a road'. Although the closest shells are bursting over the German front line, about 200 yards away, their din is terrific. Normal conversation would be impossible and the shock of each explosion, even at this distance, tugs at loose clothing and equipment.

Although Atkins does not know it, the gunners are not trying to destroy the German front line: that will take more time and metal than they have available. Instead, they seek to neutralise it by keeping its garrison underground, and so the field guns burst their shrapnel 30 feet over the German trenches, scattering them with lead balls. Most German gun positions were identified from the air in the days leading up to the attack, and the fire of the one hostile battery already in action audibly slackens as Vesta Tilley plants a monstrous high-explosive shell between two gunpits, half filling them with earth, and killing, wounding or concussing men for a hundred yards around.

At 5.15 the platoon commanders blow their whistles and the men rise to their feet and move forwards at a walk. As they breast the rise they can clearly see the bursts of shrapnel, white against the grey dawn, over the German trenches, and the German barbed wire, gapped by shelling and patrols over the past week, offers little obstacle. The leading platoons are in the German forward trench, just in front of the railway embankment, without losing a man. Once there, the drills take over.

The trench, an outpost of the main Hindenburg line, prepared the previous year when the old Somme defences lay in front of it, is good even by German standards. Its sides are stoutly revetted with wood, and thick duckboards on its floor cover a deep drainage sump. Jumping in is easy, for the firestep rises from the trench bottom along the side facing the British. Getting out will be harder, for the back wall of the trench, topped by a broad earth parados, rises up like a cliff. The only sign of human occupation is a single dead German lying on his back on the duckboards staring at the sky. But when Abraham and Jarvis throw grenades down the steps of a dugout there are shrieks from below and a desperate cry of '*Kamerad*'. Two Germans struggle up the steps half carrying a third. Kersley and Pryce-Owen, bayonet men for the bombers here, seem torn between aggression and embarrassment as they shove the prisoners against the side of the trench. Lance Corporal Henry Adnam will watch them until the company commander allocates men from one of the follow-up waves to escort them back across No Man's Land.

Atkins stands behind Abraham and Jarvis as they lob grenades over the next traverse. Two grenades, two explosions, a point so often taught but so easily and fatally forgotten. Atkins leads the way round the corner to find a short run of empty trench reeking of freshly-turned earth, wet wood and explosive. Kersley and Pryce-Owen pause at the next turning, and the bombers throw two more grenades. This time something is different. There is the scuffling of feet on duckboards before the grenades explode, and Atkins arrives in the next section of trench at the same time as a German senior NCO enters it from the other side.

Although he has been in France for about two years, most of the Germans Atkins has seen have been either dead or prisoners. There is certainly no mistaking this one's purpose or determination. He has a trim beard, and wears a cap rather than the coal-scuttle helmets of the two soldiers behind him. A thick row of silver braid round his collar marks his rank; on his left breast is an Iron Cross. He fires his automatic pistol twice: time stands still as the empty cartridge cases catch the light as they spin up and away. There is a crash behind Atkins as Abraham falls forwards, hit in the chest, and then the German's momentum carries him straight onto Atkins's bayonet. He has no time to think, but leans forward onto his rifle, setting the bayonet firmly: he then gives it a quarter-turn ('making the wound not only fatal, but immortal', as base warriors, who have never seen a trench, like to say) and tugs it out easily enough. The German falls backwards with blood pulsing from his throat, but it is a measure of his resolve that he fires once more, at the very doors of death, missing Atkins by a hair's breadth. Then he drums his heels on the duckboards and is still.

The other two Germans take the hint, drop their rifles and raise their hands, crying *Kamerad*. There is a deafening bang just behind Atkins as Jarvis shoots one straight between the eyes: only the seconds spent working his bolt to chamber another round enable Atkins to grab his rifle by the fore-end, jerk the muzzle upwards and yell: 'No, no! They've jacked!' Jarvis stops at once, like a drunk suddenly sobering up, turns to look at Abraham lying on the trench floor too obviously dead, swears, spits, slings his rifle and takes another grenade out of his waistcoat. He is just about to throw it when there is a loud shout of 'Manchester, Manchester' from behind the next traverse. And round it stalks a little corporal with a toothless grin, a grenade in his hand, and a lanky bayonet man behind him. ''Ello, choom,' he says. The junction is complete.[1]

SWITZERLAND TO THE SEA

The Western Front drew men of my grandfathers' generation to it like a malign and irresistible magnet. During the course of the First World War about 4 million British soldiers served there. From March 1916 there were never less than a million on the Western Front, and the total peaked at 1,721,056 on 1 August 1917. Although this book is concerned primarily with the British soldier, it is important not to forget that the British Expeditionary Force in France contained substantial Empire and Dominion contingents (from India, Australia, New Zealand, Canada and South Africa), and adding these to the narrowly British figure sees the total number of men under British command top two million in the summer of 1917.[2] Some 1,724,000 British officers and men were killed, wounded or reported missing on the Western Front, about five casualties for every nine men sent out.[3]

Almost 400,000 Canadians went to France, where 210,000 were killed or wounded. Newfoundland, then not legally part of Canada, lost 3,661 casualties, not including Newfoundlanders serving, as many did, in other national contingents. The Australians, with over 300,000 men in France, suffered over 180,000 casualties, and the New Zealanders, with about 90,000 in Europe, almost 47,000. The Indian Army sent almost 160,000 men to France, and some 25,000 of them were killed or wounded. Although the bulk of South African soldiers fought in Africa, more than 14,000 were killed or wounded in France. There was inevitably friction between British and Dominion contingents, with Poms v. Aussies spats the best known. The tendency for popular history to emphasise national achievements at the expense of collective effort often makes it hard to remember that this was a giant imperial endeavour. But just as there was suffering and misery enough for all, so too ought the credit to be more evenly distributed.

From Britain's point of view the Western Front was easily the most expensive of the war's theatres: Gallipoli, the next most deadly (though it lasted less than a year), killed or wounded two of every nine men sent out. Although the Second World War was a far greater tragedy in human affairs (for instance, Russian military dead probably numbered 10 million) the British armed forces lost 264,000 killed in all theatres, far less than half those killed on the Western Front a generation earlier. The Western Front thus has the melancholy distinction of being the costliest theatre in which British troops have ever fought.

And yet the front needs to be kept in proper perspective. It would be wrong to suggest that it was more dreadful, in the First World War, than Gallipoli in its scorching, stinking summer or, on the Italian front, than the Julian Alps in mid-winter. And it would be equally wrong to rank it worse than some Second World War clashes, such as 'The Kokoda Trail in New Guinea, flooded Dutch polders, the Hurtgen forest and the Reichswald, an Arakan monsoon, frozen foxholes in the Ardennes and the Apennines, the beaches of Tarawa and the putrid slime of Okinawa'.[4] But what distinguishes the Western Front is its dreadful combination of loss of life, qualitative misery and its sheer, mind-numbing scale, made somehow more strange by its 'ridiculous proximity' to Britain.

In all, nearly 750,000 British and Commonwealth soldiers, sailors and airmen died on the Western Front. They rest in more than 1,000 military and 2,000 civilian cemeteries, Over 300,000 have no known graves, and are commemorated on Memorials to the Missing like the Menin Gate in Ypres and the Thiepval Memorial on the Somme. These cemeteries and memorials mark the course of the old front line as it weaves across Belgium and down into France, with concrete pillboxes, preserved (and some more evocatively unpreserved) trenches, whilst starkly rebuilt villages trace the war's path.

The Western Front ran for about 460 miles, depending on the ebb and flow of battle, from the dunes of the North Sea coast, across alluvial Flanders, laced with drainage ditches and speckled with pollarded willows. Even the salient which bulged round the little Belgian town of Ypres had once looked handsome, as Lieutenant Guy Chapman reflected when he looked at it in the spring of 1917.

> Two mornings later we sat on the Tower Hamlets ridge and surveyed the desolation. Many months hence, I was standing on this spot with a major in the Bedfords. 'I was here in nineteen-fourteen,' he said; 'then you could not see half a mile for the woods.' It was scarcely credible. In nineteen-seventeen, it was as bare as a man's hand. It could not, one thought, ever have been otherwise. Could such destruction have been wreaked? Were these puke acres ever growing fields of clover, beet or cabbage? Did a clear stream ever run through this squalmy glen? This, the map tells you, was once a magnate's estate. Now the lawns are bare of grass. The ornamental water has been replaced by more recent landscape gardeners; it is a quag of islands and stagnant pools, over which foul gases hang.[5]

Henry Williamson, who knew the salient as a private in the London Rifle Brigade in 1914 and later as an officer in the Bedfords, observed that it:

> had the outline of a skull, with teeth trying to crack Ypres ... A fit man can easily walk round the skull's outline in a day; but in '17, could he have walked without human interference, he would have dropped exhausted, before he had finished a hundredth part of the way, and been drowned with his face under the thin top mud.[6]

Graham Seton-Hutchison, infantry officer turned machine-gunner, mused on the way that nicknames, chosen when the world was green, now veiled nameless horrors. 'God knows what cynical wit christened these splintered stumps Inverness Copse or Stirling

Wood,' he wrote. 'And who ordained that these treacherous heaps of filth should be known as Stirling Castle or Northampton Farm?'[7]

Further south came the Lens coalfield with its winding gear, slag heaps and miners' cottages, and then the escarpment of Vimy Ridge north of Arras. There the front line climbed onto the great chalk expanse of Artois and Picardy – open, confident countryside which lifted the spirits of soldiers marching down from the mud of the Ypres salient, partly because it looked like the last bit of England that most of them had seen, for it was 'effectively an extension of the Weald anticline in southern England'.[8] Lieutenant G. F. Ellenberger of the King's Own Yorkshire Light Infantry described his arrival on the uplands above the Somme in the spring of 1916:

> The poplar-lined pavés straight-stretching across the continuous plains of the North were a thing of the past; the road on which we were wound up and down following the valley on our left, on the other side of which the country rose in delightful hills; in the bottom of the valley flowed the Somme; the land we were traversing recalled the downs of Hampshire, its chalky slopes undulating and covered with coarse grass, and here and there dotted with dark copses and small woods. It was a sumptuous new world in the morning mist, seeming almost as it were home to which we had come from the flat mud of Flanders.[9]

Charles Carrington of the Royal Warwickshires thought that 'it might be Kent if it wasn't Picardy'. And Captain Rowland Feilding, fresh to the Somme from Flanders, told his wife how

> The ground is becoming strewn with a great variety of wild flowers. Few and far between are the wild lilies of the valley in bloom, which are much sought after by officers and men, and are therefore very difficult to find.
> Another common flower is a white one to which I cannot give a name. It grows from a bulb and has leaves like a daffodil, but much narrower and with a white stripe. If only you were in the country I would send you some bulbs.[10]

This charming landscape was destined to be destroyed as comprehensively as the Ypres salient had been. Second Lieutenant Bernard

Martin, of the North Staffordshires, wrote of his own fifteen months on the front that:

> The most dreadful picture in my Somme gallery is a land-scape – a wide upland slope, uniformly drab, dirty white, chalk mixed with decaying vegetation, nor a tree stump or bush left, just desolation, with a track named Crucifix Alley for men to walk round or through shell holes to the larger desolation of Delville Wood. The whole blasted slope clotted to the very edges with dead bodies, too many to bury, and too costly, the area being under constant fire from artillery. This awful display of dead men looked like a set piece, as though some celestial undertaker had spaced the corpses evenly for interment and then been interrupted. Several times I picked my way through this cemetery of the unburied. A landscape picture my memory turns up in horror.[11]

Captain Bruce Bairnsfather, infantry officer and cartoonist, noted the lethal connection between surviving landmarks and enemy fire. 'A farm was a place where you expected a shell to come through the wall at any minute', he warned; 'a tree was the sort of thing gunners took range on; a sunset indicated a quality of light in which it was unsafe to walk round'.[12]

The front line crossed the meandering Somme, still running more or less due south, before swinging eastwards to follow the high ground above the River Aisne. From there it followed the Chemin des Dames, the Ladies' Way, once a carriage road built so that the daughters of Louis XV could drive from Compiègne to the Château de la Bove, seat of the Duchesse de Nemours. Although the British passed this way in 1914 and again in 1918, from the Chemin des Dames eastwards the front was French-held. Yet the process of converting landscape to desolation was just the same, and was all the more resented because the men who fought on this blighted landscape had often lived there too. Almost three-quarters of French soldiers were peasants, and the ravaging of their land and the destruction of little villages that had stood on it for a thousand years went to their hearts. In March 1917 a French trench newspaper told how:

The ruins of the village, entirely smashed up by bombardments, scarcely made up, here and there, a few sections of wall with a sinister whiteness, from which emerged, like a sad wreck, the skeleton of a church, horribly bony, torn, murdered, mangled; a fountain and a cross remained intact, side by side, in the middle of the dead hamlet. All around, desperately white stones strewed the ground, smashed up higgledy-piggledy, piled up in heaps, amongst shell holes, plaster, burnt woodwork, with only a few briar hedges to throw their black shadows onto this livid landscape. Anyone who has not seen this little place with the straight road passing its collapsed homes, cannot understand what intense emotion, what dark and chilling sadness, what unspeakable agony is revealed by this vision of desolation.[13]

Next, the front ran across the dry, chalky plateau of Champagne – like Artois but on an even greater scale – to disappear into the mighty forest of the Argonne. It emerged on the Meuse at the little fortress town of Verdun, its bare uplands ravaged in the fighting of 1916 and, even to my English mind, still quite the most evocative spot in the whole of this belt of murdered nature. The line then followed the right bank of the Meuse past St-Mihiel, and then climbed up into the Vosges, to end, on the hills of the Swiss frontier, in geography almost as unlike that of the Flanders coast as it is possible to imagine.

John Masefield thought that the front could best be understood as a river flowing across the landscape, straight here, meandering there, sometimes wide and sometime more narrow. In some areas normality came very close to its bank. Private Robert Case of the Royal Wiltshire Yeomanry told his parents in July 1915 that: 'Back behind the lines there are, except for quantities of khaki, no indications of the biggest strafe the world has known. The land is tilled up to say 1½ miles of the firing line, and in many cases within 1,000 yards.'[14] In others, like the Somme sector in 1916–18, repeated attack and counterattack widened the front to what was, literally and metaphorically, a broad marsh. 'I cannot give you any conception of what the battlefield is like now,' wrote Masefield to his wife in October 1916, but if you will imagine any 13 miles × 9 miles known to you, say from Goring to Abingdon, raking in Dorchester, Wallingford, Nettlebed and the Chilterns above Goring, you will get a hint of its extent. Then imagine in all that expanse no single tree left, but either dismembered or cut off short, & burnt quite black. Then imagine that in all that expanse no single house is left, nor any large part of a house, except one iron gate & half a little red chapel, & that all the other building is literally blasted into little bits, so that no man can tell where the villages were, nor how they ran, nor what they were like.[15]

The Western Front was speckled with architecture which reflected its past. The great squares of Béthune and Arras, with their arcaded walks and florid house fronts – redbrick for Flanders, relieved by honey-coloured stone for Artois and Picardy – were reminiscent of the *plaças* in Spanish cities, for this was once the Spanish Netherlands. Officers and men with a literary or historical bent, and there were many, mused on architectural detail. As 4/Coldstream Guards slogged across Artois in late 1915 an officer observed 'a comic incident':

> Sergeant Melton was marching next to me. Behind us were two educated men, Sergeant Oliver and Corporal Newton – who started a discussion about the relative merits of Hazlitt and Goldsmith. To this exchange, which we could not help overhearing, Melton reacted with ill-concealed disgust. When we passed a partly-restored church Oliver and Newton discussed its date. One of them suggested it might be six hundred years old. Melton, who had good eyesight, noticed that the restored front door had a date on it. He half turned round, and, with a rictus of sarcasm, addressed Sergeant Oliver as follows: 'You great booby, how can it be that old when it has 1857 over the door?'[16]

Churches often had harsh and unpromising exteriors but were prettier inside. Captain James Dunn thought that Doullens church, though 'nondescript and unattractive without, has fine early twelfth-century detail within', as well as 'finely-preserved mid-Gothic arching'.[17] Private Frank Richards, of the same battalion, saw things with a slightly different eye. 'Stevens and I visited the cathedral,' he wrote of Rouen, 'and we were very much taken with the beautiful oil paintings and other objects of art inside. One old soldier who paid it a visit said it would be a fine place to loot.'[18] However, some private soldiers were more appreciative. Stapleton Tench Eachus, a Royal Engineers signaller, explained why he had mixed views about the church of St-Gilles at Epagnette in mid-1916.

> The church is an old one and not by any means remarkable for its structural architecture, at least that was my impression. It had however been elaborately decorated and the walls and pillars painted in divers hues. The paintings, which were hung about the building, constituted in my view the most remarkable feature to be seen in this place of worship. Perhaps however my vision in such matters may be influenced in a prejudicial direction on account of the fact that having had the privilege of visiting that most wonderful sumptuous church, St John's at Valetta, Malta, one is apt to judge readily and in so doing overlook the claims of those of less repute.[19]

Men were often struck by the way that the names of bars, hotels and restaurants reflected the area's turbulent past. A tavern on the Brussels road outside Mons, at the scene of the first clash between British and German cavalry on 22 August 1914, was named *La Reine d'Hongroie*, after the Queen of Hungary: Maria Theresa, when Mons was in the Austrian Netherlands. *Aux Armes de France* with its Valois blue with golden lilies and *L'Ecu de France* with its crown had both survived three republics, and *Le Bivouac de L'Empereur* bore the distinctive silhouette of the little corporal. The peasantry slaked their thirst in a score of establishments named *Les Cultivateurs*, and there were horses, prancing or ploughing, black and white. There was the double-headed eagle for the Hapsburg Empire and his crowned cousin for the French, and even, as a sharp-eyed army doctor recorded, *Au Grand Marlbrouck* named after the first Duke of Marlborough and *La Reine d'Angleterre* after his queen.[20]

This was a land already marked by war. Many were struck by the bizarre connection of ancient and modern. When Charles Carrington returned to the battlefields in 1923 he found:

a trench still full of the flotsam and jetsam of war. I dug an old gun out of the mud and found to my surprise that it was not a modern rifle but a Brown Bess musket, dropped there by some British soldier during Wellington's last action against a French rearguard in 1815.[21]

There was fighting there long before Wellington. In the sixteenth century the northern border of France followed the line of the Somme, as the fortifications at Montreuil, Doullens and Péronne, so familiar to British soldiers of the war, still demonstrate. Philip II of Spain built the great monastery-palace of El Escorial, just north of Madrid, to celebrate victory over the French at St-Quentin in 1557.

But the rising power of France was not to be denied, and the border moved inexorably northwards. Cyrano de Bergerac fought the Spaniards at Arras in fiction, and the future James II of England fought them in fact when Duke of York, and a lieutenant general in French service. 'I joyn'd the Army by Peronne . . .', he wrote.

> About the 16th [July 1654] . . . wee began our march towards Arras, and camp'd at a village called Sains, near Sauchy-Cauchy which lys between Cambray and Arras . . . The next day we continued our march towards Mouchy-le-Preux . . . Monsieur de Turenne's own quarter was at this place of Mouchy . . . Monsr. de la Ferté had his quarter at the right hand of our Line down by the side of the River Scarpe, at a Village called Peule.

Give or take the vagaries of spelling, James's countrymen would have recognised Cambrai and Monchy, Arras and the Scarpe, though they might have reflected grimly that a battle then cost both sides 'not . . . above four hundred . . . I remember but one Collonell, M. de Puymarais, Coll of horse, a brave young gentleman . . .'.[22] There were to be rather more brave young gentlemen stretched out on the slopes between Monchy and Arras when the British 3rd Army assaulted the place in April 1917.

The French fortified the captured ground. Vauban's *pré carré* was a double line of geometrical artillery fortresses, one running from Gravelines to Arras and on to Avesnes, the other from Dunkirk to Ypres, Menin and Valenciennes to Maubeuge. The bastions and ravelins of this fortification, built to resist the close-range pounding of heavy guns, proved surprisingly resistant to more modern artillery, and thousands of British soldiers were to retain grateful memories of casemates beneath the ramparts at Ypres, which accorded a measure of protection hard to find elsewhere in or around that blighted town. They also housed the 'offices' of one of the best-known trench newspapers, *The Wipers Times*, whose first edition had its own view on architecture:

> FOR SALE, cheap, Desirable Residence. Climate Warm: fine view. Splendid links close by, good shooting. Terms moderate. Owner going abroad. Apply Feddup, Gordon Farm, nr Wipers.[23]

There were older defences too. Coucy le Château, the finest medieval castle in France, lay on the British line of retreat in 1914. One of its lords had married Isabella, daughter of Edward II of England, and was created Earl of Bedford. His house already had the proud boast:

> *Roi ne suis, ne Prince, ne Duc, ne Comte aussi,*
> *Je suis le Sire de Coucy.*[24]

The castle's methodical destruction when the Germans withdrew from the area in 1917 offended the capable and soldierly Crown Prince Rupprecht of Bavaria, the local army group commander, who protested to his own high command that it had no military value. Henry V's men knew the castle at Peronne, and when 2/Royal Welch Fusiliers moved down south in mid 1916, they

> saw Corbie across the Somme. It cold-shouldered Henry V when he marched along its ridge, to turn at Agincourt on the host that beset him. But from what unknown church near-by did Bardolph take the golden pyx?[25]

Captain Reginald Tompson, a railway staff officer in 1914, was delighted to find himself in the village of Le Bourget, just outside Paris, the scene of a battle in the Franco-Prussian War. 'This is the very place immortalised by de Neuville in his picture *Le Bourget*', he exulted in his diary. 'I must go and see the church. They tell me the scene is exactly as in '70.'[26]

Landscape stirred more than history. Once, when 2/Royal Welch Fusiliers were on the march:

> There were few men within range of seeing who did not look wistfully at a wayside house of red brick and tiles, built to an English design, and set in an English garden . . .[27]

Men easily found familiar comparisons. The old hospital in Corbie was 'something on the lines of St Cross in Winchester', the stream running through Lumbres would make 'an ideal trout stream, if only it was properly cared for'. Scottish infantry sitting about their billets in St-Omer made it seem like a Lanarkshire town, and Aubers Ridge looked just like the Hog's Back between Guildford and Farnham.[28] The villages on the Somme were 'each . . . as big as Cholsey, reckoning from the church to half way to the asylum'. Second Lieutenant H. M. Stanford, Royal Field Artillery, told his parents that the Flanders countryside 'is very flat and full of dykes and canals but one can see fairly high hills out to the E. and N.E., otherwise it might be part of the marshes at home for the most part'. In the trenches, however, 'the mud becomes worse than the Aldeburgh River, and that's saying a great deal'.[29] John Masefield, on the Somme as a correspondent in 1916, described the Ancre running down the western edge of the battlefield, 'beneath great spurs of chalk, as the Thames runs at Goring and Pangbourne'.[30]

Most combatants wondered if the blighted landscape could ever be restored. 'We used to say that it would never be reclaimed,' wrote Henry Williamson,

> that in fifty years it would still be the same dreadful morass . . . It was said that this land . . . would not be cleared up for 100 years. But after the armistice Russian labourers came over in thousands, also Italians. I saw them digging with long-handled shovels, first collecting great dumps of wire and yellow unexploded shells. Rifles stood on thinning bayonets in places all over the battlefield in 1924, marking where wounded men had fallen. Dugouts were beginning to cave in.[31]

In some places, like the *zones rouges* at Verdun, the land was simply cloaked in pine trees after the war and left to the patient hand of nature. Some villages were so comprehensively destroyed that they were no longer worth rebuilding in a post-war France whose man-power losses had reduced pressure on the land.

When President Poincaré gave Verdun its Cross of the *Légion d'Honneur* he prophesied that 'this ravaged countryside will recover the laughing face that it wore in happy times', but the years have proved him wrong.[32] The villages of Douaumont, Fleury, Vaux, Bezonvaux, Louvemont, Ornes, Haumont, Beaumont and Cumèries were never rebuilt. Small wonder that the female figure in Rodin's bronze *La Défense*, sited symbolically outside Verdun's Porte St-Paul, is 'scream-ing in grief and anger at the sky'.[33] But elsewhere his optimism has been justified, as John Masefield prophesied while the war was still in progress.

> When the trenches are filled in, and the plough has gone over them, the ground will not long keep the look of war. One summer with its flowers will cover most of the ruin that man can make, and then these places . . . will be hard indeed to trace, even with maps . . . In a few years time, when this war is a romance in memory, the soldier looking for his battlefield will find his marks gone. Centre Way, Peel Trench, Munster Alley and these other paths to glory will be deep under the corn, and gleaners will sing at Dead Mule Corner.[34]

Major General Sir Ernest Swinton thought that Masefield was right. In *Twenty Years After* he wrote that:

> Time has worked its changes. The battle-fields today are green and gold again. Young trees are everywhere and the desolate waste of shell-hole and mud has given way to pasture-land and waving corn. Proudly on the heights stand the memorials to the fallen, and in the valleys and on hillside peacefully lie the silent cities where they rest.[35]

THE EBB AND FLOW OF BATTLE

The Western Front was created by the war's opening campaign. The Franco-Prussian War of 1870–71 had been a humiliating defeat for the French, and at its end France's two easternmost provinces, Alsace and Lorraine, were ceded to Germany. The burst of French patriotic revival which followed the defeat died away in the 1890s, its demise marked by the Dreyfus affair and the increasing use of troops against striking workers. But the French army had been modernised, with the 75-mm quick-firing field gun, the justly celebrated *soixante-quinze*, as its most visible symbol. Serious-minded officers studied march-tables at the new staff college, railway engineers threw a network of track across the countryside to make mobilisation and concentration easier, and military engineers scrawled their own geometry on the bare slopes of western Lorraine, glaring out to the new border.

But despite a properly thought-through system of conscription which filled new barracks with fresh-faced youths, France was destined to remain weaker than Germany: neither her demography nor her industry could keep pace. Part of the solution was to offset French weakness with foreign strength. In 1892 she concluded a military accord with the Russians, and the conditions of French loans to help Russian industry placed particular emphasis on the construction of railways which would help the Russian army, huge but still only part-reformed, move westwards more quickly. In 1901 the Russians agreed to launch their first attack on Germany eighteen days after the declaration of war, and to follow it with up to 800,000 men by the twenty-eighth day.

Colonial rivalry made an agreement with Britain more difficult. However, in January 1906 Colonel Victor Huguet, the French military attaché in London, called on the chief of the general staff to ask what Britain's attitude would be if the Morocco crisis, then fizzing away briskly, led to war between France and Germany. 'Semi-official' discussions between the respective staffs were authorised shortly afterwards, on the understanding that their conclusions were not binding. French overtures came at a time when the British armed services were in the process of implementing reforms following the Boer War of 1899–1902, which had gone on far longer than expected and revealed some serious flaws in the military establishment. We shall see the results of some of these reforms in the next chapter, but the essential point in 1905–6 was that the newly created general staff (soon to be imperial general staff) was testing its weight in the almost equally new Committee of Imperial Defence, which had broader responsibility for national defence.

The Royal Navy had previously enjoyed pride of place in defence planning, just as its warship-building programme gave it a stranglehold on the defence budget. But in 1906 a mixture of reticence and poor preparation lost it a succession of arguments in the Committee of Imperial Defence, and the general staff's plan for sending around 100,000 men to France in the event of war with Germany was approved. It was not to be automatic, and would still require political approval: but it formed the basis for British military planning and a series of staff talks with the French. Another war crisis in 1911 saw Major General Henry Wilson lay the army's war plan before the Committee of Imperial Defence with what Captain Maurice Hankey, its secretary, called 'remarkable brilliancy'. Nothing had been neglected. The Francophile Wilson had even included '*dix minutes pour une tasse de café*' as the troops moved up through Amiens station. The navy's opposing plan was hopeless.[36]

The improvement of their army and the construction of foreign alliances encouraged the French to forsake the defensive plans which had followed the years immediately after the Franco-Prussian War in favour of offensive schemes. The one to be implemented in 1914, 'Plan 17', called for an all-out attack into the lost provinces of Alsace and Lorraine. It embodied some characteristics which were distinctively French: 'The French Army,' declared the 1913 regulations, 'returning to its traditions, henceforth knows no law but the offensive.' The popular philosopher Henri Bergson lectured at the Sorbonne on *l'élan vital*, and Ernest Psichari wrote of 'a proud and violent army'.[37]

But it also represented a tendency which was by now marked in the tactical doctrine of European armies in general. The fighting in South Africa and in the Russo-Japanese War of 1904–5 (the latter well attended by foreign observers) had not simply reminded men that fire killed. It had warned them of the danger that fire would paralyse movement, and that war would become costly and purposeless. Count Alfred von Schlieffen, chief of the German general staff from 1891 to 1906, feared that:

> All along the line the corps will try, as in siege warfare, to come to grips with the enemy from position to position, day and night, advancing, digging in, advancing again, digging in again, etc, using every means of modern science to dislodge the enemy behind his cover.[38]

Armies believed that they had to shrug off what a French colonel termed 'abnormal dread of losses on the battlefield'. All were to enter the war convinced that the tactical offensive was the best way to avert strategic stalemate.

While the French planned a direct assault, the Germans were more subtle. Their situation was complicated by the Franco-Russian alliance, which meant that they faced the prospect of war on two fronts. Schlieffen eventually concluded that he could win only 'ordinary victories' over the Russians, who would simply withdraw into the fastnesses of their vast empire. Instead, he proposed to leave only a blocking force in the east and to throw the bulk of his armies against France. A direct assault across the heavily-fortified Franco-German border offered poor prospects, so he would instead send the majority of his striking force through Belgium, whence it would wheel down into France, its right wing passing west of Paris, to catch the French in a battle of encirclement somewhere in Champagne. The term 'Schlieffen Plan' is historical shorthand for a series of drafts revised by Schlieffen and his successor, Helmuth Johannes Ludwig von Moltke, chief of the general staff when the war broke out, and there has been a recent suggestion that it was a *post-facto* invention to account for German failure in 1914. But its essential elements were clear enough. The battle's western flank, where the German 1st, 2nd and 3rd Armies were to march through Belgium, was to be the decisive one, and it was the area of the Franco-Belgian border that would be denuded of troops by French emphasis on Plan 17. But because the Anglo-French staff talks were not binding, the arrival of a British Expeditionary Force (BEF) could not be taken for granted, and so it was precisely to this flank that the BEF would be sent.

The course of the swiftly-burning powder train that blew the old world apart in the summer of 1914 is too well documented to need description here. The assassination of the Archduke Franz Ferdinand, heir to the throne of Austria-Hungary, in the Bosnian town of Sarajevo on 28 June, encouraged the Austrians to put pressure on the Serbs, who they regarded as responsible for the outrage. The Serbs appealed to their Slav brothers in Russia, and although the Russians hoped to avoid large-scale war, their supposedly deterrent mobilisation on 30 July was followed by a German mobilisation on 1 August and an immediate French response. Early on the morning of 4 August the leading troopers of General von der Marwitz's cavalry corps, spearheading the German attack, clattered across the border into Belgium.

The British Cabinet held its first Council of War on the afternoon of Wednesday 5 August, and on the following afternoon it authorised the dispatch of four infantry divisions and a cavalry division to France: more troops would follow once it was clear that home defence, the function of the untried Territorial Force, was assured. It is clear that, whatever propaganda was milked from German violation of Belgian neutrality, British intervention was motivated by clear *raison d'état*. Sir Edward Grey, Foreign Secretary in H. H. Asquith's Liberal government, recognised that German victory would result in its dominance in Europe, a circumstance 'wholly inimical to British interests'.

The commander in chief of the British Expeditionary Force, Field Marshal Sir John French, was given formal instructions by Lord Kitchener, the newly-appointed Secretary of State for War. 'The special motive of the force under your control,' wrote Kitchener,

> is to support and co-operate with the French army against our common enemies . . .
>
> . . . during the assembly of your troops you will have the opportunity of discussing with the Commander-in-Chief of the French Army the military position in general and the special part which your force is able and adapted to play. It must be recognised from the outset that the numerical strength of the British Force and its contingent reinforcement is strictly limited . . .
>
> Therefore, while every effort must be made to coincide most sympathetically with the plans and wishes of our Ally, the gravest consideration will devolve upon you as to participation in forward movements where large bodies of French troops are not engaged . . .
>
> . . . I wish you distinctly to understand that your command is an entirely independent one and you will in no case come under the orders of any Allied General.[39]

When French was replaced by Sir Douglas Haig in December 1915 these instructions were replaced by a more forceful insistence that: 'The defeat of the enemy by the combined Allied Armies must always be regarded as the primary object for which British troops were sent to France, and to achieve that end, the closest co-operation of French and British as a united army must be the governing policy . . .'.[40] Both sets of instructions were statements of Cabinet policy, underlining the government's commitment to coalition strategy.

It is worth quoting these instructions at length because they make a crucial point about the Western Front. Start to finish, it would be the major theatre in a coalition war. Its importance was given unique weight by the fact that, from after the autumn of 1914, the Germans were in occupation of a wide swathe of French territory, which included not simply the great city of Lille, but the surrounding area of mining belt along the Franco-Belgian border. It was the land of *les galibots*, lads who went down the mine at the ages of eleven or twelve, dreadful mining accidents (1,101 miners were killed at Sallaumines in March 1906), and an area which rivalled the 'red belt' round Paris as the heartland of French socialism. Until German withdrawal to the Hindenburg line in early 1917, the angle where the front turned to run eastwards was near the little town of Noyon, which is as close to Paris as Canterbury is to London. It is easy for British or American readers to forget this now, though it was impossible for soldiers then to be unaware of the shocking damage that the war was inflicting on France or the front's proximity to the French capital.

For most of the war the BEF was not under French command. Haig was temporarily so placed for the ill-starred Nivelle offensive of April 1917, and after the German offensive of March 1918 General Ferdinand Foch became Allied supreme commander, although his role was more one of effective co-ordination than tactical command. Yet both French and Haig knew that they had to fight a coalition war, difficult, frustrating and costly though it so often was. The timing and location of the British offensives at Loos in 1915 and the Somme in 1916 were the direct result of French pressure, and the state of the mutiny-struck French army in 1917 was an element in the decision-making process which led Haig to attack at Ypres that summer.

The bulk of the British Expeditionary Force disembarked at Le Havre and moved by train to its concentration area on the triangle Maubeuge-Hirson-Le Cateau. With its commander confident in the success of the French armies executing Plan 17 it set off northwards on 21 August, and the following night halted with its advance guard on the line of the Mons-Condé Canal, just across the Belgian border. By now Sir John French was beginning to hear that the French attack had met with bloody repulse, although he had no inkling that it was in fact to cost France almost a quarter of her mobilised strength and nearly half her regular officers. On 23 August 1914 the BEF fought its first battle on the canal just north of Mons.

Although Mons was a small battle by later standards, it had a resonance all its own as the Old Army of Catterick and Quetta did what it was paid to do. Corporal John Lucy of the Royal Irish Rifles was in a shallow trench under German shellfire when German infantry came forward.

> In answer to the German bugles or trumpets came the cheerful sound of our officers' whistles, and the riflemen, casting aside the amazement of their strange trial, sprang to action. A great roar of musketry rent the air, varying slightly in intensity from minute to minute as whole companies ceased fire and opened again ... Our rapid fire was appalling, even to us, and the worst marksman could not miss, as he had only to fire into the 'brown' of the masses of the unfortunate enemy who on the front of our two companies were continuously and uselessly reinforced at the short range of three hundred yards. Such tactics amazed us, and after the first shock of seeing men slowly and helplessly falling down as they were hit, gave us a great sense of power and pleasure. It was all so easy.[41]

But both the BEF's flanks were turned, and French was reluctantly persuaded that continuing an apparently successful defensive battle would be disastrous. So that night the BEF began a retreat which took it to Le Cateau on 26 August, scene of a much bigger battle than Mons, and then on to the River Marne. The retreat from Mons tried even the Old Army to the limit, as John Lucy remembered.

> I rate Tymble for lurching out of his section of fours, and he tells me to go to bloody hell. I say: 'Shut up, cover over, and get the step.' He tells me that bastards like me ought to be shot for annoying the troops and it would not take him long to do it. I get annoyed, and moving close to him ask him what he would suppose I would be doing while he was loading up to shoot me. His comrade nudges him. He titters like a drunkard, wipes his mouth wearily with his sleeve, and says he is sorry. A bad business. Too much on the men when they begin to talk like that.[42]

By 30 August, Sir John French, his mercurial personality influenced by the losses he had sustained, the apparent collapse of French plans, and Kitchener's warning about running risks, proposed to fall back on his lines of communication to regroup, and told General Joseph Joffre, the French commander in chief, that he would not be able to fight on the Marne. An alarmed Kitchener travelled to France to meet him in the British embassy in Paris on the afternoon of 1 September. The two men did not get on, and French was especially affronted by the fact that Kitchener arrived in field marshal's uniform – not surprisingly, for he wore it every day. Although accounts of the meeting vary, it ended with a note from Kitchener which emphasised that the BEF would 'conform . . . to the movements of the French army . . .'.[43] Although the BEF played an unimportant role in the battle of the Marne, the climactic struggle of the summer's campaign, it took part in the general advance which followed the Allied victory. '[It was] the happiest day of my life,' declared Jack Seely, Liberal politician turned cavalry colonel, 'we marched towards the rising sun.'[44]

Despite optimistic chatter that the war would now follow the traditional pattern of advance, decisive battle, retreat and peace, it soon became clear that this was not to be the case. In mid-September the Germans dug in on the northern bank of the River Aisne and, although the BEF crossed the river, it made little impression on German defences. Sir John French, no military genius, but no fool either, quickly saw what had happened, and told King George V that:

> I think the battle of the Aisne is very typical of what battles
> in the future are most likely to resemble. Siege operations
> will enter largely into the tactical problems – the *spade* will
> be as great a necessity as the rifle, and the heaviest calibres
> and types of artillery will be brought up in support on
> either side.[45]

In late September French formally asked Joffre for permission to disengage from the Aisne and to move onto the Allied left flank, which would make it easier for him to maintain communications with this home base and give his cavalry the opportunity of operating against the German right flank. What followed, known to historians as 'The Race to the Sea', saw both sides shift troops northwards, feeling for an open flank. It established that, just as the southern end of the front already stretched to the Swiss border, the northern end of the front would reach the North Sea. In the process the movement northwards took the BEF to the little Belgian town of Ypres, first attacking on the axis of the Menin Road in the expectation that it was turning the German flank, and then desperately defending against strong thrusts aimed at the Channel ports.

The first battle of Ypres ended in mid-November 1914. By then the fluid pattern of the summer's fighting had set in earth, and the Western Front had taken up the line it was to retain, give or take local changes, until the Germans pulled back from the nose of the Noyon salient in early 1917. By the year's end the BEF had grown from around 100,000 men, organised in the four infantry divisions and one cavalry division that had gone to France in early August, to two armies and a cavalry corps, a total of more than 270,000 men, already more than half as many as had served in the Boer War during the whole of its duration. In the process it had lost 16,200 officers and men killed, 47,707 wounded and another 16,746 missing and taken prisoner. These dreadful figures were soon to be exceeded by more terrible casualty lists, but their impact on Britain's conduct of the war goes beyond sheer human suffering. For most of these casualties had been incurred by the regular army and, as we see later, the destruction of trained manpower in the early months of the war was to haunt the British army for the entire conflict.

Early in 1915 French initiated planning for an attack on the La Bassée–Aubers Ridge, on the southern end of the British sector. It was held by General Sir Douglas Haig's 1st Army, and he had altogether more confidence in Haig than in Sir Horace Smith-Dorrien of 2nd Army. In part this reflected the fact that Haig had served under him in the past, and the two apparently got on well: he would have been horrified to discover that Haig regarded him 'as quite unfit for this great command at a time of crisis in our Nation's history'.[46] French found Smith-Dorrien far less sympathetic, resented the fact that he had been sent out without consultation to replace the commander of II Corps when he died of a heart attack on his way to the concentration area the previous August, and likewise felt that his decision to fight at Le Cateau had been unwise.

The attack was intended to be part of a wider Allied venture, but Sir John was unable to guarantee sufficient high-quality reinforcements to take over a section of the French front, upon which Joffre withdrew his support.

The British attacked anyhow, at Neuve Chapelle on 10 March. Their initial assault went well, largely because they had one gun for every 6 yards of front, and, because they were short of ammunition, they fired what they had in a rapid bombardment just before the attack. The Germans managed to prevent a breakthrough, though the British gained a maximum of 1,000 yards on a front of some 4,000. French hoped to repeat the process as soon as he could, but lacked sufficient artillery ammunition to do so. On the 18th he told Kitchener that:

> If the supply of ammunition cannot be maintained on a considerably increased scale it follows that the offensive efforts of the army must be spasmodic and separated by a considerable interval of time. They cannot, therefore, lead to decisive results.[47]

The Germans responded to Neuve Chapelle by rejecting the pre-war defensive doctrine of 'one line, and that a strong one', and by beginning the construction of a second defensive position, itself composed of several trenches, far enough behind the first to compel an attacker to mount a distinct assault on each. The British found the battle's lessons less easy to discern. One critic recalled seeing follow-up waves 'packed like salmon in the bridge-pool at Galway' as they awaited the word to go forward, and the battle did highlight the serious problem, never fully solved during the war, of how to establish effective communications between attacking troops and their reserves. The high concentration of artillery was actually higher than that achieved at the beginning of the Somme offensive in the summer of 1916, and it was to transpire that what was eventually to become known as a lightning bombardment was actually more effective than a more methodical preparation.

The logic that encouraged the Allies to attack on the Western Front, to recover friendly territory, worked in reverse for the Germans, and persuaded them to remain on the defensive, holding gains which would prove useful bargaining counters if there was a compromise peace. They made only three major exceptions, in 1915, in 1916 at Verdun, and in the spring of 1918. The first was on 22 April 1915, when the Germans launched an attack north of Ypres, just west of the junction between British and French troops, behind a cloud of chlorine gas. Like the British at Neuve Chapelle they were unable to exploit the very serious damage done to the French defenders. The very gallant stand of 1st Canadian Division helped check the exploitation, and there followed a broken-backed battle as the British launched repeated, badly-coordinated counterattacks. This second battle of Ypres cost the Allies over 60,000 casualties, most of them British. It cost Smith-Dorrien his job, largely because of Sir John French's long-standing prejudice. He was replaced by Sir Herbert Plumer, under whose direction the British held a much reduced salient east of Ypres.

The British attacked again that spring. On 9 May 1915 they assaulted Aubers Ridge, in a movement designed to support a French offensive further south, losing 11,500 men for no gain. This time Sir John French squarely blamed is failure on lack of shells: he had been ordered to send 22,000 to Gallipoli, and *The Times* correspondent, Charles Repington, a retired officer who was staying at French's headquarters, supported his line, declaring on 19 May: 'Need for Shells: British attacks checked: Limited supply the cause: A lesson from France.' French also sent two of his staff to London to pass documents to David Lloyd George, a member of Asquith's Cabinet, and to opposition leaders. The government might have survived the shell scandal had it been an isolated problem, but the resignation of Lord Fisher as First Sea Lord persuaded Asquith to form a coalition government. Lloyd George took up the newly-established portfolio of Minister of Munitions, but, although he made a point of appointing 'men of push and go' who could 'create and hustle along a gigantic enterprise', the first consignment of ammunition ordered by the new ministry did not arrive until October 1915: the heavily-criticised War Office had in fact succeeded in generating a nineteen-fold increase in ammunition supply in the first six months of the war.

On 16 May the next British offensive, at Festubert, just south of

Aubers Ridge, fared little better, gaining 1,000 yards on a front of 2,000 for a cost of 16,500 men. Another attack, this time at Givenchy, went no better, and Lieutenant General Sir Henry Rawlinson, whose IV Corps had played the leading role in all these spring attacks, found himself passed over for command of the newly-formed 3rd Army, which went instead to General Sir Charles Monro, who extended the British line further south as far as Vimy Ridge.

French and Joffre met at Chantilly on 24 June and declared themselves committed to continuing offensives on the Western Front: without them the Germans could shift troops to another front for an attack of their own. Passive defence was, therefore, 'bad strategy, unfair to Russia, Serbia and Italy and therefore wholly inadmissible'. An Anglo-French meeting at Calais on 6 July gained Kitchener's somewhat grudging support for a large-scale offensive, and a full Allied conference at Chantilly the following day confirmed the principle of a co-ordinated Allied attack on all fronts. Joffre's strategy for the Western Front had actually changed little. Previous British attacks had been designed to support French thrusts further south. And now he proposed that the BEF should attack at Loos, in the shadow of Vimy Ridge, with one French army attacking just to its south and the main French blow falling around Rheims in Champagne.

Sir John French was not happy. On 12 July he looked at the Loos sector, and thought that 'the actual terrain of the attack is no doubt difficult, as it is covered with all the features of a closely inhabited flourishing mining district – factories – slag heaps – shafts – long rows of houses – etc, etc'.[48] He proposed to fight chiefly with artillery, but Joffre demanded 'a large and powerful attack . . . executed in the hope of success and carried through to the end'. Then Kitchener threw his weight into the balance: Sir John was ordered to help the French, 'even though, by doing so, we suffered very heavy losses indeed'.[49] Once he had received this unequivocal order French's spirits lifted, and he hoped that gas, which would now be available to him in retaliation for German use of gas at second Ypres, would be 'effective up to two miles, and it is practically certain that it will be quite effective in many places if not along the whole line attacked'.[50]

The battle of Loos was to be the biggest fought by the British army in its history thus far. First Army was to attack with the six divisions of I and IV Corps, with the newly-formed XI Corps, comprising the Guards Division and two inexperienced New Army divisions, in reserve to exploit success. Early on the morning of 26 September Haig gave the order to launch the gas from its cylinders, and the infantry went forward at 6.30. On the southern part of the front there was considerable success: Loos itself was taken, and the German first position overrun. However, it proved impossible to get the reserves up in time to exploit these gains. French, probably concerned that Haig might commit them prematurely, had unwisely retained control of them, and it was typical of his old-fashioned style of command that when he heard of the break-in he drove up to see the corps commander and give his orders in person. Precious time was wasted.

The two New Army divisions, moving up along busy roads with rain hammering down, were not in fact ready to go forward till mid-morning on the 26th. When they reached the intact German second opposition they were very roughly handled: the twelve attacking battalions, some 10,000 strong, lost 8,000 officers and men in under four hours. The history of the German 26th Infantry Regiment is deservedly much-quoted.

> Never had machine guns had such straightforward work to do, nor done it so effectively; with barrels burning hot and swimming in oil, they traversed to and fro along the enemy's ranks unceasingly; one machine gun alone fired 12,500 rounds that afternoon. The effect was devastating. The enemy could be seen literally falling in hundreds, but they continued their march in good order and without interruption. The extended lines of men began to get confused by this terrific punishment, but they went doggedly on, some even reaching the wire entanglement in front of the reserve line, which their artillery had scarcely touched. Confronted by this impenetrable obstacle, the survivors turned and began to retire.[51]

A subsequent attack was described by Captain W. L. Weetman, one of the few surviving officers of 8/Sherwood Foresters, in a letter to his former commanding officer.

We got across the open to attack a well-known spot [the Hohenzollern Redoubt] which you probably know of, though I think I had better leave it nameless . . . Of course they heard us coming and we soon knew it.

Young Goze was the first down, a nasty one I'm afraid. Then Strachan disappeared along the trench and I fear was killed. Young Hanford fell, I don't know when but was killed at once and I saw his body later on after it was light . . . Becher was outside before the attack directing us with a flashlight and got a bullet in the thigh – explosive – and lay out for nearly 2 days. Before we had finished Ashwell and Vann got nasty ones through the shoulder, and that left only the CO and myself . . .

About half an hour before the relief was finished our dear Colonel was killed instantly by a sniper, whilst trying to locate Becher's body, as we then thought he had been killed. It was the last straw and I took on the remnants to Rescue Trenches and then broke down. I thank God I was spared, but it is awful to think of all those brave fellows who have gone.[52]

Loos cost the British more than 43,000 men, including three major generals and the only son of the poet and writer Rudyard Kipling. It was the end for Sir John French. Haig ensured that the papers on his handling of the reserves were circulated in London, and French's political support, waning since the spring, at last collapsed. He left France on 18 December, resentful and embittered, returning home to a peerage (he quipped bitterly that he might take his title from the town of St-Omer, which had housed his headquarters, and be Lord Sent Homer) and the post of commander in chief of home forces. Haig replaced him, and General Sir William Robertson, French's chief of staff since early 1915, became chief of the imperial general staff in London, where he staunchly supported Haig's insistency on the primacy of the Western Front. Lieutenant General Sir Launcelot Kiggell, previously assistant to the CIGS, replaced him at Haig's headquarters.

The failure of the September offensive did not deter Joffre, and Haig inherited the requirement for another Allied offensive. This time it was to take a new form, elaborated at a meeting at Chantilly on 14 February 1916. Instead of the familiar two-pronged attack, with an Anglo-French jab in Artois in the north and a French thrust in Champagne in the south, the two armies were to attack side by side on the River Somme. The British took over the front from Arras to Maricourt, just north of the Somme, in early 1916, forming a 4th Army, commanded by the happy Rawlinson, in order to do so. Haig was especially anxious to relieve French troops because, on 21 February, the Germans had begun their attack on the French fortress of Verdun. Although it is impossible to be sure of the motivation of General Erich von Falkenhayn, who had taken over from the exhausted Moltke as chief of the general staff in the autumn of 1914, it is likely that the traditional view remains correct: he was attacking at Verdun not in the hope of making territorial gain, but with the deliberate intention of provoking an attritional battle which would 'bleed the French army white'. Haig had never had any realistic alternative to the place of that summer's Allied offensive: and now, with the attack on Verdun, he was to be constrained in time too.

In April general headquarters was moved south from St-Omer to Montreuil, better placed to watch over the extended British front, and on 26 May Haig entertained Joffre in his (remarkably modest) quarters in the nearby Château de Beaurepaire. All too well aware that many of his New Army troops, upon whom the battle would largely depend, were not yet fully trained, Haig suggested that he might not be able to attack till August. Joffre exploded that there would be no French army left by then. Haig soothed the old gentleman with some 1840 brandy, but it is clear that he fully understood the coalition dimension of the battle: on 10 June he told Kiggell that 'the object of our attack is to <u>relieve pressure on Verdun</u>'.[53]

We have already seen how soldiers' spirits lifted when they left Flanders for the wider horizons of the Somme, and Rawlinson's reaction was no exception. 'It is capital country in which to undertake an offensive when we get a sufficiency of artillery,' he recorded in his diary, 'for the observation is excellent and with plenty of guns and ammunition we ought to be able to avoid the heavy losses which the infantry have always suffered on previous occasions.'[54] The same rolling landscape that so cheered men moving to the Somme provided the Germans with admirable ground for defence, and Rawlinson faced two well-prepared lines, with a third in the early stages of construction. The front line, with the Roman road from Albert to Bapaume slashing obliquely across it, incorporated fortified villages like Serre, Beaumont Hamel, Thiepval, and Fricourt, and the pattern of spurs and re-entrants provided admirable fields of fire.

The chalk enabled the Germans to construct deep dugouts, some more than 30 feet deep and effectively impervious to destruction by all but the heaviest guns. These were no surprise to the British, who had already captured one near Touvent Farm, in the north of the attack sector. Rawlinson and his chief of staff devised a plan of attack based on the methodical reduction of strongpoints by artillery and the step-by-step advance of infantry; but this 'bite and hold' project did not please Haig, who wanted something bolder, 'with the chance of breaking the German line'. There is, though, evidence that Haig did not see a breakthrough as the battle's most likely option. His head of intelligence, Brigadier General John Charteris, wrote in spring that: 'DH looks on it as a "wearing-out" battle, with just the off-chance that it might wear the Germans right out. But this is impossible.'[55]

The eventual plan of attack was a compromise. It embodied a week's bombardment which saw Rawlinson's gunners firing a million and a half shells, the explosion of mines beneath selected points of the German line, and a massed assault by 4th Army's infantry behind a creeping barrage. Two divisions of General Sir Edmund Allenby's 3rd Army were to attack at Gommecourt, just beyond Rawlinson's northern boundary, to distract German attention from the main effort. Finally, Lieutenant General Sir Hubert Gough's Reserve Army (renamed 5th Army towards the battle's end) was on hand to push through the gap. On 22 June, with his artillery bracing itself to unleash the heaviest bombardment thus far delivered by British gunners, Rawlinson warned his corps commanders: 'I had better make it quite clear that it may not be possible to break the enemy's line and push the cavalry through in the first rush.'[56]

Much of what went wrong on that bright, bloody morning of 1 July 1916, the British army's most costly day, with 57,470 casualties, 19,240 of them killed and 2,152 missing, was determined before the first shot was fired. Rawlinson's initial deductions were correct, though even his 'bite-and-hold' scheme would have been costly. But a methodical bombardment which forfeited surprise and yet failed to deal adequately with the German front line, and scarcely at all with the second, out of range to Rawlinson's field artillery in its initial gun-lines, meshed unhappily with Haig's insistence on the need for rapid exploitation. Rawlinson's artillery density, with one field gun to every 21 yards of trench and a heavy gun for every 57, was less than had been achieved at Neuve Chapelle. And although a recent historian has described subsequent criticism of the plan as 'hindsight, untroubled by any understanding of the realities of the time', it did not require lofty strategic vision to suspect that the artillery would not do all that was expected of it.[57] Rifleman Percy Jones of the Queen's Westminster Rifles (waiting to attack at Gommecourt with 56th London Division) wrote: 'I do not see how the stiffest bombardment is going to kill them all. Nor do I see how the whole of the enemy's artillery is going to be silenced.'[58]

The strategic imperative which had taken the British to the Somme ensured that there could be no let-up despite the heavy casualties and disappointing gains of the first day. Rawlinson bewilderingly decided to jettison the normal military principle of reinforcing success in favour of consolidating the ground he had gained in the south – where the whole of the German first position on Montauban Ridge had been taken – and renewing his attack on untaken objectives further north. Haig overruled him, placed Gough in command of the northern sector of the battle, and told Rawlinson to press matters south of the Albert-Bapaume road. It took 4th Army a fortnight to secure positions from which it could assault the German second line on the Longueval-Bazentin Ridge, and the gruelling process involved a bitter battle for Mametz Wood in which 39th (Welsh) Division would be badly mauled.

Rawlinson's next major attack was delivered under cover of darkness early on 14 July 1916. Crucially, the artillery density was far higher than on the first day of the battle – 'two-thirds of the number of guns . . . would have to demolish only one-eighteenth of the length of trench'.[59] Darkness limited, though because of 'fixed lines' did not wholly negate, the effect of the defenders' machine guns, and the final five minutes of intense bombardment added psychological dislocation to the considerable physical destruction achieved over the previous three days. The attackers secured the ridge, although, crucially, they failed to take High Wood and Delville Wood, both of which sat like sponges on the crest and would enable the Germans to seep troops forward over the weeks that followed. The plan for cavalry exploitation did not work, less because of the cavalry's inherent limitations than the familiar problem of initiating exploitation as soon as an opportunity was identified.

Fourth Army spent the next two months on Longueval Ridge, fighting what Robin Prior and Trevor Wilson rightly call 'The Forgotten Battles', a series of local offensives in which Rawlinson never brought his full weight to bear. It does not require hindsight to recognise this. Company Quartermaster Sergeant Scott Macfie of the King's Liverpool Regiment told his brother that:

> The want of preparation, the vague orders, the ignorance of the objective & geography, the absurd haste, and in general the horrid bungling were scandalous. After two years of war it seems that our higher commanders are still without common sense. In any well regulated organisation a divisional commander would be shot for incompetence – here another regiment is ordered to attempt the same task in the same maddening way.[60]

But however correct we may be to criticise an army commander who was all too evidently still learning his trade, to grasp the true texture of the Somme we must look at the Germans too. Their rigid insistence on regaining captured ground meant that British attacks were followed by German counterattacks, often as futile as they were costly. Artillery ammunition was now arriving in unprecedented quantities, and the British rarely expended less than a million rounds a week that summer, more than they had fired in the first six months of the war. In the week ending 20 August they fired no less than 1,372,000 shells, and the Germans, still locked in a death-grip at Verdun, were losing the artillery battle.[61] Lieutenant Ernst Junger, who was to become not only Germany's most highly-decorated officer but one of the conflict's longest-lived survivors, recalled that his company was led forward by a guide who had 'been through horror to the limit of despair' and retained only 'superhuman indifference'. Once on the battlefield, Junger saw how:

> The sunken road now appeared as nothing but a series of enormous shell-holes filled with pieces of uniform, weapons and dead bodies. The ground all around, as far as the eye could see, was ploughed by shells. Among the living lay the dead. As we dug ourselves in we found them in layers stacked one on top of the other. One company after another has been shoved into the drum-fire and steadily annihilated.[62]

The Reserve Army made better, though costly, progress, and the capture of Pozières by the Australians on 7 August not only gave the British possession of the highest point of the battlefield, but established this battered and stinking village as a landmark in Australian history, scarcely less momentous, in its way, than Gallipoli. Here, as the inscription on the memorial on the hummocky and windswept site of Pozières Mill records, Australian dead were strewn more thickly than on any other battlefield of the war. And, though anglophone historians too often forget it, the French 6th Army, its contribution reduced but by no means removed by the continuing blood-letting at Verdun, made significant gains on the British right. Sadly, one of the consequences of the wholly logical policy of a firm boundary between British and French troops meant that neither participant in this quintessentially coalition battle fully recognised quite what the other was about. One French soldier wrote home that he had been on the Somme with the British: '*c'est à dire* without the British'.

There could be no denying that the battle was causing what Robertson reported to Haig as disquiet among 'the powers that be'. In part it was the toll of casualties (some 82,000 for 4th Army alone that summer) and in part a dislocation of public expectation as the Big Push, from which so much had been expected, failed to deliver on its promises. Although the Germans had now definitively lost the initiative at Verdun, the French were anxious to recover the lost ground, and Joffre demanded the continuation of the attack on the

Somme. And he went further. In June the Russians, as loyal to the alliance in 1916 as they had been two years before, had launched a sharp offensive of their own, named after its author, General Aleksey Brusilov. This had compelled the Germans to shift troops to support the stricken Austro-Hungarians, but if the Allies let up on the Somme Joffre feared that the Russians would be punished for their resolution.

Haig had few doubts about the need to continue. Charteris told him, not wholly over-optimistically, that the Germans were suffering appallingly. The weather would permit one last big effort, and Haig, aware since Christmas Day 1915 of the development of armoured fighting vehicles under the cover name of tanks, wrote in August that 'I have been looking forward to obtaining decisive results from the use of these "Tanks" at an early date.'[63] The question of whether Haig was right to compromise the security of tanks in order to use them on small numbers on the Somme that summer remains unresolved, but given the state of the battle, and the political and alliance pressures on him, it was certainly not unreasonable. Rawlinson, characteristically laying off his bets with fellow-Etonian Colonel Clive Wigram, the king's assistant private secretary, admitted on 29 September that:

> We are puzzling our heads as how to make best use of them and have not yet come to a decision. They are not going to take the British army straight to Berlin as some people imagine but if properly used and skilfully handled by the detachments who work them they may be very useful in taking trenches and strongpoints. Some people are rather too optimistic as to what these weapons will accomplish.[64]

On the morning of 15 September the British attacked on a broad front from the Bapaume road to their junction with the French, in what the Battles Nomenclature Committee, its logic not always clearly comprehensible to veterans, was later to call the Battle of Flers-Courcelette. There were forty-nine tanks available for the attack, and thirty-two actually went into action. By the end of the day the British had not only overrun the remaining German strongpoints on Longueval Ridge, but had taken a great bite out of the German third position on the slopes beyond it. It was certainly a telling blow, but fell far short of being decisive, and 4th Army alone had lost almost 30,000 men.

Amongst them was one of the prime minister's sons, Lieutenant Raymond Asquith of the Grenadier Guards. He had met his father only a week before.

> I was called up by the Brigadier and thought that I must have committed some ghastly military blunder (I was commanding the Company in Sloper's absence) but was relieved to find that it was only a telegram from the corps saying 'Lieut. Asquith will meet his father at cross roads K.6.d at 10.45 am.' So I vaulted into the saddle and bumped off to Fricourt where I arrived at exactly the appointed time. I waited for an hour on a very muddy road congested with troops and surrounded by barking guns. Then 2 handsome motor cars from GHQ arrived, the PM in one of them with 2 staff officers, and in the other Bongie, Hankey, and one or two of those moth-eaten nondescripts who hang about the corridors of Downing Street in the twilight region between the civil and domestic service.[65]

Hard hit during the Guards Division's attack near Guillemont on the 15th, Raymond Asquith nonchalantly lit a cigarette so that his men would not be disheartened by seeing that he was badly hurt: he died on a stretcher. Arthur Henderson, secretary of the Labour Party and a member of Asquith's Cabinet, had already lost a son on the Somme.

These politicians' sons joined the growing toll of men from across the whole of British society. Lieutenant W. M. Booth of the West Yorkshires, a Yorkshire and England cricketer, had died on the first day of the battle; Lieutenant George Butterworth, composer of the lyrical *The Banks of Green Willow*, had been killed at Pozières on 5 August, and Lance Sergeant H. H. Monro of the Royal Fusiliers (better known as the writer Saki) was to be killed by a shell in November, his last words: 'Put that bloody light out.'

Sergeant Will Streets of the York and Lancaster Regiment, a

grammar-school boy who became a miner to support his family and went on to be a war poet of some distinction, died trying to rescue one of his men from No Man's Land on 1 July. In Flat Iron Copse Cemetery, under the shadow of Mametz Wood, are three pairs of brothers: Privates Ernest and Henry Philby of the Middlesex Regiment; Lieutenants Arthur and Leonard Tregaskis; and Corporal T. and Lance Corporal H. Hardwidge, all of the Welch Regiment. Lieutenant Henry Webber of the South Lancashires, hit by shellfire on 18 July, was, at sixty-eight, the oldest British officer to die on the Western Front. He had three sons serving as captains, and would proudly salute them when they met. Sergeant G. and Corporal R. F. Lee, father and son, of the same battery of field artillery, were killed on the same day and lie in the same cemetery.

There is scarcely a village in Britain not marked by the Somme. John Masefield, who was there in 1916, caught its unutterable poignancy in a brief history written shortly after it was fought.

> The field of Gommecourt is heaped with the bodies of Londoners; the London Scottish lie at the Sixteen Poplars; the Yorkshires are outside Serre; the Warwickshires lie in Serre itself; all the great hill of the Hawthorn Ridge is littered with Middlesex; the Irish are at Hamel, the Kents on the Schwaben, and the Wilts and Dorset on the Leipzig. Men of all the towns and counties of England, Wales and Scotland lie scattered among the slopes from Ovillers to Maricourt. English dead pave the road to La Boisselle, the Welsh and Scotch are in Mametz. In gullies and sheltered places, where wounded could be brought during the fighting, there are little towns of dead in all these places: 'Jolly young Fusiliers, too good to die.'[66]

A church near my home in Hampshire contains a cross brought back from a Somme cemetery in 1925, with a nearby inscription commemorating Lieutenant Colonel the Hon. Guy Baring, MP for Winchester, killed commanding 1/Grenadier Guards on 15 September. It had been 'placed in the church of his beloved childhood home by his mother, brothers and sister'. Guy Baring lies in the Citadel New Military Cemetery near Fricourt, not far from Captain A. K. S. Cuninghame of 2/Grenadier Guards, the last surviving officer of his battalion who had landed in France in August 1914, and Brigadier General L. M. Phillpotts, commander Royal Artillery of 24th Division.[67] So much for senior officers being safe.

I point to this tiny tip of a massive iceberg because it is important to balance the undoubted achievements of the Somme against its cost. When the battle ended in mid-November the British had shoved the Germans almost back to Bapaume (which was to have been taken in the first week). The Allies had suffered 600,000 casualties, more than two-thirds of them British. They had inflicted what Sir James Edmonds, the British official historian, estimated as 660–680,000 casualties on the Germans. Accurate comparisons are impossible because German casualty figures did not include 'wounded whose recovery was to be expected in a reasonable time'. Many historians argue that Edmonds's estimate for this proportion unreasonably inflated the German total, and they are probably right.[68] Even so, it is hard to estimate German casualties at very much lower than 600,000, and Captain von Hertig declared that: 'The Somme was the muddy grave of the German field army and of the faith in the infallibility of the German leadership . . .'.[69] Charles Carrington, who saw the battle's rough edge as an infantry platoon commander, was sure that:

> The Somme raised the morale of the British Army. Although we did not win a decisive victory, there was what matters most, a definite and growing sense of superiority over the enemy, man for man . . . We were quite sure we had got the Germans beat: next spring we would deliver the knock-out blow.[70]

Paddy Griffith is right to maintain that the Somme 'taught the BEF many lessons and transformed it from a largely inexperienced mass army into a largely experienced one'.[71] A mass of official tactical pamphlets appeared in its wake, providing army schools in France and Britain with the basis for their teaching and supplying individual officers and NCOs with more reliable material for private study than some earlier privately-produced material. New weapons and equipment arrived and were mastered. David Jones, in his wonderful prose-poem *In Parenthesis*, declared:

> The period of the individual rifle-man, of the old sweat
> of the Boer campaign, the 'Bairnsfather' war, seemed to
> terminate with the Somme battle. There were, of course,
> glimpses of it long after – all through in fact – but it never
> seemed quite the same.[72]

The Somme is a watershed in the history of the British army in the war. It was a strategic necessity, fought to meet a coalition requirement, and was an Allied victory on points. Some veterans never found its price worth paying. R. H. Tawney, a future professor of economic history serving, entirely characteristically, as a sergeant in a New Army battalion of the Manchester Regiment, wrote, while recovering from his wounds in England:

> You speak lightly, you assume that we shall speak lightly,
> of things, emotions, states of mind, human relationships
> and affairs, which are to us solemn or terrible. You seem
> ashamed, as if they were a kind of weakness, of the ideas
> which have sent us to France, and for which thousands of
> sons and lovers have died. You calculate the profit to be
> derived from 'War after the War', as though the unspeak-
> able agonies of the Somme were an item in a commercial
> proposition.[73]

It confronts the historian with an unavoidable clash between head and heart: the only honest conclusion is to acknowledge the validity of both these irreconcilable imperatives.

The Allied plan for 1917 was sketched out at another conference at Chantilly on 15 November 1916. It was resolved that Germany still remained the main enemy. When Romania, badly misjudging the equipoise of fortune, joined the Allies that summer she had been roundly defeated by a German army commanded by none other than Falkenhayn, dismissed as chief of the general staff in the wake of failure at Verdun. He had been replaced by the old but wily Field Marshal Paul von Hindenburg, closely assisted by Lieutenant General Erich von Ludendorff. The Allies proposed to maintain 'general offensive action' in 1917, and to elaborate detailed schemes later. By the time these plans were produced, however, there had been a far-reaching change in personalities. Asquith was replaced as prime minister by Lloyd George in early December 1916, and at the month's end Joffre was succeeded by General Robert Nivelle, who had masterminded French recovery of Fort Douaumont at the close of the Verdun fighting.

These two changes were to have a significant impact on the British armies in France. It was already clear that Haig and Lloyd George did not get on. Haig had already told his wife that 'I have no great opinion of L. G. as a man or a leader,' and Lloyd George later declared that Haig was 'brilliant – to the top of his army boots'. John Charteris recognised that the two were fundamentally incompatible.

> D. H. dislikes him. They have nothing in common. D. H. always refuses to be drawn into any side-issues in conversation, apart from his own work. Lloyd George seemed to think this meant distrust of him. It is not so much distrust of him personally as of politicians as a class.[74]

Haig seemed to get on better with General Nivelle, initially reporting that he seemed 'straightforward and soldierly'. But his plan for 1917 worried Haig. He proposed to strike a mighty blow on the Chemin des Dames, and to gain the troops required for it he requested that the British should extend their front southwards, from the Somme to the Oise. They were also to launch subsidiary attacks to pin down the Germans and prevent them from concentrating to meet Nivelle.

Haig questioned this strategy. He was in favour of attacking a German army palpably weakened by the Somme, but had long believed that Flanders, where a short advance could bring the German railhead of Roulers within his grasp, offered better prospects than attacks further south. Moreover, he had been warned by Robertson that the government was gravely concerned by the damage being done by German submarines based at Ostend and Zeebrugge on the Flanders coast, and in April 1917 Admiral Sir John Jellicoe, the First Sea Lord, told an American colleague that 'it is impossible for us to go on with the war if [merchant shipping] losses like this continue'.[75] On 6 January 1917 Haig announced that he could not assist Nivelle unless some sort of provision was made for clearing the Flanders coast. He was spectacularly overruled. In late

February Lloyd George met Nivelle at an Allied conference at Calais, and agreed to place Haig under his command for the duration of the offensive. Haig wrote to the king, offering to resign, but the monarch's private secretary replied:

> I am to say from His Majesty that you are not to worry; you may be certain that he will do his utmost to protect your interests; and he begs you to work on the most amicable and open terms with General Nivelle, and he feels all will come right.[76]

As the Allies discussed their strategy, the Germans acted. Successes in the East, and growing war-weariness in Russia, enabled them to shift troops westward, a process which accelerated as the year wore on. And they prepared to fall back from the great apex of the Western Front salient onto a carefully-prepared position known as the Hindenburg line, a shorter length of front which would free some twenty divisions. In the process they devastated the area between the old front line and the new one, in an operation named Alberich, after the spiteful dwarf in the Nibelungen saga. The influential war correspondent Philip Gibbs thought it a telling comment on German national character that destruction like this could be carried out by men who had lived for the past two years with the population they now dispossessed.

> 'They were kind to the children ... but they burnt our houses.' – 'Karl was a nice boy. He cried when he went away ... But he helped smash up the neighbours' furniture with an axe.' – 'The lieutenant was a good fellow ... but he carried out his orders of destruction' ...

Gibbs concluded that 'on the whole, the Germans behaved in a kindly, disciplined way until those last nights, when they laid waste so many villages and all that was in them'.[77] John Masefield, not easily persuaded by anti-German propaganda, was shocked by what he saw:

> He has systematically destroyed what he could not carry away ... Bureaus, mirrors, tables, sofas, have been smashed with axes, fruit trees have been cut, looped or ringed. Beds have been used as latrines, so have baths

& basins ... Houses, churches, cottages, farms, barns &
calvaries have been burnt, blown up, pulled down or gut-
ted ... They are the acts of men. They are the acts of
beasts.[78]

One German left a sign in English reading 'Don't be angry: Only
wonder' in the wreckage of a town: it can be seen in the *Historiale
de la Grande Guerre* in Péronne. Captain Rudolf Binding, a German
staff officer, admitted that: 'The expulsion of the inhabitants from
their little towns and villages was a heart-rending business, more
ghastly than murder,' though he added that it was 'to the eternal
shame of the English' that they did not inflict losses following up
the Germans.[79]

Such destruction horrified men inured to war. One soldier agreed
that, though they might have left the Germans a desert to live in,
the British would not have systematically destroyed the orchards,
and an officer distinguished between damage done by 'honest shells'
and arsonists. 'The ruin was everywhere complete,' wrote Edward
Spears, a liaison officer with French troops who went forward into
the liberated area.

> Although there were touches which showed that more
> time had been available at some places than at others; the
> will was nowhere lacking, but the vandals had been hurried
> in some villages, that was all. It was as if Satan had poured
> desolation out of a gigantic watering-can, carelessly spray-
> ing some parts of the land more than others ... Every-
> where in these ruined villages women's clothing lay about,
> underwear so arranged as to convey an indecent sugges-
> tion, or fouled in the most revolting way.[80]

Spears's French driver, distressed almost beyond speech, kept muttering: 'The swine, the bloody swine.' Spears saw French soldiers
bruised not simply by the physical destruction but also by the inevitable consequence of a long, and not always brutal, occupation.
Some men, away from home since August 1914, found anguished
wives nursing a new baby or a flaxen-haired toddler. 'Can you love me
still, who have loved you always?' they begged. 'No physical suffering I
saw or heard of during the war equalled or even approached that

raw agony,' wrote Spears.[81] There is more to the Western Front than ground lost and gained and the evolution of tactics. Just as men changed the front, so it changed them, and both the German gas attack of April 1915 and the destruction levied during the retreat to the Hindenburg line helped set iron into the soul.

The German withdrawal left Nivelle wrong-footed, for part of his offensive, now as passionately oversold to politicians as it was to soldiers, had been aimed at some areas that had been evacuated. On 4 April the Germans captured a copy of the attack plan, and thoughtfully distributed details to their waiting batteries. When French infantry attacked on 16 April, into icy rain which turned to sleet, they were cut to ribbons. Spears saw wounded coming back in despair. 'It's all over,' they told him. 'We can't do it. We shall never ever do it. *C'est impossible.*'[82] When Nivelle called off the offensive on 9 May he had lost some 100,000 men. He did not simply lose the confidence of his government, which replaced him with the big, wintry-faced Philippe Pétain, who had held Verdun in the dark days of early 1916. He did something far worse: he had pushed his men beyond endurance. The army which had endured Verdun had been a matchless amalgam of

> steel-skulled Bretons, calm and obstinate men from the Auvergne, clear-eyed men from the Vosges, Gascons talking like d'Artagnan, idle men from Provence who put their back into it at the right moment, wolf-hunting men from the Isère, cynical and dandified Parisians, people from the plain or the mountain, from the city or the hamlet.[83]

The Nivelle offensive snapped its frayed tendons, and it began to mutiny.

The British contribution to the offensive was an attack at Arras intended to fix the Germans in Artois and prevent them from turning to face Nivelle. On 9 April the Canadians, four fine divisions fighting side by side for the first time, took Vimy Ridge in one of the war's slickest set-piece attacks. Further south, the remainder of Allenby's 3rd Army sallied out across the landscape around Monchy-le-Preux, described by James II so long before.

The battle started well, not least because of steadily-improving artillery techniques, and Ludendorff ruefully admitted that British gains were 'a bad beginning for the decisive struggle of the year'. But as the attackers passed their first objectives, beyond pre-planned artillery fire, they found themselves, as had so often been the case in the past, taking on intact defences without adequate support. Lance Corporal H. Foakes, a medical attendant with 13/Royal Fusiliers, saw the consequences of advancing into observed artillery fire.

> Over a wide belt the high explosive and heavy shrapnel came continuously and without ceasing. Amid a terrific din of roars and explosions the high explosives pitched in the ground with a shaking thud, to explode a fraction of a second later with a roar (which I always likened to the slamming of a giant door) throwing up a huge column of earth and stones and blowing men to pieces. Continually, too, came the high explosive shrapnel. A big shell, known to the troops as a 'Woolly Bear', bursting with a fierce whipping 'crack' about one hundred or two hundred feet from the ground, they rained down red hot shrapnel and portions of burst shell case.[84]

A battle which had started with great promise was soon stuck fast, but Haig was compelled to continue it to deflect German pressure from the French. It is not a battle that features prominently in British folk memory, but it should. Its average daily loss rate, between 9 April and 17 May, of just over 4,000 men, was higher than that of the Somme.

Haig knew that the French army was in 'a very bad state of discipline', and the gossipy Lord Esher drove up from Paris to GHQ and told John Charteris that 'the morale of the whole nation has been badly affected by the failure of their attack'. But the French, understandably, kept quiet about the full extent of the mutinies, and Pétain – 'they only call me in catastrophes' – vigorously wielded stick and offered carrot to restore his army to reliability.

We cannot prove that Haig embarked upon his forthcoming campaign in Flanders simply because the French had mutinied, tempting though it would be to believe it. It is, however, clear that that he had long been committed to attacking in Flanders when the opportunity offered. When the printed version of his dispatches omitted this firm declaration which had formed part of the original, he had it inserted as an addendum:

> The project of an offensive operation in Flanders, to which I was informed His Majesty's Government attached considerable importance, was one which I had held steadily in view since I had first been entrusted with the Chief Command of the British Armies in France, and even before that date.[85]

An Allied conference in May concluded that a major war-winning offensive would have to wait until the Americans, finally drawn into the war by Germany's adoption of unrestricted submarine warfare in February 1917, were present in France in strength. There were many who presciently feared that the Germans, now increasingly able to concentrate on the Western Front, might win the war before this happened, and by remaining on the defensive the Allies would hand the initiative to the Germans.

Finally, as we have seen, Haig was under pressure to get German submarines off the Flanders coast. In May he showed Pétain a sketch-map which showed a phased advance from Ypres to Passchendaele, and then out to Roulers and Thorout. As the second phase of the land advance began, there would be an amphibious hook along the coast, with a landing near Ostend. 'Success seems reasonably possible,' he told the War Cabinet that month.

> It will give valuable results on land and sea. If full measure of success is not gained, we shall be attacking the enemy on a front where he cannot refuse to fight, and our purpose of wearing him down will be given effect to. We shall be directly covering our own most important communications, and even a partial success will considerably improve our defensive positions in the Ypres salient.[86]

The third battle of Ypres was thus the child of mixed strategic parentage, as soldiers' bitter descriptions of it so accurately recognised.

As a curtain-raiser to the main battle, entrusted to Sir Hubert Gough's 5th Army, Sir Herbert Plumer's 2nd Army was to take Messines Ridge, south of Ypres. Plumer was 'Plum' to his contemporaries, 'Drip', because of a long-term sinus problem, to irreverent subalterns, but 'Daddy' to his men. His hallmark was meticulous planning and careful briefing: it is no accident that the future Field Marshal Bernard Montgomery was serving as a staff officer in one of his corps, saw the Plumer method first hand, and learnt much.

On 7 June nineteen mines (nearly a million pounds of high explosive) exploded beneath Messines Ridge. A German observer tells how:

> Nineteen gigantic roses with carmine-red leaves, or enormous mushrooms, were seen to rise up slowly and majestically out of the ground, and then split into pieces with an almighty roar, sending up many-coloured columns of flame and smoke mixed with a mass of earth and splinters, high into the sky.[87]

Plumer's chief of staff, Sir Charles 'Tim' Harington, recalled that the next morning he found four dead German officers in a dugout without a mark on them: they had been killed by the shock. Plumer's infantry advanced to secure almost all their objectives on the first day. Although Plumer lost 25,000 men, he captured over 7,000 prisoners and killed or wounded at least another 13,000 Germans. It was an impressive victory, marred only by a tendency for the infantry to lack initiative: the German 44th Infantry Regiment, just back from the Eastern Front, regarded the British infantry as lumpier than the Russian.

The local German army group commander, Crown Prince Rupprecht of Bavaria, thought that the capture of Messines Ridge presaged an immediate attack on his vital ground, the Gheluvelt Plateau, crossed by the Menin Road due east of Ypres. But Haig was unable to follow his right hook with a straight left. It took time to swing resources up to 5th Army, further north, the French requested more time to prepare their 1st Army, which was to attack on the British left, and in any event Lloyd George, who had serious doubts about the coming battle, was reluctant to allow it to proceed. Formal permission arrived only six days before the attack began. The delay between the capture of Messines Ridge and the opening of the main battle was ultimately fatal, primarily because the weather broke just as Gough's men went forward.

Third Ypres, like the Somme, was marked by tensions between GHQ and army headquarters. Gough, selected because he was the youngest and most dashing of the army commanders, did not know the salient well, and later agreed that it had been a mistake to send him to 'a bit of ground with which I had practically no acquaintance'. However, he hoped 'to advance as rapidly as possible on Roulers', and then push on to Ostend: he always believed that this was Haig's intention too. However, Haig agreed with their opponent that the Gheluvelt Plateau was indeed crucial, and wrote: 'I impressed on Gough the vital importance of the ridge, and that our advance north should be limited until our right flank has been secured on the ridge.'[88] The French 1st Army would attack on Gough's left, and Plumer's 2nd Army would mount smaller diversionary attacks on his right. When the moment was right, Rawlinson, his 4th Army headquarters commanding a much smaller force than it had the previous summer, would launch the amphibious assault.

The bombardment began on 16 July, and in its course the British fired 4,500,000 shells into the carefully-layered German defences opposite Ypres. It began the process which was to reduce the area to an abomination of desolation, doing serious damage to German positions but in the process destroying the land drainage system. The Tank Corps maintained a 'swamp map' to show those areas which were impassable to tanks, and whose extent was soon expanding alarmingly. Haig is sometimes accused of wanton disregard for weather conditions in Flanders, but it is clear from John Hussey's painstaking work that the British were to be extraordinarily unlucky with the weather: both August and October were abnormally wet.[89] Nor is it true that commanders were unaware of the conditions at the front. The story of a senior officer (generally identified as Kiggell, Haig's chief of staff) asking: 'Good God, did we really send men to fight in that?' and then breaking down in tears has been comprehensively debunked, but still retains wide currency.[90]

On 1 August Haig noted in his diary 'a terrible day of rain. The ground is like a bog.' And in October John Charteris, well forward to watch an attack, acknowledged: 'the saddest day of the year. It

was not the enemy but the mud that prevented us from doing better
. . . Yesterday afternoon was utterly damnable. I got back very late
and could not work, could not rest.'[91] Finally, this chilling description
comes not from one of Haig's critics, but from his own despatches.

> The low-lying, clayey soil, torn by shells and sodden with
> rain, turned to a succession of vast muddy pools. The
> valleys of the choked and overflowing streams were speed-
> ily transformed into long stretches of bog, impassable
> except by a few well-defined tracks . . . To leave these tracks
> was to risk death by drowning, and in the course of the
> subsequent fighting on several occasions both men and
> pack animals were lost in this way . . .[92]

Gough's infantry went forward early on the morning of 31 July.
By the day's end they had advanced an average of 3,000 yards at a
cost of 30,000 casualties. With an ugly foretaste of what was to come,
the weather was appalling, and by nightfall a gunner officer reported
that some of the infantry were up to their waists in water. There were
successive attacks through July and on into August, characterised by
determined German resistance and the growing dominance of
British artillery. A snapshot from a single action, officially part of
the Battle of Langemarck, though we may doubt if this would have
been clear to the men who fought in it, describes what the fighting
was like for one particular unit, 12/King's Royal Rifle Corps, a New
Army battalion of 20th (Light) Division.

> Aug 15th 12 noon – 8.00 p.m.
> Battalion paraded in full Battle order, and marched inde-
> pendently to the assembly place, A/Capt A.D. Thornton-
> Smith DSO, had marked out with tape the alignment for
> each platoon and no difficulty was experienced in forming
> up. Battalion HQ were established in a small house 400
> yards short of the STEENBEEK. The enemy was shelling
> fairly hard and B Coy sustained casualties at this point.
>
> Aug 16th 4.45 a.m.
> ZERO HOUR – The barrage which was terrific at this
> moment, lifted at Zero – 5 and the Oxfords were busy
> mopping up AU BON GITE, with the 6th KSLI on our

Right and the 12th King's Liverpools on our Left we advanced to the BLUE LINE, about 3/400 yards short of LANGEMARCK. During this advance and a 20 minute halt in the BLUE LINE, we were subject to very heavy Machine gun fire and suffered many casualties to both Officers and men, including the CO Lt Col R. U. H. Prioleau MC (Wounded). Capt T. Lycett, our Adjutant, was then in command, and noticing a Concrete Blockhouse on our left which was holding up the advance of the 61st Brigade, and was also causing heavy casualties with MG fire to our own men, he ordered Sergt Cooper, who was in command of a platoon of A Coy (Lieut E. D. Brown having been killed) to go for it. Sergt Cooper with four men, got to within 100 yards of the Blockhouse, through a perfect hail of bullets and tried to silence the guns with Rifle fire. Finding this of no avail, he dashed at the Blockhouse, and captured it with 45 prisoners and seven machine guns, a most gallant deed for which he has been recommended for the VC . . .

The barrage 'started to creep forward' once more at 5.45, and the battalion advanced in 'artillery formation' company by company, with men well spaced, to the Green Line just east of Langemarck. There it shook out into line and assaulted the Red Line, and took its final objective at 7.50. Just after midday a counterattack rolled in.

Fire was brought to bear on them with good effect and the Brigade were informed of the situation. Orders were issued that our positions were to be kept at all costs . . . the SOS was sent at 4.15 p.m. Our guns responded immediately but the enemy were in very superior numbers. The weight of the counter-attack seemed to be directed against the 12th King's Liverpools on our left and, after a gallant fight, they were forced to give ground. This let the enemy in on our left and our advanced posts had been driven in. The enemy bombed up our trench and our left Company B was practically wiped out – Capt T. Dove MC was killed, 2/Lt W. F. Munsey severely wounded and a few men were taken prisoners. A defensive flank was thrown back and touch again established with 12th King's

> Liverpools ... Consolidation was continued during
> the night ...

The battalion was relieved by 10/Welsh on the morning of
19 August, and returned to Malakoff Farm whence it had departed
on the 15th. 'Very tired but cheery,' reported its diarist, 'and after
a good meal everyone turned in for a good sleep.' It had lost five
officers killed, one died of wounds, two wounded and missing and
three wounded. Forty soldiers were killed and another seventeen
died of wounds: forty-seven were missing, and 134 wounded. Sergeant Cooper duly received his Victoria Cross and died in his bed
as a retired major. Arthur Thornton-Smith did not live to see his
acting captaincy confirmed, but was killed in the first advance. He
has no known grave, but is commemorated, with so many of his
regiment's dead, on the Tyne Cot memorial.[93]

The weather continued to be filthy. On 27 August Corporal
Robert Chambers of the Bedfordshire Regiment wrote in his diary:
'Raining like fury. Everywhere a quagmire. Fancy fighting the Germans for land like this. If it were mine I'd give them the whole damn
rotten country.'[94] In the middle of the month Gough visited Haig
to announce that 'tactical success was not possible and would be too
costly under these conditions', and recommended that the attack
should be abandoned. Haig disagreed. Buoyed up by Charteris's
assertion that German manpower was wilting under the strain, he
was determined to continue the battle, but decided to entrust the
main thrust to the methodical Plumer.

The next phase of the battle began well. The weather improved,
and 2nd Army's careful preparation helped the first attack, launched
on 20 September, to take most of its objectives and break up German
counterattacks with artillery fire. On 26 September the Australians
took Polygon Wood, squarely in the middle of the battlefield, and
on 4 October Plumer's men pressed even deeper, with 5th Army
keeping pace on their left. By now both the army commanders felt
that the weather made any continuation of the advance impossible,
and told Haig so. Haig disagreed again. This decision is even more
controversial than that of mid-August. Although the balance of historical opinion is now set against Haig on the issue, the Australian

Official History suggests. 'Let the student, looking at the prospect as it appeared at noon on 4th October, ask himself: "In view of three step-by-step blows all successful, what will be the result of three more in the next fortnight?" '[95]

The last phase of the fighting, formally christened the battles of Poelcappelle and Passchendaele, eventually took the British onto Passchendaele Ridge: the village was taken by the Canadians on 6 November. By now it was clear that no further advance could be expected. The project for the amphibious landing, already badly disrupted by German artillery attack on British positions at Nieuport, was shelved in October when Haig realised that its essential precondition, British capture of Roulers, would not now take place. By the end of the battle both sides had lost around 275,000 casualties, although there is the customary dispute over precise figures.

Passchendaele, like the Somme, represented a British victory on points and, also like the Somme, provides the historian with another stark confrontation between head and heart. It played its part in the wearing out of the German army, was not an unreasonable response to the situation confronting Haig in early 1917, and, given good weather and limited objectives, might have produced a respectable tactical victory: it is hard not to speculate what might have been the case had Plumer been in command from the start.[96] Yet it did not produce a breakthrough, impose such a strain that the Germans collapsed, or prevent the Germans from launching, in March the following year, an offensive which so nearly won them the war.

And while its cost in human terms was actually lower than that of the Somme, it did more serious damage to British morale. Philip Gibbs wrote that: 'For the first time the British army lost its spirit of optimism, and there was a sense of deadly depression among the many officers and men with whom I came in touch.'[97] Charles Bean, then a war correspondent and later the Australian official historian, assessed that his countrymen were reaching the end of their tether. After attending a conference given by Plumer's chief of staff in October he wrote: 'They don't realise how very strong our morale had to be to get through the last three fights.'[98]

However, two official surveys of censored mail concluded that morale remained sound, though one observed that in 2nd Army 'the favourable and unfavourable letters were almost evenly balanced'.[99] There was no sudden rise in infractions of discipline, and in the case of 5th Army, whose records are complete enough to enable us to form an opinion, convictions for self-inflicted wounds, desertion and absence without leave remained low. An unnamed young officer summed up the harsh paradox of 1917: the army was better trained but less confident.

> I am certainly not the same as I was a year ago. I can no longer write home to you, as I once did, of victory. We just live for the day and think of little else but our job, the next show, and our billets and rations. I may be a better soldier and know my job better than I did, but I dare not think of anything beyond that. After all, just imagine my life out here: the chance of surviving the next battle for us platoon commanders is about 4 to 1 against![100]

First-hand accounts leave us in no doubt of the horror of Third Ypres, but also hint at the mixture of natural discipline, loyalty and sheer endurance that kept men going. On 27 August Lieutenant Edwin Campion Vaughan of 8/Royal Warwicks advanced on a German pillbox, nicknamed Springfield, with the remnants of his company.

> Up the road we staggered, shells bursting around us. A man stopped dead in front of me, and exasperated I cursed him and butted him with my knee. Very gently he said 'I'm blind, sir,' and turned to show me his eyes and nose torn away by a piece of shell. 'Oh, God! I'm sorry, sonny,' I said. 'Keep going on the hard part,' and left him staggering back in his darkness . . . Around us were numerous dead, and in the shell-holes where they had crawled for safety were wounded men. Many others, too weak to move, were lying where they had fallen and cheered us faintly as we passed: 'Go on boys! Give 'em hell!' Several wounded men of the 8th Worcesters and 9th Warwicks jumped out of their shell-holes and joined us.
>
> A tank had churned its way slowly round behind Springfield and opened fire; a moment later I looked and nothing remained of it but a heap of crumpled iron: it had

been hit by a large shell. It was now almost dark and there was no firing from the enemy; ploughing across the final stretch of mud, I saw grenades bursting around the pillbox and a party of British rushed in from the other side. As we all closed in, the Boche garrison ran out with their hands up; in the confused party I recognised Reynolds of the 7th Battalion, who had been working forward all afternoon. We sent the 16 prisoners back but they had only gone a hundred yards when a German machine gun mowed them down.[101]

The inside of the pillbox was filled with 'indescribable filth', two dead Germans and a badly wounded one. He soon noticed that his servant, Private Dunham, was carrying, in addition to rifle, bayonet, and a 'Christmas tree' of webbing, a mud-soaked sandbag. 'What the hell are you carrying in there, Dunham?' he asked. 'Your rabbit, Sir!' he replied stoutly. 'You said you would eat it on Langemarck Ridge.'

Private Albert Bullock was in the Hampshires when he arrived in France that September. He was posted to the Royal Warwicks at Rouen, and joined the 8th Battalion at Ypres on the 29th, two days after the exploit described above. 'Colonel Carson gave us a talk on the attack,' he wrote. 'Didn't understand it much.' He was in action the next day.

> Lay on ground for some time and could feel cold breeze from shells that were going overhead . . . 7 o'clock move up over Steinbeek Stream supposed to be but more of a stinking cess-pool. Got in a hole with three others. 6-inch shell pitched 6ft away gave me clout in the back with lump of dirt and half buried us but didn't explode. Counter barrage falling heavily 20 yards behind us . . . 12 o'clock move up to original front line in reserve, can see Germans moving about easily on Passchendaele. Am shaking from head to foot through concussion of so many shells, feel very anxious to see all that's going on so keep from feeling windy.

He lost his platoon commander five days later:

> He was only 19 same as myself and was walking about on the top with only a stick, dressed in an ordinary private's

clothes as were all officers so as not to be picked off by the snipers – heard later that he was shot through the heart just after I saw him.

Sent back through the mud, Bullock

reached Winchester Farm after a struggle. It was an Advanced Aid Post, and was like a slaughterhouse. The RAMC corporal asked us to take a blind Gloster down to Habnor Farm, he was an old chap and seemed to know what was up with him, it was very pathetic.

Creature comforts and curiosity helped keep Bullock going. He became more cheerful when a 'B Coy chap . . . daft with fear' bolted and abandoned his pack after a shell half-buried them. 'We dug ourselves out and went through his pack,' he wrote. 'Found 200 Woodbines.' Things were even better when he was out of the line a few days later, guarding some prisoners. 'Helped prisoners raid truck of rations,' he wrote. 'Applied for transfer to R[oyal] F[lying] C[orps]. Some hopes.'[102]

Gunner Aubrey Wade, a Royal Field Artillery signaller, crossed the Steenbeek on

a bridge, composed of a compact mass of human bodies over which I stepped gingerly. I was not at all squeamish, the sight of dead men having long lost its terror for me, but making use of corpses, even enemy corpses, for bridge-building purposes seemed about the limit of callousness. The Major said nothing, but stopped to light his pipe on the farther bank of the stream.[103]

When he got back to the gun-line he saw a sight as characteristic of the artillery battle as widespread lines of men were for the infantry.

A few yards away the guns were incessantly firing, their barrels red-hot, their breechblocks jamming and having to be opened with pickaxes for the next round; the gunners, faces blackened with oil-splashes and smoke, mechanically slamming home the shells and staring sore-eyed through the sights.[104]

But his spirits lifted as soon as his battery came out of the line.

> What did it matter that we were rotten dirty and crawling
> with lice, that we had not shaved for weeks, that our socks
> were all in one with our feet and boots, that our clothing
> stank of cordite and gas and mud, and that we were desper-
> ately tired, haggard with fear and nervous with kittens
> from incessant shell-fire?[105]

A bath, clean clothes and a visit to the fleshpots of St-Omer proved
remarkably restorative. He visited the infamous 'No. 4', purely, he
assures us, as a spectator. It was

> easily as large as the average 'boozer' . . . a wide, thickly
> carpeted staircase of perhaps half a dozen steps, at the
> foot of which stood the proprietress of the place, a middle-
> aged, shapelessly fat woman, with black hair greased down
> over her forehead . . . Her skirt terminated half-way to
> her knee, and was raised still higher as she slipped small
> bundles of notes into her bulging stocking; the 'customers'
> paying before they ascended the staircase. On a short land-
> ing at the head of the stairs were ranged the women and
> girls whose bodies could be purchased, as the varicose-
> veined proprietress announced, for the price of fifty francs
> in one hand . . .[106]

One of Haig's motives for bringing Passchendaele to a conclusion
was that Sir Julian Byng, who had taken over 3rd Army when Allenby
was sent off to command in the Middle East after the failure of Arras,
had produced a plan to attack the Hindenburg line at Cambrai.
Brigadier General Hugh Elles, commanding the Tank Corps, and
his energetic chief of staff, Lieutenant Colonel J. F. C. Fuller, wanted
the chance to let their tanks loose on more favourable ground than
Flanders. And Brigadier General Hugh 'Owen' Tudor, commander
Royal Artillery of 9th Division, had developed a technique of marking
artillery targets without the need for pre-battle registration by fire
which all too easily gave the game away. Gun positions were precisely
surveyed, and the development of flash-spotting and sound-ranging
meant that German batteries could also be plotted with accuracy.
Although Tudor met with considerable opposition he was backed
by Byng, whose plan for a large-scale tank 'raid' embodied this 'new
artillery' which would make surprise possible.

Two of 3rd Army's corps, supported by 378 fighting tanks and more than 1,000 guns, achieved total surprise when they attacked west of Cambrai on the morning of 20 November 1917. They captured 7,500 men and 120 guns, and pushed more than three miles on a six mile front. In comparison with what had been going on at Ypres, it was indeed a famous victory, and the church bells in England were rung for the first time in the war. But yet again it proved impossible to sustain early promise. Over half the tanks were out of action after the first day, and the fighting focused on a long and bitter struggle for Bourlon Wood. When the Germans counterattacked on 30 November, diving in hard against the shoulders of the salient, they came close to enveloping many of the defenders, but an attack by the Guards Division recaptured Gouzeaucourt and stabilised the situation. In all both sides lost around 40,000 men at Cambrai, and if the British retained part of the Hindenburg line at Flesquières they had lost ground to the north and south. It was a thoroughly unsatisfactory end to a grim year.

There was never much doubt as to what would happen in early 1918. On 11 November 1917 Ludendorff met a select group of advisers at Mons to elaborate plans for the coming year. Their discussions were overshadowed by the knowledge that American entry into the war would eventually change the balance of forces on the Western Front. Although a peace treaty was not to be formally signed till March 1918, Germany could capitalise on Russia's effective departure from the war by shifting still more troops to the west. In the first months of 1918 the Germans would still enjoy quantitative superiority, and the development of 'storm-troop' tactics for the rapid advance of lightly-equipped infantry supported by a swift and savage bombardment would give them a qualitative edge too. Ludendorff was not only convinced that Germany must attack, but that she must attack the British. Victory over the French might still leave Britain in the war, now with the might of the United States at her elbow and able to continue her naval blockade.

Ludendorff's staff developed several plans, many with suitably Wagnerian names. In the event he decided to use three variants of 'Michael', attacking the British from Cambrai to the south of the

Somme. The main weight of the blow, which comprised seventy-four divisions attacking on a front of fifty miles, would fall on 5th Army in the south, its front recently extended by taking over more line from the French, taking the British front down to the River Oise. The British army was overextended and short of men. On 1 March 1918 Haig's infantry was just over half a million men strong, constituting only 36 percent of his total strength instead of the 46 percent it had made up six months before. In January he warned the government that the next four months would be 'the critical period of the war'. He was not wrong.

The Germans attacked on the foggy morning of 21 March 1918 behind a bombardment of unprecedented weight and ferocity: over 3 million shells were fired in three hours. Lance Corporal William Sharpe of 2/8th Lancashire Fusiliers recounted the effect of the shelling on the young soldiers under his command:

> My section included four youths just turned 18 years, who had only been with our company three weeks and whose first experience of shell fire it was and WHAT an experience. They cried and one kept calling 'mother' and who could blame him, such HELL makes weaklings of the strongest and no human nerves or body were ever built to stand such torture, noise, horror and mental pain. The barrage was now on top of us and our trench was blown in. I missed these four youths, and I never saw them again, despite searching among the debris for some time.[107]

When the German infantry loped forward on the heels of the barrage they made good progress on 5th Army's front, moving like wraiths through the lightly-held forward zone and slipping between the strongpoints of the battle zone. As the front was penetrated, so sinews of command and control were cut and men were fighting blind. Gunner J. W. Gore, behind the line with the administrative echelon of a heavy trench-mortar battery, recorded:

> *Mar. 21st.* Got up and found the attack had started with thousands of gas shells. About mid-day we were told to get all maps and papers ready for burning. The road full of walking wounded and ambulances coming down the line.

We made plenty of tea for the poor chaps on the road . . .
Later Bombardier Cartwright came down. He had his jaw
tied up and tried to mumble as best he could with what
seemed to be a broken jaw that Jerry was advancing and
that all our battery except four were killed or captured
. . . Somebody got a GS [General Service] wagon and we
put on it our kits and one blanket per man and marched
back behind the wagon to Nobescourt, where we slept in
a large hut by an ammunition dump. We felt lost and
homeless, most of our pals gone and all the stores left
behind for Jerry to loot.[108]

The British lost 38,000 men that day, 21,000 of them taken prisoner. For the next week 5th Army was bundled backwards, and 3rd
Army, to its north, gave ground too. On 26 March Haig saw most
of his army commanders at Doullens, and was then summoned to a
conference in the town hall where Lord Milner, a member of the
British War Cabinet, and Sir Henry Wilson, who had replaced
Robertson as chief of the imperial general staff, were to meet a
French delegation. Pétain, commander in chief of the French army,
was characteristically pessimistic, but Ferdinand Foch, a tough-
fighting general now serving on the staff, burst out: 'We must fight
in front of Amiens, we must fight where we are now. As we have not
been able to stop the Germans on the Somme, we must not now
retire a single inch.'[109] Haig at once took the cue, saying: 'If General
Foch will give me his advice, I will gladly follow it.' A paper was
drafted giving Foch authority to co-ordinate the Allied armies on
the Western Front. He was still something less than commander in
chief, and although his powers were later extended he never enjoyed
the authority of Eisenhower a generation later. But his strength and
determination, rather than any notable tactical or strategic skill,
made him the man of the moment, and the coalition braced up in
its hour of greatest need.

The Doullens agreement did not win the battle, which still rolled
westwards across the Santerre Plateau towards Amiens. On 11 April
Haig issued a general order warning that his men had their 'backs
to the wall', and 'each one of us must fight on to the end'. High-
sounding prose does not always strike the intended chord, and

thousands of humorists at once inquired where the wall might be, for they would be glad to see one. On 24/25 April the German advance was checked on the long ridge of Villers-Bretonneux with the spires of Amiens, the crucial railway link between the British and French sectors, in sight on the horizon. In all the Germans had taken more than 90,000 prisoners and 1,000 guns, and had snuffed out all the gains so hard won on the Somme. They had inflicted a very serious defeat on the British army, and recent research suggests that had Ludendorff clearly identified that the offensive's most valuable objectives were railheads (Amiens in the south and Hazebrouck in the north), the Germans might indeed have broken the Allies on the Western Front, with the French withdrawing cover to Paris and the British falling back to the coast. But Ludendorff was no master of what modern military theorists call the 'operational level' of war that links battles together to produce a worthwhile strategic outcome, and opportunism rarely wins wars.

Ludendorff tried again in April, mounting Operation Georgette in the Neuve Chapelle sector, breaking an overextended Portuguese division and knocking another deep dent into British lines. Foch sent French divisions north to replace some exhausted British divisions, and the latter were placed with the French 6th Army on the Chemin des Dames, quiet for a year. It became very unquiet when Ludendorff attacked again in late May, creating yet another large salient. But a pattern was now establishing itself. Each offensive showed less promise than its predecessor, and although the Allies were bent they were not broken. General John J. Pershing, commander in chief of American forces in France, was determined that his men would fight only as a unified force, not scattered under British or French command. But he was prepared to allow them to check the German advance in early June and then to mount a counterattack of their own at Belleau Wood, near Château-Thierry. Ludendorff knew that his time was up: two last attacks, in mid-June and mid-July – the last portentously nicknamed *Friedensturm*, the Peace Offensive – fizzled out.

The failure of the offensives which had begun with such promise on 21 March was not merely a tactical setback. Ludendorff had correctly recognised that American entry into the war would inexorably swing the balance of numbers against Germany, and his attacks had done nothing to alter that balance. Indeed, if the British had lost heavily in prisoners, the Germans had lost scarcely less heavily in killed and wounded, and Ludendorff's policy of putting the bravest and the best into assault divisions meant that his losses – over half a million for the first half of the year – fell precisely where he could least afford them.

And in the background, the Allied blockade, obdurate and unseen, was slowly throttling Germany. There were food riots across the land in 1916, and widespread misery during the 'turnip winter' of 1916–17. A shortage of horses saw six-gun teams reduced to four, and lack of good leather was emphasised by the frequent removal of boots from British dead. The blockade no more broke German civilian morale in the First World War than did strategic bombing in the Second, though this has not stopped some historians from suggesting, in an argument pressed with fierce passion though wholly unencumbered by evidence, that 'the Royal Navy . . . played the most decisive part in winning the war'.[110] It did not. It contributed to a growing sense of desperation, made it harder (though never impossible) to obtain essential strategic raw materials, and by the summer of 1918 it combined with the disappointment of empty victories to erode morale at the front. Nor was life comfortable in England. The depredations of German submarines had seen the introduction of rationing in 1915, and by 1918 many soldiers who went home on leave were shocked at the shortages they found there.

The first major Allied counterattack was delivered by the French in mid-July. The British had already launched a smaller-scale venture, when the Australian Corps carried out a slick assault on the village of Hamel, near Amiens, using tanks and a lightning bombardment in a plan that presaged later, larger ventures. Gough had been replaced as a consequence of his army's 'failure' in March, and a restructured chain of command saw 5th Army disappear, to be replaced by a restructured 4th Army under Rawlinson. He conceived of a much larger attack, using principles proved at Hamel, and although both Foch and Haig tinkered with the scheme it retained features which mark it out sharply from what had gone before. There were sufficient aircraft to ensure Allied air superiority over the battlefield and even (though the experiment was not wholly success-ful) to drop ammunition to advancing units. Rawlinson had almost 350 new heavy Mark V tanks, and enough guns (2,000 to perhaps 500 German) to give him a density of one per 22 yards of front attacked. And this front was not well dug and wired, like the old Somme front or the Hindenburg line: it was the high-water mark of a tired army running short of men.

At 4.20 on the morning of 8 August 1918 the attack began, and by nightfall the Australians and Canadians attacking south of the Somme had penetrated 8 miles and inflicted 27,000 casualties. There were moments when the battle seemed to be opening right up, and the activities of some British tank crews have a very modern ring to them. Lieutenant C. B. Arnold took his light 'whippet' tank 'Musical Box' deep into the German rear, mangling gun-lines as he did so.

> I turned hard left and ran diagonally across the front of the battery at a distance of about 800 yds. Both my guns were able to fire on the battery, in spite of which they got off about eight rounds at me without damage, but sufficiently close to be audible in the cab and I could see the flash of each gun as it fired. By this time I had passed behind a belt of trees running alongside a roadside. I ran down along this belt until nearly level with the battery, when I turned full right and engaged the battery in rear. On observing our appearance from the belt of trees the Germans, some 30 in number, abandoned their guns and tried to get away. Gunner Ribbans and I accounted for the whole lot. I continued forward, making a detour to the east and shot a number of the enemy who appeared to be demoralised, and were running about in our direction.[111]

Rawlinson thought that 'we have given the Boche a pretty good bump this time', and he was quite right. The German Official History was to acknowledge 'the greatest defeat which the German army had suffered since the beginning of the war'. Ludendorff himself admitted that: 'August 8th was the black day of the German army in the war'.[112] It is a telling reflection on the way the war is remembered in Britain that 1 July 1916 is reverently commemorated: I always find myself blinking hard as the pipes shriek out, at 7.30 in the morning, year on year, at Lochnager Crater on Pozières ridge. But 8 August is not: yet it was not simply an important victory in its own right, it was, in the most profound way, the shape of things to come.

Over the next three months the British elbowed the Germans back across northern France. Theirs was not an isolated effort. The French and the Americans attacked further south and south-east, called on by Foch's ringing *'Tout le monde à la bataille'*. The Americans pinched out the St-Mihiel salient in mid-September, and then swung north-wards to slog through difficult country against a stout defence in the battle they call Meuse-Argonne. Yet it is no reflection on Allied valour to observe that, during the war's last three months, the British took twice as many prisoners, and almost twice as many German guns, as the Americans, French and Belgians put together. And lest it be thought that the British were simply snapping up exhausted Germans who were now too tired to fight, let Private Stephen Graham of the Scots Guards assure us otherwise.

> The brave [German] machine-gunners, with resolute look in shoulders and face, lay relaxed beside their oiled machines . . . and beside piles of littered brass, the empty cartridge cases which they had fired before being bay-oneted at their posts . . . On the other hand . . . one saw how our men, rushing forward in extended formation, each man a good distance from his neighbour, had fallen, one here, another there, one directly he had started for-ward to the attack, and then the others, one, two, three, four, five all in a sort of sequence, here, here, here, here, here; one poor wretch had got far, but got tangled in the wire had pulled and pulled and at last been shot to rags; another had got near enough to strike the foe and been shot with a revolver.[113]

The breaking of the Hindenburg line by 46th (North Midland) Division in late September caused particular satisfaction, as these Midlanders had been badly mauled on the first day of the Somme.

The last Hundred Days of the war cost the British army over 260,000 casualties, well over twice the total strength of the British regular army at the time of writing.[114] The headstones in the comet's tail of cemeteries that trace the army's path from Santerre across to the Belgian border tell the story all too well. In York Cemetery near Haspres, between Cambrai and Valenciennes, lie a company's worth of the York and Lancaster regiment, with, up by the back wall, most of the machine-gunners that killed them.

The whole agonising mixture of triumph and tragedy that constituted the Hundred Days is nowhere better summed up than in the Communal Cemetery at Ors, not far from Mons. It contains the graves of two Victoria Cross holders, Second Lieutenant James Kirk, commissioned from the ranks into the Manchester Regiment, and Lieutenant Colonel James Marshall, Irish Guards by cap badge but killed commanding a Manchester battalion. It is also the last resting place of Lieutenant Wilfred Edward Salter Owen MC of the Manchesters, killed when his battalion crossed the Sambre Canal on 4 November 1918. His parents received the official notification of his death as bells were ringing to announce the armistice.

II

FLESH AND BLOOD

ONE WAR, FOUR ARMIES

In one sense there was not really a single British army in the First World War, more a collection of regiments, drawn together in loose association into brigades and divisions which had personalities of their own. As we look at infantry battalions across the best part of a century we might be tempted to assume that the Old Army 1/Grenadier Guards had much in common with the territorial 4/Queen's or the New Army 11/East Lancashire. To be sure, on one level they did look alike. All were commanded by lieutenant colonels, had four companies, and formed part of brigades which had four battalions apiece. But on another they had different histories, traditions, compositions, attitudes and aptitudes. Although the remorseless corrosion of casualties meant that, especially after mid-1916, these characters began to change, this was an army which, start to finish, revelled in an extraordinary diversity.

There were allegedly rurally-recruited regiments which marched past to *A Farmer's Boy* and cultivated close contact with the county's gentry, but actually drew their strength from mean streets and smoky factories. There was a single battery of artillery which shot two of its soldiers for striking a superior, and whole regiments which shot only enemies. One cavalry private always called his troop sergeant 'Charlie': in another regiment such flippancy might have seen him strung up to a wagon wheel for two hours a day. There were

Englishmen who wore the kilt with all the panache of a native-born Highlander; a much-wounded Belgian, Adrian Carton de Wiart, who won the VC as a British officer; and an ex-Boer guerrilla, Denys Reitz, who commanded a battalion of Royal Scots Fusiliers.

There were some officers who would have fitted comfortably into a Wellingtonian mess: and others who might have sold the great duke his coal. And then there were ex-officers who served as private soldiers because they had no other way of getting to the front. Arthur Arnold Crow resigned his captaincy in the Loyal North Lancashire Regiment because of ill-health in 1916. When he recovered he found that he could not regain his commission without giving up hope of foreign service: he enlisted and was killed as a private in the Essex Regiment in 1917. J. B. Osborne, invalided out as a lieutenant, rejoined as a private in the Argyll and Sutherland Highlanders and was killed in October 1918. And the Hon. M. F. S. Howard, son of the 9th Earl of Carlisle and once a lieutenant in the 18th Hussars, died as a private at Passchendaele, and has no known grave. There were ex-privates who commanded battalions, ex-convicts honoured with His Majesty's commission, sexagenarians who soldiered on and boys, like Private Reginald Giles of 1/Gloucesters, killed on the Somme at the age of fourteen, who died in the trenches when they should have been at school.

Reality sometimes confounded expectation. Some veterans argued that the territorial 5th Scottish Rifles was more reliable than one of the regular battalions of the same regiment. Alan Hanbury-Sparrow, who went to war as a regular lieutenant in the Royal Berkshires in 1914 and commanded a Berkshire battalion at Passchendaele three years later, reckoned that most temporary officers were good as long as their units were well commanded, and 'many were better than regulars'.[1] One officer with the rare combination of Distinguished Conduct Medal (won as a corporal in South Africa) and Military Cross (won as an officer on the Western Front) was never a professional soldier, but fitted both conflicts into a long and successful career as a tea planter in India. Sidney Farmer MM, seventeen times wounded, with a record that many a regular might have been proud of, served only for the duration of the war. After it, like so many others, he returned to the community from which he had sprung, running the Golden Lion in the Herefordshire town of Knighton, though troubled by the occasional appearance of shrapnel which travelled down his body to emerge from his feet.[2]

Although the casualties of the Somme created a demand for reinforcements which helped blur many old distinctions, British regiments remained resolutely different. The Grenadiers, the senior regiment of foot guards, trace their origins back to the Low Countries in the 1650s, when they were formed to guard Charles II, and in consequence have an enduring rivalry with the Coldstream Guards, who trace their descent from General George Monck's (Parliamentarian) Regiment of Foot. Three regular battalions strong in 1914, the Grenadiers raised a 4th battalion during the war. As one of the regiment's historians observed, 'they did not have a monopoly of discipline, smartness and professionalism in the BEF, but as an elite they did believe in the highest standards in all three, believe in them, demand them and maintain them whatever might be the circumstances and whatever the cost'.[3] A regimental history written forty years before the war had suggested that:

> The soldier in the hour of need and danger will ever be more ready to follow the officer and gentleman whom education, position in life, and accident of birth point out to be his natural leader . . . than the man who, by dint of study and brainwork, has raised himself (much to his own credit, certainly) from the plough or the anvil. In no profession should the feeling of *noblesse oblige* be more recognised than in the army . . .[4]

Noblesse indeed: one of the marked social changes in the army of the nineteenth century was that noblemen, once scattered widely across the army, had tended to concentrate in the Foot Guards and Household Cavalry. Of course there were exceptions. Major Christopher de Sausmarez, a peer's nephew, commanded 108th Heavy Battery Royal Garrison Artillery in 1914, and a baronet led one of his sections of two 60-pounder guns. The RGA had many distinctions but social exclusivity was not one of them, and a heavy battery gun-line was unfamiliar earth for sprigs of nobility. In 1914 the Grenadiers' officers included Lieutenant Colonel Lord Brabazon, Major the

Hon. Hubert Crichton, Captain Lord Guernsey, and Captain Lord Francis Montagu-Douglas-Scott. It was as understandable that Raymond Asquith, the prime minister's son who would die on the Somme, should join the Grenadiers as it was that the Prince of Wales should do the same. The officers

> all knew one another well; many, like Lord Bernard Gordon-Lennox, had married the sister of a brother officer (in this case Lord Loch); and many, like George Cecil, had succeeded their father in the regiment or, like Eben Pike or Bernard Gordon-Lennox again, were succeeded by their sons and grandsons.[5]

These ripples widened across the Household Division as a whole, as Rowland Feilding, then a captain in the Coldstream, discovered when he did his first tour of trench duty in May 1915.

> On either side of me I found relations. On my immediate left Percy Clive [a cousin] commanded a company of Grenadiers, and the Coldstream company on my right was commanded by Rollo [another cousin]. I visited Percy at 4.30 on the morning after our arrival. The last time I had seen him was at dinner in the House of Commons, and I was very glad to meet him again. While I was shaving, Rollo brought Henry Feilding [yet another cousin] to see me. He is with a squadron of King Edward's Horse, which is acting as Divisional Cavalry to a Territorial Division near here, and was paying a visit to Rollo in the trenches.

Rollo (later Lieutenant Colonel Viscount Feilding) survived the war. Captain Percy Clive MP was killed on 5 April 1918, and Captain the Hon. Henry Feilding died of wounds on 11 October 1917.[6]

Nor was this sense of identity confined to the officers. There were Grenadier families amongst the rank and file, and the warrant officers' and sergeants' mess was held together by bonds no less powerful than those which linked members of the officers' mess. It might take a guardsman two years to get his first promotion, and he would be lucky to make sergeant in less than ten. A regimental sergeant major's tour of duty was five years, and it was not unknown for Guards RSMs to ask for extensions, arguing that there was still more to be done with the battalion.[7]

The Grenadiers had a tangible quality, even to its rivals. Its soldiers were nicknamed Bill-Browns, as opposed to the Coalies, Jocks, Micks and Taffs of the other foot guards regiments. Private Stephen Graham, an educated man serving in the ranks of the Scots Guards, saw the Grenadiers assault stoutly-held German defences at the very end of the war.

> There were heavy losses suffered there by the attackers, especially by the Bill-Browns, whose discipline, courage and fame committed them then, as ever, to doing the impossible in human heroism and endurance. I lost a whole series of comrades or friends wounded or killed. C—, who had filled up a blank file with me in Little Sparta, was killed; S—, recruited from the S.E. Railway, a jolly, happy middle-aged man, who always hailed me as Steve and had a cheery word, was killed. H—, the American boy who used to dance all night at New York was wounded.[8]

In contrast, 4/Queen's was a territorial battalion of the Queen's Regiment, with a regular adjutant, regimental sergeant major and small permanent staff of regular NCOs: its other members were civilians, who soldiered in their spare time. It originated in a company of rifle volunteers formed at Croydon in 1859 in response to the threat of French invasion which had Tennyson earnestly declaiming 'Form, riflemen: riflemen, form . . .'. A second company was added in 1860 to form the 1st Surrey Administrative Battalion; this became the 2nd Surrey Rifle Volunteers seven years later and the 1st Volunteer Battalion the Queen's Royal West Surrey Regiment in 1881. It sent a company of five officers and 200 men to the Boer War, and in 1908 it was swept up in R. B. Haldane's creation of the Territorial Force to become 4th (Territorial) Battalion The Queen's Regiment, swapping its rifle-green uniforms for the scarlet of the line. Its historian suggested that it was the first territorial battalion to receive colours, presented by Lady Eldridge and Mrs Frank Watney, the wife of the commanding officer – a prominent local brewer when not engaged in his military duties.

Its men trained on weekday drill nights, one weekend each month and at a fortnight's annual camp. There were perennial problems in ensuring that employers gave men time off for camp, and compromises between day job and military identity meant that in the battalion's first year, 22 officers and 418 men attended the first week of camp at Brighton but only 13 officers and 241 men the second. In 1914 it found itself at camp, marching from Bordon to Salisbury Plain as part of a large territorial exercise, when war broke out. Mobilised on 5 August, it was sent to Chattenden, near Chatham. Like other territorial battalions it split, forming a first-line battalion, 1/4th, which rapidly departed for India, where it spent the whole war, seeing active service on the North-West Frontier. A second line, 2/4th, which included some men from the 1st Battalion who had not volunteered for foreign service and some wartime volunteers, eventually fought on the Western Front in 1918.

The third-line, 3/4th Queen's, containing officers and men from the other two battalions as well as wartime recruits, spent much of its war in southern England. In December 1914, D Company was billeted on the premises of Caleys, the court dressmakers, in Windsor High Street when a fire broke out: the lights failed, but men of the company escorted the seamstresses out of the dark and smoke-filled building, earning a fulsome letter of thanks from Mr Hugh Caley, the managing director, and less formal expressions of gratitude from the ladies. The battalion always had an easy style. When it was billeted in Reigate in January 1916 an earnest (though wisely anonymous) well-wisher told his commanding officer that:

> Refering (sic) to the health and cleanliness of this Battalion which has been very well kept up in the past, I must add that a certain Company are allowed to get dirty owing to the inconveniences of Local Baths going wrong. This Company has a bath room and are not allowed to use it. Trusting that this will soon be remedied.
>
> I remain
Yours obediently[9]

Private Richard Whatley persuaded his brother, a driver in the Army Service Corps, to apply to join the battalion, whether because of a genuine desire for life in the infantry or because he was in France and 3/4th was in Reigate it is impossible to say. Driver Whatley's letter was written in pencil and sent in a green official envelope which meant that it was not subject to censorship within his unit – a wise precaution as its contents might not have been regarded as a vote of confidence in his current management.

> Dear Sir   5/6/16
> I, Driver J. Whatley (T/94354) No 1 Company 4th Divisional Train A.S.C. British Expeditionary Force, France, take the great liberty of writing these lines to you in reference of my brother Private Richard Whatley (23729) B Company of your most noble regiment. I take the liberty of asking you if you could transfer me to the same regiment as that of what my brother belongs & also to the Same Company as I wish to soldier with him if it is at all possible as I think that it would be to our own advantage as well as that of the most noble Country we are fighting for. My enlistment age is 25 7/12 years but my proper age is 18 7/12 years. I enlisted in May 1915, & my height about 5: 6 or 7 inches & chest measurement just over 30 inches. Any more details I would be very pleased to send you, & hoping that I am not trespassing on your valuable time I close my short letter & remain
>
>   Your Umble Servant
>   Driver J Whatley[10]

The battalion at last went to the Western Front in 1917. It fought its one major battle at Zonnebeke in the Ypres salient on 4 October: all the twenty officers who attacked that day were killed or wounded, and so much of the fabric so carefully nurtured over two years was torn apart for ever. The commanding officer's typewritten list of officers and their next of kin bears repeated manuscript annotations showing killed and wounded. The same list reveals that by the time it went to France the battalion was already losing its regional character: only fifteen of its forty-four officers actually had next of kin in Surrey although there was a clear majority from south London and the Home Counties. There were two Irishmen, a Cornishman, and the padre (who already had a MC and was to add a DSO at

Zonnebeke) hailed from Newcastle. Most of the Surrey contingent came, like the commanding officer, from Croydon, and 3/4th Queen's enjoyed a warm relationship with the borough, whose citizens 'continued, as in the past, to take a great interest in the doings of this battalion . . . and among other benefits given, the receipt each Christmas in England and abroad of puddings and tobacco was much appreciated by the battalion'. Christmas 1917 was the battalion's last. It had turned over in killed, wounded and missing almost as many officers and men as had arrived in France seven months before (a worse casualty rate over such a short time than was sustained by some regular battalions), and was disbanded in February 1918, its soldiers posted off to other battalions.[11]

Lastly, 11/East Lancashire, proudly known as the Accrington Pals, was a New Army (properly 'Service') battalion, raised in late August and early September 1914 as a result of the mayor of Accrington's communication with the War Office, which accepted his offer of a locally-raised battalion. Recruiters set to work in Accrington, Burnley, Blackburn and Chorley, and all the powerful links within these bustling communities accelerated the process. For instance, H. D. Riley of Hawks House, Brierfield, Burnley, mill-owner and justice of the peace, had founded the Burnley Lads' Club for working-class boys in 1905: it had a library and reading room, and offered wide sporting opportunities. On 19 September Riley placed an advertisement in the *Burnley Express*, announcing that a Lads' Club Company was to be formed. Riley and seventy ex-members of the club enlisted the following Wednesday. There were not enough to form a full company, but the club members became part of D (Burnley and Blackburn) Company.

At this stage officers were nominated by the mayor, and Riley (hitherto without military experience) first became a lieutenant and the company's second in command, rising to captain and company commander a few days later. An eyewitness described how the company first formed.

> Miners, mill-hands, office-boys, black-coats, bosses, school-boys and masters, found themselves appearing before Mr Ross and the medical officer. Young men who should have been tied to their mother's apron-strings took home their

first service pay – 1/9d in coppers – and nearly broke
their mothers' hearts. Men of mature age, patriotic or
sensing adventure or to escape from monotony were ready
to have a go at anyone who should pull the lion's tail. The
thing was done! 250 men of good spirit and willing in
body assembled in the Drill Hall to be patiently told how
to 'form fours'.[12]

There were few trained officers or NCOs. Colonel Sharples, the
commanding officer, was sixty-four, and had joined the Rifle Volunteers over forty years before. RSM Stanton was sixty years old, had
once chased the Sioux with George Custer, fought the Zulus and
the Boers, and left the army in 1905; in 1914 this old soldier
answered the call for trained men, and he was to die of natural
causes the following year. Most of the officers were the sons of prominent citizens, and included one of the mayor of Accrington's grand-
sons. There was a sprinkling of ex-regulars among the NCOs, but
most had no military experience, and many were promoted before
they even had uniforms to sew their stripes to.

A. S. Durrant, who joined a New Army battalion of the Durham
Light Infantry at just this time, recalled that:

> I was sergeant six weeks after I joined up. You see, Kit-
> chener's Army was being built up, anybody with half a
> brain of common sense could get one stripe in no time.
> Your 2 stripes, 3 stripes. I tell you I was first a private and
> then a sergeant and I was put in charge of a hut.[13]

To the inexperienced young were added the all-too-veteran old, as
Lancelot Spicer discovered when he joined a New Army battalion of
the King's Own Yorkshire Light Infantry. He found that:

> All the men were in civilian clothes and all we had for
> training were wooden rifles. Apart from the officers, the
> only ones in uniform were a few non-commissioned
> officers who were regulars. The Commanding Officer was
> Lt. Col. Holland, a retired Indian Army officer . . . a pleas-
> ant enough old boy, but his soldiering appeared to us
> young raw recruits to be of the Indian Mutiny – in battalion
> parades he would ask in a loud voice. 'Mr Butler [the
> adjutant], how many white officers on parade?'[14]

The Accringtons were sent to Carnarvon in early 1915, and Colonel Sharples was quickly replaced as commanding officer by a regular, Major (temporary Lieutenant Colonel) A. W. Rickman of the Royal Northumberland Fusiliers. Rickman immediately made a good impression, as Lieutenant Rawcliffe observed:

> We were brought up to attention as Colonel Rickman rode up the street towards us. He had to pass a motor-lorry parked outside a shop. This narrowed the street and his horse shied. We all thought it was going through the shop window. Colonel Rickman beat the horse hard with his stick . . . to make it pass the motor-lorry. What a real display of strength and will-power. What an entrance! I thought, we're in for it now![15]

Private Pollard agreed. 'He was very smart, a true professional,' he declared. 'We were looking at a real soldier for the first time. We knew he would sort us out.'[16]

The battalion, in khaki uniforms which had replaced its original blue melton, spent much of 1915 on the move, from Rugely to Ripon, from Ripon to Larkhill and then, in December, to Devonport for the voyage to Egypt. It spent three undemanding months guarding the Suez canal before being sent to Marseilles for its railway journey to the Western Front. Part of 31st Division, it was allocated a leading role on the first day of the Somme, assaulting the village of Serre at the northern end of 4th Army's line.

What happened to the Accringtons that morning was to be matched in so many other places further down the front. The men went over the top, after shaking hands and wishing each other good luck, to find uncut wire, intact machine guns and a creeping barrage which they could never catch. Lance Corporal Marshall watched the destruction of his battalion and the changing of his world:

> I saw many men fall back into the trench as they attempted to climb out. Those of us who managed had to walk two yards apart, very slowly, then stop, then walk again, and so on. We all had to keep in a line. Machine-gun bullets were sweeping backwards and forwards and hitting the ground around our feet. Shells were bursting everywhere.

I had no special feeling of fear and I knew that we must all go forward until wounded or killed. There was no going back. Captain Riley fell after thirty yards ... the message passed down the line, from man to man – 'Captain Riley has been killed.'[17]

The Official History, its prose rising nobly to meet the occasion, reported that the attackers in this sector, pals' battalions from Hull, Leeds, Bradford, Barnsley, Durham and Sheffield, continued to advance even after the German SOS barrage crashed down.

There was no wavering or attempting to come back. The men fell in their ranks, mostly before the first hundred yards of No Man's Land had been crossed. The magnificent gallantry, discipline and determination shown by all ranks of this North Country division were of no avail against the concentrated fire effect of the enemy's unshaken infantry and artillery, whose barrage has been described as so consistent and severe that the cones of the explosions gave the impression of a thick belt of poplar trees.[18]

The German defensive barrage briefly switched to Serre itself. This may have been because the gunners knew some of the attackers had actually got that far. Skeletons in khaki rags were found there when the Germans pulled back from the village in 1917: some bore tarnished brass shoulder titles which read 'EAST LANCASHIRE'. The Accringtons lost 7 officers and 139 men killed, 2 officers and 88 men missing, believed killed, and 12 officers and 336 men wounded.[19] The battalion remained on the Western Front for the rest of the war, and while avoiding the disbandments of early 1918, and the fate which befell 3/4th Queen's, it was never the same as it had been at 7.30 on the morning of 1 July 1916. And neither, for that matter, was Accrington, which had lost too many of its dearest and its best that day.

These three battalions were not simply different in origin, tradition and composition. They behaved differently, in the line and out of it. The relations between their officers and men were different, and their approach to the war was different too. Second Lieutenant P. J. Campbell was appointed artillery liaison officer to a Grenadier battalion in 1917 and joined it in the trenches. Its commanding officer asked whether he had been to Eton and whether he was a regular: on receiving a negative answer to both questions:

> He appeared to take no further interest in me as a person, but I was impressed by him and what I saw that night. The discipline of the Guards was very strict and their behaviour even in the line very formal ... The Grenadier Guards went out, an English county regiment came in, and the difference was perceptible immediately. There was an atmosphere of warm-hearted banter, cheerful inefficiency; packs and gas-masks, revolvers and field-glasses were thrown about anyhow. Now we were all civilians who hated war, but knew that it had to be fought and would go on fighting until it was won.[20]

Major Charles Ward Jackson, an Etonian and Yeomanry officer serving on the staff, made the same point in a letter to his wife in June 1916. Some battalions seemed good enough.

> But we had not seen the Guards. You never saw such a difference. In the first place the officers all looked like gentlemen, and the men twice the size, and in the second their discipline is extraordinary. Different altogether from other regulars. Not a man sits down as you pass, no matter how far off you may be.[21]

Soldiers from other regiments who failed to salute properly as the Guards Division passed on the march were arrested and taken with it. At the day's end they were interviewed, had the error of their ways pointed out, and were invited to return whence they had come. Saluting improved for miles around. The Old Army's discipline could survive stern shocks. In the chaos following the battle of Le Cateau in August 1914, Lieutenant Roland Brice Miller, a regular officer in 123rd Battery Royal Field Artillery, described how:

> A private soldier of the Bedfordshire Regiment, grey with fatigue, approached me, came smartly to the slope [-arms]

and slapped the butt of his rifle in salute. 'Can you tell me a good position to retire to?' he asked. One man![22]

A battalion like 3/4th Queen's or the Accrington Pals was perfectly capable of laying on a smart formal parade, and there was a latent dandyism in many soldiers that found military ritual perversely satisfying. But guardee smartness was not their concern, and their discipline continued to reflect pre-war relationships. Private Bewsher of the Accringtons remembered that his company sergeant major, revolver in hand, had checked the shelters in the front-line trench for laggards before the attack on 1 July. 'He had no need to do that,' complained Bewsher. 'All the lads were ready to go.'[23] And while the regulars accepted robust discipline as a matter of course, territorials and New Army men, far more conscious of what they had once been, and, God willing, would be once again, were far less prepared to tolerate its more extreme manifestations such as Field Punishment No. 1.[24]

Sergeant Jock Chrystal of the Northumberland Hussars, a Yeomanry (territorial cavalry) regiment, reproved by his RSM, told his officer that he resented the rebuke. 'Now, Sor, did ye ivvor hear such cheek?' he asked. 'Him, Halliday, a Sergeant-Major jaist, an' me, the Duke's Forester, talkin' to me that way?'[25] It was not a remark which would have gone down well in the Grenadiers.

The different identities of regular, territorial and New Army units were blurred, though rarely wholly obscured, but casualties and the sheer caprice of battle meant that some units survived the war with their identity intact while others lost it relatively quickly. Captain James Dunn, that 'doctor with a DSO, and much unmedalled merit' who compiled the history of 2/Royal Welch Fusiliers, recorded his unit's evolution as its regular content steadily diminished. In early 1915 there were still enough old sweats about to delight the corps commander, Lieutenant General Sir Richard Haking, when he inspected the battalion: 'He chatted and chaffed, pinched their arms and ears, asked how many children they had, asked if they could be doing with leave to get another . . . When it was over he said to the GOC, "That's been a treat. That's the sort we've known for thirty years."'[26] Dunn reckoned that the battalion then had about 250 originals left, mainly in transport, drums, signals and amongst the NCOs. But by the summer of 1918 he admitted 'we were a regular battalion in name only'.[27] This is scarcely surprising, for the battalion suffered 1,107 killed, and four times as many wounded, amongst its non-commissioned personnel during its four years on the Western Front, getting through the whole of its 1914 establishment strength five times over. It was actually luckier than the New Army 10/Royal Welch Fusiliers, which lost 756 soldiers *killed* in only two and a half years at the front.

The Royal Welch Fusilier regimental depot at Litherland held officers and men from the regular, territorial and New Army battalions of the regiment, who had come from hospitals, long courses or recruiting offices. As Second Lieutenant Lloyd Evans discovered in 1916:

> They would be sifted and trained, and detailed singly or in batches to all fronts where Battalions of the Regiment were serving. In the huge mess were officers who had served with one or more of these battalions. There were 'returned heroes', so I thought of them, from the First and Second. Some struck me as being really heroic. Others were the talkative sort who worked to impress on 'these Service Battalion fellows' that 'of course it was somewhat different in the Regular Battalions'.

He had mixed feelings about being posted to the 2nd Battalion because 'it used up subalterns by the dozen', but found himself very happy in it.[28]

During the process of drafting the Welsh content of 2/Royal Welch Fusiliers seems to have increased. There had been a substantial Birmingham contingent in the pre-war battalion which led to outsiders, careless of their dentistry, calling it 'The Brummagem Fusiliers', and Captain Robert Graves recalled his CSM, a Birmingham man, giving a stern talking-to to a German prisoner caught with pornographic postcards in his pack. Dunn observed that a July 1917 draft comprising largely young South Wales Miners was 'much the best that has come to us of two years'. Nonetheless, only 37 percent of the battalion was Welsh-born.[29]

A survey of another regular battalion, 2/Durham Light Infantry, makes the same point. It mobilised at Whittington Barracks, Lichfield, in 1914, and took 27 officers and 1,000 men to France. A single day that September cost it more men than the entire Boer War, and during the whole of the First World War it suffered 5,313 casualties, which included 30 officers and 1,306 men killed.[30] The 2/Green Howards lost 1,442 officers and men killed in the war, 704 of them regulars, regular reservists or members of the Special Reserve. Of these experienced soldiers who were to be killed in the war just over half were killed in 1915, and over three-quarters had died by the end of that year.[31] Ralph L. Mottram, driving across the Somme back area in 1916, 'overtook an infantry regiment that bore my badge, and I looked in vain for any face I could recognise. But from out the ranks of the rear company rose a cheer, and I found that a few knew me. It was my own battalion, nearly all strangers . . .'.[32]

The pre-war regular infantryman who fought on the Somme was relatively uncommon, and the one who fought at Passchendaele was rarer still. But somehow battalions which the *Army List* described as regular did their best to behave like regulars. Lord Moran, Churchill's doctor in the Second World War, was medical officer to 1/Royal Fusiliers in the First. He noticed how: 'The battalion kept changing, seven colonels came and went and I could never school myself to grow indifferent to these gaps.'[33] The battalion was sorely tried on the Somme, but as it came out of the line:

> On the road we passed a Kitchener Battalion going up, they were resting by the roadside.
> 'Them's the First,' one of them remarked, and the men hearing the words straightened up and covered off.[34]

The first three armies that fought on the Western Front – Old, New and Territorial – were founded on voluntary recruiting. No less than 5,704,416 men – about a quarter of the adult male population of the United Kingdom – passed through the army during the war. Just under half, 2,446,719, were volunteers, and the remainder were conscripted by one of a series of Military Service Acts. The first came into force on 27 January 1916 and the vice was progressively tightened as the war went on.

The conscript army had no separate identity. The majority of its soldiers were infantry: the infantry was easily the largest single arm on the Western Front, and suffered the highest casualty rate of any major branch of the army.[35] Its soldiers were trained in the United Kingdom in battalions which, from the summer of 1916, steadily lost any genuine regimental identity: the 12th (Reserve) Battalion of the Welch Regiment became the 58th Training Reserve Battalion, the 230th (Graduated) Battalion and eventually the 51st (Graduated) Battalion of the South Wales Borderers.[36] As we have already seen, soldiers were trained wearing one cap badge, and then re-badged, as the demands of the front required, in the infantry base depots at Etaples. The regional identity of units in the other three armies was steadily eroded also. This reduced the damage done to British communities which had been such a feature of the early stages of the Somme, but it deprived battalions of some of the bonds which had linked their members in the past.

It is not surprising that the decline of regional recruiting affronted members of the Old Army. Company Sergeant Major Ernest Shephard of 1/Dorsets, as regimental as the proverbial button-stick, wrote on 21 August 1916:

> In the evening a lot of our old hands now attached to 2nd Wilts (who are in billets just over the bridge) came to see us. They are terribly upset on account of having to serve with the Wilts (some of them are men slightly wounded on July 1st) and they went to see our Adjt to ask whether they could not come back to their own regiments. Adjt promised to apply for them, but it will be useless. Why the responsible authorities do these things I cannot imagine. If a certain Regt is required to be reinforced quickly and none of their own are available, the matter is explained. But we well know that after our smash on July 1st strong reinforcements were sent for us, and on arrival at the Base they were diverted, some to 2nd Wilts, some to Hampshires, etc., and we received men of Hampshires as reinforcements instead of our own. And so the merry game goes on. Some big pot is drawing a large salary for such muddling work as this, ruining the one thing which

has kept our army going so well, i.e. 'Pride of Regiment', 'Esprit de Corps'.[37]

The 2/Royal Welch Fusiliers had its losses in the fighting at High Wood on the Somme made up by 540 reinforcements, volunteers and conscripts, many 'unlikely to stay the more exacting rigours of service in the field'. There were Cheshires, Shropshires and South Wales Borderers, who, as Captain James Dunn of the Royal Welch Fusiliers wrote, 'arrived restful of their transfer and resented by us'.[38] An old soldier of 1/Black Watch, widely known as Black Jock, returned to his battalion after being wounded. He was soon posted as a deserter: it transpired that he had deserted from Etaples to get back to his battalion, fearing that he might be sent amongst strangers. And his battalion, knowing well that tartan was stronger than regulations, duly expunged the 'crime'.

The war's voracious appetite for infantry led to soldiers from other arms being compulsorily transferred. This led to difficulties because, for instance, well-qualified private soldiers in the Royal Engineers drew more pay than sergeants in the infantry. Sapper George Swinford records that in mid-1916:

> I passed all my exams in sapping, mining, knots and lashings, demolitions and bridge building, and was waiting to go to the River Conway to do pontoon bridging which was the last thing. Then on Sunday morning notices were put up that every man in the camp was to be on parade at ten o'clock . . . away we all went to Kenmel Park where were attached to the Royal Welch Fusiliers.[39]

News that the sappers were entitled to extra pay unsurprisingly caused bad feelings amongst the infantry sergeants, 'who said that they would make us earn it'. After large-scale collective absenteeism, which produced a week's worth of trials, Private (as he now was) Swinford was rebadged again and sent to France, where he joined 11/South Lancashire, spending the rest of the war with that battalion.

Sometimes the process of assimilation was rough. Norman Gladden joined 7/Royal Northumberland Fusiliers on the Somme in September 1916. 'To add to our discomforts,' he recalled,

The new draft was received by the battalion without cere-
mony or any sort of induction. We were absorbed by our
company like bodies being sucked down into a morass
and made to feel as if we had no rights at all.

Posted to 11/Royal Northumberland Fusiliers a year later when he
returned to the front after being invalided home, he was much
happier: the Lewis gunners he joined were 'a likeable group, who
made me feel at home straight away'.[40] Often the new policy worked
better than many old sweats would have expected. Men needed the
sense of belonging, and battalions which took the trouble to make
new arrivals feel welcome usually reaped the benefit. Lieutenant
Colonel Eric Segrave, who commanded 1/15th London Regiment
until promoted to command a brigade in August 1918, made a
point of shaking hands with all new arrivals, regardless of rank, and
left a first-rate battalion to his successor, Rowland Feilding, who
immediately told his wife:

> They are like little lions – these London men ... The
> standard of courage among these London lads is so high
> that men who would be considered brave elsewhere do
> not seem particularly brave here.[41]

In contrast, Corporal Clifford de Boltz, posted to 1/Norfolk in
France from 2/6th Norfolk, a cyclist battalion, found his draft 'given
some rations and told to lie in a field for the night'. They 'gradually
merged into the Regt.'[42]

We cannot even tell to which regiment Percy Smith was posted
in 1917, but we do know that he was not happy when he arrived in
France. On 18 September he told his family that: 'if the relatives
and wives of us boys knew the real state of affairs out here they would
worry more and more and most likely there would be an unrest in
the country', and he prayed his brother Vic might be spared his fate.
But he was proud of his battalion:

> The Regiment I am in is a fighting Regt & we are always
> on the move we never stay at one place long, it was the
> first Regt out here when war was declared & we have some
> fine fellows. Fritz sure knows when we are about.[43]

Frederick Hodges attended Northampton Grammar School, and followed the fortunes of older boys and masters who had joined the army: one came home 'full of shrapnel . . . We were thrilled.' Hodges was later 'amazed how attractive all this information about the war was to under-age boys . . . One thing was certain . . . we must, we MUST be fit, so that we would pass A1 when the long awaited day came'.[44] He joined the Northamptons in July 1917, and was sent to France, with so many other eighteen year olds, in the crisis following the German offensive of March 1918. On arrival in France:

> We were lined up in a very long single line. We were then counted off into groups destined for different battalions. Friends who stood in line next to one another were parted by a hand and an order, and marched off to different Regimental Base Headquarters. There were bell tents in a long line, where particulars were taken, and to our surprise, new regimental numbers were given to us . . .
>
> In this peremptory way, I and about 300 others suddenly became Lancashire Fusiliers, while some of our friends became Manchesters or Duke of Wellington's or East Yorkshires . . .

He was posted to 10/Lanashire Fusiliers, where he was well received by the fiercely Irish Company Sergeant Major Doolan, 'a regular soldier, one of the very few of the original British Expeditionary Force who had survived to this stage of the war'. He was soon calling his battalion 'T'owd Tenth', and was anxious to get his new cap badge.

Hodges finished the war a corporal, and proudly returned home to Northampton in full fig.

> My khaki uniform was stained and worn, but my belt shone, my buttons gleamed, and my khaki tunic bore the colourful insignia of my regiment, brigade and division. On my epaulettes I wore the green and black tabs of battalion gas NCO with the brass fusilier bomb and the brass letters LF.
>
> On my upper arms above my Corporal's stripes, the Battalion sign, an oblong yellow flash and the 52nd Brigade sign, a green square 52, and above these and just

below my epaulettes, the 17th Divisional sign, a white dot and dash on a red background. My mother said it was quite colourful.[45]

In his assessment of the reasons for the Allied victory, Frederick Hodges suggested that 'the dogged courage and will to win at whatever the cost' was more important than 'superior military arts and skills'. He identified 'unquenchable spirit, the sticky and the earthy wit of the infantryman at war, who, though he was a mere pawn in the plans of generals, yet remained an individual who served ideals; and for those ideals, faced death daily at some chance or mischance of war with courage in the line of duty'. Hodges may have been more idealistic than many, but he came close to identifying the qualities which helped keep what was now a national army together in the last year of a long war.

OLD WORLD, OLD ARMY

'Then the "Dead March", and what a nightmare,' wrote Will Fisher.

> We draw on leather gloves, lift a body onto a sheet of brattice cloth, wrap it up, then tie it to a stretcher. 'Off with it, boys', and what a journey, even to us ... And the stupefying heat and bad air, causing the sweat to pour down one in streams, and to add to the romance the sickening stench, rising all the time to the face of the man behind. In one place, wading to our knees in water, one man fell with the stretcher. Some bodies are heavy too, our wrists giving out before the two miles are covered ... 'Who is it?' 'Don't know, indeed', on we go ... Twenty have so far been buried unidentified, owing to melting ...
>
> The pity of it all, that flesh should be so cheap.[46]

This could so easily be a scene from the Western Front, perhaps in a flooded trench at Festubert in the spring of 1915, or on the northern slopes of Longueval Ridge at the end of the Somme, but it is not. Will Fisher is describing the Senghenydd mining disaster of 1913, in the heart of the South Wales coalfields, in which 439 men died. Fisher had just come off shift, but immediately went underground again to help with the rescue operations. We will meet him again, lifelong socialist but successful and committed soldier: there was less inconsistency in that than some would have us believe. For the moment, though, let him usher us into the cramped and sweaty basement of what Barbara Tuchman called 'The Proud Tower', the world that went to war in 1914.

It is easy to romanticise Edwardian England as just one long afternoon where it was always strawberries and cream at Henley, shooting parties at Sandringham, dinner at Quaglino's and a breathless hush in the close as young Corinthians laid willow to leather. A gentleman could travel from London to Paris and on to Berlin and St Petersburg in the comfort of his Pullman carriage with the minimum of formalities and little risk. Churches were well attended, though earlier talk of a national religious revival now seemed misplaced. Sensible chaps like Alfred Hale could live quiet but comfortable lives on investment income. There might be a morning in the library, lunch in the club in St James', then a first-class carriage on the ever-reliable 4.48 from Waterloo to Petersfield, and a cab from the station to find a glass of nut-brown Amontillado and one of Mrs Ling's pies, in all its savoury splendour, waiting at home.

Even a little further down the social scale a satisfying and predictable routine could be found. J. B. Priestley left school to become a junior clerk in the wool trade, working for Helm and Co. in Swan Lane, Bradford. His day began at 9.00 and ended at 6.00, 6.30 or even 7.00 p.m., though if he stayed that late there was an extra 6d in the pay packet for 'tea away'. He smoked Cut Black Cavendish in his pipe, 3½d an ounce from Salmon and Gluckstein's, and wrote prose and poetry at home, enjoying the 'irregular rhythm of effort and relaxation'. Looking back on his youth he could not disguise his affection for the old world. 'I belong at heart to the pre-1914 North Country . . .' he wrote; 'something at the core of me is still in Market Street hearing the Town Hall chimes'.[47]

But we do not need to look very much harder to see the cracks in the masonry. The labour movement was growing stronger by the year: there were 422 strikes in 1909, 834 in 1912, and 1,459 in 1913: there would have been a General Strike in 1914 had war not intervened. Class divisions within Britain were still accepted by many, though there was growing rancour. On 23 January 1917 Corporal

Will Fisher, already feeling the symptoms of the tuberculosis that would kill him, wrote:

> Want to go through to the end, feel fit enough. Anniversary of enlisting two years ago. DEATH OF MY BOY GEORGE. The lad is better off; he is free from wage slavery and the insults of class rule.[48]

John Simpson Kirkpatrick, one of the heroes of the Australian fight for Gallipoli, was a merchant seaman from Tyneside who jumped ship in Sydney in 1909. In 1912 he told his mother:

> I wonder when the work men of England will wake up and see things as other people see them. What they want in England is a good revolution and that will clear out some of the Millionaires and lords and Dukes out of it and then with a Labour Government they will be almost able to make their own conditions.[49]

And if the Bradford community described by J. B. Priestley was 'closer to a classless society than anyone born in southern England can ever understand', there was a desperate underclass which even junior clerks seldom saw. John Cusack's mother brought up five children in two ground-floor rooms in a Glasgow tenement. There was no bathroom, and just a cold water tap and grate in the kitchen. His father and mother slept in the bed, and the children on the floor of a room eight feet square. The family went to a public wash house once a week. After his father emigrated to America the family was barely able to survive.

> For dinner at midday we'd probably have some broken biscuits which you could buy for a ha'penny a packet or we might have a ha'penny worth of hot chips from the fish and chip shop. A portion of fish cost tuppence, which was too dear for dinner . . .
>
> I hardly ever wore any shoes. I used to wear short pants made of corduroy for a Sunday otherwise of flannel. They were never new, unless you were the eldest child. You simply fell into your brother's clothes. I would wear a little flannel shirt of a dark colour, a jacket and what we'd call

a bonnet or hookerdon, a cap which I pulled down well over one eye.[50]

Underwear was uncommon – John Cusack's comrades found their army issue vests and drawers items 'previously unknown to us'. In working-class households where it did exist it had to last a full week between washes. It is small wonder that wartime rationing significantly improved the diet and health of families such as these.

In July 1901 Arthur Osburn was a medical student at Guy's Hospital, just back from serving as a volunteer private in the Boer War, an experience which helps account for the bitter flavour of his memoirs. It was decades before the founding of the National Health Service, and the very poor depended for their medical treatment on the charity of doctors and senior medical students. Osburn was on duty in a Bermondsey slum. 'Outside in the shabby court the heated air quivered,' he wrote:

> Odours of hops, tanneries, horse dung and wood pavement inextricably blended. The mean tumbledown dwelling I was in buzzed with flies, while the frowsy smell of unclean bedding was everywhere; here and there the familiar chain of brown vermin crawled from the loose and half-rotten skirting boards upwards onto the greasy walls. A thin wailing sound was coming down the steep rickety staircase from a room above – one of the spate of unwanted infants which plague the slums and which I had helped bring into the world, wondering at the time whether the snuffling, puling bundle of misery would not have done better to have got itself born in an African jungle.
>
> 'That makes fifteen, and I've buried nine, sir,' the mother had said. The midwife, nodding confidentially at me, had suggested a bootlace or lying the unwanted one down on a blanket. Full of youthful rigidity and righteousness I had sternly threatened her with the coroner if the child was not alive the next day.[51]

William Woodruff grew up in a Lancashire cotton town about ten years later. His father worked in the mill, and family life was typical of that of many manual workers, a notch up from the tenement underclass but still with precious little room for financial manoeuvre.

My brother Dan and I shared a bedroom with our parents. There were two metal beds with straw mattresses resting on thin metal slats . . . Dan and I slept in the same bed. We slept so close to our parents that we could touch them. The nearness of our bodies made us feel safe. I accepted my parents' love-making long before I understood it. It was as natural as somebody using the pisspot . . . It didn't disturb me, or confuse me, or revolt me. Like my father's deep snoring, I ignored it. Living in such a confined space meant everybody shared in everybody else's joys and sorrows.[52]

Joseph Garvey, born in Halifax in 1888 to an Irish immigrant family, was four years old when he lost his father in a quarry accident. There were no benefits, just a collection from fellow workers and the proceeds of a benefit dance which brought in less than £10, and his mother had to raise six children. 'It was a hard life for her,' he reflected, 'all work and no play, no rest. She was a small woman with long dark auburn hair, and a fresh complexion. Good looking, but she was not built on strong lines.' She died in 1902, and Garvey eventually got a job as an assistant machine minder at 24 shillings a week, good money indeed.[53] Dover-born George Fortune, one of nine children,

left school at fourteen and got a job as a lather boy. It was a first class shop, they used to charge 4d for a haircut . . . My wages were 3/6d a week – 8 am to 8pm, Saturday 8 am till midnight. I cleaned all the windows, scrubbed out the shops, cleaned two copper urns, one for morning, one for afternoon. I never had metal polish to clean them with – paraffin oil and whitening . . .

I used to do this kind of work in the cellar. It was very dark there – he would not let me have a light during the day. He liked me to sweep up after customers and brush them down; take his little boy to school and bring him home; tease out dirty old combings that old ladies used to bring to have them made up into wigs; set the razors.[54]

If life was hard in the shadow of dark satanic mills, the countryside was not always green and pleasant for its occupants. Life on the land was changing as machines began to replace men, eventually 'to sacrifice the community and the connected way of life on the twin altars of speed and greed'.[55] H. J. Massingham wrote of 'the ruin of a closely-knit society with its richly interwoven and traditional culture that had denied every change, every aggression except the one that established the modern world'.[56] In *Lark Rise to Candleford* Flora Thompson described her own village, Juniper Hill in North Oxfordshire, unaware that hers was a picture of a world that was changing for ever. Most men in the village lived off the land, with their own hierarchy of farm labourers, ploughmen, carters, shepherds, stockmen and blacksmiths, and nicknames like 'Bishie', 'Pumpkin' or 'Boamer'. Labourers received 10 shillings a week, skilled workers 2 shillings more. They ate one hot meal a day, usually stewed vegetables reinforced with a little bacon, for all households maintained a family pig, killed, bloodily and noisily, during the first two quarters of the moon, for the meat from a pig killed beneath a waning moon was believed to shrink in cooking.

Many farming youngsters were 'thickset, red-faced men of good medium height and enormous strength . . .'. Their older workmates 'stooped, had gnarled and swollen hands and walked badly, for they felt the effects of a life spent out of doors in all weathers . . .'. Endurance was their favourite virtue: 'Not to flinch from pain or hardship was their ideal.' Their womenfolk were as tough, and 'a young wife would say to the midwife after her first confinement, "I didn't flinch, did I? Oh, I hope I didn't flinch."' They did not begrudge their employer his beef and port: he was 'Not a bad 'ole sort . . . an' does his bit by the land.' Their rancour was reserved for his bailiff, '"Muster Morris" to his face but "Old Monday" or "you ole devil" behind his back.' Boys sometimes did a stretch in the army before returning, or going off to seek work in a town. In 1914 Juniper Hill, like so many other villages, did not flinch, and sent its young men, Flora's brother among them, to the war. 'Eleven out of that little community never came back again,' lamented Flora.

> A brass plate on the wall of the church immediately over the old end house seat is engraved with their names. A double column, five names long, then, last and alone, the name of Edwin.[57]

Illegitimate births were unknown in 'Lark Rise' in the 1880s, but became frequent soon afterwards. They generally passed without much comment, but when young Emily blamed the son of the house where she had been in service for her condition there was widespread support for her. The youth was able to prove that he had been away from home at the relevant time, and Emily went on to raise a large family without benefit of husband. In Glasgow there was an overall illegitimacy rate of 7 percent in 1913, and in the very poor Blackfriars district this rose to 15.6 percent of all births. The city's Medical Officer of Health reported that year that he feared that about 8 percent of poor children were infected with syphilis.[58] About 200 per 1,000 infants failed to survive the first year of life in many of Britain's large industrial towns, and many that did grew up with hollow chests and rickety limbs. Overall, 60 percent of volunteers for the Boer War had been rejected as physically unfit, and even in 1918, when military medical standards were at rock bottom, over a million men were graded unfit for front-line service.[59] There was a close correlation between social class and physical fitness. A pre-war survey of Cambridge undergraduates found 70 percent in the fittest group, Class I; 20 percent in Grade II, 7.5 percent in Grade III and just 2.5 percent in Grade IV. But in Britain as a whole in 1917 only 34 percent of recruits examined were actually Grade I, and those from urban areas with high infant mortality rates fared even worse.[60]

Thomas Atkins was no stranger to death. His siblings died in infancy from illnesses which would now be prevented by vaccination or cured by antibiotics. His workmates perished from a variety of accidents and diseases, and the prevalence of infection meant that even a simple cut could prove fatal. Most people then died at home, and in many households bodies were laid out in open coffins before burial. Funerals were rituals of enormous significance, for they said much about the status of the bereaved family and, by extension, of the neighbourhood.

> The cut of the mourning clothes and of the funeral baked
> meats, the number of mutes and the number of plumes,
> the wreaths – who sent them and how much they cost: all
> the details evoke families anxious to provide as impressive

> a display as possible, and neighbours determined to see
> that they did.[61]

Most working-class families paid into burial and sick clubs, the latter to ensure a basic income if the breadwinner fell ill, and the former to avert the crowning insult of a pauper's funeral.

Although most working-class communities generated a powerful sense of identity and shared values, they were by no means as crime-free as they appear in rosy retrospect. Drunkenness and its frequent concomitant wife-beating were common, and there was frequent violence, often on a small scale but sometimes, especially in Glagsow, where Catholic versus Protestant riots occurred, on a much larger scale. Even the small Hampshire brewery town of Alton (where I spent my middle years) was once so violent that policemen patrolled in pairs. The police were widely unpopular, and at least one of the reasons for widespread suspicion of the Military Police amongst First World War soldiers was an attitude forged in civilian life.

There were urgent political issues too. Lloyd George's radical 'Peoples' Budget' of 1906, which raised taxes to pay for social reforms, including old age pensions, had been passed at the cost of confrontation with the Lords, whose powers were reduced by the 1911 Parliament Act. Suffragettes campaigning for votes for women risked death for their beliefs. The apparent imminence of Home Rule for Ireland encouraged thousands of Ulstermen to arm and drill, and the so-called Curragh Mutiny of March 1914 originated in the possibility that the army might be used to coerce the North when Home Rule was granted. In June 1914 David Lloyd George, chancellor of the exchequer (and as unreliable a prophet of the future as he was to prove a commentator on the past), assured London's business leaders that the international skies had never been bluer. The government was far more concerned about domestic issues, and there seemed little doubt that it was right.

The Old Army mirrored this divided world. It had never been the mass army that French or German conscripts would have recognised, with middle-class men serving in rank and file alongside industrial workers or farm labourers. French infantryman Henri Barbusse tells us how:

> Schoolteachers are rifle company NCOs or medical order-
> lies. In the Regiment, a Marist friar is a sergeant in the
> medical section; a tenor, the major's cyclist; a lawyer, the
> colonel's secretary; a landlord, mess-corporal in head-
> quarter company.[62]

Stephen Westmann, a German medical student called up in 1914,
described his own army as:

> a kind of mixing bowl, where young men from all classes
> of the population met and had to adjust themselves to an
> extremely rigid discipline. The aim was to create a team
> spirit; of course, there were square pegs who did not or
> would not fit into round holes and who let their side
> down.[63]

In addition to being polarised by class, the British army was small.
In August 1914 it had 247,432 regular officers and men against an
authorised establishment of 256,798. The army reserve, ex-regulars
who had completed their service but were liable to recall in
the event of war, numbered 145,347. The Special Reserve, whose
members had carried out six months' full-time training, topped up
with two weeks a year, was 63,933 strong, and the Territorial Force
had 268,777 officers and men against a theoretical strength of
316,094. The grand total, including the Channel Islands Militias and
the Bermuda and Isle of Man Volunteers, was 733,514[64] – tiny by
the standards of Britain's allies and opponents alike. Germany had
a standing army of 700,000 men in peacetime, inflated to 3.8 million
on mobilisation, and French figures (in her case swollen by colonial
troops) were roughly comparable. The French and German armies
would receive regular reinforcements as successive classes of conscripts came of age; both were used to training and equipping men
on a large scale, and had thought (though their conclusions were
different) about how best to integrate reservists and regulars.

They were, in short, armies which reflected the societies from
which they sprang, and were geared to continental war. The British
army did neither of these things. While British generals of the
war have been subjected to persistent critical attention, some justified and some not, the politicians who both supported a military

rapprochement with France, likely to produce British involvement in a major war, and maintained exactly the sort of army suited to wage small wars rather than large ones have been let off more lightly. Osbert Sitwell, aesthete and foot guards officer, was inclined to be less forgiving. 'Even today you see references to the immense achievements of the Liberal administration of 1906–14,' he wrote,

> but can any government whose policy entails such a lack of preparation for war as to make that seeming solution of difficulties a gamble apparently worthwhile for an enemy, and this leads to the death or disablement of two million fellow-countrymen . . . Can any government which introduces old age pensions, so as 'to help the old people' and then allows half the manhood of the country to be slaughtered or disabled before it reaches thirty years of age, be considered to have been either benevolent or efficient?[65]

The BEF of 1914 was sired by the Boer War out of the redcoat army that Wellington would have recognised. After peaking at around a quarter of a million men in the year of Waterloo, the army had settled down to an annual strength of around 180,000 men, about a third of them stationed in India. The purchase of commissions was abolished in 1871, branding was also abolished that year and flogging (except in military prisons) in 1881. Edward Cardwell, Secretary of State for War 1868–75, embarked upon a series of reforms which were completed by his successor. To boost recruiting, perennially sticky in peacetime, enhance the status of the soldier in society, and create a system which would link battalions serving abroad with their training and recruiting bases in the United Kingdom, the old numbered regiments of the line, with loose regional affiliations, were combined into county regiments.

The first twenty-five line infantry regiments already had two regular battalions and were left untouched: the remainder were amalgamated. Usually the marriages were logical, if not always happy: the 37th (North Hampshire) was amalgamated with the 67th (South Hampshire) to form the Hampshire Regiment, and the 28th (North Gloucestershire) was a logical bedfellow for the 61st (South Gloucestershire). There were some ruffled tartans elsewhere: the 73rd (Highland) was swallowed by the 42nd (Royal Highland) in the Black Watch, and the 75th (Stirlingshire) was devoured by the 92nd (Gordon Highlanders). We cannot be quite sure what the 99th (The Prince of Wales's Tipperary Regiment) made of its amalgamation with the 62nd (Wiltshire) to form the Duke of Edinburgh's Wiltshire Regiment, but we can guess. Depots, many of them red-brick pseudo-keeps, sprang up in many towns. Le Marchant Barracks in Devizes, named after a hero of Salamanca, housed the Wiltshires; Brock Barracks in Reading, commemorating Sir Isaac Brock, who brought some much-needed lustre to the War of 1812, accommodated the Berkshires, and Roussillon Barracks in Chichester, named after a French regiment whose plumes had allegedly been captured at Quebec, was the Royal Sussex depot.

Cardwell's army with its linked battalions, one at home and one abroad, was optimised for Queen Victoria's little wars. It was less well suited for a long war against the Boers. There were too few regulars, and although that hardy perennial, a combination of patriotic sentiment and local economic recession, encouraged tens of thousands of young men to volunteer, the performance of some war-raised units was patchy. Kipling wrote of:

> Cook's son, Duke's son,
> Son of a belted Earl,
> Forty thousand horse and foot
> Going to Table Bay . . .

The reality was less splendid. Wags quipped that the brass IY shoulder-title worn by the Imperial Yeomanry really stood for 'I Yield', and the lugubrious ditty 'The Boers have got my Daddy' became all too popular in music halls. It is probably true to say that neither the German nor the French armies, many of whose officers gained a good deal of pleasure from watching the lion's tail getting twisted, would have done much better, and the eventual British victory owed much to the experience of colonial campaigning elsewhere. But it was clear that the army required thoroughgoing reform. It had been compelled to field almost 450,000 men to win, losing 5,774 killed in action and 16,168 to disease or wounds.

Reforms, however, were sporadic. In the immediate aftermath of the Boer War Field Marshal Lord Roberts, the commander in chief, pressed ahead with the development of the Short Magazine Lee-Enfield rifle and the quick-firing artillery which the army was to take to war in 1914, giving a crucial impetus to marksmanship training. But William St John Brodrick, the Secretary of State for War, had a rougher ride. He had a grandiose scheme for a substantial increase in the size of the army, but his Cabinet colleagues would not allow him to consider conscription in order to sustain this new force and it became clear that voluntary recruitment would not meet its needs. Brodrick departed, his only legacy the bitterly-unpopular peakless cap which bore his name. 'We thoroughly detested this new cap,' recalled Frank Richards,

> which the majority of men said made them look like bloody German sailors, but we much preferred it to the poked cap which followed it ... When this cap first appeared the men said that the War Office was being run from Potsdam. They were rotten caps to carry in a man's haversack.[66]

Brodrick was replaced by Mark Arnold-Forster. He initially hoped to save money by sharply reducing volunteer and auxiliary forces (how history repeats itself), but was seen off by opponents in both Houses, and although he had more success with his 'New Army Scheme', based on a mix of long and short service, the Conservative government fell before substantial changes could be made.

Yet the period was by no means sterile. Although the report of the Royal Commission on the South African War was delivered in 1903 at the time of a political crisis which limited its impact, Lord Esher, one of its members and a close associate of the king, had chaired a small committee which made several useful proposals. Amongst them were the strengthening of the Committee of Imperial Defence and the addition of a permanent secretariat; the restructuring of the army's command structure by the abolition of the post of commander in chief and the creation of an Army Council with a chief of the general staff as its professional head with the adjutant general, quartermaster general, master general of the ordnance, permanent under secretary and financial secretary as its members. The three main branches of the general staff were created – the directorates of Army Training, Staff Duties and Military Operations. Indeed, the general staff thus created remains recognisable at the time of writing.[67]

R. B. Haldane, Secretary of State in Asquith's Liberal Cabinet, was a German-educated lawyer who brought formidable intellectual gifts to his task. At the first meeting of the Army Council after taking office, Haldane was asked what sort of army he envisaged. 'An Hegelian army,' was his reply, and with that, he observed, the 'conversation rather fell off'. Indeed, there was a philosophical logic to his scheme. He hoped to create a genuinely national army, with its regulars constituting 'a sharp point of finely tempered steel', its Special Reserve providing immediate back up, and the Territorial Force furnishing a basis for expansion and support. Haldane was lucky in several respects. His government could expect to run a full term, so time was not pressing; he chose as his military advisers Gerald Ellison and Douglas Haig, who had a very good grasp of organisational politics; and the Esher reforms were already beginning to bear fruit.

Although Haldane later argued that his reforms were overshadowed by his knowledge of the Anglo-French staff talks, the instrument he created was not forged with a specific purpose in view, but was simply the best he could do within his reduced budget. It would consist of two distinct entities: a regular element, geared to producing an expeditionary force of six infantry divisions and a cavalry division, and a part-time Territorial Force, formed by combining the various militia, volunteer and auxiliary forces, which would take responsibility for home defence, thereby freeing up the regulars for foreign service. He reverted to the Cardwell terms of enlistment, seven or eight years' service with the colours and four or five on the reserve. Haldane's reforms did not please everyone, and the National Service League loudly proclaimed that nothing but compulsory service would do. Such a step was politically unacceptable to what was, at least by the standards of the age, a left-leaning Cabinet, and Haldane had done the best he could within his constraints.

Wellington would have recognised the regular army that emerged from Haldane's reforms because, in many key respects, it had changed little since his day. The majority of men who enlisted as private soldiers were unemployed when they joined, and few even laid claim to a trade on their enlistment papers. One 1913 recruit admitted frankly that it was 'unemployment and the need for food' that encouraged him to join. John Cusack enlisted in the Highland Light Infantry when he was fourteen, telling the recruiting sergeant he was eighteen: urchins shouted 'beef and a tanner a day' as the recruits marched past, suggesting that that was why they had joined the army.[68] His mother reclaimed him and took him home, but three weeks later he signed on again, this time in the Royal Scots Greys.

What is striking about those pre-war regulars who have left some record of their motives is just how many were attracted by more than a full belly and a good pair of boots. Herbert Wootton recalled that he was:

> Very keen on becoming a soldier. I had two uncles, both regulars who had served through the South African War of 1899–1902. As a youngster I was thrilled with their stories. I became a keen reader of G. A. Henty's books on war, and later read Rudyard Kipling's books. I loved to be in the company of old soldiers.[69]

R. A. Lloyd 'had always wanted to be a soldier, and a cavalryman at that'.[70] Frank Richards grew up in the South Wales coalfield, and his cousin David joined the army during the miners' strike of 1898. But despite 'all the Socialist propaganda' he was 'a rank Imperialist at heart', and joined the Royal Welch Fusiliers because:

> they had one battalion in China, taking part in the suppression of the Boxer Rising, and the other battalion in South Africa, and a long list of battle honours on their Colours, and . . . they were the only regiment in the Army privileged to wear the flash. The flash was a smart bunch of five black ribbons sewed in a fan shape in the back of the tunic collar, it was a relic of the days when soldiers wore their hair long, and tied up the end of the queue in a bag to prevent it from greasing their tunics.[71]

Uniform also helped attract R. G. Garrod. He was a junior clerk when he saw 'a gorgeous figure in blue with yellow braid and clinking spurs and said to myself "that's for me . . .".'[72] William Nicholson, whose grandfather had charged with the 13th Light Dragoons at Balaklava, 'was attracted by the full-dress uniform of mounted regiments', and joined the Royal Horse Artillery in 1911.[73] John Lucy and his brother Denis went 'a bit wild' after their mother's death and duly joined up.

> We were tired of landladies and mocked the meaning of the word. We were tired of fathers, of advice from relations, of bottled coffee essence, of school, of newspaper offices. The soft accents and slow movements of the small farmers who swarmed in the streets of our dull southern Irish town, the cattle, fowl, eggs, butter, bacon and the talk of politics filled us with loathing.[74]

They were 'full of life and the spirit of adventure . . .'. Joseph Garvey, too, was:

> obsessed with a desire to get out into the world . . . I was looking to the new life with joyful anticipation. Being fit, strong and athletic I could not see anything that would prevent me from enjoying the life of a soldier. So ended one phase of my life, and despite all the head shaking at my foolishness in throwing up a good job, I had no doubt in my own mind that I was doing the right thing.[75]

Training was hard. John Lucy thought its strain 'so hard that many broke under it'.

> The military vocabulary, minor tactics, knowledge of parts of the rifle, route marches, fatigues, semaphore, judging distance, shooting, lectures on '*esprit de corps*', and on the history of our regiment, spit and polish, drill, saluting drill, physical training, and other, forgotten subjects were rubbed into us for the worst six months of my life . . . In time we effaced ourselves. Our bodies developed and our backs straightened according to plan . . . Pride of arms possessed us, and we discovered that our regiment was a regiment, and then some.[76]

A man survived easiest if he set out to conform. Joseph Garvey joined the Scots Guards, and found himself on the sixteen-week-long recruits' course at Caterham.

> The drill was exacting, no slackness was permitted on or off the square. I began to understand the reason for iron discipline and fell into line at once, and tried to make myself a good soldier. Handling arms was not easy the way they had to do it, but it soon became natural and at the end of the sixteen weeks I was quite ready to take over the guard duty . . .
>
> We proved to be a good squad and we passed out with credit. The Sergeant and Corporal were pleased with us.[77]

Cavalrymen had the added challenge of mastering horse as well as arms. 'Each of the horses had a number,' recalled R. G. Garrod,

> And mine was 52, and I suppose I then and there fell in love with her. She was under fifteen hands, had the heart of a lion, would try to jump anything possible and if a sword was cut down the side of her eyes would never flinch or run.

She had to be groomed twice a day. 'First sponge out eyes, nose and dock,' wrote Private Garrod, 'then pick out feet, then start to brush, using only the brush on the horse, while the curry comb, held in the left hand, was only used for cleaning the brush.' He was reminded that horses were more important than men: 'they could get a new man for 1/- a day, but a horse cost £40'.[78] After passing off the recruit ride he was promoted to the first-class ride, with sword, spurs, rifle and the two reins of his double bridle. By the end of it 'we were extremely well trained in horsemanship, doing attack riding, vaulting, which entails jumping off your horse at full gallop and leaping up again into the saddle. We took jumps with no reins and no stirrups, just with folded arms.'

Most cavalrymen had only one horse to look after, but drivers in the artillery had two, and two sets of tack. William Nicholson was delighted to become an artillery signaller, 'which put me on the battery staff and relieved me of my two sets of draught harness which was a great day for me'. Harness did not simply have to be clean,

British and Empire dead who had no known grave were commemorated on Memorials to the Missing. This is the Ypres (Menin Gate) Memorial, bearing the names of 54,896 men lost in the Ypres salient before 16 August 1917. It was unveiled by Field Marshal Lord Plumer in 1927, and local buglers have sounded the Last Post beneath it every night, with a brief interlude in 1940–44.

Immediately after the Armistice the British sector was divided into small zones each repeatedly combed by 12-man search teams: by September 1921 they had recovered over 200,000 bodies. The company sergeant major on the extreme right appears to be wearing the ribbon of the Victoria Cross.

Hooge Crater Cemetery lies on the southern edge of the Menin road just outside Ypres, near the crater of a large mine exploded by the British and on a spot which saw the first German use of flame-throwers against British troops in July 1915. This photograph was taken in the 1920s.

RIGHT Hooge Crater Cemetery in the 1980s. In the 1920s graves were marked with wooden crosses, but by 1937 600,000 headstones had been erected. All but the smallest cemeteries contain a Cross of Sacrifice, here seen at the top left, alongside the Menin Road. This peaceful scene is a tribute to the work of the Commonwealth War Graves Commission.

BELOW The fate of the prosperous little Belgian town of Ypres (Ieper) typified the misfortunes of the towns and villages in war's path. To the rear are the ruins of the famous Cloth Hall, with the remains of limbers and horses caught by shellfire in the foreground.

Figure in a ravaged landscape, 5 November 1917. Château Wood, just along the Menin Road from Hooge, was taken by Plumer's 2nd Army in September 1917 as part of the Third Battle of Ypres. This 'corduroy' track has been created by laying timber in the mud.

The Somme from two hundred feet. Infantry moving across downland laced with trenches and pitted by shells, August 1916.

The village of Passchendaele, on a long, low ridge east of Ypres, was an intermediate objective for the British 1917 offensive. It was eventually secured by the Canadians in early November. The left photograph depicts this little agricultural community at the start of the fighting: the right photograph reveals how it became an almost-obliterated part of the artillery landscape.

The Accrington Pals on parade at Ellison's Tenement in Accrington, 1914. It often took months for uniforms to reach New Army battalions, and at first men drilled in civilian clothes.

ABOVE The territorial 4/Queen's leaving its headquarters in Croydon on mobilisation. This unit was subsequently split to form several new battalions, one of which was 3/3 Queen's, commanded by Lieutenant Colonel U. L. Hooke, the right-hand mounted officer, a major when this photograph was taken. He was killed near Arras in 1917 and the battalion, badly mauled at Passchendaele, was disbanded the following year.

ABOVE RIGHT A private of the Grenadier Guards holding up his 1908 pattern webbing 'marching order'. This contained 150 rounds of .303 ammunition in the front pouches, water bottle and entrenching tool (on his right) haversack, bayonet and entrenching tool handle (on his left). The pack with greatcoat, groundsheet and a variety of personal items is in the centre.

The issue of uniform was an important rite of passage. These recruits are putting on their uniforms for the first time. Thick, collarless 'greyback' shirts are tucked into high-waisted khaki serge trousers, kept up by braces. Some men revelled in the first new clothes and decent boots they had ever worn. Others found harsh texture and unpredictable tailoring the first of many shocks.

Potential recruits were medically inspected: height, weight and chest expansion had to fall within prescribed limits. In 1914, when this photograph was taken, standards were usually rigidly applied. It was soon clear that many useful soldiers were being excluded. 'Bantams' were men of good physique whose height fell below the normal army minimum of five feet three inches, and in 1915–16, for instance, they constituted the infantry of the 35th Division.

Pipers accompanied some Scots and Irish units into battle. Here the pipe band of 8/Black Watch plays in Carnoy Valley on the Somme after 26th Brigade of 9th (Scottish) division returned from the capture of Longueval in mid-July 1916.

Brigadier General Frank Crozier (sitting, second from left) speaking to a French liaison officer in a posed 1918 shot of the staff of 119th Infantry Brigade. All wear brassards, and officers permanently appointed to the staff have red collar tabs too. The common staff practice of wearing light-coloured shirts, ties or breeches irritated regimental officers: Siegfried Sassoon was warned by his tailor that 'You can't have them too dark.'

LEFT The headquarters of 108th Brigade of 36th (Ulster) Division, February 1918. This elaborate multi-storey structure near Essigny had been taken over from the French when the British 5th Army moved south of the Somme.

RIGHT The *Ecole Militaire* at Monteuil housed the central office of British general headquarters from 31 March 1916 for the remainder of the war. Other staff branches were scattered around this pretty hilltop town.

This dugout near Hill 60, in the Ypres salient, contained the headquarters of an artillery group in August 1917. The duty officer (left) mans the telephones that connect him with the batteries, and has trench-maps, covered in transparent talc, to view. Steel helmets and trench coats (some no doubt the eponymous Burberry) hang from the central pillar.

Off-duty soldiers in a dugout near Ypres, 1 November 1917.

RIGHT The commanding officer and headquarters staff of 12/Royal Irish Rifles outside their dugout, 7 February 1918. A shortfall in British doctors was made up by US Army doctors: the regimental medical officer of this battalion, identifiable by his hat, is American.

LEFT War by timetable. In August 1914 most of the British Expeditionary Force landed at Le Havre and went by train to Maubeuge. Here British officers, in their start-of-campaign finery, stretch their legs at Rouen station.

LEFT Light railway, often known as Decauville after its French inventor, helped carry troops and stores from railheads to the front. Here 11/Durham Light Infantry, pioneer battalion of 20th (Light) Division, moves through Elverdinghe on its way to the Ypres front, 31 July 1917.

RIGHT Men of a midland regiment entraining after a spell in the trenches. They are wearing field service marching order, with their large packs on their backs: for short periods in trenches these were often replaced by the lighter haversack, worn in the same place. The company sergeant major, cutting about on the far right, has evidently been in the battalion's '10% reserve', left out of the line.

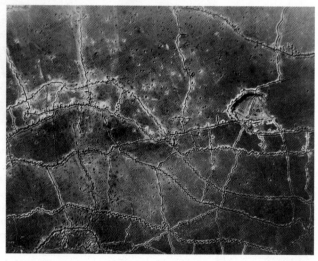

An aerial view of German trenches in the Auchy sector, between Loos and La Bassée, 14 November 1915. Fighting trenches, their 'Grecian key' design clearly visible, run across the photograph, and communication trenches, their angles less sharp, run up and down.

but polished, with leather and brasswork shining. Metalwork, like bits and chains, was unplated steel, and was burnished bright. Sometimes this was accomplished by shaking it up in a sack with old newspaper, but often there was no alternative to rubbing with the 'burnisher' – a piece of leather 3½ inches square, with interlocking links of chain sewn to one side that resembled chain mail.

Recruits, like trained soldiers, lived in barrack rooms which housed between twenty and forty men, so that all the private soldiers in an infantry platoon or cavalry troop lived together. There were thirty-two in John Cusack's recruit troop, with two old soldiers, Tom Hood and Chokey Bone, who showed them how to clean their kit and muck out. They lived in screened-off 'bunks' at the end of the barrack room, which gave corporals some privacy in trained soldiers' accommodation. The barracks of the Cardwell era had separate wash houses and latrine blocks, and, though some had had water closets fitted subsequently, most Edwardian soldiers, like their grandfathers, relied on the spooneristically-named sip-pot. John Cusack and his comrades rose at 5.00 in the summer and 6.00 in the winter, and their day began with:

> emptying the enormous piss-tub outside our barrack room. Mucking out – breakfast – PT – first drill. 1100 – stables (changed into canvas) and groomed till 1200 – then fed them and went for lunch. 1400 square for rifle or sword drill. A long time to get prepared – little time for meal.

Infantrymen did bayonet training with padded jackets and 'rifles' with spring-loaded plungers where the bayonets would have been, and cavalrymen fenced with blunted swords. 'Sergeant Croft was a real brute,' thought Private Richard Chant of the 5th Dragoon Guards. 'When one was fencing him one could always be sure of a few bruises, even through the padded jacket. But after all Sergeant Croft made men of us in the drill he conducted, and we all sang our praises of him afterwards.'[79] Training went on till 4.00, when it was time for stables again, then the 'tea meal' – lunch was still the main meal of the day – kit-cleaning and bed. Pyjamas were so rare that a man would risk bullying if he wore them. Most men slept in a grey-back shirt and long johns, or gym shorts in the summer.

Once a man had 'passed off the square' as a recruit and could 'pass the guard' – that is, satisfy the orderly sergeant at the guardroom that he was fit to be seen in public – then he could 'walk out' in his best uniform. Cavalrymen carried regimental whips and infantrymen regimental canes. As late as 1915 a puzzled New Army recruit at Aldershot found himself inexplicably rejected by the guard until he bought a Rifle Brigade cane.

Men spent hard-earned money in order to look extra smart. Experienced cavalrymen bought overalls (tight trousers) of superfine cloth which clung to the leg, had fine leather stitched to the tops of their issue boots, bought chrome-plated spurs and had coins fitted to the rowels to make them jingle. The weekly church parade in full dress was a ritual no less striking than a Zulu war dance or monastic mass. A large garrison like Aldershot, Catterick or the Curragh might see a whole brigade in the same church, and even the irreligious were stirred. 'The uniforms were wonderful, wonderful,' mused Richard Chant, 'could such a thing happen that they all came back again, but I'm afraid it's all wishful thinking.' But, he added, 'should my memoirs be read by anyone, believe me, each man was proud of his regiment, be it Cavalry, Royal Horse Artillery, Royal Field Artillery or Infantry.'[80]

Regimental pride went deep. Recruits had the lineage of their regiment, its battle honours, regimental days, and quasi-masonic practices drilled into them. Soldiers in the Queen's Royal Regiment, for instance, would know that theirs was the senior English regiment of the line, as such junior only to the Royal Scots, the 1st of Foot. 'First and Worst,' opined Queensmen to Royal Scots, who made clear their disagreement, with boots and belt buckles. Raised in 1661 to garrison Tangiers, the North African enclave brought to the English crown as dowry by Charles II's wife, the Portuguese princess Catherine of Braganza, the regiment was once nicknamed 'The Tangerines'. The Queen's bore Catherine's cipher of two 'C's interlaced within the Garter on its colours, and continued to carry a third colour, with the cipher on a green background, long after all other infantry regiments in the army had been reduced to two colours. Its

Paschal lamb badge and the name of Colonel Piercy Kirke, who commanded it at Sedgemoor in 1684, then gave it the nickname 'Kirke's Lambs', an ironic reference to its less than lamb-like gentleness to West Countrymen captured fighting for the Duke of Monmouth. By the time of the First World War it was often known, because of the lamb and flag on its badge, as 'The Mutton Lancers', or, in Cockney slang, as 'The Pork and Beans'. Members of the East Surreys spoke of it as 'The Other Surrey Regiment', which is precisely what Queensmen called the East Surreys.

From 1837 to 1881 the regiment marched passed the saluting base to a tune called *The Old Queen's*, which included part of the national anthem. In 1881 this tune was played when 1/Queen's paraded before Queen Victoria at a review at Aldershot. The queen asked whether special permission had been given for use of the national anthem, adding, unamused, that unless it had, the practice must cease. No authority could be found, and so for a short time the regiment made its feelings clear by passing the saluting base without music, earning the nickname 'The Silent Second'. In 1883 Lieutenant Colonel Kelly-Kenny, then commanding the 1st Battalion, wrote to the Portuguese embassy explaining what had happened, pointing out the regiment's connection with the House of Braganza, and asking if a Portuguese air could be used. The result was the fine march *Braganza*, actually a free adaptation of the air *O Patria*, the Portuguese national anthem at the time. Soldiers inevitably put words to it:

> Here we come, here we come
> Bloody great bastards every one . . .

Officers, in the post-prandial conviviality of a dinner night, accompanied the band with a more genteel version:

> I absolutely *do* refuse
> To be ordered about unless I choose . . .

The Queen's Royal Regiment's battle honours began with 'Tangier 1662–80', and included scores of others, from 'Dettingen' to 'Corunna', 'Cabool 1842', 'Sobraon', 'Sevastopol', 'Pekin 1860' and 'South Africa 1899–1902'. On 1 June 1794 a detachment of the regiment had served as marines aboard Lord Howe's flagship *Queen Charlotte* at his victory over the French of Ushant, and this was commemorated as the regimental day. HMS *Excellent*, the naval gunnery school on Whale Island, Portsmouth, inherited the traditions of *Queen Charlotte*, and there was a strong connection between the regiment and HMS *Excellent*, with an annual cricket week. Regimental treasure included a huge silver wine cooler, officially the Jerningham-Kandler wine cooler but known, to generations of irreverent young officers, predictably preoccupied by some of the female figures embodied in its rococo decoration, as 'The Flying Tits'.

In 1902 1/Queen's won the Punjab Open polo tournament, and five officers commemorated it with a silver horse statuette: two were wounded and two killed in action during the First World War. Another trophy, the Army in India Efficiency Prize, was won by 1/Queen's in 1905. The competition required all soldiers in a battalion, except those actually in hospital, to compete. It was so savage, including a thirty-mile march in full kit (one veteran believed that he carried 150lbs in all), and with a variety of tests, that some men died. The event was not repeated, so the battalion was allowed to retain the trophy. Hardened drinkers took comfort from the fact that 2/Royal Welch Fusiliers, the runners-up, lost five men on the march, all of them teetotallers.[81]

If the Queen's could boast a longer history than most regiments, there was nothing genuinely unique about it, for the old army was a rich repository of history (real and invented), traditions and artefacts, making regiments social organisms as distinctive as Scots clans or Native American tribes. We must, though, guard against uncritical assumption that the sheer visibility of the regimental system, reinforced most poignantly by cap badges engraved on headstones in Commonwealth War Graves Commission cemeteries, means that it was the main reason for men fighting. It certainly mattered hugely to pre-war regulars, especially to officers and senior NCOs, who might spend the whole of their working lives in the same peripatetic community, soldiering together from Catterick to Calcutta and from Kimberley to the Khyber. Herbert Wootton, a pre-war member of the Royal Horse Guards, told me that he fought for 'the Regiment and its traditions, also my comrades'.[82] Alan Hanbury-Sparrow was a thoroughly committed regimental officer – 'I always felt it my duty to be with 1/Royal Berks at the front' – but felt that the value of the regimental system diminished as the war went on. 'The casualty lists put an enormous strain on these traditions,' he wrote. 'I became increasingly cynical about their value.'[83]

There were some things men were less proud of, for, as Frank Richards described it, 'booze and fillies' were a constant preoccupation for regular soldiers. It was a hard-drinking army: in 1912–13, 9,230 men were fined for drunkenness, and this does not include the many more given drills or other punishments by officers or NCOs. Lieutenant George Barrow, a cavalry officer carrying out a brief attachment to the infantry in 1884, found himself serving with the 88th Foot, the Devil's Own, then properly known as The Connaught Rangers. 'Drink was the besetting sin of the Connaught men,' he wrote.[84] In the dimly-lit regimental 'wet canteen' men could buy weak beer known as 'swipes': 'one could drink a great many glasses of this sort of beer without feeling the effects of it'. Men drank steadily and sang songs of studied and refined vulgarity, such as 'The Girl I nearly Wed':

> I wake up sweating every night to think what might have been,
> For in another corner, boys, she'd stored the Magazine,
> The Magazine, a barrel of snuff, and one or two things more,
> And in another corner, boys, was the Regiment forming fours.[85]

Philanthropists and reformers had done much, over the previous thirty years, to ensure that soldiers had some alternative to the 'wet canteen'. The 'Garrison Institute Coffee Shop' and 'Sandys Soldiers' Home' offered heat, light and daily papers, and cheap 'char and a wad' (tea and a sandwich).[86] The Army Temperance Society encouraged men to give up alcohol altogether, and there was a strong thread of religious Nonconformity and temperance running through the army, especially amongst NCOs. But they were never more than a respectable minority, mocked as 'tea busters' or 'bun wallahs'. Many soldiers would go to great lengths to get alcohol, whatever the risks. When the 11th Hussars arrived in France in August 1914 two zealous troopers discovered that the huge cotton warehouse that housed their brigade also contained the BEF's rum casks. Their binge cost them three months' imprisonment apiece.

Men brawled drunk, and they brawled sober. Within the regiment they were encouraged to settle matters with their fists, but when dealing with outsiders 'the buckled ends of belts were used, also boots'. John Lucy's Royal Irish Rifles had an 'old and sworn enemy' in a nearby English regiment, and he noticed how: 'The Englishmen in our own regiment forgot nationality and beat up their own countrymen in the supposed defence of the honour of their chosen corps.'[87] The Essex and Bedfordshire Regiments had a feud dating back to the Boer War, when an encircled Essex patrol had allegedly not been rescued by the nearby Bedfords, who were just falling in for church parade. Percy Croney, who served in 12/Essex, knew that: 'when an Essex man sees a Bedford badge, in memory of that patrol he must call: "Thou shalt not kill," and the Bedford man, in honour of his regiment, must fight.'[88] Pubs in garrison towns were the scenes of large-scale inter-regimental fights. 'Christmas always meant a damned good tuck-in,' wrote Frank Richards, 'with plenty of booze and scraps to follow.' Inter-regimental brawls were common. Highland Regiments could be provoked (though for no easily-discernible historical reason) by asking for ''arf a pint o' broken square'; a member of the York and Lancaster Regiment would respond vigorously to a cheery greeting of 'The Cork and Doncaster, I presume'; and 'scholars' made insulting translations of high-sounding Latin mottoes and then ducked to avoid the bar stool.

The Welch Regiment had a long-running feud with the Royal Marines, its memory kept green in many a beery den. Frank Richards, as a soldier and Welshman bound to go to the aid of a brother in need, heard the traditional pre-fight patter in a Plymouth pub. A Welshman greeted a marine in 'a friendly sort of tone':

> 'Pleased to meet you, Joey, let's you and I have a talk about old times.'
> 'What old times, Taffy?' asked the marine, suspiciously.
> 'That sea-battle long ago – I forget its name – where my regiment once served aboard a bloody flagship of the Royal Navy.'

'What as? Ballast?' asked the marine, finishing his beer before the trouble started.

'No, as marines, whatever,' answered the Welshman. 'It was like this. The Admiral wanted a bit of fighting done, and the sailors were all busy with steering the bloody ship and looping up the bloody sails, see? And the marines said they didn't feel like doing any bloody fighting that day, see? So of course he called in the Old Sixty-Ninth to undertake the job.'

'Never heard tell before of a marine who didn't feel like fighting,' said the marine, setting down his empty mug and jumping forwards like a boxing kangaroo.

In a moment we were all at it, hammer and tongs, and the sides being even, a decent bit of blood flowed: fortunately the scrap ended before murder was done, by the landlord shouting that the picket was on the way.[89]

The subject of women was just as contentious. The army began to build quarters for married soldiers and their families towards the end of the nineteenth century, but soldiers required permission to marry 'on the strength' and at the turn of the century had to have five years' service and be twenty-six years of age before being considered. 'A man who married off the strength,' observed Frank Richards, 'had to keep his wife on his own shilling a day; she lived outside barrack and he inside, and they met whenever they could, but officially she did not exist'.[90]

Single men in barracks, as Kipling accurately observed, did not grow into plaster saints, and, deprived of much chance of marriage, made other arrangements. Prostitutes thronged about in garrison towns, and the Contagious Diseases Act of 1864, which vainly sought to control venereal disease by medical inspection and compulsory treatment, covered towns like Aldershot, Colchester and Woolwich in England and Cork in Ireland. Also included was the great military camp outside Dublin, the Curragh of Kildare, where girls and women known as 'wrens' lived rough outside the camp. Occasionally, when girls got into barracks, things got out of control; in 1896 soldiers of a Yorkshire regiment were involved in a gang rape, and three of them were sent to prison. There were more comfortable arrangements for officers, who could not be expected to rough it in huts out on the furze, and the future Edward VII was gently initiated into what became a life-long preoccupation at the Curragh in 1861.[91] Regiments stationed in India maintained *lal bazaars*, essentially regimental brothels, and there were also many private establishments. Frank Richards recalled that 'a magnificently built half-caste prostitute of fifty years of age' decided to celebrate her retirement by giving:

> free access to her body between the hours of 6pm and 11pm. Preference was given to old customers. She posted a notice to this effect on the door of her room and if I related how many men applied and were admitted and went away satisfied in those short hours, I should not be believed.[92]

Girlfriends were smuggled into barracks too. One of Richards' corporals briefly kept a woman in his bunk, an arrangement which led to predictable difficulties over an alternative use to which one of the company's tea buckets was put. The architects who designed the ornamental iron railings surrounding Cardwell barracks had inadvertently spaced them so widely that sexual commerce could comfortably be carried out between them.[93]

It is important that we do not follow the Duke of Wellington and believe that *all* regular soldiers were 'the scum of the earth, enlisted for drink . . .', however. There was a sprinkling of gentleman-rankers, who had joined for a variety of reasons and usually kept quiet about them. Sometimes there were tragedies that we can only guess at. In 1909 Private John Vivian Crowther of the 18th Hussars shot himself in barracks. He was described at his inquest as 'a cultured and educated Oxford graduate who had inherited a large property'.[94] John Lucy tells how:

> There was a taciturn sergeant from Waterford who was conversant with the intricacies of higher mathematics . . . There was an ex-divinity student with literary tastes, who drank much beer and affected an obvious pretence to gentle birth; a national school teacher; a man who had absconded from a colonial bank; a few decent sons of farmers.

And there were the properly ambitious. Lucy declared that: 'Promotion . . . is my mark' and was speedily made a lance corporal. He found that the first promotion was the hardest to bear, for he was at once separated from his comrades and for the new NCO 'every order he has to give to an old friend is a pain'.[95] Frank Richards decided that the price of promotion was too high, and obstinately declined it throughout his eight years with the colours and the whole of his wartime service. There were many like him: in 1918 young Frederick Hodges found himself in command of Private Pearson MM – 'a short, sturdy little man . . . nearly twice my age'. Pearson had a long-running gag about the tinned pork and beans which were a common ration issue ('I say, where is the pork?'). And he always called Hodges 'Corp'.[96]

A hard-working regular soldier, who took his military training and army education seriously, might become a lance corporal in a year or two and corporal in three. He would be unlikely to make sergeant in his first enlistment – although promotion had speeded up during the Boer War – and the prospect of a third stripe and the more comfortable life of the sergeants' mess was dangled out to persuade men to sign on after their first term. It was possible to get promoted from sergeant to colour sergeant (in the infantry) or staff sergeant (in other arms) and on to warrant officer in ten years, though this was fast work. *King's Regulations* specifically guaranteed that warrant officers would be able to complete twelve years' service, which entitled them to a small pension. Senior NCOs and warrant officers were likely to be able to complete twenty-one years' service, increasing their pensions, as long as they remained fit, and could serve even longer with their commanding officer's support. The Northamptons boasted a private soldier who had joined the regiment as a boy and died in harness just before the Boer War at the age of fifty-five. There were always jobs around the battalion which old soldiers like this could do: running the store which held the privately-purchased sports kit, helping break in recruits ('Leave to fall out, trained soldier, please?') and, of course, looking after the young gentlemen.

Most of the officers came from what Edward Spiers has called 'the traditional sources of supply', and even that arch-traditionalist the

Duke of Wellington would have been struck by how little the officer corps of 1914 differed from that he had taken to Waterloo 101 years before. The peerage, gentry, military families, the clergy and the professions provided its bulk, with a minority coming from business, commercial and industrial families.[97] In practice social divisions were more flexible than they might seem, with families who had made good in trade setting the seal on their gentility by buying land, marrying their daughters into the aristocracy and sending their sons into the army. Many a young man with a good education, crested signet ring and commission in a smart regiment was only two generations away from the shovel or the counting house.

Military families played as important a part in the army of 1914 as they had in Wellington's: no less than 43.1 percent of the fathers of cadets entering Sandhurst in the summer intake of 1910 were 'military professionals'. In the winter of 1917 this had sunk to 17.9 percent, but by the winter of 1930 it was an astonishing 62.4 percent.[98] The future Field Marshal Lord Wavell, commissioned into the Black Watch in 1901, remembered that:

> I never felt any special inclination to a military career, but it would have taken more independence of character than I possessed at the time, to avoid it. Nearly all my relations were military. I had been brought up among soldiers; and my father, while professing to give me complete liberty of choice, was determined that I should be a soldier. I had no particular bent towards any other profession, and I took the line of least resistance.[99]

Alan Brooke came from a long line of soldiers originating in Ulster, and initially wanted to be a doctor, but military blood was thicker than medical water, and off he went to Woolwich to become a gunner. It was as well for Britain's conduct of the Second World War that he did, although even at the height of his powers the slight, bespectacled Field Marshal Lord Alanbrooke had, perhaps, a touch of the consulting room to him.

Just as Wellington's officer corps contained a good many young men whose only fortune was their sword, so too the army of 1914 had many officers who were just on the right side of the borders of gentility. This often made for an uncomfortable life, for although the purchase of commissions had been abolished a generation before, being an officer in the British army was an expensive business. In 1903 a War Office Committee reckoned that an officer needed a minimum of £160 a year in addition to his pay to be able to survive in the infantry. Life in the cavalry was more expensive, for a subaltern needed to provide himself with at least one charger and could hardly avoid hunting and playing polo: he could just scrape by with £300 a year, but the average private income of cavalry officers was £6–700. In 1912 Major General M. F. Rimington warned that it had once been possible to find rich young men to join the cavalry because they were not expected to work hard. But now they were expected to work till 1.00 or even 3.00 in the afternoon: who would pay to serve in the cavalry and have to work too?[100] The Hutchinson Committee of 1905 was inclined to agree. It believed that many young men would like to join the cavalry if only they could afford it, and urged that the government should make it cheaper for young officers to maintain themselves in the cavalry by providing chargers and saddlery at public expense.

Alan Hanbury-Sparrow joined the Royal Berkshires in 1912 with just £175 a year, and found it hard going. In the following year E. G. W. Harrison survived in the Royal Artillery with only £18 a year which brought his total income to £92. 'Mess bill without a drink or a cigarette [was] £6 monthly', he wrote, 'soldier servant and washing £1 monthly, so a penny bus fare was a matter of deep consideration'.[101] Towards the other extreme, Osbert Sitwell's father (advised by the wonderfully-named Major Archie Gowk) gave him £530 a year in 1912 as a Yeomanry officer attached to a regular cavalry regiment, but stressed that if young Osbert received any pay he would expect to be given it. But some officers survived despite the odds. William Robertson had joined the army as a private in 1877 despite his mother's declaration that she would rather bury him than see him in a red coat. He reached the rank of sergeant major before being commissioned, and managed to survive on his pay, though he acknowledges the kindness of his brother regimental warrant officers who clubbed together to buy him his saddlery. He became chief of the imperial general staff during the First World

War, making the British army unique amongst allies and enemies in having as its professional head an officer commissioned from the ranks.

Officer training reflected old traditions. Officers destined for the Royal Artillery and Royal Engineers, the 'gentlemen of the Ordnance', went to the Royal Military Academy at Woolwich, known as 'the shop', which had trained them since the eighteenth century. Entry was by competitive examination: the young Alan Brooke sweated blood at an army crammer's, eventually passing in to Woolwich 65th out of 72. The entrance exam included compulsory papers in English, French or German, and mathematics, and a choice of two papers from further mathematics, history, German, Latin, French and science. Those who passed out with the highest places in the final order of merit tended to go to the Royal Engineers, and the remainder to the Royal Artillery: in the December 1909 list numbers 1–11 became sappers and 12–36 gunners.[102]

Officers for the cavalry, infantry, Indian army and Army Service Corps went to the Royal Military Academy Sandhurst, which had existed since 1799, though it had not trained the majority of officers until after the abolition of purchase. Entrance to Sandhurst too was by competitive examination, and its final order of merit was no less important than that at Woolwich. Officers who hoped to go to the Indian army, where they could live on their pay, had to pass out towards its top. Young Bernard Montgomery (already under a cloud for setting fire to a fellow cadet's shirt-tail) passed out too low to be admitted to the Indian army and joined the Royal Warwickshires instead. It is fashionable to decry the standards attained at Sandhurst: one scholar has observed that it amazing what a young man did not have to know to get into the cavalry or artillery. However, anyone choosing to look at their examination papers would be struck by the fact that these were no brainless hearties.

While Woolwich trained 99 percent of artillery and engineer officers, Sandhurst trained only 67 percent of the officers destined for the infantry and cavalry. Some 2 percent were commissioned from the ranks. These were combatant commissions, whose holders would take rank and precedence alongside their comrades from public school, as opposed to the holders of quartermaster's or riding master's commissions, appointed to honorary commissions for specific jobs. Of the remainder, about half came from universities, where they had undertaken some training in the Senior Division of the Officers' Training Corps: the Junior Division – 'the Corps' – comprised contingents in public schools. Most of the others had entered the army through 'the militia back door'. Officers holding a commission in the militia or Yeomanry (or the Special Reserve or Yeomanry from 1908) could bypass Sandhurst altogether by taking a competitive examination for a direct commission. This was how Field Marshal Sir John French, who had started his career in the navy, had got into the army, and Henry Wilson, his deputy chief of staff in 1914, had followed the same route.

Rory Baynes, considering a military career, confessed that:

> I much preferred the idea of sporting a militia officer's magnificent uniform than that of going to Sandhurst, where in those days I would have had to spend almost two years in what was a rather strict public school atmosphere.

He was accordingly commissioned in 1906 into the 3rd Bedfordshire Militia, a 'strange and exclusive crowd': no experience was necessary, but the personal approval of the regiment's colonel, the Duke of Bedford, certainly was. Young Baynes trained with his battalion, spent some time attached to a regular battalion of the Bedfords, and studied for the militia competitive examination with Major Heath, an army crammer in Folkestone, a distinctive character with Kaiser Bill moustaches, and duly came top in the 1907 examination. Although he was by then a full lieutenant in the militia, he had to revert to second lieutenant on joining his preferred regular regiment, the Cameronians.[103] Osbert Sitwell found it all arranged for him by his forceful father:

> Even Henry, who usually appeared to possess a special insight into the workings of my father's mind, could not help me . . . Then, one morning, I found out: for I read, suddenly turning a page of the newspaper that had just arrived, that a 2nd Lieut. F. O. S. Sitwell had just been granted a commission in the Yeomanry, and was, from the Yeomanry, attached to a famous regiment of Hussars.

Osbert duly reported at Aldershot in the foggy winter of 1911–12, and his first shock was getting in to his mess kit, then worn for dinner on weeknights: officers relaxed in the down-market black tie for dinner at weekends.

> Every part of the body had to be dragged and pinched and buttoned, and the boots were so tight that one could neither pull them on nor take them off, and remained for many minutes in a kind of seal-like flipper-limbo as to the feet. Only by the kindness and perseverance of Robbins – my new servant who, as I write, some thirty-three years later, is still with me ... was I able to encase myself in this unaccustomed glory.[104]

In November 1912 he transferred to the regular army, and joined the Grenadier Guards at the Tower of London. Here he was interviewed by the regimental lieutenant colonel who seemed to be:

> the improbable realisation of an ideal; an ideal cherished by a considerable number of contemporaries, including most officers and all the best tailors and haberdashers, hosiers, shoemakers and barbers in London, indeed in England ... At a single glance it might be deemed possible by the inexperienced, such was the apparent sincerity and straightforwardness of his self-presentation, to know all about him, even to write a testimonial, *strong sense of duty, hard-playing (golf, cricket, polo), generous, brave, fine shot, adequate rider, man of the world, C. of E.*

He remembered the great royal review of the Brigade of Guards on 28 April 1913 as 'a final salute from an old order which was to perish, and constituted for those taking part in it – and how few survived the next two years! – a sort of fanfare, heralding the war'.[105]

SATURDAY NIGHT SOLDIERS

There were part-time soldiers in Britain long before the foundation of the regular army in 1660, and the London's Honourable Artillery Company, once the Guild of St George and then part of the London Trained Bands, can trace its origins back to 1537. By Haldane's time there were three distinct strands in the volunteer and auxiliary forces of the Crown, and the Norfolk Committee, one of the bodies which had investigated British military performance in the Boer War, had concluded that between them they were neither fitted for taking the field against regular troops nor for providing a framework of future expansion. Yet part-time forces provided relatively large numbers of inexpensive manpower at a time when the regular army was under-recruited; they had powerful political support, most notably in the House of Lords, where militia colonels were firmly entrenched; and they seemed to offer a real prospect of widening military service so as to create that 'real national army' that Haldane sought.

The militia was founded on men's common law obligation to provide home defence, and was not obliged to serve abroad. Originally selected by ballot from lists of able-bodied men maintained by parish constables, its efficiency ebbed and flowed with the danger of invasion. It had spent much of the Napoleonic period embodied, that is called up for, full-time service, but in the nineteenth century it slipped back into its old torpor, its members turning out for infrequent training. In social composition the militia looked much like the regular army. Those who did not wish to serve could hire substitutes to do so on their behalf; militia officers were chosen by Lords Lieutenant of counties from the gentlemen of the shire, and there was a steady flow of both officers and men into the regular army.

The volunteers, first formed to meet the perceived threat of revolutionary France, had been revived by the invasion scare of the 1860s. They were wholly distinct from the militia. Members of volunteer units were required to purchase their own uniforms and much of their equipment. In many companies officers were elected, and they received their commissions from Lords Lieutenant rather than the monarch. This was Mr Pooter under arms, and as such a favourite butt of *Punch's* cartoonists. In 1899 the volunteer Lieutenant Tompkins, 'excellent fellow, but poor soldier', was asked by an inspecting general:

> Now, Sir, you have your battalion in quarter column facing south. How would you get it into line, in the quickest possible way, facing north-east?
> Well, Sir, do you know, that's what I have always wondered.[106]

Victorian volunteers were wonderfully bearded, favoured baggy uniforms of French grey, and took their marksmanship very seriously, spending weekends at Bisley ranges tending their muzzle-loading Enfield and new breech-loading Snider rifles and smelling powerfully of black powder, gun oil and cheroots. Regulars doubted whether these hirsute tradesmen were really soldiers at all, and had little doubt that they would not stand the onset of French infantry. Matters were not helped by the fact that the green-ribboned Volunteer Decoration, awarded for long service, carried the post-nominal initials VD, displayed with a pride which puzzled some regular soldiers.

The Yeomanry were different yet again. The first units of 'gentlemen and yeomanry' had been raised in 1794. They were volunteers who needed to own, or at least have regular access to, a horse, and this socio-economic distinction made them useful to a government which lacked a police force. Yeomanry were involved in the Peterloo Massacre of 1819: part of what went wrong that day was occasioned by the poor training of men and horses, and part by the fact that the yeomanry were middle-class men with an animus against the 'mob'. The Yeomanry, like the volunteers, saw a revival as a result of the invasion scare of the 1860s, and there were thirty-eight regiments in existence in 1899. Many yeomen volunteered, as Imperial Yeomanry, to fight in the Boer War, no less than 178 companies grouped in 38 battalions, and after the war more regiments were raised, some of them from urban areas with few real links to the horse-owning farmers of yesteryear.

Yeomanry regiments had little in common with volunteer battalions. Their officers could (and so often did) fit comfortably into regular cavalry regiments, and many of their troopers were scarcely less well-heeled. They carried out their fortnight's annual training in the grounds of the great houses of the land, where things were done in proper yeoman style, as a correspondent reported of the Hertfordshire Yeomanry in camp at Woodhall Park in 1903.

> The camp is pleasantly situated on sloping ground in front of the mansion, and close to the River Beane . . . There are 90 bell tents, four men to each, though the officers, of course, have one to themselves. The tents all have boarded floors and folding iron bedsteads are provided. The baths and chests-of-drawers have this year been dispensed with, and if the men want a 'dip' there are the inviting waters of the Beane close by . . . The stables are wood and canvas structures . . . Messrs Lipton are again catering for the officers and Sergeant Buck and his son Trooper Buck are again supplying the regimental mess. A Morris tube shooting range has been fixed up by Mr Buck for the amusement of the men and there are also a skittle alley, reading room, ping-pong board and other forms of recreation.[107]

The Middlesex Yeomanry enjoyed an even more elegant camp on the very eve of war, as Trooper S. F. Hatton remembered.

> Reveille about 7.00, hot coffee by specially engaged cooks, the early grooming, water and feed. A two-course breakfast

in the Troopers' mess – (the damned waiters are a bit slow this morning) – then dress for parade . . . A morning's drill or manoeuvring on the Downs, and back to camp, grooming, watering, feeding; the regimental band in full-dress uniform playing all the time during 'stables'. A wash, change into mess kit . . . Luncheon, beautifully served by hired mess waiters on spotless linen . . . In the afternoon saddlery and equipment were given over to a batman to clean for the morning – it was customary for four or five Troopers to run a 'civvy' batman between them during the camp – and then change into grey flannels for the river, lounging, sleeping or anything else Satan found us to do.[108]

Sir John French had served as adjutant of the Northumberland Hussars, and his foreword to the 1924 regimental history is a vignette of a vanished age.

They were commanded by the Earl of Ravensworth, than whom no better sportsman ever lived. The officers were all good sportsmen and fine horsemen, and to those who can look back fifty years such names as Crookson, Straker, Henderson and Hunter will carry conviction of the truth of what I say. Two of them were Masters of Hounds, but my most intimate friend was Charley Hunter, a born leader of cavalry, whose skill in handing £50 screws over five-barred gates I shall never forget.[109]

Yeomanry officers were as active in both Houses of Parliament as they were on the hunting field. Major Winston Churchill MP was in the Queen's Own Oxfordshire Hussars, and Lieutenant Colonel the Hon. H. C. Henderson MP commanded the Berkshire Yeomanry. The Hon. Walter Guinness was Conservative MP for Bury St Edmunds and a major in the Suffolk Yeomanry: when war broke out B Squadron, whose command he had just relinquished, 'had recently been taken over by Frank Goldsmith, who was Member of Parliament for the Stowmarket Division'.[110] B Squadron was graced by Sir Cuthbert Quilter, MP for Sudbury. Brigadier General the Earl of Longford was to die commanding a Yeomanry brigade at Gallipoli.

Haldane's reforms swept up militia, volunteers and yeomanry.

They turned militia battalions into Special Reserve battalions, which trained part-time just as the militia had, but would provide drafts to reinforce the regular battalions of their regiments in the event of war. Their composition, too, mirrored that of the militia: well-to-do officers and soldiers who could have fitted easily into the regular army. Some young men used the Special Reserve as a way of testing the water. George Ashurst was born in the Lancashire village of Tontine in 1895. 'We were a poor family,' he recalled. 'My father worked in a stone quarry about a mile from the village, and his wages were rather poor. To make things worse, he kept half of his wages for himself and spent them at the village pub.'[111] He became a colliery clerk on 12/6d a week, but when he lost his job his father warned him that if he took on manual work 'I will break your bloody neck.'

Ashurst went to a recruiting office to sign on. He said that he wanted to sign on for seven years, but the sergeant, kinder than many, replied: 'When you get into the army you might not like it, so I will tell you what to do. Join the Special Reserve, which means that you will do six months in the barracks and seven years on the reserve, with just a month's camp every year.' He joined the 3rd (Special Reserve) Battalion, The Lancashire Fusiliers, and trained at the depot at Wellington Barracks, Bury. 'I got on very well as a soldier,' he recalled,

> except for little reminders from the sergeant-major that I was a soldier now and 'Take your hands out of your pockets, stick your chest out and your chin in' as I walked across the barrack square. I felt really fit, too, with cross-country running and the gym exercises we had daily, and I loved the musketry lessons and the shooting on the firing range with the .22 rifles.
>
> There was also a school and a teacher in the barracks where one could go in the afternoon and sit at desks with pen and paper to improve one's education. There were examinations, and we could get a third-class certificate. If you were also a first-class shot with the rifle you got six-pence a day on your pay.[112]

Haldane faced a far greater challenge in forming the Territorial Force, which came into being on 1 April 1908. It was organised in fourteen mounted brigades each consisting of three regiments of yeomanry, a battery of horse artillery and a field ambulance, and fourteen infantry divisions, each with three four-battalion infantry brigades, artillery, engineers, transport and medical services.[113] He hoped that it would both support and expand the army, first providing home defence, thus freeing the regulars of the BEF to go abroad, and then, after six months' post-mobilisation training, being fit to take the field abroad itself. But the Territorial Force was the child of compromise. The National Service League was right to see it as a means of avoiding conscription, and by 1913 the Army Council was itself in favour of conscription. Yet in order to persuade men to sign up, they were not to be liable for foreign service unless they volunteered for it. Because he rightly believed that, given a chance, the regular army would drain territorial funds in order to finance itself, he created County Territorial Associations which maintained the Territorial Force property, with drill halls and rifle ranges, and supplied units with much of their equipment. These not only went some way towards protecting the Territorial Force from regular army pillaging, but, with the active co-operation of King Edward, swung county hierarchies solidly behind the new force. Lords Lieutenant were ex-officio presidents of their associations, and *The Territorial Year Book* for 1909 shows just how successful Haldane had been in linking landed wealth, local military experience and big employers in his associations.

But the experiment was not wholly successful. The Territorial Force peaked at 270,041 officers and men in 1909, and was only 245,779 strong by September 1913. Wastage ran at 12.4 percent per annum compared with the regular army's 6 percent, and while the old unreformed auxiliary forces had represented 3.6 percent of the male population in 1903 the Territorial Force represented only 0.63 percent of it ten years later.[114] Its equipment was obsolescent: infantry had early marks of the Lee-Enfield rifle, not the Short Magazine of the regulars, and artillery, organised in four rather than the six-gun batteries of the regular army, had 15-pounder guns and 5-inch howitzers. When the regular infantry restructured from eight companies to four in 1913, the territorials did not follow suit. Many employers were no more helpful about releasing men for service with the Territorial Force than they had been with the volunteers. While some regiments took their territorial battalions to their hearts, others did not. There was a long-running dispute about the wisdom of giving territorials artillery at all, and eventually territorial gunners wore the Royal Artillery cap badge with a blank scroll where regulars bore their battle honour 'UBIQUE'.[115]

The territorials had their own marked differences. 'I was commissioned into the 5th Scottish Rifles in February 1911,' recalled John Reith. 'The social class of the man in the ranks was higher than that of any other Regiment in Glasgow.'[116] The London Regiment, which consisted of twenty-eight battalions, all territorial, ranged from the very smart 28/London (Artists' Rifles) which had been commanded by Frederick, Lord Leighton and had been formed for men with artistic leanings, to the rather less smart 11/London, the Finsbury Rifles according to the *Army List* but known, from the location of its drill hall at the top of Penton Street and the alleged propensities of its members, as the Pentonville Pissers. When young Alan Harding, a post-office clerk, decided to join the territorials he chose 11/London precisely because he was able to get a commission: he would have had little chance in, say, the 13/London (Kensington) or 14/London (London Scottish). He was a lieutenant colonel with a Military Cross in 1918, joined the regular army and died Field Marshal the Lord Harding of Petherton.[117]

Bryan Latham agreed about the difference between battalions. 'Amongst foremost London clubs before the war,' he wrote,

> could be numbered the headquarters of half a dozen of the leading Territorial battalions. Such regiments as the Artists' Rifles, Civil Service Rifles, the HAC, the London Rifle Brigade, London Scottish and the Kensingtons ... Friends would join the same battalion, almost on leaving school; I was in my nineteenth year when I enlisted in 1913, my brother Russell 18, and my cousin, John Chappell, the same age.[118]

Latham joined 5/London, the London Rifle Brigade, whose headquarters in Bunhill Row included offices, stores, a large drill hall (also equipped as 'a first-class gym'), messes, canteens and a billiard room. The athletic club met there once a week. There were shooting matches at Bisley, and an annual marching competition, with a thirteen-mile route through the outer suburbs. Men wore full equipment, and had to complete the march in under three hours to have any chance of winning. For weekend training the eight companies would parade on Saturday afternoon at Waterloo station and travel by train to Weybridge. They marched to the local drill hall, and had supper at a restaurant, followed by a singsong: 'at such affairs every member of the LRB, whatever his rank, met on the basis of comradeship; on parade army discipline and routine took over again'. There was an early reveille, breakfast, and then manoeuvres on Weybridge Common. 'These took the form of long lines of skirmishers extending to three yards, instantly advancing by short rushes, one half of the company giving covering fire while the other half moved forward,' recalled Rifleman Latham. 'The whole culminated in fixing bayonets and charging a hill.' The battalion returned to Waterloo at about 8.00 on a Sunday evening:

> Everybody was brown and felt fit; it had been, of course,
> a lovely sunny weekend, but then all weekends before the
> war seemed to be sunny, or perhaps it is merely the
> thought of them in golden retrospect.[119]

The London Regiment was unique: territorial infantry battalions were generally part of regiments which included regular battalions too. Most followed the pattern of the Queen's Royal Regiment. In 1914 both regular battalions were in England, 1/Queen's at Bordon in Hampshire and 2/Queen's at Lyndhurst in the New Forest. The Special Reserve battalion, 3/Queen's, was based at the regimental depot, Stoughton barracks in Guildford, and there were two territorial battalions, 4/Queen's, with its headquarters at Croydon, and 5/Queen's at Guildford. Most of the half-dozen or so regular permanent staff instructors attached to each of the territorial battalions were regular Queensmen, although the adjutant of 4/Queen's, unusually, was Captain P. H. C. Groves of the King's Shropshire Light Infantry. Battalions of the London regiment had regular affiliations, the London Rifle Brigade with its regular homonym, for instance. The Queen's was associated with 22/London and 24/

London (The Queen's), based in Bermondsey and Kennington respectively, which wore its cap badge and had many Queensmen on its permanent staff.

There were inevitably exceptions to this pattern. Some counties, such as Cambridgeshire and Herefordshire, were too small to have their own regiments. Regular recruits went to a nearby regiment – the Suffolks for Cambridgeshire, and the King's Shropshire Light Infantry for Herefordshire. Larger counties, such as Surrey, could maintain two regiments, in this case the Queen's and the East Surreys. And three regiments with exceptionally good recruiting areas, the Royal Fusiliers (City of London), Middlesex Regiment and Worcestershire Regiment, had three regular battalions, which skewed subsequent battalion numbering. New Army battalions, as we shall soon see, numbered after the territorial battalions of the same regiment. The foot guards had only regular battalions, three each for the Grenadiers and Coldstream, two for the Scots and one for the Irish. There was, as yet, no Welsh Guards: the regiment would not be formed until 1915, mounting its first guard on Buckingham Palace on 1 March, St David's Day, that year.

Haldane had stuck steadfastly to the principle that the Territorial Force should contain all arms, and so it did. The fact that it attracted many middle-class men who would have been unlikely to join the ranks of the regular army meant that many of the men who joined specialist units such as the Tyne Electrical Engineers – formed to maintain searchlights and communications in the Tyne defences – already had skills which the army could use. It was harder to create purely military skills in the training time available. Norman Tennant enlisted in 11th Battery, 4th North Riding Howitzer Brigade, in 1913, with several friends from Ilkley Grammar School. In August that year his unit camped at Aberystwyth. 'To this day,' he mused, 'the smell of crushed grass, which is always to be found inside marquees, reminds me of the rough and ready meals on the bare trestle tables, slightly flavoured with smoke from the cookhouse fires . . .'. He found that the experience was useful in more than a military sense.

It was natural that groups of school friends should be drawn together, in addition to making new contacts, and this continued throughout the war. In due course we came to appreciate the sterling qualities of some of the rougher local types and responded to their innate friendliness but here in our first annual camp we felt rather shy and tended to associate with those we already knew so well.

Horses presented a real challenge, especially his 'spare wheeler' –

a vast immobile brute with thick hairy legs and drooping head; it seemed quite happy to spend much of its existence standing perfectly still, an occasional tremor of its lower bearded lip indicated that life was still present.

Tennant served in the same battery throughout the war, and recalled 'the care and devotion to his men by the battery commander, Major P. C. Petrie DSO MC, who helped raise it, train it and commanded it till the end of the war'. Its discipline, he believed, 'was derived more from a sense of comradeship than from the methods normally employed by the Regular army'.[120]

Haldane also formalised the Officers' Training Corps (OTC). The forerunners of these had been founded in Victorian times as rifle volunteer corps attached to universities or public schools. Some of the latter took their corps very seriously: the Eton College Rifle Volunteers had a regular adjutant and turned out in a natty shade of the French grey. Enough members of Cambridge University Rifle Volunteers volunteered to fight in the Boer War for the unit to earn a 'SOUTH AFRICA' battle honour. Haldane established junior divisions of the OTC at public schools and some grammar schools: successful cadets earned Certificate B, a very basic certificate of military knowledge. Senior divisions were at universities, and their cadets could earn Certificate A, which was believed to fit them for a territorial commission. More broadly, the scheme was expected to attract men and boys of 'the intellectual and moral attainments likely to fit them for the rank of officers', even if they did not immediately put these qualities to use. Between August 1914 and March the following year, 20,577 officers were commissioned from OTCs, and another 12,290 ex-OTC men were serving in the ranks.[121]

NEW ARMY

That arch-regular Lord Kitchener, appointed Secretary of State for War in the summer of 1914, had a low opinion of the Territorial Force. In part it stemmed from his experience of the Franco-Prussian War, when he had served briefly with Chanzy's Army of the Loire and had been less than impressed by French irregulars. In part it reflected the fact that he had spent most of his career abroad, and had been wholly untouched by Haldane's advocacy of a national army. Indeed, he admitted to the formidable leader of the Ulster Unionists: 'I don't know Europe; I don't know England; and I don't know the British Army.' And in part it embodied his own instinctive mistrust of the amateur: on the morning that he took over the War Office he declared that 'he could take no account of anything but regular soldiers'.[122] And to raise a new one he decided to bypass the territorial system altogether.

Kitchener's decision has been widely criticised, but it was not wholly illogical. Many territorials immediately volunteered for foreign service: F. S. Hatton proudly remembered that in his unit 'the men who did not wish to volunteer for foreign service were asked to take a pace to the rear. The ranks remained unbroken.'[123] The Northumberland Hussars affirmed that all its men had already accepted foreign service as a condition of their enlistment. But the picture was far patchier elsewhere. Walter Nicholson, a regular staff officer in what was to become the very good 51st Highland Division, admitted: 'We were very far from being a division fit for defence.'[124] Some men immediately volunteered for foreign service; some officers automatically assumed that their men would volunteer, and unwisely took this assumption for assent. Others would not serve abroad. 'It was not cowardice that decided them to say they wouldn't fight,' wrote Nicholson, 'it was the belief that the Government had broken faith with them . . . The Territorial had not joined for foreign service, but to defend his country.' One of the division's officers observed that: 'There must be something wrong if employers go out to fight alongside Regular private soldiers.'[125] In the Suffolk Yeomanry the officers of one squadron, an MP amongst them, told their men not to volunteer for foreign service and not to give way to the government's blackmail.

The overwhelming majority of territorials did indeed undertake to serve abroad (perhaps 80–90 percent of many units), and some were fighting in France as early as October 1914, when the fine performance of the London Scottish at Messines showed that territorials went into battle, and to their deaths, with the same determination as regulars. But a few did not, and there remained a slightly curmudgeonly rump of territorials who stuck defiantly to their rights until the changes in the law in 1916 rendered them liable for foreign service anyhow. Nicholson also felt that the problem of post-mobilisation training had not been thought through by the War Office. Adjutants were immediately returned to their regular battalions (and often as promptly killed in action), and this, Nicholson reflected, was: 'a blow from which the Territorial divisions did not recover for many months . . . It is very easy to be wise after the event, but in this case no great wisdom was necessary.'[126]

And there was also the question of the County Associations. These did not control the Territorial Force once it was mobilised, but their responsibility for the supply of some equipment led to frequent difficulties. Nicholson's servant was a regular soldier, and so could not draw equipment from the association, but had to apply for a new shirt to his old company of 1/Argyll and Sutherland Highlanders, by then in the trenches in France, which was palpably absurd. Procedures for pay and allowance were not the same as those in the regular army, and as Nicholson saw first-hand, many territorials were paid less by the army than they had been in civilian life, and got into difficulties. One officer on the divisional staff: 'was for ever digging deeper and deeper into his capital to keep his business going in the East End, till the war slowly froze him out. He had no time away from his military duties, save to sign his money away.'[127]

The legislative defence against incorporating territorials, individually or collectively, in units other than the ones they had joined, which had made good sense to Haldane and his associates prior to 1908, was far less logical during a major war. It caused constant problems as men complained to their MPs that they were being transferred against their will or their units were being broken up; in 1919 the War Office felt compelled to issue a formal defence of its actions.[128] Lastly, the Territorial Force had been formed for home defence, and it was not immediately clear what the extent of the German threat to the mainland of the United Kingdom would actually be: even Winston Churchill, then First Lord of the Admiralty, admitted that 'the period of maximum danger' would extend until early 1915.

On 13 August 1914 Kitchener told Lord Esher that he was perfectly happy to use territorials either to reinforce the New Armies or to release regulars from overseas garrisons. But he had already decided that he would deviate from Haldane's concept of using the territorials as a basis for military expansion. He would bypass the Territorial Force, with its different terms of service and County Associations, and raise troops through the adjutant general's branch in the War Office.[129] In August 1914, therefore, a young man wishing to join the army had three choices. He could become a regular on pre-war terms of service: the Royal Military Academy Woolwich and Royal Military College Sandhurst, for instance, continued to train regular officers throughout the war. Or he could become a territorial, accepting or declining foreign service. Lastly, he could become a regular for the duration of the war by joining the New Armies, so intimately linked to their instigator as to be called Kitchener's Armies.

His decision would be influenced by a number of factors. Many (but by no means all) local authorities, as we have seen in Accrington, threw their weight behind the New Armies. There was a widely-held belief – so marked that New Army recruiting meetings were occasionally disrupted by jealous serving territorials – that the New Armies would get abroad first, and the young and bold often chose to join them for that reason. But on the other hand, some of the cautious and far-sighted deduced that by enlisting in the Territorial Force but (crucially) not accepting liability for foreign service they were more likely to survive the war. That this was likely to produce an avoidable muddle is beyond question. Rather than joining in the rush to blame Kitchener, autocratic, opinionated and obdurate though he was, we might more reasonably criticise a government which had not put in place a mechanism for raising troops to meet the demands of the continental war in which its foreign policy was likely to involve it.

It was Kitchener's achievement to give Britain an army capable of meeting the demands of war on an unprecedented scale. Just over 5,700,000 men served in the army during the war, almost two million more than in the Second World War, and the army of 1914–18 was 'the most complex single organisation created by the British nation up to that time'. Just under half its men were volunteers: by the end of 1915, 2,466,719 had voluntarily enlisted, more than the nation was able to obtain by conscription in 1916 and 1917 combined, and the number of conscripts enlisted in 1918 was only 30,000 more than the number of volunteers enlisting in September 1914 alone.[130]

On 6 August 1914 Kitchener sought parliamentary approval for increasing the size of the army by 500,000 men, and the following day newspapers carried appeals for 'an addition of 100,000 men to His Majesty's Regular Army . . .'. Volunteers were to be between nineteen and thirty years old, and were to sign on for three years or the duration of the war. Five days later the War Office gave details of the 'First New Army', or K1, which was to comprise six complete divisions: the infantry component, by far the bulk of the force, was, as we have seen, to form 'service' battalions of existing regiments.[131] On the first day of the appeal, 7 August, *The Times* reported that the press of men outside the Central London Recruiting Office in Great Scotland Yard was so big that mounted police had to hold it in check. Although there was no wild cheering or excitement there was, perhaps more tellingly in the British context, an 'undercurrent of enthusiasm', and those who failed their medical examination were obviously disappointed. One former officer in the Rifle Brigade was so mortified at being found unfit for service that he shot himself.

Extra recruiting offices were opened to make the process quicker, and extra clerks and doctors were found to speed up the bureaucracy of attestation and medical examination. The campaign gained momentum in its second week, and Tuesday 19 August set the record, thus far, for a single day with 9,699 enlistments. News from the front, where the BEF had just fought the battle of Mons, coupled with steadily-improving procedures brought in more than 63,000 men in the week beginning 25 August. On 28 August Kitchener appealed for another 100,000 men. Although he initially intended to use these troops to reinforce the rapidly-forming divisions of K1, it was soon decided to form another New Army, K2.[132] There had already been a flurry of complaints in the press about fit men excluded by the previous limits (Admiral Sir William Kennedy gruffly told *The Times* that his butler, a fine shot, had been rejected because he was thirty-two), and so the upper age limit was increased to thirty-five for men without prior service, forty-five for ex-soldiers and fifty for ex-senior NCOs.

The widening of age limits, improved procedures, and the establishment of a Parliamentary Recruiting Committee to help the government bring together all the agencies involved, all helped. The alarmist 'Amiens dispatch' which appeared in *The Times* on 30 August – greatly overstating the damage incurred by the BEF on the retreat from Mons – persuaded many that there was a very real need, and numerous firms generously agreed to supplement the army pay of men who enlisted. Recruits flooded in, establishing records which were not to be broken for the rest of the war: on Thursday 3 September 1914, a staggering 33,204 men (equivalent to almost one-third the strength of the BEF in France) joined the army. Having formally declared the creation of the 2nd New Army on 11 September, the War Office quickly agreed to a 3rd and then a 4th New Army.[133] The 5th and final New Army was sanctioned in October: in less than three months Kitchener had laid the foundation for no less than thirty new divisions.[134] It was an achievement wholly without precedent in British history.

If Kitchener's achievement was unprecedented, the army's radical expansion was wholly unplanned. There were no weapons, uniforms or equipment for most of these men; few experienced officers and NCOs who could train them; no proper living accommodation, cookhouses or medical centres; too few rifle and artillery ranges; no draught animals, harness or vehicles; and no commanders and staff for the new divisions or the brigades that made them up. Raising and training the New Armies represented improvisation on a staggering scale. It is worth contemplating the result of a comparable increase in other professions. School registers would quadruple in size, though accommodation would not, and long-retired teachers would join untrained newcomers in the classroom. Three-men-and-a-truck London building firms would each receive a hundred new workers (many of them fishermen from the Western Isles) and be invited to embark upon complex construction projects for which no materials were yet available. And small-town banks would be invited to take on three dozen new staff, many of them innumerate and a few unreliable, to finance complex local ventures being run by the inexperienced, the overambitious and the idle.

It had never been easier to get a commission in the Special Reserve, New Armies or territorials: a young man simply had to find a commanding officer who was prepared to take him on. When F. P. Roe was at his school's OTC camp in July 1914 his contingent commander handed out applications for temporary commissions with names already filled out: they simply required signatures. 'We all of us signed,' he recalled,

> and the forms were dispatched to the War Office the same day. Understandably, in view of the fact that the same sort of procedure was going on all over Britain we heard nothing at all . . . With determined disregard for the usual channels and with renewed enthusiasm I sent a telegram to the War Office: 'Have been accepted for a commission in the 6th (Territorial) Battalion The Gloucestershire Regiment.' I later read in *The Times* of 1 October a copy of *The London Gazette* appointing me to a commission as a second lieutenant in that unit. Later on our early applica-

tions must have caught up for I was antedated in my rank
to 31st July 1914 on my birthday . . . Much later I received
the parchment of my actual commission.[135]

C. H. Gaskell, with the benefit of OTC experience, simply went to
Bulford Camp on his motor bike 'to see what could be done in the
way of getting a commission in the army'. Having failed to strike
gold there, he roared on to the Wiltshire Regiment's depot in
Devizes, where he presented himself 'to Col Stewart who treated me
with great kindness and seemed hopeful of getting me a commission
right away'. Two days later he was in 3/Wiltshire, the Special Reserve
battalion, under the congenial command of Lord Heytesbury. 'We
had a few parades to attend, some trench digging, and an odd lecture
or two,' he wrote, 'with plenty of time off for bathing and having
tea in the town and singsongs in the evening.' In a month he was
in France, commanding a platoon in 1/Wiltshire on the Aisne. As
he went into the line for the first time one of his men shouted 'Are
we downhearted?' and a weary soldier on his way out replied 'No,
but you bloody soon will be.'[136]

In September 1914 Graham Greenwell, instantly commissioned
into the infantry, told his mother that: 'I am having great fun and
enjoying it all immensely.' The only setback, though, he wrote, was
that: 'I can't get a sword or a revolver for love or money, though
Harrods are getting me one.'[137] One fond mother earnestly adver-
tised in *The Times* for a loan to buy a revolver for her officer son,
promising donors that the best possible references supported her
application. North Whitehead feared that his mother might not be
so supportive. He wrote from Rugby school that he was persuaded,
'not only by the leader writers but by letters written by officers', that
all able-bodied men really should join. He knew that she would worry
about him, but assured her that:

> our navy will play the chief part in our share of the war.
> A man who has just joined the army is nearly useless at
> first, although I can handle a service rifle . . .
> Darling Mummy, remember that in all probability I
> shall never go beyond the drill ground & that if I do I
> shall in all probability never be more than a reserve.

He was commissioned into the Army Service Corps, Special Reserve and was in France by the month's end. 'The officers who have just got their commissions owing to the war are markedly less pleasant than the regular officers who are simply charming,' he wrote. 'In active service the relations between officers of different ranks is much easier than in peacetime.' There were some pleasant surprises. 'It is almost impossible to pay for anything in the shops, they want to make a gift of everything,' and: 'The foreign soldiers all salute one as if their lives depended on it.'[138]

Family connections were useful. Julian Tyndale-Biscoe was at OTC camp on Cannock Chase when war broke out, and gleefully reported that there was a huge inter-fight to celebrate the news. When the guard charged the offenders in an attempt to restore order, 'they were soon thrown to the ground and parted from their rifles and hats'. He wired his cousin Victor, commanding King Edward's Horse, who replied: 'Regiment full strength – join something.' His uncle Albert, commanding a brigade of field artillery at Woolwich, suggested that he apply for a regular commission in the gunners. But the war, he thought, might be over by then, so instead he wrote to the War Office. There was a brief interview: 'When he heard that I had Certificate A and was in the shooting eight, etc, etc, he gave a grunt and told me that he would arrange for me to be gazetted in the next week or so.'[139]

Tyndale-Biscoe happily went off in his OTC uniform with hasty alterations to the sleeve for his new badges of rank. But he received a rude shock when he joined his battery at Deepcut in Surrey.

> Where were the guns and horses? All I could see was a large crowd of men in their civilian clothes marching unendingly to the voice of various sergeants, on a gravel square, much to the detriment of their boots. The Major said, 'Here is the Battery – I want you to train these men.' When I told him that I had no artillery training, he said 'Oh, that does not matter, you just watch the others do it, and do it yourself.'

He managed to get posted to Woolwich for some proper training, and the other officers he met typified the young men commissioned by these rough and ready methods. 'I have met a lot of nice fellows here,' he told his father. 'Apart from Paul, there are two from Cambridge – one shared the same staircase at Jesus with Harold [his brother] and the other who is in my battery stroked the Trinity boat.' Posted back to a battery at Aldershot with some decent training under his belt, he found that he had fallen into the clutches of a battery commander of the horsier persuasion. 'I don't believe in all these angles and things,' he announced. 'What I say is – "Gallop up to the top of the hill and poop off".'[140]

On 1 December 1914 Second Lieutenant Jim Mackie of 2/4th Somerset Light Infantry, himself only commissioned in September that year, told his brother Andrew:

> I heard the Colonel saying this morning that he wanted one more subaltern so I at once approached him and said that I had a younger brother who would like to join. He jumped at the idea at once and said that he should be delighted to have a younger brother of mine in the regiment . . .
>
> I asked you to send your birth certificate and medical certificate tonight because the Colonel is sending to the War Office to-morrow & if your certificates are sent up you will get gazetted more quickly . . . As the Colonel has definitely decided to take you, you need not wait till you are gazetted before you get your uniform but can begin at once.[141]

When the battalion sailed for India there were three Mackie brothers in its officers mess.

In August 1914, Harold Macmillan, the future Prime Minister, enlisted in the Artists' Rifles and was speedily commissioned into a New Army battalion of the King's Royal Rifle Corps. Sir Thomas Pilkington, his CO,

> with his white hair, rubicund complexion, and aquiline nose . . . was a figure from the past. He treated us with kindness, but seemed somewhat surprised at the strange collection of officers, non-commissioned officers, and men of which he was the Chief . . . I can see him now, with well-cut uniform, smart polished boots, and spurs, gazing mournfully at a number of men – some of whom had tunics but civilian trousers, others with khaki trousers but civilian coats – all constituting a formation of troops which

must have struck him as extremely unlikely ever to become soldiers.[142]

It struck young Harold that he could get to France quicker with a better regiment, and after an interview with the regimental lieutenant colonel found himself translated to 3/Grenadier Guards, whose legacy never left him. 'I have preserved the habit of being five minutes early for appointments,' he acknowledged in later life.

This spate of commissioning went on into 1915. Bernard Martin, still at school, was summoned by his headmaster to be told:

> 'You, and some of your friends, will be interested in a War Office pronouncement that I've just received. The regular Army has a Special Reserve of Officers; something to do with filling unexpected vacancies in the Indian Army . . . Applications for commissions in this reserve are now invited from school cadet corps members. It is not like Kitchener's Army volunteers, serving for the duration. These special reserve commissions are permanent . . .'. He picked up a paper from his desk. 'Applicants must be recommended by someone of good standing who has known the applicants personally for at least three years. The age limit is eighteen.'
> 'Nineteen, sir,' I murmured in polite concern.
> 'Nineteen for Kitchener's Army,' he explained. 'The Special Reserve for Officers is eighteen . . .' So a miracle came to pass. On the 25th April 1915, one day after my eighteenth birthday, I was gazetted a Second Lieutenant in the reserve battalion of the 64th Regiment of Foot in the regular army, an infantry regiment which boasted a long list of battle honours . . .[143]

A public school boy who wanted a commission could scarcely fail to get one. But when R. C. Sherriff was being interviewed he gave the name of his school, only to discover that it was not on the approved list: the fact that it was a grammar school with a long and distinguished history did not help. His interviewer regretted that there was nothing that could be done, and Sherriff duly signed on as a private, to gain his commission the hard way.

Not all public school boys, students or graduates wanted commissions. Sometimes this was a matter of principle. Frederick Keeling ('Siberian Joe') was twenty-eight in 1914, a Cambridge graduate and a member of the Independent Labour Party. He enlisted in 6/Duke of Cornwall's Light Infantry, and refused a commission, though he rose steadily through the ranks to become a company sergeant major in 1916. That summer he wrote to his mother-in-law:

> I may be knocked out in the next few days. If so, this is just a line to you, dear. I don't contemplate death, but it is all a bloody chance out here. If there is any sort of survival of consciousness, death can hardly fail to be interesting, and if there is anything doing on the other side, I will stir something up. Nirvana be damned!

He was killed at Delville Wood on 18 August, and never knew that he had won the Military Medal, gazetted the following February.[144]

Richard Henry Tawney, a devout Christian, socialist and distinguished economic historian, enlisted in a New Army battalion of the Manchesters at the age of thirty-four, also declined a commission and was wounded as a sergeant on the Somme. A general visited him while he was in hospital and warned the sister in charge of his ward that she was looking after a national treasure. Shocked, she asked Tawney why he had not told her that he was a gentleman. Leslie Coulson, assistant editor of the *Morning Post*, joined 2/2nd London in 1914, refusing to apply for a commission. 'No, I will do the thing fairly,' he declared. 'I will take my place on the ranks.'[145] He fought in Gallipoli, and was then transferred to 12/London. By now a sergeant, and recommended for the commission he felt he had to earn, he was killed when 56th Division assaulted Leuze Wood on 7 October 1916. By then he had established himself as a poet of some distinction and, like so many poets, expressed a rage in his writing that was absent from his military persona.

> Who made the Law that men should die in meadows?
> Who spake the word that blood should splash in lanes?
> Who gave it forth that gardens should be boneyards?
> Who spread the hills with flesh, and blood, and brains?

Even more volunteers wanted to stay in the ranks because that was where their friends were. Some units, like many of the London battalions constituting 33rd Division, were filled with men who might more naturally have been officers. The division included five public school battalions, 18/ to 21/Royal Fusiliers and 16/Middlesex; an 'Empire' and a Kensington battalion of the Royal Fusiliers; a West Ham battalion (13/Essex); the 1st Football Battalion (properly 17/Middlesex); and the Church Lads' Battalion (16/King's Royal Rifle Corps). Even the divisional pioneer battalion, best, if bluntly, described as military navvies, was 1st Public Works (18/Middlesex).[146] The Sportsmen's Battalion (23/Royal Fusiliers) included in its ranks two England cricketers, the country's lightweight boxing champion and the former lord mayor of Exeter. A member of the unit described his hut in the battalion's camp at Hornchurch:

> In this hut the first bed was occupied by the brother of a peer. In the second the man who formerly drove his motor-car. Both had enlisted at the same time at the Hotel Cecil . . . Other beds in the hut were occupied by a mechanical engineer, an old Blundell School boy, planters, a mine overseer from Scotland, . . . a photographer, a poultry farmer, an old sea dog who had rounded Cape Horn on no fewer than nine occasions, a man who had hunted seals, a bank clerk, and so on. It must not be thought that this hut was an exceptional one. Every hut was practically the same, and every hut was jealous of its reputation.[147]

Many of these men subsequently did earn commissions – some 3,000 from 33rd Division alone – but many more were killed or crippled before they did so.

Even getting into the ranks could prove tricky. Stuart Dolden was 'absolutely shattered' when he was turned down at his enlistment medical because his chest measurement was two inches under requirement. He immediately went to a 'physical culture centre' in Dover Street, whose proprietor told him that his course, of ten half-hourly sessions, would cost 30 guineas, and had been taken by many famous people including the Archbishop of Canterbury and Field Marshal Sir John French. Dolden riposted that 'I was not concerned with these gentlemen since it was my father who would have to foot the bill', and managed to get it reduced to 6 guineas. The exercises worked, and Dolden joined the London Scottish, paying a pound for the privilege of doing so. It was a good deal easier for Anthony French, signing on at Somerset House, with a grunted monologue from the medical officer:

> Hmm ... Shirt off, trousers down ... mmm ... Cough ... mmm ... Not very tall ... mmm ... Scales over there ... mmm ... Silly business war ... mmm ... Just ten stone ... shouldn't have thought it ... Hmm ... Chest measurement ... mmm ... expand ... mmm ... Blast the Germans anyway ... mmm ... two-and-a-half inches ... elastic lungs ... mmm ... try the Navy next time ... Hmm ... Mouth open ... wider ... mmm ... Say aahhh ... mmm ... ninety-nine ... mmmmm ... General Service ... Next man, Corporal ... mmm.
>
> I took my shilling and departed.[148]

I. G. Andrew enlisted in the Glasgow University Company of 6/Cameron Highlanders. He found life in a tented camp near Aldershot 'almost unendurably hard', though it ridded him of 'a certain priggish donnishness'. The bonds of mateship came quickly. He and three comrades 'marched together, drank together, ate together and at night slept next to each other wherever it might be – tent, hut, billet or under the open air of heaven'. His company sergeant major was no ordinary man, but 'a Roberston of Struhan, the son of a Colonel, the grandson of a major-general and an undergraduate of Magdalen College, Oxford'. Roberston had been a captain of rifle volunteers, a justice of the peace in India, and gave his profession on enlistment as 'actor'. Officially too old for the front, Roberston nonetheless managed to engineer his way to France, where he was wounded at Loos. There was initially too little khaki to go round, and most New Army units wore 'Kitchener Blue', deeply unpopular because it made them look like bus drivers. 6/Camerons, however, had red tunics with white facings, postmen's trousers, and, as Andrew found, 'cap comforters closely resembling tea cosies'. The full majesty of the kilt did not come till 1915.

One night in camp Andrew's pal John Irish sang 'that grand old song *The Trumpeter*'. It is the most poignant of the old army's tear-jerkers, with the trumpeter urging his comrades to:

> ... Tread light o'er the dead in the valley
> Who are lying around, face down to the ground
> And they can't hear me sounding the Rally ...

'It is a solemn moment,' he reflected, 'when a young man first senses his own mortality,' and many sensed it then. Offered a commission through the good offices of a friendly MP, he turned it down and went to France as a lance corporal. John Irish departed to be a second lieutenant in the Argyll and Sutherland Highlanders, and the farewell was painful.

> I was never to see him again, and when he met a soldier's death at Arras a year later, I felt that something quite irreplaceable had gone out of my life. [John Irish stood] with the tears streaming down his face as he sobbed, 'Good-bye Tubby, and the best of luck.'

Andrew's battalion was part of the exceptional 9th Scottish Division. Second Lieutenant R. B. Talbot Kelly, a regular gunner in one of the batteries supporting it, remembered how:

> Our Scottish infantry created an enormous impression on our minds. Never again was I to see so many thousands of splendid men, the very heart and soul of the nation. These were they who, on the outbreak of war, had rushed to enlist, the best and first of Kitchener's New Armies. And here we saw them, bronzed and dignified, regiments of young gods.[149]

The Camerons went into action at Loos 820 strong and emerged with two officers and seventy men: Lance Corporal Andrew, himself wounded, saw Regimental Sergeant Major Peter Scotland standing over the commanding officer and asked if he should fetch stretcher-bearers. 'It's no good,' said the RSM, 'the old man's dying.' Andrew at last felt able to take a commission and, while convalescing, wrote to the commanding officer of 5/Scottish Rifles, who agreed to take him. 'A man of means' thanks to his outfit allowance, he went to the best tailor in Glasgow for his uniform, but when he reported for duty at Catterick he discovered that 'second lieutenants were two a penny'.[150]

Not all Pals' battalions broke the old army's rules quite as dramatically as units such as 23/Royal Fusiliers or 6/Camerons, with their high proportion of educated men serving in the ranks. The 31st Division presented a fairer social cross section, though even here there were far more artisans, students and office workers than ever appeared in the old army. The division's 92nd Brigade had four battalions of East Yorkshires, known as the Hull Commercials, the Hull Tradesmen, the Hull Sportsmen and, for want of a better name, the Hull T'others. In 92nd Brigade were three West Yorkshire battalions, the Leeds Pals and 1st and 2nd Bradford Pals, as well as 18/Durham Light Infantry, the Durham Pals. The third brigade, 94th, contained 12/York and Lancaster (The Sheffield City Battalion, with many university students in its ranks), 13/ and 14/York and Lancaster (1st and 2nd Barnsley Pals) and our old friends 11/ East Lancashire (The Accrington Pals).

The divisional pioneer battalion, T'owd Twelfth (one of several northern battalions to use that name), was 12/King's Own Yorkshire Light Infantry, many of them miners from Charlesworth Pit who had streamed into Leeds to enlist in 1914.[151] Its composition underlines another important point about the New Armies. Many volunteers came from working-class areas with a tradition of industrial militancy: these were not the products of a cowed, deferential society. But by mid-1915 over 230,000 miners, about one-quarter of the workforce, had volunteered. 'The compatibility of class consciousness and patriotism,' observed J. M. Winter, 'could have no better illustration. Of course, we should never completely discount the desire of some miners to get out of the mines, but sentiments about nation and empire rather than discontent, were behind mass enlistment in the industry.'[152]

Wide variations in regional enlistment can barely be summarised here, and so I pass lightly over the rich tapestry of the New Armies. But three specific divisions deserve early mention. In late September 1914 a Welsh National Executive Committee was formed, with the aim of raising a Welsh Army Corps of two divisions for inclusion in the New Armies. David Lloyd George had already given the concept his eloquent support.

> I should like to see a Welsh Army in the field. I should
> like to see the race who faced the Normans for hundreds

of years in their struggle for freedom, the race that helped
to win the battle of Crecy, the race that fought for a generation under Glendower against the greatest captain in
Europe – I should like to see that race give a good taste
of its quality in this struggle.[153]

The committee, along with the numerous individuals and corporations already recruiting in Wales, made a serious attempt to attract
Welsh-speaking officers and men. Recruiting posters, in both Welsh
and English, bore calls to arms from Prince David, 'Brother of
Llewelyn, the last Prince of Wales', though there was no historical basis
for the words. A short-lived attempt to clothe the troops in Welsh grey
homespun cloth called *Brethyn Llwyd* was marred by a shortage of cloth
and the fact that the grey jackets at £1 apiece were more expensive
than khaki at 14/7d or Kitchener Blue at 14/2d: and in any event
officers and men preferred khaki. There were sharp clashes between
Kitchener, who complained that the army could not be 'a political
machine', and Lloyd George, inflamed by Kitchener's refusal to allow
Welsh to be the language spoken on parade and his reluctance to
shift other Welsh units into the new corps to bring it up to strength.

It was soon clear that there would be too few volunteers to raise
a full corps, and in December the single division that could be
brought to full manning was called 43rd (Welsh), and renumbered
38th (Welsh) in April 1915. Local politics was generally well to the
fore when it came to raising the New Armies: indeed, it is hard to
see how it could have been otherwise. But several factors, such as
Welsh nationalism, concerns about the impact of Nonconformity
with its strong element of pacifism, and the personality of Lloyd
George, all played a greater than usual part in colouring the composition of 38th Division. One of Lloyd George's sons was aide de camp
to the divisional commander, and some senior commanders owed
their selection more to their political backing than their military
ability. And the division seems to have suffered more than most from
the slow arrival of its equipment, another consequence of the army's
rapid expansion: 16/Welsh (Cardiff City) received its first eighty
working rifles in August 1915, and it was not until October that
enough rifles were available for men to fire at their range course at
Winchester prior to embarking for France. The divisional artillery

had no horses till April that year, and even then its gunners were still drilling on tent poles mounted on wheels.[154]

But how painfully hard the division tried in its first big battle. On 7 July 1916, in the early stages of the Somme, it was sent in to clear the great slab of Mametz Wood, jutting down from Longueval Ridge and the German second position. It was unutterably confusing fighting in a wood in full summer foliage, and would have tried more experienced troops and staffs. 'I could not push a way through it,' wrote Captain Llewelyn Wyn Griffith,

> and I had to return to the ride. Years of neglect had turned the Wood into a formidable barrier, a mile deep. Heavy shelling of the Southern end had beaten down some of the young growth, but it had also thrown large branches into a barricade. Equipment, ammunition, rolls of barbed wire, tins of food, gas-helmets and rifles were lying about everywhere. There were more corpses than men, but there were worse sights than corpses. Limbs and mutilated trunks, here and there a detached head, forming splashes of red against the green leaves, and, as in advertisement of the horror of our way of life and death, and of our crucifixion of youth, one tree held in its branches a leg, with its torn flesh hanging down over a spray of leaf . . .
>
> A message was now on its way to some quiet village in Wales, to a grey farmhouse on the slope of a hill running down to Cardigan Bay, or to a miner's cottage in a South Wales valley, a word of death . . .[155]

His brother Watcyn, a private soldier in the same Royal Welch Fusilier battalion (unthinkable in the old army), was killed. 'I had not even buried him,' lamented Griffith as he left this charnel place, 'nor was his grave ever found.'

At the very end of the fighting in the wood the division's Welshness was still painfully evident. 'I crouched with some men to shelter,' recalled Griffith. 'We talked in Welsh, for they were Anglesey folk; one was a young boy, and after a thunderous crash in our ears he began to cry out for his mother, in a thin boyish voice, "*mam, mam . . .*".'[156] The division lost over 4,000 men, and was so badly jarred that it was not engaged in another major battle till the first day of Third Ypres, 31 July 1917. It suffered 28,635 casualties in the whole of the war, but somehow Mametz Wood is the right place for its memorial, a proud red dragon glaring out across Happy Valley towards the blank-faced wood and Flat Iron Copse Cemetery full of the division's dead, with ripped-up barbed wire in its claws.[157]

It was not easy for all Welshmen to reconcile nationalist politics of the Chapel's reservations about violence with service in the British army. However, the problems confronting many Irish recruits were even more serious. The long-running issue of Home Rule had not simply divided Ireland but had infected British politics more broadly, and had produced the Curragh 'mutiny' of March 1914, when the officers of the Curragh-based 3rd Cavalry Brigade, under Brigadier General Hubert Gough, declared that they would resign their commissions rather than march north to compel Ulster to join a united and independent Ireland. Indeed, so heated were passions on both sides of Ireland's cultural divide that it has been well argued that the outbreak of war in 1914 actually prevented a civil war in Ireland which seemed inevitable if the British government pressed ahead with Home Rule.

But if the outbreak of a large war did indeed delay a smaller one, it nonetheless faced Irish nationalists with a cruel dilemma. Should they take the view, as some of their ancestors might have done, that England's difficulty was Ireland's opportunity, or should they support the war in the hope that by doing so they would demonstrate their responsibility and maturity? The nationalist leader John Redmond immediately declared that the war was:

> undertaken in defence of the highest principles of religion
> and morality and right, and it would be a disgrace for ever
> to our country, and a regret to her manhood, and a denial
> of the lessons of history, if young Ireland continued her
> efforts to remain at home to defend the shores of Ireland
> from military invasion, and shirk from the duty of proving
> on the field of battle that gallantry and courage which has
> distinguished our race across its history.[158]

Sinn Féin propaganda had declared that an Irishman who joined the British army was 'a traitor to his country and a felon in his soul', though this had not stopped 9.1 percent of the regular army of 1914 from being Irish. However, the decision of constitutional nationalists to encourage enlistment sharply divided them from their more extreme brethren, and led to many Irishmen ascending history's old Calvary, and fighting bravely in the ranks of an army to whose political principles they were firmly opposed.

With the active support of Redmond and his colleagues, Irishmen were enlisted into New Army battalions of Irish regiments. Many professional men who had been officers in the National Volunteers volunteered: indeed, there were so many good potential officers that some were sent off to England to help officer the Tyneside Irish. John Wray, solicitor and son of a nationalist election agent, was given an immediate commission in the Connaught Rangers and brought in 200 of his own volunteers. The 7/Leinsters maintained a cadet company for potential officers, and of the 161 men who had passed through its ranks by December 1915, thirty-five were to be killed in action. Three hundred and fifty rugby players from Dublin, white collar and tie men, paraded at Lansdowne Road rugby ground and then marched through the city to the Curragh, where they joined 7/Royal Dublin Fusiliers, where they became known as 'Toffs in the Old Toughs'. A full company of Dublin dockers enlisted, and were known as the Larkinites after their union leader James Larkin, no friend of the British government or capitalism. And, as was so often the case that heady summer, there were odd phenomena: six officers and 225 men of the Royal Guernsey Militia, many of them French-speaking, volunteered for 6/Royal Irish, as they had been so impressed by the Royal Irish battalion which had been in garrison on their island. Two divisions were soon formed, 10th (Irish), in 1st New Army, and 16th (Irish), part of the 2nd New Army. Neither was ever wholly Irish, still less wholly nationalist, but there was a solid and unmistakable streak of Irishness running through both formations.

Ulstermen, too, faced a dilemma when war broke out. The Ulster Volunteer Force was 80,000 strong, and many of its units, organised on British military lines, were well armed and well drilled. There were initial doubts about throwing the considerable weight of the UVF behind the British government (against which it might so easily have found itself fighting), but these were soon resolved after discussions between Kitchener and Sir Edward Carson, the Unionist leader. The formation of what was to become 36th (Ulster) Division began in September 1914, and many of its battalions were firmly based on units of the UVF. Frank Crozier had been forced to leave the army in 1908 after bouncing cheques, which one astute commentator has called 'a lifelong habit'. In 1914 he was, as he put it, 'a hired mercenary' training Carson's UVF, and was quickly re-commissioned into the British army to be second in command to 'my Shankhill Road boys', now transmuted into 9/Royal Irish Rifles. Before the transition was complete he watched a regular battalion of the Norfolks leave for France, seen off by a guard of honour of the UVF's West Belfast Regiment. 'Five months previously,' mused Crozier, 'these very men of the Norfolks had quitted Belfast for Holyrood, owing to the menace in their midst of the very men who were doing them honour now, and from whom they evidently felt disposed to accept the compliment.'[159]

The iconography of 36th Division made its origins clear. The divisional sign was the Red Hand of Ulster; some units wore badges which harked back to their UVF origins, and when the division took immortality by storm on 1 July 1916 (the anniversary, in New Style, of the Battle of the Boyne), there were orange sashes in evidence and the old bark of 'No Surrender!' in the air. The division scored the only significant success north of the Bapaume road that day, and Ulster Tower, a copy of Helen's Tower at Clandeboye, near Belfast, where the division did much of its training, stands on the ground it captured at the cost of 5,000 of its officers and men.

Yet we must be careful not to jam 10th and 16th Divisions on the one hand, and 36th on the other, into the obvious political niches. Some Irish regiments (notably the Royal Irish Rifles) had always recruited both Catholics and Protestants, and there was more than a little sense of a deep and common Irishness that expunged more superficial divides. 'Once we tacitly agreed to let the past be buried,' observed an officer in 10th Division, 'we found thousands of points on which we agreed.' The same music could speak to both. When the pipes of the Royal Irish howled out *Brian Boru*, that tune 'traditionally played by some Irish Regiments to lift hearts and square shoulders', in the assault on Guillemont on 15 September 1916, a man did not have to come from the South to feel his spirits soar. And when a northern-raised battalion of Irish Rifles met a southern battalion on the march with its band playing the old rebel air *She's The Most Distressful Country*, there were cheers of approval.[160]

The apotheosis of the fighting Irish came on 7 June 1917 when 16th and 36th Division attacked side by side in 2nd Army's great assault on Messines Ridge. John Redmond's brother, Major Willie Redmond MP, who had last spoken in the House of Commons just a month before to demand immediate Home Rule, was, at fifty-six, too old for front-line service. But he begged to be allowed back to his old battalion, 6/Royal Irish, and was hit as he walked forward with it, and the 36th Division's stretcher-bearers picked him up. The wound would probably not have killed a younger, fitter man, but it was too much for Willie Redmond. A Roman Catholic chaplain told how:

> He received every possible kindness from Ulster soldiers. In fact, an Englishman attached to the Ulster Division expressed some surprise at the extreme care that was taken of the poor Major, though no Irish soldier expected anything else, for, after all, Ulstermen are Irish too.[161]

Father Willie Doyle of 8/Royal Dublin Fusiliers, killed soon afterwards, enjoyed a reputation which went far beyond those who shared his faith. 'Father Doyle was a good deal amongst us,' wrote an Ulsterman.

> We couldn't possibly agree with his religious opinions, but we worshipped him for other things. He didn't know the meaning of fear, and he didn't know what bigotry was. He was as ready to risk his life to take a drop of water to a wounded Ulsterman as to assist men of his own faith and regiment. If he risked his life looking after Ulster Protestant soldiers once, he did it a hundred times in the last few days. The Ulstermen felt his loss more keenly than anybody and none were readier to show their marks of respect to the dead hero priest than were our Ulster Presbyterians. Father Doyle was a true Christian in every sense of the word, and a credit to any religious faith . . .[162]

The stone tower that now stands in the Irish Peace Park on the southern end of Messines, heavy with Celtic symbolism, gives Protestant and Catholic soldiers the recognition they deserve: a recognition mired too long in politics.

The period between the raising of the 1st New Army in August 1914 and the departure of the first of the New Army divisions to France a year later was marked by shortages of weapons, equipment, accommodation and ammunition, and men remembered the sharp contrast between enthusiastic enlistment and the confusion and boredom that often followed. Even joining was not always easy, as Percy Croney discovered when he reported to the recruiting office in December 1914. 'I took my place in the queue outside,' he recalled.

> Allowed in eight at a time by a smart sergeant, we stood in a row, stripped to the nude and a medical officer gave us a swift examination. The great majority seemed to be passed fit, and redressing we made our way to tables where soldier clerks sat.
>
> 'What regiment do you wish to join?'
>
> '7th Essex, please, all my mates are in that.'
>
> 'Sorry, 7th Essex is long ago up to establishment, why not join the R.E.s, much better pay and conditions than the infantry.'
>
> 'No, I want to be a soldier.'
>
> 'What about the Royal Field Artillery then, or the Garrison Artillery, a gunner's life is good and interesting.'
>
> 'No, I want to join my County regiment.'
>
> He at last admitted that the 12th Battalion was not yet quite up to establishment, and I was seen out into the street again, the King's shilling and 2/9d, one day's subsistence money and pay rattling in my pocket, and holding in my hand a railway warrant to carry me to Warley Barracks on the morrow.[163]

The Rain brothers, trying to enlist in a regiment of their choice before conscription overwhelmed them in early 1917, found it even harder. They were too short for the Royal Marine Artillery. Rejected by a Territorial Royal Field Artillery battery at Islington, they went on to try RFA units at Moorgate and Camberwell 'besides several others'. They managed to pass the medical at Woolwich and then 'by means of tips' secured a promise to be enlisted into the Royal Horse Artillery. But they turned out to be too young for that: and the Field Artillery there was full too. Eventually they struck lucky with the Queen's Westminsters, even if the stew they were served for dinner was 'so unwholesome that we were unable to eat it'. It was a happy choice, for their training battalion was still sending men to its 1st Battalion in France, and there was a real sense of family feeling and, by this stage in the war, no shortages of weapons or accommodation. Their company commander, Captain Gordon, 'was an officer of exceptional popularity', soon to be killed at Cambrai.[164]

Young Harry Ogle, still undecided about his future (which was in fact to see him go to the front as a private and return as a decorated captain), thought that:

> A wave of fear seemed to have spread over the country and young men not in uniform were presented with white feathers by young women (also not in uniform). Men over forty, thinking themselves safe behind 'important' jobs, urged those to enlist who were too young to have anything to lose but their lives. The elderly and painfully religious couple whose lodger I was were cold to me, loudly praising Ted Pullen who, as the newspapers had it, had gallantly 'placed his young life at the service of the Nation'. My fellow lodger, no less liable to military service than I was, openly asked me why I didn't enlist. I answered nobody, for my own thoughts were forming.[165]

In September 1914 Clifford de Boltz was 'accosted by a young lady in Great Portland Street' and presented with a white feather. 'I felt quite embarrassed,' he admitted, 'and threw the feather away in great disgust.' But he enlisted in 2/6th Norfolk, a territorial cyclist battalion, soon afterwards. The battalion was already straining its resources, and he spent his first night in the army on a pub billiard table, and regretted that: 'it went on like this for days and nobody seemed to know what to do next'. As his was a territorial battalion there was at least some uniform, but 'whether it fitted or not did

not seem to matter to them but we all felt very uncomfortable. Boots
– asked for size 5. CQMS "we haven't got any bloody boy's boots,
take these size 7 and wear three pairs of socks and you will be
alright".'[166]

Much depended on *what* men joined, and falling into the dark
maw of a freshly-raised New Army unit, with few trained officers or
NCOs, no proper accommodation, no clear sense of regional identity and pre-war kinship, was probably the worst fate. Bill Sugden
told his future wife Amy on 28 October 1914: 'Well, I've done it
now and am a regular soldier in the RFA. I write in the Main Railway
Station Sheffield having got my ticket for Newhaven and am proceeding there. I am afraid with all the excitement my hand is somewhat
shaky.'[167] On arrival he found that:

> Everything is rough. The camp is like a quagmire, and no
> floor boards in the tent . . . Had a shave with difficulty
> and cold water. Truly last night I wished I was dead.
>
> Sardines and bread for breakfast and we had to fight
> for it. The food is very roughly served. The other fellows
> have to eat their meat with their fingers which I would
> most certainly have to do was it not for my little darling's
> knife and fork.[168]

Soon he was reporting that: 'The life is harder than an outsider
would believe,' with incessant rain, wet blankets, and fatigues like
peeling potatoes and emptying urinal buckets, 'a rotten filthy job'.
Press reports of German conduct in Belgium, though, filled him with
anger and determination. 'The outrages on women and children in
Belgium have been terrible,' he wrote. 'Fancy if Amy had to fall into
their hands . . . I only hope I shall have the chance to have a smash
in return for the way our men have been treated, hands cut off and
wounded shot.'[169] Training seemed both pointless and brutal. 'Our
sergeant major is an absolute pig,' he declared.

> He swears and strikes the men . . . It is a cowardly thing
> to do as he knows the men dare not strike back . . . It
> makes my blood boil when I see it, and if he ever kicks
> or strikes me I shall go for him whatever the consequences
> and half kill him before they get me off . . . They seem to

forget we have all given up our jobs to do our best for the country, and do not expect to be treated like a lot of rifraf.[170]

In November he wondered 'why this Army is without system. If the names of 2 or 3 have to be called out they will have the whole regiment on parade for 2 hours. We are always waiting. Wait, wait, wait and always in the rain.'[171] 'All the men are keen to get on with their duty and it seems a dispiriting thing to me the way we are held back by silly fools of officers,' he wrote on 1 December. 'These men have bought their commissions. They are wealthy, brainless fools.'[172] Things picked up when he was sent to Tynemouth for gun training, and when 21st Siege Battery Royal Garrison Artillery formed there he was already a trained signaller: 'It's quite a classy job and the best educated men are naturally picked out for it.' He was promoted steadily, and in early 1917 announced from France that he was now 'the only New Army man in the battery who has risen to the rank of sergeant ... We have many regulars and I have been promoted over their heads.'[173] Eventually selected for officer training, he was commissioned in April 1919.

Other private soldiers echoed Bill Sugden's chief complaints: bad living conditions and poor food, and training and discipline that seemed inappropriate for citizen soldiers eager to learn a new trade. And experienced officers admitted that it was difficult to make bricks without straw. Captain Rory Baynes, just back from the Royal West African Frontier Force, was sent off to train a New Army Cameronian battalion. His men were an odd mixture, with an early batch of 'pretty rough' unemployed, then a batch who had just given up their jobs, and then a good sprinkling of ex-NCOs. They had no rifles and drilled with broomsticks. 'You'd see a man for instance in a rifle tunic and tartan trews, wearing a straw hat,' he wrote, 'next to someone else in a red coat and some civilian trousers.' He thought that the battalion had reached a reasonable standard by early 1915 when he was passed on the march by two companies of the regular 1/Cameronians and 'saw immediately that our standard of NCOs and everything else was far below what it really should be'.[174]

J. B. Priestley was never altogether sure why he enlisted in

10/Duke of Wellington's Regiment. 'I was not hot with patriotic feeling,' he admitted, and:

> I did not believe that Britain was in any real danger. I was sorry for 'gallant little Belgium' but did not feel as if she was waiting for me to rescue her. The legend of Kitchener, who pointed out at us from every hoarding, had never captured me. I was not under any pressure from public opinion; the white feathers came later. I was not carried to the recruiting office in a herd of chums, nobody thinking, everybody half-plastered. I went alone.[175]

He shared the familiar misery of tented camps, 'sleeping twelve to a bell-tent, kneeling after Lights Out to piss in our boots and then emptying them under the flap. The old soldiers told us that this was good for our boots, making them easier for route-marches'.[176] And like so many New Army men he resented his Kitchener Blue, 'a doleful convict-style blue outfit with a ridiculous little forage cap and a civilian overcoat'. But as khaki uniforms arrived, the weather improved and the battalion knitted together, he too felt the pride of arms which coursed through the New Armies in the spring of 1915. 'We looked like soldiers now,' he wrote.

> All four battalions had a band; and along all the route we were waved at and cheered, not foolishly either, for an infantry brigade marching in full equipment with its bands booming and clashing is an impressive spectacle. This was my idea of soldiering – constant movement, unknown destinations, fluttering handkerchiefs and cheers – and I enjoyed it hugely, sore feet and bully beef and trips on hard ground and all.[177]

Although he would later blame his sense of class consciousness on the war, Priestley still spoke up warmly for the New Armies in their prime: they were emphatically not 'a kind of brave rabble'. But it was not until the summer of 1916 that this promising amalgam of diverse humanity was ready to take the field, and even then inherent weaknesses caused by its rapid growth were too ready to make themselves evident.

Not all the flesh and blood required by the burgeoning army was human, however. The army needed huge quantities of horses. In 1914 it sent a strong cavalry division to France, with almost 10,000 horses, and each of the infantry divisions required nearly 6,000 to pull its guns and wagons and to mount its senior officers. There were 25,000 horses on the army's strength in August 1914, and at least another 120,000 were required to meet immediate demands. Because the army's peacetime requirement for horses was so small, Britain had no state breeding programme, but bought about a thousand horses a year from the trade. Most cavalry horses were 'of hunter stamp. Height 15.2 hands, cost £40 in Ireland, a black gelding'. The Household Cavalry needed something bigger, 'A real nice-looking heavyweight horse with plenty of bone,' which was likely to cost £65 as a four year old.[178]

The Boer War had already shown that the army could not hope to rely on normal commercial channels to obtain horses on mobilisation, and in 1914 its purchasing officers were equipped with justice's warrants which entitled them to obtain horses by compulsory purchase. Most tried to pay sensible sums (£70 was the guideline for an officer's charger), neither overspending nor robbing the sellers. B. E. Todhunter mounted B Squadron of the Essex Yeomanry, travelling over 900 miles to get all the horses he required. 'Essex has been pretty well skinned of her horses,' he told the remount officer in Brentwood on 14 August, 'and I had to go poaching in Suffolk before I could get the six I sent you yesterday.'[179] But not all purchasing officers were as astute. Irish dealers unloaded some questionable stock, 12 percent of which had to be sold on immediately as unsuitable.

Many private individuals, hunt stables and corporations gave up their horses voluntarily. The historian of 11th Hussars recorded that: 'Colonel Pitman's brother sent eight hunters all of which came through the war successfully. The master of the Meynell Hunt sent a number of hunt horses, and others came from Mr Fernie's and the Pytchley.' Weymouth Corporation was so generous with its omnibus horses that there were too few left to pull the buses. But most horses were compulsorily purchased. Captain James Jack of the Cameronians had already been mobilised when he heard that his two remaining hunters, 'Ardskull Boy and Home Park, have been taken for the army – the first war wrench'. When remount sergeants visited the Buckinghamshire village of Tysoe in August: 'Every farm-house ... had some shock and grief that day.' Kathleen Ashby's family lost their much-loved aged carthorse Captain, who was still useful 'if you humoured him and knocked off promptly after his stint of work, but under new men and at hard tasks he must break down'.[180] The disappearance of Sammy and Rob Roy, Titan and Jupiter, cast an early shadow over a land still unused to loss, and some families, proud that their boys should go, could not bear to lose their animals. Three Lancashire children, 'troubled little Britishers', wrote to 'Dear good Lord Kitchener' with a picture of their pony and begged that she might be spared. Two others had already gone, and three of the family were 'now fighting for you in the Navy. Mother and I will do anything for you, but *do, do please* let us keep old Betty.' Kitchener's private secretary, no less, immediately replied that he had spoken to Kitchener and 'if you show the enclosed note to anyone who asks about your pony he thinks it will be left to you quite safely'.[181]

Newly-purchased horses went to remount depots where officers entitled to a charger could take their pick. James Pennycuik of the Royal Engineers tells how:

> An enormous horse depot was formed at the Curragh racecourse to hold wonderful animals requisitioned from all over ... Ireland, a sight never to be forgotten in that green land of horses. We young officers had great fun picking our requirements, and it was a great time for any-one with an eye for a horse.[182]

Henry Owens, a hunting doctor instantly commissioned into the RAMC, collected 'a nice horse, a long-tailed bay, well bred, nice mouth and manners and nice paces'.[183] And Major Tom Bridges of the 4th Dragoon Guards secured 'one Umslopagaas, a powerful weight-carrying hunter with a wall eye, who could jump railway gates'.[184] The unlucky Private Garrod, however, lost his favourite horse, who had to be destroyed when she broke a leg, and was allocated the worst horse in the troop, 'who was such a bastard that he was known as Syphilis' because nobody wanted to catch him. He kicked out and broke the farrier sergeant major's arm when the horses were being embarked at Southampton, and then reared back 'over the dock into the water and was never seen again'.

By June 1915, long before it began to conscript men, the army had taken 8 percent of the heavy horses in use on the land, and 25 percent of saddle horses had gone from farms. At one point in 1917 the army had nearly a million animals on its strength, with 436,000 of them in France. It is small wonder that fodder was, by a narrow margin, the heaviest single item shipped to France, heavier even than ammunition. The pressing need to supply and feed horses helped break down the barriers that had hitherto kept women, apart from nurses, out of uniform. The Women's Forage Corps, which had 6,000 members by 1918, worked at baling and transporting hay, and the Women's Remount Depot played a valuable part in breaking in newly-bought horses. There were the inevitable suggestions that women would not be up to the heavy work, but, in the event, they did it very well, freeing men for military service. Edith Maudslay, a farmer's daughter, joined the Women's Remount Depot in 1915, worried about her gunner brother (reported missing in March 1918 after returning alone to his battery's gun-line to try to amend the day's fortunes with his revolver), and lived on to drive an ambulance in the London Blitz in the Second World War.[185]

The sheer weight of fodder shipped to France must not be used as evidence of the logistic burden imposed by the cavalry. By 1917 only about 27,000 of the British horses on the Western Front (falling to some 16,000 by early 1918) mounted the remaining cavalry. The overwhelming majority pulled guns or wagons, just as they did in the French, German and United States armies at that time. In December 1918 the BEF fed a total of 394,443 animals. Of these just 25,414, riding and draught horses, were in the Cavalry Corps, and 48,822 served on the lines of communication. The number of motor vehicles on the Western Front grew enormously: in August 1914 the Army Service Corps had just 507 motor vehicles at its disposal, and in January 1918 it had almost 22,000 trucks in France alone. However, for the average infantry soldier 'transport' invariably meant *horse* transport, usually the 30-cwt General Service wagon, drawn by two horses, whose load might comprise 100 blankets, twenty double tents, four hospital marquees, forty-five boxes of small arms ammunition or 900 groundsheets.

Nobody who has had much to do with the horse can deny the beast's extraordinary perversity. Lieutenant Alan Lascelles of the Bedfordshire Yeomanry admitted that:

> He debars you from spending the night anywhere in the neighbourhood of civilisation, because he takes up such a lot of room, so that where you have hoped for a roof, you get only a bivouac; he keeps you standing about two hours longer than you need after a long march, because he is unable to clean or feed himself, and will leave you altogether unless firmly secured; he drags you miles, two or three times a day, through mud that he has churned up with his feet and then refuses to drink at the end of it; he wears a mass of impedimenta with an unlimited capacity for getting dirty and unserviceable; he will bite or kick you on the smallest provocation, and at night he will keep honest men from their beds, because, unless closely watched, he will either hang himself or savage his neighbour.[186]

Yet men grew very fond of their horses, and it was a commonplace for men, inured to the passing of their human friends, to record their grief at the death of horses. An unnamed poet in 156th Heavy Battery RGA lamented the loss of the battery's 'pet', 'Billy the Stallion, killed by Hostile Aircraft, 5 July 1917.'

> He was only a bloomin' heavy,
> Only a battery horse,
> But if there's a heaven for horses
> Billy will not be lost . . .

Third Ypres was in full swing, and the army was losing thousands of men every day, but 156th Battery remembered a long-faced chum. In a base hospital the Reverend Charles Doudney talked to a young Canadian who had lost 'his nose, one eye, all one cheek, upper jaw on one side'. Despite these terrible wounds, he had not left his horse, hit by the same shell: 'His fore leg was smashed, so I could not leave him. Had him all the time since we left Canada.'[187] Only with the horse mercifully shot did he deliver his urgent demand for more ammunition. And only then did he seek medical aid. Captain Sidney Rogerson, gratefully out of the line on the Somme in 1916, saw his battalion HQ wagon, 'drawn by the two beautiful chestnuts which were the apple of the driver's eye and which I am last to see side by side in death as in life beside the bridge at Pontavert in May 1918'.[188] Old army or New, it never lost this tug of sentiment, and is none the worse for that.

III

BRAIN AND NERVE

CHAIN OF COMMAND

Whatever segment of the army Thomas Atkins joined, his world was defined by his unit. And this, for the majority of soldiers, meant the infantry battalion, a lieutenant colonel's command of something under 1,000 men. Atkins's life in the line and out of it, his chances of promotion and leave, the tautness of the discipline that bound him, his day-to-day relationships on and off duty, and even the way he wore his uniform, all reflected his unit's culture. But battalions themselves, however huge they seemed to the men in them, were small parts of a huge and complex machine. They were combined into formations – in ascending order: brigades, divisions, corps and armies. These were commanded by generals, assisted by staff officers, collectively known, from their distinguishing collar-patches, as 'red tabs'.

Formation headquarters – just four officers and twenty-three other ranks for an infantry brigade in 1914 to the 3,000 souls that constituted general headquarters by the war's end – needed offices, living accommodation and stabling. In the early months of the war large schools provided good temporary headquarters (though there were complaints about the size of desks), but soon big houses of one sort or another accommodated entire brigade or divisional headquarters, or parts of corps or army headquarters. These residences were often called châteaux, though the word covers a multitude of buildings from stately homes, through large country houses and modest farm-houses, to suburban residences with lofty titles but poky rooms. Although the First World War initiated the expression 'château generalship', commanders of previous centuries had usually lived in just such buildings, and even in 1944–45 Allied generals in France and Belgium were often housed in châteaux for perfectly good reasons. However, Field Marshal Montgomery, anxious not to attract the damaging publicity aroused by tales of comfortable life in well-appointed houses in an earlier war, initially lived in a caravan in the garden of a Normandy château, though eventually the autumn weather drove even the ascetic Monty inside.

The generals of the war remain one of the most controversial groups in the whole of British history, and some memoirs and diaries certainly seethe with criticism of them. Gerald Burgoyne, a regular officer in the Royal Irish Rifles, wrote from Belgium in early 1915 that:

> the whole time I have been out here I never once saw any of our Brigade or Divisional Staff come up to the trenches, and the ground around is to all the staff a kind of *terra incognita*. I have heard so many troops in other divisions say the same thing. In the five months I was in the trenches, I only once saw one of our Brigade Staff visit us, and not once did any of the Divisional Staff come near us. After a time we dreaded the idea of making attacks knowing it would mean heavy casualties and failure.[1]

He later reported of an incident where one British battalion fired on another that it was:

> Rotten staff management and all caused by the staff never coming near the trenches ... The consequence was that the staff were never in touch with the regimental officer – never in sympathy with him and appeared rather to look down on him for being shabby in apperance and at times very dirty. And nothing irritates the Regimental Officer more than the sight of Red Tabs, which have become the insignia of hopeless inefficiency.
>
> Luckily there are exceptions to this, as to every other

rule; but, unfortunately, this is the general opinion of the
British army at present.[2]

Lieutenant Lancelot Spicer told his mother that Loos was 'rather
chaotic. In fact the chief thing to be gathered is that our men fought
pretty well (64th Infantry Brigade, 21st Division) ... but that the
Divisional and Brigade Staffs were absolute wash-outs.'[3] In March
1915 Lord Stanhope, commanding a company of Grenadier Guards
– but shortly to become a brass hat himself – declared that: 'These
Brass Hats (as the regimental officer calls the staff) know very little
about the other end.'[4]

Postwar assessments grew increasingly vitriolic. Brigadier General
Frank Crozier, in an account written in 1937 when resentment was
at its height, his funds were low, and the generals he criticised by
name were dead, declared that senior officers were:

> all branded with the same mark – incompetence and
> self-satisfaction. Haig, in his later days, thought that the
> mantle of the almighty had fallen on him in order that
> he might win the war of God against the barbarians ...
> Horne could seldom do anything save touch his hat!
> Rawlinson was a circus clown! Robertson was a good troop
> sergeant-major ...[5]

And Eric Hiscock, writing in the 1970s, gives us what has become
enshrined as the private soldier's view of it all.

> Haig (how we hated him and all his lot) had certain disas-
> trous failings. An optimist of optimists he refused to
> acknowledge failure. In a daft way he was an inspired
> man, with the dire conviction he was never wrong. 'The
> well-loved horse,' he said, years after the cataclysm of the
> Kaiser's war, 'will always be important in war.' ... Stupid
> sod, he should have been up to his navel in mud and
> water, with nothing but chlorinated tea to drink and dog
> biscuits and bully beef to eat, and have to piss in the place
> where he slept. He might then have noticed that the men
> under his sad command had dropped shoulders, bulging
> eyes, unshaven faces, and that they staggered more often
> than they stepped, on their way to the jaws of death.[6]

But it is equally true that what officers and men wrote during the war was far less critical that the views attributed to them subsequently. Gestures that seemed theatrical fifty years on were appreciated at the time. Private Frank Hawkings recalled that on 22 April 1915 his exhausted battalion began to recover from Second Ypres.

> We halted in a field near the road . . . and after relieving ourselves of our packs and equipment, stretched our weary limbs and lay back on the dusty grass, some to snatch a little sleep and others to smoke and chat.
>
> At noon General Smith-Dorrien suddenly appeared on the scene. The battalion hastily rose to its many feet and shook itself into ordered ranks. The general then congratulated us on our achievements on Hill 60.[7]

Lieutenant F. P. Roe always retained an affectionate memory of Rawlinson issuing orders: 'He was the very epitome of a distinguished soldier.[8] Ernest Parker, a platoon commander in a Royal Fusiliers battalion inspected by Haig, thought that his 'kindly eyes looked into my own as he passed along the ranks . . .'.[9] Bernard Martin, a survivor of the Somme, no longer had any illusions about official plans or reports, but was delighted to salute Haig as his battalion came out of the line.

> We were an exhausted remnant, torn uniforms, rifles slung over our shoulders anyhow, boots uncleaned for weeks, puttees slack, but remarkably content to be alive.
>
> 'Thirteen Platoon . . . eyes right.' I made my personal salute as smart as I could. But it was a poor show really, too thin, not enough of us – in my platoon only me and four men. All the same I felt I was acting in a bit of a drama. I had saluted the C in C . . . and was proud to have done so as I think my four men were proud . . . For me the honour of saluting the C in C was the finale of a large experience.[10]

The Reverend Julian Bickersteth, an experienced army chaplain who had lost a brother in the Leeds Pals on 1 July 1916, quietly observed that there was an inevitable tension between the two sides of battle's equation. 'Returning from the battlefield to this atmosphere always makes me unhappy,' he wrote from a headquarters on 30 August 1918,

> because I see so clearly the cleavage between those who direct operations and those whose duty it is to carry them out. This is as true in civilian life, of that I am sure. The employer of labour, however sympathetic, can never really appreciate the sweat of the men ... until he lives their life ...[11]

James Jack, doyen of tough-minded infantry officers, had seen more of the war's rough edge than most, but resented: 'unjust, malicious slurs on my old commanders, despite any mistakes they have made'.[12] 'Let sleeping dogs lie,' recommended a former sergeant. 'The generals are all dead now and it is notable how most critics waited until they were dead before taking them to pieces.' H. E. L. Mellersh, a twice-wounded infantry officer, complained that his war was misrepresented on two counts by its critics.

> They sometimes ... paint the picture in colours of too unrelieved gloom. One of the curious things about a nation at war – one of the tragedies too – is that life is intensified. There is much happiness in wartime, much that is spirited, much that is admirable, much that is just jolly ...
>
> The second misrepresentation when it occurs is more serious. It stems largely from a mistaken conviction that in World War I the troops were supremely badly led. And from this unfair conviction there issues sometimes an outlook even more unfair; that the war was one vast useless, futile tragedy, worthy to be remembered only as a pitiable mistake.
>
> I and my like entered the war expecting an heroic adventure and believing implicitly in the rightness of our cause; we ended greatly disillusioned as to the nature of the adventure but still believing that our cause was right and we had not fought in vain.[13]

Often a sense of honest incompatibility emerges from contemporary accounts. Some people did jobs and lived lives which were unlikely to endear them to others: generals and their staffs usually slept dry, and the men they commanded, all too often, did not. In order to consider the experiences of Thomas Atkins we need to give some thought to the men who commanded him, and to the machinery in which he found himself a small and often rather muddy cog.

The British Expeditionary Force that went to France in 1914 was expected to consist of six infantry divisions and a cavalry division, although in the event one division (4th) arrived after the fighting had begun, and another (6th), initially retained in Britain to provide a measure of home defence until the Territorial Force was fully mobilised, did not set off for France till early September. During the whole war Britain raised sixty-five infantry divisions; there were four Canadian and five Australian divisions, and one Australian and New Zealand (later exclusively New Zealand) division. Most of them served on the Western Front, and a snapshot at the end of the war shows fifty British, four Canadian, five Australian and one New Zealand division in France and Belgium.[14]

The most numerous combat arm was the infantry, and its structure was the scaffolding around which everything else was built. The establishment of an infantry division fluctuated as the war went on, but a look at its organisation in early 1916 gives some sense of its structure for the war as a whole. Commanded by a major general with a small staff, a division comprised three infantry brigades, three brigades of field artillery, a howitzer brigade and a heavy battery, and an assortment of administrative services including three field ambulances and a divisional train – actually a horse-drawn transport column. An infantry brigade, commanded by a brigadier general with a tiny staff, had four battalions of infantry, each with a war establishment of thirty officers and 977 men. Battalions of the same regiment did not necessarily serve together: indeed, in the old army it was unusual for them to do so. The infantry strength of a division, twelve battalions, was around 12,000 men.[15] This might be reduced by as much as half by battle casualties and sickness, and the losses incurred by a division fell most heavily on its infantry. When the 34th Division (New Army, with a brigade of Tyneside Scottish, a brigade of Tyneside Irish, and a brigade with two Scots and two English battalions) suffered an appalling 6,380 casualties on 1 July 1916 it actually lost well over half of its attacking infantry.

An artillery brigade consisted of three batteries, and was commanded by a lieutenant colonel: it had much more in common with an infantry battalion (also commanded by a lieutenant colonel) than with the much bigger infantry brigade. Batteries of field guns and howitzers had six weapons apiece, but heavy batteries only four. So a division boasted thirty-six 18-pounder field guns, eighteen 4.5-inch howitzers, and four 60-pounder heavies. The whole of the divisional artillery (which included a heavy artillery ammunition column and an ammunition column for each artillery brigade) was commanded by a brigadier general, properly known as the commander Royal Artillery, but CRA in common parlance, and 'guns' (just as individual artillery liaison officers were often called 'guns' by the infantry battalion they supported) to a bluff divisional commander.

Field ambulances were also lieutenant colonel's commands, although they were much smaller, with just nine officers and 224 other ranks, than infantry battalions or artillery brigades. They answered to an assistant director of medical services (ADMS) at divisional headquarters. This gentleman, a full colonel, wore distinguishing maroon collar-patches rather than the red of the general staff. Although the division's engineers, two field companies and a signal company, were less numerous than their infantry or gunner comrades, they too were commanded by a full colonel, the commander Royal Engineers (CRE) at divisional headquarters. The sappers recognised his importance by roaring out their trademark song *Hurrah for the CRE!*, redolent of the veldt and pre-war Aldershot, on suitable occasions.

> Good morning Mr Stevens and windy Notchy Knight
> Hurrah for the CRE
> We're working very hard down at Upnor Hard
> Hurrah for the CRE . . .
> For we're marching in to Laffan's Plain,
> To Laffan's Plain, to Laffan's Plain,
> Yes we're marching on to Laffan's Plain.
> Where they don't know *mud* from clay . . .
> Oolum-da cried Matabele
> Oolum-da away we go.
> Ah, ah, ah, ah, ah, ah, ah, ah,
> Shuush . . . HURRAH![16]

The division was the common currency of all armies on the Western Front, although there were always differences between British, French and German divisions. In the French army, for instance, brigades, two to a division, consisted of two regiments, each with three battalions, and it was the numbered regiment – 66th of the Line, or 3rd Zouaves – that carried the weight of identity borne by single battalions in the British army. The Germans, for their part, removed the brigade (two regiments again) from their divisional structure in 1915 in a successful attempt to speed up tactical response by removing a link which made no unique contribution to the chain of command. The British army maintained only one brigade that did not fit naturally into the divisional structure. In August 1914 the four infantry battalions on lines of communication duties were swept up into the newly-constituted 19th Infantry Brigade, which thereafter enjoyed a peripatetic existence, moving between divisions.

In the British army the division was the highest formation with which a soldier could reasonably identify. A battalion might stay in a single division for the whole war, though there were sometimes changes, often for good reason. The mauling of the two New Army divisions, 21st and 24th, that attacked so disastrously on the second day of Loos, prompted GHQ to carry out transfers of complete brigades between three recently-raised New Army divisions and three regular divisions in France, to try to ensure that experience was more evenly spread. It was right to do so, for formations like 21st and 24th divisions clearly demonstrated the weakness of the New Armies. Only one of the two divisional commanders, two of the eight brigadiers and one of the twenty-six battalion commanders were serving regulars: the rest were 'dug-outs' brought back from retirement when war broke out. Just thirty of the regimental officers in the two divisions had regular experience: the rest were wartime volunteers with no more than a year's service, all but a few weeks of that in England.[17]

The 34th Division required substantial reconstitution after the first day of the Somme and again in the summer of 1918. Lieutenant Guy Chapman, whose brigade was loaned to the division in the first week of July 1916 to compensate for its shocking 1 July losses, recalled his men hooting when they heard that the divisional commander, Major General Ingorville-Williams, had been killed. They did not know him, though he was popular with units in the division from the start. Chapman wrote that 'it was reported [wrongly] that he had been souvenir hunting. And why not hoot? What was this Hecuba to them?'

In the winter of 1917–18 there was a large-scale reshuffle, and infantry brigades were reduced from four battalions to three. Captain James Dunn reflected on the impact that this change had on his own 2/Royal Welch Fusiliers, which moved from 19th Infantry Brigade in 33rd Division to 100th Brigade in 38th (Welsh) Division in January 1918.

> We go with mixed feelings, though the men seem pleased
> enough. The 19th Brigade, as an improvised formation at
> the outset, has been the step-child in every division to
> which it has been attached or of which it has been a part.
> It has never been given a place in the glow of the footlights
> in Great Shows except La Boutillerie, where it acquitted
> itself in a way second to none . . . We are going to a division
> begotten in Welsh parish politics: one on which the War
> Office looked askance until it had to send it overseas, and
> which has been in G.H.Q.'s bad books since the Mametz
> muddle – though some excellent officers have been given
> command of its units.[18]

Moving a battalion from a division in which it was comfortable caused not only dissatisfaction but also practical inconvenience. Divisional standard operating procedures were all different, and a great deal of the military grammar of periodic reports and returns which units had to submit to brigade and division had to be re-learnt. A unit's status and reputation, carefully polished in one division, might be dulled if it moved to another, as Private Frank Hawkings observed. 'We have been told that the Q[ueen] V[ictoria] R[ifles] are to be withdrawn from the 5th Division,' he wrote on 28 January 1916. 'We are most fed up and sick at having to leave the regiments with whom we have been ever since 1914. The regulars too are very sorry that we are going. In 1914 they looked on us as their pet Territorial regiment and we were very popular with them.'[19] And personalities played their part. The one benefit of 2/Royal Welch Fusiliers' leaving

33rd Division was that its commander, Major General Reginald Pinney, in Haig's view one of his steadiest generals, was 'a devout, non-smoking teetotaller who banned the rum ration in his division'. An appalled Private Frank Richards thought him, in consequence, 'a bun-punching crank . . . more fitted to be in command of a Church Mission hut at the base than a division of troops'.[20]

Reshuffles were the exception, not the rule, and many divisions retained much of their original composition throughout the war. They built up distinctive identities which embodied an alchemy of differing qualities: regional bonding and the argot that came with it; a blend of regimental friendships and tensions; a pride in past performance (often real but sometimes imagined); a confidence in (or sometimes unifying disdain for) the divisional commander and his staff, and an amalgam of other things besides. Divisions quickly adopted distinguishing patches worn on the sleeves or backs of tunics. These were sometimes 'tribal', like 16th (Irish) Division's shamrock or 36th (Ulster) Division's red hand; sometimes featured numbers, such as the swastika-like three sevens, joined at the base, for 21st Division; letters, like 51st Division's 'HD', for Highland Division; or sometimes a symbolism whose origin is now lost, like 11th Division's key of life or 19th Division's butterfly. They meant a good deal to the men that wore them, as the newly-commissioned Second Lieutenant Huntley Gordon RFA reflected when he went up the line with the 25th Division at Ypres in 1917.

> But there is no doubt that the 25th is one of our crack divisions, what the Boche calls 'storm troops', and I am proud to wear the Red Horseshoe Divisional sign on the back of my tunic, whatever the differences [of regional origin] underneath . . . We are to be with two other famous divisions (8th and the Highland 51st) in the centre of the coming offensive.[21]

Affection for his division rarely expunged the cap-badge pride that Private Atkins felt for his battalion, though it did enable a soldier in a unit that was down on its luck to take comfort from the fact that he belonged to a decent division. This mixture of loyalties had a double-edged effect.

Cap-badge loyalty was a vital and highly constructive force which enhanced the cohesion and fighting will-power of even a mediocre battalion; yet at the same time it was also a seriously damaging obstacle . . . It tended to encourage soldiers to regard the battalion, and not the brigade or the division, as the true centre of authority and therefore of tactical planning.[22]

Friction with other divisions helped the process of definition, and there were repeated spats between Scots and English divisions. Ian Hay, writing from the perspective of a New Army officer in 10/Argyll and Sutherland Highlanders, part of 15th Scottish Division, blamed 'the flat caps on the left' for letting down his division at Loos.[23] Robert Graves of the Royal Welch Fusiliers swiped back in his 'memoir' *Goodbye to All That*, retorting that his adjutant had told him that: 'The Jocks are all the same; both the trousered kind and the bare-arsed kind; they're dirty in trenches, they skite [e.g. brag] too much, and they charge like hell – both ways.'[24] When he tried to make contact with the Scots New Army battalion on his right at Loos he was not impressed by what he saw. 'I walked down their trench some time in the morning of the 26th [September 1915] and walked nearly a quarter of a mile without seeing either a sentry or an officer. There were dead men, sleeping men, gassed men, all lying anyhow. The trench had been used as a latrine.'[25] He later acknowledged that 'this was overstating the case', and went on to admit that:

There was a particular prejudice in the Royal Welch against two Scottish battalions in our brigade owing to an incident in the first month of the war – and against the Scots in general because of a question of sportsmanship in an Army football final some years before.[26]

In any case it is clear that by no means all Englishmen agreed with Graves and his adjutant. Private Ernest Parker of the 15th Hussars declared how:

One thing I shall never forget is the sight of thousands of rhythmically swinging kilts as a Division of Highlanders swept towards us. Skirling at the head of the column strode the pipers, filling the air with wild martial music. Behind glinted a forest of rifle barrels and the flash of brawny knees rising and straightening in rhythm. Were these the freemen of yesterday, peaceful citizens who a few months ago strolled to work. These men seemed to us a crack military unit ready to carry out its mission.[27]

Robert Case, a former Wiltshire Yeoman by now commissioned into the Royal Engineers, also had a high regard for the Scots his division relieved in the Vimy Sector in 1916. 'By heavens, though,' he wrote, 'these Scotties are the finest fellows I have ever had the pleasure of meeting anywhere. Good luck to them wherever they go.'[28]

It was commonly asserted that the Germans kept a list of the fifty most reliable British divisions, and that this always included the Canadians, Australians, New Zealanders, and the Guards, together with other well-regarded formations (9th, 18th, 29th and 51st generally amongst them) and, of course, the speaker's own division. There is no evidence that such a list existed, but the frequency with which it was discussed by contemporaries points to the importance that soldiers attached to their division's reputation. Acceptance of this sort of ranking is now so frequent that serious authorities (some quite properly applauding the achievements of their forebears) often accept at face value the mythology burnished at the time.

The most common belief is that British divisions were uniformly useless and Dominion formations were all first rate. But the evidence of fighting quality is less clear-cut than is suggested by the historian Denis Winter's affirmation that whenever Haig encountered serious opposition: 'British units were pushed aside and Dominion troops put in charge.'[29] That Dominion troops were generally good, and often very good indeed, is beyond question. But Gary Sheffield's careful study of the Australians at Pozières in 1916 shows that even these doughty fighters had a steep learning-curve to ascend. Sir James Edmonds, the waspish British official historian, warned Dr Charles Bean, his Australian counterpart: 'Don't try to persuade the Australian public that the 1916 Australian Corps was the fine instrument that it was in 1918.'[30] A scholarly examination of the detailed performance of a sample of fifty divisions in the last Hundred Days of the war concluded that:

in general, ten British divisions performed at least as well as – and in a few cases partly better than – the leading six or seven Dominion divisions. It is also interesting to note in passing that, of the British divisions with the highest success rates, all, apart from the Guards (regular) and the 66th (territorial) were New Army Formations.[31]

This work points to a wide spectrum of achievement, for example with 9th (Scottish) and 19th (Western) Divisions successful in more than 90 percent of their attacks, seven divisions with a failure rate of 25 percent or more, and only twelve divisions enjoying success in less than 50 percent of their attacks.

Success depended very much on the ability of the division's cadre to convert a flood of reinforcements into useful soldiers. 'Good infantry,' suggests Peter Simkins, 'could be created by good divisions within a few months, so long as the formations possessed an experienced cadre around which it could be rebuilt.'[32] Recovery time was also important: in mid-1917 divisional commanders generally thought that a month would enable their divisions to be properly reconstituted after a gruelling spell in the Passchendaele battle. During the Hundred Days 12th Division had five prolonged episodes in battle or in the line, and lost 6,940 officers and men, 69.5 percent of its total strength and about 75 percent of its infantry. It was consistently successful, and still had plenty of bite left at the end of October. Perhaps surprisingly, longevity in command was not necessarily a conclusive factor. Both 9th and 12th Divisions were good, but while the latter had only two commanders in its entire service the former had nine.

There is certainly no easy congruence between reputation and achievement, and the frequently-derided 19th and 34th Divisions were actually quite good. And although 51st Highland stood high in the army's regard by 1918, it took some time to scale the pinnacle of glory. Walter Nicholson, one of its regular staff officers, thought that sending the division's units to France piecemeal in 1915 was 'the negation of good organisation' from which it took months to recover. It was commanded in 1915–17 by Major General George 'Uncle' Harper, and its HD divisional patch was the subject of unkind jests. When the division took Beaumont Hamel in November 1916, at the very end of the Somme, Harper was well forward, chatting to walking wounded as they made their way back. He made the mistake of asking one Highlander how the battle was going. 'Well, anyhow,' said the man, 'they canna' ca' us Harper's Duds ony mair.'[33]

Robert Graves, helping train new drafts at the Harfleur 'bullring' in early 1916, discussed divisional ranking with his fellow instructors. 'It seemed to be agreed,' he wrote,

> that about a third of the troops forming the British Ex-
> peditionary Force were dependable on all occasions: those
> were always called on for important tasks. About a third
> were variable: divisions that contained one or two weak
> battalions but could usually be trusted. The remainder
> were more or less untrustworthy: being put in places of
> comparative safety, they lost about a quarter of the men
> that the best troops did. It was a matter of pride to belong
> to one of the recognised top-notch divisions – the Second,
> Seventh, Twenty-Ninth, Guards', First Canadian, for
> instance. These were not pampered when in reserve, as
> the German storm-troops were; but promotion, leave, and
> the chance of a wound came quicker in them.[34]

Above the division, the next link in the chain of command was the corps, formally (though rarely in practice) termed the army corps, and with its number correctly written in roman numerals. The corps was a level of command with which the British army was almost wholly unfamiliar, and given its 'small-war' tradition and aptitude this is not surprising. Although Wellington's army had been divided into three corps for the Waterloo campaign of 1815, the duke allowed his corps commanders little initiative. The British did not interpose corps headquarters between general headquarters and the fighting divisions in either the Crimean or the Boer Wars, its largest campaigns in the second half of the nineteenth century. Although autumn manoeuvres in 1912 and 1913 embodied extemporised corps, Sir James Edmonds maintained that:

> it was not originally intended to have any intermediate
> echelon between the General Headquarters of the British
> Expeditionary Force and the six divisions. The decision

to form corps was – in order to conform to French organisation – made immediately on the formal appointment
on mobilisation of Field-Marshal Sir John French as
Commander-in-Chief. Thus it happened that two out of the
three corps staffs had to be improvised; and even in the divisional staffs the Peace Establishment allowed for only two
out of the six officers given in War Establishment.[35]

By the war's end there were twenty-four British, one ANZAC (its
initials, now so emotive, standing for Australian and New Zealand
Army Corps) and one Canadian Corps. However, not all British corps
served on the Western Front; in November 1918, for instance, there
were then eighteen corps and the cavalry corps in France and
Belgium.

The corps was initially little more than a very small headquarters
(just eighteen officers) under a lieutenant general, that controlled
the divisions under its command. As the war went on, however,
corps headquarters grew steadily bigger, to twenty-three officers in
mid-1916 and thirty-seven by November 1918. This did not simply
reflect a tendency for headquarters at all levels to increase in size,
partly to reflect the need, not identified by pre-war planners, to run
headquarters on a twenty-four-hour basis. But it also marked the fact
that corps steadily gained more muscle as the war went on, and saw
it become an important battle-fighting formation in its own right,
with an added weight of combat power that made it more than
simply the sum of its divisions.

By the end of the war the corps had its own heavy artillery, quite
apart from that allocated to divisions, as well as a heavy trench-mortar
battery and a wide range of transport columns and workshops. Its
senior artillery officers, now with separate headquarters for corps
artillery and corps heavy artillery, were no longer artillery advisers
but artillery commanders, able to make full use of the range and
flexibility of what was increasingly regarded as the battle-winning
weapon: the gun. The growth in status of the senior gunner at corps
headquarters was gradual. In 1914 he was the brigadier general
Royal Artillery (BGRA), simply an adviser, but by 1917 had become
the artillery commander, general officer commanding Royal Artillery
(GOC RA) with full authority over his corps artillery and its fire

planning. Structural and personal problems remained, however. Perhaps the most notorious came in VI Corps in late 1916 when the Amazon explorer Colonel Percy Fawcett arrived to take up the new post of corps counter-battery colonel. He immediately declared that he was not in the least interested in the innovative work being done on the detection of German guns by flash-spotting and sound ranging. His corps counter-battery intelligence officer was invited to 'go away and stay away'. The only counter-battery shots which he would allow, he declared, were those against targets clearly visible from British lines, or those he had personally detected on his ouija board.[36] One brother officer described him as 'probably the nastiest man I have ever met in this world', and there must have been wry smiles when he disappeared on an expedition to the Mato Grosso in 1925.

Unlike the division and the brigade, the British corps had no permanent establishment. For instance, in November 1918 there was one corps headquarters with no divisions at all, waiting in reserve; three corps with two divisions; four corps with three divisions; eight corps with four divisions, and two corps with five divisions, in addition to the three-division Cavalry Corps. Divisions shifted between corps on an irregular and apparently unplanned basis: an extreme example of the practice was the move of 51st Highland Division between three corps in a single week in 1918. The Canadian Corps and ANZAC, however, retained their corps integrity throughout, which is one reason for the consistently high achievement of their divisions. It is hard to overstate the damaging effect of shuffling divisions between corps for, just as divisional standard operating procedures were all different, so too were those of corps, and divisional staffs had to master new procedures every time their divisions moved, with the shock wave of changes in reports and returns reverberating all the way down to companies in the line.

'Reports and returns': how little this expression would have meant to anyone who had not been compelled to wring them out of tired men spread about company's trench frontage. In May 1915 Captain Rowland Feilding, then commanding a Coldstream company in the line, sent his wife a humorous example of how they fitted into a day of trench life. The messages would have been in the argot known as 'signalese', signaller's English, taken down by the company's duty telephone operator and written in indelible pencil on a message pad (Army Form C.2121), with aaa standing for a full stop.

5 p. m. Arrival in trenches. Temper normal. Half an hour spent trying to appear interested while the outgoing officer explains the enormous amount of work he has done in his time there.

5.30 p. m. Outgoing officer departs. Half an hour spent commenting with your own officers on the utter and complete absence of any sign of any work whatever having been done since you were there last.

6 p. m. Start your own work for the night.

6.15 p. m. Telephone operator reports that he has got connection with Battalion Headquarters (NB: Life in the Trenches has now started.)

6.45 p. m. First instalment of messages handed in to you. No. 1. 'You will hold respirator and smoke helmet drills frequently during your tour aaa The signal for respirators to be put on will be two C's on the bugle. Adjutant.'

No. 2. 'Report at once if you have a fully qualified Welsh miner in your company who can speak French and German aaa Age not under 18 years. Adjutant.'

No. 3. 'All respirators will be immediately withdrawn aaa The signal for putting them on will be two blasts of the whistle and not as per the last part on my message No. 1 of this date. Adjutant.'

No. 4. 'A French aeroplane with slightly curved wings, giving it the appearance of a German one, is known to be in your vicinity aaa Use your discretion in accordance with Anti-Aircraft Regulations para 1; section 5. Adjutant.'

No. 5. 'Re my message No. 4, for the word "French" read "German" and for the word "German" read "French" aaa You will still use your discretion. Adjutant.'

7.30 p. m. Messages dealt with. Dinner.

8.30 p. m. Arrival of C.O. Suggests politely that your men would be better employed doing some other kind of work. All working parties turned over to different work. Temper indifferent.

9 p. m. to 2 a. m. Answer telephone messages.

2.30 p. m. Stand to arms. Walk round and survey the result of the night's work. Find the greater part of it has been blown in by trench mortars in the early morning.

3.30 a. m. Try and sleep.

4 a. m. Wakened up to receive the following messages:

No. 115. 'All smoke helmets are to be immediately marked with the date of issue aaa If no date is known no date should be marked and the matter reported accordingly. Adjutant.'

No. 116. 'RE require a working party from your company today from 6 am to 7 pm aaa Strength 150 with suitable proportion of NCOs aaa Otherwise, your work is to be continued as usual. Adjutant.'

5 a. m. Wakened up to send in 'Situation Report'. Report situation 'Normal.'

8 a. m. Breakfast.

9 to 11 a. m. Scraping off mud in Oxford Street. Removing bits of bacon in Bond Street. Re-burying a Fritz who, owing to a night's rain, has suddenly appeared in Regent Street.

11.15 a. m. Arrival of Brigadier-General and Staff. Orders given for everything that has been dug out to be filled in and everything that has been filled in to be dug out.

11.16 a. m. Departure of Brigade Staff. Brain now in state of coma. Feel nothing except a dull wonder. Rest of day spent eating chocolates, writing letters home to children and picking flowers off the bank. Final message can remember receiving was about twelve noon:

No. 121. 'The Brigadier-General and Staff will shortly be round your trenches. Adjutant.'[37]

Walter Nicholson, who served on divisional and corps staffs and at GHQ, argued that until the very end of the war there was no generally understood definition of the difference between 'Trench Strength Returns', 'Daily Fighting Strength Returns', and 'Ration Strength Returns'. The precise information required in situation reports varied from formation to formation, making the adjutant, the battalion commander's principal staff officer, the meat in a bureaucratic sandwich. General headquarters certainly did its unyielding best to say what it wanted, and, unlike the Feilding account above, the following was not written in jest.

> Effective strength of unit should show (1) the total strength of officers of the unit, including all sick in the country, and (2) of all men, excluding only sick in L of C hospitals and wounded in hospital and missing, but including any men detailed from their unit for any purpose, a detailed note being made in the 'Remarks' column showing the units to which detached officers and men are attached.
>
> Details by arms attached as in War Establishments should show these officers and men of other arms of the Service whose attachment is provided for in War Establishments, and who are shown in the War Establishment tables in the 'Total (including attached).'
>
> Attached (not to include details shown above) should show all other officers and men of other units who are attached to the unit for any purpose, a detailed note being made in the 'Remarks' column showing the unit from which officers and men are detached . . .[38]

We can deduce from this that an 'Effective Strength Return', since it includes sick and wounded, is not the same either as a 'Fighting Strength Return' which excludes these men, or a 'Trench Strength Return' which excludes the quartermaster and transport officer and their myrmidons, the varying percentage of men deliberately left out of the line as a nucleus for reconstitution, as well as assorted 'base details'. However, a hard-pressed adjutant, working in the stale air of a dugout under shellfire, his Army Form B.213 barely visible in the guttering flame of the oil lamp, might appreciate the differences less easily. And there were many refinements. For instance, Army Service Corps units were sternly enjoined that in any rolls or returns concerning personnel 'care should be taken to insert with the regimental number the index letter which, in all cases, precedes the number: The letters are:- S., T., M., S.S., TS., A.S.R., A.S.E., S.R.M.T., S.E., C.M.T., M.S., C.H.T., and B.B.'[39] An infantry company in the line might be expected to produce five separate returns in a twenty-four-hour period, all requiring different information subject to a definition which was not only precise but liable to variation according to the whim of brigade, division and corps.

Nicholson went further, suggesting that there was a real break between division and corps. 'The battles fought with a division were personal affairs,' he believed.

> The fighting, whether success or failure, meant heavy losses in friends. When serving in a corps staff the interest shifted from this personal aspect to the mutual, to what objective we had succeeded in gaining, and the consequent effect of these objectives on roads, dumps and railways.[40]

He argued that this brought a sense of detachment which was hard to overcome. 'We might have expected some measure of good repute,' he wrote of his time on a corps staff,

> but they [the divisions] hated us. We were all business and no soul; just a damned nuisance to everyone . . . We knew none of the divisional staffs and they knew none of us; a disastrous state of affairs. There was no human touch between the corps and the division – and there never could have been until they realised its need.[41]

Corps were under the command of armies. The original BEF effectively constituted a single army with two corps, but as more troops arrived a new level of command was introduced, with 1st and 2nd Armies coming into being on 25 December 1914. Third Army followed in July 1915, as the BEF extended its line south, and 4th Army in January 1916 as planning for the Somme began. Exploitation of the hoped-for breakthrough on the Somme was to be entrusted to the reserve army, but this was committed to command the fighting north of the Albert-Bapaume road in the first week of the battle, although it was not formally renamed 5th Army till the autumn, by which time, coincidentally, any chance of it exercising the function originally envisaged by Haig had long since disappeared.

Fourth Army was radically scaled down in May 1917, much to the irritation of its commander, General Sir Henry Rawlinson, who had been hoping to be entrusted with the main attack at Ypres that summer. 'This is rather a blow for I had been looking forward to that northern attack even though it is a difficult one,' he admitted in his diary. 'D.H. said nothing about it to me direct nor did [Lieutenant General Sir Launcelot] Kiggell [Haig's chief of staff] so I only heard of it by accident in discussing matters with Tavish [Davidson, head of the General Staff's Operations Section] afterwards.'[42] In March 1918 Rawlinson was sent south to take over 5th Army, then reeling under the impact of the German offensive. Fifth Army effectively disappeared for a time, but was soon reconstituted and by the war's end there were again five British armies in France, each with three or four corps.

Like corps, armies had no fixed establishment: in the summer of 1917, 4th Army had so few troops to command that Rawlinson found it hard to occupy himself, and though he managed 'to do a bit of reading' he admitted that: 'I find it rather hard to get through the day and generally have to organise an expedition somewhere to kill time.'[43] At the same time 5th Army, attacking at Ypres, had four full corps in the line, another weak corps in reserve and a corps in GHQ reserve poised behind that, with over 2,000 guns, 216 tanks and 406 aircraft. Just as corps expanded from being little more than post-boxes for the divisions they commanded, so armies grew from a collection of corps to structures with powerful artillery assets of their own which they could shift about the front so as support the main efforts of their corps. Of particular importance was the establishment of a major general Royal Artillery (MGRA) at army headquarters. However, because the general staff insisted that artillery officers could only issue orders to units directly under their command, MGRAs never enjoyed the authority over the gunners in their army that corps artillery commanders did for those in their own corps. Major General Budworth, MGRA of 4th Army, had the chagrin of seeing his plan for 1 July 1916 followed by only one of the four attacking corps: XIII Corps followed his advice 'almost to the letter and with success'.[44]

Finally, general headquarters controlled the entire British military effort in France. In accordance with the practice of the period, still identifiable in a modern British headquarters, it consisted of three branches, under the control of the chief of the general staff.[45] This post was held at the outset of the war by the pleasant but somewhat ineffectual Major General Archibald Murray, who had made a bad recovery from a stomach wound received in South Africa. Lieutenant Edward Spears, then a liaison officer between GHQ and the French 5th Army, reported to him in the Hôtel Lion d'Or at Rheims in the scorching heat of August 1914. Murray:

> greeted me with the kindness he invariably displayed. He was worried, not so much by the situation, which he was trying to unravel on all fours on the floor, where enormous maps were laid out, as by the facts that chambermaids kept coming into the room, and he had only his pants on.[46]

In January 1915 Murray, who had suffered a breakdown during the retreat from Mons, was replaced by Major General Sir William Robertson, a hard-headed ex-ranker who had served as commandant of the staff college and did much to tighten up procedures at GHQ. That December he departed for London to become Chief of the Imperial General Staff and handed over to Lieutenant General Sir Launcelot Kiggell. Kiggell has had an almost consistently bad press. It is, however, clear that he provided the commander in chief with what was generally very sound advice. His main fault lay in his reluctance to stand up to Haig, who had little notion of the concept of loyal opposition. This was in part owing to Kiggell's belief that a chief of staff's function, as prescribed by regulations, depended 'on power delegated by the Commander', and in part owing to persistent ill-health. Lieutenant Colonel Lord Stanhope, who knew him well, thought him:

> slow-brained, with excessive loyalty to his Chief, whoever that might be, he allowed loyalty to overwhelm principles, and both character, initiative and personal drive suffered in consequence – a misfortune because he was an absolutely upright man who had studied his profession and should have been of far greater value to his country.[47]

Kiggell was discredited by the failure of Third Ypres to fulfil expectations, and, as part of a general clearing-out of GHQ, was replaced by Lieutenant General Sir Herbert Lawrence. He had left the army as a major after the Boer War, made a fortune in business, and rejoined in 1914. Possession of what soldiers called 'fuck-off money' (officers, more politely, murmured that he 'had a good position to return to after the war') meant that he was far more robust with Haig than Kiggell had ever been. He brought much new talent to GHQ, worked well with the French, and was rewarded in Haig's final dispatch with a tribute to his: 'unfailing insight, calm resolution and level judgement which neither ill fortune nor good were able to disturb'.[48]

The chief of staff was most concerned with the general staff (G) branch at GHQ, *primus inter pares* as far as staff branches were concerned, and responsible for all matters relating to military operations. In contrast, the adjutant general's (A) branch dealt with discipline, military law, the implementation of appointments and promotions, pay and personal services, casualties and ceremonial. The quartermaster general's (Q) branch was concerned with the distribution of quarters and billets, supplies of food, ammunition and most stores (perversely, medical equipment was the responsibility of A branch), remounts and postal services. Subordinate to the staff were the armies themselves, the service directors (signals, supply, transport and so on) and the substantial staff of the inspector-general, lines of communication, responsible for the burgeoning world of the rear running back to 'the base'.

The base was in practice a huge area stretching from Le Havre, the BEF's main port of entry, to Rouen and Etaples, and up to the Channel ports of Boulogne and Calais. Although the rear area had a growing appetite for men, the non-combatant proportion of the army, rising from 16.3 percent on 1 September 1914 to 33.45 percent on 1 July 1918, remained small by modern standards.[49] The 'teeth to tail ratio' of the BEF was consistently better than that of the British army of the Second World War. The latter required 84,000 men to maintain one division, while in 1914–18 the figure fluctuated between 44,600 in February 1917 and 64,100 in May 1918.[50]

The military secretary's department (MS) worked directly for the commander in chief, and originated in the days when the military secretary was the commander in chief's confidential penman. It was much more influential than its name suggests, for it was responsible for recommending those appointments, promotions and dismissals which the adjutant general's branch formally promulgated. By the war's end the department was headed by Major General H. G. Ruggles-Brise, and its twenty-two officers included five peers or peers' sons and a high proportion of cavalry or yeomanry officers, probably because its work required self-confident men who could resist external influence. The destruction of the records of the military secretary's department by German bombing in the Second World War makes it hard to discern just how the department actually worked, although correspondence surviving elsewhere gives many clues. The department maintained lists of officers recommended for battalion, brigade and divisional command, and officers in search of jobs often corresponded with contacts in the department (Sandhurst or staff college chums were always a good start) to see what was about.

Captain Reginald Tompson, a regular gunner with a Boer War DSO, found himself on the lines of communication staff in 1915. He was torn between his desire to stay there – 'I had a £550 a year job, safety and Bridgy [his wife] very large on the credit side' – and his wish to get a job on the staff of a fighting formation and play a more useful part in the war. He explained his dilemma to a friend at headquarters lines of communication and the fixing process began. After some difficult manoeuvres, briefly losing his staff pay altogether, he duly got onto the staff, where he: 'Felt an awful swell in my new red hat and tabs.' When he was posted to the staff of 7th Division he wrote: 'Such a relief I have never felt in my life.'[51]

Thomas Hutton, commissioned into the artillery in 1910 and a temporary captain in 1915, narrowly missed a staff appointment as aide de camp to Major General George Milne, just appointed to command 27th Division. 'I . . . have been trying to get you as ADC,' wrote Milne, 'but I am afraid there is no chance of the appointment being approved. They say that you are too senior and that not even temporary Captains can be allowed to take up these appointments as they cannot be spared.' However, the following year he heard from a friend in the military secretary's department, who cheerfully signed himself 'Watty': 'Do you want General Staff or to be a B[rigade] M[ajor]? Either is open to you as I understand you were recommended for the former & you are within reasonable distance of the latter.' Hutton ended the war brigade major (chief of staff) of 115th Infantry Brigade.[52] Just before Haig handed over command of the BEF he arranged that Winston Churchill, who had recently resigned from the government and come out to France as a major, should be given command of a battalion. 'I next saw the military secretary,' he wrote, 'and arranged for W. to be posted to the 9th K[ing's] R[oyal] R[ifles] in the 14th Divn.'[53]

The fixing process was not, however, infallible. In August 1916 Walter Guinness was posted to 11/Cheshire as its second in command. Given his origin as a Suffolk Yeoman he found it rather a puzzle, made all the worse by the fact that the battalion had been badly mauled on the Somme and was in a sorry state. It was only later he discovered that he had been posted in mistake for another W. E. Guinness, a major in the Manchesters, who would have been a much better choice as second in command of a Cheshire battalion. He blamed 'the AG's department, which is constantly making mistakes in this way'.[54]

General headquarters moved frequently in the first two months of the war, but settled in the little town of St-Omer in October 1914. The commander in chief, Sir John French, lived in a lawyer's modest house in the Rue St-Bertin, and the branches of the general staff were scattered about the town. It was already common for a commander in chief to split his headquarters when battle was afoot, moving up with a small tactical headquarters and leaving the main apparatus back with his chief of staff. French used this procedure during the battle of Loos, when he took a small headquarters forward to a small château near Lillers, less than 20 miles behind the lines. Although he was connected to Robertson's room at GHQ, he had no telephone connection with 1st Army headquarters, and part of what went wrong in the battle can be attributed to his attempt to fight it in the old style. He visited headquarters to brief commanders personally and, as one officer reported, was seen 'riding quite alone through the shattered villages behind the line and thanking all he met . . . wearing his familiar khaki stock around his neck and his soft gor'blimey general's hat'.[55]

In the spring of 1916 GHQ moved south to the delightful town of Montreuil-sur-Mer, on the little River Canche, inland from Etaples. The sea had long since receded, and Montreuil sat on a steep hill, with its castle embedded in a citadel built by the great engineer Jean Errard de Bar le Duc and modified by Vauban. GHQ, by now boasting sufficient staff officers and clerks to fill a small town, housed its main branches in the old *Ecole Militaire*, but spread more widely, with both telephone exchange and pigeon-loft, in perfect encapsulation of the war's ancient and modern features, in the castle. The town was surrounded by defensive walls whose ramparts enabled staff officers to step out for lunchtime exercise.

The commander in chief, now General Sir Douglas Haig, lived in the Château de Beaurepaire, about 3 miles south-west of the town. Haig was never a man for luxurious living, and the Château de Querrieu, Rawlinson's headquarters during the Somme fighting, was actually larger and more opulent. Moving to Montreuil made good sense, for Haig was now in the centre of the British front, perhaps two hours by car from Ypres, in the north, and a little less from Amiens in the south. When the war became more mobile in 1918 he split his headquarters, just as French had done in 1915 but with infinitely better results, and commanded from forward GHQ in a train behind his advancing armies.

But nowhere were the effects of the army's rapid wartime explosion in size more evident than in the case of generals and their staffs. Newly-raised formations required not only experienced commanders but trained staff officers, and because expansion was unplanned there were no significant reserves of either available. The deficit was made good in two ways. Firstly, officers were brought back from retirement. These 'dug-outs', as they were known, were a mixed bunch. Some proved very good. Herbert Lawrence, who became Haig's CGS in 1917, had left the army after the Boer War when passed over for command of his regiment, the 17th Lancers – which went instead to Haig. Within a year of returning to the army in 1914 he commanded first a brigade and then a division in Gallipoli, and in 1916 he beat the Turks at Romani, securing Sinai for the British. Resigning command shortly afterwards on a point of principle, in 1917 he headed 66th Division on the Western Front.

The trim, chain-smoking Sir Bryan Mahon, called out of retirement at the early age of fifty-two, first raised 10th (Irish) Division and was then promoted to be general officer commanding Ireland. J. M. Babington, who had previously led the New Zealand Defence Force, was sixty-one when called back, and commanded 23rd Division with conspicuous success. John Gelliband, a bright Staff College graduate, had retired to Tasmania after being placed on half-pay as a major in the South Lancashires, but commanded an Australian battalion, brigade and division during the war. His outspokenness and informality (he always wore the same uniform as a private soldier) endeared him to his men and to the Australian official historian, Charles Bean. 'He was a direct speaker of the truth,' affirmed Bean,

> never whittling down a fact or mitigating the sharp edge of a report to please a superior. 'There comes a day in the life of all young officers,' he used to say, 'when a superior will ask them for their opinion. If the youngster gives an answer which he thinks will please, he is done; he is useless. If he says straightly what he thinks, he is the man to get on.'[56]

Trevor Ternon had retired in 1907, but came back to serve on a divisional staff and then to command the 102nd (Tyneside Scottish) Brigade of 34th Division. Another brigade in the same division, 103rd (Tyneside Irish), was commanded by W. A. Collings, who had retired in 1908 after thirty-six years' service, but was remembered by one subordinate as 'a robust, breezy Brigadier'.[57]

The performance of some other dug-outs was ambivalent. R. G. Broadwood retired as a lieutenant general in 1913, but came back to command a division, usually commanded by an officer of the more junior rank of major general. Deeply upset to have been accused by his corps commander of lacking fighting spirit, he was mortally wounded while crossing a railway bridge over the Lys at Houplines in 1917. A German field gun sniped the bridge whenever men were seen crossing: Broadwood knew that his trip was tantamount to suicide but he crossed anyway, though he asked his staff not to follow him. The gun fired as he began to walk across, and his arrival at the far end coincided with that of the shell: 'Both his legs were blown to bits and he died that afternoon in the ambulance.' He asked to be buried between a subaltern and a private soldier, and lies at Sailly-sur-la-Lys between Second Lieutenant Herbert Gittins, 5/Loyal North Lancashire, and Gunner Robert Bannick, Australian Field Artillery.

But there were also some complete failures. The behaviour of an officer brought back to command a brigade in 55th (West Lancashire) Division led Lord Derby to warn General Sir Henry Mackinnon of Western Command that:

> he has managed to get the whole Brigade by the ear and has been most insulting to the Commanding Officers and to their methods of training. I want to stop it coming formally before you and so I am going up there this week to see him and I shall tell him for his own sake that he had much better resign his command. He has effectually stopped recruiting in Lancashire by his conduct and he has produced something very near a mutiny among his own officers. I suppose we can always remove him, can't we, if he won't go on his own account?[58]

Robert Graves allegedly overheard a conversation between his adjutant and the chief of staff of a New Army division (21st or 24th, though we cannot be sure which) on the eve of Loos.

> Charley, see that silly old woman over there? Calls himself General Commanding! Doesn't know where he is; doesn't know where his division is; can't even read a map properly. He's marched the poor sods off their feet and left his supplies behind. God knows how far back. They've had to use their iron rations and what they could pick up in the villages. And tomorrow he's going to fight a battle. Doesn't know anything about battles; the men have never been in the trenches before, and tomorrow's going to be a glorious balls-up, and the day after tomorrow he'll be sent home.[59]

While some officers were brought back from retirement, others were rapidly promoted to fill gaps. Brigade commanders who had proved themselves in 1914 were natural choices for commands of New Army divisions. Ivor Maxse stepped up from 1st Guards Brigade to command 18th Division; R. H. Davies moved from 6th Infantry Brigade to 20th Division; and E. C. Ingorville-Williams from 16th Infantry Brigade to 34th Division. In the same way successful infantry battalion and cavalry regimental commanders of 1914 moved on to command brigades in 1915 and then divisions in 1916. There is no better example than the flamboyant David 'Soarer' Campbell. His nickname came, not from his own rapid rise, but from the horse he had ridden to victory in the 1896 Grand National, the Irish National Hunt Cup and the Grand Military Steeplechase. He commanded the 9th Lancers in 1914 and took part in two cavalry charges, one at Elouges on 24 August and the other at Moncel on 6 September. Captain Arthur Osburn, medical officer of the 4th Dragoon Guards, was going round the battlefield tending the wounded when he spotted movement.

> Colonel David Campbell, commanding the 9th Lancers, lay sprawled out in a field of clover. Forty yards from his feet and downhill was a small copse, a hundred and fifty yards from his shoulder was a narrow belt of woodland. He had, if I remember rightly, a revolver wound in his leg, a lance wound in his shoulder, and a sword wound in his arm. This field had been the scene of a fine charge. A half-squadron of the 9th Lancers had just charged through a squadron and a half of German cavalry, and the deep clover of the field concealed many wounded horses and men of both regiments.
>
> 'I am sorry to find you like this, sir,' I said, kneeling down to dress his wounds.
>
> 'Not at all, my boy! Not at all! I've just had the best quarter of an hour I've ever had in my life!'
>
> ... within a few weeks he was back again leading his regiment. This caused no surprise amongst those who knew him. 'David,' said one of his subalterns to me afterwards, 'will someday go down and chase Satan out of hell.'[60]

Campbell was promoted to command 6th Cavalry Brigade that November, and took over the unlucky 21st Division after its commander (possibly the general we heard being vilified earlier) was sacked in the wake of Loos. He restored its battered morale and commanded it with distinction for the rest of the war, combining frequent visits to the front with personal aerial reconnaissance. It was entirely characteristic of this tough-minded officer that he protested vigorously to his French commander about the poor position allocated his division when it was sent to 'rest' on the Chemin des Dames in 1918. It did no good, and when the Germans attacked on 27 May he recorded 'the worst day I have spent in this war, which is saying a lot'.[61]

In the British army the regulars kept a tight grip on divisional commands, and no non-regular commanded a division, except as a temporary stand-in, during the whole war. This is in sharp contrast to the Australian and Canadian practice, based as it was on a tradition of a tiny regular force and a bigger citizen army. Both the ANZAC and Canadian Corps (not to mention several of their component divisions) were commanded by men who had begun the war as amateurs. John Monash was a civilian engineer with pre-war service in the Australian equivalent of the Territorial Force, who commanded a brigade at Gallipoli and then a division and corps on the Western Front. Although his career was by no means free of mistakes, his great capacity to learn helped to make him an outstanding success. The huge and profane Arthur Currie was an insurance broker, estate agent and militia officer in British Columbia, whose questionable business practices nearly ruined him just before the war. He commanded 2nd Canadian Brigade at Second Ypres and 1st Canadian Division the following year. When his corps commander, Sir Julian Byng, was promoted to command 3rd Army after the disappointing results of Arras in April 1917, Currie was a natural successor. Neither Monash nor Currie was a heroic leader in the old style, and both favoured a managerial style of command, in part a product of their civilian background.

Although we must guard against the easy 'British bad – Dominion good' assumption, which encouraged Lloyd George to opine that Monash might have succeeded Haig, it is clear that the old army has a case to answer. Indeed, the way that it retained control of the levers of power delighted Brigadier General John Charteris, senior intelligence officer at GHQ, who wrote in 1917 that: 'The amazing thing is that with the exception of the transportation and the postal service, every particular part of the organisation is controlled by regular soldiers.'[62] When a brigade commander asked his commanding officers whether any of their officers should be short-listed for battalion command, one remarked that since all his officers were territorials the question did not arise. He meant it as a joke, but the regulars around him nodded gravely and went on to consider more suitable *regular* candidates.

But if the old army kept a tight grip on the appointment of divisional commanders and, scarcely less important, of their chiefs of staff, the sheer scale of the requirement for brigadiers encouraged a far wider field of selection. Here it is worth sketching out the way officer promotion operated during the war, for this, linked with our knowledge of the way the military secretary's department worked, helps explain how generals were appointed. Formal notification of an officer's promotion, reversion, resignation or dismissal was promulgated in a periodic supplement to *The London Gazette*, the origin of the term 'gazetted'. It was repeated in the GHQ's routine orders, and finished up being recorded in the orders of the unit concerned.

The officers' nominal roll of 3/3rd Queen's, for instance, notes that Second Lieutenant R. R. B. Bannerman was allowed to retain the acting rank of lieutenant on arrival in France by virtue of GHQ 0/9218 dated 11 August 1917 and was promoted substantive lieutenant with effect from 1 July 1917 by authority of General Routine Orders Nos 2572 and 2600 of 1917, a blanket promotion of officers of specified seniority. Captain H. C. Cannon was appointed second in command by virtue of Third Army's A/A/9024 dated 6 September 1917. The same book records tragedies with equal dry formality. Lieutenant Colonel U. L. Hooke, killed in action on 21 June 1916 (he had been in France less than a month), was buried in the field, at map reference 'H.23.bb.75. Ref 1/40,000 518. Cross erected'. The battalion's heartbeat was scarcely allowed to pause: Major K. A. Oswald, the second in command, took over and was gazetted temporary lieutenant colonel on 23 August. He reverted to major with effect from 5 October 1917, the day when he is recorded as receiving a shell wound to his left arm and knee. The subsequent announcement of a DSO for gallantry in the field on 4 October may have given him some consolation.[63]

In the old army promotion took an officer from second lieutenant to lieutenant colonel by regimental seniority, with written exams regulating promotion from lieutenant to captain, and from captain to major, and then a practical examination in tactics qualifying him for advancement to lieutenant colonel. Adverse comment in one of his obligatory annual confidential reports could halt promotion or even have him removed from the army as inefficient.[64] Beyond lieutenant colonel promotion took an officer outside his regiment, with automatic elevation to full colonel after four years as a lieutenant colonel, and advancement by seniority tempered by selection thereafter. During the First World War the rank of colonel was rare, and, with the exception of medical officers and engineers, was not to be found below corps headquarters. The sighting of a pair of full colonels dining together in Bapaume, doubtless sorting out some knotty administrative problem in the rear area, was worth a diary entry by an astonished infantry officer.

The fact that the first part of this process was regimental meant that promotion moved at different paces between regiments, with a spate of resignations or casualties bringing accelerated promotion to survivors. A regular officer could not be deprived of his permanent rank save by formal administrative action, the sentence of a court martial or the Army Board's direction that he resign, a punishment inflicted in circumstances where a court martial would have been inappropriate but his continued service no less so. Lieutenant Colonel Charles Repington, *The Times'* military correspondent from 1903 to 1918, had been forced to resign his commission for involvement in a well-publicised divorce case. The old army was, indeed, quite prone to such lapses. Field Marshal Sir John French embarked upon a passionate affair with Winifred Bennett, married to a diplomat but the mistress of an officer killed at Ypres in 1914: she was almost half French's age and several inches taller. The lovers were remarkably discreet. Repington, however, had persisted in his affair after being told to desist, and had attracted precisely the sort of scandal which *King's Regulations* warned against.

Most commissions granted during the war were temporary, and would be relinquished after its conclusion. Although wartime officers received the same beautifully-engrossed vellum commission given to regulars, the word 'TEMPORARY' was stamped on the front fold to make the point perfectly clear. An officer (regular or temporary) held substantive rank within his regiment, but might be given acting or local rank to carry out a specific appointment, perhaps to step up temporarily to command a company, or to hold a senior appointment outside the regiment. This rank evaporated when the appointment was relinquished, and the officer crashed down to his regimental rank. Unless, that is, he had been thoughtfully provided with a safety net. Brevet promotion (which applied only to the ranks of colonel, lieutenant colonel or major) gave an officer rank in the army, though not in his regiment. In 1929 Thomas Hutton, who we have already seen tweaking the system in the military secretary's department to become a brigade major, was rewarded with a brevet lieutenant colonelcy, and was thus formally described as 'Major and Brevet Lieutenant Colonel'. The advantage of brevet rank was that, while it did not guarantee a job in the higher rank, it did mean that its holder would have less far to fall if any temporary rank was relinquished and, if the worst came to the worst, would retire with a more glittering prefix than might otherwise have been the case. Because lieutenant colonels were promoted full colonel four years after their previous promotion, whether they had attained it by brevet or regimental rank, it was possible to rise straight from regimental major, through brevet lieutenant colonel, to become a substantive colonel, which is just what Hutton did in 1933. It was also possible for substantive rank to be conferred for a meritorious achievement or distinguished service: 190 major generals were appointed this way during the war.[65]

An officer might hold three ranks – permanent, temporary and brevet – spread over a wide range. In perhaps the best-known example, in 1908 W. H. Manning was inspector-general of the King's African Rifles. He was a substantive captain, a brevet lieutenant colonel and a local brigadier general, and the officers who commanded his battalions were all regimental captains but local lieutenant colonels. Soarer Campbell did very well out of the system. His substantive lieutenant colonelcy dated from March 1912; he was made a temporary brigadier general in November 1915, a brevet colonel the following February and a substantive colonel in March 1916. Appointed temporary major general when he took over 21st Division in May 1916, permanent rank caught up in January 1917. He died in 1936, a full general and a knight. In contrast, Keppel Bethell, who took command of 6th Division as a temporary major general in March 1918 and, at thirty-five, was the youngest British divisional commander in either world war, never rose in regimental rank above captain during the entire war. He became a temporary major in 1915, a brevet major in 1916 and a brevet lieutenant colonel in 1917. Although the four-year rule took him to colonel in 1921, he did not get his rank of major general back until 1930.

Territorials and New Army officers were also, at least in theory, promoted by seniority within their battalions, although there was increasingly large-scale movement between battalions in an effort to achieve some balance of quality. The whole system had become highly fluid by mid-1915, though the old principle of seniority still cropped up to cause confusion. Although Special Reserve battalions did not go to war as formed units, but sent officers and men to reinforce other battalions of the same regiment, they maintained their own seniority rolls, and their officers, kept on the permanent strength of the Special Reserve but (by a subtle distinction) on the 'held strength' of the units they served with, were promoted by their seniority on the Special Reserve. Because the latter expanded in 1914, there was a rapid increase of vacancies and thus swift promotion. This could make a Special Reserve second lieutenant a captain in just a year, while a regular officer serving in the same battalion in France, commissioned from Sandhurst just before the war, might have gained no promotion at all. Robert Graves, commissioned into 3/Royal Welch Fusiliers in August 1914, was promoted captain in October 1915. He was just twenty, and well aware that his promotion took him:

> over the heads of elder officers who had longer trench service and were better trained than myself. A Special Reserve major and a captain had been recently sent home from the First Battalion, with a confidential report of inefficiency. Being anxious to avoid such disgrace, I went to the adjutant and offered not to wear my badges of rank while serving with the battalion. 'No, put your stars up,' he said not unkindly, 'it can't be helped.'[66]

Both Sandhurst and Woolwich continued to produce regular

officers throughout the war (there were some 7,000 in all), and regular commissions were offered to many temporary officers. Most, however, had to revert to second lieutenant when appointed to a regular commission, and many found the loss of pay and status a considerable disincentive. Lieutenant Julian Tyndale-Biscoe, holder of a temporary commission, was delighted to be recommended for a regular lieutenancy, but was eventually gazetted a second lieutenant. He was allowed to retain his existing seniority while serving in the same division, so did not immediately become the junior subaltern in his battery. However, he soon resigned his regular commission and reverted to his temporary lieutenancy to retain the higher pay. When Robert Graves rejoined 2/Royal Welch Fusiliers in 1916 one of the reasons for his chilly reception was the hostility of another Special Reserve officer who had reverted to second lieutenant on being granted a regular commission and now grumbled about 'jumped-up captains'. Graves quoted him a consoling poem:

> O deem it pride, not lack of skill,
>   That will not let my sleeves increase,
> The morning and the evening still
>   Have but one star apiece.[67]

The military secretary's branch at GHQ maintained lists of officers suitable for command at battalion, brigade and divisional level, and appointed from them as vacancies arose. It was possible for an officer to be senior by regimental rank but never to get onto the military secretary's battalion command list, and so, although he might serve as locum commanding officer, he could never take over on a permanent basis. Major Count de Miremont, perennial stand-in as commanding officer of 2/Royal Welch Fusiliers, was Captain Dunn's particular *bête noire*. In November 1917 Dunn wrote:

> As O.C. Works the Count is in his element, he spends the day among sheets of paper. He conceives a new trench in cubic yards, which he has reduced to feet; he has reduced subalterns and sergeants to distraction, and the work accomplished next to nothing.

He blamed de Miremont for the deterioration of the battalion's morale in mid-1918, reporting that on 5 July:

> A new C.O. arrived in the evening, Lt.-Col. J. B. Cockburn
> from the 17th Battalion. He was 'Cocky' to everyone,
> behind his back. His transfer was felt to be an effort by
> Division to pull the battalion together. de Miremont
> reverted to Acting Major, Second-in-Command.

A month later, after a successful raid on the Germans, he announced that 'since Col. Cockburn's arrival morale had been raised to a level it had not been on for a year or more . . .'.[68]

Officers sometimes went straight from regimental captain to temporary lieutenant colonel. 'Tibs' Crawshay was a captain when he took command of 2/Royal Welch Fusiliers, and put up a crown and star on assuming the appointment. However, when his brigade commander appointed him 'O.C. High Wood' after its capture on 15 July 1916, the commanding officer of the nearby 20/Royal Fusiliers declined to accept his authority, having 'entrenched himself in the Army List. "I am sainior [sic] to Major Cra'shay," he reiterated, and sat tight; and he let his men at Crucifix Corner sit tight.' The wood was lost in an unlucky fumble which allowed a German counterattack to break scattered men from a variety of units.[69]

That same month Rowland Feilding was commanding a Coldstream company when his brigadier told him that he was being recommended for a battalion. Although, as he confided to his wife, 'I would rather command a Coldstream company than a battalion anywhere else,' he knew he was too old to remain a company commander. On 6 September he was pleased to be given 6/Connaught Rangers, 'or rather the remnant of it', which had lost its CO, second in command and half its men in 16th Division's capture of Guillemont. His brigadier, the genial George Pereira of the Grenadiers, at once 'told me to put up a Major's crowns' and when his temporary lieutenant-colonelcy was eventually gazetted it was backdated to the date of his take-over that September.

Some lieutenant colonels were very young indeed. Frank Crozier had just visited a wounded officer in hospital with the man's successor, a twenty-one-year-old subaltern who had just become an acting lieutenant colonel, when 'a red-nosed major of ruddy countenance and green-banded cap' emerged from the bar of their hotel and mistook the crown and star on the youngster's cuff for two stars.

'Here young fellow,' says the major, 'don't you know a field officer when you see him?'

'Yes, I do,' says the colonel.

'Well, why the devil don't you salute, you damned young cub? What's your regiment?' says the major.

'I salute my seniors,' replies the boy quietly. The bleary eyes of the major fall on the fatal cuff. He gasps, turns and makes for the bar, there to fortify himself with another drink.[70]

Hanway Cumming was commanding 2/Durham Light Infantry in late 1916, standing in for his brigade commander, who was on leave, when he heard that he had been promoted brigadier general to command 91st Brigade of 7th Division. This promotion from temporary lieutenant colonel to temporary brigadier general was par for the course: few officers actually wore the interim rank of colonel. In order to qualify for command of a brigade an officer had to command a battalion successfully. A divisional chief of staff ('General Staff Officer Grade 1', in the parlance of the day) was a lieutenant colonel, but if he had not already commanded a battalion he had to have his ticket punched before promotion to brigadier general. For instance, F. W. Lumsden was moved from the staff to command 17/Highland Light Infantry for just six days before being appointed to head 14th Infantry Brigade. Lord Stanhope thought his success a classic example of how somebody could be no good at one level but successful at another. Stanhope thought Lumsden was useless as a GSO2 when they served together, but then he went off to 32nd Division and 'within three months of his arrival there he had won two bars to his DSO and the VC and had been made a Brigade Commander'.[71]

Not all brigadiers paid lip service to the process of ticket-punching. Frank Crozier – retired major in 1914, lieutenant colonel in 1915 and brigadier general after the Somme – had predictably firm views. He rejected:

a colonel, a charming fellow, a staff college graduate and a one-time instructor of some military subject, at some military establishment, sent to me for a month 'to quality

for a brigade'. He is unable to kick the Germans out of
his line quickly on his own initiative, and prefers to write
orders instead of doing things!

When told that 'he'll be all right with a little experience,' Crozier
riposted:

> Experience is gained here, not in offices, or on staffs: the
> chief knows that, and says staff officers are to go to bat-
> talions to get their promotion to fighting brigades. You
> seek to evade the order by wringing a recommendation
> out of me. I have two first-class colonels here, one was a
> sergeant-major in the Royal Irish Regt in 1914; the other
> was a second lieutenant in the Ceylon Planters Corps in
> the same year. They are both going to be recommended
> for brigades after the next big show – if they live.[72]

Crozier was certainly right about the two commanding officers.
The first was the legendary Freddy Plunkett. He was regimental
sergeant major of 2/Royal Irish in 1914, when he was recommended
for the VC at Le Cateau but received a DCM instead. A Military
Cross followed in 1915, and he was then commissioned, earning a
DSO and two bars and finishing the war as a temporary lieutenant
colonel and brevet major. Crozier recommended him for a VC for
'thirty hours of sustained valour' in 1918, but was exasperated to
report that it was turned down because he had 'merely done his
duty'.[73] By 1918 he was suffering quite badly from heart trouble, and
this probably prevented him from getting a brigade. Crozier detected
a streak of gentleness even in this formidable warrior. The brigade
was in garrison in Roubaix at Christmas 1918, and laid on a panto-
mime for the children. He saw how: 'Colonel Plunkett, of Mons and
Bourlon, treble DSO, MC, DCM, marches at the head of three
hundred children, while his band plays the *Marseillaise*, and his
officers and NCOs act as ushers and help on the toddlers.' Another
of the brigade's COs, Benzie, late of the Ceylon Tea Planters' Rifles,
duly got his recommendation for a brigade, but was badly wounded
in March 1918 and was unable to take it up. The other two COs in
the brigade were scarcely less formidable. One, Andrews, had run
away from school in 1900 to fight in the ranks of the Yeomanry, and

had then been involved in several revolutions in South America, and the other, Kennedy, had been a lecturer at the London School of Economics. Even the brigade machine-gun company was commanded by another unconventional but natural soldier, 'Harrison, a rubber-planter from the Malay States'. Perhaps Crozier had some reason to look askance at staff officers.

When Hanway Cumming joined 91st Brigade he found that his brigade major was Captain R. N. O'Connor of the Scottish Rifles (the future General Sir Richard O'Connor of Western Desert fame), who had been in his company when he was an instructor at Sandhurst. He got on well with Herbert Watts, the divisional commander, and found the staff 'very capable and helpful and assisted the divisional staff in making the divisional machine "go on oiled wheels"'. However, Cumming was sacked by one of Watts's successors after a sharp difference of opinion during the attack on Croisilles in April 1917. He was lucky to be appointed commandant of the Machine-Gun School at Grantham, retaining his rank, suggesting that he had been reported on as exhausted rather than incompetent, and in February 1918 he was sent back to command a brigade in France.

Officers returning from England designated for brigade or battalion command were often held in a pool at the base, in a practice not dissimilar to (though infinitely more comfortable than) the retention of drafts at Etaples until they were posted to battalions. It was not until he reached France on his return in early 1918 that Cumming was told that he was to command 110th Brigade of 21st Division, and he had some difficulty in finding out where it was. He eventually arrived at Longavesnes, behind the Cambrai sector, to meet the divisional commander, Soarer Campbell, who told him that the division was understrength and overextended, largely as a consequence of the reduction of brigades from four battalions to three because of a shortage of manpower. The division's command structure provides a fine example of the state of the army's upper echelons at this stage of the war. Campbell, its commander, we know already. Cumming himself was a pre-war regular, a company commander in 1914 and battalion commander in 1916. The other two brigades in the division, 62nd and 64th, were commanded by brigadier generals G. H. Gater and T. Headlam. Whereas Tommy

Headlam was a regular with a conventional career path, George Gater was a civilian when war broke out:

> he had never thought of soldiering before the war, but had joined up as soon as it started and worked his way up to his present rank. He was a first-class Brigade Commander, very able and quick; indeed, it was difficult to imagine him in any other capacity.[74]

By 1918, then, brigadiers came from the full span of the old, new and territorial armies, and although the system favoured pre-war regulars there were some extraordinary examples of the rise of the gifted amateur. Perhaps the most striking case of the dramatic rise of a regular is that of Roland Boys Bradford. He joined the regular army from the territorials in 1914 and was a second lieutenant on the outbreak of war. He won a Victoria Cross commanding 9/ Durham Light Infantry on the Somme, and became a brigadier general in November 1917. Bradford enjoyed his new rank for only three weeks, and was killed at Cambrai. Aged only twenty-five, he was the youngest British brigade commander in either world war. Two of his brothers were also killed, one, George, winning a posthumous VC in the raid on Zeebrugge in 1918. More common were cases like that of Arthur Johnson, commissioned into the Worcestershire Regiment in 1903 but still, with the glacial promotion after the Boer War, a very senior lieutenant in 1914. He shot up swiftly, with a longish tour in the key job of brigade major, to get his brigade in September 1917. Johnson was badly wounded only two days after assuming command, took no further part in the war, and retired as a colonel in 1937.

Some of the amateur soldiers did just as well. Arthur Hubback, an architect, late of the Malay States Volunteer Rifles and the London Regiment, commanded 2nd Brigade in 1st Division as early as March 1916. A. C. Lowe, late of the Honourable Artillery Company, Britain's oldest volunteer unit, was killed at Ypres as commander royal artillery of 66th Division in November 1917. Ralph Husey, a former trooper in the Yeomanry, later commissioned into the London Rifle Brigade, had earned a bar to his DSO, when commanding a battalion in March 1918: 'He used a rifle himself at close range and inflicted many casualties on the enemy.' He did not live long enough to enjoy his brigade, for he was mortally wounded on the Chemin des Dames in May 1918. But as far as combat commands were concerned brigadier was the amateur's ceiling, and divisional commanders were chosen from an all-regular pool.

Some contemporaries, and too many historians, alleged that the BEF was commanded by cavalry generals. 'The Army Chiefs were mostly horsemen,' maintained Lloyd George, while A. J. P. Taylor announced that 'most British generals were cavalry men' and Robert Graves went further to opine: 'All our generals were cavalry-men . . .'.[75] The official historian Sir James Edmonds, neither considering the important issue of how long generals spent in command, nor taking much trouble over his maths, wrote that 'of the nine generals who commanded Armies, five were cavalrymen, three [actually four, and one with two tours as an army commander] infantrymen and one was a gunner'.

So what is the truth? Both commanders in chief were certainly cavalry officers. But the spread is much wider amongst army commanders. Haig commanded 1st Army for most of 1915, but handed it over to Charles Monro, an infantryman, and he passed it on, in September 1916, to Henry Horne, a gunner, who commanded it thereafter. Horace Smith-Dorrien, an infantryman, was commander of 2nd Army for the first four months of its existence, and handed it over to Plumer, another infantryman, who commanded it for the rest of the war. Third Army was formed in July 1915 under Monro, who passed it on late that October to Allenby, a cavalryman. When Allenby was moved on in the wake of the Arras battle in the spring of 1917, Julian Byng, a fellow cavalryman, took over and led 3rd Army for the rest of the war. Fourth Army was commanded by Rawlinson, an infantryman, for most of its existence. Fifth Army was headed by Hubert Gough, a cavalryman, in 1916–17, briefly by Rawlinson in 1918, and then by the cavalryman William Birdwood at the end of the war. In short, both 2nd and 4th Armies were always commanded by infantrymen; 1st Army was commanded by a cavalryman for only one year of its three-year life; and both 3rd and 5th Armies were predominantly commanded by cavalrymen, although the latter was only in existence for the second half of the war. If we look at this in rough terms of 'months in command of armies', then cavalrymen commanded armies for about one-third of the time.

The spread is even wider at the corps level. Andy Simpson's pains-taking work identifies forty-seven corps commanders on the Western Front. Of these 60 percent came from the infantry; 19 percent from the cavalry; 17 percent from the artillery and 4 percent from the engineers. Although cavalry officers were indeed over-represented, he suggests that if time in command is considered then the cavalry officers in his more detailed sample of nineteen corps commanders actually commanded for less time than their peers and therefore 'can be assumed to have been (on average) less influential as corps commanders'.[76] There is not yet a study of comparable quality for divisional commanders, but in November 1918 the proportion orig-inating in the infantry was far higher than this, with just five cavalrymen commanding infantry divisions. In short, although there were more cavalry major generals and above than would have been the case if command appointments had been allocated simply on the proportion of officers in the pre-war army, the disproportion was not excessive. Though we now have more detailed statistics than were available to John Terraine when he first wrote on this issue in 1980, it is impossible to deny the truth of his assertion that: 'The overwhelming majority of generals actually handling troops in battle came, as one might expect, from the arm which produced the over-whelming majority of those troops, the infantry.'[77]

And what is the alleged predominance of cavalry officers meant to prove? Edmonds, himself an engineer, saw in 'the cavalry spirit' what he termed 'pressure for haste and to expectation of gain of ground incompatible with siege warfare in the field by men who had to struggle over shell-pocked ground and through deep mud'.[78] This may be a fair comment on Allenby's handling of the latter stages of Arras, though it bears no relation to 3rd Army's very careful artillery preparation for the battle, the most sophisticated employed by the British army to that date. And it may indeed be a justified criticism of much of Gough's conduct of Third Ypres. But it is an odd judg-ment on Byng, whose army produced the plan for Cambrai, the world's first large-scale tank battle.

Nor is it a complaint that can be levelled against Birdwood, who made his reputation commanding Australians, who were often critical of Pommy generals but took 'Birdy' to their hearts. The much-decorated Adrian Carton de Wiart recounts a frequently-told story:

> General Birdwood ... passed an Australian soldier who took no notice of him ... the officer told him it was his G.O.C. General Birdwood. This elicited the reply 'Well, why the——doesn't he wear a feather in his tail like any other bird would?'[79]

And in neither his tactical methods nor his personal appearance did he have much in common with the popular image of the cavalry officer. Rowland Feilding saw him in September 1918.

> The newspapers have always made such a hero of him that I was prepared to be disappointed: but he certainly has a clear eye and a talking manner with both officers and men: and he talked sound common sense in his address to the Brigade, which is more than one always hears on these occasions.
>
> In appearance he is straight and upright, and he has far less 'red tab' about him than the most junior member of his staff. He does not even wear a 'red hat'. Moreover, he is evidently not punctilious about his clothing, for the spikes of his belt were missing, and the latter was done up anyhow ...
>
> So huge is the scale on which this war is being fought that it's a great event to see one's Army Commander.[80]

It is more likely that it has simply become a gratuitous calumny to refer to an unsuccessful or unpopular general as a cavalry officer. Siegfried Sassoon gives us a vignette of Rawlinson 'as he squelched among the brown tents in his boots and spurs' in mid-1916, which induces us to forget that Rawlinson was actually an *infantry* officer.[81] Finally, the success of cavalry officers such as Campbell and Bethell in command of infantry divisions suggests that an officer's arm of origin mattered far less than his ability to find practical solutions for the myriad problems of trench warfare.

Another great myth is that generals were always remote from their men and free from their risks. Although Lloyd George cannot be blamed for starting this hare, he hallooed it on its way with more gusto than honesty, as was his way. His *War Memoirs* frankly accuse generals of reluctance to risk their skins, an odd kettle-blackening exercise for someone of Lloyd George's lack of physical courage. More recently, John Prescott's foreword to a good study of the Hull Pals described how: 'Senior officers well behind the enemy lines seldom felt the conditions of horror, or the bitter consequences of their orders, ignored the growing list of casualties and enforced a brutal discipline which saw the shooting of shell-shocked soldiers.'[82]

It is abundantly clear that British generals of the First World War were more likely to be killed in action than those of the Second. The term 'general' was technically wider in the first war, because brigadier generals had become brigadiers *tout court* by the second. But even if we start with major generals then the toll on the Western Front is very heavy indeed. Of the first seven divisional commanders to go out to France, Hubert Hamilton was killed and Samuel Lomax mortally wounded in October 1914, and Tommy Capper (a great proponent of the offensive spirit, whose death surprised no-one) was mortally wounded in September 1915. Reginald Tompson was downcast to hear of Capper's death, but agreed that 'the ambition of his life was to be killed in action, which is some consolation. A braver man & a better general never walked.'[83] In contrast, one British divisional commander (the admirable Tom Rennie of 51st Highland) was killed in North-West Europe in the Second World War, and another two in other theatres. Nine British divisions were committed at Loos, six in the first attack and three in subsequent manoeuvres: three divisional commanders – Capper, Frederick Wing and George Thesiger – were killed. Loos was a bad time for red tabs: Brigadier General Bruce was captured when his position was overrun on 25 September, Brigadier General Nickalls was killed on the 26th, Capper died on the 27th, Thesiger was killed and Brigadier General Pereira was wounded on the 27th, Wing was killed on 2 October and another brigadier was wounded the following day. On 3 October Wully Robertson, French's CGS, felt obliged to warn senior commanders that:

> Three divisional commanders have been killed in action
> during the past week. These are losses which the army can

> ill afford, and the Field Marshal Commanding in Chief
> desires to draw attention to the necessity of guarding
> against a tendency by senior officers such as Corps and
> Division Commanders to take up positions too far forward
> when fighting is in progress.[84]

This slowed but did not end the haemorrhage. Edward Ingorville-Williams fell on the Somme and Robert Broadwood in Flanders. Edward Feetham died during the German March offensive, and Louis Lipsett was killed, like so many of his soldiers, during the bloody fighting of the last Hundred Days. The Canadians and Australians each lost a major general, Malcolm Mercer and William Holmes respectively. If we add brigadier generals, then the total for general officers killed or died of wounds received on the Western Front is no less than fifty-eight. There is no accurate figure for the number of generals of all ranks wounded, though it is probably more than 300, and includes some spectacular examples like Tom Bridges (major in 1914 and temporary major general three years later), who lost a leg at Passchendaele while characteristically trudging through the mud when it was 'raining old iron'.

Around 70 percent of soldiers killed on the Western Front were the victims of indirect fire, that is, of the fragments or blast effect of shells or trench mortar bombs. But in the case of generals killed in action, where the cause of death is known, thirty-four were killed by shellfire and twenty-two by small-arms fire. The generals who died were actually more likely to be killed by small-arms fire than the men they commanded, which says much about their proximity to the front. Thus, on 21 September 1917, Brigadier General Frank Maxwell, who had won his VC at Koorn Spruit in 1900, 'whilst superintending consolidation, was killed by a sniper at 40 yards range. A born leader, he had always been regardless of personal safety, and was at the time sitting on the front of the parapet, watching wiring.'[85] Major General Lipsett was hit in the face by a burst of machine-gun fire while walking in front of his line on 14 October 1918, and Brigadier General Lumsden was killed on 4 June 1918, probably by rifle fire and certainly in the front line.

Amongst all the British generals in the war no less than ten held the Victoria Cross, the nation's highest award for gallantry; 126 held the DSO, twenty with one bar denoting a second award, two with two bars and one with three. There were just three Military Crosses (scarcely surprising, as it was only available for junior officers and warrant officers and was not introduced till December 1914), one Albert Medal, and one Distinguished Conduct Medal won while serving in the ranks in South Africa. Much can be said about the generals of the First World War, but they were certainly not physical cowards.

Many generals came from military families and had relatives at the front. Walter Congreve lost his boy Billy on the Somme: Stanhope thought him 'the best staff officer of any that I have met in France'. Congreve was at a conference when the bleak news arrived, but he declined to stand down, affirmed that 'He was a good soldier,' and carried on. Herbert Lawrence lost both his sons on the Western Front. Allenby had departed to command in the Middle East by the time his only son Michael was killed, and the grief nearly broke even this iron man. The death of close friends and relatives sent rings of sorrow rippling into higher headquarters. 'Poor Sandy Wingate was killed yesterday fighting his trench-mortar battery at one of the most dangerous parts of the line,' lamented Charteris from GHQ on 19 October 1915.

> He and I were friends from the age of 10 onwards . . . He was doing well. It is the best of the nation who are called to die. He was one of the best. Only one name on a list of the killed – but a name I have had in my mind from my earliest youth – the name of a dear friend of my whole life.[86]

Generals were not just in danger from German shells and bullets but from their own superiors. Even the very senior were not safe from being 'degummed' (from the French *dégommé*, unstuck), or, in reference to the town to which unsuccessful commanders were posted in the Boer War, '*Stellenbosched*'. Horace Smith-Dorrien was dismissed as commander of 2nd Army during Second Ypres, ostensibly because, in French's words, he had 'failed to get a real "grasp"' of the situation, and his messages were all 'wordy, "windy" and unintelligible'.[87] In fact French's dislike of Smith-Dorrien went back before the war. French was a flamboyant cavalryman and Lothario, and Smith-Dorrien a strait-laced, happily-married infantryman. When Smith-Dorrien arrived in France in August 1914 to replace Lieutenant General Sir James Grierson who had died of a heart attack on his way to the concentration area, French was not pleased to see him. He had asked for Plumer instead, and was irritated to hear that Smith-Dorrien had been asked to correspond personally with the king. Although most historians regard Smith-Dorrien's decision to stand and fight at Le Cateau on 26 August that year as the right one, French, in private, thought that he had endangered the army by fighting instead of continuing the retreat.

French himself was replaced in December 1915, and Haig's leaking of papers on the handling of the reserves at Loos played its part in bringing him down. It is unlikely that Haig himself would have survived beyond the winter of 1917 had a suitable alternative been available. Lloyd George sent the South African premier Jan Smuts and the Secretary of the War Cabinet Maurice Hankey on a visit to see who might take over, but they reported that there was no obvious candidate. However, French, now commander in chief of home forces, was bitterly resentful of the role that Haig had played in his own downfall, and lost no opportunity to intrigue against him. When the Germans attacked in March 1918 there was the customary search for a scapegoat, and French, just back from a War Cabinet meeting, confided to his diary: 'Expressed myself very strongly as to the necessity for an immediate investigation into the question of *adequate command* . . . As regards the Chief Command I expressed the strong conviction that *Haig* should be replaced by *Plumer*.'[88] Not all Haig's critics took the view that the moment was ripe. General Sir Henry Wilson, Britain's senior representative on the Allied Supreme War Council, told Lloyd George that 'the Government would not get anyone to fight a defensive battle better than Haig, and that the time to get rid of him was when the German attack was over.'[89] In the event Haig dismissed Gough, whose 5th Army had been most heavily bruised by the attack. He is said to have admitted that somebody would have to go, and believed that the army could stand Sir Hubert's loss better than his own.

A serious tactical error, real or reported, could end a general's career, but he might survive it if he retained the confidence of his superiors. Lieutenant General Sir Edwin Alderson was an infantry officer of horsey disposition: he wrote *Pink and Scarlet, or Hunting as a School for Soldiering*, and he gave a wonderful series of Lionel Edwards paintings – 'dedicated to the young soldier-sportsman, for whom he wrote' – to Sandhurst. After commanding 1st Canadian Division at Second Ypres he was promoted to command the newly-formed Canadian Corps, but was replaced in March 1916 after a setback at St-Eloi, on the southern edge of the Ypres salient. So much for the official version. In practice, though, Alderson had clashed with the ferociously energetic Sam Hughes, Canadian Minister of Militia. Hughes was a great advocate of the Canadian Ross rifle, whose virtues did not include handiness in trench warfare, and Alderson sensibly favoured the more practical Lee-Enfield. Alderson might have survived St-Eloi, but he was finished without the top cover which Hughes would not dream of providing.

Another example of the vital importance of 'top cover' is the case of Major General Joseph Davies, who commanded 8th Division in Rawlinson's IV Corps in early 1915. Rawlinson blamed him for failure to exploit success at Neuve Chapelle, and agreed with Haig, then commanding 1st Army, that Davies should go home. But Davies had no intention of going quietly. He collected evidence which suggested that Rawlinson himself had been involved in the handling of 8th Division's reserves. Rawlinson very creditably forwarded the information to Haig, who had just told French that Davies should be replaced. Haig was furious, and French considered sacking Rawlinson instead. He seems to have been dissuaded from doing so by Haig, but Rawlinson was formally warned that further attempts to shift blame onto his subordinates would result in his immediate removal. Rawlinson knew that he had Haig to thank for his survival, a sense of inferiority which did not enhance his disposition to argue with Haig over the planning or execution of the Somme.

A general did not have to be wrong to be sacked, as the case of Smith-Dorrien shows. In 1916 Major General Sir Charles Barter commanded 47th London Division, part of Lieutenant General Sir William Pulteney's III Corps. Although Pulteney had been a corps commander since September 1914 his continued survival was a source of surprise to his subordinates, not least to his chief of staff Brigadier General Charles Bonham-Carter, who called him 'the most completely ignorant general I served under during the war and that is saying a lot'. Barter's division had been allocated four tanks for its attack on High Wood on 15 September. Barter spoke to the tank officers, who suggested that they should skirt the wood and fire into it, but Pulteney thought that they were being 'sticky' and ordered them straight in.

Although the attack on the wood was eventually successful, the division lost over 4,500 men during the battle. One tank was destroyed by shellfire but the others all became bogged in unsuitable ground, just as their crews had predicted. There was an added note of tragedy, because the crew of one tank, disorientated by the stumps and craters in the wood, machine-gunned some of its supporting infantry. The tank commander was so upset by this that some brother officers attributed his subsequent death to suicide. A few days later Barter was sent home 'at an hour's notice'. He demanded an official inquiry, but never received one. However, the divisional association always invited him to its annual dinner as an honoured guest. Pulteney's corps was roughly handled in the German counterattack at Cambrai, though it was not until early 1918 that he was at last replaced. It is hard to see how he managed to survive for so long, though his old army connections probably helped: he was a Scots Guards officer, 'Putty' to his many well-placed friends. It was also suggested that he was so incompetent that his corps staff was specially selected to make up for his many deficiencies, and this, paradoxically, may have contributed to his longevity.[90]

Yet another Somme wood cost a major general his job. Ivor Phillips was relieved of command of 38th Division after his 115th Brigade failed to attack Mametz Wood on 7 July. The division's war diary maintained that the undergrowth made the timescale laid down impossible, and, as we have seen, the Welshmen fought bravely, but the situation in the wood became chaotic. Wyn Griffith, sent up to replace a wounded staff captain, soon found that the brigade major had been hit too, and he was therefore a one-man brigade staff. He saw the brigade commander, already hit in the arm, in utter despair, unable to communicate with his division yet still under orders to press his attack, when a British barrage crashed down on his own troops. There was an artillery observer in a shell hole but, as another officer acidly pointed out, 'he can't see twenty yards in front of him, and all his [telephone] lines are gone. He might as well be in Cardiff.' 'This is the end of everything,' the brigadier told Griffith.

> . . . sheer stupidity. I wonder if there is an order that never reached me . . . but that Staff Officer should have known the artillery programme for the day. And if there is another order, they ought not to have put down that barrage until they got my acknowledgement. How can we attack after our own barrage has ploughed its way through us? What good can a barrage do in a wood like this?

The brigadier, at fifty-seven very old for this sort of thing, was given immediate leave of absence and then relieved of his command on 28 August. He had already prophesied what would happen. 'You mark my words,' he told Griffith, 'they'll send me home for this. They want butchers, not brigadiers. They'll remember now what I told them, before we began, that the attack could not succeed unless the machine guns were masked. I shall be in England in a month.'[91] Phillips was sacked too. He had not planned the difficult task of attacking the wood with much skill, and the fact that he was Lloyd George's protégé was, under the circumstances, more hindrance than help.

Brigadiers came and went easily: Sir James Edmonds claimed that Haig had told him that he had sacked over a hundred. Often the pretext, as it was with divisional commanders such as Phillips, was 'stickiness', that is a reluctance to push attacks home. On 28 August 1916 Brigadier General Frederick Carleton wrote to tell his wife that he had been *Stellenbosched* from command of 98th Infantry Brigade. He was a dug-out who had returned to the army in 1914, commanding 1/4th King's Own from December 1915 to June 1916, when he was promoted. His divisional commander, Major General H. J. S. Landon, tersely reported on his dissatisfaction with the progress of the sector under his command and asked Horne, the corps commander, to replace him. Pending Horne's formal action, added Landon, another brigadier had already been ordered to take over

Carleton's sector. Carleton was shocked, depressed and ill: 'I want no sympathy nor do I want to see anyone, for at the moment I am almost done to all the world.'

However, he prepared a length dossier in his own defence, and it is so useful in explaining the relationship between brigadiers and divisional headquarters that I quote it at length. His conflict with divisional headquarters began in July, not long after he had assumed command. On a date he fails to specify, but which must have been on or just after 14 July, he was with his brigade in the Somme village of Bécordel.

> At about 4.30 p.m. [Lt] Col. Simons, GSO 1. of the 33rd Division, arrived in a motor car in search of me. This officer, who appeared to be in a state of excitement and some hurry, asked me to enter his motor car. He immediately produced a map, and said: 'We want you to make an attack with your brigade tonight.' He then explained that the objective I was required to take was a portion of the Switch Trench of Bazentin le Petit Wood [running north of the wood, just beyond the ground gained in the night attack of the 14th] and that it must be carried out by 7.30 p.m. After a glance at the map, I turned in great surprise to this Officer and I said, 'Do you know the distance from here to the point from which you asked me to make the attack?' Col. Simons replied, 'No, I have not measured it.' I laid off the distance on the map in front of this Officer, making it about 10,000 yards in a straight line. I then said 'An attack under such conditions as you suggest is out of the question. The roads are congested with traffic, the ground is entirely unknown, I should have to have my orders to give and convey to the whole brigade before the attack could be made, and there could be no possibility of arriving at the position in the stated time.' Col. Simons proceeded to contest the point that the attack could be made. I then turned to him and said, 'Simons, you were at Staff College with me and you know as well as I do that what you are asking is an impossibility. It is now 4.30, and if I could now move off the head of my brigade it would be 5.30 before the tail of it would be

leaving the ground. How can you possibly, under such
circumstances, expect me to carry out such instructions?

He said that he could not attack before 8.30 p.m. at the earliest,
and with that Simons departed, saying that it was no use, and giving
Carleton 'the impression that I had wilfully obstructed him'. Once
his brigade entered the line it was dogged by misfortune. German
shelling destroyed the tapes laid to guide working parties forward,
and: 'In the case of the 20th Fusiliers, although this battalion had
previously occupied the line, they appeared to have been unable to
find their way, and did not put in any appearance at all.' Finally,
Landon interviewed him and made it clear that corps was pressing
for completion of the work and that: 'No excuse for failure to comply
with this order will be accepted.' He received notice of dismissal the
following day.

Carleton's dossier, submitted to GHQ on 12 September, was so
effective that Haig's military secretary, at the time Major General
W. G. Peyton, replied on the 16th that 'the Commander-in-Chief is
prepared to consider your re-appointment to command of an Infantry Brigade in the field when your services are again placed at his
disposal'. In a classic instance of the subtle workings of the military
secretary's department he added a personal note:

> My dear Carleton,
> No report has gone home about you, so as soon as you
> have been passed fit you will be returned to us and
> reappointed to a brigade, but give yourself a sufficiently
> long rest or you will probably break down again.
> Yours as ever etc

He was indeed reappointed to a brigade, but in Salonika, where his
health quickly broke down and he was invalided home. He died after
a heart attack in 1922, having declared that his experiences on the
Somme had taken ten years off his life.[92]

The process of losing a superior's confidence might be little more
than a matter of personality. On 1 May 1916 Brigadier General
Charles Gosling, of 7th Infantry Brigade, was hit by shrapnel – a
bullet in each leg and another in the head, though he was not very
badly hurt – on his way out of the line to get a bath. The senior

battalion commander stood in until a replacement, Brigadier General Charles Heathcote, arrived a week later. Heathcote was sent home on 30 August by Major General Bainbridge, who had assumed command of 25th Division that July, as 'unfit for command'. Alexander Johnson, his brigade major, was very angry. 'It is the most unjust thing I've ever heard,' he wrote, 'and the whole Brigade is simply furious . . . the Brigadier is sent home simply because he does not get on with the Divisional Commander.'[93] Heathcote came back out as a lieutenant colonel, commanded a battalion, was invalided home, returned to command a battalion again, and got a brigade back in May 1917, retaining it for the rest of the war.

As a general lost his commander's confidence he was often presented with make-or-break tasks. In 1916 Walter Nicholson, then a senior staff officer in 17th Division, heard that one of the brigadiers was 'for the high jump' if he did not succeed in the next attack. He failed, and was duly sacked. 'It was a change of command which could not have been worse staged,' he wrote. 'The brigadier was popular in his brigade, and the brigade took his dismissal as a drastic reflection on their action in the battle. They had a right and proper hatred of the authorities.' Nicholson privately agreed that the brigadier was not, in fact, up to his job, but thought that the timing was disastrous. 'It is scarcely an exaggeration to say that nine out of ten commanders who were relieved of their command had a justifiable grievance as regards the particular occasion,' he added, 'but would have none if they had been *dégommé* at least half a dozen times previously.'[94]

Rawlinson was painfully slow in dispensing with Lieutenant General Sir Richard Butler, demonstrably the weakest of his corps commanders in 1918. He was already unhappy with Butler before the Amiens attack of 8 August, and three days later the over-strained officer was placed on sick leave. When he returned the following month Rawlinson went up to III Corps headquarters and wrote on his return:

> I am pretty sure the Aust and IX Corps will do their jobs but am not so confident about the III Corps . . . They do not seem to fix up their plans with the same precision

as the other Corps & I think Butler does not keep his Div
Cmdrs in enough order. I suppose he has not the
practical experience to make decisions and to shut them
up when they begin talking rot. If they make a mess of
this show I shall have to talk seriously to Butler for it will
be his fault.[95]

Butler duly failed his trade test, and Rawlinson agreed with Haig to
have him relieved. He was, though, still formally in command of
III Corps when the war ended. There was good reason for Rawlinson's hesitancy, for Butler was a Haig protégé. He had served under
Haig before the war, and had then been his chief of staff in 1st Army
and deputy chief of the general staff at GHQ: he was actually Haig's
preferred choice for CGS when Lawrence was appointed. If Rawlinson was to shift him without risking personal damage then he needed
abundant evidence.

Subordinates had mixed views about the replacement of their
superiors. In November 1917 Rowland Feilding was very sorry to
lose his brigadier, George Pereira, who was simply worn out. 'He is
about fifty-three,' thought Feilding, 'but has got to look like an old
man. He is, I think, the most loyal and faithful and brave and
unselfish man I have ever met, and I feel a great personal loss in his
departure.'[96] Lord Stanhope saw Haig arrive in early 1916 to sack
his corps commander, Lieutenant General G. D. H. Fanshawe, who
knew at once that the game was up. 'Well, sir,' he declared, 'you
obviously do not want to hear what I have to say, and I had better
go.' He was replaced by his gunner brother E. A. Fanshawe, regarded
by Stanhope as 'a less good soldier'. In contrast, Stanhope thought
that 32nd Division was poor largely because its commander, Major
General Ryecroft, 'did not act happily with either his staff or his
brigadiers'.[97] He was eventually dismissed.

The issue of the dismissal of generals goes straight to the heart
of the war's mythology. Some historians seem unaware of the ease
with which incompetent commanders were in fact replaced, while
others fasten on the removal of the likes of Phillips as evidence
that GHQ knew exactly what it was doing. The truth reflects the
theme expounded at the beginning of this book: this was an army

of extraordinary diversity, and resists any attempt to superimpose easy generalisations upon it. So for the moment let us leave our red tabs vulnerable both to the enemy's fire and the military secretary's pen, and consider now what they did, and what their subordinates made of them.

ONE LONG LOAF?

It was one of the most popular jokes in that most British of all popular entertainments, the music hall. The stand-up comedian, cheeks rouged and hair gelled, eased forward to the hissing footlights and asked the audience, with the finely-timed rhetoric of his craft: 'If bread is the staff of life, what is the life of the staff? One long loaf.' His listeners would have bayed with almost as much delight in 1966 as they had in 1916, and even today it is very hard to separate the real performance of formation headquarters from what people thought of their occupants.

The general staff was a recent arrival in the British army, instituted only in the wake of the Boer War. There was a strong case for making it what was termed a 'blue ribbon' staff, loosely modelled on the German general staff, and open only to officers who had passed through the army's staff college at Camberley. They would then alternate between staff and regimental appointments to ensure that they blended theoretical knowledge with practical understanding. The blue ribbon campaign foundered in 1906 after Sir John French managed to get Algy Lawson, not a staff college graduate, appointed to the post of brigade major of the 1st Cavalry Brigade. Thereafter it was possible to go onto the staff without having been to staff college. And when he became chief of the imperial general staff in 1912 French made it clear that: 'It is the duty of the Staff to present all the facts of the situation to a commander and then to take the necessary measures for carrying his decisions into effect.'[98]

British chiefs of staff were always to lack the wide authority enjoyed by their German opposite numbers. And the fact that the British army's cultural centre of gravity remained the regiment can be gauged from the fact that in 1914 there was a scramble for staff officers to get back to their battalions, although by doing so they lost the staff pay which they earned in addition to the pay of their regimental rank. About half the army's staff college graduates were killed or crippled in the first nine months of the war, often falling gallantly at a place where they should not have been. Even Maurice Hankey, mainstay of the Committee of Imperial Defence and then of the War Cabinet, made several attempts to go on active service, but neither Asquith nor Lloyd George would let him. His deputy returned joyfully to regimental duty and was promptly killed.

However, if the reformers had lost the argument over the blue ribbon general staff, the staff retained the tribal markings invented when it seemed likely that it would indeed be an exclusive and expert group. German general staff officers wore distinctive carmine double trouser-stripes. The British army decided to distinguish its general staff officers by modifying the red and gold collar-tab already worn by generals to produce a red tab with a thin line of red cord running from a button at its apex. General staff officers were also, like generals, to wear a red band round their caps. Officers on special staffs had their own distinguishing tabs and hat bands, like the purple of medical staff and the green of intelligence.

In addition, staff officers and commanders wore armbands which identified their level of command and function. Thus we could identify an approaching lieutenant colonel with red tabs on his collar and a red band on his right arm as the chief of staff of an infantry division, shortly before he asked us what the devil our general service wagons were doing blocking his road. Were he on a corps staff the band would have been red, white and red; it would have been red, black and red for army staff and red and blue (red uppermost) for GHQ. There were elaborate prescriptions for all, down to Inland Water Transport staff officers, who gave the game away by wearing a white brassard with a blue anchor, and servants to military attachés who (partly as a means of self-protection, for a Romanian general's groom might find it hard to justify himself to a Scots sentry in Montreuil) wore yellow armbands.[99]

Though there was functional logic to all this, its effects were wholly baneful. Staff officers looked strikingly different, and the fact that red tabs and brassards were worn by all general staff officers, even the subalterns and captains acting as aides de camp to generals, increased the apparent size of the staff. These trappings were certainly not universally welcome to those who had to wear them. Major Arthur Smith of the Coldstream Guards, then on the staff of 38th Division, found himself sheltering from shellfire in a trench full of troops. 'I admit that I was frightened,' he wrote, 'but what bothered me most was that that I should show I was frightened, or that the men lining the trench should see I was a staff officer.'[100] Maurice Hankey always wore uniform in Whitehall, 'but some instinct warned me that it would be better to stick to my regimental uniform than to obtain authority to wear the red tabs of a General Staff Officer'.[101] Indeed, it is no surprise that the postwar abolition of the rank of brigadier general (it was briefly replaced by the hybrid colonel commandant and then by brigadier) was accompanied by the removal of red tabs from all staff officers below full colonel.[102]

Commanders and their staff at GHQ and army level worked in headquarters which moved infrequently and (save for GHQ itself) were usually located in medium-sized châteaux. They lived in nearby private houses, the châteaux themselves, or purpose-built 'garden suburbs' like that in the grounds of 1st Army's headquarters at Hinges Château in 1915. Corps were more mobile, with frequent moves up and down the front in 1915–17 and then some substantial shifts in 1918. They too favoured a château if one was handy, but for major offensives the corps commander would usually move up with a small staff and signallers to try to remain in contact with his divisional commanders. Lieutenant General Sir Thomas Morland of X Corps had, for instance, a forward command post in a wooden gantry up a tree in the western edge of Aveluy Wood, in the centre of his sector, on 1 July 1916.

Day-to-day business at corps level and above was done by telephone, letter and at conferences. The radio grew in importance as the war went on, but although it made a real difference in some areas (such as the control of counter-battery fire from the air) it had little real impact on upper level of command in any of the combatant armies on the Western Front. The distinguished military historian Martin van Creveld has poured scorn on the use of the telephone in the First World War. During the Somme, Haig, he maintains, was 'positioned at his headquarters where he hoped to have all the facts at the end of a telephone wire . . .', but instead he 'ended up by having none at all, and . . . was one of the worst informed men on the Somme'.[103] But on 1 July Haig did not have 'no information at all'. He had a good deal, for 4th Army told him what it thought was happening. The fact that 4th Army was often wrong reflected the fact that communication between attacking divisions and their corps had often broken down completely, leaving Rawlinson himself in the dark. Well aware of the limitations of the telephone, Haig went forward to see Rawlinson on the second morning of the battle, and directed him to press his attack where he had been successful the previous day, south of the Albert-Bapaume road. There was indeed a serious communication problem. But it was not at the upper end of the chain of command, between GHQ, army and corps, but down below corps level.

If corps headquarters moved occasionally, then divisional head-quarters moved frequently – 51st Highland no less than eighteen times between July and December 1916 – and there were wide variations in their accommodation. Where possible they would spread themselves around a farm or two in Flanders, where big farmhouses, with their buildings on three sides of a square, were so characteristic of the landscape. Walter Nicholson described a Flanders farm occupied by the headquarters of 51st Highland Division in 1915.

> It is built four-square and round a great 'midden'. One side, a single-storeyed building on a raised brick founda-tion, is the dwelling of the farmer and his family; above the living room runs a long loft. Barns form the other three sides; one for pigs, poultry and cattle. The other two filled with straw or empty according to the season. In the 'midden' manure is piled high, and as may be imagined the whole surroundings are in summer black with flies

and in winter a swamp. But the farm, impoverished in appearance, frugally furnished, provided in fact the best of all billets. The officers who had experience chose its kitchen in winter to any room in the château; while the barns, after we had repaired them, were far better than bare boards.[104]

Further south, in Artois and Picardy, the pattern of land use was different, and villages and modest châteaux were more common than the 'Spanish farms' of Flanders. When 51st Highland Division moved into the Picardy village of Senlis, with fifty or sixty houses, its headquarters was established in the best house in the village (known to the Jocks as the 'chotoo'), but sadly it was:

designed for show and not for comfort, with two or even three stairs to overtake the great one-storey farms. Built of brick, with a great dignity of iron railings and of florid decoration within, the floors are highly polished and the windows tightly shut, dust sheets are over all the carpets. They look and feel as dead as mutton . . .[105]

A proper château in Hermaville turned out to be little better, for although it was 'elegant in design', the big reception rooms 'caught all the winds of France through the badly constructed great French windows; the many smaller rooms were scruffy and unventilated'. To make matters worse the baron who owned it, an irascible former cavalry officer, shouted *'Pas des chiens dans la maison'* as the enormous dog Rip strolled in on the heels of his master, 'Uncle' Harper, the divisional commander. The beast 'may have had endearing qualities, but no sense of humour', and the baron was right to watch his step.[106]

Staff officers lived and ate in a number of messes, depending on the accommodation available. Divisional practice varied, but usually the commander, his chief of staff and aide de camp would constitute No. 1 Mess, with other senior staff officers in No. 2 Mess and separate messes for the artillery and engineer staff. When divisions moved up onto the abomination of desolation that constituted the old Somme battlefield they were forced to improvise amongst the 'dolls' houses' cobbled together in the ruins, with names like *The Palace, Evergreen House* and *Windy Corner.* Engineers soon brought a degree of comfort to such surroundings, and in early 1918 Hanway Cumming found 21st Division in 'a series of the usual wooden huts on the sheltered side of a low ridge and provided with mined dugouts as a protection against aerial bombing, which at the time was common in this part of the line'.[107] Improvisation and resource improved stark surroundings. 'Theft,' thought Nicholson, 'is an individual affair, not communal,' and therefore useful items were simply 'borrowed'. A small house in the village of Daours was soon turned into a very acceptable mess. 'We no longer ate off bare boards,' he confessed,

> pictures from the illustrated papers decorated our walls, and we had thrown away our enamel ware. Tastes had been developed in local wines and liqueurs, which were purchased from neighbouring towns whenever conditions such as the loan of a car permitted and officers returning from leave came laden. 'Long' Perry ... [brought] two hares and a grouse, Weston returned with pheasants and hares. But my gift of a salmon, the last of the season from Harrods, was marred by three days fog in the channel.

However, the commander Royal Artillery's mess was unaccountably spartan: 'They had stew for lunch and cold bully beef for supper; tea, bread and jam at all meals.'[108] Nicholson declared that staff messes were always empty except at mealtimes: there was simply too much work to do.

The central figure in all this was the divisional commander, a major general aged anywhere between thirty-five (for the precocious Keppel Bethell) and his late fifties (for Bannatyne Allason, the first commander of 51st Highland, who wore the ribbon of the Kabul-Kandahar Star from Lord Roberts' 1880 campaign). Many officers agreed with Nicholson that it was good for generals to be exposed to the gentle banter of the young, but when he joined 17th Division he found that different rules applied.

> I joined a mess at which the divisional commander sat at one end of a long table and an uncouth spotty second-lieutenant at the other extremity ... There was no general conversation, no laughter among the eighteen officers

present. One meal in such a mess would have convinced a visitor that the division 'Hadn't a hope'.[109]

Major General Pilcher, the divisional commander, already had a reputation for unhandy relations with his subordinates. Stanhope was delighted to recall an incident when Pilcher was out and about, upbraiding officers and men who were not carrying respirators. He had borrowed one himself just before the trip, and when he took it out to show a harassed subaltern how it should be put on, he discovered that the case contained only 'an old and dirty pair of socks'. He was replaced by Major General Philip Robertson: soon the food in the mess improved, the place was spotless and laughter was the rule. 'We treated him as an older equal,' wrote Nicholson, 'which is the best sedative you can give any commander.'

The division's chief of staff (General Staff Officer Grade 1) was, almost without exception, a regular officer and staff college graduate. His relationship with the commander was crucial, as Brigadier General Archibald 'Sally' Home admitted when he went to be GSO 1 of 46th North Midland Division on the Somme front in April 1916. Home had already been chief of staff to the cavalry corps, and this apparent step down was intended to give him the familiarity with infantry work which he would need if he was to go further on the staff. Indeed, he was 'wondering what an infantry division is like, luckily a sahib commands it ... Luckily I know him as he is Cis Bingham's brother-in-law.' 'I don't think I know very much about infantry,' he confessed, 'so I have to look wise.' This wisdom included being surprised by the life led by the infantry. 'A man has a pack weighing 56lbs on his back,' he wrote, 'and how he gets along at all is a marvel to me.'[110] Home had moved north to become brigadier general, general staff to the testy Lieutenant General Hamilton-Gordon of IX Corps (whose temper was ruined, it was said, by the fact that he could not taste anything), probably following the career pattern sketched out by the military secretary's department, by the time 46th Division attacked on 1 July, meeting total failure in its diversionary attack on Gommecourt. The next division south, 56th London, advanced much further, though at greater cost, and accusations of stickiness were not slow in coming.

The commander of 46th Division, Major General the Hon. Edward Montagu-Stuart-Wortley, was speedily sacked following an unfavourable report from his corps commander, Lieutenant General Sir Thomas Snow.

> His Division showed a lack of offensive spirit in the recent operations and I attributed this to the fact that Stuart-Wortley was not on account of his physical condition and age able to get about the trenches as much as was necessary for a Divisional Commander to do in this sort of war.

Haig informed the military secretary at the War Office that he was not prepared to have him back in France as a divisional commander. The general at once protested, but although he was given an understrength division in Ireland he was never employed again on active service.[111] Home admitted that 'the failure has been a great blow to me as I helped in the preparations and was responsible for the preliminary work'.[112] It is hard to resist the conclusion that Montagu-Stuart-Wortley, past his fighting best at fifty-eight, would have profited from experienced infantry advice in planning his attack, one of the most difficult on the first day of the Somme because its left flank was wide open.

It was helpful for a chief of staff and his commander to have different personalities: if one was a generalist, the other should be a man of detail; if one was taciturn, the other should be outgoing. 'To get the best out of a combination of men,' suggested Nicholson, 'you must have diversity; all high cards, but no pairs.' Allenby of 3rd Army had not earned the nickname 'the Bull' for nothing, and when he left his headquarters the staff would warn subordinates with the Morse letters BBL for 'Bloody Bull Loose'. Lord Stanhope, who grew to like him, thought that though 'to some extent he consulted his subordinate commanders, they were nervous of expressing an opinion as he was liable to be severe of anything he thought foolish'. His chief of staff, Hugh Jeudwine, had what his obituarist called 'a firm, uncompromising outlook' and Stanhope thought the combination altogether too tough. The only man who could bend Allenby seemed to be his pleasant aide de camp Captain Dalmeny – 'the bull pup' – who 'used to take him out for a walk and bring him back in a peaceful frame of mind'. Plumer and his chief of staff Major General Sir Charles 'Tim' Harington worked together so well that Charteris thought it impossible to see where one ended and the other began. Sometimes Harington would rough out a plan and pass it to Plumer for comment, or sometimes the process would work in reverse, with Plumer initiating the scheme and passing it round for the view of his staff. Stanhope, with his extensive experience of headquarters, thought him 'much the best of our higher commanders'.[113]

The 'rule of differents' also applied at divisional level. Lieutenant Colonel Jack Collins, GSO1 of 17th Division, 'had all the fire and enthusiasm the general lacked', and it was an index of the quality of his staff, which worked with broad direction but little detailed supervision, that an artillery brigade attached from another division 'gave us the unstinted meed of praise that, of the nine divisions that had shot over, we were the only division who really looked after them'.[114] But his successor was a man for detail and the mood changed at once.

> Previously G2 rang up for buses. 'That you, Quack, one bus forward, please.' 'OK,' replies Philips, and his OK is absolutely safe. Too trivial a matter for me [the division's senior administrative staff officer] to know anything about. Now the telephone rings. 'The GSO(1) would like to see the AA&QMG.' The G1 looks up, but keeps writing; then 'I need a bus, please; it's got to be at Hinges at exactly 1500 hours. Will you see that it doesn't fail?' It's a pinprick, of course; he ignores me but then I deal in many big problems and have a numerous staff for the trifles. So I go back. 'Underline it, Quack.'[115]

In all headquarters it was important for the staff branches to pull together. They were usually in different rooms or huts, and it was easy for them to drift into the backwaters of specialisation. Some staffs maintained a rule of personal contact, which decreed that as much business as possible would be done face to face, and that even unexpected visitors would always be met by an officer with a clear view of the big picture. When Lord Stanhope went to XIII Corps he found a state of 'armed neutrality' between the G and Q staffs.

His commander, Lieutenant General Sir Walter Congreve, was so involved with the troops that he made himself unpopular with his divisions and brigades, and was so worn out by this that he seemed unaware of what was wrong with his headquarters.

When Stanhope moved on to III Corps, under Lieutenant General Sir Claude Jacob, he found things altogether better. This was, he thought, because Jacob never went up the line, and 'was thus better able to keep a wide view ... While not a clever man he had sound common sense and good judgement. His staff advised him, and Divisional Staffs liked and trusted him, as did the troops.' Jacob was also not prepared to allow himself to be browbeaten by army commanders. When Gough criticised a plan of attack during Third Ypres, Jacob replied 'that he must carry out his attacks in his own way or he had better resign and hand over command of III Corps to someone else. Sir Hubert Gough replied that this was the last thing he wanted and let him carry out the attack as he planned it. The attack was a wonderful success.'[116] Walter Guinness, then serving on the staff of one of Jacob's brigades, thought him 'a very good soldier, but there is little confidence in our Army Commander (Sir Hubert Gough)' whose staff, by comparison with those of Second Army, 'struck one as haphazard in its methods'.[117]

There were functional differences between all these levels of command. Armies prepared large-scale plans of their own either within the context of a campaign plan laid down by GHQ, or on their own initiative. The scheme for Cambrai resulted from ideas put forward by the headquarters of the Tank Corps, with its laterally-thinking chief of staff, Lieutenant Colonel J. F. C. Fuller, and the ground-breaking concepts of Brigadier General Hugh 'Owen' Tudor, CRA of 9th Scottish Division. Byng backed the radicals, and persuaded Haig to let him try. It was arguably Haig's readiness to allow the battle to become attritional after its initial success, rather than to order Byng to cut his losses, that paved the way for the depressing setback which came with the German counterattack. The attack on Messines Ridge was contrived and executed by 2nd Army on the direction of, but with minimal interference from, GHQ.

The corps was the lowest level at which major plans could be formulated, largely because it boasted artillery assets which could reach deep into German defences and focus a real weight of fire-power in support of its attacks. We have already seen that the British had no experience of this level of command before the war, and it is striking to see how little uniformity there was in the function of corps throughout the conflict. Some army commanders tended to use their corps simply to transmit orders to divisions, while others allowed corps commanders more latitude in planning to achieve a broadly-defined aim. Corps themselves treated their divisions in just the same way, and 'the flexible style of command, where more authority was delegated to divisions (where possible) than had been the case since 1915, was crucial in the offensives of the Hundred Days'.[118]

But it is striking how contemporaries often perceived the corps as the rain cloud over their heads. Charles Carrington thought that:

> The remoteness and anonymity of a corps headquarters was such that the Corps Commander, inevitably, was blamed. Heaven knows, we grumbled and joked about brigade and division, but within reason. Knowing them, we made allowance. Corps we did not know and since battles in France were mostly disastrous, the Corps Commander was rarely popular.[119]

Walter Nicholson believed that Lord Cavan of XIV Corps was 'one of the rare corps commanders who was known by name to more than divisional commanders'. Carrington thought that while 'my colonel, brigadier and divisional commander were men I could respect [and] every man in my company knew Brigadier Sladen and General Fanshawe by sight I doubt if one in ten knew the corps commander's name'.[120]

Occasionally a corps commander's attempt to be well known mis-fired. Lieutenant General Sir Aylmer Hunter-Weston of VIII Corps always introduced himself by his full name and title, proudly adding 'MP' after being elected to Parliament (for North Ayrshire) in October 1916. In the bitter winter of 1917–18 'Hunter-Bunter' decided to wish troops departing on leave trains a merry Christmas. An aide de camp would open the carriage door and the general would intone: 'I am Lieutenant General Sir Aylmer Hunter-Weston MP, your Corps Commander, and I wish you a Happy Christmas.'

From the smoky fug of one carriage a disembodied voice declared: 'And I'm the Prince of Wales, and wish you'd shut the bloody door.'

The brigade, at the very bottom of our pile, had a comparatively hands-on headquarters. When Frank Crozier took command of his brigade in 1916 his divisional commander advised him, as they parted, to: 'Treat your new brigade like a big battalion.'[121] However, experienced staff officers recognised that successful brigade commanders needed a wider grasp of military matters to command a brigade successfully. Walter Guinness described one recently-arrived brigadier as 'a very nice person and a most dashing leader of men, but completely ignorant about all Staff Work and the detail of running a brigade'.[122] However, his sheer good sense in arranging matters so that his staff were not frequently disturbed meant that the headquarters actually worked much better than it had under his more experienced predecessor. Brigade headquarters were birds of passage. A division holding a sector of front might rotate its brigades so as to have two in the line and one out, and brigades did much the same with their battalions. In the hard winter of 1916–17, for instance, Crozier's brigade did seven days in the line before being relieved.

In 1914 an infantry brigade would have had only three red-tabbed officers on its staff, the commander, his brigade major and a staff captain. However, it was impossible to control four battalions in a twenty-four-hour battle with such a tiny staff, and so as the war progressed brigade headquarters was fleshed out with more officers and clerks. Walter Guinness, flagged up for a brigade major's appointment, was sent on a six-week staff course at Hesdin in late 1916. Most of those attending were brigade majors, staff captains or GSO3s, and he:

> learnt almost as much from discussing matters with them as from the lectures and exercises. In the morning we generally had certain control operation orders of either armies or corps given to us and proceeded from them to work out our orders in syndicates in which we daily changed places and fulfilled different posts. In the afternoons we had conferences and criticisms of our own and the instructors production and the evenings were generally spent at a lecture by some expert from the outside.

In February 1917 he was appointed brigade major to 74th Infantry Brigade under Keppel Bethell. 'Instead of the usual Brigade Mess of about ten,' he wrote, 'we had only five – Bethell, M—— (the Staff Captain), an Orderly Officer . . . a Signalling Officer . . . and I.'[123]

On the eve of the attack on Messines this brigade headquarters moved up into a newly-constructed dugout just 600 yards from the front line. It was all too obvious, and 'Bowyer, the QM of the 11th Lancashire Fusiliers had his head taken off [by a shell] just as he was coming into the door of our dugout.' The dugout itself was 30 feet below the surface, with 'endless passages, five entries and eight rooms . . . also electric light. One only hears a very dull thud when a heavy shell lands on top.' Later that summer, after Plumer's 2nd Army had taken direction of attacks up the Menin Road, Bethell's brigade headquarters was in a deep dugout at Birr Cross-Roads, half a mile north of the site of Hooge Château. 'The dugout was one of the most disgusting places I have ever lived in,' admitted Guinness.

> It was only kept habitable by continual pumping and when the pumps broke down one was generally up to one's ankles in water. Besides ourselves in the dugout, there was a dressing station and a good deal of accommodation given up to signals. The result was that our quarters were fearfully cramped and M—— and I had to do all our work on a table about two feet by three on to which water was continually pouring down from the ceiling. Bethell had another little cubby hole on the other side of the passage and the five days which we spent before the attack were, I think, the most unpleasant of the whole of my time in France.[124]

Bethell was notoriously testy and impatient, and 'became absolutely impossible' so that he had to eat his meals alone.

In March 1918 Hanway Cumming's brigade headquarters at Saulcourt, just behind the line, was approached by a sunken road and 'consisted of a series of "elephant shelters" dug into the bank of the road with a mined dugout below them, altogether very snug and comfortable quarters, as things went.'[125] He commanded from the dugout, he and his staff wearing gas masks for much of the day, when the Germans attacked on 21 March. In the fluid battle that followed he spent much of his time on the move. He was riding back with his orderly from another brigade headquarters (staff cars were not issued below divisional level), which was in telephone communication with divisional headquarters, 'when suddenly he was fired at comparatively short range, one bullet hitting the horse just in front of the saddle'. He galloped clear, though both horses died later: he acknowledged that he owed his life 'to the gallant way in which, although badly wounded, the horses had kept up sufficiently to carry them out of danger'.[126]

Later that year the brigade had moved south to the French sector in Champagne, with its headquarters 'accommodated in a dugout, tunnelled into a bank on the hillside and, being in the middle of the wood, was beautifully screened from aerial observation. The wood itself was delightful, full of lilies of the valley and wild spring flowers . . .'. Cumming did not relish the prospect of living in the dugout and so 'had a small wooden hut built for himself'.[127] Again his headquarters was overrun by a German offensive, and again he commanded from horseback. During the steady advance of the last Hundred Days he was often without a static headquarters at all. The perennial problem remained communication. Although his signallers were often able to get lines in quickly enough to speak to division, it was always hard to reach battalions, and on 26 August he managed to stop an attack, cancelled at the last moment by division, by using two 'young and active' staff officers to sprint forwards. At this stage in the war some brigadiers were very far forward. Private Albert Bullock of 8/Royal Warwicks encountered his brigade commander in the front wave of an attack. Brigadier General Fryell 'collected about 20 of us and we pushed up the valley with the General, who had a rifle and said he was coming with us . . . Just as I got up to go my leg went dead and I fell down . . .'.[128]

Frank Crozier, his brigade rushed forward to help stem the German counterattack at Cambrai, found a dugout to command from – where a visiting hussar caused concern by upsetting a bottle of port and six glasses. Pulled out of the line, he found his headquarters accommodated in a family vault in Havrincourt. The Germans had cleared out the coffins and their contents, but the place still smelt 'diabolical'. Crozier saw that his staff were lying in the coffin niches, and asked his servant how they could do it. 'They'd sleep anywhere, they're nearly dead themselves,' snapped his forceful orderly Corporal Starrett; 'you lie down now as you are, here's some tea coming, and go to sleep.'[129]

Being on the staff of a fighting formation was certainly no sinecure. However, there were safe and predictable staff jobs, and, particularly on the lines of communication staff or at the base, a cunning or unfit officer could find himself an easy billet. J. B. Priestley, who joined a New Army battalion in 1914, was eventually commissioned in 1917, gassed and then medically downgraded to B2, 'unfit for active service but fit for something'. He finished up at the Labour Corps depot at Rouen, running what was effectively a labour exchange that specialised in trades that were decidedly not run of the mill. 'If Fourth Army wanted two comedians, three conjurers, a couple of female impersonators it sent us a wire saying so,' he wrote, 'then we paraded the most likely specimens, tried one or two out on the stage, and packed them off by the next train.'[130] Another temporary officer who would become an author, R. H. Mottram, spent much of his war on liaison duties with the French civil authorities, and described how rear headquarters grew.

> Far more general was the continual change in organisation. The Administrative Chiefs now came back to Headquarters, and the Mess was subdivided. Laundry and Salvage, Sanitation and Gas Officers were being appointed, and soon the non-regular, untabbed personnel of the staff outnumbered the brass hats as per establishment. Expeditionary Force canteens made their appearance, and there was a tendency to specialise hospitals, create remount depots, innumerable 'schools' and baths. This kept me so busy, for there was hardly a yard of ground or a barn that the inhabitants were willing to part with, that the short rest-period soon passed. Nor was this wonderful. I ask myself what I would have thought if, coming home on leave, I had found my home full of French troops from the Pyrenees and my garden arranged for a bull-fight. Yet such would have been exact parallels to the demands we made.[131]

Soldiers on their way to and from France, on duty or on leave, tended to see far more of horsey railway transport officers ('Engines a bit frisky this morning?' asked a muddy colonel in *Punch*) or corpulent assistant embarkation officers than they did of their own formation staffs. Lieutenant Colonel Arthur Osburn, writing in 1932, by which time the staff had few friends, wrote of how:

> With each stage backwards towards the Base and the shores of old England there was an increase of the tendency to an irritable form of unreasoning obstruction, a crabbing kind of jealousy. Commandants of rest camps and other back areas, town majors, and so forth, harried the fighting man who came back for a brief respite with all sorts of restrictions and obligations . . . As one left the War behind there was also more pomposity and more fussy discipline . . .
>
> I began to realise this Back-Area spirit on the platform of Abbeville station, where a Railway Staff Officer calmly informed me that R.A.M.C. meant 'Rob All My Comrades'. I had never before heard that stupid libel.[132]

An officer of the Scottish Rifles echoed this experience. Having come out of a hard battle:

> I was detailed to ride 10 miles back to Corps H.Q. to get pay for the troops from the Field Cashier. Having got the money we were informed by the M.P. that this beautiful untouched town was out of bounds for anyone not on the corps staff. We were not allowed to get even a cup of tea although the tea shops and cafés were full of staff officers and their clerks. We were all but put under arrest.[133]

Perceptions apart, there was not much loafing at GHQ and on formation staffs. John Charteris wrote that: 'There are few, if any, officers who do not work a fourteen-hour day, and who are not to be found at work far into the night.'[134] Most general staff officers there did some work before breakfast, took an hour for lunch, perhaps taking a turn round the ramparts for their health, and then worked on to dinner, returning to their offices afterwards. Men collapsed at their desks with the strain, and the 'accidental' drowning of one exhausted brigadier general was widely believed to be suicide.

However, the war correspondent Philip Gibbs, who himself did so much to help shape attitudes, remained unsympathetic towards them. 'Within their closed corporation,' he wrote,

> there were rivalries, intrigues, perjuries and treacheries like those of a medieval court ... They worked late into the night. That is to say, they went back to their offices after dinner at mess ... and kept their lights burning, and smoked more cigarettes, and rang each other up on the telephone with futile questions ...[135]

The canard that staff officers had no idea of front-line conditions is often repeated. But even if Charteris is not a sympathetic figure it is evident that he knew just what the Ypres salient was like in 1917, for he visited it several times. On 4 August 1917 he wrote that: 'Every brook is swollen and the ground is a quagmire.' 'The front line now baffles description,' he wrote later, 'it is just a sea of mud churned up by shell-fire.' On 10 October, after watching the failure of an attack, he lamented: 'Yesterday afternoon was utterly damnable. I got back very late and could not work, and could not rest.'[136]

Many junior staff officers knew exactly what front-line conditions were like. Reginald Tompson, then on the staff of 7th Division, wrote in his diary on 30 July 1916 that:

> The conditions in the trenches which are in great part obliterated & non existent are indescribable. It takes 2 hours to go 300 yards in places, & they are up to their thighs in liquid mud, & unceasing rain continues, & where there are trenches they are often only 2ft deep. The battalions will be relieved tomorrow. 48 hours is the maximum they can stand. The food is drenched with rain before they can eat it.

Nor was he unaware what all this was doing to the division. On 1 September he 'went to Knight's funeral before starting. 3 graves, Knight ... Crawford and Stroud. Knight was only a small parcel. Stroud didn't turn up as he was never found.' Four days later he recorded:

> One of the blackest days we have ever had. We were pushed out of Ale Alley & the losses against CUINCHY

are very appalling, & nothing whatever was accomplished as far as one can see. The GOC went in to see the Corps Commander to protest at the way in which the division was being butchered for no purpose.[137]

Arthur Smith was one of the two surviving staff officers in 38th Division at the end of the Mametz Wood battle.

> In the early morning, about 5am, I was exploring an out of the way trench to see where it led to, when I came across a young lad who was wounded. He told me that he had been lying there for two days, and no one had seen him. He had a hole about the size of a shilling in the right portion of his chest, and of course he could not breathe with the right lung ... I plugged up the hole with a field dressing, and gave him a drink of water. He was so grateful. I then noticed a bible sticking out of his breast pocket, and he told me it was the best thing he had got ... I gave him the following verse to think about, 'I will never leave thee nor forsake thee,' and then went off to find some one to help me carry him away ... He will be in Hospital now, and I think he will live.[138]

The following year Smith himself needed the bible. He was badly wounded in the foot and the surgeon gave him a choice: 'I could leave your foot on and you may get blood poisoning, or I could take it off, but that would be the end of your service. Let me know tomorrow what you'd like.' He opened his bible at a page containing the phrase: 'The Lord is thy consolation and shall keep thy foot from being taken.' He declined the operation and lived to write his memoirs.

Lord Stanhope believed that the staff were blamed for what had certainly been a failing early on: 'all through the early part of the war it was very rare for generals or staff officers to be seen in the trenches'. Indeed, when he was commanding a Grenadier company in the first winter of the war he saw his own commanding officer in the trenches only four times in three and a half months. But by the time he was on the staff of V Corps in 1917 'I and the GSO2 were in the front line practically every day.' He went on to suggest that the process might have been overdone, 'and whether the Staff would not in many cases have been of more value to the fighting troops if they had thought about more fully in their offices the information they had received from reports and from personal information.'[139]

We may never get to like them, these GSO1s, deputy assistant adjutants and quartermaster generals, brigade majors and staff captains. Perhaps the glacis plate of historiography is now too thick to let us get close to them as they worry about their reports and returns, or deal with billeting problems in Hazebrouck or Albert. But let us at least judge them for what they were: by and large honest, brave and hardworking, sometimes promoted above the level of their competence, all too well aware of the consequences of their mistakes, and by no means ignorant of what they were expecting men to do or the circumstances in which they had to do it.

However, let us not imagine that Thomas Atkins and his comrades thought about them nearly as much as historians do. When the Reverend Harold Davies joined his division as a padre on the Somme he observed that:

> There is a certain difference in the interest which is taken in generals at DHQ and lower down in the brigades and battalions. At DHQ they were full of him and would talk of nothing else. In the battalion nobody talks of the general of the Div nor cares a hang about him. At present I am one of the very few in the 4th Bedfords who knows his name.[140]

And it is to this world in which red tabs counted for so little and comradeship for so much that we now turn our attention.

IV

EARTH AND WIRE

A VIEW FROM THE PARAPET

It is a truth too rarely acknowledged that the British army was not surprised by that most visible characteristic of the Western Front, the trench. The 1909 *Field Service Regulations* declared that trenches were an essential ingredient of defence, and went on to warn that they must not be sited in exposed positions, should be provided with covered communications and backed by deep shelters for supporting troops.[1] *Infantry Training 1914* repeated much of this verbatim, and emphasised that all ranks should be taught 'the general principles of the siting of trenches, the construction of overhead cover, and the circumstances in which trenches are required'.[2] The July 1914 final examination at the Royal Military Academy included detailed questions on the entrenchment of an infantry company and a detached outpost, and the 1914 edition of the *Field Service Pocket Book* had diagrams of several sorts of trenches and covered gun positions, and a table aimed at helping an officer calculate how long entrenching a position would actually take.

Not only was the trench itself not new, but there was ample precedent for trench warfare. It was not invented in 1914, but had been a feature of sieges across the ages. The English Civil War song *When Cannon are Roaring* speaks of 'Engineers in the trench/earth, earth uprearing'. Sappers, the traditional nickname for Royal Engineers (as well as the rank-title of the engineers' equivalent of a private), derived their name from the business of sapping – digging zigzagging approach trenches in the formal siege of fortresses. In 1864–5 the Confederates burrowed a complex network of trenches around the Virginia town of Petersburg, and Union forces sought to deal with them in ways that would be familiar half a century later, and which included exploding a huge mine beneath them. Trenches were dug in Boer War sieges, and the Russo-Japanese War featured trench warfare on an even wider scale. Indeed, the war on the Western Front had much in common with a traditional siege, with men taking to the earth to shelter themselves from the enemy's fire, and devising a variety of methods to make their own lives more comfortable and the enemy's less so.

The Western Front soon went to earth. As early as August 1914 soldiers scratched 'lying trenches' with their entrenching tools, out-lining an oblong 6 feet by 2; and rolling the turf forwards to provide some cover and a rest for the left arm to make the user's rifle fire steadier. Early that autumn there were short sections of disconnected trench, simple and primitive by later standards and not unlike the two-man foxholes of the Second World War. By Christmas trenches were continuous where the lie of the land permitted.

What was new about the Western Front was not the simple fact of trench warfare, but its scale and duration. As we saw in the first chapter, a line of field fortifications ran all the war from the Swiss border to the North Sea. There was not, as one might perhaps think, a single line of trenches along which an individual could walk all that distance, because geography and man interposed obstacles. In parts of low-lying Flanders it was impossible to dig proper trenches because the water table was too high, and so both sides built up rather than dug down. Private W. G. Birley of 21/London recalled 'breastworks built of sandbags instead of trenches' at both Neuve Chapelle and parts of the Ypres salient.[3] F. P. Roe agreed that:

> the trenches were not literal trenches at all but were in reality sandbag fortifications all above ground. The terrain made it impossible to build dugouts in the parados and the only shelter possible was a shallow inlet in the sandbags of the parapet, promptly given the name 'funk hole'.[4]

Second Lieutenant Edward Underhill, writing from Ploegsteert Wood, south of Ypres, in November 1915, admitted that:

> The conditions here are appalling. I never knew what
> mud was till I got here . . . We have had about three days
> continuous rain, and the result is the trenches are flooded
> and the country round is a sea of mud ankle-deep, and
> in some places today I have been over my knees in it. I
> took 150 men to do drainage work under the R.E.s on
> the communication trenches on the left of where we were
> before we came out. It was an endless, hopeless task. The
> walls had caved in in places, and as soon as the muck was
> cleared out it caved in again, and it all had to be done
> again. The fire trenches were 2 or 3 feet deep in water,
> and they were talking of abandoning them . . . All the time
> we were working this morning shells were bursting every
> now and then. And they were unpleasantly close too.[5]

Early in 1915 Lieutenant Aidan Liddell of the Argyll and Suther-land Highlanders wrote that the opposing lines in his part of the salient were only 40 yards apart: he saw 'both sides hard at work building breastwork. German officer sitting in chair directing operations'.[6] Ghastly conditions such as these, which made simple existence difficult for both sides, encouraged a certain live-and-let-live attitude which was sometimes a feature of trench warfare.

But not always. George Coppard, a machine-gunner, was at Festubert in the winter of 1915, and by then the German use of poison gas and the losses of Loos had increased bitterness. He remembered that 'the front-line area was flooded and the communication trenches had vanished under water. There was no front-line trench. Instead, earthworks, consisting of sandbags piled on top of the original parapet, had to be made.'[7] When Coppard's detachment heard a German wiring party at work (he surmised that its members were probably careless because it was Christmas), they waded through thigh-deep water with a machine gun and set it up before firing a Very light which revealed around twenty Germans. The gunner opened fire while another member of the detachment put up another flare. 'The flare burst,' he recalled, casting its glare on the tottering ghost-like figures as they fell. Swiftly, as if wielding a two-edged sword, Snowy plied the hail of bullets. Two Jerries ran onto their wire and were killed. The ground where the enemy had fallen was raked with fire, to finish off any crafty ones who might be feigning death. The second flare had just about burnt out as the firing stopped. The whole thing lasted no more than thirty seconds.[8]

Coppard's comrades were relieved on their fifth night in the line, slopping back in their thigh boots on an exhausting ten-hour march simply to get out of the line. Roe thought that it took about two hours to cover the 200 muddy yards of his battalion's frontage.

As better pumps and more 'trench stores' – such as duckboards and revetting timber – arrived, trenches could be improved. Gerald Burgoyne wrote how:

> We have slightly improved our trenches by putting boards and fascines along the bottom of them. And in the worst places there are half tubs, with a bit of plank as a seat, nailed across. A man can sit on this and keep his feet fairly dry, or rather, out of the freezing mud and water.[9]

Although there were frequent complaints that the Germans often picked higher ground so that the water pumped out of their trenches ran in to the British, this was certainly not always the case. In November 1915 Frank Hawkings wrote:

> Have been pumping all night and most of the morning with interesting results. The water has all gone into Fritz trenches, and suddenly this afternoon we observed small parties of the enemy leap out of their trenches, run along fifty yards and leap in again. We soon got busy with our rifles and laid several of them low.[10]

Even some areas of the front that were dry most of the time could be flooded by sudden heavy downpours. Hawkings recalled that at Carnoy on the Somme rains meant that:

> the water from the two hillsides has come into the valley and filled our trench in some places waist deep. In order to keep the trench from being absolutely waterlogged we

have to pump continuously with the four pumps with which we have been supplied. As two or three of the pumps keep getting clogged with mud, this is no easy matter.[11]

Trench sides were revetted with timber supported by stakes or angle iron, frames of woven willow, or revetment hurdles – frames of timber lined with stout wire-netting which were ideal for holding back crumbling chalk. In Artois and Picardy trenches were generally drier than in Flanders, and the chalk which lay so close below the surface on the Somme meant that the trenches here tended to keep their shape better and required less careful revetting. But it was much harder to dig. Lieutenant Roe thought Somme chalk 'perfectly damnably messy and intractable when trying to shovel it after rain'. However, he agreed that it did make good trenches. His battalion took over trenches from the French when the British extended their line southwards to the Somme, and he found them:

> Very deep and dry with wide walkways between parapet and parados with very few traverses to make fire bays. The dugouts were large and deep and often dug under the parapet. As there was no constant vigilance the firesteps were not well maintained and therefore not continuous. I remember well a typically French macabre joke. Within the chalk wall at the entrance to my dugout was the top of a human skull which the French officer I relieved told me was so white and shiny because the French officers had got quite fond of it – they called it François and used to stroke it as they went in and out of the dugout.[12]

In the Vosges, towards the French-held southern end of the front where it was too rocky to dig proper trenches, both sides were forced to improvise with stone-built *sangars*, another term to add to a lexicon that few men in Britain would have understood in 1913 but which had become part of their common language two years later. Lieutenant Roe described how a trench system was laid out on the Somme in 1916.

> The trenches . . . consisted of an organized system of front line, a support line and a reserve line all properly dug and extending one behind the other in reasonable parallel.

They were connected by equally deep and well-dug communication trenches which at best were built in a zigzag design to prevent bullets and blasts of exploding shells from running straight down the communication trenches. The best made front-line trenches had traverses built back from the parapet into the trench itself and these were also designed to minimise the lateral extension of the blast. These were most effective if kept thick and strong.[13]

In an ideal world (and how un-ideal this world so often was) a fire trench would be about 6 feet deep and a minimum of 3 ft 6 inches wide at the top. A gently sloping parapet (from *para pête*, 'protect head') increased the height of the trench on the enemy side by about nine inches, with a slightly higher parados (*para dos*, 'protect back') on the friendly side. This arrangement enabled a man to walk along the bottom of the trench, on slatted wooden duckboards, with his head safely below the parapet: the duckboards generally covered the sump, a narrow drainage ditch which ran along the trench floor. But it did not allow him to engage the enemy, and this was, though it was easy to forget it, the reason for his being there.

In order to enable its occupants to look out of it a fire trench was furnished with a firestep. This stood perhaps 2 feet high and ran along the enemy side of the trench. It might have been formed when the trench was first dug, or built up later with sandbags, and with real luck might have duckboards, which made it drier to sit on. Private David Jones, who served in 15/Royal Welch Fusiliers on the Somme, tells us how:

> The firestep was the front-fighter's couch, bed-board, food-board, card-table, workman's bench, universal shelf, only raised surface on which to set a thing down, above water level. He stood upon it by night to watch the enemy. He sat upon it by day to watch him in a periscope. The nature, height and repair of firesteps was of great importance to the front-line soldier, especially before adequate dugouts became customary in all trenches.[14]

It was often a bier as well, for any body left on the trench floor would inevitably be trampled on. When an assaulting party of Royal

Welch Fusiliers on the Somme passed through the trench taken by the first assaulting wave, provided by another battalion, they found a dead subaltern decently laid out on the firestep and his surviving men in good order under the platoon sergeant, who was grimly confident of holding the trench. A man standing on the firestep of a well-constructed trench would have a narrow rest on which to support his elbows when firing his rifle, with the row of sandbags supporting the lip of the parapet just in front. The prevalence of sandbags in the manufacture of the parapet meant that the colloquial 'going over the top', for mounting an attack, was often replaced by the more intimate 'going over the bags' by those who had done it a few times.

Because the firestep ran along the enemy side of a trench, British or German, a trench could not be used by its captors immediately they seized it. It had first to be 'reversed', and a firestep constructed on the other side. It might be sliced into the trench wall, or made of sandbags filled with earth. But in any event there was no point in taking a trench unless one had shovels and sandbags to hand, and their carriage (usually by follow-up parties coming hard on the heels of the assault) demonstrates sound common sense, not the mutton-headed desire, so often identified by historians to make men as heavily laden as possible. The need to reverse a trench, a process which would take about ten minutes in an emergency and far longer if a respectable job was to be done, meant that very quick counter-attacks were often successful: the counterattacking party could throw grenades into the trench from close range, and there was little its occupants could do to defend themselves.

The most common kind of front-line trench followed a Grecian key design, with sections of fire bay connected, by two right-angled bends, to short traverses. This arrangement meant that all but the heaviest shells bursting squarely in a trench would only kill or wound the occupants of a single bay. It also made it hard for an enemy who entered a trench to fight his way along it, for the defender would keep knife-rests – wire-wrapped timber with an X-frame at either end – which he could drop into a traverse to form a defensible block called a bomb-stop. 'The proportion of this traversing, formed by bay and connecting trench', observed David Jones, 'varied considerably and might be angled or square, and exactly and care-fully revetted, or be little more than a series of regularly spaced salients in a winding ditch'.[15] It was impossible for a fully-laden man to get out of a fire trench without assistance, and there were two main methods of overcoming this problem. The first was by the construction of sortie steps and stakes. Stout stakes, preferably made of ash, were driven deep into the parapet, and in the trench wall below each one were two staggered toeholds, 'with brick or stout board for foot' – an arrangement which worked better on the train-ing fields of Britain than in the real trenches of France where wooden ladders became infinitely more common.[16]

Behind the front-line trench ran another parallel trench, the 'supervision trench' or support line, at the very least gently zigzagged, but usually with bays and traverses of its own, and by 1915 there was generally another parallel trench, the reserve line, behind this. Short connecting trenches every hundred yards or so linked these lines; the whole arrangement, covering perhaps 300 yards from front to rear, formed a single defensive system. Sometimes, especially if the front trench was on a reverse slope, fire bays might be dug forward from it, each like a large letter T, with its crosspiece on the crest-line. Many trenches had saps dug forward from them towards the enemy. These often housed listening posts which warned of enemy move-ment or gave advance notice of a raid. 'Casualties were very high,' admitted Roe, 'and the saps were almost always raided in order to wipe them out. Manning a sap was universally hated.'[17] Lieutenant Charles Douie of 1/Dorsets would not have agreed. He positioned an advance post of a lance corporal and three privates, and, 'before leaving I observed to the lance corporal that the post which he held was of great danger, and wholly isolated, to which he replied in the Dorset dialect that he would be all right so long as he did not lose his pipe.' Douie left greatly heartened, wondering what could go wrong with such steady men from a county whose ancient watchword was 'Who's Afeard?'[18]

Fire trenches were approached from the rear by communication trenches. Although these were intended for movement not for fighting, and might well have to accommodate stretcher-bearers moving in one direction and supports coming up from another, they still required either zigzags or gentler curves to limit the effect of shells bursting in them; a 1915 manual recommended the construction of machine-gun emplacements at the bottom end of straight runs of communication trenches 'to repel enemy who may gain the fire trench'. Harry Ogle described the arrangements that the British inherited from the French when they moved down to the Somme.

> The ground between the front line and the village [of Hébuterne] was cut up by long communication trenches and by support, reserve and old front and other lines disused. These had been captured by the French and we took over from them to find many bodies buried only thinly under earth and lime, some being within a yard of the trench side. The place was swarming with flies and rats and there were innumerable empty bottles. The French had named the trenches and we took them over complete with trench names painted on boards. The communication trenches, or to give them their much handier French name the *boyeaux*, had names of such heroes as Vercingetorix, du Guesclin and Jean Bart, famous men such as Pasteur, or battlefields such as Jena and Austerlitz ... Sergeant Clarke says: 'We are lucky up here. They are getting all our water through the Boy-oh Jeener into Trenchay Brisoux, and Trenchay Sour – it is flooded.'[19]

Frank Hawkings was in the same village, though by then British trench names had replaced French. 'A number of CTs [communication trenches] radiate out of the centre of the village connecting up the firing line,' he wrote.

> The most important are Yellow Street, Yankee Street and Woman Street. The latter owes its name to a certain gruesome discovery. Opposite its entrance is a pool of stagnant, putrid water which was once the village pond. One day two men noticed what looked like a sack near the edge amongst the litter of perambulators, bicycles, pictures, chairs, beds and dead cats. They drew it out and were horrified to discover that it was the half decomposed corpse of a young woman.[20]

Captain Sidney Rogerson also found himself in a French-made communication trench, though much later in the war, between the Aisne and the Marne. 'The communication trenches were particularly hot,' he wrote,

> as they were much deeper than those made by the British, chiefly, I imagine, on account of the use made by the French of small donkeys for carrying rations up into the line. The processions of ten or fifteen little 'burros' piled heavens high with sacks and boxes, stepping stiffly up a trench with the donkey-herd behind them making uncouth noises of encouragement or reproof, never failed to amuse our men.[21]

Communication trenches were ideally long enough to permit troops to enter them without being observed directly from the German lines, and on flat ground overlooked by German positions they might be very long indeed. Frank Dunham was a devout Baptist from a 'superior working-class' background, who had been a general assistant in a clothing factory before the war. After serving as a Red Cross volunteer he enlisted in a London cyclist battalion thinking that it might be fun, but would report sadly that 'there was never any issue of cycles to us'. Instead, his battalion, 25/London, fought in the trenches, and Dunham eventually became NCO in charge of the regimental aid post. He recalled that on 15 April 1917: 'We were relieved by the 8th London Regiment and came out through "Convent Lane" communication trench en route for Dickebush Huts. This was a terribly long trench, 3 miles long I was told; and it wandered about and made one feel dizzy going through it.'[22]

On 1 July 1916 Captain Billie Neville issued his company with platoon footballs marked: 'Great European Cup-Final: East Surreys v. Bavarians. Kick Off at Zero [Hour]', and became immortalised in history. A year before he had written home from Dernancourt, behind the Somme front, to describe how:

> All those trenches lead somewhere, each has its particular object, every bend & curve is made to serve some special purpose. Inside they are kept daily in perfect condition,

LEFT A shell busting amongst the barbed wire in front of British trenches at Beaumont Hamel, December 1916. By this stage in the war both sides used iron wire-pickets, with a corkscrew thread at one end and loops for the wire at the other, reinforced by angle-iron stakes.

RIGHT German razor-wire entanglement near Arras, June 1917. This wire was notoriously hard to cut: shelling often simply shifted it into impenetrable piles.

LEFT Men of 15/Royal Welch Fusiliers (1st London Welsh) filling sandbags with earth excavated from a dugout in their trench, Fleurbaix, December 1917. David Jones, author of *In Parenthesis*, served in this battalion.

A communication trench leading into a front-line trench, Laventie, December 1915. The duckboards enable men to move up dryshod, but the high water table has forced them to use sandbags to build up the trench parapet. Defences like this were easily damaged by artillery and required constant maintenance.

The infantryman's real burden. Soldiers carrying timber up a well-revetted communication trench near Ploegsteert, March 1917.

The absence of a firestep marks this out as a communication or support trench. Heavily-laden men needed help to enter or leave trenches like this: these 'scaling ladders' are being installed the day before the start of the Battle of Arras, 8 April 1917.

Australian signallers moving up a communication trench while cavalry cross it, Neuve Eglise, May 1917.

Men of the Border Regiment in a support trench well-supplied with 'funk-holes', Thiepval Wood, August 1916. The steeply-sloping ground rising up from the River Ancre was ideal for the construction of these little shelters.

Trenches were equipped with a variety of 'bomb stops' to prevent an enemy who entered the trench grenading his way along it. This barbed wire gate, in the Cambrin sector held by 1/7 Sherwood Foresters in September 1917, could be shut to bar an attacker's progress. The sentry is wearing 1914 pattern leather equipment.

A company sergeant major (right) and private of a Lancashire Fusilier battalion in a flooded communication trench near Ploegsteert Wood, January 1917. Both men are wearing issue waders and have their box respirators in the alert position.

ABOVE A company sergeant major of 12/East Yorkshire checking rockets, used for signalling to supporting artillery, in a front-line trench near Arleux, 9 January 1918. Both soldiers wear the sleeveless leather jerkin first issued in 1916.

RIGHT This photograph, from the winter of 1914, shows a captain (recognisable by his cuff badges) sitting at the entrance to his primitive shelter. In some areas, like the Neuve Chapelle sector, the water table was so high that it was difficult to make proper dugouts.

Good commanding officers inspected their trenches frequently. Here the commanding officer of 12/Royal Irish Rifles makes his way down a communication trench whose sides have fallen in because of a sudden thaw after weeks of frost. This sector, at Essigny south of the Somme, was taken over from the French in the winter of 1917–18.

Trenches were a maze to the uninitiated, and so nameplates and signposts became increasingly common.

A Lancashire Fusiliers sentry using a box periscope in a well-maintained front line trench near Ploegsteert Wood, January 1917. A section of wooden firestep is visible between the two soldiers.

ABOVE Officers of 12/East Yorkshire washing and shaving in a front-line dugout at Roclincourt, near Arras, in January 1918. It was much easier to construct dugouts in the chalk or limestone of Artois and Picardy than in low-lying Flanders.

RIGHT A sentry of the Worcestershire Regiment looking through a loophole at Ovillers on the Somme, August 1916. Loopholes like this were watched by enemy snipers, and it was important to ensure that men using them were not silhouetted by light from behind.

A ration party of 6/Queen's carrying 'hay-boxes' along a communication trench near Arras, March 1917.

LEFT Front-line soldiers usually ate a cold lunch as and when they could. These Cameron Highlanders, at the entrance to a newly-made dugout at Contalmaison on the Somme in September 1916, lunch off tinned food (bully beef or Maconochie's stew) with hard-tack biscuits and tea.

BELOW Fried bacon with tea and bread was a popular front-line breakfast, though cooking had to take place after dawn stand-to. Here a soldier cooks bacon over a brazier in a support trench near Ploegsteert Wood, March 1917.

LEFT Lancashire Fusiliers being served out with stew in March 1917. Depending on the situation, hot food might be brought forward from the unit's transport lines in insulated 'hay-boxes', or prepared in large oval 'dixies' (like the one shown here) by company cooks in support trenches.

LEFT Spare a fag, mate? Goatskin jackets first made their appearance in late 1914: these are being worn on the Somme in 1916. They were unsuitable front-line garments, smelly when wet and eagerly attracting and retaining mud.

RIGHT Up the line: 2/Gordon Highlanders marching to the front along the Bécordel—Fricourt road, October 1916.

Down the line: a Scottish battalion marching out of the line in the Loos sector, October 1915. Six months later the steel helmet would replace service caps and Scots bonnets for troops in the front line.

the drainage system would rival London's itself. All the traffic is controlled as if by policemen, timetables are kept of the time to get from say 'Roberts' to 'Drake'. The routes are marked carefully to various places & every trench is named and very often numbered as well.[23]

The system of communication trenches did not always work well even in quiet times. When Winston Churchill did his first tour in the trenches as a major attached to the Grenadier Guards, he was told that because there were no communication trenches in that sector all movement to the front line had to take place over the top, after dark. In consequence it had not been possible for any of his kit to be sent forward: his servant had, however, secured him a spare pair of socks. And during an attack even a well-ordered system might break down as the Germans bombarded communication trenches to stop reserves from moving forward, as Lieutenant Roe discovered on the first day of the Somme.

> Every single yard of the communication trench up to the front line was impassable and the confusion was indescribable. Reinforcement troops and working parties with materials and ammunition were trying to make their way forward against a stream of troops coming out of the line, including stretcher-bearers with casualties, walking wounded and exhausted troops coming out after a spell in the front line. To make matters worse, many of these sections of communication trench had been destroyed by heavy artillery fire from the German lines, and this was unceasingly active.[24]

Sometimes attacking troops, exasperated by the traffic jam, climbed out of the communication trenches to reach the front line over open ground. Roe watched this happen on the Somme: a second-wave battalion,

> in attempting to move forward into the attack five minutes after zero hour they found that the communication trenches were so blown in as to be impassable. This meant that they were compelled to expose themselves from the start by advancing to our own front line over open ground

in broad daylight. The casualties . . . were so heavy as a
result of this that only a few of the battalion reached even
our own front line.[25]

Trenches bore nameboards which served the same function as
street signs in a town. Sometimes these reflected the regional origin
of the first troops to hold them: the rides which crisscross Delville
Wood on the Somme now have stone markers with street names
from London, Edinburgh and Glasgow originally given to trenches
there by 9th Scottish Division in July 1916. When Henry Williamson
revisited the battlefields in 1925 he found Somme trenches 'half
hidden by the long wild grasses of the years – Wretched Way, Lucky
Way, Tea Trench, Coffee Trench, Rum Trench'.[26] There were
attempts to make terminology logical so that an individual would
know what sort of trench he was in, even if he was uncertain as to
where he was. Trenches called 'street' or 'way' were communication
trenches. The village of Villers-Guislain on the Cambrai front had
Glass Street, Cheshire Street, Aylward Street, George Street and High
Street fanning out from it towards the front. Cheshire Street led
through Cheshire Quarry to Bicester Alley, and then into Preston
Support and Preston Trench, and then further forward to Bleak
Support and Bleak Trench. Grove Alley, Grass Lane, Flare Alley
and Pilgrim's Way led from the Somme village of Flers to front-line
trenches whose names had a degree of connecting logic: Polish
Trench was behind Shine Trench, Petrol Lane ran in to Oily Lane,
and Scabbard Trench was in front of Bayonet Trench. Strongpoints
might simply be named after units or individuals who had fought or
died there, such as Goodwin's Post on Grease Trench (along from
Petrol Lane), near Gueudecourt. And sometimes there was a more
complex story. Frank Dunham thought it sad that 'our only casualties
should result from one shell. This fell on a post in the front line,
killing one and wounding three – all these casualties turned out to
be Jews and the post was afterwards known as Yiddish Post.'[27]

Other trench signs warned men to duck in shallow stretches where
snipers were active, enjoined them to pick up discarded items such
as picks, shovels or rifles and take them to the nearest salvage dump
for recycling, or advised them what to do if gas was detected. Gas

alarms were generally empty shell cases hung from an improvised bracket on the trench wall, and were sometimes accompanied by a signboard whose doggerel enjoined those who sniffed gas to:

Beat this gong, grab your gun
And prepare to meet the bloody Hun.

And in late 1917 Rowland Feilding recorded a sign in the Croisilles sector designed to deter rubbernecking 'tourists':

Visitors are requested not to show themselves, as by doing so they may give away our positions to the enemy. We live here. You don't.[28]

In the war's first winter dugouts were rare and funk holes hollowed out of the trench sides far more common. These could be screened with a groundsheet to give a measure of privacy, and a man might lie full-length with a modicum of cover and comfort. The practice of scraping out funk holes continued for much of the war, although it was soon officially discouraged because it weakened the sides of the trench and encouraged collapses, especially in heavy rain – or heavy shelling. Dugouts became increasingly common in 1915. Sometimes these were little more than the continuation of a funk hole, as Gerald Burgoyne reported in March 1915.

There are no officers' dugouts in my trenches so I at once started to make one in the trench I hold. I cleaned a patch about eight by five on the flank of my parapet, put some men to dig down about 18 inches, and then to build a wall of sandbags around it. I had brought down, for the purpose, six sheets of corrugated iron sheeting and some stakes.[29]

But they could also be a little more sophisticated, as John Reith discovered when he called on 1/Cameronians in November 1914.

HQ was half dugout and half hut. In it were the 1st Battalion CO and other officers . . . I was received with great cordiality . . . how odd for a regular colonel to be so circumstanced – in this hole in the ground, the mud on his clothes. It was, however, a comfortable hole. It was lit by two oil lamps; there were two tables, a bookshelf and ledges all round cut out of the clay for seats and bunks. There was, moreover, a coal fire burning in an excavated clay fireplace. They were only eighty yards from the Germans. *Eighty yards.*[30]

Proper dugouts could either be mined, that is excavated via a sloping tunnel that would, with suitable steps added, eventually constitute the dugout's entrance. Or they could be 'cut and cover' dugouts, made by the construction of a vast pit which was then roofed with timber or concrete with earth piled in on top. These could only be made in rear trench-systems, but the German practice of falling back from exposed positions onto better ones (most strikingly demonstrated in the withdrawal to the Hindenburg line in early 1917) meant that the Germans had a profusion of deep dugouts constructed by the cut and cover method.

Even British dugouts, proverbially less sophisticated than the German, could nevertheless be comfortable. In 1915 Billie Harris found some British dugouts on the Somme front:

> too killing for words. In one of them there is a lovely case of stuffed birds, a beautiful 4 poster bed, and some nice chairs, a good big table, towel horse, ivory wash hand stand etc & endless bric-a-brac. They are all furnished magnificently from the cottages here and are jolly cosy . . . Company HQ is a wonderful place . . . On the left as you come in is a marvellous 'paper-flower' white bouquet in a gilt-framed case, worn by all brides if they are not already widows, & evidently a family treasure; next to it is my 'duty roll' of officers & a time table of the times a messenger takes to get from here to all HQs or companies & our platoons, in wet or dry weather by day or night. Next again was a huge full-length mirror. With some heart-searching this morning I took an entrenching tool & scientifically smashed [it] into little pieces suitable for periscopes for our sentries by day! Then there's such a jolly old bookshelf, what's on it now? A candle, *Punch*, a tin of butter, a bottle of 'Vin Ordinaire'. A megaphone, 2 smoke helmets, some fags & baccy of [Lieutenant] Pearce's, my holdall, some powder bombs for dispersing gas if it's used, some lights corresponding to their star

shells, *Newnes Summer Annual, The Morning Post* of 5 days ago, and a water bottle, some Nestles milk, a shaving brush and two periscopes . . . We've got a hat rack & an umbrella stand next to this and then comes a map (from aeroplane photos) of the German trenches so accurate that you can follow every 'traverse' & bend in them . . . Two of our chairs have backs and the third is only used by visitors (once) . . . another table littered with red covers, mags; plates, message forms for the telephone, and a place laid for an officer on duty now, who will get some bully [beef] and tea when he comes off . . . The roof was only designed to conduct the rain into several well-defined areas on the floor . . . The Hun side is sandbagged . . . we shutter the windows at night to secure the light . . .[31]

This was evidently too flimsy a structure to sustain serious shellfire, and would not have passed muster much later in the war, but the assorted personal litter is entirely characteristic of a dugout's contents.

Edward Underhill found himself in a more typical dugout, of the cut-and-cover variety, at Mont St-Eloi in April 1916. 'I and F—— and two platoons are in support,' he wrote,

and we've one enormous dugout, fifty yards long, ten feet broad, and from eight to ten feet high. It has four entrances and ten to fifteen feet of earth on top, and is awfully strong. One end is curtained off for the officers, and then a bit for servants, orderlies and sergeants, and then the rest for the men.[32]

Company Sergeant Major Shephard thought his company head-quarters dugout on the Somme:

the best I have ever been in, about 80 feet long, 10 feet wide, 100 feet below ground, two entrances down steps. We have all the Company Staff together. Dugout is parted in three. One part for the telephone and operators, Officers' servants and trench mortar battery attached. Centre part for the Officers, and third part for the stretcher-bearers, Company and platoon orderlies, sanitary men and myself.[33]

Dugouts this big led off support or reserve lines. Less sophisticated versions were often dug below the parados of a front-line trench, and these:

> could be large enough to contain a couple of wooden bed-frames with a piece of rabbit wire stretched over the top of each frame so as to leave a level surface somewhere about eighteen inches above the inevitably wet and muddy floor. Valises or bedding rolls were laid on the wire and relays of sleepers or catnappers were able to use them. A dugout could also serve as a platoon or company head-quarters. Battalion headquarters were situated in support or reserve trenches because the length of trenches occupied by a whole battalion was several hundred yards in extent. These dugouts were gloomy affairs and were invariably very badly lit by candles stuck in a couple of bottles or fixed on top of a box in their own wax. Privacy was impossible even when, for gas protection, an army blanket was strung across the entrance from the trench . . .
>
> Sometimes we were lucky enough to get a sheet of corrugated iron to put on the sandbags covering the roof of the dugout and then to cover it with another layer or two of sandbags patterned crisscross for firmness. This reduced the noise inside the dugout and gave us a feeling of increased immunity from the smaller stuff sent by Jerry.[34]

British advances on the Somme in 1916 and at Ypres the following year brought German dugouts, so deep as to be impervious to even the heaviest shells, within their grasp. In November 1916 Edward Underhill reported that:

> H and I have moved into a relatively palatial dugout, probably a German Company Headquarters. It had been occupied temporarily by an undisciplined infantry unit, who made no attempt at clearing it out. The atmosphere nearly knocked me down on first entering. Now we have removed and burned masses of filthy German overcoats, equipment and food litter of all sorts. Even so it was two days after we had taken up residence before we discovered that a

sack, nailed across a gap in the wall panelling, contained at the bottom a dismembered human arm.

At the bottom of about twenty broad steps a filled doorway opens into a large mess room, with the roof supported by pillars over 6 feet high. Beyond this a passage with alcoves on each side leads to two large and two smaller rooms, and a broad secondary stairway. The walls throughout were originally panelled with wood in two tiers, and a horizontal strip half way up was embellished by a stencilled frieze depicting an iron cross in a shield, with acorns and leaves between the shields. The mess room walls were originally covered by tapestry, but only portions remain in situ.[35]

As the Germans discovered that trenches, however well constructed, were no match for the growing power of British artillery, they paid increasing attention to the construction of concrete blockhouses which still squat on the landscape of the old front line like huge mottled grey toads. Some were designed to house machine guns, while others were designed primarily as headquarters and troop shelters. These too were incorporated into British defensive systems after their capture, although the process was rarely a pleasant one, as Huntley Gordon, an artillery observation officer, discovered on Westhoek Ridge, outside Ypres, in 1917.

All was well when we reached here, but at 9 a.m. we were strafed for half an hour. I have a nasty feeling that the arrival of an officer and a telephonist may have been noticed by more than that sniper. We had to retire inside the concrete underground blockhouse that adjoins our little suntrap. It is without exception the most horrible place I have ever been in. It was constructed by the Boche to face the other way, and now the entrance is in front. Steps lead down to a central passage with two rooms on each side, about 10ft square. The rooms are more than half-filled with stagnant water, and we have to crouch down on planks supported at water level on a heap of corpses underneath. The stench really was awful, and we all had to smoke continuously to keep it down. It must have been full of Boches when our chaps lobbed some bombs in a few days ago. Now frequent bubbles break the surface of the oily scum. We were careful not to stir it up. Thank God, we didn't have to be in there for very long or I would have tried my luck in the open.[36]

A well-developed trench system had other features. Latrines were essential, and it was a matter of unit pride to keep them in good order and to prevent men from relieving themselves in the trench. Trench latrines, generally situated down a short sap running through the parados, might consist of a bucket or a 'deep-drop' latrine topped by a pole. Some of the latter were very deep indeed. When Sidney Rogerson's company of 2/West Yorkshire was establishing itself in the front line on the Somme in November 1917 Lance Corporal Rumbold set up two or three latrines 'as effective as they appeared hygienic'. One was certainly deep enough for them to experiment by firing captured German artillery alarm rockets into it to see what colours they were. Rumbold was the sanitary corporal, and there was one in each company, responsible for trench latrines, and for more sophisticated arrangements out of the line. Frank Dunham became sanitary corporal in 1918, and found it: 'Not a pleasant job, perhaps, but one that had advantages, for I had no parades to attend, and my time was my own. The holder of this job was invariably termed "NCO i/c shit wallers" by his fellows, which was perhaps the worst that could be said of it.' In Frederick Hodges's company of 10/Lancashire Fusiliers the sanitary man was Corporal Dean, inevitably known as Gunga Dean. Some sanitary men took pride in their duties. David Jones encountered a well-educated comrade carrying two brimming latrine buckets:

'Hallo, Evan, you've got a pretty bloody job.' He said: 'Bloody job, what do you mean?' I said it wasn't the kind of work I was particularly keen on myself. He said: 'Bloody job – bloody job indeed, the army of Artaxerxes was utterly destroyed for lack of sanitation.'[37]

Trench latrine buckets would be emptied in nearby shell holes and their contents covered with earth, and chloride of lime with a light sprinkling of fine soil was thrown into deep-drop latrines. When conditions permitted latrines were inspected not simply by commanding officers and adjutants on their rounds, but by medical staff officers from higher formations. In 1917 Major G. O. Chambers, on the medical staff of the Cavalry Corps, having inspected the trenches held by 1st Life Guards, reported: 'Latrines. Fly proof pails – sufficient in quantity. Urine tubs being in front of latrines in recess of trench – ground soiled with urine.' He recommended moving them and installing 'a splash board to prevent dripping'.[38]

When men were billeted in barns or houses behind the lines sanitary men were responsible for digging trench latrines in some convenient spot, maintaining them, and then either handing them over in good order to an incoming unit or filling them in. Men closer to the front line, but not actually in a forward trench system, enjoyed the comparative comfort of:

> a row of cubicle-type opportunities . . . with a corrugated iron roof covered with sandbags, and with canvas partitions and a wooden seat over a bucket. These were built by sappers well behind the front-line trench but still well within the enemy's artillery range. There were also the refinements of a canvas curtain across the entrance and a duckboard for the feet. There were substantial improvements but things did happen. One of the cubicles seemed to me one early morning to be overlong occupied so I took a peep and found a bloody shambles. The occupant of it was dead with a large hole in the back of his head due to a large piece of shell-casing which had come through the back. All the entrances of course faced away from the front line. The final type was more permanent in design and was at once euphoniously christened the 'thunderbox'.[39]

Front-line latrines were no respecters of rank, but the hierarchy reasserted itself out of the line. Julian Tyndale-Biscoe recalled how, on his gun position:

> One day . . . a shell hit the officers' latrine, sending the screen flying. I was shocked to see a man still sitting there on the throne and I thought he must be dead. I ran as hard as I could and arrived to find Ellison up and adjusting his trousers. He said with a grin, 'It was lucky that the shell came when it did as I was feeling a bit constipated.'[40]

With the proliferation of trench mortars in the British army from 1915 onwards special bays were required to house these short-range weapons. A purpose-built trench-mortar dugout was laid out like a letter E rotated forwards through a right angle. The mortar itself was in the right-hand arm, and the remainder was roofed in, with an ammunition bay in the central arm and a shelter for the detachment in the left-hand arm. Second Lieutenant Bryan Latham, who volunteered for the trench mortars to escape an excess of 'bull' in an infantry battalion, admitted that: 'The infantry were not always pleased with us, as they claimed that with our playthings we excited the German mortars in retaliation, which the infantry had to bear, whereas we having done our firing were entitled to take refuge in the aforementioned dugout.'[41]

Trench-mortar detachments generally arrived shortly before battle commenced. For a small-scale operation on 16 June 1916, in which his fire plan was to commence with a bombardment of the German wire at 10.30 p.m., Latham recalled: 'I think we were all of us glad when a quarter to ten arrived, and we had to be up and doing.' If there were no proper trench-mortar dugouts the weapons would be fired from short saps, and infantrymen, who were inclined not to welcome a weapon which generally attracted retaliation, sometimes sought to make mortar saps uninhabitable (or at least very unpleasant for the mortarmen) by using them as latrines.

A battalion's aid post would be sited somewhere in its sector, probably opening off the reserve trench. Manned by the regimental medical officer, this was the first port of call for a wounded man, who would make his own way there or be carried in by stretcher-bearers. In mobile operations at the beginning and end of the war aid posts were set up in whatever cover was available. Arthur Osburn worked out of limestone caves at Paissy on the Aisne in September, and Lieutenant Cyril Helm, RMO of 2/King's Own Yorkshire Light Infantry, found himself, appropriately enough, in the cellar of a doctor's house at much the same time. Once trench warfare settled in, however, purpose-built aid posts were constructed. A favourite method was to use elephant iron – half-round sections of heavy corrugated metal – to roof short saps running off either side of a reserve or communication trench. The elephant iron, which was stout enough to take the weight of earth and sandbags, offered a measure of protection to the doctor and his orderlies, and to a small number of wounded on stretchers; the proximity to a communication trench made it easier for bearers to take stretcher cases on the next stage of their journey back. But an aid post had all too small a capacity, and in a major battle would speedily be clogged up with wounded as the doctor proceeded with the grim business of triage, working out which cases could wait, which required urgent evacuation, and which were beyond human help.

No overview of trenches would be complete without mention of the trench stores which formed the permanent fixtures of the place and were handed over (and signed for) when one unit relieved another. Each company would have a reserve of small-arms ammunition (SAA in the jargon of the day) and a grenade store, sited in small covered bunkers with prominent signs. Their contents were easily accessible in the event of a surprise attack, and could be made ready on the firestep or elbow-rest if there was time available. Captain H. Blair, commanding B Company 2/Royal Welch Fusiliers, arrived in the front line on 21 June 1916 and was 'filled with a haunting unrest. I sent my Sergeant-Major to have boxes of bombs placed on the firesteps and the pins pinched ready for use, boxes of reserve SAA too were to be ready to hand.' He had just spoken to a sentry and an NCO when a mine blew up under the company's position, leaving him unconscious and partially buried. However, his precautions enabled his surviving platoon to give a good account of itself.

> When Gerry's guns lifted we could see his men coming on in three lines . . . They made a lot of noise talking, and the white armlets they were wearing showed them up. We opened up with all our rifles and Lewis guns. We could see them being knocked over and carried away by their pals. They got confused, and hesitated, and made to come on in groups by the side of the crater. We fired wherever we could see anyone. One man came right round behind us; he was spotted by his armlet and was shot before he could heave a bomb. He said, 'Oh, *Mutter*,' when he was hit.[42]

A rocket stand was generally positioned just outside the company headquarters dugout, containing rockets which would be fired to tell the artillery that an attack was in progress, and requesting fire on the SOS target, usually the front of the British wire on the edge of No Man's Land.

Barbed wire, originally devised to retain livestock in their fields, had first made its appearance in the American Civil War. It was widely used in the Boer and Russo-Japanese wars, and was available, albeit in inadequate quantities, to the British army in 1914. It became an almost inseparable feature of trench warfare. Axiomatically it should keep the enemy so far from one's own trench that he could not simply lie on his own side of the wire and lob grenades into the trench. Each side controlled his own wire, repairing it, sometimes on a nightly basis, to make good damage done by shellfire or wire-cutting patrols. Wire was originally wrapped around stout wooden stakes hammered into the ground, but the weight of the wood and the noise of hammering alike suggested that there must be a better way. In 1915 all combatants introduced barbed-wire pickets, metal posts with a long sharpened corkscrew at one end and three loops along the straight section. These were screwed into the ground, and the wire was caught in their loops. They remain one of the most durable relics of trench warfare, and are still to be found in fences doing their duty in a more pacific guise. 'A job after your own heart,' Private Erskine Williams told his father.

> Observe the corkscrew iron uprights. Great idea. Men follow on with coils of wire and place [it] through the eye holes. Very smart. I've had a go at it. This is a noiseless method instead of driving wooden posts in. Always has to be done at night.[43]

Angle-iron pickets, which had so many other uses in trenches, were also used for wiring, especially when, hammered well in and set at an angle, they were set at the end of runs of wire to maintain tension.

The layout of a barbed wire entanglement had an alchemy of its own, part art, part science. John Reith described the wire in front of his trench in July 1915.

> Our plan of wire from the enemy's side was as follows: low
> wire and tin cans; high apron; low squares and diagonals;
> trip wire; low apron; more trip wire; high apron; high
> squares and diagonals nearest the parapet. About ten yards
> of ground was wired in this way; it was pretty effective.[44]

A year later ten yards of wire would have been regarded as too
thin, and in 1917 the German wire protecting the Hindenburg line
was up to thirty yards deep – great wedge-shaped masses of rusty
metal. David Jones noted that tripwire might be used almost indepen-
dently: 'Low strand-wire at about middle shin height, set some way
apart from the main entanglement, often hidden in long grass.'[45]

Wire, British and German, was intended to blunt the force of an
assault which might otherwise overwhelm the defence by sheer
weight of numbers, to canalise attackers into the killing zones of
machine guns (for which reason it often ran in long slants, rather
than straight) and make it difficult for patrols or raiding parties
to approach trenches. It could be snipped by wire-cutters which
resembled large secateurs; cut with the aid of a steel clip which held
it to a rifle muzzle so that a shot would sever it (a much-detested
device), or by well-directed artillery fire. One of the essential require-
ments for the tank, which had made its first appearance on the
Somme in September 1916, was the ability to crush wire, and tanks
were issued with grapnels which permitted them to drag away whole
sections of the stuff.

However, uncut wire was usually fatal to any mass assault, and one
of the war's enduring images was of the corpses of dead attackers
held upright by the wire. Henry Rawlinson gave Lord Stamfordham
a graphic account of the failure of the 21st and 24th Divisions at
Loos: 'From what I can ascertain,' he wrote, 'some of the divisions
did actually reach the enemy's trenches, for their bodies can now
be seen on the barbed wire.'[46] Harry Ogle's abiding memory of the
Somme was of bodies 'entangled in or sprawling across the barbed
wire, slumped over the remains of trench parapets, or half buried
in the ruined trenches . . .'[47] Second Lieutenant John Glubb saw a
corpse at Ypres suspended in a climbing position, with 'one foot
raised and a hand stretched out . . . Except for the green colour of
his face and hand, one would never have believed that he was dead.'[48]

In 1915 James Jack, looking at Rifle Brigade dead in front of his position, observed that many were 'hanging on the German wire which they were trying to cut or surmount when killed; amongst them one whom I knew and is easily recognisable'.[49]

Even men on patrol, with the opportunity to pick their way through the wire, still found it a formidable obstacle, as Eric Hiscock discovered at Bellevue in 1918.

> The light was bad (daylight had not yet broken) and barbed wire, which should have been cut by a patrol the night before, was our first serious barrier to success. I found myself faced with what looked like a fairly impenetrable obstacle and decided to crawl under it. The khaki-coloured cartridge-filled bandolier caught in the rust spikes and as I twisted to free myself, I felt the evil things bite into the collar of my tunic and into my shoulders. Agonised, I shouted to my companions who, as far as I could see, were all safely through the wire, but only Ramsden heard my cries. He turned, threw himself flat on the ground, and crawled towards me. Calmly, as though he had been rehearsing such a hazardous chore for years until he was move perfect, he pushed my head and shoulders down and lifted the wire up, then encouraged me with (and I remember it quite clearly) the words: 'You were a silly little bugger to get caught up in this bloody stuff. You should have known better. Now keep flat on your belly and don't look up. Crawl like a fucking snake.'[50]

Ivor Gurney, who served as a private in 2/5th Gloucesters, lamented a comrade 'who died on wire, and hung there ... A noble fool, faithful to his stripes'. When an officer urged Gurney to crawl through a 'hole' in the wire he was more circumspect.

> ... I smiled, as I politely replied – 'I'm afraid not, Sir.'
> There was no hole, no way to be seen. Nothing but chance
> of death, after tearing of clothes ...[51]

Just as it was sometimes impossible to dig trenches, so too was it sometimes impossible to erect wire. Even that iron man Frank Crozier, as hard on himself as on others, realised that there was no need for wire on the blighted Somme battlefield in late 1916. 'I cannot be attacked,' he declared. 'I am in a muddy wilderness and between the enemy and me is a muddy barrier over which organised advance is impossible. I need no wire and even if I did I could not get it there.' When his corps commander – 'a goodly man whom I like and from whom I am subsequently to receive much kindness' – came forward to Crozier's headquarters to ask why he had put out no wire, he frankly admitted that he had only put up a single strand to stop men walking into the German lines by mistake. The corps commander good-humouredly riposted that the adjoining division claimed to have put out a great deal of wire, and so 'the conference ends in gas, as such things sometimes do'.[52]

When Crozier was commanding 9/Royal Irish Rifles south of Ypres he offered a young officer, Second Lieutenant Army, who had lied about finding the gap in the German wire, the chance to redeem himself, in his eyes, by bringing back a sample of the wire defending the Horseshoe – a specific part of the German line. The following morning Army's company reported him a casualty. It was only later that Crozier found out what had happened.

> Army, I find, went forward on patrol, left his men lying down and went forward to the Horseshoe. There was a good deal of stray firing at the time and no unusual sound was heard. He simply disappeared. Nine months later, when Second Army launched its successful attack at Messines, over the very spot where Army fell, his skeleton and watch were found in a lonely furrow near the Horseshoe – for good luck, perhaps. He had died for more than a bit of wire. He had saved his soul.[53]

The area between British and German wire was No Man's Land. Its width varied greatly. On flattish ground it might be as much as 3–400 yards wide (witness the great expanse of pitted greensward between the opposing front lines at Newfoundland Memorial Park on the Somme); but if the combatants were contending for a commanding feature and reluctant to give an inch it would be very much less, as the preserved Canadian and German front lines on Vimy Ridge demonstrate. Where No Man's Land represented the high-water mark of an attack, British or German, it was often littered with old wire, shell holes and corpses. But in other areas, such as the Somme front before June 1916, it might be comparatively peaceful, overgrown with grass and untended crops.

The term No Man's Land had been in use long before 1914 to refer to a piece of waste or disputed land, but during the war it acquired a significance all of its own. Although by definition No Man's Land was held by neither side, patrols had to pass through it to reach the enemy wire and the trenches beyond. In some sectors No Man's Land tended to be quiet, but in others it was regularly fought over: much depended on local custom and the preparedness of new arrivals to conform to it. Units, British and German, displayed variable degrees of hostility, with some sliding comfortably into 'live and let live', trying to avoid action that would elicit a hostile response and so ratchet up the level of local violence.

In one sector the Germans put up a sign begging the East Surreys facing them to 'Chuck it' when they broke an unofficial truce observed by their predecessors. In another a Bavarian cornet player serenaded his British listeners with *Love Me and the World is Mine* on request.[54] Other units, like 2/Royal Welch Fusiliers, made it 'a point of honour' to dominate No Man's Land by patrolling after dusk. Lieutenant Roe's battalion tried 'to keep working parties and patrols as small as possible so as to reduce casualties', but he admitted that 'the Boche on the other hand patrolled with Teutonic thoroughness'. In consequence, 'refusing to allow the enemy to dominate no-man's-land was not only a tense job but required a concentrated vigilance which I found most exhausting . . .'.[55] Private Harry Ogle was covering a British wiring party near Ypres in 1915 when he heard the thump of mallets from the German side of No Man's Land.

> Of course! That means German wiring. On the principle of 'live and let live' they take advantage of our preoccupation with our own wiring to do theirs . . . Work is in full swing, knock over there, answering knock over here like an echo, and no attempt to muffle or disguise the noise.[56]

No Man's Land was always a permeable membrane, for individuals slipped across it to desert. A sentry in Frank Hawking's company was astonished to discover a German in his trench: the man said that he had been a waiter in London, was 'a great kamerad English' and had been trying to surrender for some time.[57] Five Prussian-hating Alsatians, whose province had been French till 1871, deserted to Edward Underhill's battalion.[58] The process worked the other way too, for a few British deserters, well aware that their chances of remaining undetected on their side of the line were small, 'disappeared' from front-line trenches and gave themselves up to the Germans. Deserters often sought to ingratiate themselves with their captors, and the success of a German attack on the bridgehead over the Yser on 10 July 1917 is often attributed to information volunteered by a British deserter. But the appearance of No Man's Land gave no hint as to its secrets: to new arrivals it conveyed an air of latent, mundane menace.

Men peered across the parapet onto a strange and bewildering world. Huntley Gordon surveyed the Ypres salient from a front-line trench in 1917.

> Then over to the left, more skeleton trees, identified as Glencorse Wood, Inverness Copse, and Black Watch Corner. Easy to see the Jocks had left their mark on this piece of Belgium. Other names too spoke of those who had passed this way. Tower Hamlets, Clapham Junction and Surbiton Villas told of the Cockney and suburban resident, Maple Lodge of the Canadians, Leinster Farm of the Irish. But don't think that these places could be identified by anyone but an expert. All I could see was lines and lines of sandbags alternating with hedges of rusty barbed wire, brown earth and grey splintered tree-trunks.[59]

Most new arrivals were shocked by the sheer emptiness of the landscape. The writer Reginald Farrer, looking over a parapet during a visit to the front in 1916, admitted:

> It seemed quite unthinkable that there was another trench over there a few yards away just like our own . . . Not even the shells made that brooding watchfulness more easy to grasp: they only made it more grotesque. For everything was so paralysed in calm, so unnaturally innocent and bland and balmy. You simply could not take it in.[60]

Second Lieutenant P. J. Campbell had a gunner's eye for the ground.

> I learnt the names of every wood and all the villages, I
> knew the contours of the hills and the shapes of the lakes
> in the valley. To see so much and to see nothing. We
> might have been the only men alive, my two signallers and
> I. And yet I knew there were thousands of hidden men in
> front of me ... but no one moved, everyone was waiting
> for the safety of darkness.[61]

And for infantry officer Charles Carrington the wire defined hostility.
'This side of our wire everything is familiar and every man a friend,'
he wrote:

> Over there, beyond the wire, is the unknown, the uncanny,
> there are the people about whom you accumulate scraps
> of irrelevant information but whose real life you can never
> penetrate, the people who will shoot you dead.[62]

FIGURES IN A LANDSCAPE

At any given moment around half the total strength of British combat units on the Western Front consisted of infantry, though the losses incurred in particular battles and the slow arrival ·of reinforcements occasionally reduced this to around one-third – in July 1918 and during the last Hundred Days, for instance. From early 1916 onwards there were rarely fewer than 400,000 British infantrymen in France and Belgium. Artillery constituted the next most numerous combat arm, with around 150,000 men at any time.[63] The strength of the non-combatant element of the army also fluctuated, but it was generally about half the size of the combat element, with the Army Service Corps as easily its most numerous component.

The army's definition of combat and non-combatant was always somewhat artificial. For instance, entrenching battalions (renamed pioneer battalions in 1916) were part of the infantry, badged and organised as battalions of established regiments, but were generally exposed to less risk than infantry battalions proper, while regimental medical officers, officially part of the non-combatant RAMC, paid a very heavy price for their devotion to duty. And however often front-line soldiers linked the initials of the Army Service Corps with those of a popular music-hall artist to call it 'Aly Sloper's Cavalry', it was no joke to be an ASC driver. Horse-drawn ASC units in divisional trains often operated well within the range of, and along routes all too familiar to, the German artillery. Nevertheless, the hard truth of trench warfare was that most of its actors were infantrymen, tiny figures in a landscape increasingly shaped by the power of the gun. They called themselves, in a blend of pride and self-deprecation, the Poor Bloody Infantry, the PBI, and sang of themselves as 'Fred Karno's army, the ragtime infantry'. They were the numberless and nameless chorus of trench warfare's long-running drama, well aware that without their efforts there could be no show.

Trench warfare imposed its own pattern of life. Although major offensives, British or German, changed this pattern they did not alter its essential truth: for the infantrymen who constituted the bulk of the fighting element of the army, life was cyclical, with a repeated sequence of front-line service alternating with time spent in reserve, at rest and on the move. Gunners were less mobile, for while a line-holding division would rotate its infantry through the front line it left its gunners in situ and, moreover, sometimes handed them over (temporarily or permanently) to the division which replaced it.

The time a unit spent in the line was subject to wide variation. Divisions would be concentrated for major battles, withdrawn into rest to recover from them, or moved to garrison another sector of the front where operations were less active. In battles a division might be burned out and reconstituted repeatedly. For instance, 21st Division was so badly mauled at Loos in September 1915 that it did not fight again till 1916 when it attacked Fricourt on the first day of the Somme. After three days it was taken out of the line, partly reconstituted, and brought back again on 11 July. It fought during the remainder of the Somme, took part in the Arras attack in April 1917 and had been reconstituted sufficiently to fight at Third Ypres in September/October. It was moved down to Cambrai in the wake of the successful British attack, only to be badly clawed by the German counterattack. In March 1918 21st Division was directly in the path of the main German offensive. It was sent up to Flanders where it faced another attack and then, at the very nadir of its bad luck, it was sent down south to 'rest' in the Chemin des Dames, where it was caught by yet another German offensive in May. It nevertheless played its part in the Hundred Days, though when the armistice came into effect it was out of the line – reconstituting.

During the whole war it suffered 55,581 casualties, making it the hardest-hit New Army Division. Similarly 38th Division had been put into the line to gain experience early in 1916 but its attack on Mametz Wood that July was its first proper battle – and its last for just over a year. On 31 July 1917 it was in the first wave in the attack on Pilckem Ridge. Withdrawn, topped up, and sent back into the line it fought around St Julien and Langemarck, and was then shifted to the quieter Armentières sector. It was in reserve in the spring of 1918, but fought during the Hundred Days and was up in the line, moving forwards, when the armistice came into force. Its 28,635 casualties reflected a shorter exposure to battle than 21st Division, but nonetheless represented almost twice the division's established strength.

But offensives, common though they seem to us, were the exceptions rather than the rule. A division would spend more of its time in routine line-holding than attacking, and it was perfectly possible for an infantryman to spend two years on the Western Front without actually going over the top at all. He would, however, become very familiar with the routine stages of trench warfare. By mid-1915 a division would be responsible for perhaps 5–7,000 yards of front. It might hold its sector with its three brigades in line, or push two brigades forward and keep one back. Whichever method it followed, each of the forward brigades would be likely to have two battalions in line, one in reserve and one in brigade rest. If there was a rear brigade it would have a battalion or two in reserve and the others in divisional rest. During its time in the sector, possibly two or three months, the division would rotate its brigades between the line and rest/reserve, and brigadiers would rotate their battalions in the same way. Individual battalion commanders would generally have two of their four rifle companies in the front, support and reserve lines of the front trench system, all of them within a few hundred yards of the enemy. We shall soon see that neither 'reserve' nor 'rest' meant quite what we would expect, because most of the infantry in a line-holding division would find themselves providing working parties to repair trenches, construct new trench lines or hump an ever-increasing quantity of 'trench stores' up the communication trenches. However, rotation it was, and the whole process took on the characteristics of an eightsome reel, with muddy and heavily-laden dancers treading out their prescribed steps.

Once the rhythm of the dance was established, new arrivals were given an opportunity to step out under instruction before taking to the floor unassisted. In late 1915 Company Sergeant Major Ernest Shephard described how his battalion hosted the newly-arrived 16/ Royal Warwickshire.

> **1st day**: Officers and senior NCOs are attached. They are shown everything, and get a good idea of how to work.
>
> **2nd day**: Company arrives. They are mixed in with the men actually holding the trenches and do lookout, etc., with the experienced men.
>
> **3rd and 4th day**: The new troops are given a section of trench to hold. This is always done in the centre of the Bn holding the trenches. Here they have to do the ordinary trench routine, posting sentries, etc., and this is again supervised by the OC [of] the complete sector of trenches. On the 5th day they go out for rest, and, if considered sufficiently trained, two days later they are allotted a complete sector of trenches where they are fairly quiet in the centre of a Brigade. On this occasion they are working on their own, as a Bn, and they have officers attached to them from the Bns of the Brigade to assist and see that they understand and do what is expected of them. These officers remain for the time of holding the trenches (3 or 4 days). This completes the breaking in.[64]

Charles Carrington recalled how the dance seemed to him as a subaltern in 1/5th Royal Warwickshire, in 143rd Infantry Brigade of 48th (South Midland) Division in 1916.

> The division held a front of about four miles as the bullet flies, much longer following the trace of the trenches. All three brigades were up in the line, side by side, each with two battalions 'up', one in close support and one back in reserve . . . which meant that six battalions out of thirteen [the thirteenth was the divisional pioneer battalion] in the division held the line. Each of these two front-line battalions would normally have two of its companies 'up'

and two held back in supporting positions . . . In my battalion . . . each company had three platoons actually posted in the front trenches, and one standing to arms as an 'inlying picket' under cover, ready to act in any emergency at two or three minutes' notice. If this may be taken as typical . . . the six front-line battalions in quiet times held the whole of the divisional front with about thirty-six platoon posts, and since a platoon could rarely put more than about thirty men on duty, we may conclude that the divisional front was held by 1,000 of its, say, 10,000 infantrymen.[65]

There was always debate over the density with which the front should be held. Sidney Rogerson was an experienced company commander whose books on 1916 and 1918 were firmly based on diaries. He rejected popular accounts of 'the war of the sewers, in which no one ever laughed, those who were not melancholy were absolutely hysterical, and most of the action took place in or near the crude latrines of the period'. Yet, positive though he was about the conduct of the war, he could not forgive the staff for keeping troops 'with no strategic or tactical advantage' on ground that did not have to be held.[66] David Jones commented on the fact that: 'The German trench system as a whole was of greater depth from the front line to the rear defences, of greater complexity and better builded than our own . . .'.[67] There was certainly a rough strategic logic to this, for it was not until the end of 1917, when it seemed likely that the Germans would launch a major offensive before the Americans arrived in strength, that the British took defensive preparations as seriously as the Germans did: after all, with a big push generally imminent, what was the point of elaborate defences?

C. E. Montague was a leader writer on the Liberal *Manchester Guardian* who dyed his greying hair black so as to enlist in 1914, and served in the infantry before being commissioned and appointed assistant press censor. His influential book, *Disenchantment*, was based on a very short period of front-line service. It contains the familiar criticism of generals – 'two or three were killed' – and British conduct of the war, though it is often very telling (and surprisingly romantic) in its assessment of infantry soldiers. Montague was especially critical of the British preference for holding the front trench system so strongly, which he saw as in sharp contrast to both French and German practice. The Germans, certainly, profited from the experience of Loos and the Somme to defend in ever-increasing depth, reducing the garrison of their front-trench system because of its vulnerability to the growing power of British artillery. The French, in contrast, sometimes packed their forward trenches, even in 1918. The chief reason for the success of the German attack on the French 6th Army (with its 'resting' attached British corps) on the Chemin des Dames in May 1918 was that too many Allied soldiers had been pushed forward where they were at the mercy of the German barrage.

The reduction of brigades from four battalions to three in the winter of 1917–18 had a marked effect on the choreography of line-holding. Divisional frontages were not generally reduced, and so the infantry had to do more with less. The British had also made a significant change in tactical theory. They had decided to imitate the German system of a lightly-held Forward Zone, with machine guns and artillery observers in well-wired redoubts to break up the initial attack; a more heavily held Battle Zone, where the bulk of field guns and infantry would be found; and a Rearward Zone to provide a final measure of security. There was, however, a significant gap between theory and practice. One experienced NCO warned that: 'The British Army fights in line, and won't do any good in these bird cages.' On 5th Army's front, where the main blow was to fall, there was too little manpower available to dig the Rearward Zone, and there was a widely-held feeling amongst infantry officers that it was asking a lot of the garrison of the Forward Zone to hold until relief came.

When Hanway Cumming came up to take command of 110th Brigade of 21st Division on 18 March 1918 he found the division with two of its brigades forward and one in reserve. His own brigade sector was 2,100 yards wide, and he held it with two of his Leicester battalions, one up and one back. It took him two days to get round his front line. It was essential for him to visit it as he did not know the ground, but experienced infantry officers recognised that brigadiers who spent a lot of time visiting were away from their headquarters too often. Sidney Rogerson, in a forward company of

2/West Yorkshire in late 1916, was pleased to see James Jack, his commanding officer, arrive with the brigadier in tow, but it had taken Jack four hours to get there, and Brigadier General Fagan even longer: 'The very fact that he would be absent from his head-quarters for many hours should be some answer to those who demand to know why general officers did not put in more frequent appearances in the front line.'[68]

Cumming knew at once that his front was too thinly held, and wrote just after the war that the success of the German March offensive of 1918 sprang largely from this fact. Rowland Feilding, recovering in hospital from an injury received during the battle, blamed the 'tired and untrained condition of the infantry', the failure of the machine-gun barrage, deployment in too much depth, the fog and the lack of reserves, for British failure on 21 March. The reduction from four to three battalions was not fundamentally wrong, he thought, for it was better to have up-to-strength battalions than weak ones. However, the reduction of the division's strength by three full battalions meant that there was simply too much work to do. There was 'neither time nor opportunity' for training, and his men had become 'tired, overstrained, undertrained trench-diggers and cable-buriers'.[69]

In the first autumn of the war the British Expeditionary Force was under very heavy pressure at Ypres and its front was paper-thin. There were almost no reserves, and the British front could not have been held at all had the Cavalry Corps not fought as infantry, using its rifles with a skill which testifies to the thoroughness of their pre-war training. At the crux of the battle on 31 October, when Sir John French announced that he proposed to bring up his head-quarter guard – 1/Cameron Highlanders – lead them to where the line was broken and die fighting, he was only indulging in mild hyperbole: he had no other units in reserve. During that first winter there were simply too few troops available for proper rotation to be introduced, and battalions spent week after week in the line. On 6 November Aidan Liddell of 1/Argyll and Sutherland Highlanders wrote, with understandable satisfaction, that: 'I had my boots off and changed my socks today, the first time since 18th of September.'[70]

On 15 November Arthur Smith observed that his Coldstream battalion had so far spent nineteen days in the line: 'One man has gone off his head and committed suicide, & one officer has completely broken down with nerves.'[71]

The example of a single battalion sets the pattern for this early period. The 2/Royal Welch Fusiliers went into the line at La Cordonnerie near Fromelles on the night of 22 October 1914 and came out again on the night of 14 November, rested for seventy-two hours, and went back into the line again, this time for eleven days in freezing weather. After another short rest, during which it furnished a guard of honour for a visit by the king, it spent another twenty-four days in the line. These stints of front-line duty would have been regarded as unreasonably long later in the war, and speak powerfully for the Old Army's powers of endurance. However, snipers and trench mortars, which were to impose a growing toll on front-line troops, were still in their infancy, and 'trench wastage' was still relatively low: 2/Royal Welch Fusiliers lost only eight killed and ten wounded in its last twenty-four days in the line.

Although there were occasional gruelling exceptions (a West Yorkshire battalion spent seventy days in the front line in the Loos sector in 1915, and 13/York and Lancaster fifty-one days in the line on the Somme the following year), from early 1915 there was increasing regularity in the pattern of rotation. Charles Carrington reviewed his diary for 1916 and found that:

> I spent 65 days in the front line trenches, and 36 more in supporting positions close at hand . . . In addition 120 days were spent in reserve positions near enough to the line to march up for the day when work or fighting demanded, and 73 days were spent out in rest. 10 days were spent in hospital . . . 17 days . . . on leave . . . The 101 days under fire contain twelve 'tours' in the trenches varying in length from one to thirteen days. The battalion made sixteen in all during the year . . . We were in action four times during my . . . tours in the trenches. Once I took part in a direct attack, twice in bombing actions, and once we held the front line from which other troops advanced. I also took part in an unsuccessful trench raid.[72]

The upright and soldierly James Jack was a Cameronian captain in 1914, Sidney Rogerson's commanding officer in 2/West Yorkshire on the Somme in 1916, and a brigade commander in 1918. Between December 1914 and August 1916, while serving with 1/Cameronians, he spent 141 days in the trenches, ninety in brigade support, twenty-three in brigade reserve, ninety-seven in divisional reserve, seventeen in army reserve, fifteen days travelling, nineteen in hospital and twelve on leave.

A battalion would usually be 'warned for duty' in the trenches two or three days before it was expected to move. The twelve days so well chronicled by Rogerson began in the huts of Citadel Camp, Fricourt, on 7 November 1916 when 2/West Yorkshire received orders to relieve 2/Devon, a forward battalion also in 24th Brigade of 8th Division, on the night of 10/11 November. His battalion's experience is so typical that there is merit in following its footsteps, and reaching out to reinforce it with other examples as we do so.

By now it was standard practice to leave a proportion of the battalion out of the line, under the second in command, to act as a basis for reconstitution if the worst happened, and on this occasion one of the company commanders and two company sergeant majors (including Rogerson's sergeant major, CSM Scott) were amongst those left behind. On 8 November the battalion moved up to an intermediate position, Camp 34, between Bernafay and Trônes Woods. Normally for a daylight move a battalion would march in column of route – with the men in ranks of four, shaking out into 'artillery formation', with platoons more widely spaced, when it came within the range of German medium guns. But here the tracks were too poor to permit this, and so the battalion marched in Indian, or single, file. Rogerson did not like it, observing that:

> A very comforting sense of comradeship can be developed
> by tramping along in fours. There is a sense of close com-
> pany; the ability to talk to your neighbour, even to sing
> with him. There is the inevitable swing and rhythm of the
> column. But put men into Indian file and this corporate
> cheerfulness evaporates. They develop a spiritless shamble
> with the whole line constantly contracting and expanding,

alternatively treading on one another's heels, then panting to recover lost distance.[73]

There was no camp ready when they arrived, because the battalion which should have vacated the tents had been so badly knocked about on its tour of the line that the survivors were 'weary and shocked in body and spirit, and too dejectedly apathetic to raise themselves to any effort . . .'. Although Rogerson's men were 'in a most cheerful mood', he observed that as a man got closer to the front: 'His vision changed, he began to lose his wider view . . .'. Any sense of the scale of the enterprise disappeared, and men could not tell you what the battalion's plan was: 'but ask them to describe the Kirchner pictures on the wall of their dug out, or the particular brand of bully beef which hung on the wire, and they will find little difficulty'. Two of his soldiers scrounged 'a huge balloon tarpaulin which proved big enough of itself to house more than half the company'. Company headquarters was installed in a tent, duckboards were pilfered from the nearby Royal Engineers' dump, and a brazier was lit. 'The day closed with an issue of rum,' recalled Rogerson. 'The first stage of the relief was over.'

Men were kept busy the next day, 9 November, with 'arms drill, bayonet fighting, platoon drill, bomb cleaning, kit inspections', partly to prevent them from vegetating under their shelters and partly to help integrate men who had joined 2/West Yorkshire at Fricourt, many of them Tyneside miners with heavy Geordie accents. James Jack, spick and span as ever ('Always die like a gentleman: clean and properly dressed'), briefed his company commanders in the battalion headquarters dugout, a short length of roofed-over German trench with a table and a couple of wire-covered frames which served as beds or chairs. A and B Companies were to hold the front line with C and D in close support, and Jack took the company commanders forward at 5.00 on the morning of the 10th to look at the ground in the dawn light so that they would have a clear idea of it by the time their companies arrived under their seconds in command. Guides from the Devons met them just behind the front and kept up a helpful patter:

It's not easy to find in the darkness . . . In daylight it's all right. You follow this track till you come to a dead Boche.

Here he be, zur! ... Then you have to look for a white
tape – here, zur – and he leads you roight up to behind
the old front line. But it's easy to go wrong at noight.[74]

They crossed a low valley carpeted with dead, khaki outnumbering
field grey by three to one, and reached the Devons' position where
Rogerson was given a mug of tea. It reeked of petrol: the same tins
were used for both liquids, and although petrol tins should have
been burnt out to get rid of any dregs this was not always done. The
Devon company commander showed Rogerson the position: there
were two companies forward, in a very poor trench, on newly-
captured ground, touching on the inner flank but with their outer
flanks in the air. The enemy main line was a thousand yards away on
the Transloy-Bapaume road, but there were Germans in improvised
positions much closer. The mud was so thick that it took an hour
to walk a few hundred yards. And there was nothing to see: 'just
mile upon mile of emptiness, with never a house or tree, a hedge
or spot of green to break the austere monotony . . .'.

The takeover went well. The company came up in single file under
Captain Maclaren, its Canadian second in command. The company
sergeant major had been left behind, and so Sergeant Chamberlain
was 'acting up'. But as Maclaren stepped aside to remove his jerkin
a single shell – a random 'whiz-bang' from a German 77-mm field
gun – fell just where he had been standing and killed Chamberlain
outright. Maclaren took his papers and identity disc and moved on
before the last man in the line had time to close up and discover
the reason for the temporary stoppage. There was a hasty handover
by the Devons and the incomers signed for the trench stores 'which
they could not see, much less count'.

Once established, the company fell into the familiar pattern of
line-holding, with capricious danger, hard work and boredom
equally mixed. For the remainder of the first night it was important
to get the trenches as well dug as possible. Rogerson's company
headquarters, a hundred yards behind the front trench, was too far
back for him to control the company properly, so he posted Maclaren
forward with orders to 'dig like blazes all night and lie doggo all
day'. A soldier from a recent draft was hit by a stray bullet and sent

back as 'walking wounded'. But the work progressed: before dawn Corporal Buggy Robinson's men had their trench down to a full seven feet. The subaltern commanding A, the adjoining company, had disappeared (no sign of him was ever found), and Second Lieutenant Skett of B, going forward in an effort to find him, was killed. He was immediately buried 'as reverently as we could in the circumstances, digging a grave between bursts of machine gun fire in the parados of the forward trench'.

Half an hour before daybreak the company stood to. The procedure, its name a contraction of standing to one's arms, meant that:

> all troops in the line stood in their appointed places, their rifles in their hands, or immediately convenient, with bayonets fixed, ready for any dawn action on the part of the enemy. When it was fully day and the dangerous half-light past, the order would come to 'stand down and clean rifles'. This procedure was strict and binding anywhere in the forward zone, under any circumstances whatever. The same routine was observed at dusk. So that hour occurring twice in the twenty-four, of 'stand-to', was one of peculiar significance and there was attached to it a degree of solemnity, in that one was conscious that from the sea dunes to the mountains, everywhere, on the whole front the two opposing lines stood alertly, awaiting any eventuality.[75]

Lieutenant C. P. Blacker of 2/Coldstream Guards thought that the risk of attack was 'questionable', but added: 'A more cogent reason was that, attack or no attack, troops should be thoroughly alerted and put on their toes at daybreak and nightfall. During stand-to everyone stands in the fire-bays, alert and at the ready with bayonets fixed.'[76] Platoon and company commanders would visit their men; signallers would check communications and clear the debris of the previous twelve hours from their tables or alcoves, and company sergeant majors, upon whom so much of the minutiae of company administration depended, would check things like reserve ammunition stores and latrines. They would take the opportunity to ensure that a new platoon commander or weak sergeant felt that subtle mix of encouragement laced with gentle sarcasm. Different battalions had different rules, but in some at times like this, the sergeant major was no longer 'sir' to the non-commissioned members of the company, but 'major' to his platoon sergeants and section commanders, as formality relaxed but discipline remained. 'All set, Major,' was how Corporal John Lucy of the Royal Irish Rifles responded to a front-line order from his CSM.[77] A young officer in 2/Royal Welch Fusiliers:

> feeling none too sure of himself as the stream of shells swished overhead and burst behind ... was immensely heartened by the sight of his CSM, Dealing, leaning at ease over the parapet and looking round. 'See anything, Sergeant-Major?' he asked with what unconcern he could put into his voice. 'It appears to me, sir, that there's sweet damn-all.'[78]

After morning stand-down men cleaned their rifles, with section commanders ensuring that no more than half the weapons were stripped at the same time, and ate their breakfast. Rogerson enjoyed 'a hearty meal of "Maconochie" – tinned meat and vegetables – eaten cold and washed down with a tea-cup full of rum.' Lieutenant Colonel Jack appeared – although it was an unsound practice for visitors to arrive during stand-to, and some units banned all movement at that time – to tell Rogerson to take command of the orphaned A Company in addition to his own, and to leave him with a new subaltern to replace Skett, alive at dusk but buried before dawn.

By now men's nostrils had become accustomed, though never used to, the smell of the line. Charles Carrington wrote that: 'The smell of burnt and poisoned mud – acrid is, I think, the right epithet – was with us for months on end, and through it one could usually distinguish a more biotic flavour – the stink of corrupting human flesh.'[79] Frank Hawkings recalled the 'penetrating and filthy stench which assailed our noses and filled the atmosphere – a combination of mildew, rotting vegetation and the stink which rises from the decomposing corpses of men and animals. This smell seems to be a permanent fixture in the firing line and there is no mistaking it.'[80] The much-decorated Adrian Carton de Wiart never lost his romantic view of the war, but even he admitted that: 'My worst memory was the stench of putrefying bodies, for I could smell them still, and though death may be sublime on a battlefield, it is certainly not beautiful.'[81] Eric Hiscock reflected grimly on the smells that assailed him on his first night in the line.

> That night we lit candles and brewed strong tea from chlorinated water poured from an old petrol can (the heat came from a strange concoction in a can labelled 'Tommy's Cooker') and the fumes from this emergency fuel mingled with chloride, petrol, and the smell of decaying flesh wafting from Nomansland through the blanket door of the dugout. Those famous roses of Picardy seemed a long way away, and probably stank.[82]

The presence of unburied dead and discarded food encouraged rats. They scuttled along trenches and down dugout steps, crouched expectantly on timbers and rifled men's kit like the most experienced and persistent of looters. Their familiarity with human beings produced contempt. In a billet, Lieutenant Roe discovered:

> Corporal Arthur Major [who had been asleep] was sitting up in the straw with a fully grown rat swinging from his nose with his teeth in the cartilage. We had already experienced rats nibbling away at the back of our hair . . . The lighting was elementary, a couple of hurricane 'butties' and a torch or two and I was momentarily taken aback. Clearly I could not shoot the rat with my 0.45 inch revolver in such a confined space and equally clearly I could only open the teeth and free them from the cartilage if the rat was first killed. There was only one solution, so I borrowed [Sergeant] Appleford's bayonet and got on with the job.[83]

They were cunning: when men took to hanging their food from stout cord attached to dugout beams the rats 'soon learned to walk along the cord and pull up the food with one of their front paws'. Stuart Dolden described their depredations in the Armentières sector in 1917.

> At the rear of the trenches there were huge holes from which earth had been taken to fill the sandbags which

formed the parapets. These holes filled up with water, and at night one could see the snouts of rats as they pushed their way across. They grew fat on the food they pilfered from us, and anything they could pick up in and around the trenches; they were bloated and loathsome to look on. We were filled with an instinctive hatred of them, because however one tried to put the thought out of one's mind, one could not help feeling that they fed on the dead. We waged ceaseless war on them and, indeed, they were very easy prey because owing to their nauseating plumpness they were slow of foot. We would wait and watch for them as they left the water and climbed awkwardly to the bottom of the trench. Then with a run we would catch them squarely with a mighty kick and there would be one less to batten on us.

The officers on their nightly rounds would fire on them with their revolvers and in the morning it would be a common sight to see disembowelled rats lying amongst our barbed wire.[84]

A gunner forward observation officer found a monstrous rat blocking his view.

It sat just out of arm's reach and washed. I shouted at it, flicked mud at it, threw pebbles at it and not the slightest heed was taken. Eventually in desperation I fetched my stick and, measuring the distance carefully, was able to give it a very violent jab in the middle. It then moved to one side and continued to wash.

Eventually he shot it with his revolver.[85] But such is the whimsical perversity of the British soldier that even the much-reviled rat could sometimes touch his heart. One platoon found a three-legged, one-eyed rat, so obviously a companion in adversity that, christened Albert, it became their pet.

On that first day in the line, Rogerson had to dissuade one of his officers from going to look for his brother, killed three weeks before in nearby Dewdrop Trench: even if his body was found, it would probably have been terribly mangled. While looking across the parapet Rogerson was narrowly missed by a sniper: 'a deafening clop' in his right ear showed just how good the man's aim had been. An artillery forward observation officer with a signaller and drum of cable arrived to spot for a 6-inch battery shelling a nearby German position. 'I was not disposed very charitably for him,' admitted Rogerson, 'as so far we had gone almost unmolested, and experience had taught us that any form of artillery offensiveness promptly evoked retaliation which as often as not fell on the PBI.'[86]

The British shelling induced some Germans to bolt, and the newly-arrived Second Lieutenant Cropper, shooting fast with a soldier acting as his loader, hit four or five of them. Cropper had been commissioned from Sandhurst the year before, showed 'a surprising confidence in one so young (he was not more than twenty)' and was to be killed as the battalion's adjutant in March 1918. Surprisingly, there was no retaliation. Buggy Robinson formed up to ask permission to loot German dead behind the position (he made a tidy living out of selling souvenirs to the Army Service Corps) and Rogerson agreed to turn a blind eye provided he agreed to bring back paybooks and identity discs from British dead.

A ration party arrived, carrying sandbags full of bread, tinned bully beef, jam, biscuits, water and rum. They had lost two men killed on the way up. 'The ration carriers' was a most unenviable task, as thankless as it was dangerous', thought Rogerson. 'Rarely in those days did they complete their double journey without casualties. Occasionally the whole party was wiped out while their company waited, parched and famished, for the water and food scattered about the shell holes.'[87] In 1915 Frank Richards had been carrying rations up to the front with a ration party which included Private Bolton. One of Bolton's puttees came undone and they paused while he did it up and the rest of the party went on. No sooner had they moved off than there was heavy shelling just ahead: they saved themselves by taking cover in what they soon discovered was a latrine trench. When the shelling stopped they found their way forward to their own company and reported to Lieutenant Richardson.

> We met Mr Richardson, who was pleased to see us: the
> majority of our ration party had been killed by the barrage
> on the road. Bolton's puttees had undoubtedly saved us.
> Mr Richardson was holding his nose and inquiring what

was the matter with us, as we smelt like polecats. We
explained to him what had happened, but that anyway we
had saved the bread.[88]

It was typical of the caprice of front-line life that Bolton was killed
six weeks later trying to dismantle German shells 'which we used to
sell to men in the Back Areas who were not coming in the line'.

Occasionally men made dangerous trips like this of their own
volition. Private Edge of B Company 2/Royal Welch Fusiliers – Sunny
Jim to his mates – 'was a bit on the weak side,' recalled Regimental
Sergeant Major Boreham, 'although he had stuck all the marching
of the Retreat [from Mons], and ordinary duty afterwards until the
MO [medical officer] gave him a job on the canteen staff'. On
21 August he materialised in the front line, with no personal equipment but a full pack slung by its supporting straps. He had a slight
impediment in his speech, and when his RSM asked him what he
wanted he replied: ' "I fort the boys would want some cigawettes, so
I've bwought some up." He had come about 7 miles because he
"fort the boys wanted cigawettes." He went round the Companies,
sold his stock, and went off again as if it were nothing out of the
ordinary.'[89]

On the evening of 12 November there was a sudden and unexpected bombardment, and Rogerson fired German signal rockets (tested
in the latrine) to confuse the enemy gunners. The shelling stopped
and no casualties were caused. A chastened Corporal Robinson
returned, having got lost on the way back from his corpses. Rogerson
then slept for four hours, his first rest since leaving Camp 34 some
thirty-six hours before, lying in the bottom of the trench. He awoke
to find that Maclaren was out with two helpers issuing rum and
cigarettes to the covering party – a thin line of soldiers lying out in
No Man's Land to protect men working on the trench. 'The value
of such apparently dare-devil gestures,' he wrote, 'was evident from
the fact that the news had travelled with chuckles down the sap and
into the trench long before the three had returned safely back again.'

By dawn on the 13th the trench was in good order:

> Clear of mud, fire-stepped, deep, and continuous along
> the two-company front . . . Most of all I was proud of the

> men . . . At no other time in the war did I meet a better,
> keener or more reliable set of men than that mixed York-
> shire-Northumbrian contingent in front of Le Transloy.[90]

The company stood to at dawn, both sides of the front remaining
quiet for a while afterwards.

> For a few minutes the sun and dew distilled a faint fra-
> grance even from the freshly turned earth or the coarse
> weeds buried by the night's shelling, before the nurture
> evaporated and allowed the normal odours of trench life
> to assert themselves. Even then the all-pervading reek of
> chloride of lime would be overcome for a while by the
> homely acrid smell of the cook's wood fire and – oh, most
> welcome! – of bacon.

Company Quartermaster Sergeant Carlton arrived with the ration
party and the news that they were to be relieved the following night
by 1/Worcesters of their own 24th Brigade. The 13th passed with
men focused on domestic concerns although they could hear, only a
few miles away to the north, the sound of battle. We now know (though
they did not) that it was 51st Highland Division's successful attack on
Beaumont Hamel. 'At the time the assault was being delivered,' admitted Rogerson, 'we drank, smoke and sang with never a thought for the
thousands of lives being choked out by bullet, bayonet or bomb within
a few miles of us. We were content to know that someone else was "for
it".'[91] The men became restless after dark as they waited for relief,
and the Worcesters arrived at 11.00. Rogerson sent the company on
under Maclaren and went to report to his battalion's adjutant that
relief was complete, but got lost and eventually found himself back
with the company: it had lost no men on the way out.

It was a terrible march back to La Briqueterie camp.

> Some of the younger men could hardly walk. Officers and
> fresher NCOs took over rifles and packs from the most
> fatigued without avail. The querulous, half-mutinous
> demands for rest grew more insistent. They were the cries
> of minds tortured by over-exertion and lack of sleep.

Siegfried Sassoon had watched just such a scene, standing beside
the quartermaster (the old warrior was in 'a state of subdued anxiety'

about his battalion) in much the same place three months earlier. This time it was a whole division coming out of the line:

> The field guns came first, with nodding men sitting stiffly on weary horses, followed by wagons and limbers and field-kitchens. After this rumble of wheels came the infantry, shambling, limping, straggling and out of step. If anyone spoke it was only a muttered word, and the mounted officers rode as if asleep. The men had carried their emergency water in petrol-cans, against which the bayonets made a hollow clink; except for the shuffling of feet, this was the only sound. Thus, with an almost spectral appearance, the lurching brown figures flitted past with slung rifles and heads bent forward under basin-helmets.[92]

Rogerson eventually halted the exhausted company only to find they were just 100 yards from camp. It was only 3½ miles from Ginchy crossroads to camp, and five miles in all to the front line: less than two hours at normal marching pace. 'There is no doubt that the Somme taught us that distance is a relative term,' reflected Rogerson, 'not to be measured in yards and feet.'[93] 'Dear old Hinchcliffe, the Quartermaster' had the tents organised as if it was Salisbury Plain, and the tireless James Jack rebuked Rogerson for removing his equipment before the men had been fed. He chatted to the adjutant: 'Since we had last met two of our friends had gone west, but except for a passing reference – "rotten luck" – their names were not mentioned. We were glad to be out, to be alive, and to be together again.' He drank two mugs of whisky and soda, fell over on hitting the cold night air as he left the mess tent, and crawled back to his own tent, where he fell into a dreamless sleep until 9.00 on the morning of the 14th. It was just over four days since he had gone up the line.

Rogerson's vignette of trench warfare is studded with truths which front-line soldiers would have recognised, however much individual details might have varied. The approach march was better than many. When Second Lieutenant Joseph Maclean first went up the line with 1/Cameronians in the unseasonable spring of 1917 he reported that:

It was raining and blowing, and very cold, and the march up to the trenches was the final limit. We had to go along miles (literally) of communication trenches in the dark, and every now and then we struck a shell hole, or a bit that had been blown in and had to be climbed over, and as everywhere except the 'duckboard' was deep in slime and mud you can imagine what we were all like. The last 300 yards or so had to be done over the open across clayey ground: it was a regular acrobatic performance getting across . . . I fell into the half-frozen shell holes three or four times, and soon exhausted all the swear words I ever heard, and was reduced to vulgar blasphemy. We took five hours to get up, and arrived soaking wet, covered with filthy mud and perfectly miserable.[94]

Lieutenant Colonel Alan Hanbury-Sparrow's 2/Royal Berkshires went up the line in single file across the moonscape of the Ypres battlefield in mid-1917. Half the men got lost, and it took hours to find them again. It later materialised that Private Ailey had wearily drifted off in the wrong direction with two companies mutely following him. 'This Ailey had been the curse of the battalion for the past year,' wrote Hanbury-Sparrow bitterly. 'Feeble in body, he was feebler still in mind.'[95]

The fact that Rogerson's trench was in an unusually poor state and his front-line tour shorter than many meant that the full daily routine never had time to develop. More usual was the kind of pattern (echoing watches on a warship) that C. P. Blacker remembered.

I will describe the sequence during our tour at the beginning of July when the long hours of midsummer daylight were just beginning to shorten.

All three officers were on duty during stand-to and stand-down – from 3.15 to 4.15 a.m. in the early morning and from 9.30 to 10.30 in the later evening . . .

In addition to these two periods of standing-to, each officer in turn did a long watch and a short watch during every twenty-four hours. The three long watches of about twenty-four hours ran from morning stand-down at 4.30 a.m. to 8.30 a.m.; from 8.30 a.m. to 12.15 p.m.; and from 12.30 to 5.30 p.m. The short watches were mounted during the evening period from 5.30 p.m. to stand-to at 9.30 p.m. This evening period of three hours was divided into three short watches of about an hour and a half for each officer, thus making an evening meal, taken in turn, possible.

On the different days of the tour, I did long and short watches at different times. The best of the long watches was the first of the day, after the early morning stand-down. In fine weather it was good to see the sun rising and enjoy the cold air ... The night watches, though not longer than an hour and a half, could be tribulating because of the longing for sleep. For the sentry to fall asleep on duty was regarded as a serious crime. For an officer to be found asleep on duty was *a fortiori* about the last word. I had not properly known till this tour how intense could be the craving for sleep. It could seem almost irresistible. If you leaned against the side of the trench for more than a short moment, your consciousness would insidiously and insensibly dissolve. Your brain seemed to melt and you slid down into the region of unstable mists. When you felt yourself to be in danger of slithering into this state, you welcomed a noise of war – a shell or a rifle bullet which roused you.[96]

When Robert Graves was attached to the Welch Regiment in the trenches he was told that:

Our time-table is: breakfast at eight o'clock in the morning, clean trenches and inspect rifles, work all morning, lunch at twelve, work again from one till about six, when the men feed again. 'Stand-to' at dusk for an hour, work all night, 'stand-to' for an hour before dawn. That's the general programme ... We officers are on duty all day, and divide the night up into three-hourly watches.[97]

Bernard Adams remembered a similar routine, but this time in a support trench, and from a private soldier's point of view.

This would be a typical day, say, in April.
4 a.m. Stand to. Until it gets light enough to clean your rifle, then clean it.

About 5 a.m. Get your rifle inspected, and turn in again.

6.30 a.m. Turn out to carry breakfast up to company in front line. (Old Kent Road very muddy after rain. A heavy Dixie to be carried from top of Weymouth Avenue, up via Trafalgar Square, and 76 Street to the platoon holding the trench at the Loop.)

7.45 a.m. Get your own breakfast.

9 a.m. Turn out for working party: spend morning filling sandbags for building traverses in Maple Redoubt.

11.30 a.m. Carry dinner up to front company. Same as 6.30 a.m.

1 p.m. Get your own dinner.

1–4 p.m. (with luck) rest.

7.15 p.m. Clean rifle.

7.30 p.m. Stand to. Rifle inspected.

Jones puts his big ugly boot out suddenly, just after you have finished cleaning rifle, and upsets it. Result – mud all over barrel and nosecap.

8.30 p.m. Stand down. Have to clean rifle again and show platoon sergeant.

9 p.m. Turn out for working party till 12 midnight in front line.

12 midnight. Hot soup.

12.15 a.m. Dug out at last till

4 a.m. Stand to. And so for three days and nights.

Adams acknowledged that this was 'really quite a moderate programme'. But however much officers sought to spare their men, there were unexpected emergencies.

A couple of [German trench mortar] canisters block Watling Street; you *must* send a party of ten men and an NCO to clear it at once; or you suddenly have to supply a party to carry 'footballs' up to Rue Albert for the trench-mortar men. The Adjutant is sorry; he could not let you know before; but they have just come up to the Citadel, and must be unloaded at once. So you have to find the men for this on the spur of the moment. And so it goes on, night and day. Oh, it's not all rum and sleep, is life in Maple Redoubt.[98]

For private soldiers life in the reserve trenches generally consisted of sentry duty interwoven with digging or wiring parties and punctuated by meals. Rifleman Percy Jones described his routine during a nine-day tour of duty in reserve trenches near La Chapelle d' Armentières in December 1915.

> Reveille was at 5 a.m., stand-to with rifles and equipments until 1 p.m., draw rations for the day at 7.30, meals when you like. If free in the evening one could go to sleep for the night, but as the principal duty of men in the reserve trenches is to do fatigues, one was rarely free. The most important daily fatigues were wood fatigue to the Headquarter Farm at 6 a.m., and the star performance of the day:- ration, mail-bag and general fatigue in the Factory, a ruined building on the Armentières road, which commenced from 5.30 to 6.30 p.m. And frequently lasted to 10 p.m.
>
> The daytime was spent digging in, repairing and draining trenches, of which we had a great deal during the last few days. There was also a night trench digging fatigue at any unearthly hour from 5 p.m. to 5 a.m.[99]

In front-line trenches in daylight there was usually one sentry per platoon. From early 1915 there was an increasing trickle of mirrors, placed on the parados and adjusted so that a man sitting on the firestep could see the trenches opposite, and trench periscopes of a variety of designs which permitted better observation. Until then sentries had had to peer over the parapet at regular intervals, and German snipers took advantage of any opportunity. Private Frank Richards began the war with two particular friends, known to us only as Billy and Stevens. In trenches at Bois Grenier in 1915 Richards and Stevens were watching Private Berry standing in a pool of water with his boots and puttees off, trying to fix a pump: 'his language,' reported Richards, 'was delightful to listen to':

> Soon he slipped on his back in the water and we burst out laughing. Then suddenly Stevens too dropped down in a sitting position with his back against the back of the trench; but this was no laughing matter. A sniper on our right front had got him right through the head. No man

ever spoke who was shot clean through the brain: some
lived a few seconds and others longer. Stevens lived about
fifteen minutes . . . He was a married man with three children and one of the cleanest white men I ever met. He
was different to the majority of us, and during the time
he was in France he never looked at another woman and
he could have had plenty of them in some of the places
we were in . . .[100]

Henry Williamson had a similar experience when his trench
was sniped: 'Crack! And the man next to you stared at you curiously
for a moment. Then you saw a hole in his forehead and when he
slid down you saw that the back of his head was open.'[101] At Cambrin
in June 1915 Robert Graves was shocked to find a man hit in the
head:

making a snoring noise mixed with animal groans . . . One
can joke with a badly-wounded man and congratulate him
on being out of it. One can disregard a dead man. But
even a miner can't make a joke that sounds like a joke
over a man who takes three hours to die, after the top
part of his head has been taken off by a bullet fired at
twenty yards' range.[102]

Soldiers perished from illness or accident long before they
reached a trench: Ian Hay memorably described how his own battalion's first dead soldier was left 'alone with his glory beneath the
Hampshire pines'. Accidental death was common on rifle ranges
and training grounds in France. In August 1914 Lieutenant Roland
Miller's 123rd Field Battery RFA lost its first man to friendly fire,
'when a gunner wandered out of station [at Le Cateau], met a
French sentry, but not yet appreciating the reality of things, nor
understanding the language, tried to pass, and was shot dead.'[103] On
Easter Sunday 1915, Lieutenant Roe saw a 'scene of indescribable
horror and confusion' resulting from an explosion at a grenade-
filling unit in France.[104] Harry Ogle's chum, Billy Brown, was killed
when his mortar crew, showing off at a demonstration, managed to
load a second bomb before the first had left the muzzle.[105] Frank
Dunham's comrade George Bloomfield was cleaning his rifle in a

trench at Ypres in 1917 when it went off, killing Private Beazley.[106]
And so it went on.

Once men were within range of hostile fire, death came in a myriad
of capricious ways. After he reached the front, Private Bernard
Livermore mused on:

> Death from a sniper's bullet, death from a rifle grenade,
> death from a Minnie or a toffee apple; death from shrap-
> nel (possibly from our own guns) or from gas, if the wind
> were in the right direction. Death also might come from
> bayonet or nail-studded cosh if the Bosche raided our
> lines.[107]

But the challenge to men's fortitude came neither wholly from the
simple fact of death, nor from the shocking circumstances which so
often accompanied it. Shell or bullet converted a comrade to a
corpse, sometimes one which lacked physical integrity, and this had
to be disposed of promptly, though with as much dignity as the
situation afforded.

Men killed in or near the front line were buried where they fell,
or collected after the action for burial behind the lines. In December
1914 Captain Gerald Burgoyne was told that there was a dead man
close to his company's position at Locre.

> Went out and found (from his identity disc) he was No
> 8863, B. West, Suffolk Regiment. Lying with his overcoat
> tied over his face alongside a ruined farm. Died possibly
> from wounds. Horrid job, lifting his head to get his identity
> disc. I buried him at dusk, and said the Lord's prayer over
> him. Couldn't read any prayers as we couldn't have any
> light, and as it was three bullets came so close to us, they
> might have been aimed at us.[108]

The following spring even the energetic Burgoyne found it hard to
keep pace with death's demands.

> I saw five of the Gordons and they were smelling most
> unpleasantly. Got the subaltern of [position] H3 to bury
> two of them. On the parapet of H2 noticed the left leg,
> from the top of the hip to the foot, of a Frenchman. It
> was covered in a bit of red trouser . . . Had that buried

too. In a Jack Johnson hole full of water within 30 yards of my trench, and on the road, I noticed a body, the face above water, of a bearded German. He had been there for months. Could do nothing but fill in the hole with stones and rocks.[109]

Men felt a strong obligation to bury comrades if it was at all possible. Private Stuart Dolden was moving up towards Vermelles with the London Scottish in September 1915 when 'Walker, my own particular chum' was shot through the chest. They dressed his wound at the next halt, but there they had to leave him. The following day Dolden went back with another man:

> in an attempt to find the body of our pal Johnny Walker ... He lay there looking perfectly peaceful. In life Johnny had been a good looking boy with a bright expression and a merry twinkle in his eye, and even in death he looked serene.[110]

Private Roy Ashford of 2/16th London went into the line on the Somme in September 1916, and during his first tour of duty his friend Private Hearn was killed outright by a shell, blown backwards into the trench as he stood on the firestep on sentry duty.

> First I went through his pockets and put his treasures into his gas helmet satchel, to be returned to his relatives. Then ... we heaved the body over the parados. I decided the best case would be to scrape at the nearest shell hole, which I did with a spade the Germans had left behind ... As reverently as possible we laid the body in the bottom and scraped the earth over it ... I stuck his bayonet at the head of the grave and hung his steel helmet thereon ... Then, having done our best for our lost pal, we crawled back into the trench.[111]

Ashford immediately wrote a letter of condolence to Hearn's brother, a company sergeant major in another battalion.

The worst of improvised burials close to the front line was the near-certainty that the body would be disinterred by shellfire. The pre-war army had expected great things from cyclists, acting as bicycle-borne infantry in mobile war. In the event, while cyclists did indeed prove useful as orderlies and message-carriers, most bicycle units sent to the Western Front finished up acting as infantry. Private Jimmy Smith of the Northern Cyclist Battalion buried his best friend Ernie Gays.

> I took him by the ankles, the other two took him by the arms, and we laid him in and covered him up. I remember feeling a bit upset, for the grave was only about four feet deep. I knew he probably wouldn't be there for very long, because of the shell-fire.[112]

Frank Dunham, a stretcher-bearer, was in the line near Ypres in December 1916 when he was called to a man so badly hurt as to be beyond human aid. The man's 'inarticulate sounds ... turned to groans' which so upset his comrades that they waited some way along the trench until he had died. The body was then covered with a groundsheet, but had to be kept in the trench until it could be moved under cover of darkness.[113]

Bodies moved out of the line were often taken back in the same General Service wagons which had brought rations forward, and buried in civilian cemeteries or, as the weight of casualties grew, in new military graveyards. These were sometimes within artillery range of the front, so burials had to take place at night. The dead were usually shrouded in a blanket or sewn into hessian, although Captain Billy Congreve, a young staff officer (who would himself live only a further two years), had a rough coffin made for his divisional commander, Major General Hubert Hamilton, killed in October 1914.

> I had to take the spurs off his poor feet, though, as they would not fit, and then we nailed on the lid ... It was a pitch dark night and had been raining hard all day, so there was mud everywhere and a cold wet 'feel' in the air. The rifle and machine-gun fire was very heavy, and it sounded but a few yards away, so loud was it and so still the night.
>
> The scene was one of the strangest and most beautiful I have ever seen. The poor church battered by shells, the rough wooden coffin with a pewter plate nailed on the lid on which we had stamped his name, a rough cross of

> flowers made by the men, a small guard with fixed bayonets and the group of twenty to thirty bareheaded officers and men. Above all, the incessant noise . . .[114]

It was often impractical to dig individual graves, and bodies were laid side by side in a long trench. On at least one occasion shellfire forced the chaplain, burial party and mourners to take refuge in the trench, leading to wry jokes about 'the quick and the dead'. Bandsman Erskine Williams of the Sherwood Foresters was an artist and musician who had joined the army in 1915. His band was responsible for burying the dead at Essex Farm, just north of Ypres, in August 1917, and he tells how:

> After we had dug the grave at noon we fetched the bodies from the hospital, wrapped in blankets and carried on stretchers . . . There was a whacking great shell hole in the graveyard. Some of the bodies were just as they had been knocked out . . . but the band worked well on the job, filling the grave in with earth after a brief service to the accompaniment of screaming shells . . .
>
> The poor faces at last covered with earth – what a sad sight. I was moved more by the pitiable appearance of the victims than by the terror of their look. I was surprised to find I could carry one end of a stretcher with its awful load from hospital to cemetery; it was a duty which seemed to give me strength . . . all in drizzling rain.[115]

Frank Dunham, watching his mate Corporal Gardiner buried under sporadic fire in Chester Farm Cemetery, at much the same time, complained: 'I fancy the padre got slight "wind up" with the rest of us, for he cut the service short and was soon off afterwards.'[116]

Most soldiers became inured to the sight of death, and often made rough jokes about the dead: we would now call the process 'avoidance humour'. Henry Williamson saw a German's arm sticking out of the ground near Miraumont on the Somme, and 'a young soldier laughingly put the handle of a broken spade between the stiff fingers, saying "Now them, Jerry, get on w'it: no bluudy skrimshankin" 'ere.'[117] But the same soldiers could be reverent about graves, allied or enemy. The Reverend Harold Davies saw that some British soldiers had restored a German cemetery in newly-recaptured territory, 'and outside have written with infinite pity "Forgive us our trespasses, as we forgive them who trespass against us." '[118] In December 1917 Second Lieutenant Huntley Gordon found a cross, made from a broken propeller, just in front of his gun position.

> Round the propeller-hub is painted '2nd Lieut. J. G. Will RFC.' He was the wing three-quarter known before the war as 'the flying Scot' . . . The grave must have been made by Boche airmen – a curiously chivalrous act, for they can hardly have thought it likely that we would advance far enough to see it.[119]

At night it was safe to look out over the parapet. Robert Graves tells us that in 2/Royal Welch Fusiliers sentries were ordered to:

> Stand with their heads and shoulders above the parapet, and their rifles in position. This surprised me at first, but it implied greater vigilance and self-confidence in the sentry, and also put the top of his head above the level of the parapet. Enemy machine guns were trained on this level, and it would be safer to get hit in the chest or shoulders rather than the forehead. The risk of unaimed fire at night being negligible, this really was the safest plan. It happened in battalions which did not insist on the head-and-shoulders rule, but just let their sentries sneak an occasional peep over the top, that an enemy patrol would sneak up unseen to the British wire, throw a few bombs, and get safely back.[120]

Sentries were posted in pairs at night, and in a well-conducted platoon their two-hour tours of duty would be staggered so that one was fresh and the other experienced. There was often a corrosive monotony to sentry duty, as Harry Ogle reported, shortly after his arrival on the Somme front in 1915.

> I am standing on day sentry-go in a front line trench . . . at the moment I am doing nothing but peer through a loophole. Through this loophole, which is about a foot and a half wide and half a foot high, I can see five wooden posts which support nineteen strands of barbed wire between them. I have counted them over and over again

> to keep myself awake. The strands of wire come close to my loophole, over its right hand corner. There are seventeen barbs on them ... Right in the middle foreground of a bright though ill-framed picture lie two empty tins, one jagged lid shining uncomfortably in the morning sun. There it must stay until nightfall. These are only the nearest of hundreds in the high grass.[121]

Sleep beckoned all too invitingly. 'Sleeping at post' was a capital offence in military law, and accounted for 449 death sentences during the war. Only two of these were actually carried out, both in Mesopotamia, where a pair of sentries in 6/Somerset Light Infantry were court-martialled and (despite a plea by their divisional commander for a suspended sentence of imprisonment) shot. This very low percentage of executions reflects the fact that both courts martial and the officers who commented on their cases as they went up the chain of command for final confirmation by the commander in chief knew all too well how tired men became, and generally recommended clemency.[122] Indeed, we may suspect that the men actually charged for sleeping at post represented only a tiny proportion of those actually caught asleep by an officer or sergeant, most of whom would have understood how difficult it was to stay awake. Lieutenant C. P. Blacker admitted that sometimes it was only the sound of a bullet that stopped him from slithering into unconsciousness, and:

> The Very lights not only illuminated no-man's-land, they also alerted dozy sentries. I sometimes asked the latter if they had private means, other than the traditional expedient of pinching oneself, of keeping awake. I encouraged them to think up methods, practise them on themselves and report to me any that were effective. In retrospect [he later became a doctor] I have wondered why we did not treat ourselves with small doses of caffeine.[123]

One patent method was not without risk, as F. P. Roe reflected:

> I have seen soldiers and senior NCOs standing in the front-line trench looking over the parapet from the firestep with the point of their fixed bayonet (sharpened for active service) touching the soft flesh under the chin

and kept steady there by holding it with the thumb and forefinger of the right hand. I have over and over again seen the soldiers with a little speck of dried blood caused by a nodding head and a prick with the extreme top of the bayonet – a device guaranteed to keep the sleepiest sentries awake.[124]

At Ypres in mid-1917 Gunner Aubrey Wade, manning his battery's telephone (a post no less important on a gun-line than a sentry was to the infantry), drifted asleep and missed a call for supporting fire. He knew the dangers, admitting that:

Sleep was dangerous on my job ... The slightest relaxation, and the next thing would be the major tapping me on the shoulder and telling me I would be placed under arrest. The court-martial, and the military prison, and the final scene.

But now: 'Our battery was silent behind me while the infantry was going through it up there, and it was my fault.' Questioned the following morning, he told his commanding officer that he had been out mending the wire, and showed him a recent repair. He suddenly realised that it was not in fact his wire, but happily for him the CO did not.[125]

Sentries were often tired because of the other demands on men's energies. Working parties in the line were required to bring up trench stores such as wire, timber, trench-mortar bombs and duckboards from the rear; to repair damaged trenches and construct new ones; to bury telephone cables, and to keep wire entanglements in good order. Bernard Livermore of 2/20th London remembered how trenches were deepened. 'One man used a pick on the heavy clay for two minutes by the watch,' he wrote. 'His companion then got to work with the spade and tossed the earth up eight feet to where a third man spread it. We were so worn out that often we fell asleep, standing up, in our two minutes of rest.'[126] The sandbag was to the front-line soldier what the flint was to primitive man. 'Filling sandbags and replacing shell-shattered old ones always kept us busy,' thought F. P. Roe. 'Each sandbag was about eighteen inches long and nine inches wide and of course was filled with earth or chalk available on the spot. A filled sandbag thoroughly soaked with water seemed to weigh a ton.' The trenches Frank Hawkings occupied at St-Eloi in May 1915 were:

> almost entirely built of sandbags and as they badly needed repair they kept us very busy. To judge by the grouses of the two companies in the Scottish Wood, life there is none too easy. Every blessed night they have to supply parties to carry up sandbags and other RE [Royal Engineers] stores. To add to their discomfort, Fritz sometimes strafes the edges of the wood with whiz-bangs.[127]

As David Jones observed:

> Empty sandbags were used for every conceivable purpose. They were the universal covering. They were utilised as a wrapping for food; for a protection to the working parts of a rifle, and a cover for bayonets against rust. The firm, smooth contour of a steel helmet was often deprived of its tell-tale brightness, and of its significant shape, by means of a piece of stitched-on sackcloth. The sandbag could be cut open and cast over the shoulders against the weather or tied around the legs or spread as a linen cloth on the fire-step for a meal, or used in an extremity as a towel or dish-cloth; could be bound firmly as an impro-vised bandage or sewn together as a shroud for the dead. There remained the official use: they constituted, filled with earth, the walls, ceiling and even the floor surface of half our world.[128]

Ration items such as cheese could often be 'very hairy, imprinted with the sodden hessian's weft and warp'. Sandbags were also ideal receptacles for the personal effects of the dead. One officer, seeing a filled sandbag accompanying a body being carried out of the line, asked if it contained the man's effects, only to be told: 'No, sir: his mate.' The practice of wrapping them round the legs to prevent puttees from becoming caked with mud was universal, and its fre-quent banning in routine orders had little effect.

Lieutenant Roe recalled how wood and metal sometimes took over from hessian.

Occasionally instead of interminably rebuilding the walls of the trench exclusively with sandbags we were able to utilise fascines and gabions. A gabion is a very handy hollow cylinder of metal [or wicker] filled with earth; fascines were long faggots of wood such as short branches of trees bound round at intervals with strong cords into bundles about eighteen inches or two feet in diameter, and three to four feet in height ... The fascines were especially useful when the trench was dug well into the ground and a parapet created of undisturbed earth, rather than built up from ground level with sandbags. In some areas the undisturbed earth forming the parapet could be more firmly held on the inside with rabbit wire stretched between wooden battens but this was a job for the expert sappers of the Royal Engineers. Sometimes it was advantageous to use flat wooden devices like sheep hurdles made of strong withy-like branches of small trees. These additions were called revetments.[129]

There were times when the damage done by German artillery meant that trenches had to be rebuilt 'entirely without cessation'. On the eve of the Somme this work absorbed the energies of frontline troops, and the need to dig extra communication trenches to enable attacking units to move forward swallowed up the efforts of units notionally in reserve or at rest.

In 31st Division the 94th Brigade behind the line in reserve billets were busy providing working parties to carry forward the materials with which they spent many hours repairing and rebuilding. The brigade provided daily the large total of 1,500 troops at a time to work under Royal Engineers supervision. They too get tired out for they daily had a long route-march from their Bertrancourt billets into the line and a similar return trek at the end of the day – sometimes even at night.[130]

There were few jobs which illustrated the advantages of pre-war experience quite as much as digging. Middle-class men like Corporal Henry Ogle, an art teacher who had enlisted in the infantry in 1914, suddenly found the social order reversed as he tried to dig a small funk hole.

> I was doing a hurried dig . . . when Tom [a miner] said, 'Corp, you'm a schoo'master an' knows a thing or two that's no use in this bloody place, but when it comes to pick and shovel work why, that's <u>my</u> job. I don't say you know nowt about it, but you acts as if you don't, bein' in a 'urry, an' I'm goin' to schoo'master you . . .'. He puts his pipe in his pocket, hands me his pouch, seizing my shovel with a grip and balance acquired by daily use over long years. But he eyed it, and then me, with distaste. 'You want to keep her clean, lad. Make yourself one of these. Some call it a "minute killer" but a proper <u>mon</u> saves more minutes than he kills.' He produced a little piece of wood shaped like a spade from the top of his sand-bagged right lower leg and scraped the muddy tool clean. 'Now then!' he growled, and began at the edge of the funk hole or where he judged it ought to be. He shovelled out a hundredweight or two, placing it neatly behind the edge of the trench to make room for roof-spans, if any. While he worked he delivered his lesson, suiting the actions to the words or phrases and fixing me with that rather fierce gaze of his to make sure I was attending. 'Begin at back, an' keep your feet off till you've made a bottom to stand on. Always work from a clean bottom. Find your right level, then you slopes it up a bit towards the back unless you wants water there. There's the bottom!' (Slapping it with his shovel.) 'Now your shovel will slide, an' firm it down as you go, sweet and easy like. Now find your side walls and <u>batter</u> them. Don't forget or your edges will be falling on your 'ead when you're trying to sleep. Clear your stuff as you go, don't <u>stand</u> on it.' (Looking at me severely.) 'Now, square your back corners, dead true and clean. No, you finish your smoke – you don't get baccy like that every day an' I'm not done schoo'mastering yet! Get your right hand so it backs agin' the inside of your right knee. Now use your knee to start your shove. That's usin' your weight. Easy! Throw o'er left shoulder working right-'anded, an' right shoulder left-'anded. No, a <u>proper</u>

<u>mon</u> will pick an' shovel as good wi' one as wi' t'other.
Use body and legs to save your arms. An' <u>use your 'ead</u>
on this job, same as you uses it on your own job.'[131]

This quotation tells us much, and not just about trench-digging.
Harry Ogle, an educated man who had joined up as a private, was
now a corporal, and would end the war as a temporary captain with
a Military Cross. Tom was properly respectful to an NCO, although
'Corp' soon became 'lad'. He was proud of his skills, twice referring
to the link between hard work and manliness which was such a
striking feature of the Edwardian working man, be he urban or rural.
The chance of a middle-class man like Ogle living in close proximity
to a miner in peacetime was remote. He might have once judged
Tom as a potential striker, while Tom might easily have seen him as
a toff with more money than sense. Thousands of young men like
Harry Ogle were broadened by the experience of serving with soldiers from working-class backgrounds, and many never forgot it. We
must also forgive men like Harry Ogle their attempts to catch
regional accents in their prose: they no more meant offence than
James Dunn meant to mock the brave Private Edge's speech impediment. And while Tom and his ilk rarely sought to capture middle-
class accents in their own accounts, they were often apt at imitating
them. The practice was called 'talking Rupert', and the young
Second Lieutenant P. J. Campbell, in charge of his first working
party, was amazed just how well they did it.

The inexperienced Second Lieutenant Campbell took over a
gunner working party at Potijze in the salient from an officer who
warned him: 'Whatever you do, don't bugger the men about, that's
the only unforgivable thing. That, and having unnecessary casualties.' He was astonished by the skill of the men, and by the freedom
of their conversation as they grumbled and mimicked officers,
though in a good-humoured way, and paid no attention to his
presence.

> For the first time in my life I, a boy from a public school,
> was doing manual work beside men who were manual
> workers. In a flash of revelation, caused perhaps by a flash
> of a bursting shell outside, I saw that instead of my being

> superior to them they were superior to me. But I saw
> something else, that it did not matter which of us was
> better, what mattered was that we were working against a
> common enemy.[132]

There were differing views over whether officers should work beside other ranks. Robert Graves, serving a short attachment with the Welch Regiment, was told that 'officers must work with them, not only direct the work', but found things more traditionally organised in his own Royal Welch Fusiliers.[133] C. P. Blacker, who joined 4th Coldstream Guards, the Guards Division's pioneer battalion, in October 1915, felt uneasy about sitting in a Royal Engineer officer's tiny dugout while his working party toiled in support of engineer tunnellers.

> Life at Fosse strengthened earlier scruples about how dif-
> ferent were the active-service lives of officers and other
> ranks. The routine during No. 3 Company's attachment
> to the sappers was that the officers' duties were confined
> to marching their parties to Bout-Deville where they saw
> them embussed. The officer then came back. He took no
> part in the working day . . . While the other ranks were
> pumping water up or air down, and struggling to carry
> slimy sandbags along squalid trenches, we officers sat back
> in the fire-warmed mess doing nothing . . . I tentatively
> asked [Captain] Clive Piggott, who felt much as I did, if
> it would be possible for me to do a shift with my platoon.
> He said it was out of the question and might be badly
> received by everyone – warrant officers, NCOs and other
> ranks. The latter, he said, did not expect – or want – their
> officers to live as they did. Clive was, I am sure, right –
> at least for that time and place. There was probably less
> egalitarianism in the [Guards] Brigade than anywhere else
> in the army.[134]

Soon afterwards, sent forward with a platoon to repair a communication trench in filthy weather, Blacker found just how difficult it was to get the balance right.

> Stooping, with heads bent forward, fronting the rain with
> our tin hats, we battled our way up in pitch darkness . . .

we found that much of the trench was crumbling into a
morass. In the worst places the simplest locomotion – plac-
ing one foot into the mud in front of the other and then
lugging out the rear foot – was a task which, laboriously
and slowly repeated, somewhat reminded me of Sisyphus.
The filling of a sandbag could take up to ten minutes.
The glutinous clay stuck to your shovel so that you had to
push it into the sandbag with your hands. After about an
hour some men gave up trying to use a shovel at all. Better
to pick the stuff up with your hands. It was not long before
my heavy rubber (Cording) waterproof had let the water
through in a big way, before my glasses were opaque with
rain and mud, before my handkerchief was soaking with
the effort to keep my glasses clean. By this time the men's
overcoats were soaked through. As the unrelenting
weather continued, the work slowed down and eventually
reached a standstill. I struggled up and down trying to
help small knots of men with my Orilux torch. But after
about an hour and a half the electric light began to give
out; the men would stop working when I had passed them
with my torch. Good men who ordinarily worked well sat
disconsolately, shivering and coughing in the worsening
conditions. I then compellingly realised how awkward the
officer's task could be. I was expected to keep them at it.
But you were expecting them to do more than you could
do yourself . . . After a to-and-fro argument with myself, I
finally decided that it would be moral cowardice to keep
them sitting about for another hour and a half in these
conditions.

He spoke to the platoon sergeant, who agreed that the task was
impossible, and then marched the men home. Before dismissing
them he told the men that they were not to blame, and that the
responsibility was his. Although his company commander was 'not
entirely pleased', he agreed that Blacker had done the right thing.[135]
However, it was clear that an officer was responsible for his party's
duties even if he was not actually digging or carrying himself
and that he needed good reason for curtailing a task. In September
1916, the Hon. Bingo Pakenham, a senior company commander in

4/Coldstream, was sent home by his commanding officer after failing to ensure that his carrying party took wire and pickets over Ginchy Ridge as ordered, but instead dropped it at an improvised dump on the home side of the ridge.

What was often a moral debate for officers was sheer drudgery for NCOs and men, an inseparable feature of an infantryman's life at the front. The diaries of Ernest Shephard, whose duties as company sergeant major including detailing specified numbers of NCOs and men to meet his company's share of the battalion's tasks, are speckled with comments on working parties.

> Busy all night. The RE came up for about two hours and after doing very little returned, and we carried on the sapping, repairing parapets blown in during the day, etc, until dawn . . .
>
> In the evening we supplied a digging party of 100 men for the Norfolks . . .
>
> I find parties to carry food to the two Coys, C and D, in the trenches. What with this and various other jobs our men are fully occupied. We also have to find parties for mining. This again is a great muddle and causes a lot of grumbling, not only here but when we were at Ypres. The infantry soldier's actual pay is 1/– daily. Engineers get 3/– daily, and extra pay for a special jobs such as mining.[136]

Although Shephard exaggerated the pay differential (sappers started on a basic 1/2d a day to the infantry private's 1/–[137]), he was right to observe that the extra pay enjoyed by engineers was the source of resentment to the infantry, who responded with doggerel in which the regiment's title was almost infinitely variable:

> God made the bees
> The bees make honey
> The Dorsets do the work
> But the REs get the money.

There was sound logic for the differential pay as engineers were meant to be skilled artisans, but the spate of volunteering meant that there were many infantry soldiers with better qualifications than regular engineer NCOs and, conversely, many wartime volunteers who had joined the Royal Engineers without special qualifications but found themselves far better paid than their comrades in the infantry. In August 1914 W. H. L. Watson was an Oxford undergraduate. He replied to an advertisement in *The Times* for motorcycle dispatch riders and was immediately appointed a corporal in the Royal Engineers on 2/6d a day, as much as an experienced infantry sergeant. When men were recruited for the new tunnelling companies in 1915 some men, experienced 'clay kickers', were offered 6/– a day more than a regimental sergeant major in the infantry. There was bemusement, friction and confusion over these high pay scales from the outset and, as Alexander Barrie observed, the:

> pay muddle ... disrupted the tunnelling companies throughout most of their time. Trained clay kickers were supposed to be rewarded with the six-shilling rate, while the others, classified as mates, took two-and-twopence. In practice much confusion and discontent were caused by what were often arbitrary classifications.[138]

Albert Bullock enlisted in the Royal Engineers Railway Operating Division in July 1916 and received 2/2d a day, which he retained even when transferred to the infantry and was posted to 8/Royal Warwickshires.[139]

Not all men's work was done behind the front line. Groups sent out to repair the wire needed covering parties, lying in No Man's Land on the German side of the wire. Small patrols, perhaps an officer and one or two men, crept out after dark to check the position of enemy wire or trenches. Robert Graves believed in going on patrol often because the men respected personal courage and, if one had to get wounded, it was best to be hit by unaimed rifle fire at night, and to be evacuated at a time when the medical services were not swamped by the casualties of a major battle. Larger raids were mounted to capture prisoners so that German units could be identified: German soldiers wore distinctive epaulettes which had the same recognition function as the brass shoulder-titles worn by the British. And there was an oft-reiterated conviction on the part of the high command that raiding maintained troops' aggressive spirit and prevented too much of the comfortable fraternisation of live and let live. So raiding became a part of trench life, and like the rest of that life it had its attractions and disadvantages. In Anthony French's battalion there was no shortage of enthusiasts.

> Had all volunteers been accepted each raid would have been a major offensive. Married men with families, then those who had recently been within bayonet reach of the Boche, were automatically ruled out. Company and platoon commanders sorted out the rest. The mission determined the number. Usually it was five and a junior officer: a man to cut the wire and guide his comrades back, a bayonet, a grenade thrower, another bayonet and the last man with more Mills bombs. Often they got no further than the wire. Sometimes only one or two returned. But more often than not the wily enemy was taken by surprise, and the party was back with a prisoner dead or alive or without an epaulette or two before a merciless fire was let loose from every enemy parapet . . .[140]

This was by no means a universal view. Private Bernard Adams thought that:

> This trench raiding is a strange business. I think the infantry hate it. The major does not believe that even if they succeed in identifying the unit opposite it makes any difference to our plans. There are easier and better ways of spotting a coming offensive. Probably someone high-up and rather out of touch thinks that trench raids will keep the infantry on their toes and 'cultivate the aggressive spirit'. Out in front, they just don't believe that the results justify their casualties yet they must obey orders – PBI![141]

Frequently artillery and mortars were used to cut the wire and drop a curtain of fire around the position being attacked. Bernard Livermore wrote that on Vimy Ridge in 1916:

> Our lads, with blackened faces and hands, waited in the fire bays whilst an intensive barrage of shells and mortar bombs breached a gap in our wire and also in the Boche entanglements. The fusillade ceased at the ordained

minute. Over the parapet they clambered and disappeared into the dark.

Tensely, anxiously, we awaited their return to give covering fire if the enemy retaliated with a counterattack and chased our boys through gaps in the wire. It was a difficult business when we spotted men, some crawling, some running towards our posts. Not until they were close enough to give the password were we able to decide that they were our raiders and not the Jerries. We had to hold our fire to prevent mowing down our pals.[142]

Stuart Dolden watched a company-sized raid going out on the Somme in July 1916.

A line of figures left the trench; each man had his hands, face and knees [they were wearing shorts] blackened, and the brightness of all bayonets had been dimmed. Suddenly the line disappeared behind our barbed wire. Very soon the excitement began, for our fellows were spotted when there were about seventy yards from the German trench, and the machine gun opened up on them . . . Mr Warlock of A Company sent up a red rocket as a signal to our own artillery to open fire, as it was impossible for our chaps to get through the enemy wire. Our guns got going soon after, and so did the Germans' unfortunately for us . . .

The raiding party at last received orders to retire. They sustained only two casualties which considering the heavy fire was truly remarkable.[143]

Much could go wrong. Lieutenant F. P. Roe described how one raid failed because the long grass growing in No Man's Land had ripened and turned white, presenting the Germans with 'a perfect background for discernible silhouettes of the raiding party'.[144] Sometimes the raiders made noise on their way across No Man's Land, prompting an alert German sentry to rouse his comrades. And sometimes the plan, conceived at brigade headquarters, did not reflect the realities on the ground or current enemy practice: James Dunn wrote of how 'the plan of attack imposed on us ignored or belittled the shell-hole screen the Germans placed at night on the edge of dead ground'.[145] Even if they got into the German trench unopposed, there was no guarantee that a prisoner would be taken in the ghastly mêleé that often resulted. In early 1915 Gerald Burgoyne regretted that his neighbouring battalion had rushed the trench opposite, bayoneted twenty Germans and clubbed an officer to death. 'A pretty piece of work,' he reflected, 'as they had only one casualty. There must have been some reason why they killed them all instead of taking them prisoner.'[146] Part of the reason could have been the fact that raiders often eschewed rifle and bayonet for a variety of savage coshes, bludgeons and knives, and therefore it was all too easy to do lethal damage to a struggling opponent.

Lastly, getting back into British lines could be as dangerous as leaving them. Although flanking battalions would have been notified of the raid, disorientated raiders, coming back across No Man's Land, might not be as carefully received by another battalion as by their own. Roe admitted that 'it was not unknown for men of a patrol on returning from a raid one by one instead of together to be killed by our sentries'.[147] Siegfried Sassoon, an intrepid raider who won his MC for a desperate effort to rescue a wounded lance corporal from a shell hole on an abortive raid in 1916, was wounded in the head in 1918 by a highly-regarded sergeant who thought that his returning patrol was an incoming German raid.

Food figured largely in men's minds. Of course there was a need to ingest sufficient Calories to sustain a body engaged in manual labour, which British government dietitians reckoned required 3,574 a day. Front-line troops were expected to receive 4,193 Calories a day (the Americans enjoyed a generous 4,714 and the Germans a meagre 4,038) and those in rear areas rather less. But the preparation and consumption of food also gave a texture to long days and busy nights, provided those little mental inducements which enabled men to blunt the discomforts of the moment by looking forward to something as mundane as bully beef and biscuit, and gave a focus for the little communities, gathered round tommy cooker or wood fire. Troops in trenches might either be issued exclusively with cold rations, tinned or fresh, which they would have to cook themselves, or be partially fed by hot foot prepared behind the lines in horse-drawn wheeled cookers, one per company, fitted with dixies, large metal cooking pots heated by a fire below. Although dixies were often used to deliver food over short distances, hay boxes, oblong double-skinned containers like huge oblong thermos flasks which preserved the heat, were always preferred.

Neither method, however, admitted of much culinary subtlety, and even centrally-cooked meals, popular because they had more variety and involved less front-line labour, generally consisted of stew, with pea soup and porridge as occasional alternatives. Stuart Dolden of the London Scottish was a former public school boy and had been a solicitor before the war, but found himself manning a cooker in 1916. He describes how central cooking worked in his battalion.

> When the Company were in the trenches, the cooker remained at the transport lines, and two cooks stayed with it and daily cooked meat, bacon and vegetables, which were sent up to the trenches nightly with the rations. The other two cooks went up with the Company and made tea for the troops during the Company's spell in the line and also served the rations. Then, on the next occasion, we used to reverse the role and the two cooks who had been in the line previously stayed with the cooker and the other two went up.[148]

When his battalion moved up into the line at Hébuterne on the Somme:

> The cookers followed later and on the way up stopped at Bayencourt to pick up the Company's rations at the transport line. After dark, we arrived at Hébuterne, a village just behind the front-line trenches. Part of the Battalion was in the trenches just in front of the village, while the remainder was in reserve in the village itself. We cooked meals and fatigue parties carried the dixies up to the platoons in the front line.[149]

But there was no happy ending, for: 'When the meat arrived next day its presence was so very obvious that we had suspicions as to its goodness. We accordingly got the MO [medical officer] to have a look at it. He immediately condemned part of it, and the remainder we had to wash in permanganate of potash.'[150] And although the cookers ran smoothly on roads, they were difficult to move across broken country. When the division came out of the line:

> A wearying march followed, for the whole Division tramped across tracks temporarily laid across ploughed fields. At one spot the cooker became permanently embedded in the mud. The whole transport had to charge over a steep incline, and our cooker horses failed to rise to the occasion. At last, with a great struggle and an extra horse, we got over the hillock and we were on our way again.
>
> After tramping through thick mud for solid hours, we at last arrived at our destination – a camp situated in a howling wilderness about one and a half miles north of Bray. The cookers were drawn up in a line in front of the camp . . . Water was again the trouble, and we had to wait for water tanks to be brought up on motor lorries . . . In the evening we had to make up tea and sugar rations in sandbags and these were taken up to the battalion by the ration limbers.[151]

Exhaustion or inattention in these situations could have serious consequences. Unsupervised troops might remove the dixies and light the burners, turning the cooker into a large open-air radiator. On one occasion a soldier tethered horses to a London Scottish ration limber. They pulled the rations off it, and 'scoffed the whole of the bread and biscuit rations, and so we had nothing to eat for the whole day'. Company cookers also produced food when battalions were out of the line, although their menus could be more varied. However, a particular favourite remained bacon fat. George Coppard remembered how the cooks would shout 'roll up for your dip' and produce dixie lids full of bacon fat into which men would dip their bread. And: 'Sometimes the cooks poured an extra tin of condensed milk into the big dixies of tea. The toffee-like brew seemed delicious to my young palate.'[152]

The tommy cooker, a small tin holding a chunk of solid fuel or a pot of meths on which a mess tin full of water or tinned food was heated, came in several varieties, but was not widely available at the start of the war. A company's officers might club together to buy a field canteen like that described by Gerald Burgoyne in April 1915:

'Our scoff box arrived last week and we brought it up to the trenches with us; a box fitted with plates, cups, coffee pot, etc, for six. A "joy for ever" is the primus stove with which I have been playing, blackening my dugout with smuts.'[153] The dextrous and inventive (and there were many such) improvised. Sidney Rogerson's corporal, Robinson, would soak four-by-two flannelette cloths (issued for cleaning rifles) in whale oil (issued to rub into the feet) in a small tin in order to brew a cup of tea: his scale of operations widened when he obtained an empty German ammunition box. Rogerson remembered him:

> His lean face lit by the faint flickering of the whale-oil lamp on which mug by mug he brewed us hot drink, talking to himself the while in his curious mixed slang. '*Tray bonn, ma peach*! Now the *doo lay*! Where's the *paree*! *Bonn* for the troops! This and a little drop of "Tom Thumb" will go down grand.'[154]

Frank Hawkings wrote from Wulverghem in January 1915: 'Just made some Oxo. Heating apparatus – one tin of Vaseline and a piece of four-by-two.' Seven months later he proudly declared that such grubby improvisation was a thing of the past: 'Some of us have invested in a baby primus stove for cooking purposes when we are in the line.'[155]

Larger-scale cookers were available. Lieutenant Roe remembered that, early on in the war:

> We were issued with charcoal braziers and a regular bag of charcoal . . . The only utensils were our own individual mess tin and its lid, an enamelled mug, and a knife, fork and spoon. For quite a long time my platoon of sixty men was issued with one solitary loaf of bread a week, the rest of the ration being made up with biscuits. The usual procedure was to fill a mess tin with the very, very scarce drinking water, bring it to the boil on the brazier, and then add the very hard biscuits. When there was a nice porridgy consistency we stabbed open a tin of Tickler's jam, called 'pozzy', and mixed it all together. This was eaten with a spoon and was usually accompanied by some

cold slices of corned (bully) beef. For some reason we preferred the meat cold at that time.[156]

Braziers were a mixed blessing because when issued fuel ran out men were inclined to burn almost anything flammable to cook and keep warm. C. P. Blacker observed that:

> Trench braziers were improvised and the demand for fuel grew. The wooden crosspieces of the duckboards and the boarding of the hurdles burned well, and once the discovery was made that these materials could be prised off, they quickly disappeared. Little could be done to stop these depredations to which blind eyes were turned. No one would admit responsibility. It was worst in severe frosts. 'You won't suffer for this as long as the cold spell lasts,' people would be told, 'but after the next thaw these trenches will be impassable and you will have casualties on the top.' And so they did. But not necessarily those who despoiled the revetments.[157]

It was futile to warn men of the dangers of using braziers in unventilated dugouts or cubbyholes. In April 1918 Captain James Dunn was told by an orderly that there was 'something wrong' with his men, and found them in a fume-filled cellar.

> Sergeant Jones, 'Ol' Bill', was blue and stertorous; his assistant and '37 Jones, my servant – a faithful little fellow, were dead: they slept nearer the floor level and in the far end of the cellar. Wrapped in blankets, and laid in the open with a fresh wind blowing over him, Jones came-to in a couple of hours and fell asleep. On waking he said he feared he would not get such a good job again if he went to hospital, so I kept him; he was almost himself again in a week.[158]

Bully beef, its very name deriving from the *boeuf bouilli* developed by the Napoleonic French army, had been issued by the British army for at least half a century. Soldiers carried a tin of bully beef and another of biscuits as iron rations (many found the phrase very expressive) which could only be eaten if no other food was available: unauthorised consumption of iron rations was an offence, and they were inspected regularly. Private George Fortune ate his on the way to the front by rail in 1917 when feeding arrangements broke down completely.

> We did not have a biscuit between us, as we had lost our rations when we changed trains. Someone had forgotten to take them off, and the train went off while we were being lined up for counting. We were about three days without grub. I ate my iron rations which consisted of a small tin of corned beef and biscuit which you were not allowed to touch until you had permission from an officer.[159]

Harry Ogle remembered a ration distribution in a barn in 1915 as his battalion went up the line, at which one of the corporals produced some new biscuits to replace any iron rations that had become damaged.

> The two corporals lay out the platoon's rations on a groundsheet, dividing them into four parts, one for each section, and the lance corporals take one each to divide between their men. 'What sort of pozzy is it, Freddie?' 'Plum-and-apple as per bloody usual.' There are tins of butter and jam to open, loaves to cut, cigarettes, pipe tobacco, matches and mail to distribute, and soon everybody is occupied and there is comparative quiet till Corporal Middleton come in with a big, shiny square tin. 'There's a tin of hard tack here. Make up your iron rations from it, anything that's spoiled. Iron rations only, mind, and in case any of you lot start trading your bully tins for love or anything else you fancy, there's a kit inspection in the near future.'[160]

Corporal Middleton's warning was entirely appropriate, for rations were sometimes sold or bartered. Edward Spears maintained that a British soldier 'wishing to enjoy the favours of a young lady' would open his proposition with a tin of jam and the words '*Mademoiselle, confiture?*' This remains wholly uncorroborated but, if true, would represent a remarkable triumph for a product often derided by the men to whom it was issued. 'When the 'ell is it going to be strawberry?' snorted Bruce Bairnsfather's cartoon character Old Bill.

But there was something comforting even about plum and apple, its praises sung in a ditty rapped out in the best Gilbert and Sullivan staccato:

> Tickler's Jam, Tickler's Jam
> How I love old Tickler's Jam,
> Plum and Apple in a one-pound pot
> Sent from Blighty in a ten-ton lot.

Bully could be eaten cold with bread or hardtack biscuits, fried with onions (and sometimes crumbled biscuits) to make a hash, or, reinforced by whatever vegetables were available, it could form the basis for the all-in stew which the soldiers of all armies know so well. It was soon supplemented by tinned meat and vegetables, generically known, from the manufacturer of the most common brand, as Maconochie's. It was a welcome addition for Lieutenant Roe, who affirmed that 'previously we had subsisted on cold slices of bully, bully rissoles, fried bully and bully stew', and for Private Herbert Boorer of the Grenadiers, who told his wife in 1915 that: 'They feed us on corned beef and dog biscuits. The biscuits are alright, although a trifle hard.'[161]

The chief complaints about Maconochie's were its monotony and unreliability. A good tin, solidly filled, was a welcome friend: George Coppard declared that this 'dinner in a tin' was his personal favourite. Frank Richards thought that tins made by Maconochie or Moir Wilson could be depended upon for 'a tasty dinner', but another firm offered only 'a piece of rotten meat and some boiled rice'. Its managing director should, he suggested, 'have been put against the wall and shot for the way he sharked us troops'.[162] Soldiers complained that there was sometimes too much liquid, or pieces of meat of such speculative origin that some men were reluctant to eat it in the dark. However, at least it allowed *The Wipers Times* to run an 'advertisement' featuring testimonials from delighted customers. 'Please forward to me the residential address of Mr Maconochie,' begged Corporal Will Bashem, 'as when next on leave I wish to call and pay my compliments.' Bombardier S. A. R. Castic affirmed that: 'words are inadequate to express my delight when I observe your famous rations upon the mess table'. Private Codder declared that his mortally-wounded pal regretted dying before he had been able to meet 'your world-famed proprietor. Need I say more?'.

Bully was often so common in the trenches that men would not eat it out of the line if there was any alternative. Captain Gerald Burgoyne complained that:

> The wastage in rations is terrible. Going round the place [Kemmel, behind the Ypres salient] this morning, I saw enough tins of Bully thrown away, or simply left in their boxes, to feed a Battalion. The men really get far too much, far more than they can eat, and extra rations like tinned salmon are counted extra and the same amount of Bully is issued to the men. The same with the biscuits. Men prefer to buy bread, and tins after tins of biscuits are lying about everywhere . . .[163]

Burgoyne is the only officer I have encountered whose memoirs repeatedly criticise the men he commanded, and it is hard to know quite what this dyspeptic officer would have made of an artillery headquarters where the tent floors and paths were composed entirely of full tins of bully used as paving stones. 'I saw whole cheeses thrown to the pigs,' remembered Corporal Ronald Ginns of the Royal Engineers, 'and paths made of bully beef tins unopened, while many a good fire was obtained from army biscuits. But it was the sameness that caused us to spend our pay on French food.'[164]

Captain Joseph Maclean reported from a front-line trench in March 1918 that:

> This morning breakfast was *café au lait*, (tinned) bacon and sausage, bread and marmalade, which is pretty good going in a place like this. Breakfast is the best meal of the day. For dinner we have to fall back on bully beef, while tea is generally tea, bread and jam, or cheese, perhaps with sardines or something like that. Of course everything is more or less filthy. During the night the men get stew and tea, which is brought up for them in 'hot food containers', and also rum, and I take a share of each – and the last is not the least.[165]

Corporal Frederick Hodges of 10/Lancashire Fusiliers reckoned that:

> Our rations were adequate, provided they reached us. There was bread, cheese, jam, margarine, tea and sometimes Maconochie's, a meat and vegetable ration we called M and V. Water, which was carried up in two-gallon petrol cans, was usually flavoured with petrol and sometimes also with chloride of lime, presumably when the source of supply was suspect.
>
> The bread ration varied; four or five men to a loaf when we had recently received a new draft to replace casualties, or three to a loaf when we had recently suffered casualties but still received their rations. As the ration party came in sight, the first question we asked was 'How many to a bun?' . . .
>
> The issue of a tin of Fray Bentos was always greeted with great delight because it was the best brand, and also because bully beef was usually put directly into a stew with dried vegetables. The latter were quite a novelty; I had never seen them before and wondered what was in the two heavy sandbags I carried up one night slung across my shoulder. They were full of varicoloured small, hard pieces that swelled into larger pieces of vegetables when soaked by the cook. We liked our tea strong, sergeant-major's, we called it, especially with condensed milk. Sometimes we had porridge, always knows as *burghu* [more usually *burgoo*], which was one of the Indian names we had picked up from old soldiers who had served in India.[166]

If Fray Bentos was well regarded, W. H. Davies's bully was not. Lieutenant Edmund Blunden befriended a stray terrier in the trenches, but made the mistake of giving him this unpopular brand, 'so he may have thought me a danger' and ran away.[167]

Officers often ate better, even in the line, as Bernard Martin acknowledged.

> In fact we did supplement rations when we could, extras like sardines and tinned fruits – pears, apricots, peaches, pineapple chunks. Otherwise we ate exactly the same

rations as the men, brought up usually at night by a Ration Party. Of course they didn't always reach the front line. I remember once living for nearly three weeks on bully beef and biscuits (hard square half-inch thick, as sold for very large dogs) and jam (always plum and apple in the army).[168]

Taking supplementary rations into the line was not confined to officers, though the consequences were not always happy. Sapper Arthur Sambrook was living in a dugout behind the Loos front in 1916 when another soldier produced:

a Camembert cheese he had bought into Number 3 Section dug-out and proclaiming that it was an 'epicure's dream', but his comrades did not agree, so it was decided to drop the delicacy into the stove-pipe sticking through the roof of Section 4's dug-out . . . Our stoves were home-made affairs consisting of a large paint drum, with a pipe (made of biscuit tins hammered round a pole) let into the top, and leading straight up through the surface of the ground. Anything dropped down this pipe dropped into the fire below. After dark we scouted the position, and finding no one about the cheese was dropped down the pipe, with a turf put over the chimney-top so that the inmates below would get the full benefit of the aroma! The resulting stench and smoke compelled the Section 4 men to put their gas-helmets on![169]

Requests for food, often linked to complaints about the monotony of rations and the exorbitant prices charged in shops in the rear areas, feature prominently in letters home. Private George Adams told his parents that: 'We get plenty of tuck out here, bread, cheese and bacon and a butter issue twice a week and stew for dinner. It is a bit monotonous.' He had to pay: '3d for a cake like those you send me and 2 francs (1/8d) for a tin of ham like you get at home for about 4½d and 10d for a 2½d tin of sardines.' He thanked his mother for the cake she had sent, but asked her to wrap future cakes separately from the soap 'as it spoils the taste'.[170] In the winter of 1914 Second Lieutenant John Reith was receiving parcels of one sort or another every two or three days, including:

chocolates and sweets of all sorts. There was a large consignment for distribution among the men. And one evening a splendid box of candy arrived from a girl of whom I had never heard; others followed from her at regular intervals. It was not until the spring when, being invited to tea at my home, she explained the mystery to my parents. Shortly after we had gone overseas a photograph of the officers was published in a Glasgow newspaper. This young lady and some of her friends allocated us out among themselves with this highly satisfactory result. I never met her.[171]

Unknown well-wishers did not just confine themselves to sending food. In January 1916 Gerald Burgoyne's sergeant major was putting on a new pair of socks when he found a packet of cigarettes in the toe with a note which read:

> Dear Soldier,
>> Soon these socks will be worn out. When you want
>> another pair, write to
>> Miss Meta Kerr
>>> Mullagh
>>>> Islandmagee
>>>>> Ireland
>> A Merry Christmas and a safe return.
>>> MK[172]

Bernard Livermore received: 'Cake from my old dairyman, dainties from my people and friends; all were shared out among the members of my section.' An enormous pair of socks were christened Toulouse and Toulong, but stitched together they made a passable body belt. And a helpful aunt appended a patriotic verse written by her clergyman husband, which had found favour with a local newspaper:

> Fling out the Flag!! Fling out the Flag!!
> And fight for all that we revere.
> Fling out the Flag!! Fling out the Flag!!
> Battle for all that we hold dear.
> Fling out the Flag!! Fling out the Flag!! (etc., etc.)

He gratefully replied that what she termed 'those brave heroes, the colleagues in the trenches' had discovered that the verses could be set to the tune of *Fight the Good Fight*. But he did not add that the heroes had tinkered with the words:

> Fling out the Flag!! Fling out the Flag!!
> Fling the Old Man orf' is——Nag!![173]

Pooling the contents of food parcels was the rule for officers and men alike. 'In the early days,' wrote Lieutenant Roe,

> many members of one's family sent out food parcels regularly. They were always pooled and rationed out with the greatest impartiality. Messrs Fortnum and Mason must have flourished exceedingly thereby. Their food parcels were of excellent quality and extremely well packed, for they arrived at company headquarters quite intact and unspoiled by the long transit from Piccadilly to French Flanders.[174]

Stuart Dolden came out of the line at Loos in 1915 to find that:

> The Battalion parcel post had been kept back while we had been in action [at Hulluch], but this was now served out and amounted to seventy mail bags. I received thirteen parcels, and for days I hardly touched any rations. A new draft from Rouen was in the billet when we arrived from the trenches, and as they had been on short rations, the rest of us made a dump of unopened parcels on the floor and told the newcomers to sail into them. They thought we were the kindest fellows in the world, and never was a reputation so easily gained.[175]

Parcels sent to soldiers who had been killed were often opened and their contents devoured, smoked or worn – although one infantry section could not bring itself to eat a dead comrade's twenty-first birthday cake sent out by his mother, and gave it to the less fastidious members of another platoon.

As parcels were usually distributed when a battalion was out of the line, men appreciated a mixture of items that could be eaten at once and others that would fit comfortably into packs or pouches to go up the line. Parcels sent out by the Queen Alexandra Field

Force Fund were very popular because their contents were always eminently practical: 'Towel, Mittens, Writing Tablet, Laces, Muffler, Sleeping Helmet, Soap, Handkerchief, Box of Matches, Toilet Paper.'[176] At Christmas 1914 an oblong brass box containing tobacco and other goodies was sent out to all officers and soldiers on the Queen's behalf. It was much appreciated, not least because the serviceable box could be put to many uses, but one officer was puzzled by the enclosed card which read: 'From Mary and the Women of the Empire.' He thought that he knew most of those jolly girls at the Empire Music Hall, but could not quite picture Mary. Oxo was every bit as popular a gift as its frequent advertisements suggested. 'Just before "stand-to" Priest and I made Oxo for Captain Whitmore and Mr Swainson,' wrote Rifleman Percy Jones.

> But before the water boiled it got dark and the fire made an awful light. Captain Whitmore wanted his 'Oxo' so badly that he didn't order the fire to be put out, but partly covered it with a waterproof sheet, under which I had to crawl to blow the fire!! I came out like a smoked haddock – eyes streaming with tears!! But the 'Oxo' was magnificent.[177]

Chocolate, peppermints, slabs of rich fruitcake, curry powder to enliven the all-in stew, tinned fish and meat, gentleman's relish, processed cheese ('cheese possessed' when it became a ration issue), in it rolled, from hundreds of emporia from Jermyn Street to Arkwright's corner shop. But perhaps the most welcome single item was not food at all, but tobacco.

The British army marched less on its stomach than in a haze of smoke. Woodbines hung from pale lips, black cutty pipes jutted fiercely from beneath Old Bill moustaches and Virginia cigarettes dangled from well-manicured fingers ('stinkers' – Turkish cigarettes – were frowned on in some messes). Cigarettes and tobacco were issued free, sent out in parcels, bought from canteens in the rear areas or French shops, and traded as currency. A soldier-barber would expect two Woodbines for a haircut, and a piece of gauze, used by armourers to clear rifle-barrels but much sought after by soldiers who were expected to use boiling water ('not easily procurable'), followed by flannelette was worth a whole packet.[178] Although theft within the immediate military community was frowned upon, cigarettes might sometimes be 'won' or 'wogged' from the unguarded kit of outsiders. When Albert Bullock and his mate found themselves in a Passchendaele trench with 'a B Coy chap' who bolted when the trench was blown in: 'We dug ourselves out and went through his pack. Found 200 Woodbines.'[179]

As far as cigarettes were concerned, Frederick Hodges believed that: 'Woodbines were prized above all other brands because the tobacco was mature, whereas White Cloud and other unknown brands were hated because of the acrid taste of green tobacco which we suspected had been foisted on the government by fat profiteers who smoked cigars themselves.'[180] Sidney Rogerson wondered who had named '"Ruby Queens" or "Red Hussars" ... those weird war brands of "gaspers".' Most soldiers smoked, and most smokers preferred cigarettes. 'By far the greater number of men smoked cigarettes rather than pipes,' affirmed David Jones,

> and those who did complained bitterly of the particular blend of ration tobacco. So that the issuing of these things usually called for considerable tact on the part of the NCOs in charge, and strained the amiability of those among whom they were to be divided.[181]

Ronald Ginns agreed.

> In fact, never whilst in France was I short of tobacco & I never had to buy any. At any time I had as much as 8oz in a week & when, later on, I went on leave, I took home a pack full for my dad. But this army ration tobacco was poor stuff, most ... under fancy names, never heard of either before, or since the war. Those weeks when we had BDV [tobacco] we considered ourselves in luck.[182]

Jones caught the moment of distribution on the Somme, with pipe men eager for the more negotiable cigarettes:

> Always 'ad fags corporal, always 'av' of.
> Seen you with a pipe, Crower.
> Not me corporal.
> Who are these pipe smokers – '35 Float, you're a pipe man.

> Somehow's right off it corporal, since they brought us into
> this place.
> 'Struth – very well – one packet of *Trumpeter* all round . . .[183]

Officers and men wrote home for favourite brands. Second Lieutenant H. M. Stanford, an unusually keen pipe smoker for one so young, ended his second letter home on 7 November 1914 with a request for:

> Carlyle tobacco
> Safety matches (wooden)
> *The Field*
> *Punch*
> 2 No. 1 Brownie films.

He was soon seeking 'another pipe-lighter like the last . . . I have broken the top off mine'. And then on 16 November there was a request which did credit to his classical education: 'Please send matches and baccy *quam celerrime*'. On the 23rd he asked:

> Please send me some baccy and matches; none has arrived
> yet, though the films and envelopes arrived some days ago,
> so I am afraid it has been pinched on the way. It would
> be best when sending baccy and matches to wrap them
> up in socks or 'foodstuffs' or something . . . I will close
> now, hoping to receive your baccy and matches before
> long.

A delighted postscript added: 'As you were! 3 parcels and some papers just arrived; amongst them, baccy.'[184] Private Herbert Boorer was also a pipe man, telling his wife that:

> BDV tobacco is the best, I could do with some more and
> cigarettes. I should think 50 cigarettes and 2oz tobacco
> would do per week, together with a few that we get issued
> sometimes . . .
>   I think there will be a shortage of matches soon as
> they are dear here, so always send some when sending
> cigarettes.[185]

Alcohol was as eagerly sought but, at least as far as private soldiers were concerned, was less easily come by. The rules were clear. Apart from the rum ration, spirits were forbidden to NCOs and men on active service. As we shall see in the next section, beer and wine could be purchased in the rear areas, but it was hard, though not impossible, to smuggle them into the trenches. The rum ration, a quarter-gill (one-sixteenth of a pint) per man per day, was not a right, and had to be approved by divisional commanders on medical advice that conditions were arduous. In practice almost all divisional commanders granted the rum ration. We have already seen how Major General Reginald Pinney's refusal to do so did not endear him to the troops. In Robert Graves's opinion the sick list of 2/Royal Welch Fusiliers rose alarmingly when the rum issue ceased. 'Our men looked forward to their tot of rum at dawn stand-to as the brightest moment of their twenty-four hours,' he wrote. 'When this was denied them, their resistance weakened.'[186] Rum was drawn by battalion quartermasters in brown earthenware jars marked 'SRD'. This officially stood for 'Special Rations Department', but was popularly believed to mean 'Seldom Reaches Destination' or 'Service Rum Diluted'.

The rum ration has fuelled its own set of myths, with stories of almost insensible men going over the top and staggering across No Man's Land. While it is impossible to prove that this never happened, I have not encountered a single reliable *contemporary* source that mentions large-scale alcohol abuse in the trenches. Soldiers drank themselves into oblivion in rear areas, and sometimes individuals or small groups with access to drink did so in the front line. When asked by a young officer whether the rum ration was a good thing, Frank Crozier gave a textbook justification:

> Rum properly issued, under supervision, tot at a time to each, an officer being responsible for the issue, which must be in his presence, no man forced to take it against his wish, no pooling of tots to be put into the tea brew, each tot being drunk when issued, in the presence of an officer, is a medicine, ordered only by the divisional commander on the advice of his principal medical officer. It is a temporary restorative in times of great stress. Where the harm comes is where regulations concerning the issue of rum are not observed, or when youngsters get the taste

for strong drink by first drinking rum as a matter of routine and so acquiring the habit of it . . . Misguided people
at home have, I know, scandalised the army by saying
that we dope men with rum to make them attack. Such
utterances are utterly unworthy of the British race and a
slander on our men.[187]

Some contemporaries maintained that the rum ration was never
abused. James Jack emphasised that it was 'in no sense a battle dope',
and reprimanded Sidney Rogerson for allowing Sergeant Major Scott
to issue it to his company, as it came out of the line, without the
officer supervision demanded by reglations. Charles Carrington
maintained that officers' privately-purchased spirits were never
common enough to permit front-line drunkenness: 'Whisky – at
seven and sixpence a bottle, a subaltern's daily pay, was a rarity which
we husbanded.'[188] Frank Richards maintained that in his battalion:

we never got enough rum to make a louse drunk.
   I have seen non-commissioned officers and men drunk
in action, but it wasn't on their rum ration: it was on rum
they had scrounged from somewhere else. Our ordinary
rum ration was very beneficial to us and helped to keep
the cold out of our bodies, but any man who had an extra
drop before he went out on patrols, night raids or attacks
was looking for trouble; a man needed all his wits and
craft when he was taking part in any of those, and an extra
drop made one reckless.[189]

However, rum was certainly used to reinforce, if not to induce,
fighting 'spirit'. A former Black Watch medical officer told the 1922
War Office Committee on Shell Shock that 'had it not been for the
rum ration I do not think that we should have won the war'. In his
battalion they always tried to give the men a good meal and a double
ration of rum in coffee before going over the top. Colonel Walter
Nicholson believed that the rum ration 'saved thousands of lives . . .
It is an urgent devil to the Highlander before action; a solace to the
East Anglian countryman before the fight.'[190] In Thomas Penrose
Marks's battalion an extra ration was given before an attack. This 'is
supposed to give us Dutch courage. It might fulfil its purpose if it
were handed out in more liberal doses . . . It does not even make

us merry . . . But every one of us welcomes it.'[191] Lieutenant Vaughan, recently arrived in the line, felt increasingly nervous at the prospect of an imminent attack, 'so that I was forced to go into the dugout and dispel the images with a whisky'.[192]

Even the pious John Reith admitted that rum:

> Was a very real boon, even to an habitual char wallah like myself . . . An officer was authorized to issue a tot of rum to troops coming off sentry duty or back from a raid or patrol or after persistent shelling. Dosage required putting a couple of teaspoonfuls into a mess tin of boiling hot tea, for it was strictly forbidden to allow it to be drunk neat. It warmed us up, eased tension, and even helped soothe the inevitable toothache and abscess troubles. There were many highly exaggerated tales of soldiers being drunk on rum before going over the top during a battle, but as far as my own experience is concerned such tales are wickedly untrue.[193]

Gerald Burgoyne agreed that it was an invaluable asset to tired men.

> A drop of rum in our tea works wonders . . . Sir Victor Horsley and all the drink cranks can say what they like about the issue of rum to troops, and drink generally, but if instead of writing from the comforts of a nice cosy room they'd put in a few days in the trenches I'm sure they'd change their minds. We don't want rum in the cold, or for the cold; but we want it as a 'pick me up' when we are 'done to the wide'.[194]

Edward Underhill thought that those in Britain who were trying to stop the rum ration 'are fools, for it is the best thing out here. On a cold morning after a cold night a tot of rum is very good. The dawn is the worst time of the night for cold, and so that is when they have it.'[195] When Ernest Shephard's rum ration failed to arrive on 27 April 1915 he blamed 'newspaper agitation by cranks', and hoped that those responsible would come up the line to supply hot coffee to the troops.

But of course things sometimes went wrong. Private Ernest Parker was sent back from an outpost to draw the rum ration for his section, and:

> returned by mistake with a dixie half full. Matty Parker and the other stalwarts were loud in their praises, but soon became incoherent, retiring heavily into the shelter to fall fast asleep. Fortunately when Captain Pumphrey visited us I challenged him smartly, but to my horror I noted too late that the other sentry was asleep. Corporal Matty Parker was severely reprimanded, but when we came out of the line no one was placed under arrest and we realised that the dear old Bombing Officer had not reported us. In consequence we were all thoroughly disgusted with ourselves.[196]

Gerald Burgoyne was not as forgiving. In March 1915 he found that a platoon sergeant and his corporals had finished off a half-jar of rum intended as a St Patrick's night libation for the whole platoon, 'getting beastly drunk . . . instead of giving each man in the platoon a tot . . . But I'll have 'em for it, the swines.'[197]

Bernard Livermore was grateful that his company sergeant major was kinder. He had enjoyed an early-morning rum ration, made more generous by the fact that there had been many casualties and so there were extra tots, and shortly afterwards an officer, telling him that he looked frozen, gave him a slug of whisky from his hip flask. Then Company Sergeant Major Dawes sent him to battalion HQ with a message.

> Happy, happy day! . . . I strode off briskly but, almost immediately, my legs let me down and I crashed. The CSM came along and found me stretched out full length on the slippery duckboards.
>
> 'I told you to go to the BHQ. What's the matter with you?'
>
> 'Don't know, Major . . . slipped on duckboard . . . just can't get up.'
>
> 'How much rum did you have?'
>
> 'Quite a nice lot, Major. Jolly good stuff, that rum.'
>
> 'And I suppose you've eaten nothing since four o'clock last night? I know what's the matter with you.'

He picked me up and dumped me on the nearest firestep.

'Now don't you dare move until you have recovered. If any officer asks what you are doing . . . tell them that CSM Dawes found you ill in the trench and ordered you to rest. Have you got that clearly?
Ordered you to rest!'

A great man, our CSM. If he had run me in for Drunk in Front Line I obviously could not have mentioned the whisky in mitigation of this very serious charge.[198]

A drunken man in a forward trench could be a dangerous liability. In September 1917 a drunken soldier in 13/Royal Fusiliers yelled '"Over the top! Over the top! We're coming for you" before an early morning attack. An officer ordered: "Keep that man quiet." And presently the noise stopped. When I went along the next day I found him, very quiet. Someone had stuck a bayonet into him.'[199] A drunken officer was a more serious liability. When Frank Crozier was commanding 9/Royal Irish Rifles he regarded two other COs as 'a menace to our safety' because of their drinking.

One has just kept me waiting several hours after the relief of the line was complete, during which time I commanded his battalion in action, while finishing his port in billets! The other had become so drunk during a relief of the line that the outgoing colonel refused to hand over to him and remained in command of the toper's battalion until he had slept off his liquor.[200]

Both were relieved of their commands.

On his rounds one night Crozier found one of his company commanders, the brave and popular George Gaffikin, drunk in his dugout.

His eyelids droop, his head bends down. At last I speak. 'Look at me,' I order, and he does so. 'Will you give me your word of honour not to touch liquor again so long as you are with the battalion? I don't care what you do when you are on leave,' I say slowly. 'I will, Sir,' comes the instant reply. 'Right,' I remark, holding out my hand. We go to 'stand-to' together . . . Of course I should have 'run'

Gaffikin; but I knew him and his men. I knew it wouldn't occur again, if he said so. Of course, a court martial could only mean dismissal.[201]

Crozier was right about the court martial. Colonel Nicholson knew a commanding officer who was a regular of eighteen years' service:

He drank, but none of us knew it. His drinking culminated on the night before a battle when he was incapable of issuing orders to his unit. His second in command placed him under arrest; and the general court martial which tried him sentenced him to be cashiered.

An officer court-martialled for such an offence early in the war would be immediately discharged with ignominy, thrust into civilian life shorn of rank and pension. But once conscription was in force he was deemed to be available for service as a private soldier. 'Automatically he was reduced to the ranks and handed over to an APM's [assistant provost marshal's] escort,' wrote Nicholson. 'Thence he went to the base as a prisoner, perhaps in the charge of a lance corporal, where he was posted as a private into another regiment.'[202] Within a few days a man like this went from the peak of commanding a battalion at the front to the trough of being a private soldier in the rear, with guard duties and fatigues, and the juddering pattern of hurry-up-and-wait, all glimpsed through a haze of uncertainty.

BASE DETAILS

The term 'rear' was a relative one. To a man in a front-line trench, company headquarters, perhaps only a hundred yards away, was a safe haven where a runner would often loiter if he could, while to a company commander, battalion headquarters, three hundred yards further back, was a fretful place of sharp adjutants and busy commanding officers with an unyielding concern for ration parties, wire-pickets and leave rosters. The transport lines, with the gruff quartermaster and horsey transport officer, were as far back as a man might go without dropping out of the battalion's orbit altogether. In the transport lines men rarely wore steel helmets, but they did polish their buttons, shoulder titles and cap badges daily, while front-line soldiers were not expected to polish in the trenches. There was a short-lived attempt to dull all brass fittings with acid, but the eventual policy was for brass to be allowed to tarnish in the line but to be shined when men came back from it. Charles Carrington reckoned that his men disliked outsiders in direct proportion to their distance from the wire. There was an elaborate hierarchy, starting with 'the bloody munitions workers at home who were earning high wages and seducing your girlfriend; number four platoon in the next trench who made such a noise that they woke up the enemy gunners . . . and, of course, the staff who could conveniently be blamed for everything'.[203]

A unit out of the line might be accommodated in a purpose-built camp, housed in a large building such as a factory, school or barracks, or billeted on French or Belgian civilians. Camps were a particular feature of the base – the army's sprawling administrative area running up from Le Havre through Rouen to Etaples and its satellites. They initially consisted wholly of tents, but wooden huts quickly made their appearance, first for kitchens, cookhouses, latrines and messes but eventually for sleeping quarters too. The need for cheap and easily-built huts inspired Lieutenant Colonel Peter Nissen of the Royal Engineers to design an oblong hut with a half-round roof which bears his name. The Nissen hut could be assembled by infantry pioneers under engineer supervision, as Corporal George Ashurst of 16/Lancashire Fusiliers discovered early in 1917.

> One NCO and four men were detailed to go off to the next village and learn from the Engineers how to build these sectional huts. I was the NCO selected, and four men, one from each of the four companies, were the biggest duds in the battalion – the four company sergeant-majors, as usual, selecting the biggest dud as a soldier for a working party.
>
> I marched my four men off and we made our way to the next village, where I reported to the officer in charge of the Engineers. At once I was helping and learning how to build Nissen huts, but my men had been sent to a nearby wood and were busy cutting down trees, from the trunks of which were cut the foundations of the huts. The huts consisted of six wooden floor sections placed in position on legs driven into the ground. Then rainbow-shaped iron frames were bolted to the floors. Each end of the hut was then built up in one piece, one end being composed of the door and windows. The roof of the hut was sheets of corrugated iron bolted to the frames and then lined with tongued and grooved timber.
>
> A couple of days with the Engineers and I knew all there was to be known about the building of Nissen huts. On the other hand my men, who had made excellent lumbermen, knew absolutely nothing about the building of huts.

The ignorance of his men led to a run-in with his commanding officer when Ashurst returned to the battalion, but once the unit's pioneers were put at his disposal he quickly put up enough huts to house the battalion, and was rewarded with his third stripe.[204]

Like barracks at home, camps provided social control as well as accommodation, with perimeter fences patrolled by the guard, a guardroom at the main gate and a camp commandant in overall charge, answering to the Lines of Communication staff. These 'scarlet majors at the Base' have had a rough ride from contemporaries and historians alike. Walter Nicholson is, however, right to suggest that most of them – dug-outs or officers worn out at the front – usually did their best with unpromising permanent staff, and were fatally handicapped because they were bound to lack any real bonds with the men passing through their camps. It was the army's 'us and them' at its most extreme.

Transit camps near docks and railheads housed formed units or drafts on their way to or from the front. Most incomers landed at Le Havre, though nearby Harfleur and the Channel ports of Boulogne and Calais were also used, the latter for individuals going to or returning from leave. Some vessels went up the Seine as far as Rouen, especially early in the war, as Corporal John Lucy recalled.

> We steamed in and up the river to Rouen. All who saw us on the way rushed cheering wildly to the river bank, and every flag, public or private, in sight came down at our passing . . .
>
> We had a most embarrassing disembarkation at Rouen. The French overwhelmed us, soldiers, blue-bloused civilians, women and children charged us *en masse* and barely gave us room to form up. They pressed chocolates and flowers on us, and the women kissed us with alarming freedom . . .
>
> Our first camp in France was a misery. We were crowded, thirteen to a tent, and the heavens poured rain on us for hours on end, until the ground became a quagmire, through which we sloshed ankle-deep in mud.[205]

Frank Richards acknowledged that his comrades were not slow to take advantage of this 'alarming freedom', and when his battalion left Rouen the majority of its members 'had given their cap and collar badges to the French ladies they had been walking out with, as souvenirs, and I expect in some cases had also left other souvenirs which would either be a blessing or a curse to the young ladies concerned'.[206]

Brigadier General Count Gleichen (who later changed his name to the more publicly acceptable Lord Edward Gleichen) landed at Le Havre at much the same time. He found that his rank afforded him no protection from the weather, because:

> The ground where we were to encamp was mostly sopping. It was not easy to find in the dark, especially as the sketch-maps with which we had been provided lived up to their names . . . There was of course no baggage, nor anything to sleep on except the bare ground under the tents, with our saddles for pillows; and as a pleasant excitement all our horses stampeded at about 2.00 a.m., tore up their picketing-pegs from the soft ground, and disappeared into the darkness in different directions.[207]

The Irish Guards did not know quite what to make of their enthusiastic welcome. Aubrey Herbert MP was accompanying the battalion in an unofficial status. His tailor had run him up an officer's uniform without badges of rank, and he fell smartly into step as the battalion left its London barracks. On arrival at Le Havre he heard a Coldstream officer announce:

> 'The French are our Allies; they are going to fight with us against the Germans.' Whereupon one chap said: 'Poor chaps, they deserve to be encouraged,' and took off his cap and waved it and shouted '*Vive l'Empereur!*' He was a bit behind the times. I believe that if the Germans beat us and invaded England they would still be laughed at in the villages as ridiculous foreigners.[208]

Over the following months accommodation improved, though it remained relatively spartan. Immediately after he arrived in France with a draft, Corporal Clifford de Boltz marched up the infamous hill out of Le Havre: 'When we reached the top completely exhausted we saw a huge camp composed of tents, 10 men were allocated to each tent which did not give much room for equipment, we lay down like sardines in a tin but being properly exhausted we went to sleep.'[209] The nature of the French welcome had certainly changed by the time Private A. J. Abraham arrived in 1918:

> The natives took no notice of us until we moved off, then a number of children, carrying trays of chocolate, emerged from doorways and alleys, and bore down on us. A bright pretty little girl of about ten or eleven came prancing up to me with her tray ... She quoted me one franc for a slab of a make unknown to me ... and I was able to produce the correct amount. A man in front of me called to the same girl as she turned away from me and said that he would like a similar bar. She handed him one and he proffered half a crown which she snatched and immediately skipped away without offering him any change. As a franc of that time was equivalent to ten pence she had got herself a dissatisfied customer and he called out to her 'Here, what about my change?' This sweet little girl replied 'Garn you fuckin long barstid' and galloped off to another part of the column ... Of course we only met blood-suckers but I soon learnt not to trust any French man, woman or child ...[210]

From Le Havre troops went forward by train, direct to railheads behind the front if they had arrived as formed units or trained drafts. Although officers could expect proper passenger carriages, soldiers travelled in:

> large covered trucks with sliding doors marked on both sides *Hommes 40 – Chevaux 8!* Although we had very little moving about with fifty *hommes* in one truck we wondered whether every *cheval* took up five times as much space as one *homme* and his kit ... we trundled along very very slowly, we were side-tracked into shunting yards to allow more important traffic to pass through, there was no proper opportunity to have a proper kip down even when a journey of less than a hundred miles could take two and even three days. Waits at stations en route seemed interminable especially at night. The British RTOs [Railway Transport Officers] must have had a nightmare of a

job especially as units to which reinforcements were due to arrive were often moved so quickly as to be unable to give notice of the change.[211]

Private Abraham adds that:

> There were no facilities on the train, whenever we came to a halt men would jump down from the trucks and scramble up the embankments or make for bushes behind which to relieve themselves. Without warning the train would start to move and heads would pop up from bushes or long grass and men, hurriedly pulling up trousers, would come scrambling back into their trucks. I never saw anyone left behind.[212]

Stuart Dolden found himself even worse off.

> There were ten of us in a truck, together with eight heavy draft horses. There were four horses at each end and we were in the middle. Things looked fairly promising – but oh, 'What a night we had!' Soon after the train started the horses became restive, and at every jolt of the train there was a commotion. Every now and then one of the animals would stretch out its neck and 'playfully' try to catch one of us by the ear, or anything handy. After one especially severe jolt one of the horses fell down, and as they were closely packed it was only with great difficulty that it was possible to get it on its feet again ... Just as this horse was on its feet again, another animal fell over, and at this point the only candle alight in the truck was knocked over by another enterprising beast. Pandemonium ensued, and a stampede seemed inevitable. We, who were not in charge, took refuge on the footboard outside the truck. The drivers set about the animals and eventually restored quiet.[213]

Drafts not destined to go straight to units – the majority of men arriving in France from mid-1916 – went instead to Etaples and its surroundings, the unwelcoming world of the base depots. Between June 1915 and September 1917 over a million officers and men passed through Etaples on their way to the front.[214] Historians often write as if there was a single 'Bullring' at Etaples, but there was not.

Instead, the area east of the River Canche was paved with a mosaic of numbered infantry base depots, general hospitals and convalescent camps, and the sandy area north of the depots themselves had a long line of training compounds. Charles Douie remembered 'a great wilderness of tents and buildings. For mile on mile the camps stretched along the dunes. I was awed at the vast array which spoke of the growing might of the British Expeditionary Force.'[215]

Dotted amongst huts and tents were numerous canteens which sold food, soft drink and necessities such as writing paper and soap, at near cost price, or even distributed them free. Many letters home, now nestling in archives, bear the red triangle of YMCA note-paper, testifying to its importance for young men deeply anxious to communicate with home. Bernard Livermore looked back on these canteens with enormous gratitude.

> How the various Red Cross, Salvation Army, YMCA and other organisations did their utmost to help us, as, indeed, they did through our long 'Cook's Tour'. They made Army life, on Active Service, more bearable; we were all deeply grateful for the comforts which they had provided for us. Their huts, sometimes situated uncomfortably near the fighting line, were always crowded. Food, drinks, free writing paper, games and recreation helped at all times to relieve our depression, to rest our weary bodies and improve morale.[216]

The term 'bullring' originated in the troops' suspicion that they were being goaded into performing their drills by the permanent staff (known as 'Canaries' because of their yellow armbands) for the amusement of onlookers. There were other bullrings too. Anthony French found himself based at a depot at Le Havre, known as 'The Pimple':

> The Pimple near that historic base camp was a pilgrim's daily progress to a sort of Spartan battle school ... The precise gradient ratio of the Pimple was a matter of conjecture. The men who marched up that slope at attention on fourteen successive mornings graded it in unscientific terms. It led to the land of the Canaries. These were

regular instructors with yellow arm bands and penetrating voices.

The Canaries were a thoroughgoing lot. They were not satisfied with the reports of home battalions on the quality of their drafts. They were there to prove all things. They did this by cutting their trenches uncommonly wide and profoundly deep, by withholding the order to remove gas masks until the wearers were obliged to eat, by studiously arranging for all running courses to be uphill, by loading the men with supplementary ammunition and by the effective use of extensive military vocabularies. Our evenings were spent recuperating in the camp canteen, in salving abrasions, repairing damage arising from misdirected bayonet thrusts and writing letters home . . .

On the fourteenth day we were pronounced soldiers in the making and pronounced fit to reinforce our respective regiments in the line. At that stage I could have felled an ox with my rifle butt. Thanks were doubtless due to the Canaries but familiarity had bred contempt for both them and their Pimple. Never after that did the firing line seem so desirable as it did during that fortnight.[217]

Bernard Livermore went through the bullring at Harfleur. He recalled it as:

A vast expanse, covered with small parties of men performing various antics, all with the same end in view. We practised the most deadly, the most efficient methods of killing, or avoiding being killed. This tough finishing school was as near to the real thing as possible; stretcher-bearers stood by to cart off those unfortunates who were accidentally maimed. We rushed, with raucous yells, and stabbed straw-stuffed bodies. In . . . Out . . . On Guard. On we raced and jumped down 8ft trenches, scrambling out as speedily as possible to avoid the bayonets of the following wave. We chucked our Mills Bombs out of the trenches without mishap and learned how to fire rifle grenades and other weapons. We ran, as quickly as we could, through the dreaded Gas Chamber . . . Sheer luck saved some of us from these training hazards. On two days

I was detailed for cookhouse fatigues, a tedious and boring job doing all the work for the Sergeant Cook. He 'took a fancy' to me and said that I was a good worker. He said that if I could produce a fiver he was willing to 'use his influence' to get me a permanent base job on his staff. Rather indignantly I tried to refuse this kind offer and mentioned that I had come to fight, not to peel his spuds for the duration. 'Well, no offence meant and none taken I'm sure. But, marks my words, you'll soon be wishing you had a nice cushy job down here. It ain't too cosy up in the trenches, but there is no accounting for taste.'[218]

Stuart Dolden was encamped on the racecourse at Rouen.

The camp held about eighty thousand men, and included an Indian section and hospitals. We spent a month there during which the usual training was carried out. On the Cavalry parade ground about a mile from the camp, trenches and dugouts had been made with barbed wire entanglements in front, and there we carried out those weird and wonderful manoeuvres pertaining to Army warfare . . .

Efforts had been made to beautify the camp, and in front of the officers' quarters little gardens had been planted with flowers and vegetables, and in some cases regimental crests and badges had been worked with various pieces of coloured glass to give an artistic touch.

The water supply was somewhat erratic, a serious matter . . . because it meant that if one was absent at the proper time it would be hours before you could get a wash . . . A good deal of our spare moments were spent in the YMCA hut where we were able to obtain refreshments, play billiards and from time to time listen to concerts arranged by the various regiments and allies.[219]

In 1915 the Reverend Pat Mc Cormick was a padre at the Rouen base camp; and, with two of his colleagues, was a regular feature in camp concerts singing his party piece 'Three Jack Johnsons' – Jack Johnson being a popular term for a heavy shell, named after the famous black heavyweight boxer. One hopes it was funnier then than it seems now.

> Three Jack Johnsons
> Hark how they bang!
> They went overhead with a terrible whine;
> They kicked up a dust and a terrible shine;
> They made the three parsons go cold in the spine;
> The three Jack Johnsons!

Mc Cormick made a point of speaking to all drafts when their training was complete, before they set off to the front. He gave them 'a short talk of encouragement, a prayer and a blessing – immediately after which the command to form fours was given and off they marched to the station'.[220]

Although living conditions were better for officers, their training at the base camps was still tough. In August 1917 Joseph Maclean wrote:

> Today we had a hard time in the bull-ring. In the morning we were twice over their famous 'final assault course' in full equipment. It is a series of rushes from trench to trench, the intervening space being strewn with barbed wire, high wire, shell holes etc, and they have fellows throwing huge fir cones at you all the time to represent bombs.

Anyone found chewing gum had to run at the double to the top of a nearby hill, known as Mount Spearmint. And there was the usual rough 'humour' from instructors, such as the Black Watch bombing officer who showed them a Mills grenade, and warned: 'If this hits ye, ye'll have an awfu' bother putting yourself together at the resurrection.'[221] Some students proved the truth of his words all too quickly. When Robert Graves was an instructor at Harfleur he heard a sudden crash just after he passed a table laid out with various types of hand grenade.

> A sergeant of the Royal Irish Rifles had been giving a little unofficial instruction before the proper instructor arrived. He picked up a No. 1 percussion grenade and said: 'Now lads, you've got to be careful here! Remember that if you touch anything while you're swinging this chap, it'll go off.' To illustrate the point, he rapped the grenade against

the table edge. It killed him and the man next to him and wounded twelve others more or less severely.[222]

Graves noted that by late 1916 instructors at the bullrings were:

> full of bullet-and-bayonet enthusiasm ... Troops learned ... that they must HATE the Germans and KILL as many of them as possible. In bayonet-practice, the men had to make horrible grimaces and utter blood-curdling yells as they charged. The instructors' faces were set in a permanent ghastly grin. 'Hurt him, now!' 'In the belly! Tear his guts out!' they would scream, as the men charged the dummies. 'Now that upper swing at his privates with the butt. Ruin his chances for life! No more little Fritzes! ...'[223]

Alan Hanbury-Sparrow agreed that: 'It was all the rage, this brainless bayonet-fighting.'[224] But Lieutenant R. F. Calloway, a priest who had served as a chaplain before taking a combatant commission, found it all quite inspiring. After a lecture on 'The Spirit of the Bayonet' by Lieutenant Colonel Ronald Campbell, the army's leading ideologue of bayonet fighting, he told his wife that it was 'extraordinarily good, but to me the interest of the lecture lay not so much in the lecture itself as what the lecture stood for – the entire conversion of our whole attitude of mind as a nation ... if the war is to be fought we must fight to kill'.[225] (Calloway was killed on the Somme at the age of forty-four.) Lieutenant C. P. Blacker asked an officer responsible for training bayonet-fighting instructors how many of his qualified instructors had actually bayoneted anybody. 'Very few,' he admitted. 'But we don't insist on their telling the strict truth when asked that question.'[226]

The chief complaint about the bullrings was not the quality of their training. Indeed, although Clifford de Boltz wrote that ... the 'NCO instructors were real martinets' he thought that 'the training undoubtedly did us good although we did not think so at the time'.[227] It was their stark dehumanisation at a time when men were steeling themselves to face what lay ahead. And it was their remorseless imposition of the same soulless programme upon eighteen-year-old recruits and forty-five-year-old combat veterans: after mid-1916 all but a fortunate few went up the line by way of the bullrings, whether it was their first trip to France or whether they were wounded being recycled through the training machine. Graham Seton-Hutchison, regular subaltern in 1914 and machine-gun battalion commander at the war's end, was unquestionably a hard man. But he was convinced that the bullrings actually did more harm than good. He had no time for

> chaotic marshalling to the whim of some witless NCO. Bullies too, yelling illiterate unanswerable personal abuse . . . A thousand meaty fellows, without the humours of the circus, shouted 'We're lion-tamers 'ere!' while volunteers, young men glowing with the first flush of patriotic pride, and older men already enjoying respectability, were harassed and pushed, marching, counter-marching, in fulfilment of some ill-tempered whim – by 'staff blokes' glued like limpets to what were known as 'cushy jobs'.[228]

He believed that soldiers joining their units from the bullring needed to have their self-respect restored and to be treated like the comrades they were. Henry Williamson went through the bullrings, and put a thinly-fictionalised account of them in his novel *Love and the Loveless*. 'There was something damnable about a Base system which treated old soldiers, some with two or three wound stripes, as though they were new . . .', opined his hero Philip Maddison. 'The brass-braided wound-stripers, half dead inside their heads, three quarters of their courage expended with the death of old comrades muttered to themselves. Loos – Somme – Langemarck – they'd had enough. Keep the bullshit for the rookies, who do they think we are?'[229] Second Lieutenant Wilfred Owen froze the blank stare of the bullring for posterity, writing to his mother on 31 December 1917.

> But chiefly I thought of the very strange look on all faces in that camp; an incomprehensible look, which a man will never see in England, though wars should be in England; nor can it be seen in any battle. But only in Etaples.
>
> It was not despair, or terror, it was more terrible than terror, for it was a blindfold look, and without expression, like a dead rabbit's.[230]

* * *

There were many small-scale outbreaks of collective indiscipline in the British army of the First World War. Many might best be called strikes, because they occurred in 1918–19 and represented the firmly-expressed desire of citizen soldiers, who had been perfectly prepared to 'do their bit', to go home now that the war was over. Some of these strikes were certainly serious: in late January 1919 a strike at Calais effectively paralysed part of the base organisation. However, there were only three major mutinies amongst British troops on the Western Front: an outbreak in 12/South Wales Borderers in January 1916; another in a trench-mortar battery of 38th Division in September 1917; and one at Etaples in the same month. In addition there was an outbreak of indiscipline at Blargies military prison, near Amiens, in 1916, and an Australian mutiny in October 1918 when worn-out men refused to go up the line. Given the scale of mutiny in other First World War armies this testifies to the remarkable malleability of the British soldier. And the Etaples mutiny, in particular, demonstrates that it was generally resentment at what was seen as unfair treatment, rather than class tension or anti-war spirit, that drove men to disobey.

The Etaples mutiny came as no surprise to many experienced officers: Charles Carrington called it 'a reaction against acts of petty tyranny by tactless officers. It was always believed at the time that it began in the mixed camps where men of all units exchanged complaints and did not know the officer in charge.'[231] Captain Cyril Mason of the 60th Rifles agreed that:

> There is no doubt that the men had grievances. A base camp is utterly different from one's own battalion, where officers and men are known to each other. In a base camp the men are constantly passing through, sometimes only staying a couple of nights ... The permanent staff of officers is small. They are supposed to be helped by officers passing through, but officers passing through for one or two days cannot really be much help. In a base camp much of the routine work devolved onto the permanent base NCOs, some of whom abused their position taking bribes for privileges and leave passes into Le Havre. This, and the tension of waiting for orders, made base camp an unpleasant experience for men in transit.[232]

The mutiny began on 9 September 1917 when a military police-man arrested a New Zealand gunner. The gunner was soon released, but a crowd gathered and Private H. Reeve of the military police maladroitly fired his revolver, mortally wounding the well-respected Corporal W. B. Wood of 4/Gordon Highlanders, an innocent bystander, and also hitting a nearby Frenchwoman. There was a large-scale riot that evening, with Australians and Scots conspicuously involved in attacks on military policemen; there was a general exodus to visit the freshpots of Etaples, with further outbreaks of rioting in the days that followed.

Lieutenant Ernest Parker observed that the rioters reserved their hatred for the Canaries: 'they had no quarrel with fighting officers and during our leisure we went over to Paris Plage every day unmol-ested by the mutineers'.[233] A battalion of the Honourable Artillery Company succeeded in getting things under control on Thursday 13 September, and although some men broke camp the following day, the worst was over. Private Percy Croney believed that 'the government will be hushing the whole thing up, not wanting generals in France – who would sit on the courts martial – to find out how their men are tormented in the Bull Rings before coming up the line'.[234] In the event, only four men were actually charged with mutiny (though there were many lesser charges), and one, Corporal Jesse Short of 24/Royal Northumberland Fusiliers, was shot for mutiny.[235]

The most recent work on capital courts martial concludes that the mutiny at Etaples left some officers at general headquarters 'severely rattled'.[236] It certainly emphasised what experienced officers already knew well: discipline ultimately relied on the consent of the governed. During the retreat from Mons, Alan Hanbury-Sparrow realised that 'discipline cannot go farther than public opinion allows'. The collective opinion of most units generally supported discipline, although, as we shall see, there were aspects of it – most notably the hated Field Punishment No. 1 – which were bitterly resented. Above all the unit structure, so often imperilled, but so rarely shattered, by the impact of casualties, knitted men together. 'We were banded together by a unity of experience that had shaken off every kind of illusion, and which was utterly unpretentious,' thought Charles Carrington. 'The battalion was my home and my job, the only career I knew.'[237] The bullrings never wove these bonds of mateship, and remained, first to last, something purely mechanical in an army that relied on alchemy to turn its raw metal into gold.

For most soldiers the base remained a staging post between Blighty and the unit. Even if they went forward from the base rebadged and in drafts to a new regiment, they generally adjusted to their new identities quite easily. There were sometimes teething troubles, especially in the case of officers who were 'attached' to their new units rather than formally commissioned into them. I. G. Andrew was commissioned into the Cameronians after surviving Loos as a lance corporal in the Cameron Highlanders. He blew his £50 uniform grant on khaki doublet and Douglas trews made by the best tailor in Glasgow, regarding it as 'an extravagance I never lived to regret.' However, after his turn in the bullring early in 1916 he found himself posted, with some other Scots officers, to a Staffordshire battalion which had lost heavily on the Somme. Its commanding officer told the newcomers to dress as Englishmen, but they held a meeting and refused, as was their right. The wise adjutant put it more mildly, as a request, and while 'we objected to being ordered to divest ourselves of our emblems, we didn't mind being asked'. Andrew was wounded going up the line not long afterwards and then posted back to the Cameronians, so doublet and trews earned their pay after all.[238]

Units out of the line but within earshot of its monotonous rumble generally lived in billets. The pattern of accommodation resembled that of the staff, with large farms holding a company or two, or whole battalions scattered across big villages or in small towns, or in rest camps behind busy sections of the front like Ypres or the Somme. Camps were sometimes comfortable. In November 1917 Frank Dunham's battalion was: 'marched to Aubrey Camp, situated on the roadside between Roclincourt and Arras . . . Our camp was compact and cosy, and for the first time were were in what were known as "Cupola huts" or "Nissen huts". These had wooden floors and were quite wind- and weatherproof.'[239] But before Nissen huts became general there were some less attractive buildings, as Lieutenant V. F. Eberle discovered:

We have fetched up in a so-called camp. To get in or out of it we have to walk through liquid mud which in places comes over the top of our boots. We occupy skeleton-framed greasy huts of wood with old canvas stretched over it. The floor consists of greasy mud. At 4 a.m. this morning steady streams of water descended on eight recumbent forms – came snorts and cussing as they rose and gazed at the descending rivulets. Then somebody laughed and the situation was saved. Everything has become wintry and wet now; sheets of rain and all around us a sea of mud.[240]

However, many infantrymen preferred the worst camp to the best trench. Bernard Livermore thought that:

Our rest camps in that beautiful wood at St Eloi [behind Vimy Ridge] seemed like paradise after hell. We slept for hours in long huts with tiers of chicken-wire beds. We spent the next day clearing up, washing ourselves and our filthy shirts, socks and pants. A good breeze dried them sufficiently to make them wearable again. Our puttees and trousers were caked with dry clay and required hard brushing (with our hairbrushes) to recondition them. Letters and parcels were distributed . . . These brief holidays at Mont St Eloi were most welcome after spells in the line, but passed all too quickly. If we were not practising some stunt for the future, we had plenty of fatigue work to keep us occupied. We were usually tired by the end of the day, but it was good to climb into the tiers of beds, with chicken-wire mattresses, and wonderful to be able to take off our heavy boots before we settled down to kip.[241]

Billets were arranged through the French liaison officers, attached to each unit, who worked with British billeting officers. John Reith gives a good idea of how the system worked early in the war:

The Battalion was billeted in the villages of Helfaut and Tilques. Transport in the former. We set our carts in two rows on a kind of village green, the horses were picketed, watered and fed, and I went along to the local *mairie* where Battalion HQ had been established. I was handed a slip of paper: '*Commune d'Helfaut. Rue Camp. Maison de Mdlle*

*Obert, Julia. Nombre d'officiers à loger, 2 Nombre d'hommes –
Nombre de chevaux –* 7. *11. 14. Le Maire, E. Meynin.*' And
on the top 'Lieut Reith, Lieut Workman.' The house indicated was a small farm on the edge of the green.[242]

The system did not always work this smoothly, as Lieutenant Roe
discovered.

> We arrived in the pouring rain after dark one evening.
> Our billeting officer pointed to a farm area and pointed
> out where we were to spend the night, only to be told that
> some other unit had got there first. Our claim having been
> jumped, there was no other sheltered accommodation
> available . . . All the remonstrations of our billeting officer
> and our natural indignation were of no avail, so we just
> marched into an orchard.[243]

The inexperienced Second Lieutenant Guy Chapman was sent
ahead by rail to prepare a billeting plan for his battalion, 13/Royal
Fusiliers.

> At length . . . our train came to a considered halt . . . I was
> given a bicycle and told to follow the brigade billeting
> officer. We rode in silence down silent roads, colourless,
> wreathed in mist. At last at the entrance to a village he
> dismounted. 'This is Nortlenlinghem. You've got the
> whole village. Put your men where you like and don't wake
> the *mairie.*' . . .
>
> I walked to the crossroads and in the waking dawn
> looked up and down. Everywhere there was silence; not
> even a cock crowed. Faint misgivings as to whether I was
> or was not in the war zone beset me. It was better to be
> on the safe side. Unbuttoning my holster and loosening
> my revolver I strode into Nortlenlinghem and began to
> explore. A charming village with well-built houses and
> barns. Trees heavy with fruit bowed over walls . . . A lean
> cat came out, yawned and was friendly. A dog broke
> into passionate yelps. I chalked signs and numbers on
> doors. Still not a gun fired, not a rifle. Where was this
> fabled war?

At last there was the sound of marching feet and the battalion came in sight. I reported to the adjutant.[244]

Private Anthony French remembered that his billeting officer was 'a young and case-hardened lieutenant of exceptional thoroughness', who would move ahead of the battalion with his party, chalking numbers on doors.

> When the head of the column entered the village he would be standing there on the crown of the road, arm pointing significantly to billet number one. The first platoon would wheel mechanically towards it. Then the leaders of the next platoon would follow his steps with expressionless eyes and wait for his arm to be raised. And so till the last small group, the men who had fallen by the way but were still afoot, still in step, dragging one foot behind the other.[245]

Private Harry Ogle describes the process of moving into one of the big farms that dotted the landscape like 'weights on a green picnic cloth'. His battalion was marching at ease, pipes and fags on, and rifles anyhow, until it approached its destination and formality descended.

> The order has just been given to march to attention and the platoon wheels and marches in. As the farmyard within is occupied by the manure pit, a pump and a dog kennel, they halt in the passage. 'Number Twelve Platoon, halt. Left turn. Your billet is the barn in front of you. The garden and the orchard behind it at the gable end of the house and behind it is out of bounds. The pump must NOT be used for drinking, but it has other uses. The water cart is at Company headquarters just across the road you marched in by and its water must NOT be used for washing. Company cooker and stores are in the same yard. I have instructed Sergeant Talbot to see that any serious cases of sore feet or toes must go for treatment to Sergeant Major Cooper who will be at Company Headquarters at Seven pip-emma [signalese for p.m.]. And WASH 'EM first! . . .'
>
> The platoon streams in through a side door in the

passage . . . As the men enter, one of the corporals stands by the door. 'Hunt and Hurslton, orderly men. Rogers and Ogle, draw rations. Foss, Lines, Parsons and Wallsgrove, blankets.' In the barn the men are dumping or hanging up their equipment. 'Shears, save a place for me – here's my stuff – I'm off for the char.' 'Right-oh, Eric.' Shearsby pulls out Hunt's groundsheet, spreading it out with one end against the timber wall-sill. Then he places the equipment, pack and all, at its head and folds the groundsheet over it to keep it clean and allow movement on the floor. Private Teed unrolls his to full length, removes his puttees and loosens his boot-laces, then lies with his head on his pack, blissfully inhaling the smoke of a Woodbine. Just then Lance Corporal Plummer comes in saying, 'There's an old piece of tarpaulin over in Headquarters yard and it'll just do to stretch over those little holes in the wall. Come with me, Artie, and I'll show you before the guard's mounted!'

Meanwhile orderly men and ration carriers are crossing the road with the big black Dixie of tea and soon they are heard shouting, 'Tea up! Char!' By the time they enter the barn the platoon is ready with mess-tins or enamelled mugs. Before they are all served the blanket men arrive with their rolls of ten and throw them down while they get their tea.[246]

Billets came in infinite variety. In one barn Ernest Parker's comrades discovered 'an enormous barrel of cider. Round the barn hung great clusters of apples, while the next building in the village displayed an ancient rusty sign inviting us to sample the beverages of France.'[247] Frank Hawkings, in a part-ruined village closer to the line, helped convert a damaged house in the Belgian village of Voormezeele into a guardroom.

We have selected a café on the other side of the road, the outside of which we spent the morning fortifying with barrels of rubble. It has no roof, but the upper floor still exists. This afternoon we roamed about the village, looting furniture for the guardroom, and now, I must say, it looks very comfortable with carpets, easy chairs, pictures and tapestries on the walls and in one corner we have a pedestal on which is a large vase of roses.[248]

Lieutenant Roe once found his 'billet and the platoon office in the local public house, the saloon bar having been cleared to make this possible'.[249] Gerald Burgoyne described a March 1915 billet which was far less welcoming:

> The farmer and his wife curmudgeons, everything filthy; we slept in our 'flea bags' in preference to the dirty, filthy bed in the room. The farmer's wife won't lend us a brush to sweep the floor, or to clean up, and everything is perfectly beastly. We managed to get a bit of bread from one of our men, and we had some cocoa with us, so we had a meal of sorts, of cocoa, bread and butter and jam and a slab of very heavy rich iced cake. However, even that did not spoil our sleep. We turned in just after 2 a.m. I woke at about 6 a.m. and dozed off till 10 a.m. when I forced my servant to bring me a bucket of hot water, and I wanted it as I am getting itchy in my arms and am 'afeerd'.[250]

Later the same month Burgoyne reported of another billet that: 'the three other officers of my company and myself sleep and live in a tiny room 13 feet by 12 feet. On the floor are a double mattress and a single mattress (for Father) and the boy sleeps in a corner huddled up in a teaspoon of straw. However, he is young and has only just joined.'[251]

Officers might eat in a single battalion officers' mess, but often the companies were too widely spread to permit it and they messed by companies instead. Regular officers such as Walter Nicholson and Rowland Feilding preferred battalion messes, arguing that it was hard for a commanding officer to keep an eye on his officers if they messed by companies, and in a small company mess casualties could have a particularly dispiriting impact. Gunner officers, their batteries habitually more widely spread than infantry companies, usually messed by batteries. Subalterns generally preferred smaller messes because of their relative informality. When Julian Tyndale-Biscoe returned to France in 1917 after being wounded, he was accommodated in an artillery brigade mess, whose secretary announced: 'I want all my officers to wear moustaches and not look like a lot of smooth-faced flunkies.' 'I am afraid I can't oblige him,' wrote Tyndale-Biscoe, 'unless I wear a false one.'[252] When Robert Graves joined 2/Royal Welch Fusiliers another subaltern warned him that:

> Only officers of the rank of captain are allowed to drink whisky or turn on the gramophone. We've got to jolly well keep still and look like furniture. It's just like peacetime: mess bills are very high; the mess was in debt at Quetta last year, so they're economising now to pay that back. We get practically nothing for the money but the ordinary rations, and we aren't allowed to drink the whisky.[253]

Accounts of life in these company and battery messes run like a solid thread through officers' letters and diaries. P. J. Campbell, not long out of school, had served an unhappy apprenticeship in an ammunition column before joining his first field brigade and being posted to one of its batteries. He was warned 'not to take any liberties' with Edward, the senior subaltern, such as 'calling him by his Christian name for one thing, he keeps that for his friends'. Campbell had arrived to replace an officer who had been killed, and Edward resented the fact that 'I had usurped the place that Geoffrey had once had. I was riding his horse . . . sleeping in his bed, sitting in his place in the mess.'[254] Another new officer, Josh (regarded as an old man at thirty-two), was married, and was endlessly questioned by the other subalterns, virgins to a man, as to how one actually went about sex.

When C. P. Blacker joined 2/Coldstream Guards from the 4th Battalion in 1918 he was posted to No. 1 Company.

> The company mess was located in a Nissen hut whither I was led. A sort of trellised arbour had been erected outside the entrance, giving some shade from the midday sun. Here some officers were sitting in shirtsleeves. Among them was Tom Barnard, who introduced me to the others . . .
>
> 'Teddy' Watson-Smythe, as he was universally called, was a young-looking and intensely sociable man of middle height some two or three years older than myself. He was well off to the point of opulence and had extravagant

tastes in food and dress . . . The officer most in gear with Watson-Smythe was Tom Barnard . . . He was two-sided. On one side he was off-hand, arrogant and conceited; on the other amusing and engaging . . . Artifice may have been needed (as it is needed by most of us) to conceal misgivings at the core.

G. C. L. Atkinson was a young man who had come from the Bedfordshire Yeomanry and had been awarded a Military Cross for leading a successful trench raid during a recent tour of the line . . . He was known to the world at 'Atters' and showed an interest in boxing . . . A sturdy and dependable officer.

W. R. Scott was a middle-aged man of heavy build who had settled in South Africa and wore a South African War medal ribbon . . . Scott was slow in thought, and in speech somewhat hesitating . . . The other two officers were F. D. Bisseker who had come to the regiment at the end of October 1917 and W. Jackson. Before the war Bisseker had held a responsible post in the Imperial Tobacco Company and had lived in China. I recall him as a quiet retiring man . . . Jackson was a nice-looking young man without inhibitions. He was anxious – perhaps over-anxious – to be friendly with everyone and made the mistake of calling everyone by their Christian names too soon.[255]

Officers lived and died in the company of brother officers like this, gathered from a wider social group than would have been the case before the war. Although there were no commissioned rankers in No. 1 Company's mess, they were very familiar elsewhere. On 30 October 1914, RSM Murphy, RQMS Welton and CSM Stanway of 2/Royal Welch Fusiliers were all commissioned as second lieutenants. Murphy used to bemoan his fate: 'There was I, a thousand men at my personal control, the Commanding Officer was my personal friend, the Adjutant consulted me, the Subalterns feared me, and now I am only a bum-wart and have to hold my tongue in Mess.'[256] The future Labour politician and prime minister Clement Attlee was serving with 5/South Lancashire in 1918, and contrasted the composition of its officers' mess then with that of the battalion he had joined in 1914. In 1914 most officers came from public schools, and many from Oxford or Cambridge University, but in 1918 there was much greater variety, including a miner and an errand boy.[257]

From February 1916 most new officers were identified by their units and trained at officer cadet battalions in Britain. Promotion was open to talented men regardless of their background. Ernest Shephard, who has featured prominently in these pages as a company sergeant major, was commissioned in late 1916 and killed commanding a company with characteristic competence two months later. George Ashurst (his real ambition was to be an engine driver) was training with an officer-cadet battalion when the war ended. And Clifford de Boltz, a corporal for so long, was in the line when, on 22 March 1918, his company commander received a scribbled note still preserved amongst de Boltz's papers.

> From Ajt to OC D
> Tell Cpl de Boltz to report to Bn HQ to proceed to
> England for commission at once.

He was trained at No. 5 Officer-Cadet Battalion at Trinity College Cambridge. 'Our training was very strenuous,' he recalled, 'with private study up to 9 p.m. each evening.' There was an exam after three months, and students were returned to their units if they failed. There was a final exam, with both practical and theoretical elements, at the end of the course. The war ended before the course ended – he remembered lying hatless but happy in the fountain in Trinity's Great Court on 11 November – and he was commissioned on 2 February 1919.[258]

In 1917 Sergeant Alan Sugden was annoyed not to be put forward for a commission, observing that a man who was recommended 'was no use in the battery and I was'. But he too was sent to an officer-cadet battalion in 1918, and was commissioned early the following year.[259] Sidney Rogerson's fine company sergeant major, Scott, was commissioned, only to be killed in Ireland, and Charles Douie's CSM, Miller, 'the most sturdy and reliable of sergeant-majors', would not leave the company as long as Douie commanded it. 'Not least among the many reasons for regretting the ill-fortune which cut short my command of A Company', lamented Dovie, 'is that Jim Miller applied for and immediately obtained a commission, and died, a subaltern in the South Staffords, north of the Somme, on the darkest day of March 1918.'[260] John Lucy was commissioned, survived the First World War and commanded a training battalion in the Second. He told those who had failed their commissioning boards not to be downhearted for, as his career showed, a man could rise through the ranks.

Some traditionalists found the influx of new officers from diverse backgrounds rather hard to get used to. In September 1915 Captain James Dunn described how a new officer joining 2/Royal Welch Fusiliers fell into a flooded pit on his first visit to the trenches and 'got out unaided except for an apostrophe in the pure dialect of Birmingham'.[261] The same author contrasted two new officers:

> Casson, aged 23, had been at Winchester and Christ Church; he was a sensitive, refined youth, and an amusing gossip. Evans was about the same age, but had not 'enjoyed the same social advantages'. He was very noisy and garrulous, always licked his thumb when dealing cards, and invariably answered 'Pardon?' when any remark was made to him. That 'pardon' became a little trying at times. Equally good when tested, these two merged their social incompatibilities in the end; both were killed on September 26th [1917].[262]

Some Old Army attitudes proved to be stubbornly entrenched: Alan Hanbury-Sparrow wrote in 1917 of the 'somewhat uncouth but very willing officer reinforcements', adding 'You can't make a silk purse out of a sow's ear, but you can make a good leather one.' He insisted on having a 'properly run officers' mess' when 2/Royal Berkshire was out of the line, so that his youngsters would see how things should be done.[263] When James Jack took command of 1/Cameronians, going back to the regimental fold after his tour in command of the West Yorkshires, he immediately insisted that the officers dress in regulation uniform, and presented them all with regimental canes.[264]

There were indeed some distinctive new members of the mess. One of Cyril Mason's brother officers was Johnny,

> a tough subaltern promoted from the ranks . . . At first his general appearance and manner of speaking caused him to

be regarded askance even though he had the Military Medal and one or two other decorations. He wore an appalling gor-blimey hat and talked as if he had spent the whole of his time in a dugout getting other people to do his work. It was all a pose, and in part leg-pulling. He was one of the bravest fellows in existence masquerading as a shirk. He became extremely popular, not only in the officers' mess and throughout the battalion, but also at Brigade where he went as gas officer.

In 1917 they visited another battalion's headquarters dugout during an attack, both dressed as private soldiers. Mason was invited in for a drink but Johnny was mistaken for a private and left outside: Mason had to explain that he was an officer too. When the battalion was in Bonn at the end of the war, Johnny admitted, during a conversation in the mess, to leading a pre-war strike in a Lancashire colliery, adding that he would not have told the story had any officers of the North Lancashires been present, for he had rioted against that battalion. 'Oh I've longed to meet one of you fellows for years,' said a visiting colonel. 'I was a subaltern in the North Lancs in those days and transferred to my present regiment later.'[265]

One of the most obvious social clashes between new officers and old was that while both had servants, only those officers from traditional backgrounds felt comfortable with and knew how they were expected to behave towards their servants. The army's provision of servants for its officers was not wholly a reflection of the pre-war army's social structure, for warrant officers (universally promoted from the ranks) had them too. Strictly speaking officers had servants and warrant officers 'batmen' (the term derived from the French *bât* for pack saddle, or packhorse), but the words became interchangeable. Batmen cleaned an officer's kit, lugged about his valise (canvas and sausage-shaped part sleeping bag, part suitcase), sometimes cooked his food in the line, and often acted as bodyguard and confidential runner. A good servant could free his master's energies for the task of command, and servants make frequent appearances in officers' accounts.

Siegfried Sassoon's batman was Private Flook. 'Flook and I were very good friends,' he wrote, 'and his vigilance for my personal comfort was such that I could more easily imagine him using his rifle in defence of my valise than against the Germans.'[266] Bernard Adams agreed that: 'Our servants were good friends to have behind us, and Dixon was a man in his element.'[267] James Agate's servant was 'of the surly tyrannical sort, half childhood's nurse and half golf-caddy. I go in dread and fear of him. I eat when he thinks I should be hungry and sleep when he thinks I should be tired.' He was horrified when Agate disappeared improperly dressed: 'You do me no credit, Sorr,' he declared, 'rushing off in all your swarth and sweat.'[268] Adrian Carton de Wiart enjoyed the services of Private Holmes, 'a delightful scoundrel' who took him from the field when he had suffered one of his many wounds, materialised aboard the hospital ship, despite having been turned away by the embarkation officer, and then appeared at the officers' hospital in Park Lane. 'I never enquired into his methods,' wrote Carton de Wiart.[269]

After Harry Ogle was commissioned and posted to 1/King's Own he entered his billet, where:

> We found our valises had been unrolled, beds made with our blankets, and everything neat and tidy; at the foot of my bed, a smart, alert but somehow unsoldierlike man was waiting to speak to me or for me to speak to him. He was bronzed, moustached, dark-haired, wiry and of medium build, with a humorous eye and mouth and a very alert expression. This was my batman, Private Cecil Cockerill, in civilian life the manager of a department in a Plymouth store. He was a man of wide interests and knowledge and we soon became good friends.[270]

When Lieutenant Burgon Bickersteth's servant was badly wounded he regretted that he did not know what hospital he was at, 'so I cannot write to him, which troubles me very much'. Edwin Vaughan's batman Private Dunham was indomitable. They were in a captured German pillbox near Langemarck after a hard day's fighting when Vaughan noticed that Dunham was carrying a sack. When asked what was in it he replied stoutly that it was a rabbit that Vaughan had sworn to eat on Langemarck Ridge. However, it was then rather past its best and was jettisoned into the filthy water covering the pillbox floor. Graham Seton-Hutchison lost his batman, remembered simply as Peter, and lamented that: 'The loss of his devotion smote me sorely.' He was 'a faithful servant, a friend and counsellor, an ever-present companion to give me confidence in the darkness of a dangerous night, and good cheer, when fortune favoured a visit to battalion headquarters, and a quick run along the disused tramway from Houplines to Armentières to refresh the company mess-box.' He spoke for many officers when he declared: 'Let us now, who received their ready services, praise batmen.'[271]

Many batmen reciprocated this regard. When Lieutenant Neville Woodroffe was killed at Ypres in 1914 his servant wrote to his mother: 'But there is one I can never forget that is my late Master I shall never forget him. If it had been my own brother I would not feel so sorry as he was more like a brother to me than an officer i[n] c[harge] of me.' Lieutenant Tom Kettle, an Irish nationalist MP, was killed with the Royal Dublin Fusiliers on the Somme, and his batman, an eighteen-year-old Belfast lad called Robert Bingham, wrote to his widow.

> Dear Madam
> Writing to you in respect of my late officer which I have been servant to him since he has been out in France . . . He was a brave officer and he was like a father to me as I am myself an orphan boy . . . I was awfully sorry when God called such a brave man away . . . He told me just before his death that I was going home and he was staying where he was. With that he gave me his watch and I will be willing to forward the watch to you . . . when you write to me as I am not certain of the address . . . I remain yours sincerely, Robert Bingham.[272]

George Coppard joined 6/Queen's in 1914 and was not naturally close to officers there, commenting that the commanding officer 'might have been the Shah of Persia for all that I knew of him'. But in 1915, after his transfer to the Machine Gun Corps, he became servant to Lieutenant Wilkie. 'I soon found out to my pleasure that Mr Wilkie regarded me as a comrade and I grew very attached to him,' he wrote.

He was about twenty years old, had a boyish plumpness
and wore a tricky little moustache which I secretly envied.
I do believe he was the first Scotsman I had ever met that
I came to appreciate and understand, and his brogue
was fascinating to listen to. His home was in Sanderstead,
near Croydon, which provided something in common
between us.[273]

Alfred Hale, snatched into the army from his comfortable middle-
aged, middle-class world, was less impressed. He was posted as an
officers' mess servant to a Royal Flying Corps unit at Bedford, and
found his young gentlemen anything but considerate. 'I cannot help
blaming Captain Ross,' he declared.

If he had been a little less of an almighty tin god, thought
a little less of his own comfort and more of other people's,
things might have been very different. He might at least
have seen that his own junior officers came down at the
right time in the morning, and this set a better example
to the men.[274]

Life in the world of earth and wire was generally uncomfortable
and dangerous, but it was made more tolerable by the pattern of
rotation that kept soldiers on the move between front and rear. And
although men were killed in their trenches, by shells, mortar bombs
or sniper-fire, as well as by the myriad accidents that assail folk
working outdoors with heavy equipment in all weathers, severe
casualties came, not in the drudgery of line-holding, but in the
inferno of battle. Walter Nicholson believed that: 'Trench fighting
goes on throughout the war; but a battle comes like a hailstorm,
mows down a field of corn, and is over for a year.'[275] Let us now
turn our attention to the components of these violent and lethal
storms.

V

STEEL AND FIRE

A MILITARY REVOLUTION

Every picture tells a story. Look at a photograph of a group of British infantrymen at Mons in August 1914, or perhaps on the Aisne a month later. They are combatants defined, like their fathers and grandfathers before them, by a personal weapon. In their case it is the .303-inch Short Magazine Lee-Enfield rifle, just as, for men who fought ninety-nine years before at Waterloo (about 25 miles from Mons and within earshot of its gunfire), it was the muzzle-loading Brown Bess musket. There are only two automatic weapons for each thousand-man battalion. These are Vickers-Maxim machine guns, mounted on a tripod, their ammunition contained in canvas belts and their barrels encircled by a metal jacket containing water to cool the barrel as it cracks out its 450 rounds a minute.

The faces are a mix of old and young: youths in their first enlistment, and recalled reservists who have wet their moustaches in canteens from Dublin to Delhi. Indeed, moustaches are almost universal, as the only excuse for not having one is a boyish inability to grow hair on the upper lip. *King's Regulations* leave no room for doubt: 'The hair of the head will be kept short. The chin and the lip will be shaved, but not the upper lip. Whiskers, if worn, will be of moderate length.'[1] Military uniform has deep psychological symbolism, and amongst its traditional functions are a desire to make its wearer look taller (hence high shakos and bearskin caps); broader (epaulettes);

and more virile (codpieces, sporrans, tight overalls – perhaps reinforced, toreador-style, with a well-placed folded handkerchief-facial hair and pigtails). When two officers in the Accrington Pals shaved off their moustaches before going home on leave in November 1915 Lieutenant Colonel Rickman bellowed: 'Get off my parade and don't come back until they've grown again.'[2]

In the Old Army status had always been defined with deadly elegance. Officers wore well-cut tunics of whipcord or barathea, with buff-coloured breeches and long puttees or tall brown field boots. Badges of rank were worn on the cuffs, stars and crowns framed by a flounce of worsted braid and emphasised by braid bands, one for subalterns, two for captains, three for majors and lieutenant colonels and four for colonels. Sam Browne belts with cross-straps, their glassy sheen the pride of many a batman, supported a .455 Webley revolver on the right hip and a sword on the left. Although fashion favoured the single cross-strap over the right shoulder, some regiments (such as the Oxfordshire and Buckinghamshire Light Infantry and the Cameronians) wore two straps, crossed in the middle of the back and running straight down the front from shoulders to waist.

In the first years of the war the sword was not simply a ceremonial survival. Company Sergeant Major John Clingo of No. 2 Company 3/Coldstream Guards saw two men approach his position at Landrecies on the night of 25 August 1914. They were believed to be French officers, and Private Robson, one of the machine-gunners, rose as they approached, 'when without a moment's warning one . . . whipped out his sword and practically disembowelled poor Robson . . . [but] his assailant had scarcely turned before he and his companion were riddled with lead'.[3] John Lucy saw all the nine officers of two attacking companies hit on the Aisne: 'They fell forward in the advance waving their naked swords.'[4] Lieutenant George Roupell of the East Surreys found his sword useful for walking behind the firing-line, beating men on the backside with the flat and telling them to shoot low. Alan Hanbury-Sparrow ran a German through with his sword at First Ypres, and was wounded seconds later, which might not surprise us. When 2/Scottish Rifles attacked at Neuve Chapelle in March 1915 the commanding officer left it to his company commanders to decide whether swords should be carried, and two decided that they should. At least one infantry officer wore a sword on 1 July 1916, an adjutant who wanted to ensure that he could be easily identified by runners. But by this stage they were clearly obsolete, and a general routine order specified that they should be sent back to England 'securely fastened so that the sword cannot fall out, or become detached from the scabbard'.[5]

Look at a similar photograph from October 1918: the shape and silhouette are different, for the infantryman now resembles not the gamekeeper but the industrial worker. The faces are different, for the average age of senior officers has dropped by about ten years, though while there are twenty-five-year-old lieutenant colonels there are also forty-five-year-old corporals. Half the infantrymen in France are eighteen years old, although all too often young faces frame old eyes. The replacement of the field service cap by the steel helmet, and the wearing of leather jerkins over many tunics, makes the soldiers' silhouette very different to those squared-off outlines of 1914, and there is now a rich iconography of wound stripes, service stripes and brigade and divisional patches on tunics, with some badges painted on helmets too. It is far more difficult to make out the officers. Even those who are wearing officer-style uniforms have moved their badges of rank to their shoulders, in the style condemned by crusty majors of 1915 as 'wind-up tunics'. But most officers eschew uniforms of such distinctive colour and cut when in battles or raids, and dress as private soldiers, perhaps with the addition of stars on the epaulette, but perhaps not.

This was not a popular practice with all officers, some of whom argued that it was important to show style even at the risk of one's life. On 24 February 1917 Captain Graham Greenwell complained that:

> Our new Brigadier, among other fads, has insisted on all officers providing themselves with Tommies' uniforms as a sort of disguise: they are to be worn not only in the attack but in the ordinary trench warfare; it is a sad departure from the 'Nelson Touch' – all decorations won in battle and worn in battle.[6]

Greenwell's brigadier was, however, simply obeying orders. Pamphlet SS 135, *The Training and Employment of Divisions*, declared that 'All infantry officers taking part in an attack must be dressed and equipped exactly like the men. Sticks are not to be carried.' Some officers carried rifle and bayonet in battle early on in the war. When C. P. Blacker was searching for his brother (missing, believed killed), he discovered that 'he had been last seen carrying a rifle and bayonet well in front of his platoon . . . I came back less than hopeful'.[7] A photograph of 1/Lancashire Fusiliers preparing to assault on 1 July 1916 shows a second lieutenant dressed as a private, apart from his single epaulette star. He had evidently just been issued with his tunic, which fits so badly that he has had to turn the cuffs back, and he has not made a good job of putting on his puttees. Later during the same battle a surprised soldier saw his commanding officer go over the top dressed exactly like a private, carrying rifle and bayonet.

Moustaches had become far less common by 1918. In the summer of 1916, when one might have thought that more serious issues were pressing, an officer was court-martialled for persistently shaving the upper lip. He defended himself by saying that he was an actor in civilian life, and shaving off a moustache at the war's end might leave him with a rash on the upper lip which would make it harder to get work. He was duly convicted and sentenced to be cashiered. The adjutant general at GHQ was Lieutenant General Sir Nevil Macready, and the papers passed across his desk on their way to the commander in chief for confirmation of sentence. Macready had never much liked wearing a moustache himself.[8] He did not simply recommend that the sentence be quashed, but had King's Regulations changed, and the wording 'but not the upper lip' deleted from the Army Order 340 (3) of 1916. However, there was to be no fanciful facial hair, and so 'if a moustache is worn no portion of the upper lip is to be shaved.'[9] Many officers and men of the Territorial Force and New Armies had never paid much attention to the moustache regulation in any event. In November 1914 Gunner Bill Sugden reported to his wife Amy that his was coming along well, but: 'I am trying to be photographed with it on. I want to see what you think about it. If you say it is to come off then I shall shave it off.'[10] It did not last the month. Permission to shave the upper lip saw many razors gratefully plied, though not always with a happy outcome. The Reverend Pat Mc Cormick reported that his divisional commander had removed his, but 'it didn't improve him'.

By 1918 some wholly new weapons are in evidence. Pouches bulge with hand grenades, and box respirators are always handy for both sides now use gas as a matter of course. Sentries need to be briefed on wind direction, and wise officers check cellars and dugouts for persistent gas before allowing men to enter. And while there are still plenty of rifles about, some are now equipped to fire rifle grenades, and there are numerous Lewis light machine guns, with fat cooling sleeves round their barrels and flat circular magazines ('pans') on top. Although the Lewis gun cannot provide the sustained long-range firepower of the Vickers, the fact remains that there are more automatic weapons in a single forty-man infantry platoon as in a whole battalion four years before.

And the infantry now has its own artillery. Trench mortars are not part of infantry battalions, but are grouped in companies attached to each infantry brigade. They are mostly inaccurate and short-ranged, but are still capable of dropping their bombs (often the cylindrical 'toffee apple', its 'stick' a spigot that fits down the weapon's muzzle), into the trenches opposite with shattering effect. The Germans had enjoyed an early lead with mortars, the hated *Minenwerfers* ('minnies' to the British), whose slow-moving, fat projectiles blew in whole sections of trench. There were some very primitive British trench mortars in late 1914, developed alongside devices like giant catapults, crossbows and bomb throwers that seemed to owe more to medieval sieges than to twentieth-century war. In early 1915 Captain Newton, then a company commander in 5/Sherwood Foresters, designed several types of mortar which were built at 2nd Army workshops, which Newton later commanded.

By the end of the war there were 2-inch spigot mortars firing the 'toffee apple', 3.7- and 4-inch medium mortars, and 9.45-inch heavy mortars. But the most successful of them all (and the ancestors of the 3-inch mortar of the Second World War and the 81-mm mortar still used by British infantry) were the 3- and 4-inch mortars designed by Wilfred Stokes, managing director of Ransomes of Ipswich, a firm best known for the manufacture of cranes. His weapon was originally rejected because it did not take existing ammunition, but the intervention of Lieutenant Colonel Matheson of the Trench Warfare Supply Department and David Lloyd George, Minister of Munitions, saw it brought into service. 'Mr Stokes's drainpipe' had a fixed firing pin, and its bomb was simply a canister of explosive with a percussion fuse. At the base of the bomb was an extension fitted with a blank 12-bore cartridge, with horseshoe-shaped secondary charges round it to give increased range. When the bomb was dropped down the barrel the primer on the cartridge hit the fixed firing pin and ignited, setting the bomb on its way. It was cheap, simple and murderously effective: over 12,000 Stokes mortars were made during the war.

Heavy trench mortars were the responsibility of the Royal Garrison Artillery, but light and medium weapons were entrusted to infantry trench-mortar companies, still badged to their parent regiments, and often composed of men a sergeant-major was happiest to lose. Because mortar fire generally invited retaliation, mortarmen were not welcome guests in the front line, as Llewellyn Wyn Griffith remembered.

> At night a trench mortar officer set his guns in a derelict trench about twenty yards behind the line and carried up his ammunition, heavy globes of iron with a little cylindrical projection like a broken handle. In the morning I moved the men from the bays between the trench mortars and their target, to lighten the risk of loss from retaliatory fire. A pop, and then a black ball went soaring up, spinning round as it went through the air slowly; more pops and more queer birds against the sky. A stutter of terrific detonations seemed to shake the air and the ground, sandbags and bits of timber sailed up slowly and then fell in a calm deliberate way. In the silence that followed the explosions, an angry voice called out in English across No Man's Land, 'YOU BLOODY WELSH MURDERERS.'[11]

Nor was it good for mortarmen to be captured by soldiers they had recently bombarded. Opposite Fricourt on the Somme, 2/Royal Welch Fusiliers were repeatedly shelled by a mortar firing a two-gallon drum of explosive, which sounded 'like the Day of Judgement' when it landed, blowing in all but the very deepest dugouts. When they took the village they found 'a wooden cannon buried in the earth and discharged with a time-fuse. 'The crew offered to surrender,' wrote Robert Graves, 'but our men had sworn for months to get them.'[12] Nearby a German frantically sought to have his surrender accepted by shrieking '*Minenwerfer* man, *Minenwerfer* man' in the hope that this might make him seem less hostile, but his opponent quietly remarked: 'Then you're just the man I've been looking for,' and ran him through with his bayonet.

The transformation of the army did not stop with the infantry. In 1914 most artillery was close behind the firing line. At Le Cateau on 26 August the 18-pounders and 4.5-inch howitzers of II Corps were pushed right forward into the infantry positions. There was a heart-stopping moment at midday when the decision was taken to withdraw the guns. The six-horse teams, under cover behind a low ridge, galloped forward through the infantry of the second line to recover the guns: soldiers of the Royal West Kents rose to their feet to applaud the self-sacrificing bravery of their gunner brothers. In 1918 field artillery was tucked into folds of the ground behind the infantry, and there was a proliferation of heavier guns, lurking unseen over the horizon, with a power and range that the men of 1914 could never have dreamt of. Forward observation parties of gunner subalterns and their wire-trailing signallers abounded. There were wireless sets at all formation headquarters and some battalions and batteries had them too: cumbersome and unreliable though they were, they were beginning to enable command and control to catch up with the swiftly-accelerating technology of killing. Even some of the aircraft overhead were now fitted with wireless to enable them to control the fire of heavy batteries. Many a visitor to a war cemetery just behind the front line has mused at the apparently incongruous presence of a Second Air Mechanic Royal Flying Corps amongst the graves of RGA gunners. He was in fact their radio operator, linking their 9.2-inch heavy howitzers to an observing aircraft, and running the same risks when counter-battery fire plunged in.

Indeed, by 1918 the air was very busy: one artillery officer reckoned that he could often see fifty aircraft in the sky at any one time. Gone were the few German *Taubes* of 1914, fluttering malevolently over the battlefield, and the even rarer string-and-sealing wax aircraft of the Royal Flying Corps, engaged by harassed

British infantrymen who swiftly came to regard all aircraft as hostile. There was now a wide range of aircraft carrying out the classical functions of air power. Fighters battled overhead to secure air superiority, and to blind the enemy gunners by clearing the skies of his reconnaissance aircraft and observation balloons. Ground attack aircraft (the British were just introducing the Sopwith Salamander, named after the mythical creature which could live in fire) swooped down to bomb and machine-gun front-line positions. Ammunition was dropped (not wholly successfully) to forward units at Amiens on 8 August 1918. Light bombers reached behind enemy lines to attack road and rail junctions in an effort to interdict the flow of men and material to the front. And lastly, though the combatants in France would not have taken much notice of it, strategic bombers, such as German Gothas and British Handley-Pages, reached deeper still, with the German bombing of London, first by Zeppelin and then by Gotha, giving a grim foretaste of horrors of the next war.

Men on the ground were indeed ambivalent about the war in the air. But there was widespread admiration for the courage of individual airmen on both sides. On 7 June 1916 Frank Hawkings reported that: 'A very daring aviator has been flying over the Hun trenches all day. The troops call him "the mad major".'[13] The term was widely used, for Bernard Livermore, miles away in the Vimy sector at much the same time, saw:

> the mad major zig-zagging along in his primitive ramshackle aeroplane. Flying just above our heads, he gave us a cheery wave, climbed quickly into the sky, and departed for a hurried tour of the German trenches in front of Vimy. He dropped very low and emptied his revolver at suitable targets ... Who this courageous chap was we never found out, but he certainly improved our morale.[14]

In mid-1915 Private Raymond Grimshaw of 1/7th West Yorkshires watched a German aircraft lose a brief aerial battle.

> The 'Taube' burst into flames, and dived downwards. We expected to see it crash to the ground but with wonderful skill the German got control of his machine – although it

was blazing furiously and tried to volplane back to his own
lines. He got to within 1,000 feet of the ground, when he
was suddenly seen to jump or fall out of the machine ...
Though he was German we admired the gallant attempt
he made to get back.[15]

Even those whose lives were imperilled by the bravery of German
airmen could not but admire it. Lieutenant Arthur Behrend, spotting
for his heavy guns from an observation balloon, respected the determination of a German pilot who appeared from nowhere to shoot
down three neighbouring balloons. The passengers in the first
jumped clear as it approached.

Two tumbling bodies. Then two parachutes opened and
floated gently earthwards. An anti-aircraft battery opened
up, its white bursts dotting the sky at the right height.
Otherwise its shells were absurdly wide of the mark. The
Taube, unimpressed by them, came in a leisurely if determined way and set the next balloon alight in exactly the
same way as the first. I was pleased to see that he did not
dive to shoot up the parachutists.

Mercifully the plane flew off after shooting down the third balloon.
Behrend noticed that his experienced observer, the one-legged Lieutenant Hoppy Cleaver, checked his own parachute and then stood
expectantly in the balloon's basket rather than on its rim. After they
had landed Behrend asked him why he had done so. 'To throw you
out, of course,' replied Cleaver. 'You were my guest, and I knew you
hadn't the sense or guts to get out yourself.'[16]

Many onlookers found it hard to associate the destruction of a
distant aircraft with the death of its crew. But the reflective P. J.
Campbell recalled how:

Sometimes the plane fell like a stone, but more often it
turned over and over, fluttering to the ground like a leaf
in autumn. I was still unfamiliar with death, and was distressed to think of the man inside, even if he was a
German.[17]

Yet if soldiers on the ground admired the courage of enemy airmen
if it was directed against fellow aviators, they fiercely resented the

bombing of their own rear areas which became increasingly frequent from 1916. Huntley Gordon watched a German fighter machine-gun the lorry holding an observation balloon and then shoot up some nearby horse lines. When it was brought down by British fighters he rushed to the site.

> I got close enough to see the airman as he climbed out of the cockpit, taking his helmet off. He was fair-haired and not more than 19 or 20. If we could have got hold of him we would have killed him. Everyone was savage at the machine-gunning, we being so helpless in the wagon lines . . . a staff car drew up and he was bundled into it. There was an attempt to rush the car, but the sight of senior British officers defending it with their sticks checked us, and the car got away.[18]

There was also a widespread belief that the Royal Flying Corps pursued its own agenda instead of devoting all its energies to keeping German aircraft from attacking British infantry and guns. In an effort to restore confidence, the authorities arranged for infantry battalion and brigade commanders to go on familiarisation flights, but as James Dunn acknowledged, these were not always a success.

> They were done well by in Mess. The joy rides were adventures. [Major] Kearsley was thrown out on his head in landing. In the next course two machines collided, pilot and visitor in each being killed.
>
> The comedian of the air is a pilot transferred from a Highland regiment who will fly in his kilt. In making a bad landing he threw a brigadier out, and himself was caught by the tail of his kilt on the wing of the machine; there he hung, tucked up like the lamb of the Golden Fleece, a bare-breeched Jock.[19]

Adrian Carton de Wiart was interested to discover, after the armistice, that Germans he met thought that their own air force failed to protect them from the depredations of the RFC, and he surmised that the feeling was one of the eternal truths of war.

And yet there was no shortage of volunteers for flying duties. Even men who had seen just how perilous flying actually was were anxious to transfer. This reflected a variety of motives. Captain Dunn thought that 'transfers to the Machine Gun and Flying Corps were much discussed' when his battalion was down on its luck. But many officers and men felt that they had had enough of the trenches and wanted a change. Private Monty Goodban hailed from Clapham High Street, where his father ran a domestic store. Evacuated home after being badly wounded by a grenade in late 1915, he was commissioned the following year, and transferred to the RFC almost immediately. He returned to France in May 1917 after just under twenty-three hours' training, and lasted only twelve days before he was shot down and killed. Aidan Liddell, a scholarly man with a first from Oxford, was already a qualified pilot, and spent a ghastly winter in the trenches as his battalion's machine-gun officer, earning a Military Cross in the process. While on sick leave in Britain he transferred to the RFC. He was awarded the Victoria Cross in July 1915 for an extraordinary display of fortitude in bringing a crippled reconnaissance aircraft home despite hideous wounds, from which he died a month later.

There was cavalry in evidence on the Western Front from first to last, often a good deal more useful than is generally recognised. But by 1918 some of its traditional functions were being undertaken by the tank, a weapon which the men of 1914 would have regarded as so much science fiction. In much the same way that Napoleonic heavy cavalry had charged to break the enemy's line, so heavy tanks crushed wire and crossed trenches, breaching the defensive barrier so that the infantry could pass with relative ease. They moved at a walking pace and were a generation away from providing the key ingredient in the *blitzkrieg* that featured so prominently in 1940–41, but they had already begun to make a difference. And 'whippet' light tanks (we saw something of Lieutenant Arnold's legendary whippet 'Musical Box' earlier) were beginning to take on the cavalry function of exploitation, but although they could move much faster than their heavy cousins they too were prevented, by mechanical fragility and logistic dependence, from making the bold, slashing strokes that came a generation later.

There had been a military revolution between the first and last photograph, a change in the conduct of war as profound as anything that had happened since gunpowder made its noisy and foul-smelling appearance on the battlefields of the late Middle Ages. It compelled all combatants to change doctrine, organisation and practice in order to keep pace, and for the British army (and eventually the American army too), there was the added problem of growing a small peacetime army into a big one for war. There were three distinct elements to the challenge, and theorists would now term them the components of fighting power. The first was physical, involving the weapons and equipment used; the second, so closely related, was conceptual, and concerned the evolution of military doctrine; and the third was human, and centred on the myriad of complex factors that made men fight. Finally, the army's medical services had to contend with problems of their own, as new weapons and tactics proved their terrible capacity to damage body and mind.

BROTHER LEAD AND
SISTER STEEL

The Short Lee-Enfield rifle had entered service in 1902, though in 1914 it had not yet completely replaced its predecessor, the Long Lee-Enfield. The short rifle weighed 8lb 10½oz and was 3ft 8½ins long. Its magazine held ten rounds, quickly loaded in two clips of five rounds each which the soldier thumbed in from above. The Boer War had emphasised just how important marksmanship was, and infantry training paid careful attention to it. Soldiers fired an annual range course on rifle ranges from sandy Aldershot to marshy Purfleet and rocky Glencorse, and this determined their shooting classification. The trained soldier's course consisted of 250 rounds fired at ranges from 100 to 600 yards, with the firer kneeling or lying, sometimes with his bayonet fixed, and with a 'mad minute' when he fired fifteen rounds at a target 300 yards away. Part III of the classification shoot decided a man's marksmanship standard. He fired fifty rounds, from various ranges, at a target with three scoring rings, earning four points for a bull (24 ins wide), three for an inner and two for an outer. The highest possible score was 200 points, and to qualify as a marksman a soldier needed 130 points; 105 made him a first-class shot, and 70 a second-class shot.[20]

Marksmanship did not simply consist of shooting on the range, but also included judging distance and understanding enough theory of small-arms fire to be able to aim off for wind or at a moving target, and to understand what was meant by the 'beaten zone' covered by fire at any particular range. Rifles were zeroed to individual firers, and the rifle's butt number (stamped on a circular brass plate screwed to the stock) was recorded in a soldier's personal record, his 'small book'. Like many soldiers, David Jones grew to love and understand his rifle:

> You know her by her bias, by her exact error at 300, and
> by the deep scar at the small, by the fair flaw in the grain,
> above the lower sling-swivel.[21]

There was far less emphasis on the security of weapons than would later be the case, and keen soldiers spent hours in the barrack room practising loading with drill rounds, checking their point of aim by sighting at an aiming disc held by a comrade, and balancing a penny on the foresight protector to ensure that their trigger-squeeze was smooth: jerk the trigger and the penny would fall off.

In the Old Army officers took shooting very seriously. *Musketry Regulations* ordained that 'Subaltern officers will fire the range practices . . . with their companies.'[22] Major General Tommy Capper, killed at Loos, believed that there were 'few things as disgusting' as an officer who was a second-class shot. When the young George Ashurst, a Special Reserve recruit, scored four bulls and an inner at 600 yards during his training at Brackenber Moor near Kendal, his colonel declared: '"I have never seen such shooting in my life. Nineteen points out of a possible twenty, and by a recruit too. Here, take this, my boy", and he gave me five shillings.'[23] In March 1917 Private Albert Bullock wrote that 'Colonel Peters offered £1 and Coy Officers 10/- to every marksman [but there was] only one marksman.'[24]

Marksmanship badges of crossed rifles were worn by all marksmen below the rank of warrant officer, and there were special distinctions for the best shot in each company or battalion. Good shots received a proficiency bonus, with a marksman receiving an extra 6d a day. This led to a certain amount of fiddling, and old soldiers would often make a point of squaring the man responsible for scoring on their target: small fortunes could be made with a sharply-jabbed pencil. Private Snailham of the Accrington Pals fired his range course 'in the most dreadful wind and rain imaginable. It was a farce. We couldn't see the targets, let alone hit them. By a miracle – or a fiddle – we all passed with good marks.'[25]

Even allowing for the occasional bit of fruitful dishonesty, the musketry scores turned in by the Old Army were remarkable. The commanding officer of an infantry battalion with less than 50 percent marksmen would have an embarrassing interview with his brigadier, and would return the favour, with interest, to his company commanders, who passed the bad news down with added emphasis. Some cavalry regiments were every bit as good, and in 1908 the 14th Hussars had 354 marksmen, 212 1st class shots, thirty-five 2nd class shots and just four 3rd class men. The *Field Service Regulations* of 1909 defined ranges of 600 yards and under as 'close', 600 to 1,400 as 'effective', 1,400 to 2,000 as 'long', and 2,000 to 2,800 (which required a special long-range sight) as 'distant'. An enemy who presented himself at ranges of less than 600 yards to the men of 1914 was in very serious trouble. Corporal John Lucy's men had already stopped massed attacks with their fire at Mons, but found themselves pinned down in the open on the Aisne.

> By lucky chance or instinct I saw the enemy machine gun.
> There it was, mounted daringly on the roof of a cottage,
> about six hundred yards away, and directly to my front.
> With all my strength I shrieked the range, described the
> target, and ordered five rounds rapid fire ... In about
> four seconds some thirty bullets were whistling about that
> dark spot near the chimney as we slammed in our rapid
> fire, glad to have work to do, and gloriously, insanely and
> incredibly the German machine gun stopped firing ...[26]

Marksmanship training of this quality was one of the casualties of the first few months of the war. The army expanded so quickly that old standards could not be maintained. There were too few experienced instructors, too little range-space in Britain, and, at least until early 1916, such a limited supply of rifles that some recruits graduated from wooden dummies, through a series of stopgaps like the Long Lee-Enfield, the Canadian Ross and the Japanese Arisaka, to the Short Lee-Enfield. It took a year for the Accringtons to get their Short Lee-Enfields (SMLEs), and they were luckier than many. By 1917 some drafts had not even seen an SMLE on their training, but handed in their Arisakas when they left Britain and were issued with SMLEs when they arrived at base in France. These weapons had been recycled through the salvage system, which saw many items recovered from the battlefield brought back to the base for repair, renovation and reissue. Albert Bullock arrived at Rouen on 18 September 1917. 'Issued with service rifle and bayonet – got a beauty and made a [highest] possible [score] on miniature range . . .'[27] The miniature range was a 30-yard range, popular at the base and infantry depots because it made the best use of limited space. Nevertheless, it was a mere travesty of pre-war musketry training, and this, with the constant turnover of trained men, meant that for the last eighteen months of the war the once-famed British musketry was probably little better than that of the European armies which, without the imperative of the Boer War, had taken it less seriously. Worse still, in July 1916, 2/Royal Welch Fusiliers received some drafts who had received just six weeks' training, in the course of which they had fired 'only five rounds of ball cartridge' and whose weapon handling was so poor that they were a danger to themselves and others.

The decline of shooting standards in the British army was also an inevitable consequence of the rifle's diminishing utility in trench warfare. In contrast, grenades ('bombs') had become increasingly important. Lieutenant Colonel Croft of 11/Royal Scots saw that on 14 July 1916 his soldiers seemed incapable of hitting the enemy in the open only 200 yards away, and he wrote bitterly that the archers of Crecy would have done far better. Private W. H. A. Groom agreed, admitting that 'troops under counterattack even forgot to use the rifle at long range and waited until the enemy were well within bombing range'.[28] An official pamphlet published in July 1916 warned that:

> It must be realised by all ranks that the rifle and bayonet
> is the main infantry weapon. Grenades are useful for clear-

ing small lengths of trench and for close fighting after a
trench has been rushed; but no great or rapid progress
will ever be made by bombing, and an assault across the
open after adequate preparation will usually be a quicker
and in the long run less costly operation than bombing
attacks on a large scale.[29]

However, many experienced officers recognised that reducing a soldier's reliance on the grenade and improving his marksmanship
could easily become counterproductive in the attack, as it might
encourage a static firefight rather than a decisive assault: there was
a balance to strike.

And this, of course, raised the emotive issue of the role of the
bayonet. The Short Lee-Enfield was fitted with a foot-long sword-
bayonet. Pre-war infantry training manuals described how a company
attacking would be divided into a firing-line and supports. The firing-
line, reinforced from the supports as the occasion demanded, was
to establish fire superiority over the enemy, in a process that generations of British soldiers has come to know as 'winning the firefight'.
Artillery would make its contribution, the object being 'to demoralize
the defenders and reduce the volume of their fire'. However, the
firefight was a means and not an end, for:

> **The object of fire in the attack, whether of artillery, or
> machine guns, or infantry, is to bring such a superiority
> of fire to bear on the enemy as to make the advance to
> close quarters possible . . .** as the enemy's fire is gradually
> subdued, further progress will be made by bounds from
> place to place, the movement gathering renewed force at
> each pause until the enemy can be assaulted with the
> bayonet.

At the appropriate moment the local commander would order the
assault.

> The commander who orders the assault will order the
> *charge* to be sounded, the call will at once be taken up by
> all buglers, and all neighbouring units will join in the
> charge as quickly as possible. During the delivery of the

assault the men will cheer, bugles be sounded, and pipes played.[30]

The bayonet had always been seen as much as a means of injecting psychological shock into the battle as actually killing the enemy, and the main purpose of bayonet training throughout the First World War was to give soldiers confidence to take their steel to the King's enemies. The bayonet generally receives short shrift from historians: for instance in her *Brief History of Killing* Joanna Bourke surmises that bayonet training has survived in armies largely because of their inherent conservatism. The bayonet caused only 0.32 percent of one sample of 200,000 British casualties, although this may be a reflection of the fact that the Germans placed less reliance on it: Charles Carrington affirmed that he had never seen a German soldier with his bayonet fixed. Contemporaries were divided as to its merits. Alan Hanbury Sparrow complained that 'it was all the rage, this brainless bayonet fighting' and said that he had never seen a man killed with the bayonet[31], and Rowland Feilding, another experienced infantry officer, was equally sceptical. Some officers' low regard for bayonet fighting reflected their irritation that training for it took up so much time in depots in Britain and at the base. It was easy to receive drafts well schooled in the short jab and the butt-stroke (essential ingredients of bayonet drill) but ignorant of marksmanship, and this in turn reflected the fact that bayonet training was easy to organise when ammunition and range-space were lacking.

There is no doubt at all that bayonets were used in combat on the Western Front, albeit less often than rifle fire or hand grenades. The battalion history of 2/Royal Welch Fusiliers described 'tense moments with the bayonet' in November 1914, and bayonet fighting on the Somme in August 1916. Aidan Liddell wrote of a night attack on his battalion by 224th Bavarian Reserve Regiment in December 1914. It was pressed home with such careless determination that he believed that the attackers were 'fired up with rum'. As they were in the middle of the battalion's position and 'wouldn't stop firing, they had to be bayoneted. An astonishing show altogether'.[32] A survivor of the Mametz Wood battle told Robert Graves that he saw a soldier of 14/Royal Welch Fusiliers 'bayoneting a German in parade-ground style, automatically exclaiming: "In, out, on guard!"' Graves himself saw the corpses of a man of the South Wales Borderers and one of the Lehr Regiment who 'had succeeded in bayoneting each other simultaneously'.[33] Graham Seton-Hutchison, armed with rifle and bayonet as a company commander at High Wood on the Somme, bayoneted two Germans: 'I was a murderer, breath coming in short gasps, teeth set, hands clenched round my rifle, nerves and sinews tense with life.'[34] When the Welsh Guards attacked Ginchy on 10 September 1916 its men:

> used their bayonets to great effect. 1,656 Pte. William Williams was seen to dispose of several of the enemy, until with a furious thrust he completely transfixed a German and was unable to free his bayonet. He knocked another down with his fists, and seized yet another by the throat, when they both fell into a shell hole. More Germans rushed up, and the gallant Williams did not rise again.[35]

And when 3rd Australian Division took Windmill Hill, near Zonnebeke in the Ypres salient, on 4 October 1917, there was such sustained large-scale bayonet fighting that the Official History commented on the fact.

Charles Carrington illuminated a fundamental truth when he wrote that 'the sword-bayonet was an essential part of our armament even though the deaths it inflicted were few. I never knew the enemy to stand if your men with their long gleaming blades could get within charging distance.'[36] Lance Corporal F. Heardman of 2/Manchester Pals was advancing on 1 July 1916 when:

> I came face to face with a great big German who had come up unexpectedly out of a shell hole. He had his rifle and bayonet 'at the ready'. So had I, but mine suddenly felt only the size of a small boy's play gun and my steel helmet shrank to the size of a small tin lid. Then, almost before I had time to realise what was happening, the German threw down his rifle, put up his arms and shouted 'Kamerad'. I could hardly believe my eyes.[37]

This is a vivid example of what could happen when armed men met at close range on the battlefield: one surrendered or ran away, and determination to take those last few steps was often the deciding factor. But if bayonet training gave men confidence to press on at moments like this, it often went further, and made them reluctant to show mercy.

Frank Crozier argued that the bayonet put killing spirit into a man.

> 'Mercy, mercy,' shouts a German ex-waiter on the left, as he sees the cold steel of a North Staffordshire potter quivering above his head, for he has just been felled by a rifle-butt swing by a Wolverhampton striker of past four-and-forty years. 'Mercy be damned,' shouts the potter, whose blood is up, and he thrusts to the windpipe in the most up-to-date manner.[38]

A soldier in this frame of mind was unlikely to accept surrender, especially if he had something to avenge. In the summer of 1915 Captain Billy Congreve was at Hooge, in the centre of the Ypres salient, and wrote in his diary that:

> They killed a lot of Boches during the attack. The Durhams were especially fierce (the Zeppelin [bombing raids on England] was it, or the cruiser shelling [of east coast towns]?). About fifty Boche were found hiding in the crater and they were all dealt with most unmercifully. Dads [his father, the then Major General Walter Congreve] tells a nice (?) story. He was going round some of the DLI [Durham Light Infantry] – one old man he asked, 'How are you now?' 'I be all right, thank'ee, sir. Slept foine last night, better than night before.' 'Why, how was that?' 'Well, you see, I come to a trench and in I tumbles, roight on top of two other blokes. One of 'em was dead, t'other aloive. The aloive one 'ad a great long whoite beard as long as my granfeyther's!' 'Well, what did you do then?' 'Do!' (unutterable scorn). 'Whoi *do*; put 'un on the point, o'course.'[39]

One soldier on the Somme was so enraged that his best friend had been buried alive by a shellburst that he bayoneted three Germans in a matter of minutes. The Germans, for their part, went round No Man's Land in the sector attacked by the Accrington Pals: 'They kicked one or two of the bodies; any showing signs of life were shot or bayoneted.'[40]

The ever thoughtful Lieutenant C. P. Blacker suggested that however strong the logic for the spirit of the bayonet, it was no easy matter to convert its theory into practice on the battlefield. 'It was, of course, splendid that our forceful corps commander should tell us that the real business of war was done with the bayonet and the rest was mere by-play,' he wrote. 'But bayonets would not stop the autumn rains or dry up the waterlogged crater-fields.'[41] Nor would they stop hostile machine-gun fire or shelling: the pre-war emphasis on the spirit of the offensive had undoubtedly made too much of what the bayonet could achieve in physical terms. Both British and French bayonets began the war with their quillons (the guard between grip and blade) hooked so as to catch the enemy's blade in bayonet fighting, enabling it to be snapped with a smart twist of the rifle. Hooked quillons disappeared during the war as it became evident that elaborate fencing like this would never happen. Yet, start to finish, the bayonet played its part in steeling men to face the battle of the last five yards.[42]

German infantry carried hand grenades at the very start of the war, partly because they expected to have to deal with French and Belgian fortifications. The grenade proved so useful in trench warfare that the British quickly developed their own, though once again they faced the problem of introducing new weapons at precisely the same time that they were expanding the production of old ones to equip a burgeoning army. For the first eighteen months of the war private ingenuity vied with official manufacture as the army struggled to produce grenades that were both lethal to the enemy and safe to their users. Some early versions were so delicate or unstable that their users – 'bombers', first grouped as a platoon within the battalion, and eventually spread more widely so as to constitute 'a nucleus of one officer and eight men' per company – shared with the crews of early trench mortars the discouraging nickname 'Suicide Squad'. The first grenades were empty jam tins – Mr Tickler making a further contribution to the war effort – filled with guncotton or the more effective and more stable ammonal. A detonator was inserted into the guncotton and ignited by a length of safety fuse which the thrower ignited with a match or lighter before hurling it at the enemy. The Official History advised its readers how to make one.

> Take a jam pot, fill it with shredded guncotton and ten-penny nails, mixed according to taste. Insert a No 8 deton-ator and a short length of Bickford's fuze. Clay up the lid. Light with a match, pipe, cigar or cigarette, and throw for all you are worth.[43]

By early 1915 there was even an up-market version of the jam-tin bomb with a friction primer.

Gerald Burgoyne first met the jam-tin bomb on Hill 60, outside Ypres, in May 1915:

> The Brigade bomb officer showed us some bombs he was going to use this morning, huge spherical affairs like cannon balls, about 7" to 8" in diameter, he also showed us what up till now we'd only heard of: the 'jam tin bomb', a tin the size of a 1 lb tin of jam, with a piece of fuse on top and on the fuse a cardboard cap, which the operator forced down, giving it a sharp turn; this caused a friction spark to ignite the fuse which was timed to burn five seconds.[44]

Private Harold Dolden was then a bomber in the London Scottish.

> Six of us, including myself, were Company bombers and we were issued with eight cricket ball bombs which were carried in pockets in an apron strapped round our kilt. The bombs had a detonator jutting out of the top covered with a piece of sticking plaster. On our wrist a band was worn, to which was attached the striking part of a box of matches, and we were also provided with matches. The procedure was as follows – to take the bomb from the pocket of the kilt apron, tear off the sticking plaster on the detonator, strike a match on the wristband and light the charge, hold the bomb for three or four seconds, then throw as far as possible. I do not know what genius devised this bomb with its farcial method of ignition, but I am very doubtful whether he ever spent a night in the pouring rain and tried to strike a match on his wristband . . .

> I have a further criticism to make; when one 'belly-flopped' these eight bombs strung over one's kilt caused considerable pain in our most sensitive parts, and when we were wearing gas masks our eyes watered so much that we could not see out of the goggles. Of course one must be fair, and the underlying idea might have been that the enemy would have been so intrigued by our antics that he would have forgotten to fire.[45]

The obvious disadvantages of the jam-tin bomb and other early grenades encouraged a plethora of inventions, and the War Office departments and committees responsible for such things – including the Trench Warfare Department, the Trench Supply Department, the Munitions Inventions Department and assorted committees – received thousands of suggestions for new weapons of one sort or another. The Munitions Inventions Department alone received over 100,000 from servicemen and members of the public between May 1915 and August 1918, commenting on all of them and commissioning full reports on 3,549.[46]

There were too many grenades adopted for service to be included here, but they fell into three main types: percussion, ignition and mechanical grenades. Percussion grenades, such as Hand Grenades Nos 1 and 2, had percussion detonators secured by removable safety pins, and cloth streamers which ensured that the bomb fell nose downwards. The pin was removed and the grenade was thrown. 'Care should be taken that the streamers do not get entangled,' warned a pamphlet. 'The bomb should be thrown WELL up into the air.'[47] Percussion grenades were the cause of frequent accidents, usually because the thrower hit the rear of the trench with the grenade as he drew his arm back to throw it. James Dunn, medical officer of 2/Royal Welch Fusiliers, saw that 'so many of our wounded are the victims of our own bomb accidents',[48] and Cyril Helm of 2/King's Own Yorkshire Light Infantry agreed that 'they caused heavy casualties among our own men'. Ignition grenades included Hand Grenades Nos 7–9, and the Battye, Ball, Picher and Oval grenades. These were lit by a variety of patent lighters, often a friction lighter like a large version of the striker on a box of matches, and the pamphlet was generous enough to observe that some were 'somewhat complicated, and special instruction should be given . . .': 2/Royal Welch Fusiliers reported that their strikers were 'so wet as to be useless' at the battle of Loos.

However, the future was destined to lie with the mechanical grenade, which embodied a spring-loaded mechanism igniting a fuse which exploded a detonator and thus the bomb itself. The Hand Grenade No. 12 'Hairbrush pattern' looked like a large hairbrush, with the explosive where the bristles would normally be, and a wooden handle to assist throwing. The Mills Hand Grenade No. 5 was the now-familiar 'pineapple' grenade, with a serrated cast-iron case containing a spring-loaded striker, explosive cap, fuse and detonator, weighing 1½ lbs. The thrower ensured that he had a firm grip of the grenade and its long, flat lever, removed the safety pin, and threw the grenade. As it left his hand the lever flew upwards and away, allowing the striker to shoot down and hit the cap. This ignited the fuse, which usually had a burning time of four seconds before it set off the detonator and exploded the bomb.[49]

The Mills bomb was easily the best of the wartime grenades, but it had numerous teething troubles, and as late as mid-1916 there was still one accident for every 3,000 grenades. Sometimes grenades exploded prematurely because of a manufacturing fault, but sometimes soldiers overdid the process of pinching the safety-pins so that they would pull out easily, and pins simply slid out. This may be what caused the most celebrated grenade accident of the war. Rifleman Billy McFadzean of the Royal Irish Rifles was carrying a box of grenades forward early on the morning of 1 July 1916 on the Somme when he heard the pop of an igniter cap within the box. He knew that there would be an explosion, lethal in a packed communication trench, in just four seconds, so he flung himself on the box to absorb its force: he was awarded a posthumous Victoria Cross.

Soldiers (then as now) were often nervous of throwing their first grenades, and Sergeant George Ashurst of 16/Lancashire Fusiliers had a narrow escape when one of his recruits dropped a grenade with the pin out during training in France in 1917. 'Quickly in the few seconds left to me before it exploded,' he wrote, 'I picked the bomb up and threw it out of the trench, but even as it was in the air above the trench it exploded, scattering the metal all about.'[50] Mills bombs could be carried in pouches, specially-made canvas bombers' waistcoats, or even canvas buckets, and were generally regarded as being easier to carry than the German potato-masher grenade, with its long handle, which could be clipped onto, or tucked inside, the waist-belt, but was generally bulkier. However, the handle gave the potato-masher 'a much longer range than the Mills bomb, which was rather big and heavy for many to grasp'.[51]

It was a short step from the hand grenade to the rifle grenade. The Rifle Grenade No. 3 – usually known as the Hale's Rifle Grenade – was a small grooved tube filled with explosive and fitted with a detonator. It was attached to a long tube which was slipped down the barrel of the rifle. The firer loaded a special cartridge containing extra cordite but no bullet, and the gases produced on firing sent the grenade on its way. The Mills grenade was modified, by the addition of a steel rod fitted to its base-plug, to be fired in the same way. A cup-discharger, fitted to the muzzle of the rifle, was issued to the British army at the rate of four per company in September 1916, and there were sixty-four per battalion at the war's end.

As the development of grenades improved the infantryman's lethality in one direction, so the introduction of the light machine gun did so in another. The British Expeditionary Force went to war with two belt-fed machine guns per infantry battalion or cavalry regiment, making eight machine guns per brigade. The Germans, in contrast, had a machine-gun company in each three-battalion regiment, six guns in 1914, rising to fifteen in mid-1916 – and extra machine-gun companies in addition. But it was not the sheer numbers of their machine guns that gave the Germans an advantage: it was in their organisation. A German regimental commander, disposing of roughly the same resources as a British brigadier, could centralise his firepower if he wished to do so, with 'the German concentration of fire giving the impression of superior numbers'.[52] If a British brigade was holding the line with two of its battalions up and two back, then the machine guns of the two reserve battalions would probably be out of the line. This suited the machine-gunners, as Guy Chapman discovered when he became his battalion's machine-gun officer. 'I was liking my new job,' he wrote. 'The machine-gunners considered themselves the elite of the battalion. They lived apart from the companies and except in emergency were excused fatigues. In trenches they were responsible only for their immediate surroundings.'[53]

However, the unsatisfactory nature of this arrangement was very clear to George 'Boss' Lindsay, a Boer War veteran and pre-war instructor at the Small Arms School at Hythe, who argued strongly that 'centralised control of the whole machine-gun belt' was essential if the best use was to be gained from these weapons.[54] Machine guns were occasionally massed in 1915; the practice had become widespread a year later, and by then organisational form had changed to conform with tactical function.

The Machine Gun Corps was brought into being by Royal Warrant on 14 October 1916, with its depot at Harrowby Camp, Grantham and (though not till March 1916) a training school at Etaples. George Coppard, wounded on the Somme, passed through Grantham on his way back to the front, and discovered that: 'We ex-wounded types were quickly told to forget any experience acquired in France, as it counted for nothing at Harrowby.'[55] Belt-fed machine guns were now concentrated into brigade machine-gun companies, numbered the same as their brigades, each commanded by a captain, the senior of the four section commanders making them up. The Machine Gun Corps had three proper branches, MGC (I) for the infantry, MGC (C) for the cavalry, and MGC (M) for light motor machine guns. The Heavy Branch of the MGC was the cover for what soon became the Tank Corps.

Coppard had been a machine gunner in 1/6th Queen's, part of 37th Brigade in 12th Division. In February 1916 he found himself in 37th Company of the Machine Gun Corps with a new regimental number, new identity discs and a new cap-badge. 'I had some regrets about losing the Queens's badge with the lamb,' he wrote, 'but welcomed the new one with the two crossed Vickers guns surmounted by the British crown.'[56] In late 1915 Burgon Bickersteth, commissioned into the Royal Dragoons early in the war, was his regiment's machine-gun officer, his two guns and forty men forming part of the brigade machine-gun squadron. The following year he wrote that his men had had to display Machine Gun Corps badges. 'I hate it, but I suppose it is inevitable,' he wrote. 'Of course officers have not had to change.'[57] Officers certainly should have changed, but such was the lure of the regimental system that many avoided doing so. The Guards Division preserved its own distinctive approach by not accepting members of the Machine Gun Corps, but by forming the Guards Machine-Gun Battalion, its cap badge showing a star of machine-gun bullets.

The next step was to bring brigade machine-gun companies together into divisional machine gun battalions, and this made it easier to produce even greater concentrations of fire, most notably with the machine-gun barrage, with guns firing at distant targets identified from the map. Although machine-gun battalions did not appear until the last year of the war, the trend towards centralisation and volume was clearly evident. On 24 July 1916 Graham Seton-Hutchison's guns of 100th Company Machine Gun Corps fired just twenty-five rounds short of one million: one gun fired 120,000 rounds. Simply keeping the guns topped up with water became a major logistic feat, using all available petrol tins filled with water and the company's individual water bottles into the bargain.

Seton-Hutchison spent the last year of the war commanding a machine-gun battalion, which behaved much as an infantry battalion might, save that its companies were sometimes more widely spread. Many of the problems he encountered were old rather than new. One of his company commanders, 'an officer of virile type, with the Military Cross . . . told me frankly that he did not feel confident of taking his Company into action again, a confession most difficult to make'. Seton-Hutchison sent him home to train drafts for three months, and when he returned he did very well indeed. And during an attack 'a dishevelled Signaller from Headquarters' staggered up with a sealed message. He tore it open, expecting orders for the advance, but discovered instead 'an order that I should report forthwith the number of tins of plum jam consumed by units under my command since the last report'.[58]

But if senior officers of the Machine Gun Corps were burdened by the sort of bureaucracy that other commanding officers knew all too well, the establishment of the corps made a real difference to the ordinary soldier. For a start, as a corps in its own right the Machine Gun Corps could enlist its own recruits, and was no longer dependent on drafts from other regiments which, as was the case with trench mortars, tended to produce men unwanted by anybody else. In fact, some of these rejected candidates did well. Seton-Hutchison recalled a private with a DCM who had been reduced from the rank of sergeant. He was given temporary command of a company which had lost all its officers, in a sudden crisis, and 'NCOs and men alike rejoiced in his leadership'. He gained a bar to his DCM that day, and was soon commissioned.[59] But the diversity and improved quality of recruits was also evident. In 1916 George Coppard was given two new gun-numbers. One had been born in Argentina: 'He had a university education and spoke perfect English, and I never understood why he wasn't an officer . . . Any man who travels over 6,000 miles to fight for his father's homeland is no ordinary man.'[60] There was also a growing pride in the corps' professionalism. In late 1917, when Coppard briefed Lieutenant Colonel Dawson of 6/Royal West Kent on the machine-gun plan he 'felt a warm satisfaction that a battalion commander acknowledged the authority of the Machine Gun Corps and accepted this without question from one of its very junior personnel'.[61]

The centralisation of the big belt-fed Vickers guns which had previously constituted a battalion's automatic firepower was made possible because the smaller Lewis light machine gun entered service.[62] It was a wholly new departure. Designed by the American Colonel Isaac Newton Lewis, its barrel was air cooled, so it did not need the water container which burdened Vickers crews, and its ammunition was contained in a flat 47-round magazine that fitted on top of the weapon. It was reasonably reliable, though like most weapons jammed if it got too muddy. Most infantry officers thought it a poor exchange for the Vickers because the magazine could be emptied all too quickly: a brave soldier in Rowland Feilding's Connaught Rangers battalion fired a full magazine in one long burst to destroy a German raiding party. Lieutenant Charles Carrington thought that it was hard to fill Lewis magazines (there had been a handy belt-filling tool for the Vickers) although their whole contents could be squeezed off in a few seconds. Captain Dunn regarded the removal of the Vickers from battalions as 'an insane act'. And many soldiers felt that the Lewis gun simply did not provide that sustained firepower, so destructive to enemies and so heartening to friends, that was characteristic of the Vickers.

The Lewis might be carried over the shoulder on the march, passed from man to man – 'Hand us that gas-pipe, young Saunders' – or put in an unpopular coffin-shaped wheeled trolley. Although normally fired on a bipod from the lying position because its barrel was heavy (the gun weighed 30lbs in all), a sturdy man could fire it standing up. Lance Corporal Irwin of the 72nd Canadian Battalion proved that he was one such at Passchendaele in 1917 when he attacked three German machine guns.

> With a bravery that was tinged with the uncanny prescience of an Indian scout, he worked behind the fated Boche gunners and, firing his Lewis gun from the shoulder, killed or wounded every member of the crews who were just going to begin to fire, and captured the three guns single-handed.[63]

The example of the Welsh Guards shows how the Lewis gun spread through the infantry. The battalion received a single gun in November 1915, another in December, six more in March 1916 and another eight that August, eight more in January 1918 and a further eight in April. By then the battalion had thirty-two guns, so many that they could not all be manned, although by that time every man in the battalion knew about the Lewis gun.[64] The February 1917 pamphlet 'SS 143' prescribed one Lewis gun per thirty-six-man platoon, with a full section of nine men carrying its ammunition, and by mid-1918 there were often two or more guns per platoon – at least eight per company.

For all the mistrust occasioned by its initial appearance, the Lewis gun played an essential part in the structure of British infantry in the last two years of the war. Ivor Maxse, commander of the 18th Division on the Somme, became Inspector General of Training in the British Expeditionary Force in 1918, and had already had widespread influence in maintaining that the platoon should form the basis for all infantry training. Although there were some who maintained that platoons could never be kept at the thirty-six-man strength demanded by Maxse, and were too often disrupted by casualties to be trained to the level he required, it is clear that by the end of the war the infantry battalion had been wholly transformed.

The historian of the Welsh Guards summed up the combination of weapons available to the infantry in 1917–18. There was the traditional rifle and bayonet, 'for assault, for repelling attack, or for obtaining superiority of fire'. Then there was the grenade, 'the second weapon of every NCO and man . . . used either for dislodging the enemy from behind cover or killing him below ground'. The rifle-bomb is the ' "howitzer" of the infantry, and used to dislodge the enemy from behind cover and to obtain superiority of fire by driving him underground'. Finally, the 'Lewis gun is the weapon of opportunity'. 'The platoon,' he concludes, 'was the smallest unit capable of combining these weapons – a section of Lewis gunners, a section of bombers, a section of rifle-bombers and a section of riflemen.'[65]

The remarkable achievements of the last Hundred Days reflected the transformation of the infantry. In 1914 it was an arm which had prided itself on accurate rifle-fire which paved the way for assault in line. By the war's end, if it could not perhaps produce thousand-yard hits which would have delighted the old sweats of 1914, it could generate a blizzard of close-range fire from rifles and Lewis guns, launch grenades, from hand or rifle, at an enemy up to 200 yards away, and develop attacks with platoons and sections shoving their way forward with fire and manoeuvre. The average age of its leaders, commissioned or not, had dropped, often by as much as 50 percent. And at least half its officers had been commissioned from the ranks. Old Atkins could still occasionally be found, with his bushy moustache and Boer War ribbons, but it was young Tommy that made up the infantry of 1918.

THE BOLD BOMBARDIER

Artillery had profited from the same sorts of technological innovation as the infantry weapon, with rifled barrels and breech loading becoming standard in the 1870s and 1880s. The replacement of black powder by the new high explosives such as melenite and Lyddite improved both the propulsion and the bursting power of shells, and the hydrostatic buffer and recuperator absorbed most of the gun's recoil and made it speedier to re-lay after each shot. By the turn of the century field guns fired faster, with greater range and accuracy, than ever before. But although there had been times (notably at the battle of Sha-ho, in September 1904 during the Russo-Japanese War) when guns had been used to provide 'indirect fire', engaging targets invisible to the gunners, their fire controlled by observers with telephones, in 1914 most artillery officers were still not persuaded that the future lay with indirect fire. Indeed, the standard British field-pieces of the war, the 18-pounder gun and the 4.5-inch howitzer, were both fitted with steel shields 'tested with a service rifle bullet at a range of four hundred yards and should not be pierced, cracked or distorted'.[66]

Although British artillery officers who had observed the Russo-Japanese War championed indirect fire, there was a powerful lobby which disagreed, and the 1911 General Staff Conference heard Brigadier General Launcelot Kiggell advocate 'lines of infantry pressing forward, bayonets fixed to close with the enemy. Lines of guns would support them at close range'.[67] The mounted branch of the Royal Artillery – the Royal Field and Royal Horse Artillery – was renowned for its robust, somewhat unscientific approach to gunnery. It was even said that some horsey officers 'never looked behind the swingletree' – the flexible coupling linking horses to gun and limber. The Royal Garrison Artillery (unkindly nicknamed the Gambardiers) favoured a more scientific approach to gunnery, but in 1914 it was the mounted branch that had the edge.

We have already seen how Royal Artillery commanders of 3rd and 5th Divisions decided to fight with their guns forward with the infantry at Le Cateau on 26 August 1914, and the consequence was a direct fire battle that would not have surprised gunners who had fought at Waterloo. Lieutenant Lionel Lutyens told his mother how things had been with 122nd Battery Royal Field Artillery, on the edge of a sunken lane towards the right flank of the British position.

> One of my No. 6 detachment was shot dead with a rifle-bullet in the first half-hour, and there were a good many whizzing about. Quite a number lodged in the little bank in front of my pit, and I could hear them 'zipping' all the time I was passing orders . . .
>
> I suppose the Germans started shelling us at about 9 a.m. and it went on consistently, shrapnel and high explosive. My own battery was very fortunate indeed. We were just under cover, and the enemy couldn't see us . . .
>
> The other two batteries suffered terribly . . . They were practically bang in the open and had a lot of men killed and wounded, limbers set on fire and guns knocked about . . . they had a really awful time. Miller told me their gun shields were a mass of silver where they were riddled with bullets, and several guns received direct hits . . .
>
> Our own bad time did not come till nearly three o'clock, I think. I was sitting in my pit, wondering how long it would go on, and when we would get a shell right into us, when I heard the 'pop-pop-pop-pop' of a machine gun and a perfect hail of bullets started coming over. The German had pushed a machine gun, or a couple, up onto

> the knoll . . . 500 or 600 yards to our right front and had
> turned straight onto the battery.

When the moment came to withdraw, the horse teams were brought
up from the rear.

> One of my teams was the only one that escaped unscathed.
> They drove straight up over the [gently sunken] road,
> limbered up and galloped away.
>
> It was very smart and good . . .
>
> My second team wasn't so lucky. They got as far as the
> sunken road and there the leaders [the two leading
> horses] jibbed. The driver flogged them into the road and
> one leader fell. A sergeant of mine and myself had just
> pulled him out of the way when the other leader fell, and
> then the driver.
>
> We were busy at the second horse when down came
> the near centre, and down came the off centre, and the
> driver. The horses fell so quietly it was hard to realise they
> were shot . . .
>
> We couldn't save the guns now, so I got what gunners
> I could on the limber and sent it away . . .
>
> When the limber was gone I ran to my horse. My groom
> had been standing waiting all the while with my two horses
> on the bank behind . . . Peel came galloping past as I tried
> to get on. I was so trembling with excitement and funk by
> now that I couldn't get my foot in the stirrup. I ran back-
> wards trying to reach it, and expecting 'Bronco' to be hit
> at any moment. However, he was not and I got up and let
> him go down the road as hard as he could gallop.[68]

The British lost thirty-eight guns at Le Cateau, a catastrophe
unequalled since Yorktown in 1781. While the circumstances of the
battle would undoubtedly have led to the loss of some guns, insistence on using indirect fire from artillery deployed so far forward
made the losses needlessly high.

Le Cateau was the last time that guns were deployed forward on this
scale, though there were times later in the war – and, indeed, in the
Second World War – when artillery employed direct fire on a smaller
scale. For instance, when 2/Devons held the Bois des Buttes on the

Chemin des Dames in May 1918 their supporting 5th Field Battery RFA, with the utmost gallantry, stayed with them to the end, firing their 18-pounders as long as they could and then defending their gun-pits with rifles and Lewis guns. The battery had three unwounded men left at the day's end, and it and the Devons received the unusual distinction of the collective award of the French Croix de Guerre. However, it was clear, from the late summer of 1914, that the future lay with indirect fire. Indeed, although it was not to reach its full flowering until radio sets became more readily available enabling easier communication between observer and guns after the First World War, the technical means of producing effective indirect fire already existed.

Field guns had a dial sight, and this, used with an aiming post, a sort of military theodolite called a director, and basic trigonometry, enabled guns to be laid out so that their lines of fire were parallel. A telephone message from a forward observer, giving the location and type of the target, would be translated, by the command post on the gun-line, into a fire order giving the type of shell required, and the bearing and elevation on which the gun should be laid. The gun's commander – a sergeant, and 'No. 1' in gunner terminology – would then salute to acknowledge the order, and repeated it so that the gun position officer would hear any error. A fire order shouted to an 18-pounder battery might sound thus:

> 'HE 105' [High explosive shell with the No. 105 fuse. Detachment Nos 5 and 6 at the ammunition limber can now begin to prepare the first round of ammunition. No. 6 will set the fuse indicator on the limber so that they will remember what fuse has been ordered if the task becomes a long one. The shell is passed forward by the No. 5 to the No. 4, who loads it into the gun's breech.]
>
> 'All guns, 1 degree 10 minutes more right' [This enables the No. 3, the layer, to set the correct bearing on his dial sight, and then to lay it on the aiming post. If the aiming post has to be moved then the No. 2, normally busy opening and closing the breech, will help him.]
>
> 'Angle of sight, 1 degree 20 minutes elevation' [An adjustment to allow for the difference in height between the gun and its target, applied by the No. 3.]

'One round gun fire' [Each gun is to fire one round.]
'3400' [The range in yards from gun to target.]
'Fire' [The No. 1 checks that the gun 'is in all respects ready' and pulls the firing lanyard.]

There were numerous variations, of course. The rounds would fall on the ground in the same configuration, usually a gentle semi-circle, as the guns were deployed on the gun-line. If they were shooting at a small target – a strongpoint or command post, for instance – it might be necessary to concentrate all guns onto the fall of shot of one particular gun, giving an 'individual correction' to each gun to achieve this. One gun might be told to register a number of targets (now known as 'adjustment') and the target information could then be passed on so that each gun could hit the target without the need for individual registration. As artillery survey techniques improved in 1917 even this could be avoided, and scrupulously-accurate surveying of gun positions, coupled with the detection of hostile gun positions by flash-spotting, sound-ranging and aerial photography, made it possible, as we saw at Cambrai, for accurate fire to be delivered without the need for preliminary registration, adding surprise to the gunner's repertoire.

British guns began the war with two types of shell: shrapnel and high explosive. Eighteen-pounder field guns and 13-pounder horse artillery guns fired only shrapnel. This, named after its inventor, Lieutenant Henry Shrapnel RA, had first been used at the end of the eighteenth century, and its popularity with British gunners in 1914 stemmed from its success in the Boer War. A shrapnel shell consisted of a forged steel body. Its base held a bursting charge – usually black powder in the British service, which gave British shrapnel a distinctive greyish-white burst, unlike the dark German 'Woolly Bear'. A thin brass tube, filled with powder pellets, ran up from the bursting charge to the fuse. Packed round the tube were round metal balls, 375 for the 18-pounder, at forty-one to the pound. There were various types of fuse, but the most common was the percussion-and-time fuse No. 80. This could be set to burst on impact, but when used with a shrapnel shell was generally set (by the gunner who removed it from the limber, using a fuse-fixing key) to burst about twenty feet above and in front of its target. The fuse would begin to burn as the shell accelerated on firing, and when it reached the setting prescribed by the gun position officer a flash passed into the brass tube and down into the bursting charge. This exploded, blowing the metal balls out like the blast from some gigantic shotgun. The forward observer would order 'up' or 'down' over the telephone to the gun-line until the point of burst was correct. To cut barbed wire, shrapnel had to burst three of four feet above it, something very difficult to get just right.

Throughout the war shrapnel remained a major killer for troops in the open. The British steel helmet was given its characteristic brim in an effort to keep shrapnel balls off vulnerable faces and necks. A low burst could shatter a man. In October 1914 Cyril Helm of 2/King's Own Yorkshire Light Infantry was near Festubert when:

> A young gunner Subaltern was on his way up to observe a machine-gun position. Just as he got outside my door a shrapnel shell burst full in front of him. The poor fellow was brought in to me absolutely riddled. He lay in my arms until he died, shrieking in his agony and said he hoped I would excuse him for making such a noise as he really could not help it. Pitiful as nothing could be done for him except an injection of morphia. I will always remember that incident, particularly as he was such a fine looking boy, not more than nineteen.[69]

Higher-bursting shrapnel was more capricious. The Reverend Julian Bickersteth heard that his brother Ralph, a lieutenant in the Leeds Pals, had:

> looked round to see if there was any support from the trenches behind and at that moment a shrapnel bullet struck him in the back of the head; a second later another bullet passed through his head, coming out through his forehead. He just rolled over without a word or a sound, and Bateman was able to see that he was quite dead, killed instantly.[70]

Very high-bursting shrapnel caused experienced soldiers little concern. In 1914 Arthur Osburn encountered some which was 'prompt and accurate enough, but bursting much too high; the bullets rattling off our boots harmlessly'.[71] Once the steel helmet was in service, the approved defence against high shrapnel was to tilt one's head in the direction of the burst. But here too caprice spun its dice. Lieutenant Julian Tyndale-Biscoe, regarding a 60-foot burst as little more than punctuation to his conversation, found that it mortally wounded an officer and the battery clerk: 'They both died within a minute – very sad – they had only one bullet each.' Gerald Burgoyne recalled an incident where the medical officer of a Wiltshire battalion was bending down dressing a wound in a crowded aid post: 'a piece [of shrapnel] entering the room, killed the doctor at once. The room was crowded at the time, but he was the only person hit.'[72]

High explosive, initially known as Lyddite after its filling, developed at the south-coast artillery ranges at Lydd in Kent, was available to British heavy guns and howitzer batteries in August 1914, but not to 13-pounders and 18-pounders. However, the abundant evidence that it was required for field guns too saw the first new high-explosive shells arrive during First Ypres. These consisted of a steel body filled with explosive, increasingly ammonal. Most were fitted with a fuse on the nosecap, which could be adjusted to give an instantaneous burst or a brief delay. However, in order to obtain the longer delay required to penetrate overhead cover, some heavy high-explosive shells were fused at their base and had hardened steel nosecaps, technology borrowed from naval warfare. They would go through the roofs of some dugouts to burst inside them, but very deep German dugouts were always too much for them.

A more serious problem was producing fuses that burst on the slightest touch, either against wire or the surface of the ground. This was not a simple matter, for such a fuse had to be stable enough to accelerate swiftly when the shell was fired, perhaps brush a camouflage net or branch near the gun muzzle, and then burst at the instant when it reached its target. The British 'No. 100 Fuse' was safe enough but, because it had an infinitesimal delay, made only a slight crater, and in wet ground might lose much of its effect. The No. 106 fuse was introduced in 1916 and was available in large numbers in 1917. It made no crater, but expended all its explosive force by bursting flat: it was not only more effective for wire-cutting than even the best low shrapnel, it was also shockingly lethal against troops. The Germans developed a similar fuse at much the same time. 'The Germans have a new extraordinarily sensitive contact fuse,' wrote James Dunn in June 1917. 'A shell makes scarcely any shell hole, so the horizontal burst is not lost; a fair-sized splinter, which hit a man beside me below the knee, had carried the better part of 200 yards with a nearly flat trajectory.'[73]

High-explosive shells sometimes killed by blast alone: a direct hit might disintegrate a body altogether, showering those nearby with a dreadful rain of flesh, blood and stomach contents. Ernest Shephard saw how 'Pte Tibble (a nice sociable man) was blown to pieces,' and later 'Pte Adams 8080 (a quiet, nice lad) and Cpl Hodges (a good chum) were blown to pieces.'[74] But blast could equally well kill by sucking the oxygen from a man's lungs and leaving his body intact. 'One 4.2 [inch] that burst among 3 men sitting in a shell hole killed them with no more visible mark than some singeing of their clothing,' recalled Captain Dunn.[75] Or men might be literally blown up, flung, whole or in fragments, for a considerable distance. When Ernest Shephard's company was hit by heavy howitzers in July 1915 the effects were appalling.

> We found two machine gunners belonging to our company who had been blown from the trench over the railway bank into a deep pool of water, a distance of 70 yards. One man, Pte Woods, was found in 8 pieces, while others were ghastly sights, stomachs blown open, some headless, limbs off, etc. Up to the present we have found 17 and buried them.[76]

A subaltern of 7/Royal Innisikilling Fusiliers, attacking Ginchy in August 1916, saw how a shell:

> landed in the midst of a bunch of men about seventy yards away on my right. I have a most vivid recollection of seeing a most tremendous burst of clay and earth go shooting up in the air – yes, even parts of human bodies – and then when the smoke cleared there was nothing left. I shall never forget that horrifying spectacle as long as I live, but I remember it as a sight only, for I can associate no sound with it.[77]

James Dunn saw a shell fall just ahead of him near Polygon Wood
in September 1917:

> two men suddenly rose into the air vertically, 15 feet per-
> haps, amid a spurt of soil about 150 yards ahead. They
> rose and fell with the easy, graceful poise of acrobats. A
> rifle, revolving slowly, rose high above them before, still
> revolving, it fell. The sight recalled, even in those sur-
> roundings, a memory of boyhood: a turn that thrilled me
> in the travelling circus at St Andrews.[78]

Small shell fragments inflicted wounds of almost surgical pre-
cision. An Irish medical officer fainted when the wounded man on
his stretcher had his face sliced neatly off and hurled, like a rubber
mask, against the side of the trench. C. P. Blacker saw a similar sort
of wound, when a man had his face removed, 'the soft parts being
detached from the front of his skull from a blow upwards ... The
image of this groping sightless figure, kneeling and pawing the air,
has often come back to me since.'[79] Larger fragments behaved like
the axe or bludgeon of a medieval executioner, lopping off limbs
or cutting men in half. The cumulative effect of death by shellfire
was all too well remembered by Harry Ogle:

> Entangled in or sprawling across the barbed wire, slumped
> over the remains of trench parapets, or half buried in
> the ruined trenches, were corpses, both grey-green and
> khaki-clad; and overall lay a covering of chalk dust and
> flies which never had time to settle before being raised by
> the next explosion. Amongst the wreckage crept wreaths
> and coils of smoke which hardly vanished before another
> shell obstructed the scene and added worse confusion.
> The days were hot and windless. The dead remained where
> they had fallen and suffered alternate burial and disinter-
> ment by shellfire ... In many places were mounds which
> indicated corpses with here and there an exposed head
> or knee. Across the parapet and parados were bodies
> either lying where they had fallen or slung there out of
> the way. I never had a strong stomach and smoked Digger
> Mixture in a corn cob until my mouth felt like pickled
> leather.[80]

It would have required great prescience to have predicted, before the war, that artillery would wield such destructive power. Guns increased in number and in calibre, and the quantity of ammunition at their disposal grew beyond all measure. In August 1914 British field guns had just 1,000 rounds per gun available in limbers and ammunition wagons at the front line, ammunition parks in the lines of communication and depots at the base. In June 1916 each 18-pounder actually had 1,000 rounds ready on its gun position, and in the summer of 1917 expenditure of 18-pounder ammunition (one type among many) regularly exceeded a million rounds a week. A single 6-inch howitzer, which arrived at the front in June 1917, had fired 20,789 rounds by the armistice, fifty-six times the rounds per gun available to these weapons in January 1915. On 1 October 1918 the British army had 10,153 guns, howitzers and mortars in France, amongst them more 9.2-inch heavy howitzers than it had possessed guns of all calibres in August 1914. However one looks at the statistics, the story is one of extraordinary expansion.[81]

Doctrine evolved as the weight of metal grew. *Field Service Regulations 1909*, which remained the army's capstone doctrine pamphlet throughout the war, had always emphasised that the gaining of superiority of fire was essential for a successful attack, and that '**the greater the difficulties of the infantry, the more fully should the fire power of the artillery be developed**'.[82] Direct fire was still favoured, the guns simply furnished support in the way that rifle or machine gun fire might have done, albeit on a heavier scale. During the first two years of the war there was (with exceptions like Neuve Chapelle, when shortage of ammunition did not permit a lengthy bombardment) a general belief that artillery should strive to destroy both enemy trenches and gun positions, by elaborate preliminary bombardment if necessary. It became apparent, however, that even the heaviest bombardment could not inflict total physical destruction. From the Somme onwards doctrine changed, with an increasing emphasis on fire which sought to neutralise – that is, to make the enemy incapable of offering resistance for a specified time – rather than to wholly destroy him. Artillery would fire a preparatory bombardment, cutting wire, neutralising hostile gun positions, and rendering the defending infantry incapable of manning their positions then the attacking infantry (itself, as we have just seen, becoming increasingly flexible) would exploit, with a creeping barrage moving in front of it.

The quicker the bombardment arrived, the better it worked. Indeed, one of the reasons why the bombardment at Neuve Chapelle had worked so well was the rapidity of its delivery. A later study suggested that a 90 percent erosion of the enemy's will to fight could be produced by six hours of bombardment with o.1lb of shell yard of front, or six minutes with 1lb of shell per yard. From mid-1916 there was increasing emphasis on rapid bombardment, both retaining tactical surprise and ensuring that the defenders were subjected to a pounding whose weight and suddenness broke their will even if it left their bodies intact. German artillery doctrine moved in exactly the same direction, attaining its apotheosis in the spring offensive of 1918. Small wonder that when the German bombardment began on 21 March, Lieutenant William Carr of 377th Battery RFA was simply stunned:

> Think of the loudest clap of thunder you have ever heard, then imagine what it would be like if it continued without stopping. That was the noise which woke us at 4.40 a.m. on Thursday, 21 March. I have never before or since heard anything like it.[83]

At precisely the same time Lieutenant Arthur Behrend, asleep well behind the front, in a dugout in the headquarters of a heavy artillery brigade,

> awoke with a tremendous start, conscious of noise, incessant and almost musical, so intense that it seemed as if a hundred devils were hammering in my brain. Everything seemed to be vibrating – the ground, my dugout, my bed . . .
>
> I do not know how long I remained in bed – it must have been nearly five minutes. I was trembling with excitement – or was it fear? – and I felt powerless to move. Besides, what was the use? There was nothing to do, and one might as well be killed decently in bed instead of half naked while struggling into one's shirt.[84]

From mid-1916 British artillery was capable of delivering fire which had exactly this sort of effect, and it became increasingly able to do so in the next two years as techniques improved and the quantities of guns and ammunition grew.

Even by 1916 it was commonplace for German prisoners, enduring, when in British hands, the fire of their own artillery, to observe that it did not begin to equal the savagery of a British bombardment. Captain Rudolf Binding, a German staff officer, saw that British bombardments drove men, quite literally, to drink: 'They have a craving for brandy which can hardly be satisfied, and which shows how badly they yearn to lose the faculty for feeling.'[85] Lieutenant Ernst Junger wrote of the Somme that:

> The power of logical thought and the force of gravity seemed alike to be suspended. One had the sense of something as inescapable and unconditionally fated as a catastrophe of nature. An NCO of No. 3 Platoon went mad.[86]

The caprice which guided German shells also inspired the British. In 1914 the German soldier Stephen Westmann stepped aside from his company, resting on the line of march, to relieve himself. An incoming British shell, probably from a 60-pounder, killed or wounded forty-two of his comrades and put a splinter clean through his pack, where his head had rested a minute before. And although the pre-Somme bombardment lacked the rapidity which later shelling acquired, it was still terrible to suffer beneath it.

> Again and again we had to dig ourselves and our comrades out of masses of blackened earth and splintered wooden beams. Often we found bodies crushed to pulp, or bunks full of suffocated soldiers. The 'drum fire' never ceased. No food or water reached us. Down below, men became hysterical and their comrades had to knock them out, so as to prevent them from running away and exposing themselves to the deadly shell splinters. Even the rats panicked and sought refuge in our flimsy shelters; they ran up the walls, and we had to kill them with our spades.[87]

The preliminary bombardment, long or short, focused on specific targets, but a creeping barrage was wholly different. It moved just ahead of the infantry, and although it was possible for the artillery to concentrate it so as to follow the outline of the German defensive system, it usually moved as a 'straight barrage' parallel with the infantry. It was first used on a large scale on the first day of the Somme, when it generally failed because it moved ahead of the infantry too quickly, allowing defenders to pop up between the departing barrage as it thundered away across the landscape, and the attacking infantry, heavily laden and moving in lines. Limited communications made it impossible to introduce flexibility into the plan below corps level, and in the early days of the Somme it was often evident that the barrage was out of kilter with the infantry attack. 'In spite of the infantry being mown down,' wrote Walter Guinness, who was then second in command of an infantry battalion, 'the prearranged attacking barrages must be followed: they are the laws of the Medes and Persians.'[88]

But in the British night attack on 13/14 July, the artillery fireplan was much more successful, largely because there were more guns per yard of front than there had been on 1 July: the preliminary bombardment was short; and the attacking infantry were 'leaning on the barrage', not trudging far behind it. Indeed, although General Rawlinson was entitled to claim credit for championing the night attack (against serious opposition from Haig, who argued that troops and staff alike were insufficiently 'experienced in such work'), after he had walked the ground he declared:

> There is no doubt that the success of the enterprise must be attributed in a very large measure to the accuracy and volume of the artillery bombardment. The enemy's wire, as well as his front and second line trenches, were smashed to pieces. The morale of the defenders had been greatly reduced by the din and concussion of the constant explosions, and it was clear from the number of dead that were found in the trenches that he had likewise suffered very heavy casualties from the artillery bombardment.[89]

Sadly, no clear and even learning curve was ascended by the British army that summer, and there were still too many times when the same objectives were attacked, time and time again, by too few soldiers behind too thin a barrage. However, the right lessons were undoubtedly learnt, although at a price. The December 1916 publication *SS 135: Instructions for the Training of Divisions in Offensive Action* (later re-issued with modifications as *The Division in Attack*) – the army's offensive bible for the rest of the war – clearly laid down the functions of the preliminary bombardment and the creeping barrage. It is full of good sense. The timing of the barrage was crucial, but 'must be regulated entirely by local conditions', from 75 yards a minute in good conditions to 15 in very poor ones. It should certainly move more slowly as the attack went on and men became tired, and if the advance was a long one then it should dwell for extra time on specified objectives to give men a chance to catch up.

In 1917 Lieutenant Colonel Rowland Feilding affirmed that:

> It is generally better to risk a few casualties from our own fire than that the artillery should shoot too much for safety. More casualties may easily be caused in the attack by machine guns of the enemy remaining in action between the infantry and the barrage than are ever likely to result from accidents from closer shooting.

However, he warned that a barrage rarely looked the same in practice as it did in theory:

> The so-called barrage 'line' is in reality an irregular and varying belt, perhaps 150 yards in width, and it requires much individual judgement on behalf of the men to advance at exactly the proper speed. It is a difficult business in daylight, and much more so in the dark, especially in the heat and turmoil of an engagement.[90]

It was officially advised that men should keep 50 yards behind an 18-pounder barrage. Varying standards of shell manufacture, and the fact that gun barrels lost minuscule amounts of rifling each time they fired a shell, thus becoming less accurate with each shot until their 'barrel life' was expired, helped widen the 'zone' of the gun, the cigar-shaped area into which its shells would fall even if it was perfectly laid for each shot. Nevertheless, many experienced infantry officers thought it worth closing up to a mere 20 yards behind the rear edge of the barrage.

It was all but impossible, even at the end of the war, to vary the speed of a creeping barrage once it had begun, so careful liaison between infantry and gunners was required in the first place. Shrapnel was originally the preferred projectile for creeping barrages, but, on 14 July 1916, 9th Scottish Division used high explosive to good effect, keeping the Germans in their dugouts until the infantry had arrived. In 1917 the new, quick-acting 106 Fuse was popular, and adding smoke shells to the barrage, first tried at Arras in April 1917, produced good results, not least because the defenders, unsure whether it was smoke or gas, donned their gas masks and lost fighting efficiency.

Defensive artillery tactics evolved in tandem with offensive tactics, with the box barrage as a common feature. This, as its name suggests, boxed off a sector of the front. It could either be an open-sided box, with friendly troops attacking into the open end, or a solid box which completely surrounded a hostile unit – for instance, a counter attack division moving up at Ypres in 1917. A standing barrage, maintained on a particular feature for a specified time, acted like a breakwater, diverting or canalising an enemy attack or protecting a friendly flank.

This steady improvement of artillery technique owed much, as we have seen, to the development of artillery staffs at division, corps and army level. It also reflected the growing expertise of artillery observers, who were so much harder to train than gun numbers. They had to know precisely where they were, no easy task in an unfamiliar trench, and if an observer's assessment of his own position was wrong his fire control was certain to be wrong too. Walter Guinness complained, in August 1916, that: 'Our gunners seem not to be a patch on the French. It is of course impossible to train artillery in a few months and I suspect that some of the trouble is due to bad work on the part of the FOOs [forward observation officers].'[91]

An artillery battery – horse, field or heavy – would always deploy with its gun-line some distance behind the trenches in a defensive battle, or the forward elements of advancing troops in an advance. Guns needed to be far enough forward to make the best use of their range – 6,525 yards for an 18-pounder and 7,300 for a 4.5-inch howitzer – but not so close to the front as to become involved in the infantry battle. For much of the war the 18-pounders and 4.5-inch howitzers would be perhaps two miles behind the front, with medium guns (such as 6-inch and 8-inch) further back, and heavies such as the 9.2-inch howitzer, tractor-drawn and transported in three large sections, up to five miles behind the front. Lieutenant R. B. Talbot Kelly emphasised that it was no use for an 18-pounder battery to be 3,700 yards from German trenches, as his was in early 1917: 'we were often unable to do anything with tantalising targets behind German lines that we saw from our OP [observation post].'[92]

Field batteries had six guns, in three two-gun sections – left, right and centre – each commanded by a subaltern, and generally deployed with the whole battery together, under the command of its major – although it was possible to detach sections, or more rarely individual guns, for specific tasks. Two to three miles behind the gun-line were the wagon-lines, commanded by the battery's second in command, the battery captain. The battery's horses, wagons and administrative staff – its sergeant-major, clerk, shoeing-smith, veterinary sergeant, storemen and cooks – were to be found there. Signallers, that special tribe with their own rights, privileges and language, were split between gun- and wagon-lines, and responsible for keeping the telephone wire going forward in good repair, and in assisting signallers from brigade to maintain those running back. 'They were a group of men apart,' wrote David Jones,

> of singular independence and resource. Excused fatigues, generally speaking, and envied by the ordinary . . . soldier. Accustomed as they were to lonely nocturnal searchings for broken telephone wires, they usually knew the geography of the trenches better than most of us. They tended to a certain clannishness and were suspected of using the mysteries of their trade as a cloak for idling. They also had the reputation of procuring better rations . . . and knowing ways and means of procuring extra comforts – such as officers' whisky, spare blankets, etc. Always, of course, consulted as to any likely new move or turn of events, because of their access to 'the wires'.[93]

Subalterns and gunners were rotated between gun and wagon-lines to rest them, and very often the battery commander and his captain swapped for the same reason. Wagon-lines were places of comparative comfort and relative safety, usually with huts and dug-outs for officers and men and hard standing for the horses. Officers messed together, and in a quiet sector one battery captain made the point that the Royal Regiment could show form even in the midst of a major war by dining nightly in his blue patrol jacket, with high-collared tunic and tight red-striped overalls.

In 1917 Second Lieutenant P. J. Campbell had just joined a battery still recognisably composed of Yorkshire territorials. His chronicling of his first few weeks with his battery, learning the rules in the wagon-lines, gives a clear picture of the pattern of a gunner's life. First, there was the element of risk, rarely wholly absent. A whiz-bang, the German 77mm (roughly equivalent to the 18-pounder) was unlikely to hurt you if it landed more than 20–30 yards away. Decent overhead cover would keep out a 4.2-inch shell, but the 5.9-inch, the 'five-nine', workhorse of German medium guns, was an unwelcome visitor, and one falling even 100 yards away would wreck many defences. Big guns like the 8-inch and 11-inch were far worse, but the Germans tended to use them only against British heavy gun positions further back.

Campbell was given command of the left section of his battery, with two experienced sergeants, Denmark and Feuerbach (the latter's German-sounding name had, it was said, prevented him from getting a commission), two 18-pounders, fifty gunners and drivers and fifty horses. Sergeant Denmark quickly put him in the picture: 'all in all the battery is good, Sir ... I don't believe there's a better one in France. Officers and men have always worked together, they trust one another, you'll never be let down by anyone in C Battery.'[94] Sergeant Thirsk, the battery's signals sergeant, was 'one of the best non-commissioned officers in the battery and one of the nicest of men. I never heard him raise his voice or speak angrily, but his signallers were so well trained and so devoted to him that they knew what to do before they were told.'[95]

Campbell was given the nightly task of taking ammunition forward to the battery, just as a subaltern's detachment from the divisional ammunition column (his previous posting on the Western Front) unloaded its ammunition at the battery's wagon-lines. He was relieved to be able to cope with being shelled, welcomed the strength and confidence of his men, and marvelled at the way his battery commander seemed to know everybody's name and chatted with an easy familiarity without ever compromising his authority. Campbell read his letters at breakfast after a busy night. 'I was as happy as I had ever been,' he wrote.

> I could not help it. Happy to be where I was and with the night's work safely behind me, and happy because of my home, which my letter brought so clearly before me. They took me away from Ypres, and I was relieved to be in England as I read.

He was glad to have been brought into the war so gradually, and the gun-line held few terrors when he reached it. His first task was to fire harassing missions of 250 rounds per night: bearings and elevations to random targets were worked out, and then passed to his Nos 1. This did not please the battery commander. 'Chuck the stuff where you like,' he ordered. 'You're just as likely to hit Fritzes in one place as in another. But don't take any risks with the range, don't shoot short, that's the only thing for which there is no forgiveness.' And he was to get it all over by 2.00 a.m.: 'It's the Fritzes who are to be harassed, not us.'[96]

Finally, Campbell accompanied Edward, the senior subaltern, to an observation post, just behind the forward trenches, where Edward shot the battery to ensure that lines of fire were parallel and to record targets with individual corrections for each gun. His helmet protectively tilted low over his eyes, Campbell saw his first view of the front:

> There was not much to see. Only trenches in the foreground. I could not tell where ours ended and the enemy's began. Nothing was to be seen in any of them, just a succession of trenches. But in the distance, about a mile away, country began again, and colour. I could see grass and trees on the top of a low ridge, red-brick houses and the tower of a church looking almost undamaged. It was a pleasure as well as a surprise to see these ordinary things

... The village was Passchendaele, Edward told me, but
the name meant nothing to either of us.

Forward observers, the eyes of the guns behind them, might spend
their time in a purpose-built or improvised observation post, be
attached to an infantry battalion headquarters as a liaison officer
(though here too communications were vital, and an forward observation officer without them would not be well received), or be sent
forward with an attack to organise protective fire the minute the
objective was secured. Forward observer H. M. Stanford was in a
static observation post during the first week of the Somme.

> From our OP I could see a Boisselle and could see the Divn.
> on our right who were practically bombing along through
> the village. There are practically no houses and the place
> is simply a side of a hill honeycombed with [mine] craters
> and dugouts. I saw some Bosches there so I got one of
> our guns switched round and did a bit of sniping . . .
>
> Next day I had the time of my life. I got on to Bosche
> bombing parties at short range and fairly blew hell out of
> them with shrapnel whenever they showed. I and the
> 'Hows' next door fairly stopped a counter attack which
> made our people give some ground, and I believe I made
> a bag of about 20 Huns with one round . . . One time I
> saw a Bosche bombing-party appear over the parapet and
> I hit one man plumb with a percussion [fuse], disintegrat-
> ing him and his pal alongside. Another time I got into
> the middle of six or seven firing over the parapet and the
> whole lot dropped, tho' whether all were hit I could not
> tell. Anyhow I had a real hectic day.[97]

In describing the same incident to his mother Stanford apologised
for sounding 'very beastly and bloodthirsty', but 'the whole thing is
so impersonal that one thinks no more of it at the time than shooting
rabbits. It is only afterwards, when you hear our wounded calling
for help in no-man's land that you realise the horror of it . . .'[98]

Stanford was using established communications to a well-prepared
gun-line. The German spring offensives of 1918 bit deep into the
British positions, disrupting the communications on which effective
indirect fire depended, and causing some battery commanders to

look over their shoulders earlier than they might. Lieutenant Camp-bell was sent forward as an observer on 21 March and felt unusually frightened, not just because of the shelling. 'That was nothing,' he wrote, 'that stopped as soon as the shelling stopped. This was a new fear and it was not going to stop, it lasted for more than four months, it was the fear of the unknown'. There was visible panic amongst some of the infantry, who told him: 'Jerry's through. He's in Epéhy; we've got no officers left.' Gunner Aubrey Wade, in another battery, saw broken infantry 'throwing away their rifles as they ran, coming down through the guns at the double in two and threes, hatless and wholly demoralised, calling out to us as they passed that Jerry was through and it was all over . . .'[99]

Then Campbell saw wave after wave of Germans coming in in good order, but his battery commander was reluctant to engage because he sensed the need to withdraw. Eventually Campbell was given just two guns. 'Shrapnel was the right weapon to use against enemy troops in the open,' he wrote, 'but the shells should burst fifteen feet above them, not a hundred. I corrected the fire. I had to make use of three or four corrections before the shells were bursting at the right height.' He was awarded the MC for his action that day, but for months the sight of its ribbon made him unhappy: he felt that the battery could have done better.[100]

The story was repeated all along 5th Army's front, with indirect fire first losing much effectiveness as communications were cut, and then becoming impossible as batteries were pushed off their maps. Campbell saw the men of a 60-pounder battery on their way back, and an officer told him that they would have to use the *Daily Mail* war map if they wanted to use indirect fire: they had nothing else. But good batteries kept trying. The three surviving guns of a field battery came into action near Arthur Behrend's headquarters, quickly laid out their lines of fire and 'ten minutes later they were shooting madly away'. The battery commander, a subaltern, looked so dazed that Behrend's comrades gave him a good feed. He spoke to the youngster: 'The Germans had overrun them early in the day, he said, but not before the gunners had twice repulsed them with rifles and Lewis guns. How they managed to get any guns away he didn't know – only three had been fit to move and the other three were lying smashed on the position.' When he left Behrend looked back: 'and saw the vivid flashes from the field guns firing away in the midst of our once spotless headquarters it seemed – as it so nearly was – the beginning of the end of all things'.[101]

A gunner officer sent forward with an attack would be well aware that his was a vital but dangerous job. Julian Tyndale-Biscoe was detailed to accompany an infantry attack in mid-August 1916, controlling the fire of two artillery brigades. His commanding officer told him frankly that 'the longer you stay alive the greater use you will be', and he stuffed his pockets with biscuits and raisins before setting off with two good signallers, both volunteers, and half a mile of cable on drums. He directed fire as long as he could until a sharp counterattack came in 'with German infantry zigzagging like rabbits . . . [I] picked up a rifle and had some pot shots . . . I saw several bowled over'. But by now the barrage had outdistanced the assault, and 'up popped the machine guns, with our men only half way across, and several stout Germans, standing waist-high, poured fire upon them, this holding up the whole attack'. The telephone wire had been cut, but Tyndale-Biscoe managed to save the day by telling his guns to reduce their range by flashing Morse code with an old petrol tin rigged to a rifle and bayonet. He was shot through the shoulder minutes later, but the episode earned him an MC, and MMs for the two signallers – often the unsung heroes of such stories.[102]

The other unsung heroes toiled on the gun-line, servants of machinery in the age of industrialised war, converting the shells that arrived from the wagon-lines each night into heaps of empty brass cases, recovered and sent off to the base for recycling. An infantry officer watched a field battery at work on the Somme –

> the gunners stripped and sweating, each crew working like a machine, the swing and smack of the breech blocks as clean and sweet as a kiss, and a six-foot stream of flame from the muzzle, a thunderclap of sound, and away tore the shell over the hills to the Boche trenches 5,000 yards away.[103]

There was a clear understanding in many batteries that officers concerned themselves with things like fireplans and tactics, but that

NCOs looked after daily routine. A No. 1 was very busy: he was not simply responsible for the gunners, horses, limber and wagon in his subsection, but had to do a myriad of other tasks in action, such as keeping an eye on the length of recoil every time his gun fired to ensure that the recuperator band was not too worn, watching the breech in prolonged firing so that it did not get so hot as to 'cook-off' a newly-loaded round, and monitoring the run-out adjusting valve to ensure that the barrel ran out smoothly.

Good Nos 1 jealously guarded their authority over their gunners. When Second Lieutenant Campbell tried to sort out a minor accident, Sergeant Denmark turned on him with a face like thunder: 'Who's taking charge here, are you, Sir, or am I?' He later explained: 'Don't be daft. Officers have their own responsibilities . . . How do you think it's going to help us or anyone else if you go asking to be hit?'[104] When the battery joined the preparatory bombardment for Third Ypres everybody was clear what had to be done. The creeping barrage would increase by 100 yards every four minutes, and the Nos 1 were responsible for ordering the lifts. 'There was very little talking,' recalled Campbell. 'Everyone was alert, each man had his work to do and he was doing it; he did not want to be distracted.'[105]

The layers who aimed the guns were also important men, for they needed to be able to set their sights quickly and accurately, perhaps with gas masks on or hostile counter-battery fire crashing down, so that the barrage moved at the right pace. They practised regularly, because:

> Orders came to them in degrees and minutes, and may change very suddenly when in the middle of a battle and when under fire (eg: from 3° 15' right of zero to 1° 45' left of zero, and so on). Layers are trained against a stop-watch and the figures on the gun's sights checked.

By 1918 layers were often nineteen-year-olds, with the nimble fingers and agile brains of youth, tweaking their dial sights and deftly balancing the elusive cross-levelling bubble with easy confidence. And just as regular infantry officers had often prided themselves on being good shots, so many gunner officers might have agreed with R. B. Talbot Kelly that: 'I was the equal of the best of the layers, just as I could take the place of any driver in a gun team.'[106] But the secret of good leadership lay in knowing how to do the job without crowding those whose job it was.

The Royal Artillery attracted a good proportion of steady, slightly introspective men who would never have joined the army in normal times, but took themselves and their new profession seriously. At Arthur Behrend's brigade headquarters was Gunner Freshwater, 'the hardest of hard-workers and a first-rate handyman.' He once refused to move when an officer shouted: 'Come here, carpenter.' 'Yes, I heard you,' he acknowledged. 'But I'm not a carpenter. I am Gunner Freshwater.' His devotion to his mundane duties could only have one end. On 21 March 1918 he went on with his work despite the bombardment: a shell fell nearby, and 'when the smoke and dust had cleared away we could see him lying dead on the road with his overturned barrow beside him'.[107] But there were moments when very junior soldiers simply had to carry on. At Third Ypres 134th Battery RFA was so hard hit by gas and shell that only two of its men, Acting Lance Bombardier Fisher and Gunner Monchie, were left on their feet. They knew that they *were* the battery, and that the infantry relied on them. They opened fire with a single gun at the appointed hour, and maintained the barrage lifts on their own until help arrived and Fisher, badly gassed, was carried away.[108]

THE DEVIL'S BREATH

Gas was first used on the Western Front by the Germans at Second Ypres in April 1915. Its appearance introduced a new edge of harshness into the war. Ernest Shephard's company was caught by a gas attack on Hill 60, just outside Ypres, on 1 May 1915, and even the tough-minded Shephard was shocked by what he saw.

> The scene that followed was heartbreaking. Men were caught by fumes and in dreadful agony, coughing and vomiting, rolling on the ground in agony . . . I ran round at intervals and tied up a lot of men's mouths, placed them in sitting positions, and organised parties to assist them to the support dugouts . . . When we found our men were dying from fumes we wanted to charge, but were not allowed to do so. What a start for May. Hell could find no worse [than] the groans of scores of dying and badly hurt men.

The following day he wrote:

> The bitterest Sunday I have ever known or wish to know . . . Hardly know who is dead yet, but several of my best chums are gone under. Had we lost as heavily while actually fighting we would not have cared as much, but our dear boys died like rats in a trap, instead of heroes as they all were. The Dorset Regiment's motto is now: 'No

prisoners.' No quarter will be given when we again get to fighting.[109]

Lord Stanhope was at a French headquarters near Ypres just after the initial attack, and saw a French general interview prisoners, one of whom admitted to helping launch the gas. 'Sergeant major,' said the general quietly. 'Take a file of men and take this man to the wall at the bottom of the garden.' There was a brief pause and a volley.[110]

A German officer prophesied that the Allies would condemn the Germans as uncivilised and develop gas themselves as soon as they could, which is precisely what happened. The British government immediately decided to retaliate, and in May 1915 Charles Foulkes, a regular engineer, who had hitherto known nothing about chemical weapons, was appointed to command an organisation which began as the Special Service Party, was briefly 250th Company RE, and went on to become the Special Companies and eventually the Special Brigade. Foulkes was typical of the energetic and resourceful men who would rise to meet the challenges posed by military revolutions, without allowing existing organisational barriers to stop them, but, in the process, losing much of their objectivity about the merits of their pet weapons.

The War Office wrote to universities in search of chemists, and combed the army for suitable personnel: by 30 July it had 400, 126 by transfer and 274 by special enlistment. In September, on the eve of the first British use of gas at Loos, Robert Graves's company commander was scathing about them: 'Chemistry-dons from London university, a few lads straight from school, one or two NCOs of the old-soldier type, trained together for three weeks, then given a job as responsible as this.'[111]

This was not an unfair analysis of the Special Companies' composition, although it did less than justice to the quality and commitment of many of their members. They were enlisted as corporals, Royal Engineers, on 3 shillings a day, which created predictable problems, and Foulkes asked them to revert to private soldiers. Ronald Ginns, a well-educated and democratically-inclined corporal, described how: 'the proposal was voted upon and, needless to say, rejected unanimously'. He agreed, however, that some of the Old Army NCOs were not ideal. There was a corporal with a DCM: 'reduced to the ranks for drunkenness. He looked like what he was, a drink-sodden Irishman, who was however entirely destitute of fear.' And then there was a sergeant who was:

> a regular army man from the Lancers. He was a drink-sodden bully, who claimed that he came from a good family. His most unpleasant trait was his habit of borrowing money from the corporals in his section and forgetting to pay it back. Those who objected to being fleeced, myself particularly, had extra duties found for them. I should have been heartily pleased if he had been killed.[112]

Some of the sergeants '& better-class corporals' were commissioned in the field, 'gazetted straight away and equipped in France'. And it was also quickly realised that the gas companies had an appetite for honest labour, and reserve infantry battalions in Britain produced 'some good steady workers . . .'.

Foulkes recommended that chlorine gas should be discharged from cylinders in front-line trenches, which was the method used by the Germans. He had 5,100 cylinders containing 140 tons of chlorine available for Loos. By dawn on 25 September the 1,400 men of the gas companies had lugged their cylinders into the front line, connected up their discharge pipes – a vertical pipe going up to the parapet and a horizontal pipe pointing towards the German lines. The success of the gas would depend partly on wind direction, and Haig, then commanding 1st Army, was faced with a difficult decision, for the wind was very light that morning: he asked his senior aide de camp to light a cigarette, and when he saw the smoke drift gently eastwards he authorised the use of gas. It worked well in the southern part of the attack front, but in the north the wind eddied back, blowing the gas onto the attackers. The episode is often highlighted as an example of the sheer stupidity of the high command, but the effects of the gas on British troops are overstated: in fact it killed only seven of them, and without it the substantial gains around Loos village would have been impossible.

The first appearance of gas had prompted the adoption of primitive anti-gas protection, with rags, gauze or cotton pads (French and Belgian chemists generously supplied sanitary towels for this purpose, with ear-loops already handily attached) held across the mouth and nose by tape or string. It could be kept damp with a solution of bicarbonate of soda, and some medical officers recommended urine. In late May some units were supplied 'with a flannel pad chemically treated and a pair of eye protection mica goggles'. By the end of the year most soldiers had what was officially called the 'smoke helmet' but was better known as 'the goggle-eyed booger with the tit', a grey flannel bag, impregnated with chemicals, with two eyepieces and a rubber mouthpiece. Frank Hawkings received his helmet 'made of flannel soaked in hexamine and glycerine, and fitted with a rubber mouth valve' in July.[113] Bernard Livermore was in the line near Vimy a year later when:

> Some order came round that a gas attack was expected and we had to pull our uncomfortable flannel bags over our heads. The eye goggles steamed up and we could see very little but we dared not take them off as gas might be in the trench. A new device had been issued to rid the trenches of gas; gigantic flat fans, like fly swotters on long poles. One had to walk along the duckboards, flapping gas in front of one by beating on the ground. We flapped the gas – if there was gas – round the traverse; there we met a man from the next bay flapping it stoutly into our territory.[114]

The smoke helmet had only a limited life once exposed to gas so two had to be carried. In 1917 it was replaced by the PH (Phenate-Hexamine) Helmet, which had thicker material, impregnated with alcohol, glycerine, caustic soda and sodium phenate. It had a one-way valve at the mouth piece, and two glass eyepieces, with spare glasses available.

This in turn was succeeded by the box respirator, which Lieutenant W. Drury of 4/King's Shropshire Light Infantry described in his Western Command Gas School notes as:

> A tin cylinder filled with chemicals, with inlet valve at the bottom, and connected by a rubber tube to impervious

> face mask. In connecting tube is a rubber outlet valve. The face piece or mask is made of water-proof material with 2 elastic bands attached to slip over the head & hold the mask in position ... The whole is issued in a water-proof sachel [sic].

Fresh air was drawn in through the cylinder, whose mixture of charcoal, permanganate and soda lime, in layers separated by gauze, was designed to filter gas from the air to make it breathable. The box respirator was available in five sizes, although 'Nos 1 and 5 sizes are only issued by special indent ... Every man at the front should have issued to him a box respirator, one PH helmet and one pair of goggles.' Masks were tested in gas chambers at training units in Britain and at the base, and platoon commanders were bidden to inspect them weekly for wear and tear.[115] The box respirator was a lifesaver, but men hated living in it. F. P. Roe called it 'the familiar obscene blubbery spitting object, always a major obstacle to full movement, and often uncomfortably sweaty in warm weather or if worn over a long period of time. The eyepieces invariably clouded over from the inside ...'.[116]

Anti-gas protection marched in step with improvements in gas delivery. In early 1916 the four existing gas companies expanded into the Special Brigade, with four battalions of four companies apiece, and a mortar battalion. The latter, equipped with 4-inch Stokes mortars, pointed the way ahead, for gas was now being delivered, by both sides, by indirect fire as well as cylinder. From mid-1916 gas was routinely added to bombardments. It was useful for incapacitating the horses of hostile batteries, which could be accorded only primitive protection via an equine gas mask: the very notion of trying to fit masks to terrified horses in a muddy wagon-line at two o'clock on a rainy morning beggars belief. Captain Dunn saw his first horse in a gas mask in August 1917: 'worn at the "alert", fixed to the noseband of the head-stall'. Gas could be used to drench headquarters, so that staff officers, even in deep dugouts, would be forced to work masked-up; and it could be slipped in with the morning mist to incapacitate men caught at break-of-day befuddlement.

Both the Allies and the Germans relied on two main types of gas shell, each of several different varieties, developed in an attempt to sidestep the enemy's anti-gas protection. T-shells delivered liquid (usually benzyl bromide and xylyl bromide) which vaporised into lachrymatory or tear gas, 'which causes men to weep and the eyes are made so painful that men are practically put out of action for some time'. The liquid vaporised slowly and ground contaminated by it remained dangerous for twenty-four hours or longer. K-shells were lethal, their palite or disphosgene converted to gas when the shell burst to give instant, though short-duration, effect. Sometimes K-shells had tear or sneezing gas added: the latter made it hard for men to keep their respirators in place, and if they fumbled too long the gas killed them.

Gas shells had a sound all of their own. The liquid in them – 317cc for a German 77-mm shell – slopped about as the shells spun in flight, sometimes giving them a curious hooting sound (James Dunn thought they 'twittered') as they arrived to burst with a plop which was scarcely louder that that of a dud. By the end of the war the British were using gas grenades too. One, a variant of the No. 28 grenade, filled with a coughing agent, was used for clearing enemy-held dugouts, and another variant, filled with a persistent tear agent, could be used to render abandoned dugouts uninhabitable by unmasked troops.

Mustard gas, a favourite filling for German shells in the last eighteen months of the war, was not primarily lethal but was incapacitating, spreading ugly blisters over the skin and causing temporary or permanent blindness. Captain Dunn reported the symptoms as: 'redness or blistering of sweaty parts, streaming eyes, and a few have some cough'. One doughty fusilier muttered: 'I don't mind the (obscene) gas if it'll rid me of the (obscene) lice.'[117] Dunn noted that he had a fresh batch of casualties the next morning, and it soon became clear that mustard was very persistent indeed, and that splashed uniforms had to be discarded.

And in sufficient concentration mustard was indeed a killer. Sergeant Charles Arnold of the Border Regiment was in a dugout at Ypres when a gas shell burst squarely inside:

> The men on my right and left were killed along with 15 others. I had got a slight hit in the head and was gassed.

> It was the time the Germans first started to use mustard gas. I had not been in the ambulance long before I was blind. The gas took all the skin off me and all my hair as well.[118]

One British officer, sent to decontaminate a captured German position in late 1918, saw two of his experienced sergeants, Jo Cross and Don Britton, looking at some damaged gas shells without their gas masks on.

> Though we had all been through German mustard gas bombardments and knew the smell of it and that, normally, it was not particularly lethal, this was their first experience of it in high concentration and close quarters. Alas, it was their last . . .
>
> Cross died in his billet next morning, and Britton was taken to hospital *in extremis*. And I, having inhaled comparatively little of the foul stuff, woke up the same morning, temporarily blinded, sores on the forehead and under the arms and with no voice.[119]

Familiarity often bred a dangerous contempt. When the Germans first used what was initially called 'mustard oil' at Ypres in 1917, Major Martin Littlewood RAMC saw the breezy divisional gas officer pick up an empty shell and put it under his arm. It produced an immediate blister, 'so I entered him sick. It was a great temptation to fill in his label as a "self-inflicted wound".' Littlewood thought that the new gas was very effective indeed, and believed that the Germans could not have been aware just how many British gunners had been blinded by it.[120]

From mid-1917 the mortar battalion's companies often delivered Thermit bombs, which were not conventional gas at all: their mixture of powdered aluminium and iron oxide was ignited to produce 'a metal-melting heat that doused enemy trenches with a rain of molten fragments'.[121] By then some of the best results were being obtained from the Livens projector, brainchild of William Livens, a civil engineer commissioned in 1914. His projector was basically a huge and simple mortar, usually dug-in dozens at a time, and fired at once to lob their projectiles, containing gas or Thermit, a relatively short distance. Baseplates of Livens projectors still emerge after the spring ploughing of French and Belgian fields: they look like large steel helmets trodden on by an ungainly giant.

From April to December 1917 the Special Brigade executed 348 operations, with almost 12,000 cylinders and 100,000 projectors and another 120,000 Stokes mortar bombs delivering about 2,050 tons of gas.[122] Foulkes still hoped to do better: in the last year of the war he experimented with 'gas beam attack', with railway trucks packed with gas cylinders trundled parallel with the German lines when the wind was right: in ten beam attacks Foulkes's men discharged more than 27,000 cylinders of gas.

The German scientist and ardent patriot Fritz Haber played a leading part in the development of the German chemical weapons programme, and his son Ludwig wrote *The Poisonous Cloud* (1986), one of the best works on gas in the First World War.[123] His last chapter, 'Was Gas a Failure?', demands the unequivocal response that it was. Its effects were never decisive: indeed, Fritz Haber himself admitted that once the British had developed a box respirator, gas 'was a waste of time'. It caused far fewer casualties than shells and mortar bombs, machine guns and rifles, and of the men it injured fewer (3–4 percent) actually died than was the case with most other weapons, where deaths ran at about 25 percent of all casualties.

But it made the lives of all combatants significantly more difficult: the invisible threat of a ghastly death struck at the very heart of men's ability to cope with battle. Norman Gladden reflected that gas 'inspired a fear that was out of all proportion to the damage done'. Lord Moran thought that it was a major cause of psychiatric casualties, for it exposed a man's natural unfitness for war, although he believed that most of those affected by gas were more frightened than hurt. Alan Hanbury Sparrow called gas 'the Devil's Breath'.

> It was Ahrimanic from the first velvety phut of the shell burst to those corpse-like breaths that a man inhaled almost unawares. It lingered about out of control. When he fired it, man released an evil force that became free to bite friend and foe till such time as it died into the earth. Above all, it went against God-inspired conscience . . .
>
> The gas mask makes you feel only half a man. You can't

think; the air you breathe has been filtered of all save a few chemical substances. A man doesn't live on what passes through the filter, he merely exists.[124]

Even soldiers who had seen many dreadful things found that it was the sight of gas casualties that froze their marrow years afterwards. Bernard Martin heard the gas-gong sound at Ypres in 1916 when the sentry spotted a cloud of gas moving towards the British lines.

> Blast from a shrapnel shell momentarily blew a gap in the gas cloud, and I saw several men, (unrecognisable of course in their masks) standing irresolute as though uncertain of purpose – all but one had made his purpose apparent. He was without a mask, his head bare, his white face expressing horror. Before the cloud of gas reformed I saw this man lurch sideways, arms outstretched, attempting to pull off another man's mask; a third, wielding what I judged to be a bit of broken duckboard, pressed between the two. I saw one of them fall to the ground. All over in a moment, a vivid picture in my mind for ever, and ever, and ever, and ever.[125]

Albert Bullock was moving up to the attack through a gas cloud with his company on 4 October 1918 and: 'met Griffiths crying because he had just found one of the goggles of his gas mask broken and didn't know what to do. Last I saw of him.'[126] And for James Dunn there was something almost wordlessly terrible about the effects of the gas that passed low through a Flanders farmyard:

> Horses and tethered cattle were startled and tugged at their head-ropes. A little dog on a heavy chain, unable to scramble onto the roof of his kennel, ran about frantically; hens flew onto walls and outhouses, clucking loudly; little chickens stood on tiptoe, craning to raise their gaping beaks above the vapour; mice came out of their holes, one climbed the gable of a barn only to fall back when near the top. Seedling peas and other vegetables were bleached, and wilted.[127]

BRAZEN CHARIOTS

By 1918 gas, indecisive and ghastly though it was, was firmly woven into the combined arms battle, as part of the preparatory bombardment, tucked into the creeping barrage, or to blanket areas to which the enemy was to be denied free access. Smoke, too, was widely used, delivered by shells, mortar bombs, hand-held smoke candles, smoke generators or even smoke grenades.[128] But far more portentous was the fact that this battle now contained a weapon which was beginning its ascent to the pinnacle which it was not to scale for another generation: the tank.

The Tank Corps, created by Royal Warrant on 27 July 1917, had evolved from the Machine Gun Corps (Heavy), with a strength of just 133 officers and 1,069 men in May 1916, to reach 2,801 officers and 25,498 men at the war's end. By that time it had almost exactly the same number of officers and men in France as the cavalry – 13,984 mounted troops to 13,594 members of the Tank Corps. Of the three most important types of tank, 1,015 Mark IVs, over 400 Mk Vs, and 700 Mk V* tanks had been built by the end of 1918. The story of the Tank Corps is one of remarkable expansion for an arm which did not exist when war broke out, and if the British may be blamed for losing their lead in armoured warfare in the inter-war years, they rarely receive the credit they deserve for winning the race during the First World War. Ludendorff cited Allied tank superiority as one of the main reasons for German defeat in 1918. He was being less than honest, for the history of the last Hundred Days shows that tanks were still only useful for set-piece battles, and were not yet able to achieve and maintain the sort of operational tempo which they displayed in some Second World War campaigns. They were not battle-winners on their own, but they had already shown themselves to be worthy members of the combined arms team into which the British army had so painfully evolved.

The heavy tank was debuted by the British on the Somme on 15 September 1916. Bernard Martin, hearing the noise of a nearby engine, went over to investigate and found:

> A great thing like one of those tanks for water on the roofs of big buildings, with an engine inside and I suppose men ... A kind of land battleship! As we walked over ground made uneven by big shell holes, branches of trees and stumps, I gave my thoughts absolute freedom. 'This new weapon will be irresistible, will cross No-Man's-Land, go over trenches, withstand small arms fire and machine-gun fire, perhaps even field gun shells ... Jerry infantry will be helpless!'[129]

Tanks were used again, still in small numbers, at Arras and Third Ypres the following year. On neither occasion was the ground firm enough to give the tanks much prospect of success, as Second Lieutenant Gerry Brooks, commanding the tank 'Fay' on 2 August, discovered all too well.

> The fun began when the tape we were following led through some very swampy ground. It was so wet we found it hard to swing. The four of us [tanks] got rather bunched and 'Foam' received a couple of direct hits and Harris her commander and two more of the crew were wounded. Harris was in great pain having his left arm nearly blown off from the elbow and also armour plate and rivets in his leg. We passed a good many dead who had fallen on July 31st. Soon we came up to our infantry who were hiding in shell holes with very heavy machine-gun fire. This pattered against our armour and some came through in a fine spray so that we were all bleeding from small cuts.

'Fay' became bogged down and had to be abandoned shortly afterwards. One crew member was killed as they bailed out, but Brooks managed to make his way back to British lines.[130] The injuries caused by rivets, pieces of armour plate and bullet fragments were so characteristic of tank warfare that crewmen wore leather goggles with metal grilles over their eyes and a chainmail curtain covering their face. Sapper officer Lieutenant V. F. Eberle thought that it was a hopeless venture from the start. 'I believe the number I counted was fourteen within my view from one point,' he wrote. 'In this particular area they had an almost impossible task, becoming sitting targets once they were held fast in the gluey mud.'[131]

That November tanks were used on a much larger scale at Cambrai, where the firm downland offered better going. One driver of G Battalion recalled: 'What a joy it was to be driving on good, dry ground without having to crawl in bottom gear with mud up to your sponsons.' Brigadier General Hugh Elles, commander of the Tank Corps, led the attack in the heavy Mark IV tank 'Hilda', commanded by Lieutenant T. H. de B. Leach. 'Hilda' flew the flag of the Tank Corps, its dark green, dark red and brown stripes symbolising the tanks' progression through mud, through blood, to the green fields beyond.[132] The surrounding tanks were 'Harvester', 'Harrier' and 'Huntress', for this was H Battalion, and the names of individual tanks took their initial letters of their names from that of the battalion.

The leading tanks carried a bundle of fascines – tightly-bound stout brushwood – to drop into German trenches to make them easier to cross. Operating in sections of three, No. 1 tank dropped its fascine into the front-line trench, crossed and turned left, shooting up the trench garrison as it did so. The remaining two tanks made for the second trench, where No. 2 repeated the crossing process, leaving the remaining tank free to proceed to the third trench. The infantry followed up, moving through gaps ripped in the wire and capitalising on the 'tank fright' generated by the weapons already christened 'the Devil's Chariots' by a German journalist.

There was a hold-up on 51st Highland Division's front, for which Major General Harper is generally blamed. However, the best modern research suggests that it was less the fault of infantry-tank co-operation than the inevitable consequence of the vulnerability of tanks in this sector as they breasted a rise only to be confronted by German field gunners who had been well trained in anti-tank tactics. Lieutenant General von Watter, commanding the German 54th Division, had a brother who had encountered British tanks on the Somme, and they had debated the best way of dealing with them. German gunners hauled their 77-mms out of their gunpits and fought them in the open, quickly traversing to take on the tanks as they nosed over the ridge.

The incident spawned the legend of 'the Gunner of Flesquières'. Haig's Cambrai dispatch spoke of many tanks being destroyed by 'a German artillery officer who, remaining alone at his battery, served a field-gun single handed until killed at his gun. The great bravery of this officer aroused the admiration of all ranks.'[133] A footnote to the bound version of the dispatches added that the German officer was not identified. Efforts were certainly made at the time to find his body, which would not have been the case had the incident been simply an ex-post facto invention of Haig's to excuse the temporary setback. Yet there seems no factual basis for the incident as described, although both Lieutenant Müller and Sergeant Major Kruger of 108th Field Artillery Regiment merited the gratitude of their countrymen for their bravery that day. Had Cambrai stopped after two days, as was originally Haig's wish, it would now be remembered as a fine example of excellent co-operation between artillery (the swift and accurate bombardment which accompanied the assault was a key ingredient of the success achieved on the first day), tanks and infantry. But the cavalry exploitation did not materialise, and the battle subsequently bogged down into an attritional struggle for Bourlon Wood which left the British poorly balanced to face a deftly-judged German counterattack.

British tanks played an undistinguished part in resisting the German spring offensives of 1918, although the Germans put tanks captured at Cambrai (prominently marked with large iron crosses) to good effect alongside a few of their large and cumbersome A7V tanks in these attacks. The first ever tank-versus-tank action took place near Villers-Bretonneux on 24 April 1918 when Second Lieutenant Frank Mitchell's Mark IV tank engaged a German A7V *Sturmpanzerwagen*. Some of Mitchell's crew had been so badly mustard-gassed that they had been evacuated, and the eyes of the survivors were all smarting. Mitchell spotted the German tank:

> I informed the crew, and a great thrill ran through us all. Opening a loophole I looked out. There, some three hundred yards away a round squat-looking monster was advancing; behind it came waves of infantry, and farther away to the left and right crawled two more of these armed tortoises.
>
> So we had met our rivals at last! For the first time in history tank was encountering tank!

Mitchell's tank was 'male' (that is, armed with cannon) Mk IV, with a 6-pounder gun in a sponson on each side. The 'female' was equipped with two machine guns but no cannon, and there were, predictably enough, 'hermaphrodites' with one of each. The tank was pitching sharply as it crossed the shell-torn ground, and Mitchell's right-hand gunner missed with his first two shots. The Germans replied with armour-piercing machine gun fire which 'filled the interior with myriads of sparks and flying splinters. The crew flung themselves flat on the floor. The driver ducked his head and drove straight on.' Mitchell manoeuvred so as to give his left-hand gunner, Sergeant J. R. McKenzie, a shot. McKenzie had been blinded in his right eye and was manning his gun single-handed, as his loader had already been evacuated. He missed with his first round, and Mitchell then decided to stop to allow for steadier shooting.

> The pause was justified; a well-aimed shot hit the enemy's conning tower, bringing him to a standstill. Another round and yet another white puff at the front of the tank denoted a second hit! Peering with swollen eyes through the narrow slit, the gunners shouted words of triumph that were drowned by the roar of the engine. Then once more he aimed with great deliberation and hit for the third time. Through a loophole I saw the tank heel over to one side; then a door opened and out ran the crew. We had knocked the monster out.

Although there remains uncertainly as to whether Mitchell's opponent was actually knocked out, or fell over while turning sharply to take evasive action, the significance of the clash is clear enough.[134]

At Amiens on 8 August 1918 – what would become known as 'the black day of the German army' – Rawlinson's 4th Army deployed 534 tanks, 342 of the new Mark Vs, 72 whippets, and 120 supply tanks. Captain Henry Smeddle commanded a section of three Mark V* tanks in the battle. A public schoolboy from Dulwich College, he had enlisted into the Army Service Corps in 1915 and had reached the rank of lance corporal before being commissioned into the Machine Gun Corps (Heavy) in June 1917. By now very careful attention was paid to co-operation between tanks and infantry, and Smeddle spent the days before the battle being briefed on the plan and passing the information on to his men, 'excepting the actual date, time, and location, which would only be given at the last moment'. Surprise was crucial: 'There was to be no smoking, or flashing of electric torches, and no shouting, whistling, or unnecessary noise during the march. Only tank commanders would be allowed to smoke; the glow of their cigarettes was to be the method by which they would guide their tanks whilst walking in front without undue attention.' Smeddle's tanks moved into position along guide-tapes at a slow walking pace, and he waited for zero hour in a silence that seemed like the quiet before the storm.

The barrage 'broke the silence with a terrific crashing roar . . . It was still dark, but the flashes of the guns gave out sufficient light to distinguish the forms of the gunners and guns, the nearest of which was twenty-five yards from where I was standing, and so quietly had everything been prepared that I was not aware of its presence until it started firing.' He led his section forward, using his pocket compass to keep direction through the thick mist, crossing the first-line trenches, now empty of infantry, and meeting wounded and German prisoners on their way back. He lost a man to a strafing attack by low-flying German aircraft, and found himself being filmed by 'the official cinema operators' as he reached his first objective. Smeddle's tanks were in the second wave, but they now took the lead, and Smeddle was narrowly missed by the nosecap from a shell which hit the tank two feet from his face. It was now clear just how well things were going.

The enemy were evidently quite unaware of the rapidity of our advance, for just as we were about opposite Harbonnières we saw an ammunition train steaming into the station as if nothing was the matter. It was immediately shelled by all the 6-pdr guns of the approaching tanks. One shell must have struck a powder van for suddenly the whole train burst into one great sheet of flame, reaching to a height of not less than 150 feet. Needless to say that train was stopped.

It was followed by another one, a passenger train rushing up fresh troops; this was running on another track and ran right into our lines where it was captured, complete with personnel.[135]

The development of the tank marked another step in the soldier's gradual evolution from warrior to servant of machinery. The daily intimacy of their life bound tank crewmen with a peculiar intensity. In October 1916 tank gunner Victor Archard lamented the loss of a chum, posted as missing: 'Poor Jim was my most intimate friend; he was one of God's good men and I still hope for him. I will never give a German any quarter after this, if I am not prevented by orders.'[136] Crewmen were cooped up in a hot, rattling metal box, filled with the fumes of an unreliable engine fuelled by all too easily-ignited petrol. A direct hit from a field gun might mean instant oblivion: Edwin Campion Vaughan saw a tank supporting his attack on the 'Springfield' pillbox at Passchendaele converted to 'a crumpled heap of iron' by a single heavy shell

Armour-piercing bullets, shell-splinters, or rivets dislodged by hits sped around inside the armoured carapace, and the special goggles issued to crewmen did not always prevent their blinding. Lieutenant Basil Henriques commanded a tank on the Somme in September 1916.

As we approached the Germans let fly at us with might and man. At first no damage was done, and we retaliated, killing about 20. Then a smack against my flap in front caused splinters to come in, and the blood to pour down my face. Another minute and my driver got the same.

> Then our prism glass broke to pieces, then another smash,
> I think it must have been a bomb, right in my face.
> The next one wounded my driver so badly that we had to
> stop.[137]

Henriques looked back to see his gunners prostrate on the floor and the tank's sides riddled.

If a tank began to burn, as it so often did, men faced an urgent scramble to escape. The sight of terribly burned tank crew persuaded even infantrymen out in the mud that theirs was likely to be an easier death. And Germans, initially terrified by a tank's appearance, often responded viciously if they took its crew alive. When Lieutenant C. B. Arnold baled out of his stricken light tank 'Musical Box', deep in the German position east of Amiens on 8 August 1918 he described how:

> We were all on fire. In this rush Calvey was shot in the
> stomach and killed. We rolled over and over to try to
> extinguish the flames. I saw the enemy approaching all
> around. The first arrived came for me with a rifle and
> bayonet. I got hold of this and the point of the bayonet
> entered my right forearm. The second man struck at my
> head with the butt end of his rifle ... When I came to,
> there were dozens around me, and anyone who could
> reach me did so and I was well knocked. They were
> furious.[138]

Taken to enemy divisional headquarters, he was punched in the face by an angry staff officer. Arnold recognised that his tank's achievements that day really depended on the bravery of the private soldiers in his crew, and concluded his report by affirming: 'The conduct of Gunner Ribbans and Driver Calvey was beyond all praise throughout.' New weapon: old values

SWORD AND PISTOL

Despite the efforts of some excellent scholars, the reputation of British cavalry in the First World War remains low. Stephen Badsey ruefully concluded that:

> The metaphor of the charge against machine guns, or of the incompetent Victorian cavalry general attempting to control a tank battle, has spread beyond military studies into the general vocabulary of historians and readers of history, as a touchstone of all that is reactionary, foolish and futile. It is probably too well established ever to be removed.[139]

In part this is another damaging legacy of some historians always ready to nudge a chuckle from their readers at the spectacle of silly men on funny horses galloping about amongst the mud and trenches. In part it reflects a tendency, still alive and well, to associate the British army's wartime performance with its social composition, a process bound to reflect badly on the cavalry, which demanded substantial private means for its officers. And in part it embodies the very real problem of making sense of the changing role of horsed cavalry as the military revolution gusted across the Western Front.[140]

In 1914 British cavalry was unquestionably the best, for its limited numbers, on either side. It had learned valuable lessons in the Boer

War, and almost uniquely amongst European cavalry, carried exactly the same rifle as the infantry rather than the short and less accurate carbine in vogue elsewhere. Sergeant Percy Snelling of the 12th Lancers saw French horsemen in action in August 1914, and noted that 'they do not fight much dismounted and their carbines are very unreliable', while Major Archibald 'Sally' Home thought that 'their weakness lay in the small attention that had been given to fighting on foot, and for this work the carbines they carried were an inferior weapon'.[141] There had been a fierce pre-war debate as to the relative merits of shock action, with sword and lance, and fire action with the rifle. Although the traditionalists had eventually won by getting the lance, briefly abolished as a weapon of war, reinstated in lancer regiments, the 1907 edition of *Cavalry Training* emphasised that 'thorough efficiency in the use of the rifle and in dismounted tactics is an absolute necessity'. But it went on to affirm that 'the rifle, effective as it is, cannot replace the effect produced by the speed of the horse, the magnetism of the charge, and the terror of cold steel'.

In one sense the controversy echoed discussions about the use of the bayonet by the infantry, and a belief in the enduring value of 'shock action' reflected the need to give men the confidence to close with their enemy. Even Douglas Haig, cavalryman though he was, thought that fire action was nine times more likely than shock action. In 1910 Lieutenant Colonel F. M. Edwards, another cavalryman, summed up the views of many of his comrades when he observed that: 'The *desire* to use the sabre or lance should be predominant, but it must be held in check by a thorough knowledge of the power of the firearm.'[142]

British cavalry dressed in khaki uniform like that of the infantry, but with a leather bandolier rather than webbing equipment, and had long ago eschewed the majesty of busby, lance-cap and dragoon helmet for the service-dress cap. In contrast, as Second Lieutenant Kenneth Godsell observed, the French still retained cuirassiers, with back- and breast-plates and steel and brass helmets, as their shock cavalry. These antique warriors were:

> easy to see at long distances, as the sun flashed in all directions from their shining breastplates. As the latter

were not bullet-proof, it was difficult to understand their exact function. The French cavalryman is rarely seen off his horse. He has a rooted objection to dismounting. His animals were looking very thin and tired as a result of long and trying marches in this hot weather.[143]

The German cavalry looked just as old-fashioned. Although German regulars had taken to wearing field-grey by 1914, their cavalry went to war in uniforms of traditional cut, with plastron tunics for uhlans, frogged jackets for hussars and spiked helmets of polished steel for cuirassiers. The inspector general of German cavalry frankly admitted that: 'Despite the improvements made in fighting dismounted, there was nevertheless a lack of schooling in firing practice in the larger units . . .'.[144]

Some pre-war cavalrymen had envisaged that the war would start with a big cavalry battle in which one side would seize superiority. In fact there were many clashes, on a much smaller scale, as German advance guards met British rearguards. On 22 August Major Tom Bridges's squadron of the 4th Dragoon Guards ambushed a German patrol on the Mons-Brussels road, and, as Private Ted Worrell remembered, there was plenty of old-style hack and gallop when the Germans fell back after a brief firefight:

> The chase went on for a mile but we were better mounted and caught up with them on the outskirts of Soignies and there was a proper old melee. Captain Hornby ran his sword through one Jerry and Sgt. Major Sharpe got another. I got a poke at a man but I don't know what happened to him. There was a fair old noise what with the clatter of hooves and a lot of shouting. The Jerries couldn't manage their lances at close quarters and several threw them away and tried to surrender but we weren't in no mood to take prisoners and we downed a lot of them before they managed to break it off and gallop away. Our horses were pretty blown so Capt. Hornby decided not to give chase. I suppose it was all over in five minutes but we certainly showed them that the 4th were hot stuff.[145]

On 24 August the 9th Lancers (with Soarer Campbell in command) and two squadrons of the 4th Dragoon Guards charged

German infantry and guns near Elouges to take the pressure off the infantry rearguard. The charge bought the infantry a breathing space, but did little real damage to the Germans (though this did not prevent it from featuring in a spirited and largely imaginary battlepiece by Richard Caton Woodville, now hanging in the National Army Museum in Chelsea). In contrast, on the 28th the British 3rd Cavalry Brigade, covering the gap between I and II Corps as they fell back, put in a textbook attack, with the fire of J Battery Royal Horse Artillery and machine guns and dismounted squadrons of the Royal Scots Greys covering a charge by a squadron of the 12th Lancers. The lancers went through the dragoons of the German advance guard, who had dismounted to use their carbines, rallied and returned twice more. Captain Bryant, adjutant of the 12th, had not invested in the new 1912-pattern regulation sword, the officer's version of the plainer trooper's 1908-pattern sword with its straight, slim blade and big handguard. However, his 'old cutting sword, well sharpened . . . went in and out of the German like a pat of butter'. He cut down five Germans, and another officer killed three with his sword and another with his revolver. The action 'very effectively dampened the ardour of the German cavalry' and deterred the Guard Cavalry Division from exploiting the inter-corps gap.[146]

There were other cavalry actions on the retreat to the Marne and the subsequent advance to the Aisne, with that at Néry on 1 September giving L Battery RHA its niche in the military pantheon. But it was not until First Ypres that the cavalry again played a really significant role. By now it had been reorganised, and instead of the one big division which had started the war there was now a Cavalry Corps, which was to remain in existence, with occasional restructurings and a very brief disappearance, for the rest of the war. The Corps had five divisions in September 1915, and shrank thereafter to constitute just three (under 3 percent of the strength of the BEF) by the war's end. In October 1915 the Cavalry Corps generated less firepower than an infantry division because its regiments were much smaller than infantry battalions, one man in four had to hold the horses of the other three, and the Royal Horse Artillery's 13-pounder gun was less effective than the 18-pounders of the infantry divisions.

But it fought dismounted to hold Messines Ridge against determined German attacks with courage and, no less to the point, marksmanship of which any infantry battalion would have been proud.

In late 1915 the Cavalry Corps furnished a Dismounted Division, created by producing a three-battalion brigade from each of the cavalry divisions. Every dismounted battalion was composed of three companies, one from each regiment in the parent brigade. The Division lost almost 1,000 men during a seven-week tour of trench duty, persuading 'Sally' Home that 'officers and men feel that they had done their share and there is not that restless feeling in the Corps. We are busy training now in real cavalry work in the hope that if the day comes we may be ready.'[147]

Some cavalry always remained outside the Cavalry Corps. There was a cavalry regiment in each corps, and a cavalry squadron which formed part of each division to provide its commander with gallopers, mounted escorts and a small mobile reserve. The 1/Northumberland Hussars, for instance, sent a squadron each to 1st, 7th and 8th Divisions. B Squadron announced in *Plum and Apple*, 1st Division's newspaper, that it constituted 'a gallant band of mounted navvies FOR HIRE – ALL KINDS of tasks undertaken . . . We will dig you in cheaply or do you in for nothing.' They were as surprised at the physical appearance of French cuirassiers as were some of their regular brethren, and when they were pointed out to Private Chrystal he declared: 'Gox! Wey, I thought them——wor German hoolans an' fired at the likes o' them aol day yesterday!' Private Daglish of the Morpeth Troop went some way towards making amends. When a pretty girl waved her handkerchief and shouted '*Vivent les anglais*' as his troop rode by he replied politely: 'Very canny, hoos yorsel?'

The main task confronting British cavalry and its commanders was not, however, riding errands for divisional commanders or worsening Anglo-French relations, but trying to devise ways in which the mounted arm could restore a measure of mobility to battle by capitalising on success achieved by infantry and artillery. And here its problem was wholly new. In the past cavalry had been able to find flanks to turn or gaps to exploit. On the relatively small battlefields of the eighteenth and nineteenth centuries some could be kept back, under the hand of the army commander, for prompt commitment when he saw that the enemy's line was so weakened that it might be broken by a charge, or when he thought the moment ripe to launch his horsemen in pursuit. On the Western Front there were no open flanks round which cavalry could swirl, and the difficulties of moving troops, on foot or horseback, across crowded rear areas while a battle was in progress made it difficult to bring cavalry up in time to seize a fleeting opportunity.

Much has been made of the failure of cavalry to exploit the success achieved around High Wood in the night attack of 14 July 1916 on the Somme. Both the Official History and the redoubtable Marquess of Anglesey, historian of the British cavalry, maintain that the cavalry destined to exploit success, 2nd Indian Cavalry Division, led by the Secunderabad Cavalry Brigade, simply took too long to get within striking distance, and that part of the problem stemmed from a smashed-up battlefield laced with trenches. In fact the war diaries of the units concerned make it clear that the leading cavalry regiment was on the old British front line by 7.00 that morning, and that the whole of the leading brigade, with its artillery, was there by 9.30 a.m. There was no trench-crossing problem. Portable bridges to allow cavalry to cross trenches had already been developed, and a squadron of the specialist Canadian Fort Garry Horse, complete with bridges, was attached to the Secunderabad Brigade that day but did not need to use any of them.

Nor is it true to say that the attack, when it went in late that afternoon, was a catastrophe. Lyn Macdonald quotes Second Lieutenant F. W. Beadle, an artillery officer in 33rd Division, who watched the charge of the Deccan Horse and the 7th Dragoon Guards.

> It was an incredible sight, an unbelievable sight, they galloped up with their lances and with pennants flying, up the slope to High Wood and straight into it. Of course they were falling all the way . . . I've never seen anything like it. They simply galloped on through all that and horses and men dropping on the ground, with no hope against the machine-guns, because the Germans up on the ridge were firing down into the valley where the soldiers were. It was an absolute rout. A magnificent sight. Tragic.[148]

I must begin by declaring my admiration for anyone who fought on the Somme, but it has to be said that this vivid and compelling quotation illustrates the dangers of relying on uncorroborated oral history. Although Second Lieutenant Beadle tells us precisely what we expect to hear, it is something that did not actually take place. Firstly, British and Indian cavalry did not (for perfectly sensible reasons) use lance-pennants in action in the First World War: a photograph of the Deccan Horse shows them pennantless that very day. Next, none of the infantry in High Wood, who would have been glad to see the cavalry appear, mention them charging 'straight into it', although it would not have been an easy thing to miss. A heavily shelled wood in full summer foliage was (as we saw in nearby Mametz) a tricky obstacle for even infantry to negotiate. What was the merit of the cavalry galloping into it, especially when part of it was British-held at the time?

Lastly, the war diary of the Secunderabad Brigade reveals that it lost eight men killed and less than 100 wounded all day: this was evidently not the Charge of the Light Brigade. The 7th Dragoon Guards had an officer wounded, two troopers killed and twenty wounded, and the Deccan Horse two Indian officers wounded, three troopers killed and fifty wounded. Both the brigade's machine-gun squadron and N battery RHA, which did not take part on the charge, lost more men than the 7th Dragoon Guards, who did. Robin Prior and Trevor Wilson, who use the same Beadle quote, announce that 'the cavalry were soon dealt with by German machine-gunners', but detailed analysis of the action shows that the reverse is true. When German machine guns opened up from Longueval village, the Secunderabad Brigade's machine guns duly silenced them. The 7th Dragoon Guards speared sixteen Germans and captured another thirty-two in its charge; the Deccan Horse killed some more and captured six, and both the Royal Horse Artillery and the cavalry machine guns caused casualties, though we cannot reasonably estimate how many. However, it is already perfectly clear that the cavalry killed more, probably many more, of the enemy than the enemy killed of it.

What happened around High Wood is that the cavalry failed to exploit a window of opportunity that opened at dawn and slammed shut before dusk. Once again poor communications are largely to blame. While General Rawlinson was not necessarily wrong to put the cavalry under XIII Corps for the start of the battle, he was unlucky that the gap appeared on the front of XV Corps. It was not until around 6.00 p.m. that the Secunderabad Brigade was assigned to XV Corps, and this tells us more about the nature of Rawlinson's chain of command than it does about the strengths or weaknesses of the cavalry. Ironically, on 14 July 1916 the cavalry would have done better had it shown more dash rather than less. Had the cavalry brigade or divisional commanders shown more initiative they might have short-circuited this very slow chain of command and slipped in before the window of opporutunity had shut. But the real problem that day was not the cavalry *per se*: it was the perennial difficulty confronting an attacker on the Western Front. There were times when an attacker might strike such a heavy opening blow as to damage his opponent's central nervous system, which in great measure is what the Germans achieved on 5th Army's front on 21 March 1918. But it was usually easier for the defender, pushed back onto his own communications, to recognise where he was losing the battle and to take prompt action to cauterise failure than it was for the attacker, his own communications stretched tight over the hard edge of the battlefield, to reinforce his success.[149]

Although the tactical circumstances of Cambrai the following year were very different, the blame for failure to exploit initial success was once again laid at the cavalry's door. The forward headquarters of the Cavalry Corps was just five miles behind the front when the attack began, and its commander, Lieutenant General Sir Charles Kavanagh, was in touch by telephone with his own divisions and with III and IV Corps, whose infantry and tanks were to make the attack. Although Kavanagh is often written off as a chump, Walter Nicholson, who had attended his briefing for an earlier attack, found him 'a fine fighting man with every intention of taking his corps to victory', and thought his divisional commanders were 'as good as one could wish'. He had spoken slowly and clearly, and referred to his BGGS ('Sally' Home) for confirmation when required, although Nicholson, an infantryman, thought that Kavanagh had added too much detail about horses.[150] Kavanagh's orders for Cambrai stated that: 'The order for the forward movement of the cavalry divisions from their forward concentration areas will be issued by Cavalry Corps. The order will be issued as soon as it appears that the situation is favourable and that there is the possibility of a cavalry advance.'

But early on 20 November, when the battle began, his 1st Cavalry Division was sensibly put under the command of IV Corps, through which it would move to exploit. Less sensibly there was no direct link between corps and division, so Kavanagh's headquarters had to relay messages both ways. However, despite some confusion in the transmission of orders, 1st Cavalry Division reached Ribécourt just before midday, perhaps an hour and a half after the infantry had secured it: no mean achievement. But there were further delays in orders and information as the short November afternoon slid by, and only a single squadron of the 4th Dragoon Guards managed to capitalise on German disorganisation, launching a successful charge which captured a transport column and about fifty infantrymen.

Kavanagh's other attacking formation, 5th Cavalry Division, was ordered forward by corps headquarters just before midday, and thanks to preparation by the cavalry of an approach track, it covered ten miles in an hour and a half to reach the outskirts of Marcoing. Elements of 7th Dragoon Guards crossed the canal and passed back word that the bridges there were intact, but no further action was taken that day. Further west, a tank crashed through a damaged bridge at Masnières, and it took some time to strengthen a nearby bridge to get cavalry across. Not long before 4.00 p.m. the Fort Garry Horse began to cross. Lieutenant Harcus Strachan, of B Squadron, recalled how:

> Lieutenant Colonel Paterson gave the order to 'carry on', and the squadron, taking horses in single file at a distance, crossed the bridge, which was under fire and very precarious. Several men fell into the canal and a number were drowned, but by the blessing of Providence, we reached the other side and away we went at the gallop at 3.45 p.m. We reached the infantry where they had captured the German trenches, but while cutting a passage through the old German wire, Captain Campbell [and a number of

men] were killed and command fell upon me. With a few
ground scouts as our only protection, we left the infantry
behind and proceeded at a gallop . . .

The squadron had to negotiate a long camouflage screen running
along the main road on the far side of the canal, by cutting a gap
through which the men filed, to form up on the far side. Moving
up the ridge east of Masnières, Strachan's men found themselves
facing a battery of four 77-mm guns.

Fortunately swords had been drawn before crossing the
bridge and the squadron charged the guns, each troop
column converging on them. It is interesting to note that
one gun continued to fire until the last and those gunners
probably escaped owing to the difficulty of reaching them,
whereas the remaining gunners, who ran away as soon as
we appeared, were satisfactorily accounted for almost to
a man . . .

Whilst charging the guns we were fired on by machine
guns but these also ceased fire when the guns were taken . . .

German infantry were now observed retiring in great
disorder in the direction of Rumilly, and the squadron
rode right over them as they discarded arms and equipment right and left. They offered no opposition, but they
protected themselves as well as they could by lying down
or hiding behind piles of rubbish, etc, where they could
not be reached by the sword . . . After passing them, there
was no opposition at all; everything was in the wildest
confusion and there was every indication of a demoralized
retreat on the part of the enemy . . . [151]

After a series of incidents behind the German lines Strachan's
survivors (following 'a conference of all ranks') stampeded its surviving horses to confuse the Germans and withdrew on foot. It reached
British lines with three officers, forty-three other ranks and eighteen
German prisoners. Strachan was awarded a Victoria Cross to add to
the MC he already held. There is no doubt that the performance
of the cavalry that day was disappointing. But its failure stemmed
from precisely the same factor which had prevailed on 14 July 1916:
the chain of command's slow response to a fluid situation. As long

as that situation remained fluid, the cavalry was able to act very effectively indeed. The Canadian Cavalry Brigade captured 400 men and nearly 100 machine guns that day, running a well-aimed point through the myth that there could be no cavalry charge until the last machine gun was taken. Farrier Sergeant Bert Turp would certainly have agreed, for he took part in a successful charge in mid-1918: it is worth noting the emphasis on concealment until the last moment.

> A major of the 10th Hussars gave the order to draw swords and hold them down along our horses' shoulders, so that the enemy would not catch the glint of the steel, and we were told to lean down over our horses' manes. A moment later we were wheeling into line. I can't remember if I was scared, but I know that we were all of us very excited, and so were the horses . . . Then the horses started going down but we kept galloping and the next moment we were in amongst them. Oddly enough, at the moment of the real thing I remembered my old training and the sword exercise. As our line overrode the Germans I made a regulation point at a man on my offside and my sword went through his neck and out the other side. The pace of my horse carried the sword clear and I then took a German on the nearside, and I remember the jar as my point took him in the collarbone and knocked him over.[152]

Actions like this confirm that cavalry charges could indeed succeed. On 25 September 1916, D Squadron 19th Lancers, acting as divisional cavalry, was told that the Somme village of Gueudecourt had been abandoned by the Germans. Captain FitzGerald, the squadron leader, was ordered 'to seize the high ground some 600 yards east of the village and establish a strongpoint there'. He trotted round behind Flers, crossed two trenches full of British infantry, picked up a troop of South Irish Horse (part of the corps cavalry regiment), met an infantry brigadier, who could tell him little, and cracked on at speed. He was in Gueudecourt before the Germans could react, and although heavy fire prevented his getting beyond it, he held the village until the infantry came up to relieve him. He lost three men killed and seven wounded. This time the chain of command, and the time elapsed from opportunity to exploitation, were both very short.

They were short, too, at Honnechy on 9 October 1918, when British and Canadian cavalry drove in the German rearguard after a brief conference in which the commander of 3rd Cavalry Division agreed with his brigadiers that the advance would peter out unless some life was injected into it. It was certainly no push-over, as Sergeant D. Brunton observed: 'As each squadron rode forward it was met by heavy high-explosive shell and machine-gun fire, and to make matters worse a number of enemy aeroplanes appeared and, flying low, followed the advancing cavalrymen with machine-gun bullets and bombs.'[153] During the action the 3rd Dragoon Guards galloped into Honnechy in squadron columns in extended order, under fire the whole way. Confronted by a brook 'with a bad take-off' the commanding officer, Lieutenant Colonel Leslie Rome, an Australian, jumped it 'in good old-fashioned style'. Not a horse refused the obstacle, and as the cavalry passed through the tired infantry, men 'rose with a cheer and followed in support'. The capture of Honnechy enabled the Canadians to push on into nearby Reumont, and by the day's end they had captured 400 Germans, several guns and almost 100 machine guns.

The official historian, while noting that the Cavalry Corps had captured over 500 prisoners, ten guns and about 150 machine guns on 8–10 October for the loss of 604 all ranks, sourly commented that it 'had done nothing that the infantry, with artillery support and cyclists, could not have done itself at less cost'. This was certainly not the view of Walter Nicholson, senior administrative staff officer in XIII Corps, attacking in that very sector. 'Here in this open country, with a beaten enemy, unprotected by wire or entrenchment, we failed to make a knock out,' he wrote.

> We brought up a colossal artillery force and fired tons of shells at the enemy. Our infantry continued behind this barrage to the exact point they had been ordered to take – and stopped. There was no soldierly skill . . . Our advance was the most cumbrous steam-roller affair it was possible to conceive . . . In fact they had learnt to manoeuvre; while we had not.[154]

Just beforehand, near Montbrehain, Burgon Bickersteth, on the staff of a cavalry brigade, saw:

> An embankment . . . lined with a number of listless-looking infantrymen. I walked along the railway line looking for an officer. Seeing none I shouted for one. After a short delay two curious-looking objects, subalterns, white-faced and somewhat helpless, shuffled to their feet. I asked them where their battalion HQ was. 'There,' they said, pointed to some figures . . . 'But there are no senior officers left,' they added, 'they have all been killed.' . . .
>
> A man shouted 'here they come.'
>
> I looked over to the right and about 400 yards off I saw the Boches advancing in a long straggly line and in little groups . . . Our infantry seemed to take no interest in the matter at all . . .
>
> What impressed me was the utter lack of any controlling hand. All the colonels and seconds-in-command may have been killed during the morning, and here were elements of three battalions . . . with no idea as to who were on their flanks, if anybody, very vague as to where the Boches were, out of touch with their battalion HQ, let alone the brigade . . . not frightened but hopeless, not sullen or unwilling to obey, but uncertain what to do and badly led – indeed, not led at all.

Bickersteth inspired a successful defence and was awarded the MC. 'I feel that all the men (and especially Corporal Harding) who worked with me deserve a decoration more than I do,' he admitted.[155] The episode tells us much, not least about the need for a clear controlling voice at moments of crisis with a battle teetering in the balance.

The secret, in 1918 as it had been in 1854, was tempering dash with judgement. On 8 October 1918 there were three mounted charges – the Marquess of Anglesey describes them as 'wonderfully gallant' – by the 19th Hussars and a troop of the 20th. It was clear that Lieutenant Colonel George Franks, commanding officer of the 19th, who had been responsible for a successful *coup de main* which had forced the Germans off a bridge over the Somme in March that year, had a point to prove. 'I am the man to drop the flag and off we go to *Death or Glory*,' he told his sergeants. 'If this is successful it will be a bigger thing than the Palestine affair.'[156]

Although the 19th Hussars got as far as a German battery and killed several of its gunners with the sword, they could not hold their ground when a counterattack jabbed in. Sergeant Brunton, in France since 1914, and lucky to survive the day, wrote in his diary that 'the true cavalry spirit still lives', but admitted that it was 'altogether a bad day's work for the regiment'. Colonel Franks was amongst the 111 killed, and his body was buried by torchlight in the civilian cemetery at Brancourt le Grand that night. His officers erected a fine stone cross above it, and its inscription contained perhaps a hint of reproof: 'He fell while charging some German machine guns.'[157]

These charges, in the very last days of the war, underline the fact that cavalry could be very useful if it moved fast, snatched fleeting opportunities, and made good use of the ground and supporting fire. But if it launched a frontal attack on an intact defence it was likely to lose: the difference between success and failure might be a matter of minutes, and there was little chance of recovery if the decision was wrong. It is also clear that, since time was always of the essence, cavalry was likely to do better if it was close-coupled to the divisional battle to make the best of brief chances, not held at a high level for deliberate strokes. And if the Cavalry Corps ultimately failed to deliver the strategic blow for which Haig thought it suited, the British were indeed fortunate that there was no German equivalent. The Germans had steadily reduced the proportion of their cavalry to other arms on the Western Front, and in March 1918 found themselves with nothing to exploit the promising success they achieved against the British astride the Somme. We have just seen how good German infantry could be routed by horsemen if caught off-balance, and the same thing happened, on a far larger scale, to robust Turkish infantry in Palestine. Artillery officers like P. J. Campbell and Arthur Behrend, seeing the pillars of their universe totter, thanked heaven that there was no German cavalry on hand to administer the decisive kick.

The cavalryman's life on the Western Front represented the

most extreme juxtaposition of ancient and modern. Corporal Harry Easton of the 9th Lancers charged at Elouges on 24 August 1914, and his account could almost come from the Napoleonic wars.

> I remember very distinctly seeing the whole line at a hand canter and the trumpeter of the 4th Dragoon Guards was Jackie Patterson a big friend of mine from early days in Canterbury where his parents kept a pub . . . [He galloped towards] a huge brick yard surrounded by a 12 foot high barbed wire fence we were very close when my horse fell and threw me. I am not sure whether she had been hit or stumbled.[158]

Private Ben Clouting was nearby with the 4th Dragoon Guards.

> Each Troop was closely packed together and dense volumes of dust were kicked up, choking us and making it impossible to see beyond the man in front . . . All around me, horses and men were brought hurtling to the ground . . . Ahead, the leading troops were brought up by agricultural barbed wire strung across the line of advance, so that horses were beginning to be pulled up when I heard for the one and only time in the war a bugle sounding 'troops right wheel'. I pulled my horse round and then, with a crash, down she went.[159]

The horse again made its own ageless demands, as Private R. G. Garrod of the 20th Hussars discovered in August 1914.

> My horse went lame because it had cast a shoe and I had to wait until the farrier corporal could see to it. I had no shoes left in my frog [a leather wallet attached to the saddle, with a sword-socket on its outside] and when the farrier searched his bag, he hadn't one small enough, so he used the smallest he had . . . He and I then hurried along to catch up with the regiment when the horse suddenly went lame again and we found she had cast this new shoe. Shoey told me he couldn't do anything more for me but I wasn't to ride her, but to walk and lead her . . . Needless to say I didn't walk my horse, I ran and she trotted beside me.[160]

As the front solidified into trench warfare, there were repeated attempts to replace the extemporised stabling of the first six months of the war by temporary stables which offered cover and hard-standing for horses. But there was sometimes little that could be done, as Ben Clouting recalled of the hard winter of 1917–18:

> We tried as hard as possible to give the horses shelter, often behind the walls of partly-destroyed houses, but they suffered very badly. Mules, however, proved very successful in dealing with the exceptional weather conditions. These hardy creatures proved their importance when I saw a GS wagon stuck fast in the winter mud, despite the best efforts of two shire horses to move it. In the end the shires were unhitched and a team of four mules took over and walked away with it, their tiny feet coping much better with the suction of the mud.[161]

And the war imposed extra burdens of its own, as an officer of the 3rd Hussars recalled of the Somme in the autumn of 1916.

> Working parties were our fate throughout October on that battle-field. Here are are a few of them: an ammunition dump devoid of great interest at Windy Docks one day took two officers and 47 men; upon another day the same dump at the same heaven-inspired spot took a similar party; yet another say the dump claimed 4 officers and 154 men. One night a cable was to be buried for the XIV Corps in what had been the village of Guillemont and 6 officers and 186 men went to bury it; but someone had forgotten the promised tools – some men were wounded, and the party returned in the early hours of the morning. A couple of nights later 2 officers and 101 men again journeyed forth to bury that cable, the tools were there this time, and the cable planted with the loss of some more wounded men.[162]

Hussars, once the most colourful and dashing of light cavalry, reduced to navvies in the world of earth and wire.

WITH THE RANK AND PAY
OF A SAPPER

In one sense military engineering underwent no revolution in the First World War. Sappers, then as now, helped the army to fight, move and live. When the army was in retreat they blew up bridges. The first engineer VCs of the war were won on 23 August 1914 by Lance Corporal Charles Jarvis, who worked single-handed under heavy fire for an hour and a half to destroy the lock bridge at Jemappes on the Mons-Condé canal, and by Captain Theodore Wright, who made repeated though unsuccessful attempts to blow up the nearby road bridge at La Mariette, swinging hand over hand beneath it. When the army advanced, they threw pontoons across rivers whose bridges had been demolished by the Germans. At Vailly on the Aisne, on 14 September, 'the passage of the bridge [was] kept open and controlled with great coolness' by Captain Wright, who was killed by a shell.[163] When opportunity offered they replaced pontoons with permanent structures, strengthened old bridges to bear new loads, or added fresh crossings to water obstacles which compelled the British to fight astride or across them.

Engineers provided the brains (though not always the muscle) behind the construction of everything from field fortifications to roads and camps, and many spent their time in the familiar task of trench-digging, as Lieutenant John Glubb reported in early 1916.

> During the battle last month the troops suffered heavily and were too tired to bury their dead. Many of them were merely trampled into the floor of the trench, where they were soon lost in mud and water. We have been digging out a lot of these trenches again, and are constantly coming upon corpses. They are pretty well decomposed, but a pickaxe brings up chips of bone and rags of clothing. The rest is putrid grey matter.[164]

They also constructed railways, from spurs off the full-gauge main line to the Decauville light railways that ran up to the front. On 1 April 1917 Sergeant Will Fisher wrote: 'In charge [of] party laying "Decaville" light railway, shift 12–8, for conveying ammunition to batteries. Line running through Bapaume town, advance parties levelling, demolishing walls.'[165] They were responsible for gas delivered by cylinder, projector and mortar. They diverted civilian water supplies if they were available, or drilled for water if they were not. Searchlights were their responsibility too. The Royal Engineers Signal Service laid and maintained cable for telephone and telegraph, and could do so at speed, cross-country from a cart paying out cable from huge drums. Members of the Signal Service were responsible for all wireless communications, from GHQ down to individual sub-units with heavy batteries or tank brigades. They installed and ran power-buzzers (essentially a short-range apparatus for transmitting Morse), and furnished the army with its carrier-pigeon service. They worked closely (though not always harmoniously) with the Royal Artillery in flash-spotting and sound-ranging. By the end of the war the Royal Engineers numbered over a quarter of a million officers and men, and we cannot wonder at it.

In another sense, though, even if the sappers did not preside over military revolution, much of the change they managed was nothing if not momentous. The development of wireless communication was one such example (although it had ceased to be an engineer's responsibility when it came to full flowering: the Corps of Signals was formed in June 1920 and became Royal that same August). Another crucial responsibility was surveying, mapping and printing. Twentieth-century armies' reliance on maps is so obvious that it is often scarcely mentioned. However, British sojourn in France and Belgium in 1914–18 was accompanied by the need to produce accurate maps on a previously undreamed-of scale. Some were area maps for which French and Belgian national resources provided at least a basis, although the British preferred contours rather than the height-hachuring of continental maps. Others were trench maps on a much larger scale, required in large numbers and subject to frequent change as battle ebbed and flowed.

There were only three trained survey officers in the British Expeditionary Force in August 1914, but the Topographical Sub-Section of GHQ ('Maps GHQ') came into its own in 1915, when it ordered the re-drawing of all trench maps on a scale of 1:10,000. There was the familiar tension between various parts of the army – 2nd Army, for example, retained its own series of map-sheets covering its front – and individual field survey companies, one for each army, pressed ahead with their own experiments and innovations. No. 3 field survey Company broke new ground when it brought out a privately-purchased printing machine and process camera in early 1917, which enabled it to produce daily situation maps. In June 1918 the Field Survey companies were renamed battalions, not before time as many had previously had a strength of more than a thousand officers and men. It has been estimated that more than 34 million maps of one sort or another had been issued for use on the Western Front, an accomplishment, in its way, no less remarkable than many more showy achievements.[166]

Map users certainly noticed the improvements. Lieutenant Roe recalled that early trench maps, drawn on sections of bigger topographical sheets,

> were invariably most inaccurate ... Any inaccuracies would almost certainly occasion completely unnecessary casualties. Accuracy was literally a vital necessity. Keeping these large-scale maps up to date so that they could be completely depended upon was also of paramount importance. Forward saps and listening posts, shell craters, machine-gun posts of the enemy and fixed rifle stands

had to be determined and mapped . . . We also included contours and the colour of vegetation at different times of year in no-man's-land, for yellow grasses were more dangerous than green ones, even on night patrols because of silhouette difficulties.[167]

But Bernard Martin tells us just how much better things had become by Third Ypres in 1917.

One day Watson showed me the new Trench Map to be issued to us for the Big Push. Printed by Ordance Survey, Southampton, it was the first map I'd seen which gave names to all the trenches, ours and the enemy's. Older maps gave a few names, such as farms and woods . . . and names given at various times by our men – Old Kent Road, Shrapnel Corner, Clapham Junction, Tower Hamlets and so on. The new map had names for every trench, hundreds of them; odd words without meaning as though taken from a dictionary but in groups, starting with a particular letter. For trenches in our possession the letter I (Imp Avenue, Illusive, Imperfect, Image Crescent, etc) and enemy trenches with letter J (Jehovah, Jordan, Jericho, Java etc).[168]

Before the war the army gave map references using what was known as the 'Bingo' system, which appears to have come into use in the British army in about 1885, and was certainly current in the Boer War. A pre-war order, referring to a mutually-agreed map, might be:

Enemy positions stretch along the ridge from the V in VINE HOUSE as far as the first R in CROSSROADS. Our forces will establish a battery in the wood 200 yards SOUTH of the Y in ROPLEY and push cavalry forward to the T in STREAM and 50 yards further NORTH.

The system was not foolproof: there were long-running Boer War jokes about which R in MODDER RIVER the writer actually meant.[169]

The army began the First World War with the Bingo system, as

Captain Robert Dolby, medical officer of 2/King's Own Scottish Borderers, remembered.

> The ambulance wagons were to come to Lorgies to the cross roads ... The position of these cross roads on the map coincided with the 'L' of Lorgies; hence, when special messages were sent to the field ambulance, the place of meeting was always designated by its map position in relation to one of the letters of the printed word. So much has this map reading and map designation become a feature of the service that it is told of one private soldier addressing his chum, 'Where shall I meet you, Bill?' 'At the second "o" in bloody,' was his reply.[170]

In 1915 the Bingo system was replaced by the more methodical grid-reference system, with which generations of Sandhurst cadets would become depressingly familiar. Peter Chasseaud, doyen of the war's topographical historians, tells us how it worked:

> Each 1:40,000 sheet was divided into 6,000 yard squares, described by capital letters. These were subdivided into 36 numbered 1,000 yard squares, which were then quartered into 500 yard sub-squares designated a, b, c and d. A point within a sub-square could be described by two or four figure co-ordinates taken from the SW corner, giving easting first and then northing. Each 1:40,000 sheet was divided into four 1:20,000 sheets, which in turn were divided into four 1:10,000 sheets. The map reference on all these was identical.

In practice, for a soldier wishing to find the full reference for the southern tip of High Wood on the Somme, it would work as follows: the reference would begin with the number of the 1:40,000 map sheet, in this case 57cSW3, which establishes that the map is one of those covering the general area of the Somme (57d sheets lie to its west and 57b sheets to its east). A capital letter – in this case M – defines the 6,000-yard square in which the wood lies. The 1,000-yard square is numbered 4, and the 500-yard sub-square within it is c. Within this sub-square he would first establish the position of the wood edge in eastings, estimating how far from left to right it lies in tenths. It is nine-tenths of the way along, so earns the figure 9. He would then do the same for northings: here the tip of the wood lies right on the line, so earns o. His full reference for the southern edge of High Wood is thus: 57cSW3 M4c90. This would be close enough for most sorts of work, but an even more precise definition could be found by giving the subdivisions of eastings and northings in hundreds rather than tenths, although there was little point in trying to attain this degree of accuracy save on 1:10,000 trench maps.

The same method works in reverse. We saw earlier how Lieutenant Colonel U. L. Hooke of the Queen's was buried in the field. His battalion's Army Book 120 gives the location of his grave at H.23.b.7.5, Ref 1/40,000 51b. On the 1:10,000 series this is sheet 51b NW3, and from it we can see that the colonel was buried on the southern edge of the village of Fampoux, east of Arras, just north of the Arras-Cambrai railway line. Utten Lamont Hooke, killed at the age of thirty-six and, as the cemetery register informs us, the husband of Enid A. Hooke of 50 Temple Road, Croydon, still lies there, in Plot I, Row C and Grave 35 of the Commonwealth War Graves Commission's Level Crossing Cemetery, Fampoux.

If the engineers discovered novel techniques as far as mapping was concerned, they blended old and new to take the war underground. Medieval engineers had dug beneath besieged castles, secured their tunnels with wooden pit-props, smeared the wood with pig fat and then fired it. When the props burnt the tunnels collapsed, and the fortifications above sank on their foundations. The advent of gunpowder made the business more hazardous and spectacular: chambers were packed with barrels of powder and then exploded. An attacker could blow up part of a fortress, breaching its defences, while a defender could use countermines, exploding them under attacking troops as they massed for the assault. The traditional importance of military mining is underlined by the fact that the Royal Engineers had themselves evolved from the Corps of Royal Sappers and Miners. However, even the most traditionally-minded sapper could not have guessed, in August 1914, just how important mining would once again become.

Given the resemblance of trench warfare to sieges, it is scarcely surprising that both sides took to mining. The Germans began in December 1914 by exploding ten mines beneath a sector held by the Indian Corps at Festubert. British attempts at retaliation in January 1915 failed. The sector chosen was simply too wet, and water entered the tunnels dug by 20th Fortress Company Royal Engineers more quickly than the pumps could shift it. The Germans helpfully hoisted a notice, in English, in their trenches. 'No good your mining,' it read. 'It can't be done. We've tried.'[171] In February the Germans exploded a mine beneath a battalion of East Yorkshires at St-Eloi, just south of Ypres, and the demand for retaliation grew.

John Norton Griffiths, Conservative MP and civil engineer, had already been pressing the War Office to employ what he called 'moles', labourers who had been working on a tunnelled drainage system in Manchester using a technique called clay-kicking. A man would sit with his back against a wooden rest, with a special spade between his feet. As he kicked it forward to dig out clay, his mate reached past him to drag the debris out. In February 1915 Norton Griffiths was summoned to see Lord Kitchener. He demonstrated the technique of clay-kicking on the floor of Kitchener's office, using a fire shovel from the grate, and was at once told to recruit 10,000 of his moles. He left for France immediately, and called on the BEF's chief engineer, Brigadier General George Fowke, wearing what James Edmonds – then a sapper colonel and later the official historian – called 'something between uniform and hunting kit'. He soon received formal War Office approval to raise the first Royal Engineer tunnelling companies, numbered 170 to 178.

Norton Griffiths encountered a host of problems in raising his miners. There were predictable difficulties over pay: clay-kickers were entitled to six shillings a day, their mates a mere 2/2d. Some men, enlisted, as they thought, specifically for mining duties, did not take comfortably to military discipline, and had to cope with some mining equipment that had served in the Crimea. But work was quickly out in hand, and on 17 April 1915, 171 Tunnelling Company blew the top off Hill 60, in the Ypres salient, just beating German miners, who planned to explode a mine of their own on the 19th. Although the Germans recaptured Hill 60 in the gas attack which so infuriated Ernest Shephard, the pattern was set, and over the next two years

British, Canadian, Australian and New Zealand miners grew increasingly effective. On 19 June 1915, 175 Tunnelling Company exploded the biggest mine of the war thus far, containing 3,500 lbs of ammonal, beneath Hooge Ridge on the Menin Road.

Just over a year later, mines on an even bigger scale were an integral part of the British plan of attack on the first day of the Somme. Nineteen mines had been dug beneath strongpoints in the German front line on the Somme, and one of them, which produced Lochnagar crater, which still pits the fields just south of La Boisselle, contained 66,000 lbs of ammonal in two charges 52 feet below the surface. When it was exploded, at 7.28 on the morning of 1 July, it left a crater 90 yards across and 70 feet deep, with lips 15 feet high. The explosion could be heard in London. Mines like this did not simply destroy German trenches and obliterate their garrisons, but they shook the earth so severely as to wreck deep dugouts some distance from the blast. Yet they did not guarantee tactical success. The mine beneath Hawthorn Ridge, near Beaumont Hamel, was blown at 7.20 a.m., deliberately early so that this dominating feature could be secured before the main attack began. Corporal George Ashurst, waiting nearby with 1/Lancashire Fusiliers, felt 'a queer dull thud and our trench fairly rocked, and a great blue flame shot into the sky, carrying with it hundreds of tons of brick and stone and great chunks of earth mingled with wood and wire and fragments of sandbags'.[172]

It had long been axiomatic that, as Harry Ogle reported in 1915, when a mine was exploded: 'The enemy lip of the crater had to be occupied if possible and put into a state of defence or at least denied to the enemy.'[173] At Hawthorn Ridge parties of 2/Royal Fusiliers rushed for the crater even as the debris was settling: the Germans, who had been using earphones to trace the progress of British mining, were ready, and had men in reserve to secure their own side of the crater: the Fusiliers were eventually dislodged. Corporal Ashurst, pinned down in No Man's Land with the leading elements of his own battalion, 'noticed a few of them running for their lives back to the front line' much later in the day: 2/Royal Fusiliers lost 561 men that day, including their commanding officer.

Mines were next used on a large scale when Plumer's 2nd Army assaulted Messines Ridge on 7 June 1917. Some of the mines exploded that morning had been started in 1915, and the entire mining programme showed just how large an enterprise mining had become since that first British mine had been exploded under Hill 60 just over two years before. Each army now had a Controller of Mines with a specialist staff. There were more than 30,000 men in British, Canadian, New Zealand and Australian tunnelling companies and their supporting units. In suitable areas a shallow defensive mine gallery, intended to detect and disrupt German mining, would run below the front line. Offensive mines ran deeper, their horizontal galleries generally approached by way of a vertical shaft. In the Messines area miners sinking these shafts had to contend with surface soil, then sludgy quicksand, and then a layer of blue clay which expanded on contact with the air and had to be very carefully shored up with stout timber to prevent the shaft from caving in.

Clay-kickers, lying against their wooden frames, drove the galleries forward. Their mates shovelled the spoil they excavated into sandbags and dragged them back to the start of a track which carried trolleys, and these were pushed along to the shaft. Men working at the top hoisted the sandbags to the surface, and once there they then had to be shifted far enough behind the British front line for their presence not to make the mine shafts obvious to aerial observation. Hand-operated pumps sent fresh air down into the galleries, and miners took canaries down with them, keeping a watchful eye on the bird's health as they worked. Breathing apparatus helped rescue squads to make their way to men overwhelmed by gas. Frank Dunham of 25/London found it 'most interesting to see these miners digging away, and strutting up with planks of wood as they went along. Where the width of the tunnel permitted, trolleys were used to wheel the soil away. Another strange thing was that these tunnels were lit by electric light, worked from a dynamo.'[174]

Sapper Jack Lyon of 171 Tunnelling Company helped dig one of the mines beneath Messines Ridge, exploded with such effect on 7 June 1917:

> Each shift comprised twelve men with an RE Corporal in charge. At the face were three men who were RE Sappers.

Three men worked the trolleys, one man manned the 'windjammer' or air pump. One man at the shaft-bottom kept the sump there empty and hitched sandbags to the rope from the windlass at the pithead. [There were] two men at this windlass, one man unhitching the bags and passing them back to the other, who took them to the dumping ground. At the tunnel face one man was engaged in 'clay-kicking'. Sitting with his back against an inclined plank fixed between the floor and the roof he used both feet to press a small sharp spade called a 'grasper' into the face and lever out a lump of clay. [His mate] put this into a sandbag. When full, the bag was passed to the third man who dragged it to the far end of the trolley-rails. As each man was a Sapper, they could relieve each other so the face-man 'kicked' for two hours of the six-hour shift.

It was small wonder that Plumer's chief of staff had announced that although they might not change history, they would certainly change geography. These tunnellers worked three shifts in two days and then had a day off. After fifteen days they were withdrawn 'for a bath and delousing operations, the latter being only partially successful'.[175]

Although sappers were the stars of mining, as usual the infantry provided the scene shifters, and generally complained about it. Lieutenant Ernest Parker remembered that:

Towards evening we daily journeyed to the front line and there, in shifts of eight hours, worked under the orders of a company of New Zealand sappers who were tunnelling under the German trenches. At the top of the sap, we hauled a continuous stream of chalk-filled bags, carrying them outside and unloading the chalk some distance from the sap-head. By special favour, I was sometimes allowed to crawl down the deep shaft, where I could cautiously watch the New Zealanders working at the rock face. Now and then we listened in, and heard the enemy working in their counter saps.[176]

But most infantrymen were soon convinced that they would rather be in a trench than down a mine. One of Bernard Adams's comrades told him what it was like down there.

First of all you go down three or four ladders; it's awfully
tricky work at the sort of halt on the way down, because
there's a little platform, and very often the ladder goes
down a different side of the shaft after one of these halts
... It's a terrible long way down, and of course you go
alone ... I didn't go far up the gallery where they were
working because you can't easily pass along, but the RE
officer took me along a gallery that is not being worked,
and there, all alone, at the end of it was a man sitting. He
was simply sitting, listening. Then I listened through his
stethoscope thing ... and I could hear the Boche working
as plainly as anything ... as we went away and left him,
he looked round at us with staring eyes just like a hunted
animal. To sit there for hours on end, listening. Of course,
while you hear them working, it's all right, they won't
blow. But if you *don't* hear them! God, I wouldn't like to
be an RE. It's an awful game.

'We always laugh at these REs for looking like navvies, and for going
about without gas-helmets or rifles,' reflected Adams. 'But really they
are wonderful men. It's awful being liable to be buried alive at any
moment.'[177]

Galleries ran into wide chambers that were filled (armed was the
technical phrase) with explosive, usually ammonal, contained either
in waterproof bags or tins, tamped firmly by sandbags to prevent too
much of the blast from blowing back along the line of least resistance
down the tunnel. The explosives were initiated by a pattern of electric
detonators, stretching round the chamber like the nerves of a hand,
and joined to a main cable which ran down the tunnel to a firing-
point in a trench, where an engineer officer would push the handle
of an electric exploder to fire the mine. Sometimes there was a firing
dugout further back, with a small generator providing electricity,
connected to the mine by a simple throw-over switch. Usually the
officers firing mines expressed relief and satisfaction that the mine
had exploded as planned. But one, a son of the manse, knelt and
doffed his steel helmet before he thrust down the plunger, begging
God's mercy for the men he was about to kill.

Spectators found mine explosions perhaps the most unnatural of the bizarre spectacles furnished by the front line. Bernard Adams was enjoying a mug of tea in a front line trench when:

> There was a faint 'Bomp' from goodness knows where. And a horrid shudder. The earth shook and staggered and I set my legs apart to keep my balance. It felt as if the whole ground were going to be tilted up. The tea splashed over the fire-step as I hastily put it down. Then I looked up. There was nothing. What had happened? Was it a *camouflet* [small mine] after all? Then, over the sandbags, appeared a great green meadow, slowly, taking its time, not hurrying, a smooth curved dome of grass, heaving up, up, up like a rising cake; then, like a cake, it cracked, cracked visibly with bursting brown seams; still the dome rose, towering ten, twenty feet up above the surrounding level; and then with a roar the black smoke hurtled into the air, followed by masses of pink flame creaming up into the sky, giving out a bonfire heat and lighting up the twilight with a lurid glare! Then we all ducked to avoid the shower of mud and dirt and chalk that pattered down like hail.
>
> 'Magnificent,' I said to Scott.
>
> 'Wonderful,' he answered.
>
> 'The mud's all in your tea, sir,' said Davies.
>
> 'Dr-r-r-r-r-r' rattled the Lewis guns. The Lewis gunners with me had been amazed rather than thrilled by the awful spectacle, but were now recovering from the shock and emptying two or three drums into the twilight void. I was peering over a vast chasm where two minutes ago had been a smooth meadow full of buttercups and toadstools.[178]

Gas and cave-ins were not the only dangers faced by miners. Although the Germans had lost their ascendancy by 1916, they remained capable of exploding mines of their own. As they worked, miners of both sides paused to listen, and often drove small galleries, designed to house *camouflets*, towards the enemy's work, hoping to blow in his tunnel before his mine could be armed, tamped and fired. F. P. Roe thought that:

> The last thing any infantry soldier wanted to be in was a front-line trench with our own tunnelling going on under-

A gunner with his battery's post, near Aveluy on the Somme, September 1916. The parcels probably contain things like sweets, chocolate and tinned food, usually pooled amongst the happy recipient's close friends.

LEFT Mail posted in England was despatched to Base Post Offices at Le Havre or Boulogne, and then went up the line of communication to the addressee's unit, where it was divided into company/ battery piles for distribution. Most mail reached its recipient on the second day after posting. These gunners are sorting their battery's mail near Grevillers in late August 1918.

RIGHT Out of the line officers and men were often billeted on French civilians. Here *monsieur* reads the paper while three British lance-corporals look with interest at *madame's* cooking-pot.

LEFT Time out of war. An old sweat with three long service chevrons and one wound stripe on his cuff minding the baby outside his billet at Adinkerke near Dunkirk, August 1917.

RIGHT The world of the rear. What soldiers called 'the base', the area around Rouen and Etaples, was full of stores deports, holding camps and hospitals. This motor ambulance depot at Etaples was staffed by members of the Voluntary Aid Detachment, many of them middle-class women who drove ambulances and tended wounded.

A.F.A. 2042.
114/Gen No./5248.

FIELD

POST CARD

The address only to be written on this side. If anything else is added the post card will be destroyed.

[Crown Copyright Reserved.]

Lady Mellor –
1 Embankment gds
London.
SW

NOTHING is to be written on this side except the date and signature of the sender. Sentences not required may be erased. If anything else is added the post card will be destroyed.

[Postage must be prepaid on any letter or post card addressed to the sender of this card.]

I am quite well.

~~I have been admitted into hospital~~

{ ~~sick~~   } ~~and am going on well.~~
{ ~~wounded~~ } ~~and hope to be discharged soon.~~

~~I am being sent down to the base.~~

                              (letter dated 20.23 Oct)

I have received your ~~telegram~~ ,, ———
                       ~~parcel~~   ,, ———

Letter follows at first opportunity.

~~I have received no letter from you~~
{ ~~lately~~ }
{ ~~for a long time.~~ }

Signature } V. C. O. Mellor
only }

Date 30 . 11 . 17.

Wt.W3677386. 29346. 5000m. 9714. C. & Co. Grange Mills, S.W.

Field service postcards were readily available. The writer, Lieutenant Vintcent (sic) Mellor, son of Sir John Mellor, permanent secretary at the Treasury, died of pneumonia in March 1918. When his troopship was torpedoed he gave up his place in a lifeboat to a private who could not swim, and spent five hours in the water: another private wrote that he was 'a good old sport.'

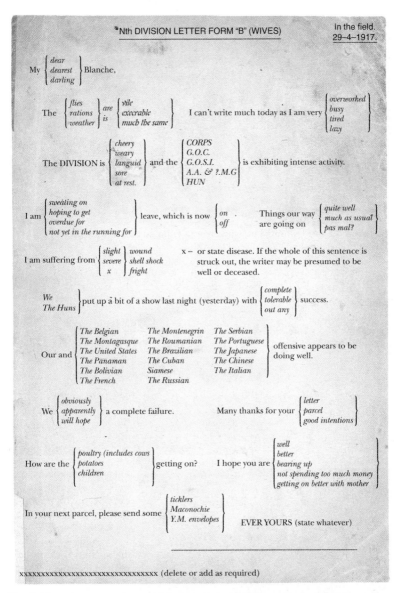

Nth DIVISION LETTER FORM "B" (WIVES)

In the field.
29–4–1917.

My {dear / dearest / darling} Blanche,

The {flies / rations / weather} {are / is} {vile / execrable / much the same} I can't write much today as I am very {overworked / busy / tired / lazy}

The DIVISION is {cheery / weary / languid / sore / at rest.} and the {CORPS / G.O.C. / G.O.S.I. / A.A. & ?.M.G / HUN} is exhibiting intense activity.

I am {sweating on / hoping to get / overdue for / not yet in the running for} leave, which is now {on / off}. Things our way are going on {quite well / much as usual / pas mal?}

I am suffering from {slight / severe / x} {wound / shell shock / fright} x – or state disease. If the whole of this sentence is struck out, the writer may be presumed to be well or deceased.

{We / The Huns} put up a bit of a show last night (yesterday) with {complete / tolerable / out any} success.

Our {The Belgian / The Montagasque / The United States / The Panaman / The Bolivian / The French / The Montenegrin / The Roumanian / The Brazilian / The Cuban / Siamese / The Russian / The Serbian / The Portuguese / The Japanese / The Chinese / The Italian} and offensive appears to be doing well.

We {obviously / apparently / will hope} a complete failure. Many thanks for your {letter / parcel / good intentions}

How are the {poultry (includes cows / potatoes / children} getting on? I hope you are {well / better / bearing up / not spending too much money / getting on better with mother}

In your next parcel, please send some {ticklers / Maconochie / Y.M. envelopes} EVER YOURS (state whatever)

xxxxxxxxxxxxxxxxxxxxxxxxxxxxxxxxx (delete or add as required)

The field service postcard was widely parodied: this Western Front spoof dates from 1917.

There was not one bull ring but many. Troops going to the front via Etaples were trained in dozens of open-air arenas like this.

RIGHT From gamekeeper . . . An infantryman in the winter of 1914. The removal of his cap-badge is the only concession to life in the line.

LEFT To industrial worker. Infantrymen carrying wire for revetting trenches along the duckboards, winter 1917. Sandbags protect their puttees from the worst of the mud.

British Officer as seen by
the Military Tailor

As he actually appears on
leaving for the front

After three weeks in the
trenches
From *Punch*, March 10, 1915

The magazine *Punch* was not far from the truth when it showed the impact of trench warfare on military tailoring.

LEFT Infantry led by an officer in a 'British warm' crossing a newly-constructed pontoon bridge over the Somme in Peronne, devastated by the Germans on their retreat to the Hindenburg Line, March 1917.

RIGHT Soldiers of 2/Argyll and Sutherland Highlanders in the Bois Grenier sector, early summer 1915. This primitive anti-gas protection was first issued to the battalion on 3 May. The bottles are supposed to contain sodium thiosulphate solution for dampening the cotton pads, though a self-produced alternative was also used.

LEFT A 9.2-inch howitzer of 2nd Australian Siege Battery, Ypres 1917. The gunners are wearing their box respirators, which gave good protection against gas. A camouflage net helps screen their position against aerial observation.

RIGHT Tanks passing through Méaulte, just south of Albert, after its capture by 12th Division, 22 August 1918. Conditions inside a tank were so unpleasant that, out of action, crew members not involved in actually driving it usually rode on top or walked behind.

LEFT Tanks were expected to crush wire and, often using ropes and grapnels, to clear avenues for attacking infantry.

BELOW Bayonet training at Etaples. These men are first making a regulation 'long point' against a 'standing' target, quickly followed by another against a 'lying' target.

Lochnagar crater, the result of the largest mine exploded on the Somme on 1 July 1916. A total of 66,000 lbs of ammonal was exploded 52 feet below the surface, leaving a crater 90 yards across and 70 feet deep with lips 15 feet high. The bang could be heard in London.

LEFT The approach to the Somme village of Beaumont Hamel was dominated by the Hawthorn Ridge redoubt, and 40,000 lbs of ammonal were exploded beneath it at 7.20 on the morning of 1 July 1916. The British were unable to secure the crater and the attack in this sector failed.

RIGHT Miners laying ammonal charges in a mine chamber on the Somme, in June 1916, pause silently while the officer on the left uses a geophone to listen for German counter-mining.

LEFT Cavalry could make a valuable contribution even in trench warfare, but only if they intervened while the battle was still fluid. These horsemen are awaiting orders to move forward at Arras in April 1917. Extra ammunition is in bandoliers round the horses' necks.

A 9.2-inch howitzer in action in the ruins of Tilloy-les-Mofflaines, just east of Arras, April 1917. The layer (third from left) is busy at his sight, and gunners on the right are setting fuzes.

RIGHT An 18-pdr field gun shooting over Montauban Ridge towards High Wood, 30 July 1916. The gun's No 1 (left) keeps an eye on his detachment while the No 4 (centre) seats a fresh round with the heel of his hand. The gun position officer (right) has a megaphone for shouting orders across the gun-line.

LEFT Gunners hauling an 18-pdr out of the mud near Zillebeke, east of Ypres, 9 August 1917.

neath us and this made us extremely apprehensive of the possibility of being blown to bits when the mine was exploded; we were scared stiff that the Germans were also busily engaged in the same important business, and that it might at any time entirely without warning blow the trench and us in it sky-high. We were sure that it was a completely devilish business.[179]

If British miners failed to intercept an enemy mine, the consequences for the infantry above could be dire. Writing from Voormezeele in the Ypres salient, Frank Hawkins told of the explosion of a British mine, followed shortly by that of a German.

> **15 July 1915**. We hear that a mine which the REs have been preparing beneath the Mound of Death for some time past is due to be exploded shortly.
>
> **17 July 1915**. The mine was exploded at dawn this morning, but a little later the enemy exploded counter-mines beneath trench Q1. We had a shocking lot of casualties, and all the troops stood to arms and kept up a rapid fire to ward off a possible attack. They say that fortunately the enemy mine blew up short of the trench, but in spite of this there are nineteen killed and three or four times that number wounded. A bad show.[180]

On 9 April 1916 2/Royal Welch Fusiliers were holding the line near Bethune:

> At 8 a.m. the Germans blew in yet another small mine on our part of this much-mined area. Five miners were caught underground; four or five of our men were more or less buried in the collapse of our part of the trench; a broken leg has been the worst injury. It has been an exciting affair for the miners. They could hear the German miners only an estimated 10 feet off, so there was a race against time to get a charge tamped and fired. The *camouflet* that was blown there yesterday morning obviously failed to wreck the German work.[181]

In June that year the Germans exploded a much bigger mine beneath the same battalion, leaving a scar 120 yards long, 70–80 yards wide and 30 feet deep, with a smaller crater proper within it.

The explosion cost B Company two-thirds of its trench strength, including 'two very recently joined young officers and its fine sergeant-major'. The Germans who attacked in the aftermath of the blast were driven off by a brisk counterattack led by Captain Stanway of C Company (sergeant major in 1914 and battalion commander in 1918). Frank Richards thought that much credit was also due to Private Hammer Lane, whose platoon commander panicked and yelled: 'We'll have to surrender.' 'Surrender my bloody arse!' shouted Lane. 'Get your men to meet them front and rear!' It was 'a glorious summer morning next day' and, hearing that a staff officer was coming to inspect the crater, some of the fusiliers propped up a dead German officer on the firestep, with a lighted candle in one hand and a small bible in the other. Just before the red tab appeared they put a lighted cigarette in the corpse's mouth. Richards maintained that this was not done to insult the dead German, who was decently buried soon afterwards, 'but just to give the Staff officer a shock'.[182]

There were shocks underground too when miners broke into one another's galleries and fought with pistols, knives or coshes. British miners unable to obtain a revolver would occasionally cut most of the butt and barrel off a rifle, leaving them with a stubby weapon whose bullet could penetrate more earth than a pistol-bullet.

But the most dreaded fate was not sudden extinction in an underground brawl, but slow death at the end of a gallery blown in by a German *camouflet*. In June 1916 the main tunnel of Petit Bois, one of the mines aimed at Messines Ridge, ran for 1,600 feet to a fork where it divided into two chambers to contain explosives. On 12 June the ground above shook and there were two spouts of earth from No Man's Land: the blue-rimmed craters showed that the German *camouflets* had been driven deep. Twelve miners were walled up at the far end of the tunnel. Rescuers frantically dug a new tunnel to bypass the destroyed section, but when they reached the trapped miners four days later they found them all dead. Or so they thought. One of them, Sapper Bedson, an experienced miner from Whitehaven, had picked a spot at the tunnel face where the ground was slightly higher, removed the glass from his watch so that he could feel the time, put his water bottle to hand, and dozed fitfully while his mates gradually suffocated around him. He was unconscious when they got him out, but came to and muttered: 'It's been a long shift. For God's sake give me a drink.'[183]

Despite this setback, Petit Bois was brought back into service, pushed forward to 1,800 feet, and again split to allow two huge charges to be placed. There were eventually twenty-four mines loaded with a total of a million pounds of ammonal under Messines Ridge.[184] The largest, laid by 1st Canadian Tunnelling Company near St-Eloi, contained a remarkable 95,600 lbs of ammonal, 125 feet below the ground, and was finished only nine days before the battle started. Nineteen of the mines were blown at 3.10 on the morning of 7 June 1917 with a blast so thunderous that the professor of geology at Lille University, more than 12 miles away, sprang from his bed thinking that there had been an earthquake, and the earth tremor was registered by a seismograph on the Isle of Wight. Some defenders were vaporised; others were buried beneath earth and rubble; still others were found intact but dead in their dugouts, the breath sucked from their bodies by the explosion. Philip Gibbs thought the sight:

> The most diabolical splendour I have ever seen. Out of the dark ridges of Messines and Wytschaete and that ill-famed Hill 60 there gushed out and up enormous volumes of scarlet flame from the exploding mines and of earth and smoke all lighted by the flame spilling over into mountains of fierce colour, so that the countryside was illuminated by red light.[185]

There were many ways in which the war pointed the way ahead, but in the gigantic mine, its pillars of fire reaching up to an affronted heaven, there was a destructive ingenuity not to be rivalled until the explosion of the first atomic bomb.

WOEFUL CRIMSON

The war imposed an unprecedented burden on the army's medical services. They had learnt valuable lessons in the Boer War, and the Royal Army Medical College at Millbank, founded in 1902, had done much to improve the professional education of army doctors. But their wartime expansion was staggering. The Royal Army Medical Corps grew from 1,279 regular and 1,128 territorial officers and 3,811 regular and 12,520 territorial other ranks in 1914, to over 10,000 regular officers and 98,986 other ranks, and 2,845 territorial officers and 32,375 other ranks in November 1918.[186] As almost all RAMC officers were medically qualified this enormous expansion was only made possible by luring a growing proportion of the nation's doctors into military service. The fact that the RAMC was already short of doctors when war broke out exacerbated the problem. There was as yet no National Health Service, and it was to prove anything but easy to shift doctors from secure, relatively well-paid jobs, into the army.

Some went easily enough. Dr Henry Owens heard on 3 August 1914 that doctors were required and put his name forward: he rode the mare Colleen in the horse-show at Harleston that afternoon. He reported to the War Office on 6 August, 'told them that I wanted to see something of the war, if possible & as soon as possible, & wanted some job with a horse to ride in it'. He was immediately posted to 3rd Cavalry Field Ambulance as a temporary lieutenant RAMC.[187]

However, what was easy for an enthusiastic young doctor in 1914 was less easy for others. Some volunteers were initially turned down because they were too old, while many territorial doctors needed time to make arrangements to hand over their practices. The army soon offered twelve-month contracts to doctors who volunteered, leading territorials to complain that their own terms of service were inferior but their obligations greater. The Central Medical War Committee tried to take a global view of the problem of providing army doctors while at the same time providing for the health of the civilian population, and local medical committees strove, not always with success, to ensure that those doctors who did volunteer did not have their patients filched by partners who stayed behind. Captain Robert Dolby admitted that the regimental medical officers who joined with him in the early autumn of 1914 were:

> A scratch lot . . . one of us on leave from India, where he was a doctor to an Indian Railway; another, one of the most distinguished of the younger heart specialists in London, a man for whom 'auricular fibrillation' had no terrors; two of us, much general medical knowledge but no special leanings; and myself, by way of being a bit of a surgeon. We were badly wanted; for the casualties among medical officers had been great. Regimental medical officers, with their advanced dressing posts in good positions when fighting commenced, too busy with their wounded to notice the retirement of the fighting lines in front, had awakened to find themselves in the forefront of battle . . . Many of them, to their credit, stayed with their wounded, and paid the penalty of duty with their lives or with many months in a German prison camp.[188]

There were frequent fears that the army would run out of doctors. No less than 400 were killed or wounded on the Somme, and the army in France was usually well understrength for doctors: over 500 in March 1918, for instance. Conscription never applied to doctors, but there were frequent warnings that unless doctors heeded the call and served in their medical capacities, they would find themselves

conscripted as privates in the infantry, and this may have concentrated some medical minds. The problem was eventually solved by
a combination of methods. Experienced medical students serving in
the army were discharged and sent back to medical school. P. J.
Campbell's comrade Edward, with his MC and bar, went off to qualify. Another gunner officer, recommended for a decoration at Loos
when, as a forward observation officer, he temporarily reverted to
his earlier calling to care for wounded in a front-line trench, was
sent back to complete his studies, and was then re-commissioned,
this time into the RAMC. He died bravely, still undecorated, in
March 1918. Next, female doctors took over an increasing number
of military appointments in Britain, though on shamefully unequal
terms of service, to free their male colleagues for the front. No less
than 200 nursing sisters were trained as anaesthetists, and finally,
from 1917 American doctors were posted to British military hospitals
or served as medical officers with units.

Not all the Americans were ready for the cultural shock. Guy
Chapman remembered that in 1918 his battalion's new medical
officer, 'a sturdy round-faced American doctor from Baltimore, of a
humour and an ingenuousness to smooth our churlish insularity',
was mercilessly conned by the battalion's seasoned malingerers, who
appeared on sick parade in droves and were promptly excused duty.
When told what was happening he replied with surprise: 'D'you
mean those boys have been guying me?'[189] He toughened up immediately, and the sick list shrank. In addition, several volunteer medical
organisations, of which the Scottish Women's Hospital is perhaps
the best known, took some of the pressure off military hospitals.

It took the medical services some time to adjust to the sheer scale
of the war. In October 1914 Surgeon General Sir Arthur Sloggett
was sent out to become director general of medical services in the
British Expeditionary Force, France, and established a medical cell
in GHQ at St Omer. A director of medical services superintended
the medical services of each of the BEF's armies, and there were
medical cells at corps and divisional headquarters. At the latter the
assistant director of medical services, a full colonel, controlled three
field ambulances, each a lieutenant colonel's command, which provided the essential links between the regimental medical officer and

the hospitals to which his wounded would be evacuated. A number of civilian consultants, including some of the most distinguished specialists in Britain, were given temporary rank in the RAMC to advise the director general.

The regimental medical officer, a lieutenant or captain in the RAMC, was effectively the general practitioner for an infantry battalion or unit of equivalent size in other arms. When his unit was not in the line, men came to see him at specified times, usually a morning 'sick parade', although he would deal with subsequent emergencies as they arose. When Frank Dunham became his medical officer's orderly in June 1918 he was amazed at the range of illnesses that were presented at his first sick parade: 'Impetigo, Psoriasis, ICT (Inflammation of Connecting Tissue) and others some of which I was in a mess with when it came to writing them down'.[190] The flu-like 'trench fever', pyrexia of unknown origin – or PUO to doctors – was endemic, and although many infantrymen observed that they generally felt better than they ever had at home, a doctor argued that what really counted was steadfastness in the face of constant minor illness.

> Tis easy to smile when the skies are blue
> And everything goes well with you,
> But the man who could grin
> With his boots letting in,
> With a boil on his neck
> And its mate on his chin
> With an ITC at the back of each knee
> And PUO of 103,
> Was the fellow who won the war.[191]

The medical officer's usual prescription was 'M&D' – medicine and duty, which meant that the patient would remain at work while he took the appropriate medication, often a 'No. 9 pill', a vigorous laxative which dealt well (though, in Haig's case in August 1914, volcanically) with the consequences of a diet of army biscuits and bully beef. More serious routine cases could be sent off to a specialist in a hospital behind the lines.

The regimental medical officer had two distinct responsibilities.

On the one hand he was a commissioned officer in a combatant army, bound to observe military law: but on the other he had sworn an older oath before he was attested into the army, and was aware – sometimes very well aware – of the fact that his responsibilities as a doctor might conflict with those as an officer. Medical officers were under constant pressure to keep sick lists down, and, as Lord Moran testifies, often had to send back into the line men who, by any objective standard, richly deserved rest. Lieutenant G. N. Kirkwood, RMO of 11/Border, was dismissed for over-empathising with the soldiers under his care, and his divisional commander declared that: 'Sympathy for sick and wounded men under his treatment is a good attribute for a doctor but it is not for an MO to inform a CO that his men are not in a fit state to carry on a military operation. The men being in the front line should be proof that they are fit for any duty called for.'[192]

A soldier wounded in action would walk, or be carried by regimental stretcher-bearers – soldiers in his battalion who carried no arms and were distinguished by their stretcher-bearer brassards – to the regimental aid post, in, or just behind, the front trench system. Officers and men had two first field dressings sewn beneath the front flaps of their tunics, and could give basic first aid even before the wounded man reached the regimental aid post, but only when the battle permitted. Men were ordered not to stop to help their comrades in an attack, and found it 'very distressing to have to leave friends lying on the ground without being able to do something for them'.[193] Many officers carried gelatine lamells, thin sheets of gelatine containing mild analgesic, and as early as 1915 company commanders were issued with 'a tube of ¼ grain tablets of Morphia; 1 to ease pain; 2 (or ½ grain) to cause semi-insensibility till death comes.'[194]

Many medical officers went out on to the battlefield to help the wounded themselves when the pressure of work at the regimental aid post died away, and it is an index of their courage that of the only three men awarded a bar to the Victoria Cross, two were medical officers. Captain Noel Chavasse, RMO to the 1/10th King's Liverpool, the Liverpool Scotttish, earned one VC on the Somme and the bar, posthumously, at Ypres. Arthur Martin-Leake had won his

VC in the Boer War and added its bar in 1914. Martin Littlewood knew him in 1917, and was pleased to find that he was sensible as well as brave. When they came under shellfire he declared: 'By God, this is dangerous. Run.' 'We were only too cheerful to do so,' admitted Littlewood. 'Only a very brave man can be a coward.' Martin-Leake's realism was well founded, for a medical officer did his men a disservice if he went forward when it was not absolutely necessary. Arthur Smith lamented that his medical officer, in a very tight corner at First Ypres, was 'much too brave for a doctor, they ought to keep further back. He was right up dressing our fellows' wounds when he was hit in the arm. He died two hours before our stretcher bearers arrived two days later, from loss of blood.'[195]

Good stretcher-bearers, and there were many, were highly regarded. Norman Gladden remembered Private Bell with affection and respect:

> He was a fat, lazy and easy-going person in normal times, who became a fearless, self-sacrificing hero when there was any succouring to be done. His good temper, carried almost to the limits of non-involvement, made him a favourite in the company, and he could almost get away with murder.[196]

The award to Bell of the Military Medal was universally popular, and it is no accident that the most-decorated other rank of the war, Lance Corporal Bill Coltman VC, DCM and bar, MM and bar, was a stretcher-bearer. A gardener from Burton-on-Trent, he enlisted in 1/6th North Staffordshire in January 1915, but as a member of the Brethren, a Nonconformist sect, felt unable to kill, and duly became a stretcher-bearer, one of many soldiers who were prepared to serve but not to take life. He went back to gardening after the war.

Carrying a man on a 6-foot stretcher with its wooden poles and canvas base was often sheer, backbreaking stuff, and Frank Dunham never forgot his first carry:

> It was slow work, and the mud in the wood was knee deep, we were slipping all over the place with the stretcher and I felt sorry for poor old Chambers, who gave an extra loud moan every time the stretcher bumped. We four SBs were

all done in by the time we reached the Aid Post, and we rested here a short time while the MO saw after Chambers – he had an ugly-looking wound in the small of the back. Cpl Leary was good enough to give us a mug of tea each and, thus refreshed, we returned to our dugout.[197]

Stormont Gibbs saw stretcher-bearers at work clearing Delville Wood in August 1916.

> One of these bearers had been working increasingly at getting people who were near enough to drag and now he was working further afield crawling about with bandages and iodine and a water bottle. The look in his eyes was such a contrast with what I had seen earlier in the eyes of those men who were running away. It was also a contrast with the dull expression of the people who were left. It is scarcely an exaggeration to say that the soul of this man seemed to be shining through his eyes as he went about his dangerous work of mercy. His face was beautiful.[198]

Private Albert Bullock, hard hit in the hip on 6 October 1918, shouted for stretcher-bearers after he fell, 'and saw two not twenty yards from me . . . and they came out to me without hesitation'. They were machine-gunned on the carry, but 'the two bearers stuck it like heroes till we were under cover'.[199] Anthony French was carried from the field of the Somme in September 1916 after lying for a long time in a shell hole.

> At first I was soothed by the unaccustomed motion, but when the bearers entered a narrow trench and had to stretcher bars together to follow its twisting course, I longed for the journey's end. It was the easiest journey I have ever made. Reflected on senses already distorting the known and natural were ghastly images, a vague consciousness of things unseen. Clammy vapour rising from the ground. The stench of exposed death and decay. The phantom faces of unknown soldiers speaking only in whispers, absurdly, so I thought, since the enemy was thousands of miles away . . . At regular intervals the flash and bellow of a mighty gun and the rushing sound of its dis-

gorged shell in flight, like a ghost-train cleaving the sky. A dim reddish light glowing opaquely through canvas between tree trunks. Figures moving softly hither and thither. A voice demanding: 'What's his trouble?' And somebody answering 'Right leg.'[200]

At the aid post the medical officer would make a quick assessment. This was often no easy task, for in any sort of serious action he would quickly be overwhelmed by the sheer weight of casualties. Ernest Parker had never really appreciated his MO until he saw him in a trench at Loos, 'feverishly at work, his head swathed in a blood-stained bandage'.[201] Harold Dearden's aid post near Ypres was:

> a perfect shambles of mud, rain and blood. It was quite impossible to get any cover for anyone . . . We were heavily shelled all night; and in the early morning a flight of Boche planes bombed us from very low down, and I had several of my wounded killed that way. I spent all night either in my slit [trench], sitting in quite two feet of muddy water, or else dodging round the aid post trying to explain to my poor fellows that I had no cover to give them, and had done all that was possible; but they kept asking to see me every five minutes and on the whole it was a ghastly night.[202]

Some men were so badly hurt that it was a waste of time and effort to move them further back: they would be made as comfortable as possible and left to die. Many doctors took the view that a merciful overdose was the kindest treatment for a badly-wounded man. Second Lieutenant Treffry was terribly mangled by a shell on the Somme. His comrade C. P. Blacker saw it happen, and rushed forward to find that:

> One leg had been almost blown off with the jagged end of a femur sticking out. An artery was spurting. The other leg had been twisted back to front. His uniform had been ripped open and his abdomen gaped with bowels extruding. His face and moustache were a parched yellow. Stertorous sounds and blood were coming from his mouth.

Blacker briefly considered shooting him, but instead had him stretchered back to an aid post near Guillemont, where a young RAMC officer agreed that there was: 'Nothing to do but put him to sleep . . . But Treffry had a tough constitution and did not die until nightfall.'[203]

There were times too when morphine was no use. Arthur Osburn, striving desperately to care for a group of cavalrymen hit by a heavy shell on the Aisne in 1914, found:

> One terribly wounded . . . lay with both legs partly torn away at the knee, one arm broken and other wounds; he was still conscious.
>
> 'Oh! My God! Shoot me! Shoot me!' he moaned. 'Quick!' I injected some morphia into his breast. Someone who had rushed into the yard was standing, breathless, horror-stricken, beside me. The tortured man recognised him – his brother!
>
> 'Shoot me. Tom! Oh! Shoot me! For the love of God! Shoot me, will you! WILL YOU!' he began to scream piteously.
>
> Irresolutely, the man appealed to, fumbled with his revolver and looked at me rather wildly. Then, suddenly dropping his revolver, he covered his face with his hands and staggered away.
>
> I hastily soaked with chloroform a piece of clothing that had literally been blown from one of the other wounded, and doubling it, I laid it over the mouth of the agonised man beside whom I was now kneeling . . .
>
> I was dulling pain with chloroform; morphia seemed quite useless.
>
> My knees were soiled with manure from the yard; the spouting arteries that I had tried to check had drenched the front of my tunic and accoutrements and sprinkled my face, where the blood dried. My arms to the elbows were caked.[204]

Sidney Rogerson was a very experienced company commander by the time he fought on the Chemin des Dames in 1918, but little could have prepared him for it.

> A vivid picture stands out in my mind of that moment. From the ridge in front, mutilated human beings, Englishmen and French, were being carried down on hurdles of ground sheets – such medical amenities as stretchers had

disappeared long before. Bourdillon bent over to talk to one poor devil whose stomach had been ripped open, his entrails only held in by the sopping field dressing. He came across to me. 'I can't take him in the cars,' he said, 'he's bound to die, and it would only mean pushing some one off who might recover. If there weren't so many men about I'd do what he's asking me.' 'What's that?' I asked. 'Shoot him, and put him out of pain.'[205]

Other men could be saved by swift treatment. The medical officer would do his best with them, stopping bleeding and cleaning wounds, and then stretcher-bearers, sent forward by the bearer sections of field ambulances, would carry them back to the tent section of the field ambulance in the advance dressing station, where better treatment was possible. Soldiers whose wounds were less threatening might take longer to reach the advance dressing station; scarce places on stretchers were given to those whose need was greatest. 'I know of no greater relief than that experienced by a Regimental M.O. on getting rid of the wounded,' reflected Cyril Helm.[206]

Walking wounded would be directed back, under their own steam, to a walking wounded collecting station, usually in the same vicinity as the advance dressing station. Before leaving the regimental aid post a wounded man was tagged with a label giving an initial diagnosis and specifying what drugs, if any, he had been given. 'These tickets were issued to us in book form,' wrote Frank Dunham, 'similar to a cheque book, so that we retained a complete list of all casualties passing through our Aid Post. This list we had to send to our Orderly Room daily, whence the information was passed on to the Base and thence to England.'[207] When Harry Ogle was hit in the leg by a rifle bullet which remained in the wound, he was tagged wrongly: it took him several days to persuade the doctors to X-ray his leg, so convinced were they by the tag's insistence that the wound was superficial.

Work at an advance dressing station during a major battle was unrelenting. In July 1917 Major Martin Littlewood RAMC, who had already informed his diary that 'I develop lice and a touch of scabies', wrote that his dressing station, near Ypres, received a 'constant stream of wounded and now and then some who have been out two days. Awful. Busy all night until morning.' When he got out of the line in November he was so affected by the experience that he found he could no longer sleep in sheets, and when he raised the blinds to enjoy the sensation of a naked light, thought 'of the men lying around the Menin Road'.[208]

Chaplains were also busy, taking dictation from men who wanted to send letters home, comforting the badly hurt, and often, when there was a heavy surge of casualties, helping with first aid. Julian Bickersteth, in an advance dressing station just behind Gommecourt on 1 July 1916, supervised the loading of ambulances – four lying and four sitting cases apiece – and organised hot tea or Oxo for the wounded. He wrote that:

> The worst wounded seemed often to feel less pain than
> those who had slighter wounds. The shock of a shattered
> limb seemed to destroy the nerves in that part of the body.
> One lad said to me, 'Oh, my leg is so stiff, Sir,' and the
> boy's leg was smashed altogether . . . But I heard no word
> of complaint, and scarcely a groan.[209]

Doctors often commented on the resignation of their wounded, and Lord Moran wrote that only once, during his whole time on the Western Front, did he encounter a man who was terrified of death when the moment came. He tried to give the man privacy by shoving a heavy box of dressings against the dugout door, but reflected that those who practised medicine became party to dreadful secrets.

At night Julian Bickersteth would go forward with the bearer sections of the field ambulance running his dressing station, collecting wounded from the battlefield and bagging up the identity discs and personal belongings of the dead, recording the details on a label attached to his tunic. Only his faith kept him going, he reflected, and 'comforted me with the thought that those bodies are not down here – they are above . . .'. The division's assistant provost marshal sent a squad of thirty men to dig a huge grave, 26 feet long, 6 feet wide and 4 feet deep, and on one occasion Bickersteth had to take cover in it to avoid shelling – by no means a unique experience of the close proximity of the quick and the dead. Because many of the wounded who reached an advance dressing station died there, the extemporised graveyards that surrounded so many later formed the basis for several Commonwealth War Graves Commission cemeteries on the Western Front. Perhaps the best known former dressing station is Essex Farm, just north of Ypres, where the Canadian medical officer John McCrae wrote the poem *In Flanders Fields*.

In October 1918 Albert Bullock, with his hip wound, was taken by wheeled stretcher from his regimental aid post to the advance dressing station, and although he was very cold and wanted a drink they had nothing for him. His battalion, 8/Royal Warwicks, had suffered more casualties in forty-eight hours than it had for nearly a year in Italy, and it was not alone: the system was creaking badly. So badly, indeed, that nobody had yet relieved him of the grenades and flares in his pockets and he dumped these, with his gas mask and helmet, when he reached his next port of call, the casualty clearing station. The journey from dressing station to clearing station was usually made by motor ambulance. It could be easy enough if the system was not under pressure, but Frank Hawkings, walking wounded on the first day of the Somme, saw it close to meltdown.

> Eventually we found the dressing station [actually his battalion's regimental aid post], crowded with wounded, on the outskirts of Hébuterne. While I was waiting to be attended to, I suddenly felt giddy and fainted away. When I recovered, Captain Clarke, the doctor, was trying to rouse me. He soon bandaged me up. And off I went through the village to find the field ambulance ... At the opposite side of the village I found a crowd of wounded waiting by a medical dugout for the arrival of motor ambulances. I joined this crowd ... when a hail of long-range machine-gun bullets came pattering on the ground near us ... we set off to walk to Sailly-au-Bois. [Given a lift to the ADS there] we were inoculated against tetanus (lock-jaw), and were given a mug of tea ... There were too many cases for the authorities to do more than inoculate us and dress our wounds and so it was left to us to drift on to the casualty clearing station at Couin as best we could ... Here were hundreds of men on stretchers in the cornfields where they had been dumped by the ambulance men.[210]

The casualty clearing station was a field hospital set up in tents, Nissen huts or commandeered accommodation. A station might have half a dozen doctors and as many nursing sisters, and by September 1917 there were fifty-nine of them on the Western Front, each capable of dealing with up to 1,200 cases a day. At the peak of the third battle of Ypres there were twenty-three clearing stations behind the salient, each with three surgical teams working sixteen hours on and eight off. There was a conflict of opinion over the role of the clearing station. Traditionally, army doctors argued that the main role of the medical evacuation system was to shift soldiers along it as quickly as possible. However, there were those like Sir Anthony Bowlby, brought in as consulting surgeon to the BEF, who thought that the stations should be pushed well forward and should operate as quickly as possible, as many of the men evacuated so quickly would actually die. A change in practice brought good results, though there were suggestions that it led to the capture of part of two clearing stations during the German 1918 March offensive, for it was no easy matter to move a hospital and its patients at short notice.

But with the enhancement of the medical achievements of the casualty clearing station came, some argued, a decline in its practicality. Colonel David Rorie, assistant director of medical services, 51st Highland Division, thought that the clearing station personnel were 'the spoilt children of the RAMC', arguing that they were always eager to obtain labour from the field ambulances, but slow to return it. And they sometimes complained when soldiers appeared with their pockets full of hand-grenades: 'Tommy was a casual soul, and often carried an odd bomb or two inside the torn lining of his tunic pockets or otherwise bestowed about his person.'[211] A man would probably not get out of his clothes till he reached a clearing station, revealing some unpleasant surprises. A captured German complained that he had not had his boot off for fourteen days. 'Unfortunately,' wrote Rorie, 'before I managed to leave his side he managed to get the boot off. I decided at once that he was no liar.' Some men were shocked into incontinence, or lost control of their bowels through pain or fear, and one Irish officer, in the grips of dysentery and the victim of a long carry, muttered repeatedly: 'It's not my fault . . .'

From the clearing station patients, British and German, would be moved to a base hospital or on to the French coast for transport to Britain. This part of the journey was usually made by rail, and Harold Dolby saw German prisoners, who, at least in theory, received exactly the same treatment as their captors:

> being carried by our men to the ambulance train ... Fat and smiling Germans were being carried on the shoulders of our orderlies to the train; here in clean linen on swing cots with English nurses and doctors to attend them they were going to make their way in comfort to St Nazaire.[212]

Private Alf Arnold, working at a field hospital behind the Somme battlefield in July 1916, told his parents that:

> On two trains there were about 200 German wounded. Poor beggars they were knocked about too. One or two had died on the train and others were dying. No one who has not seen, can realise how badly some of them were mutilated. I was pleased to see how kindly they were treated by the English stretcher-bearers & RAMC men.[213]

Bernard Martin, wounded at Passchendaele, remembered little of his own train journey:

> Flat on a stretcher ... a glimpse from an ambulance window of the ruins of the Cloth Hall ... mild indignation ... I could have shown them a safer route avoiding Ypres ... Somewhere before dark my stretcher was on flat ground in a field full of stretchers, as though we were a carefully cultivated crop of some choice plant ready for harvest, waiting to be reaped. My heart leaped up when I beheld an English girl kneeling beside me, gentle hands seeking where to give me an injection – then back to unconsciousness. Next, I was looking from the window of a stationary hospital train, recognising the harbour at Boulogne. Two days, I think, in a bed, a real bed, in the Casino – this time indignant to discover my legs still caked with Flanders mud ... Probably I was under sedation because I next remember being aboard a hospital ship, SS *St Denis*, in the harbour awaiting nightfall, before crossing the English Channel.[214]

F. P. Roe had the good fortune to be wounded at Shrapnel Corner, just east of Ypres, in December 1916, when there was no major battle in progress and the chain of evacuation was working well. He remembered nothing of being treated at a dressing station, and:

> When I next came to I was lying on the stretcher on a railway platform. I remember being dimly concerned that I could not tell what time it was as the wristwatch I had worn throughout my time in France and Belgium had somehow disappeared. I was later loaded into an ambulance train and was exhorted to roll off the stretcher onto the top bunk of one of the carriages ... When the train finally stopped, I was again exhorted to ... roll off the bunk and onto a raised-up stretcher ...
>
> When I woke up again I found that I had been admitted to an officers' ward of the famous No. 14 General Hospital at Wimereux which was on the French coast near Boulogne. I shall never forget my first night there. There was an officer opposite me who at intervals throughout the whole night repeatedly called out in a loud and agonized voice, 'Mabel, Mabel!' The cries towards morning became quieter and quieter and he died peacefully early in the morning.[215]

Some soldier patients remained at hospitals on the continent, convalescing in special centres, some of them so tautly run that, as Harry Ogle observed: 'they must have been designed to make soldiers desire fervently to get away ... even back to the very line itself'.[216] They were posted back to their units when passed fit. The more seriously ill went back to Britain, and were distributed about a range of hospitals and nursing homes, public and private, throughout the country. On 8 October 1918 Albert Bullock was operated on at No. 6 General Hospital in France: he came to and found that they had kindly stuck the bullet that had hit him, wrapped in muslin, to his chest. He crossed the Channel aboard *Gloucester Castle* and was in a military hospital in Weymouth on 11 October, five days after being wounded. His wound became infected and he nearly died, but he had nothing but praise for his treatment. When he was able to eat again he wrote that 'the Staff Nurses are as pleased as me, especially Nurse Beanell who was a real trump to me'.[217]

Real trumps indeed. From 1916 nurses – military nurses of Queen Alexandra's Imperial Military Nursing Services and the Territorial Force Nursing Services and a wide range of auxiliaries such as the Voluntary Aid Detachments (which had a total strength of 82,857 by the war's end) – were increasingly numerous in France, although the sight of five English nurses behind the Somme in 1916 was so unusual as to persuade all around to stop work 'to behold the fair "visions".' Sister May Tilton testifies to the fact that there was an extra dimension to female nursing. In May 1917 she was running a sixty-bed surgical ward with one VAD and 'sometimes two orderlies' to help.

> One night I discovered a Lancashire lad of eighteen crying in pain. He whimpered 'No one has been near me, and I am in pain.' I brought him some nourishment and a sedative, made him as comfortable as possible, and found time to sit beside him until he fell asleep. Holding my hand in both of his, he whispered, 'You are good to me. I feel lovely now.' He died before morning.

Bluey, an eighteen-year-old Australian with ginger hair, told her: 'Mine is not an Aussie Blighty, so of course I'll be going back again, and I know it won't be my luck to get out of it again. Will you kiss me good-bye before you go?' And when her clearing station on the outskirts of Ypres was bombed in 1917 (German aircraft were very active over the salient at night), one wounded man complained that they had no right 'to send you nurses so far up here in the danger zone', and an appallingly wounded Scot urged her to get under his bed, as she might get hit. Her patients kept in touch when they left hospital though sometimes the news was bad. 'A brave mother' wrote to say:

> Our dear boy and only son Tom has died after a haemorrhage at No 18 BH [Base Hospital] at Etaples. I try to be brave for his father's sake, who is broken-hearted. I have been helping him to work up a business for our dear boy when he returned to us, but God willed it otherwise.[218]

Second Lieutenant Mellersh, carried into a clearing station at Corbie, was surprised to find:

> A real hospital, with real beds and real army sisters in their red and grey capes and their wide, white spotless headgear.
>
> I was led to a bed and a Sister came up to me. 'Hello sonny!' she said. 'Where've you got it? Is the rain making it muddy? Can you get into bed – you'll get a hot drink in a moment.'
>
> But I found I could not undo my mud soaked puttees. I felt exhausted and found I was shivering. One orderly helped me. Then in bed I somehow could not stop shivering. The sister came back. 'That's better!' she said. 'Why, you're shivering.'
>
> 'I'm sorry,' I said, in genuine contrition.
>
> 'You poor boy!'
>
> It was so kind, so heartfelt. I was suffused with a glorious self pity and a deep feeling of worship for that sister.[219]

Lancelot Spicer, in No. 1 Red Cross Hospital, reported that it was a 'most amusing place' because its volunteer staff were rather blue-blooded: 'nothing but Duchesses and Countesses – they really are very nice and work awfully hard'.[220] And Harry Ogle found the matron of No. 6 General Hospital 'efficient, kind and friendly, interested in us as persons but had no favourites'.[221] Albert Bullock's matron wrote to his mother to report his progress, and on 15 November 1918 confessed that: 'I feel so cheerful that no more boys are being killed and maimed and we have ceased the fighting. You may be sure I will send you word of your boy very shortly. Yrs very truly, Matron.'[222]

Officers and men recovering from wounds or sickness appeared before medical boards, generally composed of three doctors, who decided whether they were fit for active service, home service, or should be discharged. Soldiers passed fit for home service only were periodically re-examined. As Britain's manpower situation worsened in 1917 and on into 1918, travelling medical boards toured the country re-examining men who had previously been placed in a low medical category: many were 'combed out' and posted to France.

War is often the handmaiden of beneficial change, and the First World War was no exception. Advances in medicine and hygiene meant that sick rates on the Western Front, at 1.3 sick to 1 wounded, were lower than on other fronts, and far lower than the 24 to 1 of the American Civil War, and 10 men died from enemy action for every 1 that died of disease, a dramatic reversal of the traditional ratio. Saline drips became routine to reduce the damage done by shock; blood transfusions, cutting-edge in 1914, were used in the clearing stations from 1917 and the advance dressing stations in 1918; gas-gangrene, common in wounds inflicted in areas where the soil was heavily manured, affected 10–12 percent of wounds in 1914 but only 1 percent in 1918, and 'meticulous primary surgery', and the delayed suture of wounds, proved real life-savers. Abdominal wounds were still hard to deal with, and their mortality rate ran at about 50–60 percent, with some specialist surgical units getting it down to 40 percent by the war's end. The army took delivery of its first X-ray machine in 1913: by 1918 they were in regular use at clearing stations and occasionally further forward. Some apparently simple inventions had profound consequences: the Thomas splint brought the death rate for fractures of the femur down from about 60 percent to some 30 percent.[223]

Venereal disease, so long a scourge of armies, was described by an official history as causing 'the greatest amount of constant inefficiency in the home commands. . . '.[224] It estimated that the admission rate of Australian and New Zealand troops was as high as 128 and 130 per 1,000 of strength compared with 24 per 1,000 amongst British troops. The British army reported 416,891 hospital admissions for VD during the war, and as a stay in hospital averaged some fifty days for a soldier with syphilis the issue was as much about manpower as medicine. Soldiers who contracted VD were obliged to declare it, and were then sent to special hospitals, where their pay was stopped: as most married men made 'allotments' to their wives, marriages were often put at risk. Failing to declare VD was an offence under military law, punishable with up to two years' imprisonment with hard labour. The establishment of early-treatment centres where men were able to disinfect themselves went some way towards helping, as did the politically-contentious use of licensed brothels.

One in Rouen was visited by 171,000 men in its first year, and there were only 243 reported cases of VD; however, opposition at home led to its closure.

Officers suffering VD were sometimes able to persuade a considerate regimental medical officer to treat them privately, but for most men there was no choice between shameful hospitalisation or untreated disease. And it was difficult for the latter to remain undetected for long due to periodic inspections. On 4 May 1918, Captain G. O. Chambers, AADMS of the Cavalry Corps, informed the camp commandant that a sapper of the topographical section:

> Has been sent to 51 CCS this day suffering from syphilis. I discovered the case during a medical inspection of the Corps to-day. From the appearance of his present condition I consider him to have had the disease from 4–6 weeks.
> He has not reported sick in this period.[225]

Most controversially, the war did much for the recognition that not all wounds were to the body. A condition broadly defined as shell shock, because it was initially believed to result from the physical impact of a nearby shell on the brain, was increasingly recognised by the authorities, although the term covered a variety of traumatic neuroses. Symptoms presented in different ways. Some men, like Private Alfred Moss in F. P. Roe's platoon, became 'withdrawn, untypically quiet for long periods, and eventually even morose'.[226] Second Lieutenant William Carr found one of his sergeants, the sole survivor of a gun detachment hit by a shell, 'in a terrible state, shaking and incoherent. We spent some time talking to him trying to calm him down and comfort him, but to no avail.'[227] Others developed hysterical conversion syndromes, in which a mental condition had physical symptoms like paralysed limbs, blindness or deafness. Some men went berserk: Frank Hawkings and his comrades were only saved from one who jumped out of his trench and fired at friend and foe alike because the Germans machine-gunned him.

At first, as R. H. Ahrenfeldt acknowledged in his history of British military psychiatry, it was almost a matter of chance whether a man with psychiatric illness was considered to be genuinely ill, a malingerer, or even a deserter. By August 1916 the BEF had its own consulting psychiatrist and consultant neurologist, and by the year's end there were psychiatric centres in every army area and 'mental wards' in base hospitals. Treatment in the United Kingdom improved in parallel, and the work of Dr William Hales Rivers, who developed treatment for 'anxiety neurosis' at Craiglockhart Military Hospital in Edinburgh, is perhaps the best known, not least because Siegfried Sassoon, declared shell-shocked after publicly protesting about the war, was one of his patients. In 1922 a War Office inquiry into shell shock concluded that physical concussion caused few cases, that exhaustion was more common, and that there was a range of wholly genuine 'war neuroses'.

Although shell shock is often seen as *the* disease of the war it was, in its various forms, less common than we might think. In 1917 psychiatric admissions ran at 1 per 1,000 for the civilian population, 2 per 1,000 for troops in Britain and 4 per 1,000 for the BEF. Some shell-shocked men did not get as far as hospital because, as the 1922 inquiry made clear, the incidence of shell shock could be reduced by good discipline and leadership within units. Wise regimental medical officers could often deal with many mild cases by resting men in safety not far from the battlefield, and giving them the firm expectation that they would recover, pointing the way ahead to the effective treatment of what modern military psychiatrists would describe as 'battleshock'.

Yet there was more than pure logic at work where this terrible response to a shocking war was concerned. The shell-shocked victim, unable to gain employment after the war, became one of the period's most enduring icons. And, as Peter Leese has written: 'The memory of shell shock has remained potent too, because it has become the first and most powerful expression of the destructive effects of industrialised warfare on the mind . . .'.[228] It marked the military revolution just as surely as the heavy gun, tank or aircraft.

VI

HEART AND SOUL

THE WILL OF AN ARMY

What modern military theorists call 'the moral component of fighting power' is always more difficult to define than its fellows in the trilogy, the physical and conceptual components. It can neither be counted and costed, nor can it be accurately assessed through drill books, training manuals or pamphlets on doctrine. In the First World War, difficulties are especially acute because the whole issue of motivation is intimately linked to our interpretation of the war more widely. For some historians, combat motivation primarily reflected a draconian code of discipline which made the officer's pistol and the firing squad the army's natural response to personal failure: for others, decent fellows, proud of their cap badge and bravely led, did their job without flinching.

Of course the truth is more complex: motivation on the Western Front reflected a whole host of factors which varied from man to man, unit to unit, place to place and time to time. It is in this area that deconstructivist history is most dangerous, because by focusing on particular aspects of this complex mosaic, perhaps to meet an understandable personal or political demand (or simply to sell more books), writers often paint a picture that the men of 1914–18 would look at with disbelief. We have already seen that they were not lions led by donkeys. But so too were they neither thugs led by nincompoops, nor weaklings coerced by brutes, nor yet warriors led by heroes. Yet if we look hard enough we can find evidence of all these types – perhaps even in the same battalion on the same day.

In *Redcoat*, my study of the British army in the eighteenth and nineteenth centuries, I focused on what I saw as the two prime factors in motivating in the army of the age, and called them stick and carrot. Under stick I reviewed the coercive aspects of morale, and under carrot its persuasive aspects. The First World War requires a wider analytical framework, including a broader assessment of what men thought about their world, themselves and their enemy.

MAN AND GOD

It was an irreverent and blasphemous army, with the conversation of soldiers larded with what David Jones termed 'the efficacious word . . . above any other . . . considered adequate to ease outraged susceptibilities'.[1] Frederic Manning, in the first edition of his book *Her Privates We*, rendered the word as 'muckin', but, in the second edition, was allowed to unveil it fully. Corporal Hamley of 7/King's Shropshire Light Infantry, in reserve behind the Somme battlefield, is not wholly content with one of his signallers, Private Weeper Smart:

> 'You shut your blasted mouth, see!' said the exasperated
> Corporal Hamley, stooping as he entered the tent, the list
> of his head, with chin thrust forward as he stooped, giving
> him a more desperately aggressive appearance. 'An' let
> me 'ear you talkin' on parade again with an officer present
> and you'll be on the bloody mat quick, see? You miserable
> bugger you! A bloody cunt like you's sufficient to demoral-
> ise a whole fuckin' Army Corps. Got it? Get those buzzers
> out, and do some bloody work for a change.'[2]

The parish priest of the Belgian village of Dickebush was frankly puzzled by it all. 'I have looked it up phonetically in my little English dictionary (*fahke*),' he wrote.

And I find, to my surprise, that the word 'fake' means 'false, unreal, or not true to life'. Why the soldiers should refer to us in this way is difficult to understand, and yet everywhere one hears talk of 'fake Belgium' and 'fake Belgians'.[3]

And for all this, American oaths were a novelty even to the British. Eric Hiscock's comrades in 26/Royal Fusiliers were shocked to hear the Germans called 'cocksucking mother-fuckers' by the new arrivals: 'no one . . . had heard such expressions before, nor knew what they meant'.[4]

Coarse language, no great surprise to men from hard, working-class backgrounds, was a shock to those from more sheltered upbringings. Rory Baynes remembered that at his prep school 'a boy called Quin was beaten with a slipper for using bad language. The depraved boy was heard to say "damn". '[5] An officer noted how he found himself in serious trouble with his fiancée for using the same word when he missed a shot at golf. Officers might, however, legitimately allow themselves to use 'bally' in public. When the popular Captain Gussy Collins, wearing his trademark monocle and carrying a cane, saw his old company of 25/London making for its objective at Messines, he shouted cheerily: 'Haven't you captured the bally place yet?'[6] But for some men serving in the ranks swearing was not least amongst the crosses that they had to bear. Alfred Hale, conscripted in April 1916, endured a perfunctory medical examination 'wearing literally nothing but my coat and walking shoes' and then went to draw his uniform at the tailor's store.

> There, with much foul language on the part of an individual who ordered us all about, with 'Take off your boots', 'Put them on again', 'Now put your khaki tunic on', etc, all shouted at the top of his voice and interspersed with such expressions as 'What the bloody hell?', 'By Jesus'; etc, we recruits gradually transformed ourselves, outwardly, that is to say, from civilians into soldiers.[7]

He later lamented that: 'One got so very wearied of hearing everything being described as f-cking this and f-cking that, the very word, with its original indecent meaning, being at length a mere stupid and meaningless vulgarity.'[8]

In one sense an army is defined by its language. Stephen Graham thought that once a man 'begins to use the army's language without wishing it he has ceased to be an individual soldier, he has become *soldiery*'.[9] Henri Barbusse wrote of how the speech of his own army, 'made of a mixture of workshop and barrack slang, and patois, seasoned with a few newly-coined words, binds us, like a sauce, to the compact mass of men who . . . have emptied France to concentrate in the North-East'.[10] The British army was linked by its oaths, its nick-names, its deliberate mispronunciations and its practice of calling acquaintances of the same rank 'chum' – cartoons in Australian trench journals rendering it 'choom' in evident testimony to the abundance of northerners. A long-eared chum was a mule and a long-faced chum a horse, as Richard Chant of the 5th Dragoon Guards reflected in a poem:

> So good luck to all the Pals I know
> That's had the life-long run
> Especially those that took the Jump
> On the back of his long-faced Chum.[11]

But a long-haired chum was altogether different, a woman. Food – itself snap, scoff or scran – had a myriad of descriptions which rival the art of modern menu-writers. When Sidney Rogerson woke up on his first night out of the line Private Parkin told him with delight that lunch was 'stewed beef and sixty-pounders, sir, and deaf'uns and custard'.[12] A 'sixty pounder' was a big suet dumpling, and a 'deaf'un' a tinned fig. Indeed the whole business could be unutter-ably confusing, and when delivered in a variety of accents we should not be surprised that young Huntley Gordon admitted that it was 'sometimes difficult for me to make out what a man is saying'. If other-rank English confused officers, the reverse was also true. A machine-gun sergeant, directed to take his men to 'Oom-bare-con' (the village of Humbercamps, just south of Arras), acknowledged the order, and then, when out of earshot, asked his men what it meant: 'Whereupon from the back of the section rose the irreverent voice of Pte Archbold. "He said Oom-bare-con; but you, poor ignorant perisher, probably call it Humber camps".[13]

Signalese, the language once peculiar to signallers, seeped into the army as a whole. There was a phonetic alphabet, to prevent misunderstandings over the telephone. And so trench mortar, abbreviated to TM, was Toc Emma. There was as yet no twenty-four-hour clock, and so p.m. was Pip Emma and a.m. was Ac Emma. Officers and men used the alphabet in everyday speech to emphasise their warrior status. To an habitué the 'Deputy Assistant Adjutant General, General Staff Officers 1st, 2nd and 3rd Grades, and Acting Assistant Quartermaster General' were 'Don Ac Ac Gees, Esses O 1, 2 and 3; Ac Ac Q Emma Gee.'[14] A trench-mortar battery, TMB, was a Toc Emma Beer; an Observation Post, OP, was an O Pip; and a machine gun, MG, was Emma Gee *tout court.*

To call the Germans the Alleyman (a corruption of the French *allemand*) or Ypres Wipers implied an early arrival at the front, and the use of such words by newcomers would earn the forcefully-expressed disapproval of old hands. Place names were shamelessly mispronounced. Monchy Breton was Monkey Britain; Auchonvillers, Ocean Villas; Bailleul, Baloo; Biefvillers, Beef Villas; La Quinque Rue inevitably La Kinky Rue; Sailly la Bourse, Sally Booze; Wytschaete, White Sheet; Ploegsteert Wood, Plug Street Wood and Albert was rendered with English pronunciation and a good hard 't'. Mouquet Farm, that evil spot on the Somme, was Mucky Farm or Moo-Cow Farm. Where local names were lacking, invention was at hand: three advance dressing stations in the Ypres salient were christened with the mock-Flemish names of Bandaginghem, Dozinghem and Mendinghem – the latter two still have Commonwealth War Graves Commission Cemeteries named after them.

Old India hands expected the French to understand them when they began to 'sling the bat'. Frank Richards, loose in Rouen with his comrades Billy and Stevens in August 1914, saw how the former:

> ordered a bottle of red wine, speaking in English, Hindustani and Chinese, with one word of French to help him out. The landlord did not understand him and Billy cursed him in good Hindustani and told him that he did not understand his own language, threatening to

knock the hell out of him if he did not hurry up with the wine.[15]

Wallah – person – had words added to define a man's trade, from Vickers-gun wallah for the machine-gun officer to shit-wallah for the sanitary corporal. A rifle became a *bundook* and a bed a *charpoy*, and knife, fork and spoon were *jury*, *chummage* and *conter*. Roti – bread – became *rooty*, and so the Long Service and Good Conduct Medal, awarded for eating army bread for twenty-one years in an aura of undetected crime was the Rooty Gong. Men were enjoined to put some *jildi* in it, or to get something done on the *jildi*, from the Hindustani for 'to hurry'. An order might have to be carried out *ekdum*, at once. A madman might be *doolally* or have the *doolally* tap (from the hospital at Deolali near Bombay, and the Hindustani for fever), or be *piache* or even stone *piache*. *Khush* was pleasant in Hindi, and from it came cushy. Soldiers going up the line invariably asked the troops they were relieving what things were like up there. 'Cushy, mate, cushy' was a reply as common as it was inaccurate.

A wound serious enough to procure freedom from future front-line service was a cushy blighty, or more commonly a blighty one. Blighty was perhaps a corruption of the Hindi *bilāyatī*, a foreign country, the Arabic *beladi*, my own country, or the Urdu *belait*, strange or foreign. John Brophy and Eric Partridge described it as meaning much more than home, but 'a sort of faerie, a paradise which he could faintly remember, a sort of never-never land'. Blighty was a place described in song:

> Carry me back to dear old Blighty,
> Put me on the train for London Town . . .

And it was an adjective too, describing not simply 'things English and homelike' but anything that was generally very good, as in: 'This is real Blighty butter.'[16] The two staples of French *estaminet* life, white wine and chips, *vin blanc* and *pommes frites*, were Point Blanc and Pomfritz, good examples of the linguistic blurring that produced Franglais. Soldiers' Franglais included two of the war's most characteristic words: San Fairy Ann (with its close relatives San Fairy and San Fairy Anna), came from *ça ne fait rien* – it doesn't matter. And for the use of 'napoo', from *il n'y en a plus*, there is no more, let us listen to Arthur Smith of the Coldstream Guards:

> It can be no more – finished – no – and almost anything
> negative. For instance 'Napoo shelling tonight' means 'no
> shelling tonight'. 'Have you any more bread?' – answer
> 'Napoo'. When a man is drunk he is considered to be
> Napoo. If a man is talking too much someone tells him
> to 'napoo' or shut up. If a man gets out of breath he will
> say, 'Napoo breath' and so on.[17]

Walter Guinness reported that a trench was fittingly called Napoo Avenue because it had been destroyed three times in six days. Then there was the jig-a-jig, for making love, and the descriptive zig-zag for being drunk. The latter led to the following badinage between a British soldier and a French girl.

> '*Marie, ally promenade ce soir?*' – '*Non, pas ce soir.*'
> After an interlude of unsuccessful blandishments: '*Moi ally
> au estaminet, revenir ziz-zag, si vous no promenade.*'[18]

Franglais joined bat to produce mongey wallah – monger from manger, thus cook.

Nicknames abounded too. Officers often retained ones awarded at Sandhurst or staff college (Archimedes Edmonds, Apple-pie Allenby – The Bull came later – Wombat Howard-Vyse, Putty Pulteney and Sally Hume) or were awarded them on first joining their units. Frank Dunham's company commander, Captain A. R. E. Watts, was Nellie to the troops because of 'his girlish face and swanky ways'. An officer in the Gloucesters 'from his first appearance on parade until he left the regiment twenty years later was known as "Agony".'[19] Lieutenant General Sir Aylmer Hunter-Western was universally Hunter-Bunter, and Rawlinson was so well aware of his abbreviation Rawly that he kept a pet boar of the same name. Plumer was affectionately Daddy to his troops but Drip, because of a long-running sinus problem, to irreverent subalterns. There was a long tradition of nicknames that accompanied certain surnames. These were sometimes logical, like Dusty Miller, Spud Murphy, Spokey Wheeler or Chalky White. Historians in the ranks might have known that the original Charley Peace was a nineteenth-century burglar, and that

Tom King had been a notorious highwayman. The connection between Fanny Fields and Lottie Collins and the music-hall singers of the same name would have been clear, as would Brigham Young from the Mormon leader. But what of Daisy Bell, Knocker White, Pincher Martin, Rattler Morgan and Smoky Holmes?

A commanding officer or company commander, even if in his twenties, was the Old Man, and a regimental sergeant major was the reg'mental. The quartermaster, commissioned from the ranks and often the former regimental sergeant major of his battalion, was spoken of as the quarter bloke by soldiers and quarters by officers. But as Henry Williamson's character Philip Madison discovered, a new subaltern addressing a senior quartermaster to his face as 'quarters' was likely to have his vocabulary quickly and helpfully broadened. Newly-promoted second lieutenants were 'one-pip wonders', and officers more generally might be defined by the stars they sported on cuff or shoulder:

> There were one-pippers, two-pippers, three-pippers too,
> Just hanging about with fuck-all to do . . .

To his servant an officer was simply 'my bloke'. The company quartermaster sergeant could, like his superior at battalion headquarters, be known within the company as the quarter bloke. He might, from his rank of colour sergeant, be termed the colour bloke or colour bundle.[20] Or, from the commodity he so often dispensed, he might be called the soup-dragon. Sergeant was more rarely abbreviated to 'sarge' than novelists would have us believe: the contraction 'sarn't' was far more common, both up and down the chain of command. Corporals were 'full screws' and lance corporals 'lance jacks'. The rank of lance private did not feature in *King's Regulations*, but old hands granted it, in mock despair, to new arrivals.

Weapons had nicknames of their own. A Lazy Eliza was a long-range shell, probably destined for a distant battery, that rustled harmlessly overhead. But Pissing Jenny and Whistling Percy were shells from German 9-inch naval guns, and the Wipers Express was a heavy gun notably used at Second Ypres. A whiz-bang or a pip-squeak was the shell from a German 77-mm field gun, often fired at such close range that the whistle of the shell's arrival almost coincided with the sound of its explosion: Sidney Rogerson wrote of 'the double-tap of a Hun 5.9 inch or the Whiz-Bang! of our eighteen pounders.' A Coal Box or a Jack Johnson was a heavy shell which burst with a cloud of black smoke. Five-nines and nine-twos were German 5.9-and 9.2-inch guns, the decimals generally omitted by those who had heard the brutes. Two German machine guns near Festubert were christened Quinque Jimmy and Blighty Albert. A rifle, when not a bundook or a shooting iron, might be a hipe, from NCOs' practice of mispronouncing words when giving orders to give extra snap, as in: 'Order . . . hipe!' A bayonet could be a tin-opener, a toothpick or a pigsticker.

Soldiers often sang on the march. Unlike their German opponents or their French allies, as they tramped the pavé they had a marked aversion to overtly patriotic songs (though these had their place at concerts) and preferred a mixture of the mawkish and sentimental, the pop songs of the day, borrowed from music halls, and the obscene and irreverent. Captain Dunn believed that:

> The best-known snatches are short, four-line pieces that some vocal, inglorious Milton has been delivered of suddenly. They are fitted, as a rule, to a metrical or psalm tune. They can hardly be called songs, they're not songs. Their drollery makes them catch on, and they get an extraordinary circulation just to be hummed or trolled at odd times, with more or less variation according to individual taste and ingenuity . . . Here is one that is merely vulgar; it illustrates the inconsequence and clowning that give most of them their distinctively English flavour.
>
> *You can wash me in the water*
> *In which you've washed your dirty daughter*
> *And I shall be whiter*
> *Than the whitewash on the wall.*
>
> She may be the 'Colonel's', 'Quarter's', or 'Sergeant's' daughter.[21]

The French sometimes produced bands and colour parties just behind the lines to give a stirring welcome to troops coming out of the line. But as one British soldier wrote:

> One of our younger officers copied the idea; and we were
> to sing; and about a minute later we were to stop singing.
> We had not got the thing right, it seemed ... We all
> sang with extremely improper versions to the tune of 'We
> Wanted to Go Home'.[22]

Such frivolity could offend the serious-minded. Captain Robert
Dolby, captured when his regimental aid post was overrun by the
Germans at First Ypres, heard, in his prison-camp, how:

> The [German] recruit however sings all the time; on the
> march he is ordered to sing. One can hear the Sergeant-
> Majors shouting '*Singen Sie*'. And their songs are simple,
> homely subjects as a rule; of home, of peace, of quiet
> farms, of golden harvests. There are, of course, the more
> arrogant songs like 'Deutschland über Alles' and the
> 'Wacht am Rhein'. But on the whole one cannot fail to
> be struck with the quality of the verses. German songs
> are melodious, simple, and speak of noble subjects. The
> French songs, barring the 'Marseillaise' are trifling and
> often vulgar; but our English songs are futile: American
> rag-time and the odious 'Tipperary'. If songs be a test
> of national character, then the German has much to his
> credit.[23]

It's a Long Way to Tipperary was indeed a favourite throughout the
war, with alternative words beginning, 'It's the wrong way to tickle
Mary . . .', and ending rather worse. There was the supremely lugubrious *We are Fred Karno's Army*, its words readily adaptable to fit the
names of many units, sung to the tune of *The Church's One Foundation*:

> We are Fred Karno's Army, the ragtime infantry,
> We cannot shoot, we cannot fight, what bloody use are we?
> And when we get to Berlin, the Kaiser he will say,
> 'Hoch hoch! Mein Gott, what a bloody useless lot'
> The ragtime infantry!

And there were endless variations on *Mademoiselle from Armentières*.
One told how:

> Three German officers crossed the line
> *Parlez-vous,*

Three German officers crossed the line
Parlez-vous,
Three German officers crossed the line, fucked the women and
   drank the wine,
With an inky-pinky *parlez-vous* . . .

Or perhaps singers preferred the more respectable:

> Madame, have you any good wine,
> *Parlez-vous,*
> Madame, have you any good wine,
> *Parlez-vous,*
> Madame, have you any good wine,
> Fit for a soldier of the line
> Inky-pinky *parlez-vous* . . .

Or then again there was the subversive:

> The Sergeant-Major's having a time
> *Parlez-vous,*
> The Sergeant-Major's having a time
> *Parlez-vous,*
> The Sergeant-Major's having a time,
> Fucking the girls behind the line
> Inky-pinky *parlez-vous.*

With its variants like:

The ASC have a jolly fine time . . .

Some units preferred 'Skiboo! Skiboo!' and concluded 'Ski-bumpity-bump skiboo'.

Mademoiselle . . . was popular partly because it allowed different voices to take up the lead down the ranks of a marching company, sometimes mimicking officers or NCOs. Thus a subaltern with a stammer and an officer's use of expletives might be gently sent up:

They c . . . c . . . came across a wayside inn,
Parlez-vous,
They c . . . c . . . came across a wayside inn
Parlez-vous,

> They came across a wayside inn, and kicked the b ... b ... bally
>   door right in,
> Inky-pinky *parlez-vous* ...

Indeed, the best songs allowed for the natural inventiveness of their
singers. George Coppard's battalion of the Queen's was particularly
fond of one which opened with the confident solo:

> Today's my daughter's wedding day,
> Ten thousand pounds I'll give away.

The chorus riposted with gusto:

> Hooray! Hooray!

The solo then changed his mind:

> On second thoughts, I think it best,
> To store it in the old oak chest.

This allowed the chorus, so often denied a legitimate expression of
its dissent, to yell, with more feeling than metre:

> You stupid old bastard!
> You dirty old bleeder![24]

'Some of the songs we sang on the march gave vent to our private
feelings,' wrote Frederick Hodges;

> ... we always laughed when we sang the old favourite 'I
> want to go Home, I want to go HOME! Don't want to go
> to the trenches no more, where there are whiz-bangs and
> shrapnel galore. Take me over the sea, where the Allem-
> ande can't get at me! Oh my! I don't want to DIE. I wa'ant
> to go HOME!' Nostalgia or homesickness was expressed
> in many popular sentimental songs of the period. 'The
> roses round the door make me love Mother more. I see
> my sister Flo, and the folks I used to know.'
>   Another favourite was 'Roses of Picardy' with its sad
> haunting tune. Also 'There's a long trail a'winding to the
> place of my dreams' and 'Keep the home fires burning,
> while the hearts are yearning. Turn the dark clouds inside
> out, till we all come home'.[25]

The king of all marching songs, rightly described in Francis and Day's song annual for 1917 as 'The British Army's Battle Cry', was *Here we are! Here we are! Here we are again:*

> Here we are! Here we are! Here we are again!
> There's Pat and Mac and Tommy and Jack and Joe,
> When there's trouble brewing, when there's something doing,
> Are we downhearted? No! Let 'em all come!
> Here we are! Here we are! Here we are again!

It could be sung in cheery insouciance or with gentle disapproval. The Welsh Guards' historian admits that when the battalion moved up to Loos:

> There was some confusion in orders and billeting arrangements. The battalion passed through Haillicourt, wandered about in the country beyond, and eventually returned to the village, which, being recognized by the men, although it was dark, was greeted with the song, 'Here we are! Here we are! Here we are again!'[26]

And it could be flung in the teeth of the worst the war had to offer. A crippled battalion coming out of the line, its men muddied and filthy and its strength left on the battlefield, somehow braced up as it reached the village where it was billeted, and found courage to bark out the old words 'Here we are! Here we are! Here we are again . . .'.

But despite the bawdiness and cynicism of much of what they sang, soldiers, perverse as ever, could sometimes sing so sentimentally that they moved others to tears. The Reverend Julian Bickersteth, looking out through the inverted V of his tent flap in a bivouac behind the Somme battlefront in September 1916, could see twenty men round a bright camp fire.

> The fire lights up their faces, and the sound of their voices singing well-known songs comes clearly across to us. 'Keep the home fires burning' is one of them, and I wonder how many of them will ever gather round a home fire again. A full moon fills the top of the triangle and completes the picture.[27]

Welsh-recruited battalions often sang beautifully, and there is a heart-stopping account of a battalion moving up in the dark singing that most beautiful of hymn tunes, *Aberystwyth*, until the voices were lost in the sound of shellfire. The Welsh Guards choir came second in the male voice competition at the Welsh National Eisteddfod in 1918; but its finest hour had probably come earlier, as the regiment's historian, an eyewitness, remembered:

> The really effective singing did not come from the choir standing in a body on a rough platform, but from the heart of the battalion when going into battle or after the fight. 'In the sweet bye and bye, we shall meet on the beautiful shore,' after the engagement at Gouzeaucourt, when the shattered battalion was withdrawn to a wood behind the village, brought a hush over the camp. The singers were hidden amongst the trees in the moonlight and the air was frosty and still. This was not a concert, but a message, a song of hope and faith.[28]

So what hope and faith moved this vast assemblage of the proud and the profane, the cynical and the contemptuous, that constituted the British army in France? The question is a complex one, all the more so because it is bound up in the role of the military chaplain, an individual who has generally had a poor press. Religion and those who championed it divided men's opinion, but there was a far more powerful spiritual undertow on the Western Front than we sometimes think. The Reverend Harold Davies was struck by the paradox inherent in a battery of artillery he visited. They were:

> The most foul-mouthed lot that I have struck since I came to France. Yet after nauseating me for an hour this afternoon with their 'poisoned gas' they suddenly began to sing hymns with real feeling and piety. There is some real religion deep down in the hearts of these lads – one cannot call them godless because no sooner has one come to this conclusion than some spark of the Divine flashes out of them. The difficulty is to seize it and kindle a real fire within them.[29]

The Church of England was not simply England's established church, but was the religion given on attestation (sometimes with supreme cynicism) by the great majority of soldiers. It is important not to view the Church through the prism of the early twenty-first century, but to remember that a century ago it exercised a much more prominent role in national life, and that clergymen were comparatively well paid. Church attendance was substantially higher than it is now: in 1911, 98 per 1,000 of the population of England took Holy Communion in Church of England churches on Easter Sunday, a figure that had shrunk to 73 in 1939, 42 in 1973, and is now much lower. Perhaps most significantly for the men who went to war, three-quarters of children in England and Wales attended Sunday school in 1888, so that: 'the religion of the average private soldier had been formed in the Sunday and day schools, not by adult worship in church'.[30] Other Protestant sects had a very strong following in Wales, Scotland, Northern Ireland and parts of England. And Roman Catholicism, for all the disadvantages under which it had laboured for so long, had a powerful hold on the southern counties of Ireland and footholds in England too.

In short, there was a wider sense of spirituality than is the case today. But increasingly it was expressed, not with any theologically-precise certainty, but with that generalised sense that encouraged one sergeant major to tell a padre: 'to most men religion means nothing, except the notion that there was one above, a sense of duty to live cleanly, and a belief that there would be a reckoning sometime'.[31] Indeed, this tendency to move towards 'a non-dogmatic affirmation of general kindliness and good fellowship' was precisely what the Liberal MP C. F. G. Masterman had identified in his 1909 book *The Condition of England.* Padre Julian Bickersteth was detailed to pass the night with a man due to be shot for desertion the following morning. The victim, from the poorest of the poor in London's East End, had lost his father young, been sent off by his mother 'to do what he could for himself' and was in prison by the time he was twenty: there was no sign of a conventional religious background. He gave 'great heaving sobs' when Bickersteth explained what must happen at dawn. But he rallied after tea, bread and jam and a pipe of tobacco, and they sang together for three hours.

He chooses the hymns. He will not sing one over twice. He starts the hymn on the right note, he knows the tunes & sings them all perfectly . . . Oh how we sang! – hymn after hymn . . . After half an hour away for some dinner, I returned to the little room . . . we agreed to close the singing, but he wanted to sing one of the hymns he had already sung, a second time as a last effort. So we sang 'God be with you till we meet again' . . . he said 'We haven't finished yet: we must have God Save the King,' and then and there we rose to our feet, and the two Military Police who had replaced the ordinary guards . . . had to get up and stand rigidly to attention . . . a few seconds later the prisoner was asleep.

At dawn Bickersteth walked the 300 yards to the post, stood beside the bound and blindfolded soldier, whispered 'Safe in the arms of Jesus' and heard him repeat the words clearly. The assistant provost marshal silently motioned him away, and the volley came a few seconds later. Bickersteth, believing that his duty lay with the living, followed the members of the firing party out of the yard, spoke to them and gave them cigarettes.[32]

If the Church of England gained much from being the established church, it lost much too. In the 1906 Church Congress a bishop supported Christian Socialism by arguing that: 'The bishops' incomes linked them with the wealthy. The clergy sought their friends among the gentry and professional people. So clerical opinions and preferences reflected those of the upper and middle classes, not those of the wage-earners.'[33] It was said that after Cosmo Gordon Lang became archbishop of York in 1908 he never again entered a shop. The alignment between the established church and the ruling elite more widely is underlined by the family links between regular officers and clergymen before the war. In 1900 some 10 percent of regular officers had clergymen as fathers: the future Field Marshal Montgomery, subaltern in 1914 and temporary lieutenant colonel in 1918, was a bishop's son, and Major General Feilding, commander of the Guards Division for much of the war, had a brother in the Church.

The connection continued during the war. Samuel Bickersteth, vicar of Leeds in 1914, and his wife Ella had six sons, two of them in holy orders. All served in the army or the War Office. One was killed as a subaltern with the Leeds Pals on 1 July 1916, and two were awarded Military Crosses, one, Julian, for his courage as a padre and the other, Burgon, for bravery as a cavalry officer at the very end of the war. A. F. Winnington-Ingram, bishop of London and perhaps the war's most vocal supporter on the bench of bishops, was a chaplain to a territorial battalion, and gave some of his most rousing appeals in uniform, sometimes speaking from a wagon decked in Union Jacks.

Archbishop Randall Davidson had refused to see a party of unemployed men who had marched to London in 1907 under the auspices of the Christian Social Union, and the incident heightened the tension between the conservative and more radical elements within the established church which pre-dated the war. Many wartime observers felt that the fact that many Church of England chaplains came from middle-class backgrounds made it hard for them to empathise with the soldiers to whom they ministered. In contrast, Roman Catholic chaplains often came from working-class backgrounds. Father Willie Doyle was the youngest of seven children of a devout Irish Roman Catholic family, and three of his brothers became priests. Cardinal John Heenan, Roman Catholic archbishop of Westminster in 1963–75, was fond of relating that he had been at seminary with ex-Lance Corporal Masterson, later archbishop of Birmingham, and ex-Sergeant Griffin, later Archbishop of Westminster.

But the sheer diversity amongst chaplains of all denominations warns us yet again that there is no easy categorisation. Nor should we forget that, while clergymen were never formally conscripted during the war (though they came close to it in 1918), many clergymen volunteered to serve as officers or in the ranks. In September 1916 Julian Bicketsteth celebrated Holy Communion with two other clergymen, one a private and one a lance corporal, in his tiny dugout. 'We could just three of us kneel in comfort,' he told his parents. 'Every few seconds the blast of one of our guns would shake the whole air, but nothing disturbed us. I never felt so close to you in my life.'[34] Earlier he had reported that there were four clergymen serving in the ranks of 56th London Division, two RAMC privates and two others. Father Hubert Northcott enlisted as a gunner with his bishop's permission. 'I now no longer wonder why men are not particularly moved by matters of religion,' he wrote. 'You know what it feels like to be a convalescent after an illness. Every faculty seems dormant save the physical . . .'.[35] Some clergymen serving in the combat arms proved formidable soldiers. The Reverend Dr Bruce M'Ewen, minister of the second charge of St Machar's Cathedral in Old Aberdeen, joined the infantry at the age of thirty-eight and ended the war as a major in the Machine Gun Corps, returning to his pastoral duties (now as minister of the first charge) when hostilities ended.

In Stephen Graham's Scots Guards battalion there was a sergeant, later company quartermaster sergeant, who had served in the regiment in the Boer War and returned to civilian life when his enlistment expired. He had attended theological college, been ordained and had a Church of England parish in Surrey when war broke out. He was recalled as a reservist and joined without protest. 'I soon learned that he was very much pained at the brutality of the conversation,' wrote Graham, 'which was so much worse at the front than at home. Or than it had been in the Boer War, and he found difficulty in accustoming his mind to the flow of brutal talk which covered his ears day and night.' His habit of looking at the world from beneath a lowered brow gave him the nickname 'the Creeping Barrage', but although 'he was laughed at for many things, he was in secret and sometimes also openly, greatly admired because he lived what he preached. "I will say this about the Creeping Barrage," said one; "He lives the life".' In contrast, Graham believed that 'the padres, being officers, lived at ease; and whereas the men had poor food, they ate and drank in the company of officers. I could not help feeling how badly handicapped the padres were'.[36]

Frank Richards raised another criticism of chaplains, widely echoed elsewhere. It was not simply that they were officers, but that they encouraged combat without participating in it themselves. He thought them 'a funny crowd: they prayed for victory and thundered for the enemy to be smitten hip and thigh, but did not believe in doing any of the smiting themselves'. He believed that 95 percent of his comrades 'thoroughly detested' church parades on Sunday, though they amused themselves by putting some unauthorised words to *O God, our help in ages past*

> John Wesley had a little dog,
> It was so very thin,
> He took it to the Gates of Hell,
> And threw the bastard in.[37]

The army's bureaucratisation of religion through compulsory church parades certainly did not help. Bernard Martin, who came from a Nonconformist family, 'soon learnt in the army that anything but Church of England was called "Fancy religion".'[38] Private Eastwood, in Stuart Dolden's company of the London Scottish, claimed to be Roman Catholic, thinking that this would get him off church parade. But on Sunday he was marched off with other Roman Catholics to a service five miles away, and changed his religion the next day. 'I have never seen such a dramatic conversion,' remembered Dolden, 'and all without the aid of prayer.'[39]

C. E. Montague thought that the soldiers he knew hovered on the threshold of religion, 'prepared and expectant', but were driven away by a chaplain who could not grasp their fleeting spirituality.

> As soon as his genial bulk hove in sight, and his cheery robustious chaff began blowing about, the shy and uncouth muse of our savage theology unfolded his wings and flew away. Once more the talk was all footer and rations and scragging the Kaiser, and how 'the Hun would walk a bit lame after his last knock'.[40]

Siegfried Sassoon chided a chaplain's facility for finding the wrong word. 'And now God go with you,' he had told a group of men bound for the front. 'I will go with you as far as the station.'[41] The dockers' leader Ben Tillett added cowardice to the charge-sheet, and asked a 1916 Trades Union Congress meeting why those 'who were so fond of talking about heaven should be so afraid to go through its gates'.[42] Most chaplains knew that there was at least a modicum of truth in all these accusations, and many wrestled regularly with what they perceived as the most serious, the Church's support for the war and the relative importance of the spiritual and the temporal in their task.

Their status, however, was clear. Padres were officers holding the King's Commission, although their rank was relative, with the chaplain general, at the top of the tree, ranking as a major general, down to the most junior, a chaplain to the forces 4th class, as a captain. The chaplain general was always a priest of the Church of England until the appointment of the Reverend James Harkness, a minister of the Church of Scotland, significantly also an established church, in 1987.[43] They were to be addressed 'both officially and otherwise by their ecclesiastical title or official appointment and not by their relative rank or military title', although, as Arthur Osburn complained, some preferred to use military ranks. In August 1914 there were 117 chaplains, 89 of them Church of England, 11 Presbyterian and 17 Roman Catholic. By August 1918 this had grown to 3,416, with 1,941 Church of England, 298 Presbyterian, 643 Roman Catholic, 246 Wesleyan, 248 United Board, 11 Welsh Calvinist, 14 Jewish and five Salvation Army. By the end of the war there were seventeen chaplains in each division, and a varying allocation to hospitals. Above divisional level the hierarchy reflected 'a dual organization, one for Chaplains of the Church of England and a parallel one for those of other denominations who are administered as one unit . . .'.[44] This produced a deputy assistant chaplain general (Church of England) and a deputy assistant principal chaplain (other denominations) at corps headquarters, an assistant chaplain general and an assistant principal chaplain at army headquarters, and a chaplain general and a principal chaplain at general headquarters.

Bishop J. Taylor Smith, the London-based chaplain general of the army, was an evangelical with a missionary background who had served as bishop of Sierra Leone. He had been attracted to the post because 'being a great missionary, he might be nominated to a position which would give him the chance of dealing with the largest missionary society in the world, namely, the soldiers of the British army'. Critics suggest that he had no real theological insight, and his words tripped too easily off the tongue, while Stephen Louden, himself a senior Roman Catholic chaplain, observes that the 'notion of the British soldier as missionary was an enduring one but curiously unimpeded by most of the evidence . . .'.[45]

A much more significant figure was the deputy chaplain general, Llewellyn H. Gwynne, bishop of Khartoum, and brother of H. A. Gwynne, editor of the *Morning Post*. From July 1915 he was responsible for the Western Front, and had a remarkable impact on chaplains and generals too. The Reverend F. R. Barry admitted that:

> Many of us, I think, would have gone under or suffered shipwreck of their faith had it not been for the patient care and guidance of the great and saintly Bishop Gwynne, Father in God to a whole generation of young men . . . I have used the word 'saintly' deliberately. For he made it easier to believe in God. He was a commanding figure of that period.[46]

Julian Bickersteth, too, admired him from the moment they first met on his arrival in France.

> The Bishop could not have been pleasanter. He explained a good deal about the work to be done and how he thought it best to attempt it, and obviously wanted to be considered not just a superior officer, but a real Father-in-God; it will not be difficult to feel that he is indeed the latter. We had three or four minutes prayers together.[47]

Gwynne got on well with Haig, who told him that 'a good chaplain is as important as a good general', and he used his connections to build a better framework for support and the spread of good practice. He approached General Plumer in search of accommodation for 'a bombing school for chaplains'.

> 'A what?' exclaimed Plumer.
> Gwynne went on to elaborate his idea and said how necessary it was to bring back the chaplains from time to time for a 'gingering up'. 'You have refresher courses for machine gunners and others. Why should I not have one for chaplains?' Plumer thought the idea was a good one and offered to put at his disposal a chateau with extensive grounds and beds for twenty chaplains.[48]

From 1916 chaplains, conferences were organised under the auspices of the senior chaplain to 1st Army, and the following year Bishop Gwynne's 'bombing school' was established at St Omer with the Reverend B. K. Cunningham as warden. It was concerned less with 'gingering up' chaplains than ensuring that, as 'BK' put it, the chaplain did not 'lose his bearings'.

It was easy enough for a chaplain to lose his bearings in the maelstrom of the Western Front. In 1915 Bishop Winnington-Ingram made a passionate demand for the men of Britain to:

> band together in a great crusade – we cannot deny it – to
> kill Germans. To kill them, not for the sake of killing but
> to save the world: to kill the good as well as the bad; to
> kill the young men as well as the old; to kill those who
> have shown kindness to our wounded as well as those
> fiends who crucified the Canadian sergeant, who superin-
> tended the Armenian massacres, who sank *The Lusitania*
> – and to kill them lest the civilization of the world should
> itself be killed . . .[49]

This was not a view confined to bellicose bishops: Geoffrey Studdert Kennedy, later the celebrated chaplain 'Woodbine Willie' but then a vicar, wrote in his parish magazine in September 1914: 'I cannot say too strongly that I believe every able-bodied man ought to volunteer for service anywhere. There ought to be no shirking of duty.'[50] Even Conrad Noel, the socialist vicar of Thaxted in Essex, supported the war because it promised to help small nations against Prussianism.

The view of the war as a great crusade did not often survive contact with its harsher realities. Julian Bickersteth worked in an advance dressing station on the Somme.

> One poor fellow, a gunner, died in my arms in the aid-post,
> whither he had been brought by his comrades, hoping
> that it might be possible to save his life. The doctor looked
> at him, shook his head, and passed to another patient. It
> wasn't even worthwhile dressing his wounds. The morphia
> tablets helped him to bear the pain, but he was conscious
> up to the end. The doctor left me alone with him, so we
> were able to have prayers together and a little talk, and I

administered to him the last Sacrament. The roof of the little dugout was low and the place was dark and he tried to raise himself to look out of the narrow doorway as if to have a last look outside. Grey and pitiful enough was that scene.[51]

The Reverend Michael Stanhope Walker went straight from a Lincolnshire parish to the Western Front, and was at a casualty clearing station on the Somme: he buried 900 men in three months. On the first day of the battle he wrote:

> We have 1,500 in and still they come, 3–400 officers, it is a sight – chaps with fearful wounds lying in agony, many so patient, some make a noise, one goes to a stretcher, lays one's hand on the forehead, it is cold, strike a match, he is dead – here a Communion, there an absolution, there a drink, there a madman.[52]

The Reverend Charles Doudney described the smell of the once-pretty garden of Potyze Chateau, near Ypres, home to an advance dressing station.

> The flowers are gone, and their perfume is replaced by the all-pervading stench that one is even beginning to become accustomed to – of putrefaction fraught with chloride of lime; in some parts of the ground one has the predominance, in some the other. But it's the smell of a charnel house, and in places is added the strange effluvium, indescribable, of newly-shed blood.[53]

Some chaplains collapsed under the impact of such things. On 17 August 1916 the level-headed Reverend Harold Davies reported:

> Found a new Chaplain ... in No I Field Ambulance. Apparently he was suffering from dysentery and shock. As usual he had no previous military experience and had just been sent out here. Someone had sent him to the 108th Brigade at Bully Grenay, where he was not really wanted and he had seen bad sights, which had unnerved him.[54]

Alan Hanbury-Sparrow thought that 'the priests, with the exception of the Roman Catholics, did not seem sufficiently equipped to withstand, without harm to themselves, the arguments of an earnest doubter'.[55] At its worst the experience of the front could break a chaplain's faith, as Bishop Gwynne had seen all too clearly.

Many chaplains who survived the physical and psychological assaults of the front rejected the Winnington-Ingram view of the great crusade. Harold Davies admitted 'I shall never be a soldier' after being chided for holding an impromptu service in what turned out to be the trench-mortar bomb store, putting his congregation somewhat closer to their Maker than he had intended. But he was firmly committed to the war, and was perfectly prepared to help doctors usher numerous unwounded stragglers out of the Royal Naval Division's casualty clearing station during its attack on Beaumont Hamel in November 1917: 'It's worse than the tramp ward of a workhouse', a surgeon told him. However, he agreed with a gunner officer in wishing that 'the chattering magpies of our English Parliament who draw £400 a year and talk so much hot air could have been compelled to spend an afternoon in this valley of horrors'.[56]

Father Francis Drinkwater, a Roman Catholic, spent much of the war at the front, was wounded and gassed, and emerged with his strong faith undimmed. But on 2 July 1916 he wrote that: 'I shall soon be a pacifist and a conscientious objector – to modern warfare anyhow. It becomes more impossible every month, and the ghastly mangling of human beings en masse seems disproportionate to any conceivable object.[57] Julian Bickersteth also saw the war out to the end, but it strained even his determination. He wrote at the end of 1916:

> Oh! To get this wretched business over. There is only one question that no Tommy is ever tired of asking, 'When do you think it will end, Sir?' Yet I do think it is true that no one wants to see the business half done. Peace must not be returned to Europe for a year, but if possible for all time ... Who can stick it longest? That is the question.[58]

And in 1918 he acknowledged that:

> The war becomes more terrible and soul-corroding as month succeeds month ... It has lost all the romance of some years ago. It is now a perpetual round of dull, prosaic murder, with one desire in the hearts of all – to keep alive

a little longer and to see an end to the business. No one has any heart in it ... We are in it and we can't get out of it now, even if it costs the lives of all who are now in France.[59]

The crusade of 1914 had become, four years later, a matter of sheer endurance.

Many soldiers, and indeed some Anglican priests, felt that Roman Catholic chaplains' requirement to be on hand to administer the extreme unction encouraged them to spend more time in the front line. Robert Graves argued that if Anglican regimental chaplains

> had shown one-tenth of the courage, endurance and the other human qualities that regimental doctors showed ... the British Expeditionary Force might well have started a religious revival. But they had not, being under orders to avoid the fighting and to stay behind with the transport. Soldiers could hardly respect a chaplain who obeyed these orders, and yet not one in fifty seemed sorry to obey them. Occasionally, on a quiet day in a quiet sector, the chaplain would make a daring afternoon visit to the support line and distribute a few cigarettes before hurrying back ... [But] the Roman Catholic chaplains were not only permitted to visit posts of danger, but definitely enjoined to be where the fighting was, so that they could give extreme unction to the dying.[60]

Guy Chapman echoed similar sentiments.

> These Catholic priests impressed one. [Father] Leeson never dropped a word of religion in my hearing; but one felt a serenity and certitude streaming from him such as was not possessed by our bluff Anglicans. Already there was a growing dislike of the latter. They had nothing to offer but the consolation the next man could give you, and a less fortifying one. The Church of Rome sent a man into action mentally and spiritually cleaned. The Church of England could only offer you a cigarette. The Church of Rome, experienced in propaganda, sent its priests into the line. The Church of England forbade theirs forward of Brigade Headquarters, and though many, realizing the

fatal blunder of such an order, came just the same, the publication of that injunction had its effect.[61]

And Julian Bickersteth confessed that: 'It makes me despair of the Church of England. Rome makes no mistakes . . .'.[62]

Yet many Anglican chaplains recognised, as did Bickersteth himself, that they would only gain men's respect if they entered the crucible with them. 'I must admit that I find it increasingly difficult to face enemy fire,' he wrote, 'but our task is absolutely nothing compared to what the brave lads in the trenches have to endure when they take part in an attack.' He made a practice of carrying a pyx containing Sacrament in one kind, bread marked with wine, and going forward to give it to the wounded and dying. The universally-admired Reverend Theodore Bayley Hardy, a fifty-five-year-old Church of England clergyman, earned the MC, DSO and VC during a year's service at the front and was eventually killed in action. On one occasion he spent two days in the mud with a half-buried soldier, working with the men who were trying to extract him. Other chaplains shared similar risks. Anthony French was lying wounded in a crater in September 1916.

> I heard movement coming my way and I thought of rats, bloated rats, and felt weak and defenceless. I lay stork still. Dimly I saw a figure passing to and fro, here and there, bending low. My heart beat uncontrollably.
>
> His head was bent over mine. I stared unbreathing. I saw a white collar and the familiar tin hat. He spoke in cultured English, and his voice had a deep, rich timbre.
>
> 'Are you asleep?'
>
> 'No, Padre.'
>
> 'Badly hurt?'
>
> 'Not really.'
>
> 'Could you walk?'
>
> 'Afraid not, but I can crawl.'
>
> 'Better lie still. You're some way off, but I'll try to send the stretcher bearers. They're all busy just now, but be patient and lie still.'
>
> I thanked him. But he had gone, and I feared for him out there when the rattle of fire was resumed.[63]

Father Drinkwater particularly admired Canon Scott, Church of England padre to 1st Canadian Division, who certainly did not conform to the stereotype of the stay-back padre. 'He wanders round all the most dangerous parts with a tin of bully and a biscuit; reads his own verses to the men in the trenches,' wrote Drinkwater. Scott lost his son, an infantry officer, and found his body in a fresh shell hole 'where the Canon recognized his son's hand (by the ring) sticking out of the earth'.[64]

A few chaplains went much further. In 1918 Frank Crozier encountered a Welsh Nonconformist chaplain 'indulging in rapid fire from a shell hole at fleeting enemy targets'. He disapproved, because these were 'circumstances which called for no emergency'. Crozier disarmed the chaplain, gave him lunch, and told him that he should never have been a clergyman at all. 'He renounced his vocation,' wrote Crozier, 'and joined up as a private. He did quite well, and I was told that he had the finest flow of language in the regiment which, being Welsh, was saying a great deal.'[65]

However, because chaplains carried the authority of a commissioned officer there were rare moments when a commanding officer might expect his padre to exercise military command. Father John Groser, trained in the tradition of Catholic socialism at Mirfield, and later a great East End priest, was ordered to take command of a party of men who, so his CO thought, would only stand if led by an officer. He refused. 'I reminded him of the scores of men he knew who had fallen that day after doing their utmost,' said the colonel,

> and I was conveying to him – in what words I cannot remember – my despair of a religion that could teach that such a patronizing stand-offish attitude was the right one, when my words were drowned by a terrific burst of fire from our guns, who had spotted a counter-attack forming up. When the firing was over Groser told me that he would do what I wanted provided he didn't carry arms. To that I readily agreed.[66]

Father Groser was awarded the Military Cross, and wounded and sent home in 1918. On 8 October 1918, 2/Royal Welch Fusiliers lost its Nonconformist padre, killed in action.

The padre should not have gone with A Company in the early morning. He was told that he would be an embarrassment to them, but he was impulsive, he insisted on going, and was killed while seeking an MC to please some fool of a girl in Liverpool who had taunted him with having no decoration.[67]

Many chaplains were unsure whether their main role was spiritual or temporal, whether they were, as one put it, 'Mr God or Mr Cinema'. It was easy to slip into the latter role, and to concentrate on providing the troops with much-needed welfare support, like tea and cake at the base or cigarettes in the front line, or to offer advice with problems that arose at home. The majority of private mail, except that in strictly-rationed green envelopes, had to be censored by an officer, and padres – often less busy than combatant officers – were frequently busy reading soldiers' letters, which gave them a few useful insights. The Reverend John Sellors, a working-class Anglican sent to France in 1917, was delighted to find that one of his letters had been written by

quite a wag. He said his doctor had ordered him a holiday abroad, and here he was, but he could give no answers as he had not decided what hotel to stay at. He could not say much owing to the censor, but he would tell one secret ... 'I am determined to finish this war' ... I could not resist the temptation to put 'Good old sport (censor)' on the letter although I am told that this is strictly against orders.

The Reverend Pat Mc Cormick, an Anglican who had served in the Boer War, was amused to censor a letter betokening a fleeting relationship just before the writer left for France:

Dear Molly,
A Happy Christmas. I am sending this to my aunt to forward to you as I do not know the address. Please tell me your name when you write as I have forgotten it.
Yours, Dick[68]

Slipping between the roles of welfare officer and priest did not come easily to many. Sellors had been advised by a friendly sergeant that he would be best advised to 'mix with the boys, join in their lives and interests and see the boys made more contented and happy'. And Sellors hoped that by mixing with them in this way he could indeed help 'bring them to higher things, the things of God'. But his was not an easy road. His diary makes it clear that he was gently teased by the NCOs, who asked him to speak to the other officers and get them to acknowledge salutes more politely. And then over dinner in the mess many officers suddenly affected 'a bleating kind of laugh; all eyes turned in my direction and I assumed it was meant to imitate me . . .'.[69] The real question of whether he ever managed to be more than a decent sort who gave cigarettes to the boys must remain unanswered.

When the Reverend Theodore Bayley Hardy arrived in France he spoke to the more experienced Studdert Kennedy.

> He asked me about purely spiritual works. I said there is very little: it is all muddled and mixed. Take a box of fags in your haversack and a great deal of love in your heart and go up to them. Laugh with them, joke with them. You can pray with them sometimes but pray for them always.[70]

But even Studdert Kennedy, eccentric and outgoing as he was, questioned his own role.

> What the bloody hell is the Church doing here? An amateur stretcher bearer or an amateur undertaker? Was that all a Christian priest could be in this ruin of a rotten civilisation? I have pondered as I sat down after singing a comic song to the men at rest. An amateur comedian struggling to make men forget for one short hour the horrors in the midst of which they live and are called upon to die; always an amateur, always more or less inefficient and untrained, I was typical it seemed to me of the Church I loved and served.[71]

And in *The Unutterable Beauty*, the volume of poetry he published in 1927, he acknowledged the burden:

> Of unpaid – unpayable debt,
> For the men to whom I owed God's Peace,
> I put off with a cigarette.[72]

It was perhaps in their ability to shift easily between roles that Roman Catholics had the greatest advantage. They were, suggests Stephen Louden, 'able to minister as priests, dispensing not fags but forgiveness, not just cheer but communion'.[73] Sacramental rituals were at their most valuable when men confronted the terrifying unknown, and there was something 'commendably professional' about the average Catholic padre. Irish regiments containing an overwhelming majority of Roman Catholics sometimes celebrated the sort of *grande messe militaire* once seen in the French army, whose drummers beat the long roll of *au champs* at the elevation of the Host. Rowland Feilding's Connaughts heard High Mass in the village church at Locre on 17 December 1916.

> Three priests officiated. Soldiers, accompanied by a sol-
> dier organist, composed the choir, and the battalion
> bugles sounded the 'General Salute' during the Elevation.
> All was very impressive and, considering that they are only
> out of the trenches for a few days' rest, the smart and
> soldierly appearance of the men was very remarkable. But
> there is never any difficulty – no matter what the circum-
> stances – in getting a good Irish battalion to turn out well
> to go to Mass.

'The intensity of their religion is something quite remarkable,' he reflected later, 'and I had under-estimated it.'[74] Father Francis Glee-son, mounted, with a stole over his service dress, gave absolution to 2/Royal Munster Fusiliers at a wayside shrine as the battalion moved up to attack Aubers Ridge in May 1915: the men, heads bared, within sound of gunfire, then sang the *Te Deum*. The Munsters lost nineteen officers (including their commanding officer and adjutant) and 374 men the next morning: only eight were taken prisoner. The incident formed the basis for Fortunino Matania's well-known painting *The Last Absolution of the Munsters*.

But not all approved of the line taken by Roman Catholic clergy-men. C. P. Blacker attended Mass with the Irish Guards and was shocked to see how the congregation was visibly horrified by Father Leahy's description of hell. 'I could not overcome a feeling of dis-taste,' he wrote, 'over the picture of this group of fine men weeping and striking their breasts when what they really wanted was a renewal of faith and a message of comfort.'[75]

Many Church of England chaplains had to improvise. The Reverend Victor Tanner was in a trench at Passchendaele.

> After another shell fell close I said 'Now, lads, I am going to ask you to do something which perhaps you have not done yet. I am going to ask you to close your eyes and pray that God will protect and keep the boys in the front line, and that He will extend the protection to us,' and every man closed his eyes. We could scarcely hear one another's voices amid the whistling and bursting of the shells. But God heard those prayers. That very trench was blown in during the afternoon and several men were killed or wounded.[76]

But if Anglican clergymen could not produce anything to equal the Connaughts' High Mass, it is clear that the good ones could indeed engage the spirituality of their flock. Julian Bickersteth put considerable effort into preparing willing soldiers for confirmation, though he noted sadly how death constantly raided his flock. When Charles Doudeney was mortally wounded by a shell fragment his widow received letters which testified to the fact that her husband had given men much more than cigarettes. Corporal R. W. R. Bond of the Military Police told her that:

> Your dear husband was the means of getting a party of us ready for our Confirmation for which we all owe an allegiance to our dead comrade. He is greatly missed by us all – a brave and plucky gentleman. We will do our best to get to your dear husband's resting place, and do our best to make it up properly. While I am writing these lines I must thank you for the copies of the C. F. N. [*Christian Fellowship News*] which I distribute among my comrades, who find a very healthy bit of literature very acceptable in this awful place.[77]

And there were Scots and Welsh battalions where Protestantism was firmly founded. On Easter Sunday 1915 John Reith attended Communion with officers and men of 5th Scottish Rifles:

On this occasion the Minister took service behind the bar of a common drinking shop; silver flagons were ordinary bottles, chalices were tumblers. For long years this grey-haired padre had ministered to a congregation in a Scottish border town. He had dispensed a hundred Communions but never one so solemn as this, for all its undecorous setting. It had a circumstance of its own, a dignity and a compelling pathos. Drone of an aeroplane overhead, intermittent gunfire, rattle of a passing limber, these the organ undertones. As at home, we sang the 35th paraphrase to the tune Rockingham, but with new and pregnant significance. I looked from Minister to congregation, a hundred or so mostly very young, but with five months of war strain.[78]

Charles Douie attended a service in a barn at Henencourt at much the same time.

The night was quiet, apart from the incessant muttering of the distant guns. A few candles gave a flickering light. All round the barn men's equipment and rifles hung on the shadowed walls. The Communion table was a rough wooden packing-case. Yet the service was impressive, had indeed a splendour often absent in formal surroundings.[79]

And Walter Nicholson had the highest regard for Chaplain Rushby, a Wesleyan, who 'went over the top with the leading company' at Fricourt, and reported 'a pleasurable excitement I shall never forget, nor ever be able to deserve'. 'I never met a finer Christian,' reflected Nicholson,

but he never paraded his religion. He had a complete and utter faith in the goodness of our soldiers; glorying in their courage, endurance and cheerfulness. It was clear to him that they had a deep regard for divine things and that one of his battalion was linked to Cromwell's ironsides in piety and courage.

In Nicholson's experience 'when the padres were good, they were very very good; but when they were bad they were awful'.[80]

* * *

In 1917 Anglican chaplains produced the report *The Church in France*, based on the results of 300 questionnaires. Neville Talbot, one of the chaplains who responded, affirmed that: 'The soldier has got religion, I am not sure that he has got Christianity.' There was a widespread feeling that Jesus was respected as a heroic fellow-sufferer, but little support for turning the other cheek. Many chaplains who responded thought that the war had broken down social barriers, and there was surprisingly little hatred of the Germans. However, it affirmed that priests needed to do more than simply to reach soldiers through their 'Tommy-ness': 'There are things beyond Tommy, and the minute he wakes up to this primary fact, we shall have a sign that he is saved.' In 1919 an inter-denominational group of seventeen chaplains published *The Army and Religion*, which reached some similar conclusions. The war, it declared, had shown many of the clergy to be amateurs because of their unwillingness to discuss spiritual issues man to man.

Chaplains' familiarity with the opinions of their soldiers through their censorship duties would have enabled them to see, as a modern researcher can, just how deep a current of belief flowed through the army: it certainly gives the lie to Robert Graves's suggestion that: 'Hardly one soldier in a hundred was inspired by religious feeling of even the crudest kind.'[81] For some, belief was a reflection of pre-war teaching and feel for liturgy. Second Lieutenant Huntley Gordon reflected on the Psalms at Hellfire Corner, just outside Ypres, in August 1917.

> In this strange world, the Psalms can be a very present help in time of trouble; particularly as they were written by a fighter who knew what it was to be scared stiff. It's really amusing to find how literally some of them apply to life in the Ypres Salient in 1917. 'I stick fast in the mire where no ground is.' (Psalm 69) 'The earth trembled and quaked: the very foundation also of the hills shook.' (Psalm 18) 'The clouds poured out water, the air thundered: and the arrows went abroad.' (Ps 77) 'Thou shalt not be afraid for any terror by night: nor for the arrow that flieth by day . . .' (Ps 91) But David was obviously whistling to keep his courage up. Well, there are moments

when it's something to be able to whistle at all. But this is surely to regard God as your lucky mascot; and that won't do nowadays.

One has to accept that one's own survival cannot be the first consideration. We have got to beat the Boche, whatever the cost. But this suppressing of one's instinct for safety is not easy, particularly at moments when your stomach turns over and won't go back into its place; 'Our belly cleaveth unto the ground' (Ps 44) when the 5.9 cometh! All I hope is that, whatever happens, we may still be able to say 'Our heart is not turned back: neither our steps gone out of thy way: No, not when thou hast smitten us into the place of dragons, and covered us with the shadow of death.' (Ps 44).[82]

And in August 1916 Private Alf Arnold RAMC told his parents that he had just heard a very good sermon comparing the nurse who looked after the patients in his ward to Jesus Christ: 'I think that is very beautifully explained,' he wrote.[83]

But for far more soldiers belief was a conviction akin to fatalism, where God was indeed a mascot and prayers became more fervent as danger loomed. Some officers saw God as a sort of celestial commander in chief to whom they would eventually have to give an account of their operations on earth. Brigadier General Johnnie Gough, Haig's chief of staff until he was killed in 1915, told a padre that:

> I believe that I shall stand before Almighty God. There are many things which I have done which I ought not to have but I think he will say: 'Look here, when you have honestly known a thing to be your duty have you failed to do it?' I really think I shall be able to say, 'No'.[84]

Others, officers and men alike, simply trusted that God would do his best for them. Private George Taylor of 1/Grenadier Guards told his mother how much he hoped for her prayers, and concluded: 'May Jesus in his great love and compassion please grant that we may be spared to meet each other again. Give my love to all my friends . . . Yours in the Pink, George.'[85] Private Roy Ashford reported that services at the base were 'better attended than any I have seen in the Army', and was glad to be blessed by a chaplain before he went up the line.[86] Driver Len Doust RFA admitted to the desperate prayer so common before danger: 'Oh God, for Christ's sake, don't let me be killed or maimed; don't let me lose my arms or legs.'[87] Another soldier told his sweetheart:

> I know a lot of men here before the war were great sinners but I know that they often pray now, it is the time the Germans are shelling our trenches that they think there is a God. I am not saying that I said my prayers before the war because I did not, but I don't believe I have missed a night since I have been out here and ever since the battle of Neuve Chapelle I have believed there is a god because I prayed to him before the battle to keep me safe and He did, I had some marvellous escapes.[88]

On the eve of the Somme a major in the London Scottish told Julian Bickersteth that he was quite confident that he would be safe because he knew that his young son prayed so hard for him: 'The faith of my little boy is so real . . . God could not disappoint a faith like that.' 'I never saw him again,' wrote Bickersteth sadly. 'He was shot dead in the advance next morning.'[89] But the current of belief flowed in two directions. W. H. A. Groom, religious when he went to war, lost his faith: 'my belief in a church which condoned killing faded away'.[90]

Religious belief, so fervent when shells whined overhead, was coupled with the selflessness which was so common in good units to encourage some chaplains, like David Railton, to 'hope for such great things from the war'. But the war did not produce the national religious revival they prayed for, and the replacement of comradeship by selfishness was one of the unwelcome features of men's return to civilian life. 'It was just too wonderful for words to be a civilian again, free from orders and restraints,' exulted Roy Ashford, 'but just one thing was missing, and that was the comradeship and helpfulness one received from "chums" in the army'.[91]

Practical experience of the way the war broke down social barriers encouraged several clergymen to pursue Christian fellowships after the war. The Reverend Philip 'Tubby' Clayton was invited by Neville Talbot, senior chaplain of 6th Division, to establish a rest house for soldiers. Talbot found a suitable property in Poperinghe, and called it Talbot House after Neville's brother Gilbert, killed when the Germans first used flamethrowers against the British at Hooge in 1915. It was universally known as 'Toc H' (signalese for TH) and became an oasis offering comfort and sanity, where men could drink tea, read newspapers and, if they wished, pray in the 'Upper Room'. A notice at the door warned all who entered to abandon rank: Toc H was one of the few places where an officer could meet a non-commissioned brother in comfort. Talbot re-established Toc H in London in 1920 and it became the centre of an international movement. The original Toc H still survives in Poperinghe, and its quiet and simple Upper Room always seems to me to be heavy with the presence of the thousands who knelt there and prayed that their cup might pass.

Sometimes men's spirituality was enhanced by the landscape. It was not always blighted and blasted, and nature struggled on in the most surprising ways. R. B. Talbot Kelly spent much of his time in observation posts, with ample opportunity to savour nature. He wrote that:

> The very spirit of the trees sank deeply into me . . . to me half the war is a memory of trees; fallen and tattered trees; trees contrasted in summer moonlight, torn and shattered winter trees, trees green and brown, grey and white, living and dead . . . Beneath their branches I found the best and worst of the war; heard nightingales and smelt primroses, heard the scream of endless shells and breathed gas; rested in their shade . . . cowered in their roots.[92]

C. P. Blacker had a keen eye for nature, which he put to good use as he wandered through a wood near his battalion's camp at Corbie:

> The floor was ablaze with white, yellow and blue flowers. The luxuriance was so unexpected as to make me feel that, as in a fairy story, I had inadvertently broken into some secret and privileged place where I had no business to be. The white flowers, pinkily nodding in the sunlight, as if in timid recognition, were of course wood anemones; the yellow flowers were lesser celandines and primroses . . . As I picked my way through the trees I came to a

concealed clearing thick with wild daffodils, mostly in bud but a few in flower.

He later sustained an out of body experience near the same wood.

> The experience lasted, I should say, about thirty seconds and seemed to come out of the sky in which were seemingly resounding majestic harmonies. The thought: 'That is the music of the spheres' was immediately followed by glimpses of luminous bodies – meteors or stars – circulating in predestined courses emitting both light and music. I stood still on the tow-path and wondered if I was going to fall down. I dropped onto one knee and thought: How wonderful to die at this moment. I put my hand over my forehead as if to contain the tumult and fend off something. Wonder, awe and gratitude mounted to a climax and remained poised for a few seconds like a German star shell. Then began the foreknown descent.

Blacker, an intelligent and well-read man who went on to become a doctor, thought deeply about the incident, and eventually concluded that it had been religious rather than pathological. And when he revisited the Somme with a brother officer in 1960 he saw a dark cloud hanging over the battlefield, 'rimmed and shot through with light . . . The cloud came from the infernal regions; the illumination, which came from elsewhere, honoured the multitudes of dead.'[93] Charles Douie linked the rhythm of the seasons with the pattern of men's lives.

> I watched the coming of spring in the woods, and the young corn in the fields, and the men, the flower of every shire in Britain, on the march towards the chalk uplands of the battlefields. I wondered often how many of those whose eyes were delighted by the glory of the fields would see the harvest, and I thought of that other harvest which death would reap.

In the late spring of 1916 he spent much of his time in a dugout west of Thiepval, 'looking out over the broad marshes of the Ancre and the great trees of the wood beyond'.[94]

In the very midst of Third Ypres Private Groom found his spirits touched by dawn: 'It was a marvellous sunrise and I remember the huge red ball of the sun resting on the top of a distant pillbox.'[95] Fred Hodges admitted that:

> Certainly I have never lived so close to nature since, nor been so acutely aware of life. Between the wrecked villages, the crops lay ungathered, and nature, uncontrolled by man, was a riot of scent and colour; oats and barley mingled with cornflower and poppies, with the song of a lark in the blue sky.[96]

And P. J. Campbell thought that the roses at Gibraltar Farm, not far behind the front, 'were as beautiful and smelt as sweetly here as in a Oxford garden,' and watched daily as a pair of swallows reared five young in a nest on the beam of a shelter.[97]

There was always an extraordinary poignancy in discovering that even a battlefield remained home to animals and birds. A mole fell into Sidney Rogerson's trench on the Somme, and he thought it 'one of Nature's miracles that this blind, slow creature could have survived in ground so pounded and upturned'.[98] Charles Douie was struck by the spectacle of two mice playing hide-and-seek behind a dud shell in his trench. Lieutenant Edwin Campion Vaughan's platoon found a dead pigeon 'and buried him, railing his grave with little sticks and chains of sedgegrass, and in his coverlet of pimpernels we erected a tiny white cross'.[99] In the spring of 1916 Captain Dunn 'avoided treading on little frogs in Cambrin trenches,' and shortly afterwards he heard a nightingale.[100]

FRIEND AND FOE

There was widespread agreement that, as Robert Graves observed: 'Patriotism, in the trenches, was too remote a sentiment, and at once rejected as only fit for civilians, or prisoners. A new arrival who talked patriotism would soon be told to cut it out.'[101] An infantry officer remarked on 'how much more seriously the company would take the war were the [Ypres] Salient around Preston, or Bolton, or Manchester'.[102] And another commentator discerned 'no self-conscious patriotism among the rank and file . . . The word itself meant nothing to them.'[103] Yet there was certainly a conviction, often expressed in letters home, that the war had to be won to keep Britain safe. In August 1914 Sergeant Bert Fielder assured his wife that:

> If I go away you must not worry if you don't get my letters because you must understand it is all for the good of England, and the English soldier is not only fighting for his country but to save his own home from destruction and being ruled over by the Germans.[104]

Men at the front, many of whom genuinely believed that they were fighting to preserve the mother country, were irritated to learn that their views were not shared by those they thought they were defending. In October 1915 Second Lieutenant Edward Underhill wrote bitterly that his countrymen had no idea what the war was about.

> I don't believe you in England realize what was is, and invasion is the only thing to do it. I am not at all sure that invasion wouldn't be the best thing to happen to England. All this fuss about recruiting is very galling to us out here. We are firm believers in National Service and would like the slackers out here for a week or two. Nobody can realize what it is like unless they have heard shells rushing over-head, and have seen all the ruins of farms and houses, or been deliberately shot at by one's fellow man, even though they are a different nationality. It is ghastly to me who has only seen a little bit of what it is like. What it must be with gas and liquid fire added, and then on top of all a heavy bombardment. I hate shells; they are awful and give me the jumps, or as we say out here 'they put the wind up me'.[105]

He was right to be concerned: a shell-splinter hit him in the back of the head, just under his steel helmet, as he rallied his company at Stuff Redoubt, near Thiepval, on 12 October 1916, and killed him: he was twenty-one.

Many veterans detected a sense of national superiority which had little to do with the immediate aims of the war and was not patriotism in any conventional sense. 'If the Germans won and invaded England,' declared one, 'they would still be laughed at in the villages as ridiculous foreigners.' 'I did not think it occurred to us that we could ever be defeated,' opined another, 'so great was our faith in the British Empire with all its great traditions.'[106] C. E. Montague later wrote of the unreasoning national pride that characterised the New Armies, adding wearily that: 'the high unreason of faith that would move mountains in 1914 seems to be scarcely able to shift an ant-hill today'.[107] Although some cynics observed that the only Empire the average soldier knew was the Hackney music hall of the same name, there was a powerful alliance between public-school commitment to an empire with a civilising mission (and, in a more practical sense, a huge network of jobs providing outdoor relief for the middle classes) and working-class music-hall patriotism with its noisy affirmation that British was best and foreigners were funny. In his *Spanish Farm* trilogy Ralph H. Mottram wrote of the soldiers' affection for 'the football fields and factories, the music halls and seaside excursions that they talked of, and hoped to see once again'.[108]

And there was often a striking contrast between the shared values of the front and the increasingly distant world of Blighty. 'London irritated me beyond expression,' wrote John Reith of his leave in 1915; 'was this what one was fighting for: loafers, profiteers, the whole vulgar throng on the streets'.[109] Bernard Martin found it irritating to be acclaimed as a hero, but 'the word meant nothing in front-line trenches' back at home:

> More than once strangers patted me on the back and offered to give me a drink in a pub; but even these good-natured people did not want to learn how heroes live and die. Exceptionally, I was asked: 'Do the French women wash your clothes and mend them?' and a man said, 'When it's too dark to go on fighting – are you free for the evening, can you get to a cinema?'.[110]

H. E. L. Mellersh, home on leave in 1916, discovered that:

> The general atmosphere at home ... made me feel, on this leave and all subsequent leaves, that I did not any longer fit in. Inevitably I was out of sympathy with the old way of life that in any case had changed, while I too had changed ...
>
> Nevertheless, when all that is said and done, I did, in those days of my first return home from the front, consider myself as someone apart, as someone belonging – even though I had been with them for so short a while – to the Second Battalion, The East Lancashire Regiment, and no longer to this cosy, suburban, restricted, uninspiring Clarence Road, St Albans.[111]

Motivation often changed as experience grew. Many was the man who, like Eric Hiscock, felt patriotic enough until he found out what the war was really like.

> The Oxford glamour of donning uniform was at last in shreds, the mud and fearful noise and incomprehensible

action that was surrounding me had stilled for ever any semblance of Elgar's Land of Hope and Glory running through my stupid brain. War, I knew at last, was run for fools by fools on office stools, and the sooner I got out of it the better for all concerned, which meant me, my parents in Oxford, and the girl I left behind me – a plumpish flapper called Doris who sold bags and suit-cases over the counter of a smart leather-merchant's shop in Oxford's Queen Street.[112]

But as big issues slipped away, smaller ones grew. Playing the game mattered. Second Lieutenant W. E. Giffard, already one-legged, and with two brothers killed in the war, was offered a ground job which would have spared him the danger of more ascents in an observation balloon. He declined on the grounds that: 'I do not think it is playing the game.'[113] What was 'playing the game' to a public-school boy was 'finishing the job' for a working man. At the very end of the war one of Private Stephen Graham's comrades told him:

> I am a married man . . . I have four children. I've been out here three years, and it's been hard. But if the armistice were called off tomorrow, I'd gladly go on fighting. Why? In order that we might make a clean job of it. All that I care for is that my boys should not have to go through what I've gone through.[114]

What an Australian memorably termed 'the bonds of mateship' set rock-hard to link men in what one wise analyst has called 'trench households', small groups such as an infantry section, machine-gun detachment or the officers of a rifle company, who lived in close proximity, pooled privately-obtained food or drink, and wrote to console the relatives of the killed.[115] Charles Carrington thought that:

> A Corporal and six men in a trench were like shipwrecked sailors on a raft, completely committed to their social grouping, so that nobody could have any doubts about the moral and physical failings of his pals since everyone's life depended on the reliability of each.[116]

C. E. Montague used precisely the same simile. Front-line life was:

> very domestic, highly atomic. Its atom, or unit, like that
> of slum life, is the jealously close, exclusive community
> life of a family based in an urban cellar . . . Our total host
> might be two million strong, or ten millions; whatever its
> size a man's world was his section – at most his platoon;
> all that mattered to him was the one little boatload of
> castaways with whom he was marooned on a desert island
> making shift to keep off the weather and any sudden attack
> of wild beasts.[117]

Sometimes the small group encompassed those whose rank
might be presumed to exclude them. Second Lieutenant Richard
Gale broke down in tears when trying to wrap up the remains of
his batman, dismembered by a shell, and was taken back to
recover, not with his fellow officers, but to the men's dugout: 'Their
comradeship meant everything to me . . .'[118] Montague argued that
this sort of relationship was not simply founded on mutual survival,
though that counted for much: most NCOs and men in the line
simply believed that it was up to them and the junior officers to win
the war.[119] Alan Hanbury Sparrow thought that the real focus of
loyalty came slightly higher, in what he called 'regimental will. For
we no longer rely on unknown forces, but upon what we know
ourselves.'

What so many observers noticed were resolution and endurance
which often had little to do with military discipline but often
reflected qualities that men brought into the army, whether they
came from mean streets or big houses. Siegfried Sassoon summed
them up well when describing the soldier, Christ-like with his load
of shouldered planks, in *The Redeemer*.

> No thorny crown, only a woollen cap
> He wore – an English soldier, white and strong,
> Who loved his time like any simple chap,
> Good days of work and sport and homely song;
> Now he has learned that nights are very long,
> And dawn a watching of the windowed sky.
> But to the end, unjudging, he'll endure
> Horror and pain, not uncontent to die
> That Lancaster on Lune may stand secure.[120]

J. R. R. Tolkien, author of *The Lord of the Rings*, served on the Western Front with 11/Lancashire Fusiliers, and wrote that Sam Gamgee, Frodo's sturdy and long-suffering companion on his journey to Mount Doom, was a portrait 'of the English soldier, of the private and batman I knew in the 1914 war, and recognized as so far superior to myself'.[121] Occasional official reports into the army's morale were conducted on the basis of censored letters, and revealed a broad spirit of endurance that was bent, but not broken, by suffering. In November 1916, in the aftermath of the Somme, one concluded that: 'the spirit of the men, their conception of duty, their Moral[e] has never been higher than at the present moment', though their earlier enthusiasm had been replaced by 'dogged determination to see the thing through at any cost'.[122]

And even in November 1917, as Passchendaele squelched to its close, a report based on an analysis of 17,000 letters written by combat troops concluded that: 'The Morale of the Army is sound ... there is ample ground for the belief that the British Army is firmly convinced, not only of its ability to defeat the enemy and its superiority man to man, but also of the dangers of a premature peace.'[123] C. E. Montague, for all the disenchantment which was to give his post-war memoirs their title, wholly agreed. He had little time for the way the army was run, and was critical of staff and chaplains alike.

> But the war had to be won: that was flat. It was like putting out houses on fire, or not letting children be killed; it did not even need to be proved; that we had got to win was now the one quite certain thing left in a world of shaken certainties.[124]

Humour helped men endure. Some of it was decidedly dark, like the practice of giving a cheery shake to the dead hands which sometimes protruded from trenches, or infuriating, like drifting small paper boats, carefully ignited, along the long water-gully beneath the seats in base latrines. Some jokes reflected a belief that the war would prove very long. In 1915 it was said that a subaltern in a battalion on the Ploegsteert front visited a comrade in the line near Kemmel. 'You will notice,' said the Kemmel man, 'my men are planting daffodils on the parapets to hide 'em. We hope to have the line quite invisible in the course of time.' 'Humph,' replied the Ploegsteert man: 'You are a lot of blooming optimists. *My* men have planted acorns in front of *our* trench.'[125] There was sometimes a fine edge of humour to the relationship between company commanders and their sergeant majors, or platoon commanders and their platoon sergeants. A Royal Welch Fusiliers company commander was in his dugout in a heavily-shelled front line when the sergeant major pounded down the steps with a face like thunder. 'Tell me the worst, sergeant major,' said the officer, expecting news of a disaster. 'Well, Sir, I'm not sure that I should mention this,' replied the CSM, 'but I have just seen your servant stirring your tea with his finger.'

There was also repeated badinage between units, as Anthony French of 15/London remembered:

> One spark of humour could set a whole column alight.
>
> We approached a signaller industriously repairing a broken line and a voice cried: 'Some say "Good old Signals!"'' to which a second voice replied: 'Others say "... old Signals!"'' The verb was irrelevant and its execution biologically absurd, but the couplet was invariable whoever might be the 'good old this' or 'good old that'. It was always the curious colloquial adjective 'old' that preserved the affection.
>
> The signaller took no heed.
>
> 'He's going up the "line,"' someone suggested.
>
> 'Lend 'im your button 'ook,' said another.
>
> The signaller turned and shouted with feigned surprise 'Oh! It's the bloody infantry. What *you* doing up the line, anyway?'
>
> 'We're looking for the GPO.'
>
> 'Lookin' for bloody trouble, you mean,' said the signaller, raising a fist.
>
> Another voice shouted: 'What did you do in the Great War, Daddy?' and from somewhere came the oft-repeated quip: 'Hold your tongue, son, and polish up those medals!' ...
>
> 'Medals?' cried another; 'I've spat 'em before breakfast!'
>
> Someone tried to sing 'Give me the switch Miss for

Ipswich, it's the Ipswich switch which I require,' but metre
and pace failed to register, so Maxwell raised his voice
and set the column singing:

'Kitty, Kitty, isn't it a pity in the City you work so hard
With your "One, two, three four five six seven eight Gerrard?".'
Kitty, Kitty, isn't it a pity that you're wasting so much time
With your lips close to the telephone when they might be close to mine?'

> My last sight of the field-telephone man was of his face
> wreathed in smiles and his hand waving a friendly
> farewell.[126]

C. E. Montague regarded laughter as 'the deadliest solvent of
hatreds', with his comrades quipping about 'old Fritz' or 'the good
old Boche', 'as if he were a stout dog fox or a real stag of a hare'.[127]
To soldiers he was Fritz or the Alleyman, to officers more often the
Boche (in a variety of spellings) or the Hun. Indeed, Private Stephen
Graham maintained that 'the German was never Bosche or Hun
to the rank and file, but always "Jacky" or "Jerry" or "Fritz".'[128] To
the thoughtful David Jones he was something more sinister, for his
field grey

> seemed always to call up the grey wolf of Nordic literature.
> To watch these grey shapes moving elusively among the
> bleached breast works or emerging from between broken
> tree-stumps was a sight to powerfully impress us and was
> suggestive to us of something of what is expressed in those
> lines from the *Ericksmal* . . . 'It is not surely known when
> the grey wolf shall come upon the seat of the Gods.'[129]

Jones wondered what the German made of British 'ochre coats and
saucer hats'. But to many he was bewilderingly elusive. When Sidney
Rogerson saw German prisoners after his battalion had come out of
the line on the Somme he admitted that:

> Few of them were our idea of 'square heads'. Some were
> mere boys, others myopic bespectacled scarecrows. Many
> were bearded, some having the fringes of whiskers framing
> their faces after the manner of the great crested grebe.
> All wore the long-skirted field grey coats, the trousers
> stuffed into clumsy boots. It gave us a strange feeling to

see our enemies at close range. Except for dead ones, for
an occasional miserable prisoner dragged back half-dead
with fright from some raid, or for groups seen through
field-glasses far behind their lines, many of us had never
seen any Germans.[130]

And Charles Carrington heard wagon wheels, wiring parties, coughs
and sneezes and even a sergeant major, his voice at full throttle,
before he actually saw his first German.

Two general truths define the British soldier's relationship with
his enemy on the Western Front: the first is that he generally had a
high regard for the Germans, and the second that the fighting man
rarely felt a high degree of personal hostility towards them. There
are, though, striking exceptions, and it is typical of the way the war
has been approached that some historians choose to emphasise the
divergences rather than the norm. Officers, in particular, often
admired the Germans' sense of discipline and duty. In October 1914
Lieutenant Billy Congreve searched the bodies of Germans who had
been killed attacking Gordon Highlanders.

> A good many of them had been bayoneted. Horrid wounds
> our bayonets make, and these Germans must have put up
> a good fight. It is all rot the stuff one reads in the papers
> about the inferiority of the German soldiers to ours. If
> anything the German is the better, for though we
> undoubtedly are the more dogged and *impossible* to beat,
> they are the more highly disciplined.[131]

'Newspaper libels on Fritz's courage and efficiency were resented
by all trench-soldiers of experience,' maintained Graves.[132] 'Had we
but had NCOs like the Germans,' argued Alan Hanbury Sparrow,
'we could have built dugouts like the Germans and saved countless
casualties'. He thought that their high standard of pre-war training
meant that the Germans could use NCOs where the British had to
use officers, and so 'thousands of promising young officers were
killed doing lance-corporal's work'.[133]

In part this did indeed reflect the fact that the German army was
a conscript force structured for major war. In part, too, it reflected
the fact that German senior NCOs often commanded platoons and

acted as seconds in command of companies.[134] (In the late 1930s the British sought to imitate the German practice by introducing the rank of warrant officer Class 3 – warrant officer platoon commander – but it was not generally a success and the project was speedily abandoned.) There was wide agreement that British troops, even in very good battalions like 2/Royal Welch Fusiliers, generally required the presence of an officer to make them stand. When the British lost control of High Wood on 14 July 1916 it was partly because some of the men in scattered units drifted back, 'not demoralised, just leaderless'.[135] In contrast, the German infantry mopping up one flank of the wood were commanded by an NCO, as humanitarian as he was brave. He marched the prisoners his detachment took to the rear, and: 'About two miles back he halted them at a canteen, went in and bought a box of cigarettes and a bottle of brandy; each prisoner was given six or seven cigarettes and a pull at the bottle.'[136] A month later Lieutenant Stormont Gibbs reflected of another failed attack that:

> It seems hardly credible anyhow for Suffolk yokels to get as far as an objective with at the most two officers – who were both probably wounded . . . It may be suggested that the sergeants and other NCOs should have held the men together. But the suggestion would not come from anyone aware of the ineffectiveness of the average NCO under shell-fire. There are exceptions – and then they ought to be officers. This may' only apply in the infantry where promotion is so rapid owing to continual casualties. It may also apply to 'regulars'. Our high-class parade-ground company sergeant major, an old regular soldier, could not be taken into the line or he inspired panic.[137]

In May 1917 a British attack on Tunnel Trench in the Hindenburg line narrowly failed. One experienced sergeant blamed 'panic among men without enough training and discipline', and another said that success 'only wanted running forward instead of running away': it was significant that 2/Royal Welch Fusiliers had only one unwounded officer in action.[138] In an earlier action a sergeant reported that things got out of hand when his platoon commander was killed (knifed as he went for three Germans) and the men rather lost heart: 'If there had been an officer about it would have been all right, someone to give an order and take no back-chat.'[139] Corporal Fred Hodges was inclined to agree. 'The Germans were always referred to by us as "Jerry bastards" but we all respected their courage, professional skill and determination,' he wrote. 'Their NCOs, and some of their private soldiers, displayed great initiative; more, I sometimes thought, than we did when not being led by a determined officer.'[140]

The problem also reflected the British army's reluctance, rooted deep in its history, to give NCOs wide responsibility out of the line. Sidney Rogerson's Company Sergeant Major, Scott, was:

> Quiet-voiced, phlegmatic to a degree, with sandy hair, ruddy face, and blue eyes ... the antithesis of the bellowing warrant officer beloved by cartoonists. A man of considerable education and marked gentleness of manner, he got results by the affectionate regard in which he was held by officers and men rather than by obvious resort to discipline.[141]

Scott was commissioned, captured towards the end of the war, but killed fighting the IRA in Dublin immediately after it. For all Scott's evident quality, when Rogerson allowed him to issue rum to the company after it emerged from the line, Lieutenant Colonel James Jack rebuked him for permitting it without an officer present. Yet when the battalion had to be moved by rail, the business of entraining was left to the regimental sergeant major and the company sergeant majors working on the adjutant's direction. British NCOs and warrant officers were expected to get on with a wide range of purely mechanical tasks, and the army could not have been run without them: they never enjoyed the executive authority of the *Unteroffiziere mit Portepee* on the other side.

But who can doubt the potential of the best of them? Edmund Blunden paid handsome tribute to Company Sergeant Major Lee, 'tall, blasphemous and brave'.[142] Siegfried Sassoon affirmed that: 'CSMs were the hardest worked men in the infantry; everything depended on them, and if anyone deserved a KCB it was a good CSM.'[143] Arthur Behrend wrote with affection of 'the excellent sergeant major'. When a shed full of reinforcements was hit by a shell (they were killed before they had formally joined the brigade and appeared on its ration strength, and Behrend soon had to deal with letters asking if he knew what had become of the writer's son), it was the sergeant major, 'always at his best at times such as this' who sorted the ghastly business out.[144] And when R. B. Talbot Kelly was observing for his battery at the very end of the Somme battle he saw spectacular heroism displayed by Corporal Barber of the Black Watch. He was:

> A truly heroic figure. When he returned the first time the whole of the front of his chest and legs were scarlet with blood, the result of a German bomb bursting near him, and although he assured us that his wounds were only scratches, his appearance was quite terrifying . . . I would say that this corporal showed the most exemplary courage throughout this action, cheering-on and encouraging the wretched private soldiers who were helping him, and keeping the coolest of heads . . . this NCO's actions must have been largely responsible for restoring the situation on this little bit of the front.[145]

There was often admiration at the way the enemy fought. When Norman Gladden's comrades moved past a dead German, large and fully accoutred, who had been killed making a single-handed stand in an advance post, 'a murmur of approbation went down the file, not, for once, for the death of an enemy but in admiration of a brave man'.[146] In August 1918 William Carr, at thirty-one rather old for a gunner subaltern, was observing for his battery of 18-pounders.

> All along the trenches coal scuttle helmets appeared. I spotted a machine gunner at the near end as he got his gun into position.
>
> Keeping my eyes on him I sent another message to our guns.
>
> 'Ready any minute now.'
>
> The machine gunner was absolutely still. Did he guess that over a mile away six guns were pointing in his direction? Did he banish thoughts of wife and children as he

concentrated on the target appearing up the spur? A red spurt of flame flashed from his gun.

'Fire!' I shouted.

'Fire!' the signallers repeated the order.

Within seconds we could hear shells going over and immediately the trench disappeared from sight as duck-boards shot into the air. We were dead on target.

'Repeat,' I shouted before the last round had arrived. Now for the other half of the trench.

'Switch two minutes right, five rounds gun-fire.' Some shells were falling short.

'Add twenty – three rounds gun-fire.'

As the trench became visible again I saw the machine gunner. He was covered in blood, terribly wounded, yet he was struggling to get his gun back into position. I'd have to silence him.

'Left section only, return to target one, five rounds gun-fire.'

A minute or two passed as the guns were re-aligned. Through my glasses I could see Jerries running along the trench but the brave machine gunner stayed at his post . . .

Every Remembrance Day during the two minutes silence I can see him and recall the moment when he disappeared in a shower of rubble.[147]

Captain Robert Dolby had been told that the Germans were auto-mata 'incapable of separate independent action', but soon saw how wrong this was when his battalion was overrun at First Ypres:

They poured out of the ends of the trenches, spread out into the most perfect open order and advanced at the double: nor was any officer visible. Some ran and dropped, so that I thought the whole line had been wiped out by our fire, but these men were foxing; and those who fell face downward soon got up to run forward again. Not so with the killed or wounded, they lay on their sides or, spinning round in the air, they fell supported by their packs . . . Taking cover of every natural object, they got behind trees or wagons or mounds of earth; so they advanced up to within 100 yards of our position, and our

field of fire not being good, there they found shelter.
The under officer was particularly gallant, for he ran to a
mound of light soil, laid his glass on the top and closely
examined our trenches with his elbows spread upon the
top. From time to time he would turn his head and speak
to two orderlies who crouched beside him like spaniels.[148]

Beating off this sort of attack brought a mixture of emotions.
Corporal Charles Arnold reported that when the Germans attacked
in mass at Mons:

We then had revenge for poor C Company. I think the
Germans will always remember my company, A Company,
1st East Surreys. They came at us in hundreds and we
poured rapid fire into them until our rifles became too
hot to hold and we were sick of killing. Just before we
retired, I had a last look round. I saw the German dead
piled up in heaps, the sight sickened me.[149]

Most officers and men saw more Germans after capture than they
did in the line, and found them a very mixed bag. Lieutenant Joseph
Maclean thought prisoners taken at Ypres in 1917:

A very poor looking crowd – thin and small and some very
young – but there are boys of the other sort, and in fact
the average Bosche seems to be a very well set up sort of
fellow. Yet most of them are sick of the war, much more
than we are.[150]

Many prisoners worked at labouring duties behind the lines under
the command of their own NCOs. J. B. Priestley thought that 'they
were far more frightened of their own sergeant-major characters –
iron men with Iron Crosses, Kaiser moustaches, terrible rasping
words of command – than they were of us, the utterly amateur
British'.[151] German doctors and stretcher-bearers generally carried
on with business as usual after capture, often going back onto the
battlefield, without orders from their captors, to help clear the
wounded of both sides. But perhaps the best example of proper
behaviour on the part of prisoners was a very docile group which
was sent back across the battlefield with a single escort. He fell into

a shell hole and accidentally ran his bayonet through his leg, but his charges loyally carried him the rest of the way.

Burgon Bickersteth could not deny his admiration for a captured officer who would disclose no confidential information. He was 'an extraordinarily nice fellow I thought. He would tell me nothing except his regiment and division. He was good looking and well-dressed and perfectly calm and collected.'[152] Edward Vaughan chatted to a badly-wounded German in a captured pillbox with an officer-to-officer courtesy which somehow made light of circumstance, and the German offered him the only hospitality at his disposal: a piece of sugar, crumbling and so bloodstained that Vaughan could not face it, but 'slipped it into my pocket while pretending to eat it'.

Dead officers sometimes struck a spark of admiration too. Billy Congreve thought that Lieutenant Meyer Zu Wambergen, adjutant of the 57th Regiment, 'died an Iron Cross death all right, leading his men inside the enemy's line . . . I wonder if I shall ever have the chance of finding out more about him?'.[153] Charles Carrington spent several hours in a shell hole on the Somme in the company of a dead German officer, a well-dressed and handsome man about his own age: he removed the Iron Cross from the body, somehow not as a trophy, but for reverend safe keeping.

Soldiers speedily discovered just how heterogeneous in composition the German army was. In May 1916 Edward Underhill wrote that:

> A few nights ago four Huns came across and gave themselves up to the battalion on our left. They were fine great men, and were pleased at getting safely through. They were Alsatians, and very much objected to being called Prussians . . . They belonged to the Guard, probably the Reserve Guards Division, and deserted because they had been addressed by their generals, who told them they mustn't mind going over the top nor dying for the Fatherland. They had relieved the Bavarians on May 4th, who had gone to Verdun. They also told us about several new mines, and quite a lot of information was obtained from them.[154]

A year later Bernard Martin's company was commanded by:

> an old Captain who had just come to us from a Kitchener
> army unit [and who] said contemptuously, 'By all means
> give the Hun his due, serve him right, all Huns deserve
> to die, descendants of that butcher Ghenghis Khan.' This
> was a sentiment not general at this period of the war. Most
> PBI [Poor Bloody Infantry] recognised that Germans were
> not all alike – Prussians were aggressive bullies, others
> from Bavaria, Saxony, Württemburg, might be 'good'
> Germans.[155]

George Adams had enlisted underage into the Middlesex Regiment and survived Loos: 'I am sorry to say that nearly all the fellows I knew have gone and Dad, Jack Badrick, the bricky who used to work for Harry Rooney has gone as well.' He told his parents on 30 October 1915 that they had 'a kind of arrangement' with the Germans opposite: 'They are Saxons you see they are club waiters and barbers and they don't like the war and are decent fellows. Now the Prussians, who they relieved, if you show your head an inch above the parapet you get it, they are *no bon* as the French say.'[156] Lieutenant Graham Greenwell wrote on 4 June 1915 that the Saxons hated the Prussians far more than the British, 'and when they are relieved by them they call out: "Give it them hot tomorrow, it's the Prussians".'[157]

In many sectors opposing trenches were so close that it was easy for shouted conversations to take place. Bernard Adams, then serving in the ranks, affirmed that at Cuinchy in November 1915:

> The Germans opposite us were very lively. One could often
> hear them whistling, and one night they were shouting to
> one another like anything. They were Saxons who are
> always at that game ... It was quite cold, almost frosty,
> and the sound came across the 100 yards or so of No
> Man's Land with a strange clearness in the night air. The
> voices seemed unnaturally near, like voices on the water
> heard from a cliff. 'Tommee – Tommee. *Allemands bon –
> Engleesh bon.*' 'We hate *ze Kron prinz.*' (I can hear now the
> nasal twang with which the 'Kron' was emphasized) 'D—
> the Kaiser' '*Deutschland unter Alles.*' I could hear these

shouts most distinctly: the same sentences were repeated again and again. As 'Comic Cuts' [the name given to the daily Intelligence Reports] sagely remarked, 'Either this means that there is a spirit of dissatisfaction among the Saxons, or it is a ruse to try to catch us unawares, or it is mere foolery.' Wisdom in high places! . . .

The authorities now try to stop our follows answering. The entente of last Christmas is not to be repeated.[158]

The entente in question was, of course, the celebrated Christmas truce of 1914, when there was widespread fraternisation. Second Lieutenant Bruce Bairnsfather of 1/Royal Warwickshire exchanged two of his buttons with a German officer; a soldier in the London Rifle Brigade swapped a tin of bully beef for a German spiked helmet (he was asked to return it the following day, and sportingly did so); and near Fromelles a joint burial service was conducted by the chaplain of 6/Gordon Highlanders and a German divinity student. There may even have been a proper football match – the Lancashire Fusiliers' history reported a 3–2 victory – but it is more likely that there was the occasional less formal 'general kickabout'.[159] There was nothing on the same scale thereafter, largely because outraged officialdom issued severe warnings that, as Wyn Griffith put it, 'we must confine our goodwill not to fellow Christians, but to Christians of allied nationality'. However, even then there was a good deal of shouting 'Merry Christmas Tommy' and 'Merry Christmas Fritz', and some bartering of souvenirs went on in No Man's Land.[160]

Yet if large-scale fraternisation was rare, small-scale contact was common. In front of Guy Chapman's battalion,

'Hallo Tommee' cried a German voice, 'are you soon going home on leave?' 'Next week,' the Englishman shouted. 'Are you going to London?' was the next question. 'Yes.' 'Then call at two-two-four Tottenham Court Road and give my love to Miss Sarah Jones.' 'I'll go round all right and I'll jolly well . . .' The fate of the lady was eclipsed in a roar of laughter from our side and the angry splutter of a machine gun from across the way.[161]

One British infantry section was surprised to hear a German shout: 'It is I, Fritz the Bunmaker of London. What is the football news?'

'A blurry supporter of blurry Chelsea,' muttered Bill – hitherto the most aggressive man in the section. ''e must be a damned good sort of sausage eater.'[162]

Billie Neville wrote from the line near Albert in late 1915 that:

> We have a rather sporting crowd of Huns opposite, as when we shell them they crawl out next night & put German flags in the shell holes! Also this morning they stuck up a white flag of sorts and a big dummy man, we all blazed at it & they signalled the shots, bullseyes, inners & magpies with another flag![163]

On another occasion the Germans mounted a raid with artillery support; however, 'They did not come as a fighting patrol . . . but carried placards which they dropped into the bays, and in big bold letters the placards read: "Deutschland welcomes the 29th Division to France." They must be a sporty lot over there.[164] The Germans often demonstrated a good knowledge of the units opposite them, and V. F. Eberle, an engineer officer near Ploegsteert in May 1915, observed that: 'The Germans opposite are now more chatty. On our battalion relief nights the incoming troops are greeted with "Hullo, the Blanks".'[165] Sometimes, less well informed, they called across to ask what the relieving unit was. Scenting the chance of a wind-up, soldiers usually replied with something dramatic but untrue, like 'First Black Watch' or 'Th'Oirish Guards'.

There were times when it was difficult to feel much real hostility to the men in the trenches opposite. When Brigadier General Count Gleichen was told by a sentry that he often saw a German not far away, he asked why the man had not shot him. 'Shoot him,' said the man, 'why, Lor' bless you sir, 'e's never done me no harm.'[166] One of Frank Dunham's comrades gave just the same reply when a sergeant asked him why he had not fired at a German who had just looked over the parapet: 'No, I couldn't kill him, for he ain't done no harm.'[167] Even Frank Crozier, not backward when it came to killing, could not see the sense in sniping ordinary Germans when there was no battle on: the practice revolted him and he gave it up.

Soldiers on both sides periodically deserted by creeping across

No Man's Land, though it was always a tricky business. Gerald Burgoyne was shocked to report that:

> A young German, 18 to 19 years of age came across to the Wilts line the other day to give himself up. He asked for bread and wanted to give himself up. The men let him come within 20 yards and then riddled him with bullets. I call this nothing less than murder.[168]

Another, who tried the same with Frank Hawkings's battalion, was luckier.

> At dusk this evening a Hun appeared and slid over C Company's parapet, much to the astonishment and fright of the adjacent sentry, who, however, soon recovered when the German informed him in fairly good English that he had come over to surrender. We crowded round him, and while he told us that he was 'a great *kamerad* English' and that he had been a waiter in a London hotel before the war, we relieved him of his buttons and badges as souvenirs.[169]

The hunt for souvenirs was universal – 'rather like looking for mushrooms' – and prisoners and the fallen were routinely pillaged of cash and collectibles. Those, British and German, who knew the rules ensured that watches and other valuables were easy of access at the moment of capture in order to avoid a dangerous scuffle as captors sought their dues: one British officer was told that his men had been 'given' watches by their prisoners out of sheer gratitude, but was realistic enough to wonder. The 2/Royal Welch Fusiliers, reprimanded by their brigade headquarters when a German prisoner claimed his watch had been stolen, 'sent down two dozen for him to choose from'. Prisoners often showed their captors photographs of their wives and children to make the point that they too were family men whose deaths would spread rings of sorrow: one fell on his knees and babbled to Edward Vaughan of his wife and '*zwei Kindern*'. There was a 'natural utilitarian morality' which encouraged men to loot bodies, both British and German. 'A tin of bully in a dead man's pack can't help him,' affirmed George Coppard, 'nor can a packet of cigarettes.' But the business of going through the wallet of a German brought him up sharply: 'There were wives and children, parents, old chaps with big whiskers, nearly all dressed in black, as if attending a funeral. Respectable, clean and tidy was the general impression.'[170]

There were occasional local truces, usually dictated by the need to bury the dead or recover wounded, and these continued despite official disapproval. Often men would not fire on stretcher-bearers or doctors clearly going about their business, and one British soldier, bravely caring for the wounded just in front of the German parapet, was eventually asked by a German officer if he wanted to 'come over'. When he replied that he did not, the German firmly told him that he would have to go back to his own lines or be shot: he walked back unmolested. In February 1917 the Germans allowed Rowland Feilding's men to recover their wounded, and he walked forward to supervise the operation. 'I found Germans – almost shoulder to shoulder,' he told his wife, 'leaning over their parapet, exposed from the waist up: on our side it was the same. All were intensely interested in the stretcher-bearers at work in No man's land.' He then discovered that there had recently been a divisional order forbidding precisely that sort of thing: 'In short, our methods henceforth are to be strictly Prussian; the very methods to abolish which we claim to be fighting this war.'[171]

This pattern of respect illuminated by flashes of chivalry was wreathed with darker clouds. First, there was no guarantee a man's surrender would be accepted. If he maintained a brave defence to the last moment and then threw down his arms he was likely to be killed out of hand, sometimes with a gruff: 'Too late, chum,' as the bayonet went in. Charles Carrington explained that:

> No soldier can claim a right to 'quarter' if he fights to the extremity. But if in a lull of the battle the enemy show a white flag and comes out of their position unarmed and with raised hands, crying '*Kamerad, Kamerad*!' . . . then by the conventional law of arms they are entitled to mercy.[172]

Thomas Penrose Marks, a private and then an NCO in the infantry, was disinclined to show mercy to machine gunners who surrendered at the last moment:

> They are defenceless, but they have chosen to make themselves so. We did not ask them to abandon their guns. They only did so when they saw that those of us who were not mown down were getting closer to them, and the boot is now on the other foot.[173]

Ernst Junger, on the other side of the line, argued that:

> The defending force, after driving their bullets into the attackers at five paces' distance, must take the consequences. A man cannot change his feelings again during the last rush with a veil of blood before his eyes. He does not want to take prisoners but to kill.[174]

Private Stephen Graham was taught that when trench-clearing: 'The second bayonet man kills the wounded . . . You cannot afford to be encumbered by wounded enemies lying about your feet. Don't be squeamish. The army provides you with a good pair of boots: you know how to use them.'[175] George Coppard reported 'an unexpected bonus' when two German wagons left it too late to get away from the front line with the sun coming up behind them and were ruthlessly machine-gunned, 'but there was genuine regret about the horses'.[176]

Next, successful surrender usually depended on a brief but clear break between combat and capitulation. Even then it was a dangerous time, as Guy Chapman discovered when talking to a moody company commander:

> 'What's the matter, Terence?' I asked.
> 'Oh, I don't know. Nothing . . . At least . . . Look here, we took a lot of prisoners in those trenches yesterday morning. Just as we got into their line, an officer came out of a dugout. He'd got one hand over his head, and a pair of field-glasses in the other. He held out the glasses to S—, you know, that ex-sailor with the Messina earthquake medal – and said, 'Here you are, sergeant, I surrender.' S— said, 'Thank you, Sir,' and took the glasses in his left hand. At the same moment, he tucked the butt of his rifle under his arm and shot the officer straight through the head. What the hell ought I to do?' . . .
> 'I don't see that you can do anything,' I answered slowly. 'What can you do? Besides, I don't see that S—'s really

to blame. He must have been half mad with excitement by the time he got to that trench. I don't suppose he ever thought what he was doing. If you start a man killing, you can't turn him off again like an engine. After all, he is a good man. He was probably half off his head.'

'It wasn't only him. Another did exactly the same thing.'

'Anyway, it's too late to do anything now. I suppose you ought to have shot both on the spot. The best thing now is to forget it.'

'I dare say you're right.'[177]

An experienced sergeant in Fred Hodges's battalion, wounded, his platoon cut off by a box barrage and badly outnumbered, told his men: 'You can't do anything, lads. Put up your hands and cry *Kamerad*.'[178] Prompt surrender saved their lives. On 28 March 1918 the Rain brothers, both privates in the Queen's Westminsters, realised that their position had been encircled – a nearby company of the London Rifle Brigade, seeing the way things were going, had already given in 'with practically no resistance' – and concluded that surrender was the best option. They dumped their kit in their trench, and then walked over the parapet with their hands high above their heads.

> A German officer motioned us with his walking stick to the rear. It was with some difficulty that we found our way to the German trenches, the ground being almost unrecognisable. The place was crowded with Germans coming across in full marching order, who took little notice of us, & seemed extremely jubilant at their so-called victory.[179]

Particularly detested adversaries might well be killed on the spot: we have already seen the fate of the *Minenwerfer* man who fell into the hands of the Royal Welch at Fricourt. When Alan Hanbury Sparrow's battalion was clearing a village in 1914 it was ordered that all concealed snipers and machine-gunners were to be killed out of hand: 'the only way to stop it is to let these fellows realize it means certain death'.[180] Some Germans lay up in shell holes on the Somme as the mid-September attack rolled over them.

> These scattered Germans were always a nuisance. A single
> man would lie in a shell hole and be passed over, and
> would then calmly snipe runners, or any single or couple
> of men who approached him. To a bigger party he would
> surrender if in danger of being discovered, and if it was
> not convenient to detach a man to take the prisoner back
> he would often be told to get back himself, but at the first
> opportunity he would slip into another shell hole and start
> sniping again.

Lieutenant Stephen Stokes, Welsh Guards, was grenaded by one of
these men, but the bomb left him uninjured. It was the German's
last weapon, and he then tried to surrender:

> but Stokes refused to accept it, and without argument shot
> him. It may be argued that it requires brave men to do
> these deeds, but as brave men they must be prepared to
> accept the logical consequences of their action.[181]

And there were periods when men were disinclined to accept
almost any sort of surrender. The German gas attack of April 1915
caused widespread resentment amongst British and French alike,
and it was not a good time for a German to be captured. Captain
Arthur Smith saw few prisoners then, 'because most of them were
killed before they had a chance to surrender & also the British
soldier is none too keen to make prisoners of them after this gas
business'.[182] Captain Lord Stanhope saw a French general interview
a prisoner, discover that he had been involved in the gas attack, and
order: 'Sergeant major . . . take a file of men and take this man down
to the wall at the bottom of the garden.'[183] Tempers had worn thin
on the Somme by 26 July, as Graham Greenwell wrote: 'feelings run
a bit too high to make the unwounded prisoner's lot a happy one.
A whole crowd who came towards our own trenches with their hands
up were mown down by their machine guns as well as ours.'[184] In
April 1917 a group of German prisoners detained in a quarry just
behind the Arras front unwisely applauded a successful counterattack, and were immediately grenaded by their infuriated escort.
And while most front-line soldiers had a healthy scepticism about
tales of German barbarism, rare first-hand experience of real atroci-

ties put iron into the soul. In November 1918 Guy Chapman's company:

> Went back to Louvignes ... We buried those who had died at Ghissignies. The faces of the section killed in the orchard had been mutilated by the enemy. The instrument, a knife lashed to a stick, was found beside a corpse, the eyes of which had been gouged out.[185]

Simply having his surrender accepted did not guarantee a man's life. Both sides sent men captured in major attacks back across No Man's Land under escort. Often there was a barrage falling between the high-water mark of the attack and friendly trenches, and escorts sometimes concluded that it was too dangerous to take their prisoners back, and killed them. Crozier believed that: 'The British soldier is a kindly fellow and it is safe to say, despite the dope, seldom oversteps the mark of barbaric propriety in France, save occasionally to kill prisoners he cannot be bothered to escort back to his lines.'[186] Sometimes prisoners were killed by accident. The war diary of 10/ Royal Inniskilling Fusiliers tells how, on 1 July 1916, prisoners taken by the first attacking wave were so anxious to reach the safety of the British line that they ran back, collided with the second assaulting wave coming forward, 'and many were bayoneted in the heat of the moment'.

But sometimes it was deliberate. Frank Richards saw one of his comrades escorting six German prisoners towards Clapham Junction on the Menin Road during Third Ypres. The man left him in no doubt as to what was to happen.

> 'Look here, Dick. About an hour ago I lost the best pal I ever had, and he was worth all these six Jerries put together. I'm not going to take them far before I put them out of mess.' ...
>
> Some little time later I saw him coming back and I knew it was impossible for him to have reached Clapham Junction and returned in time ... As he passed me again he said: 'I done them in as I said, about two hundred yards back. Two bombs did the trick.' He had not walked twenty yards beyond me when he fell himself: a shell-splinter had gone clean through him.

Richards remarked that while he had heard of such things happening, this was the only case that he could vouch for, and added that 'the loss of his pal had upset him very much'.[187]

Fury at friends lost could indeed drive moderate men over the edge. At Ypres in 1917 Norman Gladden watched: 'two of our runners sniping at German prisoners . . . Both were normal, kindly fellows in ordinary times, loving fathers of families . . . the particular incident was unusual in my experience, the aberration of individuals under incalculable stress.'[188] An 'old time sergeant' in Stephen Graham's Scots Guards battalion approached his officer, who was 'a poet, and wrote some very charming lyrics and had a taste in art,' saluted and asked: 'Leave to shoot the prisoners, sir?' He declared that it was to avenge his brother's death, and duly shot the Germans one after the other. Some men approved, but others were clearly shocked.[189] And there were soldiers who enjoyed killing, in a boyish, destructive, self-willed way. On 10 June 1915 one private soldier wrote that:

> I saw a Hun, fairly young, running down the trench,
> coming down the trench, hands in the air, looking terri-
> fied, yelling for mercy. I promptly shot him. It was a
> heavenly sight to see him fall forward. A Lincoln officer
> was furious with me, but the scores we owe wash out any-
> thing else.[190]

Such incidents demonstrate just how much depended on officers setting a standard of behaviour. Some battalions had an unofficial policy of discouraging the taking of prisoners. Private Arthur Hubbard of the London Scottish told his mother from the Somme that:

> We had strict orders not to take prisoners, no matter if
> wounded. My first job was when I had finished taking some
> of their wire away, to empty my magazine on 3 Germans
> that came up out of one of their deep dugouts, bleeding
> badly, and put them out of their misery. They cried for
> mercy, but I had my orders, they had no feeling whatever
> for us poor chaps . . .[191]

Such cases were the exception rather than the rule, and even a hard man like Frank Crozier insisted that prisoners should be protected.

On 1 July 1916 he watched 'an advancing crowd of field grey . . . fall like grass before the scythe' and forcefully intervened when he could see that they were prisoners.[192] But he admitted that there were times when it was simply not possible to accept surrenders. While supervising the collection of wounded from the front line on the night of 1 July 1916 he recalled how he was

> suddenly challenged by a German sentry. I pull out my revolver, fire and miss him; but my orderly, who is behind me, sums up the situation and fires a Very light pistol he is carrying, hitting the Boche in the head and blowing it off. There is another German behind who puts up his hands and shouts '*Kamerad*'. The dark is lit up by the burning German whose uniform is on fire. We can take no chances, so I kill the other German with my second round.[193]

When the fury had passed, men could be extraordinarily kind to prisoners. Henry Williamson retained one dominating image of breaking the Hindenburg line in 1918. It was:

> the sight of a Saxon boy crushed under a shattered tank, moaning '*Mutter, Mutter, Mutter*,' out of ghastly grey lips. A British soldier, wounded in the leg, and sitting near by, hears the words, and dragging himself to the dying boy, takes his cold hand and says 'All right, son, it's all right, Mother's here with you.'[194]

Ernest Parker led a party which captured a German in a night raid near Ypres, and: 'When we arrived at the Canal bank dugouts . . . the men fell out with their prisoner to have breakfast . . . we were amused to discover the troops regaling the German prisoner with rum and cigarettes'.[195] Edward Vaughan captured a bedraggled group of Germans near Langemarck on 27 August 1917. He could not spare a man to escort them back, 'so I put them into shell holes with my men who made a great fuss of them, sharing their scanty rations with them'.[196] And when Crozier's men captured two German electricians near Cambrai in 1917, his batman, David Starrett, at once started a conversation with them in pidgin French, gave them cigarettes and tried to scrounge them some food.

Starrett (to the cook) 'Have you got some tea and steak for these two Jerries?'

Selbwy: 'No, not *** likely; there's not enough for ourselves.'

Starrett 'We can't let them starve.'

Selbwy: 'Well, you've got some tea and steak yourself. Give 'em yours.'

The prisoners got their tea and beefsteak, some bread, margarine and jam. And they devoured the food like hungry hounds.[197]

Starrett's kindness was handsomely rewarded, because the prisoners then revealed that there was a large booby trap in the cellar: had they been summarily executed it would never have been discovered till it destroyed Crozier's headquarters.

MORALE AND DISCIPLINE

The glue which holds armies together has a complex and variable composition, which includes not only major components like belief in a nation's war aims and hostility towards the enemy, but small, and often more powerful, ones like the bonds that link men in their sections, companies and battalions. The formal structure of the military hierarchy, backed by the constraints of discipline, also plays its part, and wise leaders recognise that the stick of discipline must work alongside carrots such as sport, entertainment, decorations and leave.

When a man joined the army he became subject to a code of discipline enshrined in the annual Army Act and *King's Regulations for the Army*, a legal code explained by *The Manual of Military Law*. The latter emphasised that 'in all times and in all places, the conduct of officers and soldiers as such is regulated by military law'.[198] It was pervasive and intrusive, and created a wide range of offences which had no civil equivalents. Although discipline had a wholly formal aspect, it was hedged about with unofficial sanctions. Thus while it was an offence under military law for a superior to strike an inferior, many units tolerated unofficial violence. Captain Gerald Burgoyne told his company NCOs in 1914 that 'I could not be bothered with petty crime, they must make the men obey them, how I did not care; and that I would back them up in all they did.' Not long afterwards he saw a fatigue party, 'the men all over the place, no discipline, and the corporal in charge, useless . . . I ran out and gave him two under the jaw.' And when a man was late on parade, pleading that 'I was just getting a drop of tea wetted,' Burgoyne 'lifted him a couple of the best and kicked him till he ran.'[199]

In December 1914 a company quartermaster sergeant in 2/Royal Welch Fusiliers found that a corporal – 'a smart-looking man but a poor non-commissioned officer' – had been seen striking a brave but scruffy soldier. The company quartermaster sergeant duly laid him out. The corporal complained of assault, but the company commander decided that justice would be done if the CQMS knocked the corporal down once more.[200] Corporal Charles Arnold was cheeked by a man in his section, but 'instead of putting him in the guard room which was the right place for him I gave him a good hiding . . . Perhaps you may call me a cruel bounder [but] the fellow thanked me afterwards because if I had put him in the guard room he would have got about three months imprisonment.'[201] Unofficial punishments were often winked at by officers. In 1914 Captain Lord Stanhope's company contained a man who was:

> always late and always filthy, and the men disliked him as much as I did. I suggested one day that when he came up for punishment that the company should see that he washed properly at the baths. On the next visit that we made, I heard the most frightful yells and, looking round the corner from my bath, found the men cleaning him with a hard scrubbing brush which was followed by a pail of nearly boiling water.[202]

Some regular NCOs maintained that they did not need to go to these lengths: it was possible to 'sweat a man' quite legally so that he would get ever deeper into trouble and finish up in military prison.

A soldier of the rank of corporal or below formally charged with an offence (rather than being simply cuffed round the head or being told to clean out the latrines) would appear before his company commander. The company commander might either deal with it himself, or remand the soldier to the commanding officer. Fines (for instance, the second offence of drunkenness rated 2/6d and the third 5 shillings) and periods of CB (confined to barracks) were the most common penalties at this level. 'Company orders' ('company memoranda' for the Guards) could be very rough justice indeed, with a presumption of innocence often replaced by the unstated conviction that the man would not have been charged if he was not guilty. In 1917 Private William Albery, under training in England, was brought up before his company commander for a trivial misdemeanour.

> 'Kep orf.' Quick march, Halt. Left Turn. Company Commander. 'Have you anything to say?'
> 'Please Sir –'
> 'Hold your noise' shouted the sergeant, 'Seven days CB' ordered the captain. 'Seven days CB' echoed the sergeant. So that was that.[203]

In addition to being confined to barracks 'CB' involved performing 'fatigue duties to the fullest possible extent, with a view to relieving well-conducted soldiers therefrom'.[204] And there were extra parades, including pack drill, under the provost sergeant, who supervised the regimental police. Harry Ogle experienced it himself:

> Seven soldiers, in full marching order but without rifles, file through a gate and approach the burly figure of the Provost Sergeant, who stands at ease, his silver-topped cane under his left arm in the middle of a small field. The straggling party has nearly reached him when suddenly he springs to attention and yells at the nearest man: 'You there, right marker, Halt!' and then to the remainder, 'Fall in on the left of the marker at the double. Halt! Answer your names.' The Provost Sergeant delivers every order and every homily in a loud hoarse yell, without the least sign of strain or even effort, and without a pause for either breath or punctuation. There is seldom more than ten paces marched without either a change of direction or formation. 'Into file, right turn. Quick march. On the left form squad. Forward. When you joined the army you joined a body of MEN. If you behave like kids you TAKE

THE CONSEQUENCES. About turn. By the left. Change
direction left. Left form. Forward.'[205]

A soldier who went before the commanding officer appeared on
battalion orders, this time with the regimental sergeant major marching in the capless prisoner between a two-man escort. The CO's
powers of punishment were wider than those of a company commander: he could detain a man, or award him Field Punishment
No. 1, for up to twenty-eight days, and could reduce corporals and
lance corporals to the ranks. A man could elect for trial by court
martial, or be remanded by the CO, and senior NCOs and officers
alike were sent for court martial for all but the most minor offences,
for the commanding officer could neither imprison them nor
deprive them of their rank.

Flogging in the army had been abolished in peacetime in 1868,
on active service in 1881 and in military prisons as recently as 1907.
The old army believed that there remained a requirement for a
campaign punishment which was exemplary and yet did not result
in an individual escaping from duty. The result was Field Punishment
No. 1, which could be awarded by either a CO or a court martial.
A prisoner sentenced to it forfeited his pay, could, as the *Manual of
Military Law* explained, be kept in fetters or handcuffs so as to prevent his escape, and 'may be attached for a period or periods not
exceeding two hours in any one day to a fixed object, but he must
not be so attached during more than three out of four consecutive
days, nor during more than twenty-one days in all'. He could be
subjected to 'labour, employment and restraint' as if he was
undergoing a sentence of hard labour. Field Punishment No. 2 was
precisely the same, but did not include the daily attachment to a
'fixed object'.[206]

Field Punishment No. 1 was awarded on 60,210 occasions during
the First World War, and was thus infinitely more common than the
death penalty: an average of about one soldier in fifty serving in
France received it, although this figure does not reflect the fact that
several men received it more than once. There were 3,080 death
sentences, of which 346 were actually carried out, all but 37 of them
for offences which attracted the death penalty only under military

law. We ought, perhaps, not to be surprised that Field Punishment No. 1, so very visible, features far more frequently in letters and diaries than the death penalty. The latter aroused powerful emotions, though men were divided over it. Both Rowland Feilding and Julian Bickersteth were amongst the many who deplored it. However, Private Arthur Moss of 1/Royal Fusiliers thought it 'very severe but it is done as an example to maintain discipline in the service',[207] and Frederic Manning's comrades agreed that 'Miller the deserter' ought to be shot for leaving them in the lurch.

Field punishment, however, attracted almost as much resentment amongst officers, who were not subject to it, as amongst soldiers, who were. It was regarded as degrading, primitive and wholly out of place in a citizen army fighting a great war. Lieutenant F. P. Roe was amongst the many young officers shocked by their first encounter with it.

> One of my early memories was the sight of a garrison artilleryman on a very hot day handcuffed to the gun wheels of his battery's gun carriages, a heavy howitzer battery. He was sweating profusely and was covered with flies . . . The experience haunted me for a long time.[208]

Handcuffing to a wheel met the remit of regulations, but some units tied a man with his arms outstretched, earning the punishment the nickname 'crucifixion'. In August 1916 Victor Archard, a tank gunner, noted that one of his comrades was given fourteen days' Field Punishment No. 1 for 'swearing about an officer in his absence and to his own fellow gunners,' and soon afterwards:

> I saw No. 1 Field Punishment being inflicted for the first time. The prisoner has been standing for hours against the railings of the main entrance to camp, with his arms tied to the rails about a foot above his shoulders. This is given to him every other day, and lasts two hours.[209]

In Arthur Moss's regular battalion field punishment was made even more severe by 'tying a man to a wheel & turning same round ever so long until the head is downwards. Shocking punishment & nasty to look at . . .'[210]

As we might expect, unit tolerance of field punishment varied.

Australians sometimes released British soldiers they encountered tied up, and threatened the regimental sergeant major or the regimental police if they tried to re-attach them to wheel or fence. Private Marshall of the Accrington Pals described an incident during the battalion's brief sojourn in Egypt in 1915–16.

> We were at Al Kantara and marching past a Regular Army camp. Two men were strung up on a gun-wheel in the sun . . . 'Potty' Ross, (Z Company Commander) said: 'That's what happens if you misbehave.' The reply came back, 'It won't, tha' knows. If you did that to any of us, t'others would cut him down.'[211]

He was scarcely exaggerating. In some units the practice was so universally abhorred that it was simply ritualised, and the culprit was shut in a hut with the handcuffs thrown in after him.

But there remained an argument that commanding officers needed a severe and immediate sanction at their disposal. Douglas Wimberley, reflecting on his time as machine-gun company commander, affirmed that:

> Field Punishment No. 1 I never had to give, though in my judgement it is very valuable and necessary on active service. Field Punishment, in my opinion, if given should be carried out by the letter of the law. Some units, especially MG Companies and the like, without a provost Sergeant, carried it out very slackly. It was frequently given and treated almost as CB and meant little more than the pay forfeited and an ugly mark on the man's [conduct] sheet. If I gave F. P.2, I always tried to ensure that it was properly carried out as it was meant to be, that is, as a severe punishment. And a severe punishment it is – the man loses pay, goes down any fixed number of places on the leave roster, is fed on bully and biscuits, gets no cigarettes or rum, and has those cigarettes he owns, and his money, kept from him during the punishment; and he is kept hard at work at manual labour or unpleasant sanitary duties. If it is carried out like this, it need seldom be given and does not lose its hold as an enforcer of discipline.[212]

And in 1917 the humane Rowland Feilding complained of:

> A tendency to commute all sentences of imprisonment
> which, for obvious reasons, are served out of the line, to
> Field Punishment, which is served in it. But, in the latter
> case, the punishment falls so flat that the hardened
> offender cares nothing for it.[213]

Of the types of court martial prescribed by the *Manual of Military Law* the Field General Court Martial (FGCM) was that which applied on active service on the Western Front. It consisted of a president, an officer not below the rank of captain, although a major was preferable, and two other officers who had held commissions for at least a year. The officer who convened the trial could not sit on the court, nor could any witness or individual involved with the investigation of the case. The accused could object to the composition of the court, was entitled to speak in his own defence and could be assisted by a 'prisoner's friend'. When the court discussed its verdict the most junior officer voted first in an effort to prevent a dominant senior officer imposing his will. Sentences, including recommendations for mercy, were passed on up the chain of command for confirmation by the commander in chief. A FGCM could try officers, and had at its disposal the full range of penalties prescribed by the Army Act, but there had to be unanimity if the death penalty was to be imposed.[214]

This form of court martial had the stated aim of providing 'for the speedy trial of offences committed abroad or on active service in cases where it is not practicable . . . to try such offences by an ordinary general court-martial'. The major difference between it and the general court martial was the absence of a legally-qualified judge advocate who advised the court. However, from early 1916 the post of court-martial officer was introduced. These personnel were drawn from experienced lawyers already serving in the army, and were expected to 'keep the court straight on matters of law and procedure'. Despite assertions that these were 'kangaroo courts' it is evident that they were bound by strict rules of procedure, and abundant evidence suggests both that their members took their duties seriously, and that formation commanders and eventually the commander in chief looked hard at their proceedings. Nor is it true to say that courts martial were generally composed of officers without front-line experience sitting in judgment on men from the trenches.

The case of Private James Haddock of 12/York and Lancaster is not untypical. When he was court-martialled for desertion in September 1916 two members of the court had gallantry awards and the third, also with front-line experience, was later killed in action. The court sentenced him to death and he was shot. The case is doubly informative because Private Haddock had deserted on his first day with the battalion. His CO, to whom he was a stranger, would have had no compunction in sending him for trial, and the fact that all three members of the court were in his regiment would have been more likely to harm than to help him.[215] And it was not a good time to desert at the end of a long battle, when formation commanders and the commander in chief, all aware of the need to buttress discipline, were more likely to favour a more draconian approach than might have been the case in quieter times.

None of this meant, however, that courts martial did not sometimes commit injustices. Firstly, their members were all too well aware that they were small but important cogs in the disciplinary machine. Charles Carrington remembered that when he was being instructed on courts martial he was taught that 'the first duty of the court was to ensure that the prisoner had every advantage to which he was legally entitled', but that 'the court should not hesitate to pronounce a heavy sentence if the case was proved . . .'. Although Carrington retained a generally positive view of the war, he admitted:

> A memory that disturbs me is the hint or warning that
> came down from above . . . that morale needed a sharp
> jolt, or that a few severe sentences might have as good
> effect. It was expedient that some man who had deserted
> his post under fire was shot to encourage the others. Some-
> times discipline would be screwed up a couple of turns:
> death sentences would be confirmed and executed.[216]

Frank Crozier rebuked a major for excessive leniency as court martial president. When he began to say: 'I thought a life sentence sufficient . . .' Crozier snapped that 'you are merely there to do justice, not only to the prisoner but to discipline. It is not for you to judge the prevalence of a particular crime.'[217]

The experience and resolution of court-martial members varied immensely: some prosecuting officers were good at their jobs while others were not; some defendants were well represented while others simply threw themselves on the mercy of the court. Guy Chapman first sat on a court martial in 1916:

> The accused was an elderly pioneer sergeant of the 6oth [Rifles]; the charge 'drunk in trenches'. He was duly found guilty. As he was marched out, I hurriedly turned the pages of the *Manual of Military Law* and found to my horror that the punishment was death, *tout court*. So when Major the Hon George Keppel turned to me as junior member of the court and demanded my sentence, I replied, 'Oh death, sir, I suppose.' Major Keppel blanched and turned to my opposite number, Gwinnell. Gwinnell, who was as young and unlearned in experience as myself, answered, as I had, 'Death, I suppose.' Our good president looked across from the top of his six feet and groaned:
>
> 'But my boys, you can't do it.'
>
> 'But, sir,' we protested in unison, anxious to justify our-selves, 'it says so here.'
>
> It was only after a moving appeal by the president that we allowed ourselves to be overborne and to punish the old ruffian by reduction to the rank of corporal in the place of executing him; but we both felt that Major Keppel had somehow failed in his duty. Perhaps as a retribution for this bloodthirsty exhibition, I was thrown on my way home.[218]

Bombardier Bill Sugden also had reason to be grateful to a wise president. He had 'gone a bit potty' when sent round to the ser-geants' mess with a message.

> They were all drunk and started saying things. They were all regulars and jealous of Kitcheners. What possessed me I don't know. I flew into the most intense rage and went for the whole lot. About six of them put me in the clink with a soldier with a fixed bayonet over me.

He was remanded for court martial and warned that 'you are liable to be sentenced to death'. However, the president declared that a sober man with his excellent record must have been unreasonably provoked, and dismissed the case. 'Then he ordered me outside and talked like a father to me,' wrote Sugden. 'I was absolutely flattened out.'[219]

Striking a superior officer could indeed get a man shot. Two members of 72nd Battery RFA were shot on the same day, 3 October 1916, for unrelated acts of striking superiors, in one case a subaltern and in the other the battery sergeant major. Lord Cavan, the corps commander, wrote tellingly on documents on the case that: 'I recommend that the death sentence be carried out as discipline in this battery is bad.'[220] But the overwhelming majority of soldiers executed (266 out of 346) were shot for desertion, a crime which the army regarded particularly seriously. During the war the overall desertion rate ran at 10.26 per 1,000 men, more than a division of troops for the average size of the army on the Western Front. Circulars were issued warning officers against excessive leniency. Nonetheless, in order to convict the court had to be certain that the defendant was not simply absent without leave but had formed the intention of never returning to his unit. Walter Guinness found himself president of a Field General Court Martial in October 1916, and although there was 'palpable desertion' the 'half-witted youth prosecuting . . . never attempted to produce the necessary evidence'. In consequence, 'we came to the conclusion that as the prosecution did not attempt to deal with the question of intention we could only find the man guilty of absence without leave'. He added that he was 'particularly grateful' not to have to sentence the man to death.[221] Not everyone was pleased at such even-handedness. On 25 January 1915 Gerald Burgoyne wrote 'the man I ran in for sleeping at his post has just been remanded for a Field General Court Martial. I fear he will be shot . . . I fear this fellow will have to be made an example of.' But not long afterwards he added that the man: 'got off with three months owing to a technicality. He was very lucky.'[222]

Early in 1915 it became clear that many men regarded a sentence of imprisonment, either in a military prison in France or Britain, as preferable to repeated tours of trench duty, and in April Parliament agreed that military sentences could be suspended: capital sentences by the commander in chief, others by army commanders. Many men sentenced to imprisonment were returned to their units, and an increasing number of those sentenced to death had the sentence commuted to a suspended sentence of five years. Feilding thought that suspended sentences were a good idea:

> First, the soldier had a sword of Damocles hanging over his head, and secondly, the better man, whose trouble had come upon him from some momentary lapse (an ever-present possibility in war, as in peace) had a chance of atoning for his delinquency, and often, by good behaviour or a gallant act on the battlefield, he earned a complete reprieve.[223]

Many capital sentences inflicted in the second half of the war were on men already under suspended sentence for a previous offence. For instance, Private Evan Fraser of 2/Royal Scots deserted within a month of his first conviction, escaped from custody to desert again, was duly sentenced to death and was shot – becoming the first man under suspended sentence to be executed for reoffending.

A further area of controversy was the mental state of men tried for capital offences. The diagnosis of psychiatric illness caused by the war was in its infancy, and it was still a matter of some chance as to whether a soldier displaying a severe reaction to his experiences was treated as a patient or a criminal. Even in 1914 a man could be examined by a sympathetic doctor who diagnosed psychiatric breakdown. Private William Dunbar of the London Scottish 'became a casualty with a complete collapse of my nervous system' in the autumn of 1914. He was evacuated to England, and recovered well enough to be commissioned into the Royal Field Artillery.[224] But medical officers were under great pressure to report men as being fit for duty for as long as possible. Lord Moran described how a man reported sick for the second day running, saying: 'It's no good, sir ... I can't stand it no longer.' Moran examined him, found that 'there was nothing wrong with him physically and he was sane enough. He was simply tired – but so were others. Once more I sent him back and the next day he was killed.' Here Moran felt that there was little choice. But he was critical of a colleague who went off to do a brief examination of a man facing a death sentence. 'There's a fellow over there run away from the trenches,' said the doctor briskly, 'they are going to shoot him and want me to say that he's responsible. I shan't be long.'[225]

Several soldiers were shot after pleading that they had been suffering from what was then termed 'shell shock'. Lance Corporal William Moon of 11/Cheshires had been traumatised by what his company sergeant major described in court as 'an incident that occurred on 31st December 1915 when a shell burst close to him and blew part of a comrade's head and brains into his face'. He went into hospital, but was 'nervous' when he came back to the battalion, and deserted shortly afterwards. The defence did not call evidence from the doctors who had treated him in hospital, and his regimental medical officer told the court, not unreasonably, that he could offer no evidence on his mental state as he had not seen him since the incident. Although the brigadier recommended clemency, other formation commanders were not as benevolent, and William Moon was shot.[226] Private John Docherty of the Black Watch, a veteran of Loos, tried for a second offence of desertion, was examined by two medical officers whose report stated: 'Although not of unsound mind, he is suffering from a marked degree of neurasthenia. Whether this is the result of shell shock or of recent onset, we are unable to state.'[227] The authorities were unimpressed, and on 15 February 1916 John Docherty was one of eleven men shot, with ghastly appropriateness, in the abattoir at Mazingarbe just behind the Loos front.

Three officers were executed during the war. One, Second Lieutenant John Patterson of the Essex Regiment shot a military policeman who was attempting to arrest him for desertion. Sub-Lieutenant Edwin Dyett of the Royal Naval Division was shot for desertion, as was Second Lieutenant Eric Poole of the West Yorkshires. The latter's brigadier wrote that he had previously been in hospital for shell shock, and was 'of nervous temperament, useless in action, and dangerous as an example to the men'. An RAMC officer concluded that he was 'of a highly-strung, neurotic temperament, and I am of the opinion that excitement may bring on a condition which would make him not responsible for his actions at the time'. At his court-martial the battalion's quartermaster declared that Second Lieutenant Poole was 'very confused indeed' when apprehended, and his regimental medical officer also testified that he was 'more liable to shell shock that a normal man'. Brigade, divisional and corps commanders recommended leniency, but Plumer, the army commander, wrote that he would have recommended Poole's execution had he been a private, and 'in view of the inherent seriousness of the offence when committed by an officer' he supported the death penalty. Haig took precisely the same view, adding that all ranks must realise that the law applied to officers as well as privates, and confirmed the sentence. The adjutant general told 2nd Army that the promulgation of sentence of death did not involve cashiering. Eric Poole was accordingly dressed as an officer when he was shot at Poperinghe on 10 December 1916.

Once a death sentence was confirmed by the commander in chief it was read out to the condemned man. Harry Ogle described such a soldier having his sentence read out in the middle of his brigade, drawn up in hollow square, in the autumn of 1916.

> In the middle of the square was a small group of officers
> and drummers and one figure who was already little more
> than a ghost. A minute ago he had been a private soldier
> in a regiment of the line, wearing the regiment's badges
> and buttons and all honourable military identity and was
> now under sentence of death. He was to be shot at dawn
> the next day ... I was one of the many who sympathised
> but acquiesced, unable to think of an alternative. Now he
> was drummed out of the service and marched away to wait
> for the dawn.[228]

Sometimes the sentence was announced before representatives from each unit in the brigade, or perhaps, as with the case of James Crozier described below, it was a battalion parade. The moral effect of death sentences was magnified by their promulgation in routine orders, so that soldiers across the whole of the British Expeditionary Force were well aware of what might just happen to them too. Normally a condemned soldier was told of the confirmation of his sentence the day before it was put into effect. He was already detained, either by his own regimental police or by the military police, within a short walk of the scene of execution. A single execution was likely to be carried out under regimental arrangements, with the assistant provost marshal from division in attendance. Soldiers from the victim's unit, under the command of an officer, constituted the firing party, and both the regimental sergeant major and provost sergeant would be on hand to ensure that the dreadful ritual went smoothly. A medical officer would pin an aiming mark – a piece of white cloth (rifle-cleaning four-by-two flannelette was convenient) – to the man's tunic over his heart while the man was being tied to the post. Sometimes the firing party arrived to find rifles ready, one of them unloaded, but this gentle deception was rare, for a man would know that his rifle had not fired, or notice the absence of a live round's sharp kick if it had been replaced by a blank. It was important that the firing party should be sober and as steady as possible, and above all to know that they would be doing their comrade no favours if they fired wide. Stage management was all, and one provost sergeant reported, with no hint of malice, that things had 'gone off *champion*'.

On his last night before execution the victim would be offered the consolation of a chaplain, and given a good feed if he wanted it. Sometimes he was encouraged to drink himself into oblivion. Frank Crozier wrote of one of his soldiers, Rifleman James Crozier (no relation), who 'was brave. He showed no malice. He was cheerful almost to the end – but not quite to the bitter end. I made him drunk some hours before the execution, to ease his living misery.' Crozier then carefully briefed 'a certain junior officer . . .':

> 'You will be in charge of the firing party . . . the men will be cold, nervous and excited. They may miss their mark. You are to have your revolver ready, loaded and cocked; if the medical officer tells you that life is not extinct you are to walk up to the victim, place the muzzle of the revolver to his heart and press the trigger. Do you understand?' 'Yes Sir,' came the quick reply. 'Right,' I add, 'dine with me in my mess to-night.'!
>
> I wanted to keep this young fellow engaged under my own supervision until late at night, to minimize the chance of his flying to the bottle for support.

In this case the victim was carried to the stake, too drunk to walk, and tied on 'like dead meat in a butcher's shop'. The men of the firing party came up to the aim on a silent signal, and fired when the officer dropped his handkerchief. It was 'a nervous ragged volley, yet a volley', but the doctor signed that life was not extinct, so the subaltern stepped forward steadily to administer the *coup de grâce*. Afterwards Crozier had the battalion formed up just outside the little garden where the execution had taken place, and then: 'We march back to breakfast, while the men of a certain company pay the last tribute at the graveside of an unfortunate comrade.'[229]

The Reverend Julian Bickersteth, who helped two men through their last hours on earth, wrote how one of them, who had joined underage in 1914 and had done three years at the front:

> gave me all his little treasures to give to this friend or that. He wrote a letter to his sweetheart and sent her his letter with all its photographs and trinkets, a lucky farthing which she had given him for a keepsake, his last 'leave' ticket and other small things. He sent a letter to his best chum in the regiment and said he was sorry he hadn't made good, and wished them all a Happy New Year and hoped they would get home safe after the war . . . As they bound him, I held his arm tight to reassure him – words are useless at such a moment – and he turned his blind-folded face to me and said in a voice which wrung my heart, 'Kiss me, Sir, kiss me,' and with my kiss on his lips, and 'God has you in his keeping' whispered in his ear, he passed into the Great Unseen.[230]

The papers relating to the majority of capital courts martial are now available for consultation, and formed the basis for the government's 1998 decision not to grant a blanket pardon to all those executed. The most that one can say is that the overwhelming majority were justly convicted *by the law as it then stood*. Indeed, in some of the most-publicised cases, like that of Lance Sergeant Willie Stones of 19/Durham Light Infantry, it is hard to see how the court could have decided otherwise on the evidence presented to it. Most – almost 90 percent – of death sentences were commuted, and the cases where they were not often reflected a desire on the part of the chain of command to reinforce discipline in a particular unit or at a particular time. It was indeed a hard law, but it was, in general, fairly applied. But like so much else about this war the issue divides head from heart, and if my head applauds the logic of capital sentences, they still break my heart.

To official executions must be added an unknown number of unofficial executions where soldiers were shot out of hand by officers or NCOs. Frank Crozier wrote of such things in his breezy way, and Sidney Rogerson describes an incident in the spring of 1918, but reputable accounts are few and far between. So too are genuine accounts of the killing of soldiers by 'battle police', and it is to the army's wider coercive apparatus that we must now turn our attention.

We have already encountered the regimental police under their provost sergeant, members of a specific battalion in the line and out of it. Garrison Military Police, composed of soldiers on long attachments from their units, patrolled large towns. The Corps of Military Police, with its two branches, foot and mounted, had previously recruited only volunteers of four years' service and exemplary records, but in 1914 it began to recruit directly for the first time. In 1918 it numbered 151 warrant officers and 13,325 other ranks. It had only three officers, largely because it came under the executive authority of the provost marshal at GHQ and assistant provosts marshal at formation headquarters down to division. These were often combatant officers who were no longer fit for front-line duty: for instance, Walter Nicholson tells us that the assistant provost marshal of one of his divisions, Major E. L. Bowring of the Worcesters, had been a company commander in 1914 but was 'mentally and physically exhausted, starting at any sudden sound'.[231] It was certainly no sinecure, and in November 1914 the assistant provost marshal of 1st Division won a DSO for leading his policemen and a group of stragglers in a desperate counterattack. From time to time the provost staff were given temporary command of yeomanry regiments to help with route-signing and traffic control, and from February 1918 had two garrison battalions of infantry under permanent command.

A good deal of the work of the military police was commonplace. They investigated a whole range of crimes, from theft to drunkenness and criminal damage, many all too common where young men gather in large numbers. They enforced discipline over matters of military protocol like turnout and saluting, and in the process became, with their red-topped caps, the all-too-visible symbols of the army's authority. Their operational role was of growing importance, for they signed routes behind the front and were responsible for controlling movement along them. Most controversially, they also provided a network of 'battle stops', 'straggler posts' and 'examination posts', behind the front. These were intended to redirect genuine stragglers and to detain men attempting to leave the front without due cause, though often the distinction was not an easy one to make. For much of the war stragglers were relatively uncommon: a single corps at Messines Ridge in 1917 had forty-four men composing its straggler posts but found only nineteen stragglers. In March 1918, however, with a large-scale retreat on the whole southern part of the British front, at least 25,000 stragglers were collected, fed and put back into the fighting.

The term 'battle police' (sometimes personalised – and we can see where the argument is going – to 'Haig's battle police') has been applied variously to regimental police ordered to follow up attacking troops, and to military police working just behind the line, and there are repeated tales of stragglers being shot by 'Redcaps in the trenches'. It is hard to find first-hand accounts of such occurrences: most of those who mention it heard it from somebody else. Indeed, the mechanics of the situation should give us pause for thought. Military police were armed with pistols, and the prospect of their moving into the rear area of a battalion in action and shooting rifle-armed soldiers on the spot cannot be taken too seriously. There were certainly rare occasions when military police were authorised to use lethal force: on 25 June 1916 the New Zealand Division ordered its straggler posts to fire on stragglers who refused to stop. But in May 1918 the commander of 19th Division was refused GHQ's permission to 'confirm and have carried out' summary death sentences on stragglers. It was unwise of military policemen to break the rules, for unauthorised use of weapons could put them in the dock: the policeman whose ill-aimed shot started the Etaples mutiny was court-martialled and sentenced to three years' imprisonment with hard labour. Dislike of the military police reflected the deep unpopularity of the civil police in many working-class areas of Britain, and was exacerbated by their role in the maintenance of discipline in the rear areas when soldiers felt that 'goin' large a bit' was no more than their entitlement. But there is surprisingly little evidence to support suggestions that they were used as drovers shepherding men into battle.[232] For while coercion undoubtedly played its part in keeping men in the line, it was no more than part of a complex process.

If, on the one hand, the army coerced, it also encouraged. Although relations between officers, NCOs and men varied from unit to unit, they were often very cordial, and morale at sub-unit level was extraordinarily personality-dependent. Private S. B. Abbot of 86th Company MGC censured one of his officers, nicknamed 'the Orphan', as a 'thruster' who endangered his men's lives by excessive zeal in shooting up German positions while at the same time paying careful attention to his own safety. But Abbot wrote warmly of another officer, 'Mr Street . . . a splendid man', mourned as 'our brave and kind officer' when he was killed in April 1917.[233] Frank Gray was a thirty-seven-year-old lawyer conscripted as a private in 1917. His chauffeur took him to the recruiting office, and thereafter he endured the 'terribly hard' life of the infantry soldier under training. He was sharply critical of the way the army was run by 'the united aristocrats of an antique system'. But he dedicated his book to: 'my Commanding Officer, the late Colonel R. E. Dewing DSO, who was part (or the victim) of the system, but who possessed a fine knowledge of men, was humane, kind, and courageous, and so remained to the end'. He also recorded his debt of gratitude 'to NCOs and men who were my friends throughout, who made hardship endurable to me, and gave me the life I still retain'. His company commander in 8/Royal Berkshires 'had more the appearance of an unsuccessful poet than an officer of the British Army' but 'was a gentleman – fair, clever and brave'. Junior officers 'were in the main great' and 'even Commanding Officers, in my time recruited from without more frequently than within the system, were distinctly good'.[234]

Fred Hodges had nothing but praise for his officers, and was sad to see some of the freshly-painted crosses ready for their graves in October 1918.

I walked slowly past them, and noted that Captain Hamilton now had a posthumous MC, and that Lieutenant Gibbs was a captain ... I noticed that both these fine young officers were aged twenty-four and at the time I thought it was quite a mature age; in the circumstances of their young lives, it was.[235]

Private George Fortune of 18/Lancashire Fusiliers affirmed that:

Our officers and NCOs were wonderful the way they used to do their duty. They were always watching over us and seeing we got a hot drink. We used to have a drop of water out of our water bottles to help make the tea. One day I had drunk all mine and could not give any. I told our officer I did not want any tea. He said 'you must' and 'come and see me when we are out of the line'. I went to see him and he gave me another water bottle.

But there were flies in any ointment, and Fortune developed a dislike for Sergeant Watts. 'He made me clean the metal washbasin with sand,' he recalled. 'The water was ice cold, and the sand got into my broken chilblains ... Since 1919 I have been looking for that bastard. It's not too late yet to kill him.'[236]

Frank Hawkings was heartbroken when a well-respected officer was killed at Zillebeke in May 1915:

The adjutant, Captain Culme-Seymour, has been killed. He went up to the front line to reconnoitre and was shot by a German bombing party while he was cheering the men on. Everyone is awfully cut up. He was a regular attached to us from the KRR [King's Royal Rifles] and was very popular. The Colonel has gone sick with injuries to his face and knee. There will soon be nothing left of the old regiment. Major Dickens is now in command, but he is not so well known as the old Colonel was.[237]

After Norman Gladden's company commander was killed at Passchendale he wrote that: 'Even amidst so much human disaster ... I felt a painful stab of sorrow at this news, mixed with a great anguish at the senseless elimination of a good, brave and truly gentle man.'[238] Ernest Shephard was distraught when his company commander was killed in a needless and unplanned foray into the German trenches. 'The loss of my gallant Captain to the Battalion, my Company, and myself cannot be estimated,' he lamented. 'He was the bravest officer I have met, his first and last thought was for the good and honour on the Bn, his Coy and his men.' Sergeant Goodwillie, the pioneer sergeant, 'very well liked by the Captain', rushed out to try to help him, and was killed as well.[239] T. P. Marks helped his mates carry back the body of their platoon commander. 'The ground had been torn up and it was heavy work even with four men,' he wrote. 'But we would willingly have carried him twenty miles.'[240]

William Carr noted how the mood of his battery changed during the March retreat when its former commander returned after recovering from a wound.

> Then shouts – orders – the adjutant had arrived – move on. We staggered to our feet; it was going to be a devil of a job getting out of that field . . . I wondered whether we could manage it with men and horses so exhausted. Then a word from Gardner.
>
> 'The Adjutant tells me the Major's back. He's at HQ now – Major Sutherland is back.' The news went round 377 [Battery RFA] like wild fire.
>
> 'The Major's back – he's ah richt – he's coming back.'
>
> It was miraculous, men were on their feet, horses mounted, shovels seized and a start made to hack down the hedge. The ditch was filled with clods of earth, brush-wood – anything we could find . . . We were the first battery out of the field.[241]

P. J. Campbell saw how a good battery could be ruined by a bad commander. One was with his battery for only seventeen days, 'and in that time the morale of the battery had sunk to a lower level than ever before, far lower than after months of fighting and heavy casualties at Ypres'. But another battery commander, though reserved and unfriendly, was respected because 'we knew that he knew what to do'.[242] The efficiency of 2/Royal Welch Fusiliers had fallen off by July 1918, but a new CO soon put a spring back into its step: 'There was to be company training: parades before breakfast were to be revived . . . and servants, cooks and details used to having a slack time had to parade and furbish up their drill against a day when they might be wanted.' The regimental sergeant major, late on parade because he had 'over-slept', got 'a good choking-off'. And then the commanding officer organised a trench raid, allowing companies 'a large latitude in making their dispositions, but he supervised everything, and by a tactful gentle gingering-up soon made everyone feel that a long-absent efficient authority had been restored to the Battalion'. When the raid took place, he met the leading company as it crossed No Man's Land, and said: 'You'll have to go into the village for your prisoners; I've been down to have a look, and there aren't any outside the wire.' The whole business was 'a magnificient tonic'.[243]

Popularity was helpful, though not if too clearly courted. Brave and thoughtful young officers often knew just how to get it right. Guy Chapman heard his company servants discussing the merits of their 'blokes' in 1918.

> ''E's not a bad little chap,' said a voice.
>
> 'Little, all right,' replied my own batman, Johns, 'why 'e don't come even as high as my Titch even.' I mutely thanked him for the comparison.
>
> The voice of the mess cook took up the discourse.
>
> 'That there young Knappett, y'know, 'e's too regimental, making us all come up for the rum every night. Now young Brenchley, 'e knows 'ow to treat us. The other night, when the Sarn't wants us all one by one, 'e says – didn't 'e, Johns? – "All right, Sarn't," 'e says, "I can trust the servants." See. Trusts us 'e does. 'member when we was on the Menin Road, old Nobby an' me was lying in a shell hole. 'E comes over the top. "'Ow are yer gettin' on," 'e says; "would yer like a drop of rum?" Would we like a drop of rum! And 'e brings it over 'isself. O, 'e's my ideal of an orficer, 'e is.'[244]

Some soldiers who hated the 'boss class' as a matter of political principle were content to make an exception for their own officers. Private Mason of 2/Scottish Rifles was 'a great gaunt Clydesider' who had been recalled to the army as a reservist after spending several years as a miner.

> There he had become involved with some men of violent
> Communist opinions and at times in the trenches he
> would tell [Lieutenant] Kennedy of what he and his
> friends would do to the capitalists and bosses after the
> War. It was blood-curdling stuff, in spite of which Mason
> was the most loyal and willing soldier, and went out of his
> way to almost mother Kennedy, and to give him cups
> of tea and extra rations at frequent intervals. Apparently
> officers of his own Regiment were exempt from the fury
> of class-hatred.[245]

But there was much more to success as a leader than simple popularity. Soldiers generally preferred a hard man who knew what he was doing to a genial incompetent. In Campbell's artillery unit, Major John of D Battery was 'the man most disliked and most feared in the whole brigade' because he expected others to live up to his own high standards of courage. After John was killed, fighting an ammunition fire characteristically single-handed, Campbell wrote:

> He did not love danger or glory, he despised both. But
> he had set himself a standard and he had to live up to it.
> He could not accept anything that fell below it, never for
> himself, hardly for anybody else. He was the greatest sol-
> dier I was ever to serve with.[246]

James Jack was also not an easy man: it was typical of his self-discipline that he maintained such a rigid diet to keep himself in fighting trim that he consumed too few calories and was always cold. Rogerson wrote of how: 'In all ways he set us an example, but if asked to name his peculiar characteristic, I would say it was his determination, from which I never saw him relax, to keep up at all times and at all costs the proprieties of the old life of peace.'[247] Frank Crozier also insisted on 'proprieties', but his were rather different. In a railway carriage he ordered two subalterns to 'show kit' and open up their packs.

> The result is astonishing! Two pairs of girls' garters and
> an odd one. Two pairs of silk stockings and a chemise,
> one night-dress and a string of beads. A pot of Vaseline,
> a candle, two boxes of matches, and an envelope full of
> astonishing picture postcards, completes the list. 'Sou-
> venirs,' says one rascal. '*Tout prêt*,' says the other.[248]

There were few hard-and-fast rules about styles of command. What worked for Crozier's Ulstermen might not have done so elsewhere. P. J. Campbell though that the commander of his Yorkshire territorial battery, Major Eric, was successful because he was a Sheffield man:

> and a lot of the battery had known him before the war, they knew his family, they thought it right that he should command them, it was almost a feudal relationship; and in return the Major talked to them about their homes, he understood them, they knew that he took a personal interest in them.[249]

Relations between officers within the same unit battalion, and more particularly the same sub-unit, were often fraternal, and accounts often testify to the same sort of family atmosphere that was achieved in good infantry sections. Herbert Asquith, the second son of H. H. Asquith, served as an artillery officer for most of the war, and described life in his battery in 1917:

> The number of officers in a battery was a major, a captain, and usually four subalterns, six in all, about the size of an average family; in marches behind the line this was a pleasant number for a mess . . . Our battery commander, Major MacFarlane, was a regular soldier of exceptional qualities and a most charming companion: we were to learn in open warfare in 1918 his swift instinct for choosing positions, his great powers of endurance, and his almost uncanny intuitions as to the movements of the enemy. He presided over a family which would have been extremely happy, if Fate had allowed it, but at the battle of Passchendaele such a gift could scarcely be expected: our battery like many others had serious losses and of the three subalterns I came to know in June only one was left at the end of the battle.[250]

What was fraternal amongst officers was often paternal from officer to man. R. B. Talbot Kelly took it a step further. As he walked round his gun-pits under heavy shelling one evening:

> I felt like a mother going round her children's bedrooms in a great thunderstorm, but in this case the thunderstorm

was one of explosive and gas, and 'mother' was many years younger than any of her 'children'. Metaphorically I tucked each detachment up in bed, told them they would be all right, and in due course returned to my own niche by the roadside.[251]

One of the most moving First World War poems, Ewart Alan Mackintosh's *In Memoriam, Private D. Sutherland*, catches the full responsibility of a relationship which, in Mackintosh's view, went even beyond paternalism.

> Happy and young and gallant,
> They saw their first-born go,
> But not the string limbs broken
> And the beautiful men brought low,
> The piteous writhing bodies,
> That screamed 'Don't leave me, sir,'
> For they were only your fathers
> But I was your officer.[252]

As is often the case with family life, paternalism cut two ways: sometimes an officer's need to look brave in the eyes of the group kept him going. Vaughan was very frightened indeed before his battalion attacked at Langemarck, and had slipped into a dugout to dispel terrible images with a whisky. When the attack began:

> Dully, I hauled myself out of the mud and gave the signal to advance, which was answered by every man rising and stepping unhesitatingly into the barrage. The effect was so striking that I felt no more that awful dread of the shellfire, but followed them calmly into the crashing, spitting hell.[253]

But with the support he gained from his men came the responsibility to share their last moments. He was following Corporal Breeze when a shell burst at his feet: 'As I was blown backwards I saw him thrown into the air to land at my feet, a crumpled heap of torn flesh.' Minutes later it was clear that Breeze was not dead, for:

> I saw the stump of his arm move an inch or two ... He was terribly mutilated, both his feet had gone and one arm, his legs and trunk were torn to ribbons and his face

was dreadful. But he was conscious and as I bent over him
I saw in his remaining eye a gleam of mixed recognition
and terror. His feeble hand clutched my equipment, and
then the light faded from his eyes.[254]

An officer might expect the same from his men. At Loos a Highland private carried his wounded officer out of the line, stood with
him in the British front-line trench while the man clutched his ankles
in his death-agony, then shook himself free, collected another bag
of hand grenades, and returned, in fighting fury, to be killed in the
German position.

But officers could exasperate as well as inspire. Some battalions
insisted that subalterns marched with rifle and pack like the men,
as Rowland Feilding discovered when he marched from Winchester
to Southampton to embark: 'it was the first time I ever carried a
pack, and it felt as if it was filled with lead before we reached Harfleur'.[255] Junior officers generally marched lightly laden, with their
valises carried on the battalion's transport wagons, and commanding
officers, seconds in command, adjutants and company commanders
were mounted – a source of much ribaldry to the files immediately
behind them on the march. 'I'm sorry about that, boys,' was the
natural response of an unwise officer when his horse relieved itself,
for the inevitable response was: 'Never mind, sir, we thought it was
the horse.' Sensible officers recognised that horses could be a
communal asset on difficult marches, and during the retreat from
Mons their chargers were often festooned with exhausted men and
their kit. Alan Hanbury Sparrow saw his commanding officer lead
1/Royal Berkshires on foot: 'the old man is so weary that only his
courage gets him along'.[256] However, the CO of 11/Royal Northumberland Fusiliers did not make himself popular by chivvying tired
men from the saddle: Norman Gladden heard '"Come off that
bloody horse . . . you bastard . . .", muttered by men as the colonel's
well-groomed horse found the hill no obstacle'.[257]

W. H. A. Groom, who served in the ranks of the infantry, writing
in the early 1970s in angry reaction to the beginnings of revisionist
approaches to the war, maintained that 'the objective accounts
written by commissioned officers from generals to subalterns show
little knowledge of the real feelings of the men', and wrote with

admiration of 'the practically classless Commonwealth forces'. He thought that inspection by Haig was 'a most boring day . . . he did not even look at us, let alone inspect us'. And he vigorously challenged James Jack's assertion that 'there was little grumbling and never a whine', arguing that things would not have gone well for whiners. But he admitted that one of his company commanders was well regarded: 'he was one of the original peace-time battalion privates who had won the DCM in 1915. He had an excellent parade voice, was good looking and popular with the rankers because he always seemed to know what he was about.'[258]

Because of the growing number of officers commissioned from the ranks – the likes of John Lucy and Ernest Shephard, formerly regular NCOs – officers *were* increasingly aware of the lives of the men they commanded. From 1916 most newly-commissioned officers had served in the ranks before attending an officer cadet battalion: the granting of direct commissions had 'practically ceased' from February that year. About 229,000 new commissions were granted during the war, and 107,929 of their holders had passed through officer cadet battalions after serving in the ranks.[259] By 1918, the officer corps had become remarkably heterogeneous. It is beyond question that many newly-commissioned officers faced pressure to adopt traditional styles of officer leadership. However, many pre-war regulars would still have readily agreed with Alan Hanbury Sparrow that the 'somewhat uncouth but very willing officer reinforcements' were capable of doing a very good job, and although: 'You can't make a silk purse out of a sow's ear, you can make a good leather one.'[260]

Bravery, indeed, was the *sine qua non*. An officer could slurp his soup or even wear light-coloured shirts but his bravery atoned for much. Frank Richards went straight to the point. 'We always judged a new officer by the way he conducted himself in a trench,' he wrote, 'and if he had guts we always respected him.'[261] George Coppard agreed that: 'We took particular notice of the behaviour of officers under fire and compared our conduct with theirs. All soldiers look for and admire a brave and intelligent leader and will even put up with abuse from him providing that at a critical moment he displays courage and leadership.' One of his officers in particular was 'courageous steady and companionable, and we thought a lot of him'.[262] Although John Lucy was another who believed that regular officers were often out of touch with their men, he thought that they were 'extraordinarily gallant, and their displays of valour, often uncalled for, though thought necessary by them, coupled with the respect engendered in the old army for its corps of officers, won the greatest devotion, and very often the affection of the men'.[263] Edward Vaughan's spirits, already lifted by the bravery of his men, were stiffened by the courage of his company commander, who 'stood, eyeglass firmly fixed in his ashen face, while bullets chipped splinters from the beam beside his head'.[264]

Nevertheless an officer's reputation could be blasted by a lapse. Lance Corporal Coppard was detailed to look after a new officer, but: 'The poor devil was paralysed by fear . . . Not even the urge of nature would drive him out of the place [a deep dugout], and he did his business there. He lost his appetite and wouldn't touch the tasty bits I fixed up for him.'[265] The officer was finished: he reported sick and never returned to the front. Many found instances like this the cruellest of disparities between officers and men. Medical officers were far more prepared to certify terrified or exhausted officers as sick than they were men. Moran reckoned that by 1917 subalterns did not last long:

> The average subaltern, if he comes out here for the first
> time, does no more than sample war. A few, and these are
> the more fortunate, were hit, happily before they showed
> signs of fear. And some went on leave and did not return,
> and some went sick, and some were dispatched to the
> trench mortars or in drafts to other Fusilier battalions.

The army's chain of command, aware of the damage that could be done by irresolute or frightened officers, and of the way that such men undermined its caste system, was usually prepared to support commanding officers who gave their failures an easy way out. And there was a way out even for commanding officers who failed themselves. Moran's own CO reported sick: 'He looked old and troubled. In a quarter of a century he had been a soldier preparing no doubt for the real thing. It had come and this was the end.'[266] Yet most officers played the role expected of them. Fred Hodges had five company commanders in the seven months to November 1918.

> The first was Captain Sankey, a hard and very determined officer; he was wounded and replaced by Captain Jowett, a very much loved officer who was killed while attempting to help a wounded man who was lying out in the open between us and the Germans. Sankey returned to the battalion and was killed at Flers, and his successor was not with us long enough for me to get to know his name. He was the one who was wounded and then killed with stretcher-bearers. The next was Captain Hamilton, a natural leader, who was mortally wounded in the attack at Gouzeaucourt in September. The one who replaced him was Captain Wareham. He was wounded in our attack on Neuvilly on 12th October.[267]

Good officers were wholly absorbed in their commands. Lieutenant Colonel A. J. B. Addison of 9/York and Lancaster was mortally wounded on 1 July 1916, but lived, untended, in a shell hole for two or three days. He scribbled in his pocketbook: 'Tell the Regiment I hope it did well.'[268] In May 1918 Lieutenant Colonel Dean of 6/South Wales Borderers was carried into an artillery headquarters, appallingly wounded, unable to speak and obviously dying. He signalled for pen and paper, and scrawled his last order: 'To my battalion – Stick it, Boys,' and died within a few minutes. Regular officers, temporary officers, ex-rankers: gallant gentlemen indeed.

When the army went to war in 1914 it rewarded courage with a limited range of awards. The Victoria Cross was available to all ranks for the highest acts of valour. Officers could be appointed companions of the Distinguished Service Order (DSO), instituted in 1886, for either gallantry or rendering distinguished service. The fact that the decoration could either reflect great bravery just short of that required for a VC, or a heroic struggle amongst the files and memoranda, always left it open to criticism, and during the Boer War it was so regularly bestowed on well-connected staff officers that it was said that its initials stood for Dukes' Sons Only. Other ranks could be awarded the Distinguished Conduct Medal (DCM) for distinguished conduct in the field, and the medal's popularity was enhanced by the fact that recipients received a cash bounty. A bar on the medal ribbon (worn as a rosette when the ribbon was worn alone) signified a second or subsequent award. In addition, the various grades of orders of chivalry (most commonly the Bath and the St Michael and St George) could be bestowed upon officers. All ranks could be Mentioned in Dispatches, and officers could receive brevet or substantive promotion as a reward for distinguished service.

However, it soon became clear that the existing system would, like much else, not cope with a world war. The award of large numbers of DSOs and DCMs in the first six months of the war encouraged the creation, in December 1914, of the Military Cross (MC) for officers below the substantive rank of major and for warrant officers too, and in March 1916, of the Military Medal (MM), known, from its stripey ribbon, as a duckboard, for other ranks. In 1917 the Order of the British Empire was instituted, its five classes (from MBE to GBE) giving the opportunity of rewarding civil or military service across a wide range of ranks and appointments: a medal of the order (BEM) was added later. Allied nations conferred their own honours on selected British servicemen (a practice the British reciprocated), and men were allowed to wear such awards without the normal difficulty of obtaining royal permission to do so.

Old soldiers reacted disdainfully to the expansion of honours. 'All officers thought a lot of the DSO, and all men thought a lot of the DCM,' wrote Frank Richards, but they were less impressed by the new awards.

> There were no grants or allowances with the Military Medal, which without a shadow of a doubt had been introduced to save awarding too many DCMs. With the DCM went a money-grant of twenty pounds, and a man in receipt of a life pension who had won the DCM was entitled to an extra sixpence a day to his pension ... The old regular soldiers thought very little of the new decoration.[269]

An officer or soldier was decorated as the result of a citation initiated by his commanding officer or, in the case of a higher headquarters, by the formation commander. Decorations might be periodic, awarded in the New Year's honours or the king's birthday honours, or in the list for a specific battle. Or they might be immediate, bestowed soon after a particular act of bravery. It soon became evident that an immediate award had to be very immediate indeed if its recipient was to live to receive it, and by 1918 these awards could be issued within a week of the act which had earned them. Formal investiture with the decoration itself might, however, take some time, for the most prestigious awards were given by the king in person; divisional commanders presented the ribbon of the award, often made up with a clip so that it could be pinned on immediately. Siegfried Sassoon was recommended for an award for gallantry on a raid near Fricourt in May 1916, and his MC was announced a month later: the kindly James Dunn took the purple and white ribbon off his own tunic and sewed it to Sassoon's. In 1917 Joseph Maclean told his parents that a brother officer had just been awarded the DSO for taking a pillbox, adding that: 'The job was worth a Victoria Cross.' Two nights later he came round to Maclean's company mess to play bridge; Maclean reported 'He has his ribbon up . . .'.[270] John Cusack was awarded the MM for galloping through a village on 8 August 1918 and reporting it clear; he felt that he owed the award to the fact that the flamboyant act had been carried out under the eyes of his brigade commander. It was speedily presented by 'a general, an old character with a shaky hand'.[271]

For most of the war there was a set quota for awards. On the Western Front for the year from 1 April 1917 it was 200 DSOs and 500 MCs every month: in May 1918 the limit was removed 'provided the standard of the award was maintained'. There was no specified limit for DCMs and MMs. During the whole of the war 500 VCs (and two bars) were awarded for service in France and Belgium, with 6,768 DSOs (with 606 first bars, 69 second bars and 7 third bars); 31,793 MCs (with 2,761 first bars, 157 second bars, and 4 third bars); 21,041 DCMs (with 439 first bars, and 7 second bars), and 110,342 MMs (with 5,718 first bars, 180 second bars, and a single third bar).[272]

It was widely agreed that a man was far more likely to receive an award for a successful operation than a 'dud show'. While a commanding officer could never wholly guarantee an award, he could make it clear that he would recommend those taking a prominent part in, say, a trench raid, for decorations, if they survived. Brigadier General H. B. de Lisle, commanding a cavalry brigade in 1914, promised a DSO to the first officer to kill a German with the new pattern cavalry sword, and was as good as his word, although Captain Charles Hornby's DSO, earned on 21 August 1914, was not gazetted till February the following year. A good deal also depended on a commanding officer's skill at citation-writing (what Rowland Feilding called 'not necessarily a truthful but a flowery pen'), and his relationship with the brigadier. Feilding, constantly warned by his superiors that most decorations had to reflect 'a specific act of bravery' rather than sustained good performance, described one act so eloquently that the delighted general wanted to hear all about it from the soldier when he conferred the decoration, but the man was unable to recall the incident. Awards were scarce in Stormont Gibbs' battalion, he recalled, because the CO 'never gave anyone a good write up; the fact of his putting anyone in at all was a remarkable event'. Gibbs did his best, as adjutant, to make up for the deficiency, 'and in this manner Scrimgeour and Richards got MCs. I don't remember anyone else getting one tho' "other ranks" got a fair ration of MMs.'[273]

The system caused joy and woe in equal portions. George Coppard MM admitted that 'to win a medal of some sort was my highest ambition. There were medal-scoffers of course, who joked about medals being sent up with the rations, but I am sure that every man in his heart would have liked a medal, if only to relieve the monotony . . .'.[274] Decorations brought extraordinary pleasure: Siegfried Sassoon wrote of the preoccupation with the left-hand side of the tunic, so common to winners of the MC, and John Cusack was delighted to put up his 'duckboard'. Yet along with the honest pride engendered by a decoration came the burden of living up to it. 'After you got a decoration there was a general feeling – and a fear – that you were expected to do more in any action that was going,' thought Cusack.[275] F. P. Roe had a Royal Munster Fusilier corporal under his command who had won the VC in Gallipoli but declined to wear the ribbon 'as he had been so teased by his fellow soldiers in the regiment . . .'.[276]

On the other hand, some men became so caught up in the repeated demonstration of courage that it eventually consumed them. Company Sergeant Major J. Skinner VC DCM and French *Croix de Guerre* was wounded in action eight times and, after his investiture with his VC, given a posting in Scotland. But he evaded the order and rejoined his old company near Ypres, apparently wagered with a brave comrade as to which of them would be hit next, and was then killed in March 1918 as he went out to aid a wounded man. This very gallant warrant officer was carried to his grave by six other VC winners of the incomparable 29th Division. Towards the end of the war Lieutenant F. L. C. Jones – 'A Mons man, a Grenadier, commissioned in France', who was hoping for a regular commission – confided to a brother officer that he was 'going all out for a VC' to boost his chances. When his advancing platoon found a machine-gun post he yelled, 'Here's my chance, I'm after that VC.' 'He got twenty yards, and went down, shot through the head,' recalled an eyewitness.[277]

Not all who wanted decorations received them. Feilding wrote that: 'I have known men – good men too – eating their hearts out through lack of recognition. How petty this sounds! Yet a ribbon is the only prize in war for the ordinary soldier . . . '.[278] Ernest Shephard was infuriated to read that a baker with the Army Service Corps had been awarded the DCM 'for turning out the maximum amount of bread', and snorted: 'Ye Gods, what an insult to a *fighting soldier*, who risks his life daily. What are the authorities thinking about to award medals in this way and bring contempt on what should be a prized honour?[279] Diaries are spattered with comments about undeserved awards, and drenched with complaints about unrequited valour. Private Mayne of 6/Connaught Rangers was caught by a German raiding party, hit all over with grenade fragments and had his left arm shattered. 'Nevertheless he struggled up,' wrote Feilding, 'and leaning against the parapet, with his unwounded hand discharged a full magazine (twenty-seven rounds) into the enemy, who broke, not a man reaching our trench. Then he collapsed and fell insensible across the gun.' At that stage only the Victoria Cross and Mention in Dispatches could properly be awarded posthumously: Mayne died of his wounds, and was duly mentioned.[280]

The lavish award of decorations to staff officers caused irritation to those outside the scarlet circle. Arthur Osburn complained that 'our own generals and even some of their youngest ADCs with their rainbow breastplates of coloured gee-gaws and ribbons surpass even the Ruritanians'.[281] Regimental officers who went onto the staff knew just how much easier it was for staff officers to be recognised. When Lord Stanhope, then on a corps staff, heard that he had received a MC and a Mention on 1 January 1916 he confessed that he had always objected to the decoration of staff officers, but in this case, he mused, it was a recompense for the promotion he might have received had he remained at regimental duty. And then, eighteen months later, 'to my surprise and much to my dismay I was awarded the DSO. The Corps Commander was always most free in recommending both his own staff and those serving under him for rewards.'[282] And a general's ADC, on the staff since being shot at Loos, told Guy Chapman that the divisional commander had just offered to recommend him for an MC yet again: 'Damn it, if I couldn't get one with the Brigade of Guards I'm not going to pick it up on the way . . . It isn't decent.'[283] Lieutenant Colonel Dunnington-Jefferson, a regular Royal Fusilier who served on the intelligence staff at GHQ throughout the war, was even more frank:

> I regret to record the following awards during the Great War, all of which should have gone to somebody who had earned them by fighting the Germans instead of to somebody who saw very little of the front line:
>
> Six Mentions in Dispatches
> DSO and Brevet of Major
> Foreign Decorations – Italian Order of St Maurice and St Lazarus;
> Belgian Order of the Crown and Croix de Guerre; French Legion of Honour.[284]

Yet it was still painful when the expected award did not materialise. Reginald Tompson already had a DSO from the Boer War, but hoped to become a Companion of the Order of St Michael and St George. On 1 January 1918 he grabbed the morning papers with excitement.

> I had been put in for CMG last year, but had not got it,
> so had to wait 6 more months, when a strong recommen-
> dation had gone in, & I was told it was a certainty. How-
> ever, there was nothing. Looked down the list of Brevets
> wondering if by chance I had got in there, but it likewise
> proved blank. Felt a bit bad about it all day . . . The fact
> that most of our GHQ friends seem to have piled honour
> on honour in proportion as they have avoided risk appar-
> ently does not make it easier to bear.[285]

Foreign decorations could cause particular upset. Arthur Behrend, adjutant of a heavy artillery brigade, was asked to nominate an NCO for a French military medal. He suggested to the CO that they should recommend the pleasant but useless sergeant major, who duly received not just *a* military medal, but the prestigious *Médaille Militaire*. Some commanding officers, knowing that foreign awards were given with a set quota and were therefore relatively predictably obtained, used them as a compensation for officers and men whose British awards had not materialised. Many COs and divisional com-manders distributed congratulatory certificates on much the same basis: Sassoon knew that he was not going to receive the hoped-for bar to his MC when a certificate appeared instead.

Discipline coerced men, comradeship and leadership buttressed their resolve, and decorations encouraged them. But scarcely less important was the army's growing realisation that the conditions of the front line were tolerable only for a limited period, and that once out of the line men must be allowed to enjoy themselves – as far as the demands of trench-digging and stores-carrying allowed. Even the simplest pleasures seemed Elysian to men who had recently emerged from a world of unbelievable filth laced with mortal danger. 'Did not a mess tin of stew, a tot of rum or whisky in a tin mug, taste more like divine nectar than the best champagne drunk out of the finest cut glass today?' asked Sidney Rogerson.

> The one meal of my life that I shall always remember, and
> can even now savour, consisted of an omelette for four
> eaten by one, with half a yard of French loaf, 'watered'
> down by two quarts of French beer. The subsequent
> instant panics were soon drowned in a sleep that lasted

round the clock and several hours on, and brought an
ever greater sense of relief.[286]

Getting clean and louse-free – and having one's dignity restored
in the process – was scarcely less important than eating and sleeping.
Front-line soldiers were almost invariably infested with the body
louse, *pediculus vestimentii*. The fully-grown female of the species was
about 4mm long, and the male slightly smaller: they were generally
grey, sometimes with a blueish streak in the middle, though sharp
colour variations caused great interest to their victims. They fed off
their human hosts, causing intense irritation and broken skin as they
did so, and the females laid eggs, about five at a time, in the seams
of clothing. One unit checked the shirts of all its soldiers, and found
that a mere 4.9 percent were louse-free. Just over 50 percent had
one to ten lice, and an unlucky 2.8 percent had over 350 lice. When
the lice found in trousers were added, the average soldier was found
to be host to 14.7 of the creatures.

Lice were known as chats, and soldiers conversed – 'chatted' –
while plucking them from their garments. A heated bayonet was
invaluable for dislodging them from the seams of a kilt. They could
be cracked between thumb and forefinger, but some soldiers felt
that destruction was more certain if they were dropped, with a gratifying pop, into a tin lid heated over a candle. Ernest Parker paid
tribute to their valour and determination, for even

> deloused shirts were not what they claimed to be, for dor-
> mant under the seams at the armpits were fresh platoons
> of parasites ready to come to life as soon as they were
> taken under our protection. In this way we maintained
> that the breeds were crossed, so that they survived the
> ceaseless war we waged on them.[287]

Stuart Dolden was deeply embarrassed when he first discovered that
he had lice, but saw that his comrades were at work on the seams
of their clothes with lighted cigarettes, burning out the eggs, so he
knew that he was not alone. He plied them with Keatings, a well-
known insecticide, but they seemed to thrive on it. Anthony French
remained a 'Vinny Virgin', louse-free, for three months, but it all
ended when he anointed himself with anti-louse ointment.

Almost immediately they found me. They thrived and multiplied and gorged themselves on the pomade and then
turned their attention to me. I was never alone. I became
louse-conscious. And I joined my colonel and my comrades in the daily hunting routine.[288]

Even shaving was a delight. Although men shaved as best they
could in the front line, sometimes using a splash of hot tea to moisten
the stubble, in many trenches this was impossible and most soldiers
grew beards. Even Ernest Shephard, that tough and efficient sergeant-major, acknowledged that he and his men were bearded, filthy,
and stank like polecats. When Second Lieutenant C. H. Gaskell
joined 1/Wiltshire on the Aisne in September he noted that: 'They
nearly all had beards – officers and men – and were literally covered
in mud and wet through.'[289] Joseph Maclean wrote from his trench
in 1917 that: 'I haven't washed or shaved for a week and look like
a Boche prisoner.'[290] After getting up the morning after coming out
of the line on the Somme, Captain Rogerson shaved: 'What bliss
it was to lather up and feel the razor shaving off this unwelcome
growth.'[291]

The army quickly recognised that private ingenuity was no answer
to getting clean and louse-free. There were properly-organised
communal baths by early 1915, and within a year divisions had bathing facilities through which personnel were rotated when out of the
line. Barring bad luck and major battles, many soldiers could expect
a weekly bath, as much as might have been expected in most working-
class households in peacetime. While men had a hot bath, their
clothes were steam cleaned in an effort to rid them of lice and louse
eggs, and their shirts and underwear taken away for washing, repair
and eventual reissue. There were frequent angry protests when a
much-loved grey-back shirt, fluffy from repeated gentle washes (if
still a bit grubby and lousy), was replaced by a board-hard garment
fresh from delousing. And, as George Ashurst complained, 'the fumi-
gation had killed the lice all right and we had some relief from the
itching and scratching, but the seams of our pants and coats still
held thousands of lice eggs and we soon discovered that the warmth
of our bodies hatched them out again.'[292]

Ernest Parker visited his divisional baths in Poperinghe in 1915.

There, in batches of platoons, we handed our clothing to the orderlies and took our turn in the tubs, kept warm by continual addition of hot water. These improvised baths had been made by sawing in half the vats used for storing wine, and into each of them as many as four men would struggle with one piece of soap between them. After removing a month's dirt and thus thickening the water for our successors, we stood shivering while 'deloused' shirts and socks with our own fumigated tunics and slacks were handed over by the attendants.[293]

There was a similar establishment in a converted brewery at Pont de Nieppe, as Harry Ogle remembered.

There was little conversion necessary. The River Lys provided the necessary water, the vat room provided the bath tubs and water pipes, a storeroom was emptied for use as a dressing room, and all that was needed then was the installation of a stoving and fumigating plant. The vat room contained dozens of big wooden tubs of perhaps 200 gallons capacity, every one with water piping hot . . . The hot bath was a joyful event . . . Marching companies of soldiers in fatigue dress, carrying towels only, were a familiar sight on the Armentières road . . . They marched briskly along, always singing, arms swinging high, towels tucked under their shoulder straps.

Arrived at the Brasserie, the men filed into the big dressing room by a street door. Within they stripped naked. They put their boots on again, bundled their clothes together, leaving on the floor or on the benches only their braces, belts and service caps into which they put their personal gear. These were looked after by an NCO bath attendant. Next they pushed their bundles through a hatch in the storeroom wall and trooped, stark naked, looking and feeling ridiculous, on to the River Lys towing path. Within a few yards, fortunately, was the vat-room door. Every vat was big enough to accommodate two or three men at a time. The water was hot and deep. Soap lost was only with difficulty recovered. It was not provided by the bath people and that was the only snag.

> The rest was undiluted joy. The big, steamy room with its
> great tubs and innumerable steam pipes and water pipes
> rang with the noise of many voices raised in song or badi-
> nage or in exultant whoops of sheer delight.[294]

And in January 1918 a big ditch adjoining the dye factory at
Ribemont on the Oise was converted into a battalion bathhouse by
the stretcher-bearers of the London Scottish, but the awful weather,
coupled with the presence of dye in the water, meant that the scheme
was not a success, and its few users emerged muttering that they
were marked men.

When routine permitted, officers could expect to get away for the
day to Amiens, the mecca for units on the Somme, or Poperinghe,
for units in the salient. The two best restaurants in Amiens were
Godbert's and the Hôtel du Rhin, the latter home to many journalists
attached to general headquarters. Captain James Dunn contrasted
'the supercilious indifference with which they jostled past the mere
front-line officer ... with their alert deference when a red tab
entered the room'.[295] Second Lieutenant Thomas Nash recalled that:

> The English usually went to feed at the Hôtel du Rhin,
> where the food was not of the best, the charges very high
> and the service poor. At the Godbert the cooking was
> wonderful and every meal a work of art. It was not cheap,
> but it was jolly good. This particular day I met Papa Joffre
> having lunch there and mine was the only British uniform
> in the place. He returned my salutation very graciously
> and generously gave me his left hand to shake!![296]

In Poperinghe the military favourite was Cyril's, usually known as
Ginger's after 'the flame-headed, tart-tongued daughter of the
house'. Skindles was also popular. Although James Dunn thought
that its substantial civilian clientele helped keep its standards
higher, Henry Williamson regarded it as the classic British home
from home.

> In June 1916, an officer in the Rifle Brigade, enjoying egg
> and chips and a bottle of wine in a certain estaminet in
> Poperinghe, declared to his friends that it was as good a
> pub as Skindles in Maidenhead. The estaminet already

had a longish name painted on its front – Hôtel de la Bourse du Hoblon something or other – but no one took any notice of that. The British officers soon began to call it Skindles, and very soon the three rooms on the ground floor were crowded with tables, and the tables with bottles; and around the bottles . . . sat the British officers smoking, laughing, eating or waiting to eat, and shouting the name of Zoë, which was the name of the daughter of the 'Mother of the Soldiers', as madame was called. The officer of the Rifle Brigade was killed on the Somme a few weeks later, as were nearly all his friends; but others came, and vanished, and others after them; and many, many more stretched their booted and puttee'd legs under the tables and drank in the fug of tobacco smoke and laughter; until the guns were silent and the feet of men marching at night were rarely heard, and upon the 'Mother of the Soldiers' and her helpers fell a strange loneliness.[297]

NCOs and men found it hard to get to Amiens: indeed, the journey often involved a good deal of lorry-hopping even by officers. Poperinghe, closer to the front, and the railhead for units in the salient, was far easier. Many establishments were out of bounds to other ranks, and in any case there was a natural tendency for each to cleave to its own. Frank Richards maintained that a brief halt at Le Cateau in August 1914 was 'the only time during the whole war that I saw officers and men buying food and drink in the same café'.[298]

Although the post-conscription influx of soldiers with private incomes meant that some could indeed afford to eat where they liked – one told an officer 'I have independent means, sir, and am interested in agriculture' – most would have sympathised with George Coppard when he declared: 'My saddest memory of the war is my continual state of poverty.'[299] The Reverend Andrew Clark, a vicar from Essex, heard soldiers complaining about their pay to a hymn-tune:

> We are but little children weak
> Who only earn eight bob a week
> The more we work the more we may
> It makes no difference to our pay.[300]

Soldiers were usually paid irregularly, in arrears: their paybooks, which had to be carried at all times, gave details of entitlements and stoppages. An officer designated to pay his unit drew the money from a field cashier, and soldiers were then paid in cash, in local currency, at a pay parade, signing an acquittance roll which the officer than used to support his original draft on the cashier. Or not, as the case may be. Officers were sometimes killed or wounded before they had the opportunity to submit the roll, and the Pay Department maintained a long guerrilla war against ex-officers well into the 1920s, trying, in the perennially mean-spirited way of such departments, to find out just how Mr Snodgrass managed to mislay 12 Platoon's acquittance roll during the battle of the Somme: he must either furnish it, obtain signatures in lieu, or pay up.

A man might get less than his allotted pay because he was on stoppages – either to pay for lost kit or barrack damages, or because his pay was being docked for disciplinary reasons – and most soldiers made an 'allotment' which went straight to their families back home. Proficiency pay was added for soldiers who passed special courses, but when George Adams qualified as a machine-gunner in August 1915 he told his parents: 'We have been told that we are entitled to an extra tanner [sixpence] a day as soon as we are proficient but I expect that will go the same way as proficiency pay for firing the rifle.' He thought that he should now be on 1/8d a day, and felt 'real goosy' at the prospect of getting it. But he had been right in the first place: he received less than he expected, and was told to expect the balance of his pay in England 'after this job out here is finished'. When he finished the course he was told that the machine-gunner's qualification badge would cost him 1/9d (out of his pay) and so he asked his mother to run one up for him in white cotton on khaki instead.[301] In addition, soldiers who had been well paid in civilian life became increasingly bitter about strikes in Britain and the wages received by munitions workers, now mainly women. The Reverend Clark noted in his diary with a note of disapproval how one munitions girl had apparently just spent 18/11d on a hat.

Most of the men looking for food and drink just behind the lines were thus usually short of cash, and found a wide range of estaminets which met their needs by providing the staple of egg and chips with white wine or (notoriously watery) beer for around 1 franc, a little under a shilling. Only officers were allowed to drink spirits, but many establishments were willing to bypass the ban by surreptitiously reinforcing the coffee (with much nodding, winking and franglais), though military police would sometimes burst into estaminets to sniff cups in search of spirits. Frank Richards and his mate Paddy celebrated the award of their DCMs by escaping to an out-of-bounds café, where 'with *vin blong*, the gramophone playing, and two fair damsels to dance with, we were celebrating very well'. The fun was spoiled by the military police, 'decent chaps' but obliged to run them in because the APM was nearby, and eight days' Field Punishment No. 1 was the outcome.[302]

While most estaminets were wholly respectable, with madame and daughters running front of house and monsieur toiling in the kitchen, others were less so. At the war's end Frank Crozier found Margot, the pretty waitress at his favourite hotel in Boulogne, in floods of tears. Although, she said, she had 'loved and been loved by many British officers during the hectic days' she had fallen deeply in love with 'a good-looking young British officer, son of a noble house, who – having slept with her on many occasions – promised to marry her'. She had just been jilted, and that very night she shot herself with a German pistol given her as a souvenir by a colonel.[303] Such stories did not always have totally tragic endings. One officer knew, from censoring an NCO's mail, that the man in question had a wife in England. But at the end of the war he announced that he would stay in France and 'marry' the proprietress of a nearby fish and chip shop, with whom he had a long-standing relationship.

And some estaminets had a good deal more than Pomfritz on offer, as Lance Corporal George Ashurst found in Armentières.

> Drink flowed freely in the estaminets and cafés, and as the music and singing went on the boys danced with mademoiselles in the flimsiest of dresses, or flirted with them at the tables, using the most vulgar of expressions. All the evening Tommies could be seen either going to or coming from the girls' rooms upstairs, queues actually forming on the stairs leading to these rooms.[304]

And then there were outright brothels where sex was the main item on the menu. These ranged from the establishments described by Gunner Aubrey Wade in the opening chapter, through *Le Drapeau Blanc* in Rouen – where several young officers on a draft conducted to the front by Robert Graves lost their virginity – to a decorous house behind the Somme battlefield whose beautiful and engaging ladies bore as little resemblance to the pale and overworked women of the notorious Rue des Bons Enfants in Armentières as a regular footguards battalion did to a down-on-its-luck pioneer battalion. Haig, an abstemious man, often used to stop at a café for a light lunch during visits to units or headquarters, and on one occasion selected this most up-market of bawdy houses. He remained wholly unaware of its real *raison d'être*, and the story caused huge delight.

Most soldiers of the old regular army had a vigorous interest in sex, and the likes of Frank Richards were usually prepared to engage a fleeting target at a moment's notice. Wartime soldiers ranged from the determinedly moral to those who quickly discovered an appetite for casual sex which might have lain dormant but for the war. Patriotic girls in England were often happy to oblige departing warriors, and one of Eric Hiscock's comrades, Corporal Thomas (his real name Reginald, but universally known as John), embarked upon a lifelong obsession after a barmaid from the Eagle and Child public house in Oxford slipped into his sentry box outside the Corn Exchange to make the Ultimate Sacrifice. He constantly volunteered for guard thereafter, and would stagger off duty 'exultant but weary'. However, by 1919 he had contracted venereal disease and he shot himself rather than face the shame of a VD hospital.

For some the urgency grew in direct proportion to the danger, and one soldier's lasting memory of going up the line of Second Ypres was of a young Highlander, kilt pulled up, making passionate love to a shopgirl. Arthur Osburn wisely observed that:

> Plants and animals and men, when stress or privation threaten the extinction of their species, will hastily, even prematurely, 'cast their seed'. That last fling by the young conscript in the brothels of Swansea or Havre before he went up to the shambles of Ypres was due to an instinctive

urge: for the very young soldier it was probably his *first* fling, as it might be his last.[305]

The army's wider sexuality was much more complex than the sort of smash and grab urgency displayed by so many. Sensitive men – and there were a good many throughout the army – valued women as a symbol of decency and peacetime normality. Sidney Rogerson thought that: 'Women stood as a symbol of all that we were missing . . . The point is that the longing was sensuous as opposed to sensual.' He noted how officers bought bath crystals, hair oil and pomade behind the lines because their squalid lives made them eager for the trappings of another world.[306] In 1914–15 many young officers went from public school to the front with no opportunity to grow up in between. In peacetime married subalterns were rare, and even in mid-1916 there were often few married officers in the average company or battery mess. They were barraged with questions about how one actually went about sex, and for many a youngster the real question was whether it was best to 'play the game and stay clean' or, with death such a familiar friend, to lose their virginity before the reaper called. Charles Carrington went so far as to point to an 'anxious obsession' with sex amongst his comrades.

P. J. Campbell thought that the young men of his generation needed 'love and laughter, occasional pleasures, affectionate comradeship always'. He was deeply smitten by a French girl whose long hair accidentally brushed against his hand in a shop, though that was as far as things went. On leave in Paris a major offered to find him a 'safe, clean prostitute' for 200 francs (at about £8, no mean outlay for an officer on 7/6d a day). He declined, but bought some postcards (probably of Kirtchners' long-legged bestockinged beauties, such a favourite in officers' messes) and pinned them to the wall of his dugout.

Many soldiers fell in love, or something very like it, with French or Belgian girls, and there were many wartime marriages. And there were British women in France in growing numbers, first nurses in the hospitals behind the front, and later the uniformed drivers of the Women's Army Auxiliary Corps. The WAAC drivers were sternly ordered to have nothing to do with officers: Crozier knew that he was contravening regulations when he gave lunch to Madge, wife of a brother officer: they agreed that as he was a general they might break the rules safely. But nurses and drivers alike were hotly, and by no means fruitlessly, pursued. When the well-regarded Captain Yates, quartermaster of 2/Royal Welch Fusiliers, was looking for billets in La Panne in August 1917 he shone his torch into a doorway only to find:

> two nurses, each with a squire in very close attendance. Yates was told to 'get out' . . . 'I'm an officer, a lieutenant,' said one of the squires. 'Well,' said Yates, in his diluted Lancashire, 'I'm a captain, but I don't want to spoil sport, just to find my billet.'[307]

Charles Carrington wondered whether 'there is a homosexual element in *esprit de corps*? Was there a tendency to reject the notion of women's society to derive an emotional satisfaction from a world of men only?' There was certainly a powerful emotional undertow in the relationship between men. Captain Herbert Read looked at his company and thought of the day when the war would end and they would be separated for ever. He did not know 'What time your life became mine,' and reflected on the marches, nights in trenches, battles and 'many acts and quiet observances' that had brought him so close to his Yorkshire soldiers. And at the moment of parting:

> I know that I'll wander with a cry:
> 'O beautiful men, O men I loved,
> O whither are you gone, my company?'

It would be easy to misjudge the extraordinary tenderness that soldiers were capable of showing one another, but there was usually nothing physically sexual in such relationships. Alfred Hale observed that two old corporals in his tent slept together, and he thought nothing of it.

At the time homosexuality was an offence against civil and military law, and 8 officers and 153 soldiers were actually court-martialled for 'indecency' on active service during the war. Arthur Osburn maintained that some officers and men deliberately admitted to homosexuality in order to be court-martialled, for a conviction would result in two years' imprisonment in a British prison. He heard one officer announce, in a crowded leave train: 'I've had two years of the War, and that's as much as I can stand. I intend to get out of it this time even if I have to arrange to be caught red-handed in someone else's bunk!'[308] Osburn, by then a lieutenant colonel, did nothing at the time, but when he mentioned it to the assistant provost marshal at Poperinghe the fellow shrugged his shoulders, for the ruse was already well known. In fact the number of courts martial for 'indecency' is surprisingly low. It reflects several facts. Firstly, some homosexual officers and men sublimated their desires, at what cost we will never know. Secondly, there was often a clear understanding that soldiers in monogamous relationships ought not to be penalised. David Jones wrote movingly of a homosexual couple in his company, and at the battle's end how:

> . . . Bates without Coldpepper
> Digs like a Bunyan muck-raker for his weight of woe.[309]

And thirdly, it was often easy enough for officers to masturbate in a two-man room in a hut, or for private soldiers to do the same in the dark recesses of a tent or dugout. 'Brook, Jackson and myself all had some homosexual tendencies,' wrote Eric Hiscock, 'and in the days and nights of stress we masturbated, but kisses on unshaven faces were rare, and then only at moments of acute danger.[310] He was propositioned twice, once by an officer who victimised him for his refusal, and then by a middle-aged private on a leave train, who gave him 10 shillings to keep quiet about some sleepy fondling.

Hiscock gambled the 10 shillings playing crown and anchor on the boat back to England, and here he was in good company. Gambling was officially forbidden, but crown and anchor was as universal in the British army as the card game *skat* was in the German. The banker kept a cloth and die bearing crown, anchor, heart, club, spade and diamond. The cloth was spread, the die was rattled, and men were encouraged to step up and put their money on one of the symbols. An experienced crown and anchor man's patter was a delight.

> Come and put your money with the lucky old man. I touch
> the money, but I never touch the dice. Any more for the

lucky old heart? Make it even on the lucky old heart:
are you all done, gentlemen ... *Are you all done?* ... The
diamond, meat-hook, and lucky old sergeant-major ...
Now, then, will anybody down on his luck put a little bit
of snow [some silver] on the curse? Does anyone say a bit
of snow on the old hook? Has no one thought of the
pioneer's tool? Are you all done, gentlemen? *Are you all
done?* ...[311]

Harry Ogle thought that crown and anchor men were 'no ordinary
men', and that they must have begun early as 'newspaper boys, then
hangers-on, tipster's boys, frequenters of back-alley precincts, fetch
and carry boys on racecourses ... Their patter was continuous,
spoken with a voice always raucous, but untiring and effortless ...'.[312]

Gambling went on in billets and estaminets, but it was generally
unsafe in the great variety of canteens that sprang up in the rear
areas. Ogle remembered Lady Egerton's Coffee House at Rouen:

a large wooden hut which looked grim outside but inside
was gay with the flags of all the allied nations, hanging
from rafters and spars. There were men returning from
leave, men from hospital and men in new drafts. Some
sat at tables writing letters or field postcards, or drinking
cocoa. Others just sat patiently until some NCO came in
with shouted instructions.[313]

Then there were the bigger YMCA canteens, well stocked with pro-
visions of all sorts for those who could afford them. In the autumn
of 1916 a huge marquee appeared in Bazentin Wood, literally on
the Somme battlefield:

The canteen had a trestle table-counter stacked with *everything* ... that could be eaten or smoked or mixed for
drinking. There were biscuits, slab cake, dates in fancy
boxes, figs, chocolates and sweets, oranges, tins of sweet-
ened milk, of cocoa, bottle of camp coffee ... Hoe's Sauce
and Tomato Ketchup.[314]

And right at the other extreme were tiny, one-man establishments,
often run by clergymen charging only cost price for their wares, in
the very shadow of the front line. Rowland Feilding found one in

an emplacement on the recently-taken Messines Ridge, run by a 'fine sportsman' who was 'a Nonconformist minister. We shook hands and I congratulated him on his effort. For his cash-box he had a German machine-gun belt box.'[315]

If some pleasures, like sex and gambling, were either private or forbidden, others were officially organised, and it was here that the rich variety of the regimental system made itself felt. Regiments took pride in pushing the boat out on key anniversaries or national saints' days, and particularly on Christmas Day, when it was an army tradition that the officers waited on the men. On Christmas Day 1917 the NCOs and men of 1/1st South Midland Field Ambulance sat down to a Christmas dinner of roast pork, cabbage, onions, potatoes, apple sauce, plum pudding, apples, oranges, wine and cigarettes. The printed menu proudly announced that the chef was 'Lance Corporal Draycott', and his assistants 'Privates Hood and Raybould'.[316] The year before the junior ranks of 2/Royal Welch Fusiliers had enjoyed soup, roast meat with potatoes, carrots, turnips and onions, plum pudding, with an apple or orange, and nuts. The sergeants had whisky, port and cigars in addition, and at 5.00 p.m. there was tea with cake, candied fruit and sweets, and a canteen-full of beer for every man. The officers, dining in company messes, did even better, with *pâté de foie gras*, curried prawns, roast goose, potatoes, cauliflower, plum pudding, anchovies on toast, and dessert, the whole lubricated with Veuve Cliquot, port, cognac, Benedictine and coffee. The Royal Welch made much of St David's Day, Irish regiments paid vinous tribute to St Patrick, and the Scots duly celebrated St Andrew. On Minden Day, 1 August, the six Minden regiments celebrated the bravery of their forefathers, who had attacked a superior body of French cavalry in 1759. New traditions sat alongside old. In 1915 the London Scottish held an all-ranks lunch in a ruined factory in French Flanders to mark the anniversary of the regiment's first battle at Messines the year before, and there was 'Soup, Roast Beef, Plum Duff . . . also whisky for those that were inclined'.[317]

Etonians celebrated 4 June in proper style. Lieutenant C. P. Blacker went to the 1917 dinner with fellow Old Etonians in his battalion, and found 300 guests seated, not by army seniority, but according to the dates when they had been at school. Sadly, the evening got out of control with the sort of high spirits which would have been vandalism (with sore heads and field punishment to follow) had it occurred in a canteen. A speech by Lord Cavan was inaudible; a group climbed onto the table, 'forming a ram as in Eton football', and the table collapsed. Eventually 'everything breakable in and around the room – tables, chairs, bottles, glasses, windows – was systematically smashed'. Blacker's disgust with the performance made him feel 'out of gear with my old school'.[318]

Music halls played such an important part in pre-war popular culture that it is hardly surprising that they were quickly replicated on the Western Front in the form of divisional concert parties. Some actors were professional, others talented amateurs. The 4th Division's Follies led the way in December 1914, and soon there were dozens of others, with names like The Volatiles, The Snipers, The Duds, The Pipsqueaks, The Whizzbangs, The Lads and The Verey Lights. Their repertoire was a mixture of songs and sketches, part cribbed from the London music hall and part extemporised to reflect life at the front: men relished sentimentality, popular songs and, of course, actors in drag. Soldiers remarked that some of these were very convincing indeed, although it was acknowledged that getting the shoulders quite right was never easy. In 25/Royal Fusiliers the quartermaster, against all the odds, was transformed into a convincing woman, and had his audience 'indulging in delightful fantasies that brought them substantial memories of the girls they had left behind in London, Manchester, Glasgow, wherever.'[319]

Really good 'female' leads were so important that divisional staffs became involved in finding them. Lieutenant Colonel Walter Nicholson, then in 51st Highland Division, tried to swap Private Connell of the Highland Light Infantry, star of the 32nd Division concert party, for two radial machine-gun mountings, and when negotiations broke down, promptly 'kidnapped' him, with the army commander's approval, and transferred him to the divisional artillery. Nicholson thought that The Duds of 17th Division were 'perhaps the best in the country'. It was his policy to have a show every night, and a new one would open just a day after a divisional move. He noted sadly that his star, Isabelle de Holstuff – alias Private Plumstead – went the way of so many leading ladies, by first showing 'a tendency to slovenliness' and then growing conceited. The best of the concert parties 'reached a high level, thanks to the talent available . . . But perhaps the standard of the shows and their popularity could be counted as a measure of our mentality under strain; they might have bored us in the piping times of peace.'[320] Some officers found the material rather too near the knuckle, but John Reith, who saw The Follies in 1915, thought it 'quite elaborately done, clever, and thoroughly enjoyable'.[321]

Concert parties were more than just a cheap way to entertain the troops. Like songs on the march, they provided an outlet for resentments, and enabled soldiers to take a gentle poke at authority. Private Walkey, a machine-gunner in 1/20th London and talented lyricist until his death at Loos, set new words to a popular song.

> Hullo! Hullo! When's the next parade?
> Can't we have a minute to ourselves?
> Five, nine, three: another after tea.
> Oh! oh! oh! they've done us properly.
>
> Hullo! Hullo! What's their dirty game,
> Working us at ninety in the shade?
> It wasn't the tale they told when we enlisted,
> Now it's all parade, parade, parade.

But though flag-waving patriotism was unpopular, there was plenty of room for divisional pride; 29th Division's party would sing:

> With a roll of the drums, the division comes
> Hotfoot to the battle's blast,
> When the good red sign swings into the line,
> Oh! There they'll fight to the last.[322]

So many of the habits of peace slipped easily into war. There were divisional horse shows and race meetings, both popular and well attended. This was partly because they gave drivers and transport men the chance to show their animals off to advantage, and partly because they offered the opportunity of seeing great men in the spotlight, with sturdy quartermasters bumping along in the 'Stores Stakes', and rather more horsey officers cracking round with their battalion's hopes (and a good deal of money) riding with them. In

July 1917 Rowland Feilding finished up in hospital, telling his wife that:

> I turned a somersault with my mare over the sandbag wall at the Royal Munster Sports yesterday . . . straining and tearing some muscles in my back, and breaking a bone or two in my left hand. The last I remember was crawling away from the course, and the soldiers clapping as I picked myself up from the ground. They are always like that.[323]

Transport was provided to give men days at the beach, and when the demands of the front permitted, leave centres on the coast could accommodate parties for up to two weeks: Stuart Dolden remembered 'twelve perfectly glorious days' at 5th Army Rest Camp near Equihen, Boulogne.[324]

But it was the army's passion for football that chimed most eloquently with the old life. James Jack complained that however tired men claimed to be, they would play football whenever the opportunity arose. Bernard Martin agreed that:

> On every possible occasion the men turned to sport. We had inter-Platoon matches and inter-Company Championships, football most of the year, in summer cricket. We played in any weather, on any condition of ground where we happened to be and at all available times: for instance a match between my company and B Company only a few hours before we started a night trek to relieve a battalion of Warwicks in the front line. I wrote the score on the back of a trench map; we won 3–0, and I added, below, the names of two officers killed and three wounded during the relief.[325]

Edward Underhill admitted that a football match was 'quite good fun', even if the ball was an odd shape: 'Soccer, of course, the men only play that.'[326]

And there were quieter amusements. Men read voraciously across a literary spectrum of extraordinary breadth. There were the classics: Alan Hanbury Sparrow read Francis Bacon's *Essays* at Passchendaele, preferring it to *Handley Cross* or *The Pickwick Papers* which he normally carried. Private Norman Gladden enjoyed sentimentality, noting that authors like Charles Garvie and Elinor Glyn were always snapped up from bookshops. Lieutenant Charles Douie carried *The Dolly Dialogues*, Rider Haggard novels and *The Oxford Book of English Verse*, C. P. Blacker, who went to war with the two-volume *Principles of Psychology*, was absorbed, by August 1918, in Thomas Hardy's *Tess of the D'Urbervilles*. Blacker, spotted reading a book by Bertrand Russell while waiting for a train, was at once befriended by the railway transport officer, 'a distinguished linguist and scholar' who was working on the proofs of a book by Israel Zangwill. Private Groom 'found poetry helped . . . I took my school *Golden Treasury [of English Verse]* to France. Actually it became invaluable – it was my talisman – so much that when a whiz bang blew my haversack and its contents to smithereens I was windy for weeks until another *Golden Treasury* arrived from England.'[327] P. J. Campbell enjoyed *Framley Parsonage* because it described such a peaceful existence where getting into financial trouble was the worst thing that could possibly happen: 'that could not be so bad, I thought, as being FOO on the day of an attack'.[328] Stephen Graham saw his comrades read newspapers like the *London Mail* and *London Opinion*, and 'voraciously devour' the tub-thumping *John Bull*, while *The Times* and *Morning Post* remained 'comparatively untouched'.[329] And against all the odds, the adventure stories of Nat Gould, Jack London and Rudyard Kipling were the three most popular authors in military hospital libraries.

The army also generated literature of its own. 'Trench journals' or 'trench newspapers' appeared in ever-increasing numbers from early 1915. They generally started as newssheets published by individual units or formations and often became sophisticated productions containing announcements, news, a variety of humour, sketches and cartoons. *The Fifth Gloster Gazette*, for instance, was the journal of 5/Gloucesters, a territorial battalion which served in France in 1915–17, and fought in Italy from November 1917 to September 1918 when it returned to take part in the Hundred Days. The gazette was initially edited by the padre, the Reverend G. F. Helm MC, and one of its most notable contributors was Will Harvey, a talented poet who had joined as a private in 1914 and was commissioned after winning the DCM. Private K. A. Robertson, also later commissioned and awarded the MC, designed the cover and provided much of the artwork. Other contributors, writing under initials or pseudonyms, included Captain R. F. Rubinstein ('Fibulous') and Second Lieutenant Cyril Winterbotham ('C.W.W.'), who was killed the day after submitting his poem *The Wooden Cross*. Not all contributors were Glosters: Captain W. O. Downs MC, a promising playwright, killed in action, served in 4/Royal Berkshire, and the contributor 'Emma Kew' was Lieutenant Gedye of the Bristol Royal Field Artillery, also killed in action.[330]

Although *The Fifth Gloster Gazette* was produced in France till mid-1917, thereafter it was printed in Bristol and shipped to the front. In contrast, *The Wipers Times*, journal of the 24th Division, was generally printed 'in a rat infested cellar at Ypres'. Except for the final edition of December 1918 it was never produced outside the front-line area, and 'at one time the printing press was within 700 yards of the front line and above ground'.[331] It was edited by Captain F. J. Roberts of 12/Sherwood Foresters, and its contributors included the poet Gilbert Frankau, an officer in the divisional artillery. The printing press was rescued from a wrecked works in Ypres, and a sergeant in the Foresters, a printer in civilian life, soon restored it to working order, though the third edition was delayed because of 'the jealousy of our local competitors, Messrs. Hun and Co.' who 'brought some of the wall down on our machine' with a shell. *The Wipers Times* was unusual in that it was written, edited and printed so close to the front. Most other 'trench' journals were actually printed well behind the lines or, indeed, in Britain, and enjoyed a wide circulation amongst families and friends in the unit's recruiting area as well as in the units themselves.

Such journals contained announcements of decorations, promotions and casualties: the February 1917 edition of *The Fifth Gloster Gazette* proudly reported that Private H. W. Voller had been commissioned in the field, adding sadly that he had been 'since killed in action'. There were genuinely helpful hints on how to fill in the army-issue correspondence card or how to write to a prisoner of war in Germany, and tongue-in-cheek advice, for instance about the need for soldiers standing to attention while holding a dead rat to ensure that the creature's tail was in line with the seam of the trousers. But

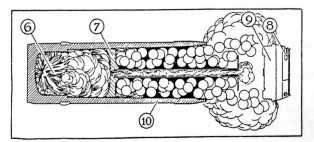

ACTION OF FLAME THROUGH CENTRAL TUBE AND IGNITION OF BASE CHARGE

(a) The setting of the time-train ring (not shown) determines the length of time the fuze will burn before exploding the base charge. Flame from this time train reaches the ignition pellet (1), exploding the magazine charge of black powder (2), whose flame flashes through the central tube (3), burning the fiber cup (4) and the cloth disc (5), and ignites the base charge (6) of loose black-powder.

ACTION OF BASE CHARGE AND FORMATION OF SMOKE BALL FROM MATRIX

(b) The ignition of the base charge and the generation of the explosive gases ejects the diaphram (7) and the balls with a velocity equal to the remaining velocity of the projectile plus 350 feet per second (the bursting velocity). This action forces the entire fuze (8) and the head (9) to strip the threads which attach them to the case (10) and fly forward. The matrix of resin, in which the balls were imbedded, is ignited and forms the smoke ball.

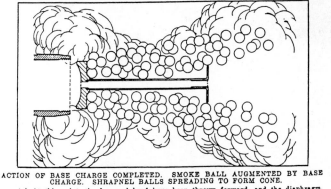

ACTION OF BASE CHARGE COMPLETED. SMOKE BALL AUGMENTED BY BASE CHARGE. SHRAPNEL BALLS SPREADING TO FORM CONE.

(c) At this point, the fuze and head have been thrown forward, and the diaphragm, tube, and balls are being acted upon by the forces of forward movement and centrifugal force to form the shrapnel cone; the empty case is retarded by the action of the bursting charge, and the smoke cloud is augmented by the white smoke from the base charge.

FIGURE 74. - ACTION OF SHRAPNEL AT TIME OF BURST.

An Ordnance School diagram showing how a shrapnel shell worked.

ABOVE Artillery forward observation officers of
12th Division, one using a periscope, direct fire
from the edge of Cuthbert Crater, near Arras,
April 1917. The two signallers are using field
telephones to pass orders back to the guns.

RIGHT A corporal of the West Yorkshires loading
a 3-inch Stokes mortar, Cambrin, February 1918.
The mortar bomb in the muzzle has had its safety
pin removed, while the bomb held ready in the dugout
still has the split-ring attached to the pin clearly visible.

BELOW The Mills bomb, the best of the British hand-
grenades, arrived in preservation wax which had to be
removed before it could be used, and grenades in
ready-to-use boxes in front trenches required regular
maintenance. This soldier is cleaning grenades outside
a dugout on the Somme, September 1916.

LEFT Map sheet 57c SW3 showing the central sector of
the Somme, 31 July 1916.

This belt-fed Vickers medium machine gun is rigged for use as an anti-aircraft weapon, Gavrelle sector, January 1918.

A Lewis gun covering the Lys canal at St Venant during the April 1918 German offensive. The No 1 is aiming the weapon and his No 2 has drums of fresh ammunition to hand.

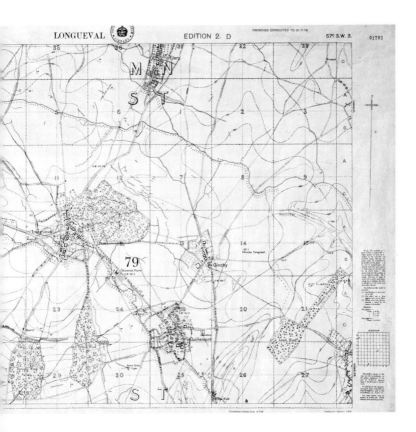

A YMCA stall at a walking wounded collecting post just behind the front during the Passchendaele battle. Stalls like this were run by clergymen and philanthropists of all sorts. One officer encountered a comrade's father, himself too old for the army, dispensing free tea and snacks close to the front in a Flanders winter.

Army Ordnance Corps soldiers enjoying a hand of cards on the Somme, mid-1916. They are sitting on a vast heap of 'toffee apples,' bombs fired from trench mortars by means of a metal spigot which fitted into the socket on the bomb and slipped down the mortar's muzzle

British and German officers in No Man's Land during the Christmas Truce of 1914. The British officers, on the right, are Second Lieutenant the Hon. Harold B. Robson and a comrade of the Northumberland Hussars.

The victim of this 1915 firing squad is described as a German spy. The photograph is probably authentic: the soldiers wear a mixture of pre-war service caps and 1915 trench caps, and their sergeant stands close behind them with his rifle smartly at the slope arms.

RIGHT An open-air canvas bath near Fricourt on the Somme, September 1916. The tails of the 'greyback' shirt were long enough to cover a man's dignity.

LEFT An advanced dressing station in a dugout near Ypres, summer 1917. Wounded, already given first aid and tagged by their regimental doctor, were given further treatment here and then moved on to a casualty clearing station. Some of these men have the coveted 'blighty one', a wound serious enough to earn evacuation but not severe enough to threaten life.

RIGHT A chaplain writing a letter for a wounded man at an advanced dressing station near Noyelles, 8 October 1918.

LEFT A chaplain, probably Father Dominic Devas, wearing the shamrock arm badge of 16th (Irish) Division, conducting a burial in a trench, 1916.

The wings of the morning. A chaplain preaching from the nacelle of an FE 2B night bomber, September 1918.

LEFT German prisoners arriving at 4th Army's main 'cage' at Dernancourt on the Somme, 15 September 1916.

RIGHT Relief shows in the faces of many of these Germans captured on the Somme, September 1916.

Vivent les alliés! British and French soldiers playing cards outside an estaminet, October 1914.

LEFT General Sir Herbert Plumer of 2nd Army decorating a woman ambulance driver for her bravery during an air-raid, 3 July 1918.

RIHT King George V presenting the Reverend Theodore Bailey Hardy with his Victoria Cross, 9 August 1918. Hardy earned the DSO and MC as well as the VC in eleven months, and was killed shortly after this photograph was taken. His daughter Elizabeth (third from left), serving in France as a VAD, had spent part of the previous evening cleaning her father's muddy boots.

RIGHT Two well turned out soldiers (cavalrymen or gunners because of their spurs) arriving on leave at a London terminus. Officers and men proceeding on leave were reminded that dress regulations must be strictly observed. They were not permitted to substitute shoes for boots, and officers were warned against omitting the cross-strap of their Sam Browne belts.

BELOW Soldiers on leave at Charing Cross station. Soldiers travelled in field service marching order, and infantrymen generally carried their rifles.

LEFT Back to the Front. Troops disembarking from the leave-boat at Boulogne, 30 January 1918. The highlander stepping ashore has four wound stripes on his left cuff, and an expression that speaks volumes.

what makes them so valuable is the insight they provide into what junior officers, NCOs and men – it is rare to find an editor above the rank of captain, and many contributors were private soldiers – actually thought about the war. Of course there were limits to comment and criticism, but the trench journals of the First World War, with their bottom-up attitudes, were quite different to other war publications, including, for instance, the Gulf War's *Sandy Times* – essentially a top-down official publication.

If *The Fifth Gloster Gazette* and *The Wipers Times* are, because of their modern facsimile editions, the best known of the trench journals, they are simply the tip of a mighty iceberg: the war reserve collection in the University Library at Cambridge comprises no less than 118 British and Commonwealth titles. Battalion journals had titles that were baldly descriptive (*The London Scottish Regimental Gazette*); humorous (*The Gasper* for the public schools battalions of the Royal Fusiliers or *The Mudlark* for 1/Bedfords) or historical (*The Minden Magazine* for the Lancashire Fusiliers). The titles of divisional journals varied from the punnish *The Direct Hit* (58th London Division) and *The Dump* (23rd Division) to the more patriotic *The Dagger, or London in the Line* (56th London Division).

Strong threads of consistency link trench journals. Overt patriotism was rare, and criticism of the government and its policy common. In January 1916 *The Gasper* satirised Asquith, then prime minister.

> O Free Man and Noble Man Asquith!
> A peerless Peer were he!
> But he clings to the lime like a principle mime,
> Spouting prodigiously.
> We may go to the wall, but were *Asquith* to fall
> 'Twere a criminal tragedy!

Nor did the Labour politician Ramsay Macdonald escape unscathed. In August 1917 *The BEF Times* described how 'Flamsey MacBonald' had addressed a great Labour meeting only to be heckled and booed: 'Mr Flamsey only looked pained and surprised at the ingratitude of the working man who grudged him his self-appointed task of doing nothing at £400 a year.'

'Are you a victim to optimism?' inquired *The Somme Times* of its readers in July 1916.

> You don't know? Then ask yourself the following questions. 1) Do you wake up in the morning feeling that all is going well for the Allies? 2) Do you sometimes think that the war will end in the next twelve months? 3) Do you consider our leaders are competent to conduct the war to a successful issue? If the answer is 'yes' to any one of these questions, then you are in the clutches of that dread disease.

England, according to *The Whizz-Bang* of January 1916, was a far-off land 'where no shells burst and no bullets fly'. *The Welsh Division New Year Souvenir* for 1917–18 described the war in an alphabet:

> E – why England! For whom we are fighting,
> Tho' it's awfully boresome and rarely exciting.

And yet there was still a regard for the Empire. As late as November 1918 *The Dagger* assured its readers that the British Empire was founded on hope and humanity, and the Canadian *Dead Horse Corner Gazette* of October 1915 affirmed that 'imperialism has ceased to be an empty phrase, it has become an actuality revitalized by national sacrifice'.

Pay was a constant theme. In July 1916 *The Fifth Gloster Gazette* set its readers a mock examination which included the question: 'A munitions worker works 5 hours a day, 5 days a week and draws £5 pay per week. Compare the scale of pay of those who make the shells and those who deliver them.' *The BEF Times* of 1 December 1916 declared:

> Here's to the lads of the PBI,
> Who live in a ditch that is never dry;
> Who grin through comfort and danger alike,
> Go 'over the top' when the chance comes to strike;
> Though they're living in Hell they are
> Cheery and gay,
> And draw their stipend of just one bob a day.

Officers and NCOs were gently sent up. A poet in the Welsh Division described a trench inspection.

> A subaltern stood in a blasted trench
> More like a field well ploughed.
> He cursed old Fritz for his dirty tricks
> And spoke his thoughts aloud:
>
> 'The Brigadier comes round today.
> What a lot of faults he'll find.
> His little book is full of notes
> And "strafes" of every kind.
> "What are these sand-bags doing here?
> Why is this place not clean?
> When did the Primus stove get lost?
> Where *has* that rifle been?
>
> Where are your men at work just now
> When did you visit your Posts?
> Why is this cook-house in this state?
> What's this? – Oh! Lord of hosts!"'

In Christmas 1916 the editor of *The Dump* commented on an unhelpful senior officer.

> I once asked a choleric Colonel
> To write something for this jolonel
> But I'm sorry to tell,
> He replied 'Go to —' Well,
> He consigned me to regions infolonel.

Poetry ranged from doggerel to dramatic and from parody to profundity. When we think of First World War poets we should consider not simply the great and the good, but the thousands of men who found in verse the only way of expressing the inexpressible. The poem *The Offside Leader* may feature in no anthology, but it says a good deal about the way field gunners thought about their horses.

> This is the wish as he told it to me,
> Of Gunner McPherson of Battery B.
> I want no medals or ribbons to wear,
> I've done my bit and I've had my share,

Of filth and fighting and blood and tears,
And doubt and death in the last four years.
My team and I were among the first
Contemptible few, when the war clouds burst,
We sweated our gun through dust and heat
We hauled her back in the big retreat,
With weary horses and short of shell
Turning out backs on them.
That was hell.
That was at Mons, but we came back there,
With shining horses and shells to spare,
And much I've suffered and much I've seen,
From Mons to Mons on the miles between.

Will Harvey had himself been posted as missing when the *Fifth Gloster Gazette* printed his tribute to his friend Second Lieutenant R. E. Knight DCM, who had died of wounds received on the Somme.

Dear, rash, warm-hearted friend,
So careless of the end,
So worldly-foolish so divinely-wise,
Who, caring not one jot
For place, gave all you'd got
To help your lesser fellow-men to rise.

But whether poetry attained such high seriousness, or was yet another parody of Omar Khayyam ('Awake! For Minnie in the Bowl of Night/Has flung the Bomb that puts the Rats to flight') it all helped make the trench journal what it was: part-funny and part-serious, proud and self-deriding, cynical yet supremely confident, an echo of a generation brought up to endure. It both reflected morale, and helped to sustain it.

The prospect of leave helped maintain morale, although, as we have already seen, it had a bittersweet tang, as so many men felt increasingly out of sympathy with the land that had given them birth. Once the leave system got into its swing in early 1915, leave was allocated by unit, with officers and men moving up steadily in a leave rota. Men received leave warrants which enabled them to travel to Boulogne and board a leave ship which took them to Folkestone, whence they travelled by train to Charing Cross or Victoria stations. Leave was normally for a week, although it was soon recognised that men travelling to the Western Isles would have run out of time by the time they reached home, so they were allocated extra days. In times of particular crisis leave was cancelled, and those still on the Continent were ordered to return to their units at once. There were frequent complaints that the system of leave allocation was unfair, and it was certainly true that generals and senior officers were able to get home far more regularly than private soldiers. One of Walter Nicholson's divisional commanders, Philip Robinson, always became irritable if he did not get back to his family every three months, while a private in an infantry battalion might well have to wait a year.

However, like so many of life's sought-after experiences, the reality of being on leave was often an anti-climax. P. J. Campbell wrote of the essential strangeness of being back in England, 'thinking about the men, wondering whose turn it was to go to the OP, and what the shelling had been like today'. When he was walking through Oxford in plain clothes, a corporal asked him if he would not rather be with the lads in France: 'a true answer would have been that I was already there, not here in the middle of Oxford'.[332] John Reith should have enjoyed dinner with his brother in London, but:

> I do not know whether it was the rich food to which one was a stranger, or the blaze of lights, or the orderly and ever-luxurious amenities; or the difference in atmosphere generally, and the crowds of young men who should, one thought, be in uniform. Anyhow it all jarred; I was out of touch with this sort of life and felt resentful of it.[333]

H. E. L. Mellersh thought that 'there was always some disappointment in these leaves, the difficulty to fit back, in so short a period, into home life, the feeling of alienation from the home front outlook. Rather, one wanted to be with one's companions but not at war: one wanted a binge, a spree, a night on the town, which meant going to "a show" which is to say to the theatre.'[334]

To the difficulty of fitting in was added the anguish of parting: it nearly finished even Frank Crozier. After saying goodbye to his wife and child at Charing Cross he declared: 'I vow to myself never to come on leave again, even if I get through.' Two days later he received a letter telling him: 'After you left . . . we went to the hotel and cried ourselves to sleep, Baba in my arms.'[335] It is small wonder that some men declined leave. 'I said Goodbye, Sir, when we left home,' said one soldier, 'I couldn't stand it again.'[336] And there was the final agony of returning to one's unit to find that familiar faces had gone. Norman Tennant 'was grieved to hear that Arthur Driver's brother and Gunner Gee had been killed at the OP during my absence. I felt very bad about this and in some way responsible for their loss.'[337] Like so many hundreds of thousands of men who made that short sea crossing he was drawn back to the front by a combination of legal obligation, the expectation of family and friends, and, above all, a sense of obligation to those he had left behind. The mixture was infinitely variable, but for most men, almost despite themselves, the carrot of mateship weighed heavier than the stick of coercion.

ENVOI

A new life began with the armistice. Captain Charles Douie declared that the soldier's abiding memory of the armistice was of silence free from gunfire, while the civilian's was one of enthusiastic noise. He knew at once that an old world had passed. 'We learned to hold in high account some values no longer of much account in a protected country – courage, fidelity, loyalty to friends,' he wrote. 'Death was to us a byword. Our lives were forfeit, and we knew it.'[1] He argued that while Britain had risen to meet the challenge of war, it was far less successful in meeting the expectations of peace, and this corrupted popular remembrance of the war, for 'the men who had never lost heart in the darkest hours of 1918' now faced the spectre of unemployment 'without the support of either the old comradeship or the old faith'.[2] Frank Richards DCM MM, still a private, having repeatedly turned down promotion, felt much the same. For him the armistice opened the door to: 'a funny world and I have come to the conclusion that the lead-swingers and the dodgers get on best in it. Since 1921 I have had a pretty tough time and have had long periods of unemployment and I expect there are thousands of old soldiers who are worse off than I am.'[3]

Even as silence replaced din on 11 November 1918, many men recognised that, as Graham Seton-Hutchison put it: 'The only life which they had ever known had come to an end; and the future opened mysteriously, offering what?'[4] T. P. Marks remembered his train journey home with veterans 'almost all of whom hoped to start a life of which they had dreamt in the trenches, in the wide steppes of Russia or on the River Piave'.[5] The blighting of these aspirations struck many veterans as the cruellest aspect of their service. Many of those who came to look upon the war as waste and sham did so, not at the time of the armistice, but through the lens of penury and disillusionment that characterised the postwar years for all too many of them.

'Only those men who actually march back from the battle line on 11th November, 1918, can ever know or realise the mixed feelings then in the hearts of combatants,' wrote Frank Crozier. 'We are dazed.'[6] Stuart Dolden was making breakfast for his company that day when he heard a gunner on a horse careering through the village yelling that the war was over. He assumed 'that the strain had been too much for him, and that something had snapped in his brain'. When the news was confirmed, he and his comrades did not 'conduct ourselves like a crowd of maniacs': they knew the Germans were doughty fighters, and feared that it might only be a truce. There was, however, a profound sense of relief: 'Frankly I had had enough, and felt thoroughly weary and in that respect I was not alone.'[7] The 2/Royal Welch Fusiliers greeted the news with 'anticlimax relieved by some spasmodic cheering . . . by a general atmosphere of "slacking off for the day" and by the notes of a lively band in the late afternoon'. One of its officers endorsed Charles Douie's reflections. 'To me the most remarkable feature of that day and night was the uncanny silence that pervaded,' he thought. 'No rumbling of guns, no staccato of machine guns, nor did the roar of exploding dumps break into the night as it had so often done. The War was over.'[8] Frank Richards, for his part, celebrated by adjourning to the cellar of a house and playing pontoon: 'About six hours later I rose up, stony broke . . . But I consoled myself with the thought that I had arrived in France broke and would leave it the same way.'[9]

Guy Chapman's comrades in the Royal Fusiliers accepted the armistice with a shrug.

> On 11th November we marched back fifteen miles to Bethencourt. A blanket of fog covered the countryside. At eleven o'clock we slung on our packs and tramped along the muddy pavé. The band played but there was very little singing. 'Before a man comes to be wise, he is half dead with catarrhs and aches, with sore eyes, and a worn-out body.' We were very old, very tired, and now very wise.[10]

Lancelot Spicer (Cambridge undergraduate four years before, and now a brigade major with DSO and MC and Bar) was overcome by sheer bewilderment. He was:

too deluged with the idea of the Armistice to write more
. . . Troops marching along the road by platoons at intervals – a fresh autumn day.

An early telegram has given the expected news 'Operations will cease at 11 a.m.'

The men cannot grasp it – they have become so used
to this soldier life, so numbed to endurance that they find
it hard to believe they can live otherwise.

At 11 o'clock, under orders (and for that reason only!)
the troops are halted and give three cheers – but there is
no enthusiasm. Of course they are glad it is all over – but
they do not realise it.[11]

Heavy casualties in the recent fighting of the Hundred Days were
uppermost in many minds. James Jack noted that his brigade had
lost two-thirds of its strength in a month, and all too many officers
and men knew of a comrade killed at the very end. Let one individual
tragedy stand for so many others. Eddie Giffard had not followed
his two elder brothers into the army, but went off from Marlborough
to help manage a sheep station in New South Wales. One brother
was badly wounded on the retreat from Mons and another was killed
at First Ypres. Eddie returned to England in 1914, joined the Royal
Artillery, and by 1918 was commanding a field battery. His last diary
entry, on 8 November, reports 'rumours of Armistice', but he never
lived to see it. He was killed shortly afterwards by one of the last
shells fired at his battery.[12]

The mood at GHQ was more upbeat: Reginald Tompson tells of
'a very cheery evening, but it was spoilt by the idiocy of the Adminis-
trator of the WAACS who refused to let them dance. A very boister-
ous evening.' Perhaps unsurprisingly, his diary for 12 November
reports: 'Rode early, with an awful head.'[13] Some units celebrated
with due formality. Burgon Bickersteth was in Leuze when the hour
struck, and: 'the trumpeters played "cease fire" and then the band
crashed out "God Save the King". The infantry presented arms, and
every cavalryman sat on his horse at attention, the officers saluting.
Then followed the *Marseillaise*, and after that the Belgian National
Anthem.'[14] The officers of William Carr's battery of Field Artillery
rode into Maubeuge and were royally entertained by the population.

After drinking a good deal they enjoyed a final sing-song, concluding with *Scots Wha Hae*, upon which they jumped on the only English officer present. 'The French were scared,' he remembered, 'I believe they feared we would kill him.'[15] Major Martin Littlewood was invited to celebrate with some Irish sappers, who had taken over a newly-liberated house. He had just enjoyed 'an excellent curry' when: 'A distraught lady in deep mourning burst into her home. She inspected our plates, and then hurried into the back garden. She came back even more upset, demanding: "But where is Henri, the children's friend?" Where indeed was the Belgian hare?'[16]

There was also ambivalence amongst those in England. H. E. L. Mellersh was on leave in London, and dropped in to see a comrade in Millbank Hospital before embarking for France. As he walked up Whitehall towards the West End, he felt strangely dissatisfied.

> I should have liked to have done a bit more since retiring
> from the March retreat; I should have liked to have won
> that MC. A munition girl passed me; and she called,
> 'What's the matter? – cheer up!!' Was I looking as gloomy
> as that? I was surprised at myself. I make no pretence that
> mine was a typical mood.'[17]

But there was certainly great rejoicing too. Captain Harry Ogle, on a course in Blackpool while recovering from a wound, was at once dismissed from his lecture, and he and his fellow students 'gave one yell and rushed out to join the others, and a surging throng of all ranks mingled with civilians to converge on the Town Hall square just when the Mayor of Blackpool announced the armistice. The town went wild with relief and joy.'[18] But many soldiers felt uneasy about entering into the spirit of it all. Lieutenant Ernest Parker drifted towards Trafalgar Square just in time for the official announcement.

> Soon lorries carrying munition workers began joy-riding
> through Trafalgar Square, the passengers dancing on the
> floors of the lorries and screaming at the top of their
> voices. Alas, I could not share their high spirits, for the new
> life which was now beckoning had involved an enormous
> sacrifice, and would be yet another challenge for those

like myself who had had the good fortune to survive the perils of the long war. Surrounded by people whose experiences had been so different, I felt myself a stranger and I was lost in thoughts they could not possibly share.[19]

The news found Robert Graves on leave in North Wales, and sent him 'out walking alone along the dyke above the marches of Rhuddlan, cursing and sobbing and thinking of the dead'.[20]

The overwhelming majority of the 1,859,000 troops in France and Belgium when the armistice came into effect were wartime volunteers or conscripts: about half of them were eighteen years old, and had known no real life before the war. As Sergeant Will Fisher observed in his diary on 12 November, there was: 'One topic of conversation now: demobilisation.'[21] A few soldiers took the view that they had automatically become civilians with the conclusion of hostilities, but were swiftly disabused. Brian Lathan, private in 1914 and now a captain lugging his baggage onto a boat for England, recalled that: 'The rank and file made it quite plain that in their opinion they had already done with the army, and demobilisation was only a formality.'[22]

There were noisier rumblings of discontent, provoked by the slowness of the demobilisation process and fears that all the jobs would have been snapped up by the first men to return, and in the winter of 1918–19 and beyond there were real fears amongst the army's high command of the spread of what it termed 'Bolshevism' in its ranks. Harold Macmillan admitted that: 'Even the high state of discipline of the Brigade of Guards was threatened, though it never yielded, by the genuine indignation which was felt.'[23] James Jack testified to 'serious insubordination in the back areas – none at the front – by the unfair way in which demobilisation is being conducted'.[24] While Charles Carrington's company remained 'soldiers, and good for any military duty, many of them were trade unionists, with a strong sense of solidarity, even if this meant a sympathetic strike'.[25] On balance, though, the 'soldiers' strikes' and other disturbances that winter were less an explosion of working-class consciousness than a firmly-expressed wish for citizen-soldiers to become civilians again.

A substantial force – over 32,000 men by August 1919 – was required to garrison the Rhineland territory relinquished under the terms of the armistice. Some units marched straight there, bands and regimental colours sent out from Britain to permit impressive entries into German cities. The army's peacetime standards of smartness were reimposed: the commanding officer of the Welsh Guards was reproved by his brigadier who had seen 'Two men going about like poets!' with long hair. Older soldiers from the Army of Occupation were demobilised individually over the months that followed, to be replaced by drafts of youngsters from England. Other units were disbanded in France, collapsing, like a deflated balloon, as officers and men were sent home for demobilisation. Units destined to be retained in the post-war army lost their wartime soldiers on demobilisation and were topped up with regulars from elsewhere. Although the men of Stephen Graham's Scots Guards battalion roared with laughter when an officer suggested that some might want to sign on as regulars, a couple of the six hundred in Guy Chapman's battalion were tempted:

> 'What do you want to stay on for, Hockley? You're married, got a family.' 'Well, Sir, do you think there's anyone else in England who'll keep my missus and kids and pay me a quid a week pocket money?' His logic was irresistible. He was re-engaged.[26]

Officers and men destined to return to civilian life were divided into demobilisation groups and each group subdivided into a range of demobilisation numbers, with different priorities for release. The first group, generally pre-war civil servants, were the demobilisers who would administer the system in Britain. The second group comprised 'pivotal men' who would, the government believed, create jobs for others. In the third category came the 'slip men' who had a slip filled out by an employer promising a job. Two remaining categories comprised men expected to find work rapidly, and those for whom the process was expected to be more difficult. All soldiers would report to one of twenty-six 'dispersal stations', where they would be given a ration book, pay for twenty-eight days' terminal leave, and a baggy civilian 'demob suit'. They could either keep their army greatcoat, give it in at the centre, or hand it in to any station master subsequently and receive £1 in return.

The system was sensible enough, but it had one serious flaw. It favoured men who had recently joined the army, because they were far more likely to be able to produce slips from potential employers or demonstrate their usefulness to the post-war economy. Men who had served longest were disadvantaged, and the dissatisfaction nerved some of the most serious disturbances, with soldiers in uniform taking part in protest marches with banners declaring: 'We Won the War, Give Us Our Tickets', and 'We Want Civvie Suits'. And there were many who agreed with Graham Greenwell that the system of numbering was decidedly odd. 'I wrote to Carew Hunt the other day and asked him to find out what was the position at Oxford,' he wrote. 'Students are "Class 43" on the demobilisation list – the last but one, whereas "Gentlemen" are in "Class 37". So it would seem better to be a mere gentleman.'[27] After the general election of 1918 the plan was effectively scrapped, and demobilisation went on at a faster pace, with 56 percent of officers and 78 percent of men eligible for release discharged in ten weeks: 14,000 men were demobilised daily at the height of the process.

Some found the business of discharge a brief punctuation in the longed-for transformation from soldier to civilian. Alfred Hale, demobilised at Fovant camp, 'a mass of corrugated iron and wooden huts' just west of Salisbury, could never again look at the branch line that took him home on the South-West Railway to Wimbledon 'without recollecting what it meant to me that afternoon'.[28] Ginger Byrne, on leave in London, fed up with the army, and well aware that 'firing machine guns and looking after them' had limited attraction to civilian employers, procured a slip from a friend of his sister's promising a job (which, like many such, never materialised). He was sent to the Machine Gun Corps pay office in Chelsea, and thence to the demobilisation centre at Crystal Place.

> I went in to the Crystal Palace a soldier with my rifle and equipment and everything on, and I came out the other a civvy – civvy clothes, civvy suit. And I drew thirty-five quid blood money – that's my gratuity, see. Out of the army and out of a job.[29]

It took Frank Dunham, another slip man, three visits to the London Records Office, but eventually his unit wired 'Release Approved' and off he went to 'Purfleet Demobilisation Camp, where I handed in all my kit and left for home'.[30]

George Coppard was convalescing at Alnwick, where he received his Military Medal from General Sir John Maxwell of Northern Command ('an exciting experience') when the war ended. 'I have always regretted that I was not in at the finish of the fighting,' he wrote. 'To have celebrated survival with those left of my old company would have been a privilege indeed.' He was demobilised just after his twenty-first birthday, with four and a half years' service, picking up a £28 gratuity and handing in his greatcoat for the £1. And then:

> I joined the queue for jobs as messengers, window cleaners and scullions. It was a complete let down for thousands of men like me, and for some young officers too. It was a common sight in London to see ex-officers with barrel organs, refusing to earn a living as beggars. Single men picked up twenty-one shillings a week unemployment pay as a special allowance, but there were no jobs for the 'heroes' who had won the war.[31]

Like so many other ex-soldiers he was bitter at the lavish grants for Field Marshal Haig and Admiral Beatty (£100,000 plus earldoms) and the £30,000 and viscountcies for the army commanders. It was the last act in the unlucky tactlessness which had so tainted the relationship between the red tabs and the rest.

For others, that swing of the hinge, as one life opened into another, grated painfully. 'My demobilisation papers came through in March [1919],' wrote William Carr. 'When it was time to go, I slipped quietly away unable to face the gunners, for the memories of all that had happened had come surging back in a great wave of emotion. The tears were streaming down my face.'[32] 'Looking back on those firm ranks as they marched into billets, to the Fusiliers' march,' wrote Guy Chapman, 'I found that this body of men had become so much part of me that its disintegration would tear away something I cared for more dearly than I could have believed. I was it, and it was I . . .'.[33] Charles Douie thought that battalions should

have been demobilised decently as formed bodies, not whittled away.
He remembered his own last parade, in the pre-dawn chill.

> I gave for the last time the familiar orders; the men dis-
> appeared into the cold and darkness. I returned to the
> mess-room and sat by the fire. I had several hours to wait
> but I had no desire to sleep again. In my last hours as a
> soldier I wanted to think, and in the firelight the memor-
> able years marched by.[34]

Young officers, so many of them 'temporary gentlemen' with wartime commissions, became increasingly aware of the impermanence
of their status. Guy Chapman recalled how:

> We were melting fast. In two months we should be down to
> cadre strength. We should be dispersed into an unfriendly
> world, Smith back at business, Whitehead sailing for Port
> Elizabeth, Gwinnell going east, Uncle in Chelsea. A com-
> mission for the employment of ex-service officers and men
> under the leadership of Sir Henry Lucy appeared at div-
> isional headquarters ... An elderly bilious person
> attended to my questions after he had explained patheti-
> cally that this was the first holiday he had taken for years.
> 'How old are you?' he asked. 'Twenty eight.' 'Oh you're
> far too old. I'm sorry. I can do nothing. Good morning.'
> Disconsolately I joined Smith and Blake outside. 'My old
> sod,' said Blake harshly, 'told me that military distinction
> was quite a useless distinction for civil life. Then I told
> him that I'd get a better job in London than he was ever
> likely to get; but that if he was going to hand out this kind
> of stuff to my subalterns, the sooner he cut his holiday
> short the better.'[35]

But J. B. Priestley, another temporary gentleman, was glad to get
out without a backward glance.

> No awards for gallantry had come – or were to come –
> my way; but I was entitled to certain medals and ribbons.
> I never applied for them; I was never sent them; I have
> never had them. Feeling that the giant locusts that had
> eaten my four and a half years could have them, glad to
> remember that never again would anybody tell me to carry

on, I shrugged the shoulders of a civvy coat that was a bad
fit, and carried on.[36]

It was soon told how 'ex-officer organ-grinders, cabmen and
railway porters became familiar objects of compassion'. In 1920 a
journal lamented:

> Ex-officers who . . . are turning their hands to many things.
> Brigadier-Generals are acting as company cooks to the
> R.I.C. [Royal Irish Constabulary]. Colonels are hawking
> vegetables. Majors are travelling in proprietary goods. Cap-
> tains are renovating derelict 'prams'. And subalterns are
> seeking anything which will keep them from having to fall
> back on charity or to beg in the streets.[37]

Alfred Pollard, a London insurance clerk who enlisted in 1914 and
was commissioned two years later, won the VC, DCM, MC and bar.
He was at one time reduced to trying to pawn his medals, but re-
couped his fortunes with the 1932 book *Fire Eater* in which he
described how much he had relished combat. Harry Carter, signals
sergeant in 2/South Staffordshire in 1914, ended the war commanding 7/South Staffordshire and earned a DSO and bar and an MC
and bar. He invested his £1,500 gratuity in a poultry farm which
failed, and then worked as a mechanic in a motorcycle factory and
as a steel erector.

Many temporary officers commissioned from the ranks returned
to their old trade and re-enlisted into the ranks. One spectacular
case was Lieutenant F. G. S. Thomas, compulsorily retired in 1924
under the 'Geddes axe' of army reductions. He immediately enlisted
as a gunner in No. 8 Mountain Battery on the North-West Frontier
of India, and was an imposing figure as his battery's right marker
on parade, with his impressive physique and MC. He was re-
commissioned in 1932, and badly wounded in 1941, winning a DSO,
as a battery commander in the Western Desert. Lastly, the demobilised officer became as much of a cliché in the novels of the postwar
years as the half-pay officer had been in books written after the
Napoleonic wars. The best-known example is Oliver Mellors, Lady
Chatterley's Lover indeed, an infantry officer turned gamekeeper.

Dissatisfaction with the new life reflected more than difficulty in

Envoi

finding jobs. 'The trouble was that so many civilian jobs seemed by comparison with fighting for one's country, unromantic, petty, even undignified,' mused H. E. L. Mellersh.

> No doubt many of us had ideas above our station: we had been somebody during the war and we expected to continue to be somebody. Perhaps it was a good thing that I had not got that MC or that temporary captaincy, for I might have felt more like that myself. Perhaps also we contributed to the disillusionment ourselves by conforming unconsciously, that is to say, to the tradition of peacetime employment, the tradition of having an unheroic cash nexus . . . one did not strike in the army, for pay or anything else. It had probably never occurred to me that I was employed, and for pay . . . There *was* a nobility in being a soldier.[38]

Some went even further. Graham Greenwell wrote that:

> The horrors of the Great War and the miseries of those who were called upon to take part have been described by innumerable writers. For my own part I have to confess that I look back on the years 1914–1918 as among the happiest I have ever spent. That they contained moments of boredom and depression, or sorrow for the loss of friends and of alarm for my personal safety, is indeed true enough. But to be perfectly fit, to live among pleasant companions, to have responsibility and a clearly defined job – these are great compensations when one is very young.[39]

Adrian Carton de Wiart, much-decorated and repeatedly wounded, agreed:

> Frankly I had enjoyed the war; it had given me many bad moments, lots of good ones, plenty of excitement, and with everything found for us. Now I had ample time for retrospection . . . Far and away the most interesting and important lesson I had learned was on man. War is a great leveller; it shows the man as he really is, not as he would like to be, nor as he would like you to think he is. It shows him stripped, with his greatness mixed with pathetic fears

and weaknesses, and though there were disappointments they were more than cancelled out by pleasant surprises of the little men who, suddenly, became larger than life.[40]

John Reith professed himself 'happy and absolutely thrilled with it', but his views might have changed had he remained in the infantry for the whole war. F. P. Roe had 'enjoyed the tremendous traditions and sense of comradeship which the army accorded' to the extent that he became a regular, served throughout the Second World War, and only in 1952 did he hang up his Sam Browne for the last time: 'It was the same unchanged belt that I had worn for nearly thirty eight years.'[41] And Charles Carrington echoed so many veterans in declaring: 'We were bonded together by a unity of experience that had shaken off every kind of illusion, and which was utterly unpretentious. The battalion was my home and my job, the only career I knew.'[42] It had of course been easier for officers to enjoy the war than it had been for ordinary soldiers: if they had more chance of being killed, they lived better out of the line. But one of Huntley Gordon's sergeants believed that most men were genuinely cheerful:

> the squalid side of the war doesn't matter to them at all, so long as they have their own friends with them and are fairly treated by their officers and NCOs. What does make them wild is to get about 2/6d a day and hear of Clydeside dockers and South Wales miners, who get at least five times as much, striking . . . to demand still higher pay.[43]

Horses, such a pride and comfort to so many men during the war, were also discharged. They were examined by vets and only the best were returned to Britain: the rest were sold locally, often for knock-down prices on a flooded market. This caused intense grief in the Middle East, where animals were harshly treated indeed. The troopers of an Australian Light Horse brigade held a race meeting one day and shot their horses the next. One summed up his feelings:

> Maybe I'll be court-martialled,
> but I'm damned if I'm inclined
> To go back to Australia
> and leave my horse behind.

Even in France and Belgium there was widespread resentment at another example of governmental parsimony. 'We stopped in the market square,' wrote Guy Chapman.

> It was the day of condemnation for our horses. They were to be examined by the ADVS [Assistant Director of Veterinary Services], and those which he cast were to be sold to the Belgians. Knowing the manner in which the natives treat their animals, we were as angry at this as at every other scheme which a vile administration was putting into practice. Hallam met me with a gap toothed grin more distended than ever. 'It's all right, sir. She's going home. Aren't you my beauty.' Ginger took her congratulations coldly. She was quite aware of her value. Home too was the sentence for Polly and the quarter-master's Bob. Something had been saved.[44]

Officers were allowed to buy their chargers if they passed the inspection. Captain Lloyd Evans of 2/Royal Welch Fusiliers:

> Negotiated for Jenny, the adjutant's hack; but my sentimental gesture fell through as she was graded 'for sale on the Continent'. Yates [the quartermaster] got Girlie . . . She was ridden with the Wynnstay Hounds, and reared a foal which was ridden with the Wynnstay; she lived until 1931.[45]

Some horses bore charmed lives. Cauliflower, a 15-hand bay mare with black points, carried Sergeant Major Lorimer of the Northumberland Hussars during the war. She returned home to take a Miss Straker hunting for fifty-three days in 1922–23 without once being 'sick or sorry'. Jones and Joubert, gun horses of J Battery RHA, out since Mons, went home in 1918 and, turned out in the stable yard of their Aldershot barracks, walked unhesitatingly to their old stalls. They had more of pre-war life to return to than many of the war's human survivors.

In strict terms the war created no 'Lost Generation'. Britain did not lose 'an entire generation of young poets, philosophers and politicians in the war', and the influenza epidemic of 1918–19 was far more destructive. But the actual death rate – one in four of men who served were under twenty-five years old in 1914 – is severe in itself, all the more so for selecting a high proportion of the bravest and the best. And, as J. M. Winter has demonstrated, the war killed a greater proportion of officers than other ranks, and 'privileged groups bore a disproportionately heavy burden of war losses . . .'[46] The war did not wipe out the aristocracy, though as C. F. G. Masterman observed shortly after the war, the aristocracy had not suffered such losses since the Wars of the Roses. David Cannadine echoed this, affirming that not since this time 'had so many patricians died so suddenly and violently'.[47] They made this sacrifice 'in the defence of a country that was gradually but irreversibly ceasing to be theirs'. The reduction in agricultural rents and the splitting up of great estates had begun well before the war: the movement was to accelerate into the 1920s and 1930s, and the loss of young aristocrats played its part in the process.

Gerald Gliddon's county survey shows how the war blighted the great houses of the land. Lord Anslow of Bangors Park in Buckinghamshire lost his son and heir in 1915; the Desboroughs of Taplow Court in Buckinghamshire lost two of their sons, Julian and Billy, in the war and a third, Ivo, was mortally injured in a car crash in 1926, and Lord Cawley of Berrington Park in Herefordshire lost three of his four boys. So it goes on, county by county and house by house.[48] A beautiful memorial chapel in St Barnabas Church, Ranmore, near Dorking, distracted my attention during a recent family wedding. It commemorates three of the four sons of Henry, 2nd Baron Ashcombe and his wife Maud. Henry was killed when the Guards Division attacked on the Somme on 15 September 1916, and Alick died with the 15th Hussars at Bourlon Wood in November 1917. William was killed charging with the Royal Dragoons near Ham on 24 March 1918 in what the Marquess of Anglesey calls one of the best examples of shock action of the whole war: up to 100 Germans were cut down and another 100 captured.

But the parish memorial plaque in the same church emphasises just how widely the burden was shared. This tiny parish lost fourteen of its men in the war, a toll multiplied, stone by stone by stone, on war memorials across the land. For in remembering the blood debt paid by the aristocracy, so well commemorated in bronze and ashlar, we should not forget how the process of volunteering early on in the war had also swept up the natural leaders of other social groups. I think particularly of militant miners, who volunteered in such numbers and died in a proportion that brings them their own hard nobility. As G. W. E. Russell wrote at the time: 'The burden of the war lies as heavy on the poor as on the rich, for neither poverty nor riches can mend a broken heart.'[49]

Amongst the 3,450 dead in the Australian Imperial Force Burial Ground, a Commonwealth War Graves Commission cemetery at Grass Lane, Flers, lie Lieutenant Colonel Charles, Earl of Feversham, Second Lieutenant Ernest Shephard and Sergeant Harold Jackson VC. Feversham left his broad acres, a pretty countess and happy children to die leading the battalion he had raised, 21/King's Royal Rifle Corps (the Yeoman Rifles to its many friends) in its first battle. Dogs were frequent visitors to the trenches and he had taken his deerhound to war: it too was killed, and was buried with him.[50] Shephard, a photographer's son from Lyme Regis, left home young and first went to sea before joing the Dorsets in 1909 at the age of seventeen. Lance corporal the next year, he was a corporal in 1913 and went to war as a sergeant, rising to company sergeant major in April 1914. He was commissioned in November 1916 and killed commanding a company of 5/Dorsets less than two months later. Professional to the last, when he saw that his position was untenable he sent a message warning a supporting company that it should not waste men and reinforce him. He lies seven miles from his 'dearest chum', CSM Sam Shapton, who went off for his last tour in the trenches in November 1915 despite being very ill. The RMO had told him that he could stay with the transport, and Shephard begged him to do so. 'No,' he told Shephard, 'I'm no quitter. I'll go with my boys.'[51] He was shot through the head. Harold Jackson was a wartime volunteer from Kirton, near Boston in Lincolnshire, who had won his VC in March 1918 but been killed on the old Somme battlefield in August 1918, underlining yet again the human cost of the last Hundred Days.

The 'lost generation' cannot simply be charted by those who were killed or crippled, although the latter definition must certainly be widened to include men who returned broken in mind rather than body: in March 1939, 120,000 men were still receiving pensions or had received awards from primary psychiatric disability. And there were many who were not disabled but whose bodies never healed: I. G. Andrew's company commander, hit at Loos, had to have his wound dressed daily for the rest of his long life. There were thousands, across the whole social spectrum, who came home unable to take much interest in things that might have excited them before the war. A. J. P. Taylor suggested that the real 'lost generation' were the men who might, but for the war, have gone into politics, and whose absence from the political stage contributed to a lack of leadership which was to cast its own dark shadow into the 1930s.

Britain had begun to remember her dead while the war was still on, with 'street shrines', the first of which was established in an east London street where sixty-five men had enlisted from forty houses. The Imperial War Museum was established in 1917 specifically to commemorate the war, and after the armistice a great range of memorials, public and private, sprang up across the land, marking a sacrifice which was wholly unprecedented. What became the Imperial War Graves Commission was established as the Graves Registration Commission in March 1915, and was responsible for the identification and burial of British and Commonwealth war dead, and for the commemoration of the missing on those huge memorials of which Thiepval and Tyne Cot are perhaps the best known. The memorialisation of the war has spun off on its own trajectory long after official memorials were completed, and the cemeteries received headstones to replace their wooden crosses in the 1930s. In recent years the Accrington Pals have received their memorial, a brick wall on the edge of the copse from which they attacked; a dignified stone commemorates the Liverpool and Manchester Pals' battalions who took Montauban on 1 July 1916, and the dragon of the 38th Welsh Division glares out at Mametz Wood. The Irish Peace Park on Messines Ridge, commemorating *all* Ireland's dead, has an imposing stone tower at its centre, and at 11.00 a.m. on 11 November each year the sun shrines straight from memorial stone to tower, like a sundial marking the passage of lives rather than time. It is a long-deserved recognition, for many Southern Irish soldiers who fought so well for Britain found themselves undeservedly mistrusted by their comrades in arms after the Easter Rising of 1916, and were later discriminated against in a newly-independent nation.

Families were allowed to add their own inscriptions to the graves of their loved ones, and these, like so much else, chart the war's ambivalence. There is pride. Private E. George of the 3rd Hussars lies beside the gentle Aisne, and his parents' inscription affirms: 'A SOLDIER'S SON, A SOLDIER'S BROTHER, HE DIED AS A SOLDIER SHOULD'. The parents of Second Lieutenant W. A. Stanhope Forbes, killed on the Somme, believed that: 'HE SAW BEYOND THE FILTH OF BATTLE AND THOUGHT DEATH A FAIR PRICE TO PAY TO BELONG TO THE COMPANY OF THESE FELLOWS'. Private Alf Goodlad of the Accringtons told his parents that: 'THE FRENCH ARE A GRAND NATION, AND WORTH FIGHTING FOR', and they have put it on his grave. Two brothers, buried near Serre, are '*UNIS DANS LE MORT COMME ILS L'ETAIENT DANS LA VIE*'. Captain M. K. Lloyd of the Grenadiers was killed on 15 September 1916, and his headstone tells us what he would have been as well as what he was, a veteran of First Ypres; he was also a baronet's only son.

There is cold fury too, like 'SCHOOL WAR DEATH' on a private's headstone at Cambrai and 'SACRIFICED TO THE FALLACY THAT WAR CAN END WAR' on a subaltern's at Tyne Cot. More often the Bible and Shakespeare play their dignified part, the latter never better than for Raymond Asquith: 'SMALL TIME BUT IN THAT SMALL MOST GREATLY LIVED THIS STAR OF ENGLAND'. Sometimes brave grief overwhelms me. What father of daughters can hope not to blink hard when he sees that a gunner captain's girls have had 'THE GOOD LORD HAS TAKEN AWAY OUR HERO DADDY' written above their father's grave. And often the graves themselves give us pause for thought. What incomprehensible fate brought Private Louis Cuckle from the Ukraine by way of Hull to die below Mountauban Ridge in a territorial battalion of the Seaforth Highlanders, and how did German-born Sergeant Major Kleinstuber, bandmaster of a Cameronian battalion, finish up in the same cemetery?

The eleventh hour of the eleventh month became the moment when the nation commemorated its war dead. The Cenotaph, a symbolic empty tomb in Whitehall, was unveiled by King George V on 11 November 1920, on the same day that the Unknown Warrior, an unidentified corpse chosen blindly from amongst the war dead, was interred in Westminster Abbey. It is hard for those of us used to the scale of modern commemoration to grasp just how well-attended Remembrance Day was, not simply in London but in towns and villages across the land, in the 1920s, as survivors and families gathered round new memorials to mourn and remember. Those who had been under fire were in a class of their own, and they knew it. They were at once grateful and guilty to have survived: 'We who are left know well that we would not be here if we had been as good men as they . . .'[52] 'As the two minutes silence ticks away . . .' wrote William Carr,

> I think of Watson at Cambrai, of Stevenson at Hangard, of a German machine-gunner and a stretcher party at Morlancourt. Armistice Day is not, as I heard one young minister of the kirk proclaim to a congregation of war veterans, an outdated glorification of war. We recall our comrades and our enemy and we pray for peace.[53]

Three medals distinguished those who had served on the Western Front in the first two years of the war. The Mons Star, or 1914–15 Star (issued depending on a the date of a man's arrival in France), the British War Medal and the Victory Medal all formed a trio nicknamed Pip, Squeak and Wilfred. Men who had arrived after 1 January 1916 received only the last two medals, small recognition for such service. At Remembrance Day in 1929, with unemployment cutting deep and too many medals gone to the pawnshop, hundreds of veterans turned out in proud defiance with their pawn tickets pinned to their lapels where the brass, nickel and ribbon used to go.

That very year Charles Douie (whose house at Rugby school had lost twenty-three of the fifty-six boys of his year) complained that: 'The war is an improper subject for conversation, and all references to it are dismissed except on Armistice Day. On one day of the year the dead at least have their meed of honour; the living are without honour even on that day.'[54] It is often said that the war's veterans never spoke about their experiences, but this is not true. They spoke freely to insiders, to comrades in national veterans' organisations, of which the British Legion, vigorously championed by Haig, became the best-known; in scores of smaller clubs and associations, and to the men remembered as 'uncles' by my father's generation, who unfailingly appeared in collar and tie on Sundays and talked about things as secret as the rites of some arcane religion. For just as wartime leave had drawn a sharp dividing line between front and Blighty, so the peace cut even deeper. There were things a man could never share, even, or perhaps especially, with those he loved the most. For how could you describe being splashed by your best friend's stomach contents, seeing barbed wire draped with entrails, or praying that the next shell would kill anyone, however much you admired them, rather than you? And how too could anyone understand the bliss of an army blanket on a stone floor, the delight of the quarter-bloke's shout of 'Gyp-oh' when the hot bacon fat was brought on, or the pleasure of listening to the fifes squealing in the little square at Corbie?

It is small wonder that we sometimes find them hard to grasp, and try to judge them by poems they never read, or cast them in dramas they would never have bothered to watch. Like so many wars, the First World War could have been averted by more astute diplomacy and waged with greater skill. Like so many peaces, that which followed it could have been better drafted or more capably sustained. Yet we must judge the men who fought the war by their motives and achievements, not by the conflict's origins or results. Let us, by all means, persist with those squabbles which will remain dear to historians. But let us never forget that generation whose courage and endurance lift my spirits and break my heart. And let us do better for their great-grandchildren than we did for them.

REFERENCES

Introduction

1 Brian Bond *The Unquiet Western Front* (Cambridge 2002) p. 26.
2 Omer Bartov 'Trauma and Absence: France and Germany 1914–1945' in Paul Addison and Angus Calder (eds) *Time to Kill: The Soldier's Experience of War in the West 1939–45* (London 1997) pp. 348–58.
3 Charles Carrington *Soldier from the Wars Returning* (London 1965) p. 264.
4 Cyril Falls *War Books* (London 1995) pp. i–ix.
5 See Frank Davies and Graham Maddocks *Bloody Red Tabs: General Officer Casualties of the Great War 1914–1918* (London 1995).
6 David Jones *In Parenthesis* (London 1961) p. xv.
7 Huntley Gordon *The Unreturning Army* (London 1967) p. 114.

The Old Front Line

1 This incident is based on an attack described in Hanway R. Cumming *A Brigadier in France* (London 1922), although I have varied the detail and changed some names. The tactics generally follow those laid down in the February 1917 General Staff Publication *SS144, The Normal Formation for the Attack.*
2 *Statistics of the Military Effort of the British Empire During the War* (London 1922) p. 64 (iii).
3 *Statistics* pp. 248, 251–2.
4 John Ellis *The Sharp End of War* (Newton Abbot 1980) p. 4.
5 Guy Chapman *A Passionate Prodigality* (London 1985) p. 187.
6 Henry Williamson *The Wet Flanders Plain* (London 1987) p. 96.
7 Graham Seton-Hutchison *Warrior* (London ND) p. 200.
8 Peter Doyle *Geology of the Western Front* (London 1988) p. 16.
9 'Arrival on the Somme', G. F. Ellenberger Papers, Department of Documents, Imperial War Museum.
10 Rowland Feilding *War Letters to a Wife* (London 1929) p. 76.
11 Bernard Martin *Poor Bloody Infantry: A Subaltern on the Western Front* (London 1987) p. 91.
12 Bruce Bairnsfather *Bullets and Billets* (London 1916) p. 238. Captain Bairnsfather was the originator of the fiercely-moustachioed cartoon character Old Bill, typical of the British regular in the early years of the war.
13 Quoted in Stéphane Audoin-Rouzeau *14–18: Les Combattants des tranchées* (Paris 1986) p. 88. Author's translation.
14 Michael Moynihan (ed) *A Place Called Armageddon* (Newton Abbot 1975) p. 128.
15 Peter Vansittart (ed) *John*

*Masefield's Letters from the Front
1915–17* (London 1984) p. 193.
16 C. P. Blacker *Have You Forgotten
Yet?* (London 2000) p. 60.
17 Capt. J. C. Dunn *The War the
Infantry Knew* (London 1987)
p. 261.
18 Frank Richards *Old Soldiers Never
Die* (London 1933) p. 13.
19 Stapleton Tench Eachus Diary
16 June 1916 on
www.wardiaries.co.uk.
20 Dunn *The War* p. 384.
21 Charles Carrington *Soldier from the
Wars* p. 136.
22 A. Lytton Sells (trans. and ed.)
*The Memoirs of James II: His Campaigns
as Duke of York 1652–1660*
(Bloomington, Indiana, 1962)
pp. 157, 189.
23 *Wipers Times* (London 1973) p. 6.
24 'Not King, nor Prince, nor Duke,
nor Count am I, I am the Lord of
Coucy.'
25 Dunn *The War* p. 223.
26 Captain R. H. D. Tompson Diary
1 September 1914, Tompson Papers,
private collection.
27 Dunn *The War* p. 236.
28 Feilding *War Letters* pp. 79, 33.
29 Second Lieutenant H. M.
Stanford to his parents, 11 and
28 November 1914, private
collection.
30 John Masefield *The Old Front Line*
(London 1917) p. 55.
31 Williamson *Wet Flanders Plain*
pp. 95, 167.
32 Ian Ousby *The Road to Verdun*
(London 2001) p. 263.
33 Ousby *Verdun* p. 269.
34 Masefield *Old Front Line* p. 11.
35 Major General Sir Ernest Swinton
(ed) *Twenty Years After: The Battlefields
of 1914–18 Then and Now* (2 vols,
London 1920) I p. 2.
36 Lord Hankey *The Supreme

Command 1914–18* (London 1961) 2
vols, I pp. 79–82.
37 Cited in Paul-Marie de la Gorce
*The French Army: A Military Political
History* (New York 1963) pp. 89–92.
The best modern scholarly study of
the French army in this period
remains Douglas Porch *The March to
the Marne* (Cambridge 1981).
38 Quoted in Michael Howard 'Men
Against Fire: The Doctrine of the
Offensive in 1914' in Peter Paret
(ed) *Makers of Modern Strategy*
(Oxford 1986) pp. 510–26.
39 Cited in Sir James Edmonds
*History of the Great War: Military
Operations, France and Belgium, 1914*
(London 1923–25) 2 vols, I
pp. 444–5.
40 Quoted in John Terraine *Douglas
Haig: The Educated Soldier* (London
1963) p. 181.
41 John Lucy *There's a Devil in the
Drum* (London 1938) pp. 113–14.
42 Lucy *Devil* p. 154.
43 Quoted in Richard Holmes *The
Little Field Marshal: Sir John French*
(London 1981) p. 233.
44 Quoted in Holmes *Little Field
Marshal* p. 239.
45 French to George V, 2 October
1914, in Royal Archives GV Q832/72.
46 Terraine *Haig* p. 79.
47 French to Kitchener, 18 March
1915, French Papers, Department of
Documents, Imperial War Museum.
48 French Diary 12 July 1915,
Department of Documents, Imperial
War Museum.
49 Haig Diary, 19 August 1915,
Haig Papers, National Library of
Scotland.
50 Minutes of 1st Army conference,
6 September 1915, Papers of
Lieutenant General Sir Richard
Butler, Department of Documents,
Imperial War Museum.

51 Captain G. C. Wynn *If Germany Attacks: The Battle in Depth in the West* (London 1940) p. 77.

52 Capt. W. L. Weetman to Lt. Col. Foljambe, 25 October 1915, private collection.

53 William Philpott 'Why the British were really on the Somme . . .' in *War in History* Vol 9 No 4 2002 p. 459.

54 Rawlinson to Colonel Clive Wigram (the king's assistant private secretary) 27 February 1917, quoted in Robin Prior and Trevor Wilson, *Command on the Western Front* (London 1992) p. 139.

55 Brigadier General John Charteris *At GHQ* (London 1931) p. 143.

56 'Report of the Army Commander's Remarks . . .' quoted in Prior and Wilson *Command* p. 155.

57 Robin Neillands *The Great War Generals on the Western Front 1914–18* (London 1998) p. 239.

58 Percy Jones Papers, Department of Documents, Imperial War Museum. Jones, a journalist on the weekly magazine *Truth*, had joined the territorials before the war and volunteered for overseas service on its outbreak. He survived, only to be drowned in an accident in 1919.

59 Prior and Wilson *Command* p. 191.

60 Scott Macfie Papers, Department of Documents, Imperial War Museum.

61 *Statistics* pp. 408–9 (shrapnel) and pp. 412–13 (high explosive).

62 Ernst Junger *The Storm of Steel* (London 1929) pp. 93, 99.

63 Terraine *Haig* p. 222.

64 Rawlinson to Wigram, 29 August 1916, Wigram Papers, private collection.

65 John Jolliffe (ed.) *Raymond Asquith: Life And Letters* (London 1980).

66 John Masefield *The Battle of the Somme* (London 1919) p. 94.

67 I cannot speak too highly of Martin and Mary Middlebrook's *The Somme Battlefields* (London 1991), a painstaking guide to these silent cities.

68 The essential analysis is M. J. Williams 'Thirty Per Cent: A Study in Casualty Statistics' in *Journal of the Royal United Services Institute* (February 1964) and 'The Treatment of German losses on the Somme in the British Official History' *Journal of the Royal United Services Institute* (February 1966).

69 Terraine *Haig* p. 232.

70 Charles Carrington (writing as Charles Edmonds) *A Subaltern's War* (London 1929) p. 114.

71 Paddy Griffith *Battle Tactics of the Western Front: The British Army's Art of Attack 1916–18* (London 1994) p. 65.

72 Jones *In Parenthesis* p. ix.

73 R. H. Tawney 'Some Reflections of a Soldier' in *Nation* October 1916.

74 Charteris *GHQ* p. 84.

75 The most scholarly recent account of the linkage between military and naval policy is Andrew A. Weist *Passchendaele and the Royal Navy* (Westport, Conn., 1995).

76 Terraine *Haig* p. 273.

77 Philip Gibbs *From Bapaume to Passchendaele 1917* (London 1918) p. 69.

78 Vansittart *Masefield's Letters* p. 223.

79 Rudolf Binding *A Fatalist at War* (London 1929) pp. 151–2.

80 E. L. Spears *Prelude to Victory* (London 1939) p 223.

81 Spears *Prelude* p. 247.

82 Spears *Prelude* p. 507.

83 Ousby *Verdun* p. 250.

84 Foakes Papers, Department of

Documents, Imperial War Museum. Lance Corporal Foakes won the Military Medal for his bravery in the battle. His account ends with the dedication:

Remembering the 13th Royal Fusiliers who fell
And very best wishes to my son, Eric

85 J. H. Boraston (ed.) *Sir Douglas Haig's Despatches* (London 1919) typewritten addendum to face p. 88.

86 Terraine *Haig* p. 310.

87 Wynn *If Germany Attacks* p. 273.

88 Quoted in Peter H. Liddle (ed.) *Passchendaele in Perspective* (London 1997) p. 36.

89 John Hussey 'The Flanders Battleground and the Weather in 1917' in Liddle *Passchendaele*.

90 It appears to have originated with Edmonds in 1927 and then been publicised by Liddell Hart, which does not augur well. It lacks the quality of evidence which might induce any reasonable bench of magistrates to award a speeding fine.

91 Charteris *GHQ* p. 36.

92 Boraston *Despatches* p. 106.

93 Battalion War Diary in National Archives WO95.

94 Chambers Papers, Liddle Collection, Brotherton Library, University of Leeds.

95 Terraine *Haig* p. 366.

96 This assessment is sustained by the careful Robin Prior and Trevor Wilson in *Passchendaele* (London 1996) which ranks, alongside Liddle's invaluable work, as essential reading on the battle.

97 Quoted in John Terraine *The Road to Passchendaele: The Flanders Offensive of 1917* (London 1977) p. 341.

98 Quoted in Liddle *Passchendaele* p. 139.

99 Quoted in Liddle *Passchendaele* p. 360.

100 Quoted in Swinton *Twenty Years* II p. 1078.

101 Edwin Campion Vaughan *Some Desperate Glory* (London 1981) pp. 224–5.

102 A. V. Bullock Diary, Bullock Papers, Department of Documents, Imperial War Museum.

103 Aubrey Wade *The War of the Guns* (London 1936) p. 55.

104 Wade *Guns* p. 57.

105 Wade *Guns* p. 62.

106 Wade *Guns* p. 64.

107 Quoted in Malcolm Brown *The Imperial War Museum Book of 1918* (London 1998) p. 46.

108 Quoted in Brown *1918* p. 14.

109 Terraine *Haig* p. 423.

110 John Laffin *British Butchers and Bunglers of World War One* (Stroud 1989) p. 170.

111 Report of Lieutenant C. B. Arnold, Tank Museum, Bovington.

112 Terraine *Haig* p. 458. See also first-rate tactical analysis in Prior and Wilson *Command* pp. 316–26.

113 Stephen Graham *A Private in the Guards* (London 1919) p. 242.

114 *Statistics* pp. 263–4. This includes battle casualties and under 2,000 deaths from illness (mostly influenza), but it does not include a large number of non-battle sick, a reflection of the influenza epidemic which was sweeping Europe.

Flesh and Blood

1 Alan Hanbury Sparrow questionnaire, compiled during research for Keith Simpson *The Old Contemptibles* (London 1981).

2 Alyn Tanner 'Sergeant Sidney Farmer MM – Seventeen Times Wounded!' in *Journal of the Orders*

and Medals Research Society, vol 41 no. 4 (December 2002).

3 J. M. Craster *Fifteen Rounds a Minute: The Grenadiers at War 1914* (London 1976) pp. 2–3.

4 Lieutenant General Sir Frederick Hamilton *Origins and History of the First Grenadier Guards* (London 1874) p. 3.

5 Craster *Fifteen Rounds* p. 5.

6 Feilding *War Letters* p. 4.

7 Graham *A Private* p. 115.

8 Graham *A Private* p. 266. 'Little Sparta' is Graham's nickname for the guards depot at Caterham, where recruits of all foot guards battalions were trained.

9 Papers of Lt Col. K. A. Oswald, Commanding Officer, 3/4th Queen's, Queen's Royal Surrey Regiment Museum, Clandon Park, Guildford.

10 Papers of Lt Col. K. A. Oswald.

11 'History of 1/4th Battalion the Queen's Royal West Surrey Regiment', Queen's Royal Surrey Regiment Museum, Clandon Park, Guildford.

12 Unpublished company history quoted in William Turner *Accrington Pals* (London 1992) p. 29.

13 A. S. Durrant Papers, Liddle Archive, Brotherton Library, University of Leeds.

14 Lancelot Dykes Spicer *Letters From France 1914–1918* (London 1979) p. xiii.

15 Quoted in Turner *Accrington Pals* pp. 67–8.

16 Quoted in Turner *Accrington Pals* p. 68.

17 Quoted in Turner *Accrington Pals* p. 145.

18 Edmonds *Military Operations, 1916* (2 vols 19) I p.

19 Turner *Accrington Pals* p. 210.

20 P. J. Campbell *In The Cannon's Mouth* (London 1986) p. 127.

21 Quoted in Michael Moynihan (ed.) *Greater Love* (London 1980) p. 115.

22 R. B. Miller account, private collection.

23 Quoted in Turner *Accrington Pals* p. 141.

24 Quoted in Turner *Accrington Pals* p. 116.

25 Quoted in Howard Pease *The History of the Northumberland (Hussars) Yeomanry* (London 1924) p. 116.

26 Dunn *War* p. 185.

27 Dunn *War* p. 484.

28 Dunn *War* p. 356.

29 Lieutenant Colonel Peter Crocker 'Some thoughts on the Royal Welch Fusiliers in the Great War', unpublished.

30 David Thompson 'The 2nd Battalion Durham Light Infantry in the Great War' in *Stand To*, The Journal of the Western Front Association (no. 65, Sept. 2002).

31 John S. Sly 'The men of 1914', *Stand To* (no. 34, Summer 1992).

32 R. H. Mottram 'Ten Years Ago: Armistice and other memories, forming a pendant to *The Spanish Farm Trilogy*' (London 1928) p. 113.

33 Lord Moran *The Anatomy of Courage* (London 1945) p. 64.

34 Moran *Anatomy* p. 134.

35 Though there are lies, damned lies and statistics: it was more dangerous to be a flying member of the Royal Flying Corps (which had a total strength of only 121,518 in January 1918) than to be in the infantry, 1,750,729 strong on the same date. *Statistics* p. 230.

36 Peter Simkins 'The Four Armies 1914–18' in D. G. Chandler (ed.) *The Oxford Illustrated History of the British Army* (Oxford 1994) p. 259.

37 Ernest Shephard *A Sergeant Major's War* (Ramsbury, Wilts, 1987) p. 124.

38 Dunn *War* p. 245.

39 Quoted in Judith Fay and Richard Martin (eds.) *The Jubilee Boy* (London 1987) pp. 89–90.

40 Norman Gladden *Ypres 1917* (London 1967) pp. 16, 40.

41 Feilding *War Letters* pp. 290–1.

42 De Boltz Papers, Liddle Archive, Brotherton Library, University of Leeds.

43 P. Smith Papers, Department of Documents, Imperial War Museum.

44 Frederick James Hodges *Men of 18 in 1918* (Ilfracombe 1988) p. 17.

45 Hodges *Men of 18* p. 216.

46 William Fisher *Requiem for Will* (privately printed, Monmouth 2002) pp. 4–5.

47 J. B. Priestley *Margin Released* (London 1962) p. 32.

48 Fisher *Requiem* p. 62.

49 Quoted in Les Carlyon *Gallipoli* (Sydney 2001) p. 270.

50 John Cusack and Ivor Herbert *Scarlet Fever: A Lifetime with Horses* (London 1972) pp. 8, 13.

51 Arthur Osburn *Unwilling Passenger* (London 1932) p. 263. But J. C. Dunn, for much of the war RMO of 2/Royal Welch Fusiliers, had also served in the ranks in the Boer War and saw the First World War in a less gloomy light.

52 William Woodruff *The Road to Nab End* (London 2002) p. 12.

53 Joseph Garvey 'Memoirs of a Nonentity', unpublished typescript, private collection, pp. 2–3.

54 Unpublished account by George Fortune, private collection.

55 Sleeve notes to Mike Nicholson *Stone by Stone*, Cilletune Music, West Chitlington, West Sussex, 2001–2.

56 Quoted in Flora Thompson *Lark Rise to Candleford* (London 1979) p. 10.

57 Thompson *Lark Rise* pp. 47–9, 54, 241. Private Edwin Timms, Canadian Infantry, was killed near Ypres on 26 April 1916 at the age of thirty-six.

58 John Baynes *Morale* (London 1967) pp. 212–13.

59 J. M. Winter *The Great War and the British People* (London 1985) pp. 50–3.

60 Jay Winter 'Army and Society: The Demographic Context' in Ian F. W. Beckett and Keith Simpson (eds) *A Nation in Arms* (Manchester 1985) p. 200.

61 Standish Meacham *A Life Apart: The English Working Class 1890–1914* (London 1977) p. 58.

62 Henri Barbusse *Le Feu* (Paris 1917) p. 23. Author's translation.

63 Stephen Westmann *Surgeon with the Kaiser's Army* (London 1968) p. 24.

64 *Statistics* p. 30.

65 Osbert Sitwell *Great Morning* (London 1948) p. 259.

66 Frank Richards *Old Soldier Sahib* (London 1936) p. 23.

67 For the structure of the general staff see *King's Regulations and Orders for the Army 1912, Revised August 1914* (London 1914).

68 Cusack and Herbert *Scarlet Fever* p. 16.

69 Herbert Wootton questionnaire compiled during my research for *Firing Line* (London 1985).

70 R. A. Lloyd questionnaire compiled during research for *Firing Line*.

71 Richards *Old Soldier Sahib* pp. 21–2.

72 R. G. Garrod Papers, Liddle Archive, Brotheron Library, University of Leeds.

73 W. J. Nicholson Papers, Liddle Archive, Brotherton Library, University of Leeds.

74 Lucy *Devil* p. 15.

75 Garvey 'Memoirs', pp. 2–3.

76 Lucy *Devil* pp. 37–8.

77 Garvey 'Memoirs' p. 14.

78 Garrod Papers, Liddle Archive.

79 R. Chant Papers, Liddle Archive, Brotherton Library, University of Leeds.

80 Chant Papers.

81 'Traditions, Treasures and Personalities of the Regiment', Queen's Royal Surrey Regiment Museum, Clandon Park, 2001.

82 Wootton questionnaire.

83 Hanbury Sparrow questionnaire.

84 Quoted in Sir George Barrow *The Fire of Life* (London 1941) p. 14.

85 Richards *Old Soldier Sahib* p. 25. The magazine was where the battalion's ammunition was stored, and forming fours was a drill movement. Soldiers of a later generation added a 17-pounder gun to the collection.

86 A wad was certainly a sandwich in 1914, though in my own time in NAAFI queues in the 1960s it had been transformed into a piece of cake.

87 Lucy *Devil* p. 59.

88 Percy Croney *Soldier's Luck* (Exeter 1965) p. 137.

89 Richards *Old Soldier Sahib* pp. 39–40.

90 Richards *Old Soldier Sahib* p. 32.

91 Con Costello *A Most Delightful Station: The British Army and the Curragh of Kildare, Ireland 1855–1922* (Cork 1999) pp. 149–74.

92 Richards *Old Soldier Sahib* pp. 109–10.

93 Private information from an RSM of The Queen's Regiment. Thank you, Jack, for this and for so much else.

94 Costello *Curragh* p. 261.

95 Lucy *Devil* p. 63.

96 Hodges *Men of 18* p. 50.

97 Ian F. W. Beckett and Keith Simpson (eds) *A Nation in Arms* (Manchester 1985) p. 39.

98 Beckett and Simpson (eds) *Nation in Arms* (p. 91).

99 Quoted in John Connell *Wavell: Soldier and Scholar* (London 1964) p. 34.

100 Major General M. F. Rimington *Our Cavalry* (London 1912) p. 18

101 Quoted in Beckett and Simpson (eds) *Nation in Arms* p. 67.

102 Order of Merit in the Papers of Lieutenant General Sir Thomas Hutton, Department of Documents, Imperial War Museum.

103 John Baynes and Hugh Maclean *A Tale of Two Captains* (Edinburgh 1990) pp. 9, 22.

104 Sitwell *Great Morning* pp. 118–19.

105 Sitwell *Great Morning* pp. 183–4, 258.

106 *Punch* 11 October 1899. Tompkins might have considered turning the battalion about, so that it would still be in quarter column, but now facing north. He would bear in mind, though, that it was now inverted, with H, its most junior company, at the head of the column and thus breaking the laws of seniority. Ordering the battalion to deploy from column into line to the right would have produced the gratifying result of markers scampering forward from the right front of each company to mark out the new line under the direction of the mounted adjutant, a regular to whom this was food and drink: companies would then take post on the markers. Deployment to the right meant that A Company would now be on the right of the line, as

was its due. The line could now be moved forward with a gentle 'right incline', and the problem would be solved. I suspect that the general might not have liked the temporary inversion, but this is the quickest practical solution. None of this would have mattered much under Boer fire a year later.

107 Quoted in J. D. Sainsbury *The Hertfordshire Yeomanry* (Welwyn 1994) pp. 118–19.

108 S. F. Hatton *Yarns of a Yeoman* (London ND) p. 22.

109 Pease *Northumberland Hussars* p. viii.

110 Brian Bond (ed.) *Staff Officer: The Diary of Lord Moyne* (London 1987) p. 23.

111 George Ashurst *My Bit* (Ramsbury 1986) p. 15.

112 Ashurst *My Bit* p. 25.

113 For detailed establishments see *The Territorial Year Book 1909* (London 1909) pp. 29–34.

114 Beckett and Simpson (eds) *Nation in Arms* p. 129.

115 Latin for 'Everywhere', and granted instead of the specific battle honours worn by regiments of infantry and cavalry. It is shared by the Royal Engineers, and cynics maintained that while it did indeed mean 'Everywhere' where engineers were concerned, for the artillery it meant, all too literally, 'All over the place'.

116 John Reith *Wearing Spurs* (London 1966) p. 17.

117 Personal information from Field Marshal Lord Harding, 1986. Although he was generally known as John, Harding was actually christened Alan Francis.

118 Bryan Latham *A Territorial Soldier's War* (Aldershot 1967) p. 1.

119 Latham *Territorial* p. 3.

120 Norman Tennant *A Saturday Night Soldier's War 1913–1918* (Waddesdon, Bucks 1983) pp. 2, 4, 6, 10.

121 Beckett and Simpson (eds) *Nation in Arms* p. 72.

122 Quoted in Beckett and Simpson (eds) *Nation in Arms* p. 131.

123 Hatton *Yeoman* p. 27.

124 Territorial divisions originally had regional titles and were not numbered until May 1915. By then regular and New Army divisions had extended divisional numbering as far as forty-one, and first-line territorial divisions were numbered in the order they went abroad as formed bodies. First was 42nd (East Lancashire) Division, and then 43rd Wessex, 44th (Home Counties), 46th (North Midland), 47th (2nd London), 48th (South Midland), 49th (West Riding), 50th (Northumbrian), 51st (Highland), 52nd (Lowland), 53rd (Welsh), 54th (East Anglian), 55th (West Lancashire) and 56th (1st London) Divisions. Second-line territorial divisions were formed from units like 2/4th Queen's, the nucleus of its soldiers left behind when 1/4th Queen's left for India. These comprised 45th (2nd Wessex), 57th (2nd West Lancashire), 58th (2/1st London), 59th (2nd North Midland), 60th (2/2nd London), 61st (2nd South Midland), 62nd (2nd West Riding), 63rd (2nd Northumbrian), 64th (2nd Highland), 65th (2nd Lowland), 66th (2nd East Lancashire), 67th (2nd Home Counties), 68th (2nd Welsh) and 69th (2nd East Anglian) Divisions.

125 Colonel W. N. Nicholson *Behind the Lines* (London 1939) pp. 15, 19–20.

126 Nicholson *Behind the Lines* p. 46.

127 Nicholson *Behind the Lines* p. 49.

128 For the effect of the political pull exercised by territorials see Kevin W. Mitchinson 'The Transfer Controversy: Parliament and the London Regiment', *Stand To* (no. 33, Winter 1991).

129 Although there were circumstances when County Associations were involved in recruiting the New Armies, general arrangements were kept 'separate and distinct', Beckett and Simpson (eds) *Nation in Arms* p. 139.

130 Peter Simkins *Kitchener's Army* (Manchester 1988) p. xiv.

131 9th (Scottish), 10th (Irish), 11th (Northern), 12th (Eastern), 13th (Western) and 14th (Light) Divisions.

132 15th (Scottish), 16th (Irish), 17th (Northern), 18th (Eastern), 19th (Western) and 20th (Light) Divisions.

133 3rd New Army: 21st, 22nd, 23rd, 24th, 25th and 26th Divisions. 4th New Army, its divisions largely made up of Pals' battalions: 30th Division (battalions from Manchester and Liverpool); 31st Division (initially numbered 38th, with battalions from Yorkshire, Lancashire and Durham); 32nd Division (battalions from Glasgow, Birmingham, Salford, Newcastle and Westmorland and Cumberland); 32nd Division (initially numbered 40th, all its battalions from London); 34th Division (battalions from Tyneside, Edinburgh, Cambridge and Grimsby); 35th (Bantam) Division (initially formed as the 42nd, and allowed to recruit infantry below the normal acceptable height.

134 The 5th New Army included 36th (Ulster) Division; 37th Division; 38th (Welsh) Division; 39th Division, 40th Division and 41st Division. In all there were seventy-one infantry divisions, regular, territorial and New Army, of which sixty-three served abroad.

135 Brigadier F. P. Roe *Accidental Soldiers* (London 1981) p. 22.

136 C. H. Gaskell Papers, Department of Documents, Imperial War Museum.

137 Graham H. Greenwell *An Infant in Arms* (London 1972).

138 N. Whitehead Papers, Liddle Archive, Brotherton Library, University of Leeds.

139 Julian Tyndale-Biscoe *Gunner Subaltern* (London 1971) pp. 3–4.

140 Tyndale-Biscoe *Gunner Subaltern* pp. 5, 11.

141 John H. F. Mackie (ed.) *Answering the Call: Letters from the Somerset Light Infantry 1914–19* (Eggleston, County Durham, 2002) p. 17. This is a wonderful account of one family's service to the county regiment.

142 Harold Macmillan *The Winds of Change* (London 1966) I pp. 62–3.

143 Bernard Martin *Poor Bloody Infantry* p. 7. The 64th had been amalgamated with the 98th to form the North Staffordshire Regiment in 1881, but old habits died hard.

144 *Stand To* (no. 5, Jan. 1998) p. 48.

145 Quoted in Tonie and Valmai Holt *Poets of the Great War* (London 1999) p. 128.

146 Martin Middlebrook *Your Country Needs You* (Barnsley 2000) p. 73.

147 Quoted in Simkins *Kitchener's Army* p. 92.

148 Anthony French *Gone For a Soldier* (Kineton 1972) p. 21.

149 R. B. Talbot Kelly *Subaltern's Odyssey* (London 1980) p. 50.

150 I. G. Andrew Papers, Liddle Archive, Brotherton Library, University of Leeds.

151 Jack Horsfall and Nigel Cave *Somme: Serre* (London 1996) p. 54.

152 Winter *Great War* p. 35.

153 Quoted in Simkins *New Armies* p. 96.

154 Clive Hughes 'The Welsh Army Corps 1914–15' in *Imperial War Museum Review* (no. 1, 1986).

155 Llewelyn Wyn Griffith *Up to Mametz* (London 1931) pp. 210–11.

156 Griffith *Mametz* p. 225.

157 The best short history of this division is in Ray Westlake *Kitchener's Army* (Staplehurst, Kent, 1998) pp. 148–54.

158 Quoted in Terence Denman *Ireland's Unknown Soldiers* (Blackrock, Co. Dublin, 1992) p. 26.

159 F. P. Crozier *A Brass Hat in No Man's Land* (London 1930) p. 24.

160 Tom Johnstone *Orange Green and Khaki* (Dublin 1992) p. 256.

161 Quoted in Johnstone *Orange* p. 278.

162 Quoted in Johnstone *Orange* pp. 290–1.

163 Percy Croney *Soldier's Luck* (Devon 1965) pp. 10–11.

164 G. and S. Rain Papers, Liddle Archive, Brotherton Library, University of Leeds.

165 Harry Ogle *The Fateful Battle Line* (London 1993) p. 10.

166 De Boltz Papers, Liddle Archive, Brotherton Library, University of Leeds.

167 Pamela McCleary (ed.) *Dear Amy* unpublished typescript of the letters of Alan ('Bill') Sugden RFA p. 4.

168 McCleary (ed.) *Dear Amy* pp. 5–6.

169 McCleary (ed.) *Dear Amy* p. 11.

170 McCleary (ed.) *Dear Amy* p. 16.

171 McCleary (ed.) *Dear Amy* p. 25.

172 McCleary (ed.) *Dear Amy* p. 28.

173 McCleary (ed.) *Dear Amy* p. 171.

174 Baynes and Maclean *Two Captains* pp. 68–9.

175 Priestley *Margin Released* p. 81.

176 Priestley *Margin Released* p. 90.

177 Priestley *Margin Released* p. 93.

178 *Types of Horses Suitable for Army Remounts* (Board of Trade, London 1909).

179 B. E. Todhunter Papers, Liddle Archive, Brotherton Library, University of Leeds.

180 Pamela Horn *Rural Life in England in the First World War* (New York 1984) p. 89.

181 John Pollock *Kitchener* (London 1998) p. 405.

182 J. A. C. Pennycuik Papers, private collection.

183 H. B. Owens Papers, Department of Documents, Imperial War Museum.

184 Tom Bridges *Alarms and Excursions* (London 1938) p. 15.

185 Happily, Lieutenant Maudslay, who had returned from Argentina in 1914 to join up, was captured. See the Edith F. Maudslay Papers in the Liddle Collection, Brotheron Library, University of Leeds.

186 Duff Hart-Davis (ed.) *End of an Era: Letters and Journals of Sir Alan Lascelles, from 1887 to 1920* (London 1986) p. 210.

187 Jonathan Horne (ed.) *The Best of Good Fellows: The Diaries and Memoirs of the Reverend Charles Edmund Doudeney* (London 1995) pp. 113, 115.

188 Sidney Rogerson *Twelve Days* (London 1933) p. 141.

Brain and Nerves

1 Gerald Achilles Burgoyne *The Burgoyne Diaries* (London 1985) p. 51.
2 Burgoyne *Diaries* pp. 217–18.
3 Lancelot Dykes Spicer *Letters from France* (London 1979) p. 5.
4 Lord Stanhope Papers, Department of Documents, Imperial War Museum.
5 Frank Crozier *The Men I Killed* (London 1937). It is instructive to compare its tone with the same author's rather more positive *A Brass Hat in No Man's Land*, published in 1930. Crozier is not always a reliable witness, nor did his literary approach bring him many friends. My copy of *Brass Hat* has an alternative title scrawled in: *A Fat Arse in No Man's Land.*
6 Eric Hiscock *The Bells of Hell go ting-a-ling-a-ling* (London 1976) pp. 81–2. The Haig quote is wrong both in substance and in date.
7 Frank Hawkings *From Ypres to Cambrai* (London 1974) p. 49.
8 Roe *Accidental Soldier* p. 181.
9 Ernst Parker *Into Battle 1914–18* (London 1994) p. 35.
10 Martin *Poor Bloody Infantry* pp. 95–6.
11 John Bickersteth (ed.) *The Bickersteth Diaries* (London 1995) p. 274.
12 Jack *Diary* p. 250.
13 H. E. L. Mellersh *Schoolboy into War* (London 1978) p. 16.
14 Order of battle in *Statistics* pp. 13–15.
15 These orders of battle are from the 1916 edition of the 1914 *Field Service Pocket Book* (HMSO 1916). Variations in unit establishment (crucial documents, for they provided entitlement to promotion, rank and pay) were issued by the Staff Duties (2) branch at the War Office and promulgated through GHQ in France.
16 In another version we have 'the old Dun Cow' catching fire, more probably a reference to an alehouse conflagration than arson in the byre, and a further version becomes more colourful still.
17 Sir James Edmonds *History of the Great War: Military Operations, France and Belgium 1915* (2 vols, London 1992) II pp. 283–4.
18 Dunn *The War* p. 440.
19 Frank Hawkings *From Ypres to Cambrai* (London 1974) p. 83.
20 Richards *Old Soldiers* p. 88.
21 Gordon *Unreturning Army* p. 52.
22 Paddy Griffith (ed.) *British Fighting Methods in the Great War* (London 1996) p. 6.
23 Ian Hay (pseud. Ian Hay Beith) *The First Hundred Thousand* (Edinburgh 1916) p. 68.
24 Robert Graves *Goodbye to All That* (London 1969) p. 131.
25 Graves *Goodbye* p. 138.
26 Robert Graves *But it Still Goes On* (London 1930) pp. 24–5.
27 Ernest Parker *Into Battle* (London 1994) p. 13.
28 Moynihan *Armageddon* p. 127.
29 Denis Winter *Haig's Command* (London 1992) p. 144.
30 G. D. Sheffield 'The Australians at Pozières: Command and Control on the Somme, 1916' in David French and Brian Holden Reid *The British General Staff: Reform Innovations c. 1890–1939* (London 2002).
31 Peter Simkins 'Co-Stars or Supporting Cast? British Divisions in the "Hundred Days", 1918' in Griffith *British Fighting Methods* p. 57.
32 Griffith *British Fighting Methods* p. 59.

33 See John Lee 'The SHLM Project: Assessing the performance of British Divisions' in Griffith *British Fighting Methods*. In the Second World War the same patch was believed to stand for Highway Decorators.

34 Graves *Goodbye* p. 152.

35 Edmonds *Military Operations 1914* I pp. 7–8.

36 Paddy Griffith *Battle Tactics of the Western Front* (London 1994) pp. 152–3.

37 Feilding *War Letters* pp. 15–17.

38 'Revised Army Form B 213 (G[eneral] R[outine] O[rder] 1175)' in *SS 309 Extracts from General Routine Orders Part 1 Adjutant General's Department*, 1 January 1917.

39 'Nominal Rolls, Returns etc (GRO 147)' in *SS 309*.

40 Nicholson *Behind the Lines* pp. 215–16.

41 Nicholson *Behind the Lines* p. 166.

42 Quoted in Prior and Wilson *Command* p. 269.

43 Quoted in Prior and Wilson *Command* p. 272.

44 Shelford Bidwell and Dominick Graham *Fire Power* (London 1982) p. 100.

45 The chief of the general staff began as head of the General Staff Branch and as such first among equals in a headquarters. By 1916, however, the organisational table in the *Field Service Pocket Book* shows him as separate and superior.

46 Edward Spears *Liaison 1914* (London 1999) p. 72.

47 Stanhope Papers, Department of Documents, Imperial War Museum.

48 See the entry in J. M. Bourne *Who's Who in World War One* (London 2001) pp. 167–8. The quote from Haig's dispatch is in Haig *Despatches* p. 350. But we should not read too much into the latter: from personal correspondence after the war it is evident that Haig and Lawrence were chalk and cheese.

49 *Statistics* p. 65.

50 Ian Malcolm Brown *British Logistics on the Western Front 1914–1918* (London 1998) p. 238.

51 Reginald Tompson Diary, private collection.

52 Hutton Papers, Department of Documents, Imperial War Museum.

53 Terraine *Haig* p. 170. In the event Churchill commanded a Royal Scots Fusilier battalion.

54 Quoted in Moyne *Staff Officer* p. 144.

55 Penney Papers, Department of Documents, Imperial War Museum.

56 Quoted in Peter Charlton *Australians on the Somme: Pozières 1916* (North Ryde 1986) p. 171.

57 Quoted in Simkins *New Armies* p. 216.

58 Simkins *New Armies* p. 217.

59 Graves *Goodbye* p. 125. Some caution is required, as is so often the case with Gravesian anecdotes, but the story has the ring of truth.

60 Osburn *Unwilling Passenger* p. 117. See also Edmonds *1914* I pp. 277–8.

61 Bourne *Who's Who* pp. 49–50.

62 John Charteris *GHQ* (London 1931) p. 209.

63 Army Book 129, 3/3rd Queen's, Queen's Royal Surrey Regiment Museum, Clandon Park.

64 See *King's Regulations and Orders for the Army 1912 Revised 1914*, especially paras 758–882.

65 *Statistics* p. 554.

66 Graves *Goodbye* p. 142.

67 Graves *Goodbye* p. 172.

68 Dunn *The War* pp. 413–14, 497, 502.

69 Dunn *The War* pp. 236–42.

70 Crozier *Brass Hat* pp. 206–7.

71 Stanhope Papers.

72 Crozier *Brass Hat* pp. 144–5.

73 F. P. Crozier *Impressions and Reflections* (London 1930) p. 202.

74 Cumming *Brigadier* p. 96.

75 John Terraine *The Smoke and the Fire: Myths and Anti-Myths of War* (London 1992) p. 162.

76 Andrew Simpson *The Operational Role of British Corps Command on the Western Front 1914–18* (PhD Thesis, University College London 1999).

77 Terraine *Smoke* p. 163.

78 Terraine *Smoke* p. 162.

79 Adrian Carton de Wiart *Happy Odyssey* (London 1950) p. 90.

80 Feilding *War Letters* p. 313.

81 Siegfried Sassoon *Memoirs of an Infantry Officer* (London 1977) p. 75.

82 Quoted in Davies and Maddocks *Bloody Red Tabs* (London 1995) p. 1.

83 Tompson Papers, Department of Documents, Imperial War Museum.

84 Quoted in Davies and Maddocks *Bloody Red Tabs* p. 6.

85 Quoted in Davies and Maddocks *Bloody Red Tabs* p. 93.

86 Charteris *GHQ* p. 118.

87 Quoted in Holmes *Little Field Marshal* p. 284.

88 Quoted in Holmes *Little Field Marshal* p. 333.

89 Terraine *Haig* p. 427.

90 Bourne *Who's Who* pp. 238–9.

91 Griffith *Mametz* pp. 206, 216, 221.

92 Quoted in Malcolm Brown *The Imperial War Museum Book of the Western Front* (London 1993) pp. 136–44.

93 Nigel Cave *Vimy Ridge* (Pen and Sword Battleground Europe Series, London 1996) p. 75.

94 Nicholson *Behind the Lines* p. 161.

95 Quoted in Prior and Wilson *Command* p. 354.

96 Feilding *War Letters* p. 226.

97 Stanhope Papers.

98 Quoted in Holmes *Little Field Marshal* p. 136.

99 Details of armbands, etc., derived from *Extracts from General Routine Orders . . . Part II, Quartermaster General's Branch*, SS 340, 1 January 1917.

100 A. F. Smith Papers, Department of Documents, Imperial War Museum.

101 Lord Hankey *The Supreme Command 1914–19* (2 vols, London 1961) I p. 167.

102 A senior general staff officer worked directly for a commander at any level of command: he was styled general staff officer grade I (GSO1) at division, brigadier general, general staff (BGGS) at corps and major general, general staff (MGGS) at army. General staff officers (GSOs) were graded 1 (lieutenant colonels), 2 (majors) and 3 (captains), and abbreviated as GSO1 and so on. Other staff officers took their titles from the tripartite division of staff functions. Thus a division had, in addition to its three GSOs on the general staff branch, an assistant adjutant and quartermaster general (AA&QMG), a deputy assistant adjutant and quartermaster general (DAA&QMG), both with responsibilities for A and Q branches, and a deputy assistant quartermaster general (DAQMG) responsible for Q matters alone.

103 Martin van Creveld *Command in War* (London 1985) p. 166.

104 Nicholson *Behind the Lines* p. 65.

105 Nicholson *Behind the Lines* p. 70.

106 Nicholson *Behind the Lines* pp. 77–8.

107 Cumming *Brigadier* p. 92.
108 Nicholson *Behind the Lines* pp. 107–8.
109 Nicholson *Behind the Lines* p. 121.
110 Brigadier General Sir Archibald Home *The Diary of a World War I Cavalry Officer* (London 1985) pp. 103–5.
111 See Ben Fenton 'Shamed general's battle of the Somme' in *Daily Telegraph*, 16 August 1998.
112 Home *Diary* p. 113.
113 Stanhope Papers.
114 Nicholson *Behind the Lines* p. 151.
115 Nicholson *Behind the Lines* p. 179.
116 Stanhope Papers.
117 Bond (ed.) *Staff Officer* p. 162.
118 Simpson *Corps* p. 224.
119 Charles Carrington *Soldier From the War Returning* (London 1965) p. 104.
120 Carrington *Soldier* p. 195.
121 Crozier *Brass Hat* p. 132.
122 Bond (ed.) *Staff Officer* p. 198.
123 Bond (ed.) *Staff Officer* p. 131.
124 Bond (ed.) *Staff Officer* p. 165.
125 Cumming *Brigadier* p. 97.
126 Cumming *Brigadier* p. 116.
127 Cumming *Brigadier* p. 163.
128 Bullock Papers, Department of Documents, Imperial War Museum.
129 Crozier *Brass Hat* p. 182.
130 Priestley *Margin Released* p. 135.
131 Mottram *Personal Record* pp. 103–4.
132 Osburn *Unwilling Passenger* p. 255.
133 Jack *Diary* p. 248.
134 Charteris *GHQ* p. 185.
135 Philip Gibbs *The Realities of War* (London 1920) p. 208.
136 Charteris *GHQ* pp. 241, 243, 259.
137 Tompson Papers.
138 A. F. Smith Papers.
139 Stanhope Papers.
140 Davies Papers, Department of Documents, Imperial War Museum.

Earth and Wire

1 *Field Service Regulations 1909: Part I* pp. 152–3.
2 *Infantry Training 1914* (HMSO 1914) p. 12.
3 'My Experiences in World War 1 by W. G. Birley', private collection.
4 Roe *Accidental Soldiers* p. 42.
5 Edward Underhill *A Year on the Western Front* (London 1988) p. 18.
6 Captain John Aidan Liddell Diary, Department of Documents, Imperial War Museum.
7 George Coppard *With a Machine Gun to Cambrai* (London 1988) p. 57.
8 Coppard *Machine Gun* p. 61.
9 Burgoyne *Diaries* p. 48.
10 Hawkings *From Ypres* p. 79.
11 Hawkings *From Ypres* p. 79.
12 Roe *Accidental Soldiers* p. 91.
13 Roe *Accidental Soldiers* p. 90.
14 Jones *In Parenthesis* p. 198.
15 Jones *In Parenthesis* p. 198.
16 Captain B. C. Lake *Knowledge for War* (London 1915) p. 50.
17 Roe *Accidental Soldiers* p. 97.
18 Charles Douie *The Weary Road* (London 1929) p. 170.
19 Captain Henry Ogle *The Fateful Battle Line* (London 1993) pp. 53–4.
20 Hawkings *From Ypres* p. 89.
21 Sidney Rogerson *Last of the Ebb* (London 1937) p. 17.
22 Frank Dunham *The Long Carry* (London 1970) p. 38.
23 Ruth Elwin Harris *Billie: The Neville Letters, 1914–16* (London 1991) p. 58.
24 Roe *Accidental Soldiers* p. 159.
25 Roe *Accidental Soldiers* p. 165.

26 Williamson *Wet Flanders Plain* p. 138.

27 Dunham *Long Carry* p. 35.

28 Feilding *War Letters* p. 206.

29 Burgoyne *Diaries* p. 161.

30 Reith *Wearing Spurs* (London 1966) p. 64.

31 Harris *Billie* pp. 63–4.

32 Underhill *A Year* p. 51.

33 Ernest Shephard *A Sergeant Major's War* (Ramsbury 1987) pp. 88–9.

34 Roe *Accidental Soldiers* p. 91.

35 Underhill *A Year* p. 106.

36 Gordon *Unreturning Army* p. 90.

37 Jones *In Parenthesis* p. 207.

38 Major G. O. Chambers *Field Message Book* 'Battle of Arras, Battle of Cambrai', Chambers Papers, Department of Documents, Imperial War Museum.

39 Roe *Accidental Soldiers* p. 90.

40 Tyndale-Biscoe *Gunner Subaltern* p. 83.

41 Bryan Latham *A Territorial Soldier's War* (Aldershot 1967) p. 49.

42 Quoted in Dunn *The War* pp. 209, 213.

43 Quoted in Daphne Jones (ed.) *Bullets and Bandsmen: The story of a Bandsman on the Western Front, written by his daughter* (Salisbury 1992) pp. 29–30.

44 Reith *Wearing Spurs* p. 199.

45 Jones *In Parenthesis* p. 203.

46 Quoted in Holmes *Little Field Marshal* p. 304.

47 Ogle *Fateful Battle Line* pp. 103–4.

48 John Glubb *Into Battle: A Soldier's Diary of the Great War* (London 1978) p. 54.

49 Jack *Diary* p. 84.

50 Hiscock *Bells of Hell* p. 30.

51 Quoted in I. M. Parsons (ed.) *Men Who March Away* (London 1969) p. 60.

52 Crozier *Brass Hat* pp. 136–7.

53 Crozier *Brass Hat* p. 125.

54 Neville *Billie* p. 109.

55 Roe *Accidental Soldiers* p. 100.

56 Ogle *Fateful Battle Line* p. 42.

57 Hawkings *Ypres to Cambrai* p. 82.

58 Underhill *A Year* p. 56.

59 Gordon *Unreturning Army* p. 42.

60 Reginald Farrer *The Void of War* (London 1918) p. 113.

61 Campbell *Cannon's Mouth* pp. 218–19.

62 Carrington *Soldier* p. 87.

63 *Statistics* pp. 64–5. Combat arms constituted: headquarters, cavalry, artillery, engineers, Royal Flying Corps, infantry, Army Cyclist Corps, Machine Gun Corps and Tank Corps. Non-combatant services constituted the Army Service Corps, Royal Army Medical Corps, Army Veterinary Corps, Army Pay Corps, Labour Corps and miscellaneous units.

64 Shephard *Sergeant Major's War* p. 80.

65 Carrington *Soldier from the Wars* p. 87.

66 Rogerson *Twelve Days* pp. xv, 5.

67 Jones *In Parenthesis* p. 200.

68 Rogerson *Twelve Days* p. 58.

69 Feilding *War Letters* p. 285.

70 Liddell Diary, Department of Documents, Imperial War Museum.

71 Arthur Smith Papers, Department of Documents, Imperial War Museum.

72 Carrington *Soldier* p. 87.

73 Rogerson *Twelve Days* p. 9.

74 Rogerson *Twelve Days* p. 26.

75 Jones *In Parenthesis* p. 202.

76 Blacker *Have You Forgotten* p. 237.

77 Lucy *Devil* p. 242.

78 Dunn *The War* p. 252.

79 Carrington *Soldier from the Wars* p. 127.

80 Hawkings *From Ypres* p. 22.

81 Carton de Wiart *Happy Odyssey* p. 91.

82 Hiscock *Bells of Hell* p. 27.

83 Roe *Accidental Soldiers* p. 87.

84 Dolden *Cannon Fodder* p. 110.

85 Talbot Kelly *Subaltern's Odyssey* p. 108.

86 Rogerson *Twelve Days* p. 49.

87 Rogerson *Twelve Days* p. 52.

88 Richards *Old Soldiers* pp. 90–91.

89 Dunn *The War* p. 253.

90 Rogerson *Twelve Days* p. 58.

91 Rogerson *Twelve Days* p. 82.

92 Siegfried Sassoon *Memoirs of an Infantry Officer* (London 1977) p. 87.

93 Rogerson *Twelve Days* p. 96.

94 Baynes and Maclean *Tale of Two Captains* p. 119.

95 Alan Hanbury Sparrow *The Land-Locked Lake* (London 1932) p. 257.

96 Blacker *Have You Forgotten* p. 237.

97 Graves *Goodbye* p. 86.

98 Bernard Adams *Nothing of Importance* (London 1988) pp. 107–9.

99 Percy Jones 'The Story of the Nine Day Trench', unpublished typescript, P. H. Jones Papers, Department of Documents, Imperial War Museum.

100 Richards *Old Soldiers* p. 77.

101 Williamson *Wet Flanders Plain* p. 169.

102 Graves *Goodbye* p. 98.

103 Roland Miller.

104 Roe *Accidental Soldiers* p. 56.

105 Ogle *Fateful Battle Line* p. 96.

106 Dunham *Long Carry* p. 38. Private Bloomfield was tried for negligence. He was acquitted, and returned to his battalion in time to be crippled for life in the next attack.

107 Livermore *Long 'Un* p. 52.

108 Burgoyne *Diaries* p. 14. Private Benjamin West's temporary grave was not found after the war, and he is commemorated on Panel 21 of the Menin Gate Memorial to the Missing at Ypres.

109 Burgoyne *Diaries* p. 118.

110 Dolden *Cannon Fodder* pp. 30, 34.

111 R. G. Ashford Papers.

112 Quoted in Holmes *Firing Line* p. 201.

113 Dunham *Long Carry* p. 21.

114 Terry Norman (ed.) *Armageddon Road: A VC's Diary 1914–18* (London 1982) p. 47.

115 Daphne Jones (ed.) *Bullets and Bandsmen* (Salisbury 1992) p. 72. The Canadian Medical Officer Lieutenant Colonel John McCrae was inspired to write the poem 'In Flanders Fields' by his experiences in the field hospital at Essex Farm. The concrete bunkers which housed it have been sensitively restored.

116 Dunham *Long Carry* p. 30.

117 Williamson *Wet Flanders Plain* p. 134.

118 T. H. Davies Papers.

119 Gordon *Unreturning Army* p. 71.

120 Graves *Goodbye* p. 114.

121 Harry Ogle *Fateful Battle Line* p. 56.

122 Cathryn Corns and John Hughes-Wilson *Blindfold and Alone* (London 2001) p. 135.

123 Blacker *Have You Forgotten* p. 237.

124 Roe *Accidental Soldiers* p. 109.

125 Wade *Guns* p. 31.

126 Bernard Livermore *Long 'Un – A Damn Bad Soldier* (Batley, West Yorkshire, 1974) p. 54.

127 Hawkings *From Ypres* p. 64.

128 Jones *In Parenthesis* p. 205.

129 Roe *Accidental Soldiers* p. 95.

130 Roe *Accidental Soldiers* p. 149.

131 Ogle *Fateful Battle Line* p. 141.

132 Campbell *Cannon's Mouth* p. 41.

133 Graves *Goodbye* p. 86.

134 Blacker *Have You Forgotten* p. 65.

135 Blacker *Have You Forgotten* p. 74.

136 Shephard *Sergeant Major's War* pp. 26, 56, 57.

137 See outline pay scales in *Field Service Pocket Book 1914* p. 179. Military pay was (and remains) more complex than it might seem, with trade and proficiency additions enhancing basic pay, and an assortment of deductions (their reason often not clear to the victim) reducing it.

138 Alexander Barrie *War Underground: The Tunnellers of the Western Front* (Staplehurst 2000) p. 40.

139 A.V. Bullock Papers.

140 French *Gone for a Soldier* p. 54.

141 Adams *Nothing of Importance* p. 86.

142 Livermore *Long 'Un* p. 58.

143 Dolden *Cannon Fodder* p. 77.

144 Roe *Accidental Soldiers* p. 34.

145 Dunn *The War* p. 300.

146 Burgoyne *Diaries* p. 62.

147 Roe *Accidental Soldiers* p. 99.

148 Dolden *Cannon Fodder* p. 100.

149 Dolden *Cannon Fodder* p. 69.

150 Dolden *Cannon Fodder* p. 79.

151 Dolden *Cannon Fodder* pp. 82–3.

152 Coppard *With a Machine Gun* p. 44.

153 Burgoyne *Diaries* p. 190.

154 Rogerson *Twelve Days* p. 50.

155 Hawkings *From Ypres* pp. 36, 75.

156 Roe *Accidental Soldiers* p. 43.

157 Blacker *Have You Forgotten* p. 70.

158 Dunn *The War* p. 471.

159 George Fortune account, private collection.

160 Ogle *Fateful Battle Line* pp. 35–6.

161 Quoted in Moynihan *Armageddon* p. 21.

162 Richards *Old Soldiers* pp. 66–7.

163 Burgoyne *Diaries* p. 96.

164 Ronald Ginns Papers, Department of Documents, Imperial War Museum.

165 Baynes and Maclean *Tale of Two Captains* p. 136.

166 Hodges *Men of 18* p. 106.

167 Edmund Blunden *Undertones of War* (London 1965) p. 98.

168 Martin *Poor Bloody Infantry* p. 79.

169 Quoted in James Sambrook (ed.) *With the Rank and Pay of a Sapper* (London 1998) p. 51.

170 Adams Papers, Liddle Archive, Brotherton Library, University of Leeds.

171 Reith *Wearing Spurs* p. 68.

172 Burgoyne *Diaries* p. 84.

173 Livermore *Long 'Un* pp. 54–5.

174 Roe *Accidental Soldiers* p. 44.

175 Dolden *Cannon Fodder* p. 48.

176 Dolden *Cannon Fodder* p. 48.

177 Jones Papers.

178 Jones *In Parenthesis* p. 203.

179 Bullock Papers, Department of Documents, Imperial War Museum.

180 Hodges *Men of 18* p. 105.

181 Jones *In Parenthesis* p. 206.

182 Ginns Papers Department of Documents, Imperial War Museum.

183 Jones *In Parenthesis* p. 75.

184 H. M. Stanford Letters, private collection.

185 Quoted in Moynihan *Armageddon* p. 22.

186 Graves *Goodbye* p. 85.

187 Crozier *Brass Hat* p. 123.

188 Carrington *Subaltern's War* p. 83.

189 Richards *Old Soldiers* pp. 100–1.

190 Nicholson *Behind the Lines* p. 291.

191 Thomas Penrose Marks *The Laughter Goes from Life* (London 1977) p. 124.

192 Vaughan *Some Desperate Glory*.

193 Reith *Wearing Spurs* p. 53.

194 Burgoyne *Diaries* p. 31.

195 Underhill *A Year* p. 26.

196 Ernest Parker *Into Battle
1914–18* (London 1984) p. 36.

197 Burgoyne *Diaries* p. 151.

198 Livermore *Long 'Un* pp. 61–2.

199 Guy Chapman *Passionate
Prodigality* p. 205.

200 Crozier *Brass Hat* pp. 128–9.

201 Crozier *Brass Hat* pp. 72–3.
George Gaffikin died bravely at the
head of his company when the 36th
Division stormed the Schwaben
Redoubt on 1 July 1916.

202 Nicholson *Behind the Lines*
p. 291.

203 Carrington *Soldier from the Wars*
p. 99.

204 Ashurst *My Bit* pp. 111–13.

205 Lucy *Devil* pp. 81–3.

206 Richards *Old Soldiers* p. 14.

207 Edward Gleichen *The Doings of
The Fifteenth Infantry Brigade*
(Edinburgh 1917) p. 14.

208 Aubrey Herbert *Mons, Anzac and
Kut* (London 1920) p. 20.

209 De Boltz Papers, Liddle Archive,
Brotherton Library, University of
Leeds.

210 Abraham Papers, Liddle
Archive, Brotherton Library,
University of Leeds.

211 Roe *Accidental Soldiers* p. 39.

212 Abraham Papers, Liddle
Archive, Brotherton Library,
University of Leeds.

213 Dolden *Cannon Fodder* p. 112.

214 Douglas Gill 'Mutiny at Etaples
Base in 1917' in *Past and Present*
No. 69 p. 89.

215 Douie *Weary Road* p. 39.

216 Livermore *Long 'Un* p. 46.

217 French *Gone For a Soldier*
pp. 26–7.

218 Livermore *Long 'Un* pp. 46–7.

219 Dolden *Cannon Fodder* p. 14.

220 Reverend Pat Mc Cormick 'My
Diary of the War to November 1916',
Department of Documents, Imperial
War Museum. Shine in this context
means noise, as in Kipling's lines:

When shaking their bustles like
ladies so fine,

The guns of the enemy wheel into
line

Shoot low at the limbers and don't
mind the shine

For noise never startles the
soldier . . .

221 Baynes and Maclean *Tale of Two
Captains* p. 95.

222 Graves *Goodbye* p. 159.

223 Graves *Goodbye* p. 195.

224 Hanbury Sparrow *Land-Locked
Lake* p. 213.

225 Calloway, Quoted in Alan
Wilkinson *The Church of England and
the First World War* (London 1978)
p. 44.

226 Blacker *Have You Forgotten*
p. 157.

227 De Boltz Papers, Liddle Archive,
Brotherton Library, University of
Leeds.

228 Seton-Hutchison *Warrior* p. 224.

229 Henry Williamson *Love and the
Loveless* (London 1958) p. 252.

230 H. Owen and J. Bell (eds)
Wilfred Owen: Collected Letters (London
1967) p. 521.

231 Carrington *Soldier from the Wars*
p. 245.

232 C. T. Mason 'War Journal',
private collection p. 85.

233 Parker *Into Battle* p. 86.

234 Percy Croney *Soldier's Luck*
(London 1965) p. 173.

235 The BBC series *The Monocled
Mutineer* gave a starring role to Percy
Topliss, although there is no
evidence that he was within a
hundred miles of Etaples at the time.

236 Corns and Hughes-Wilson
Blindfold and Alone p. 393.

237 Carrington *Soldier from the Wars* p. 199.

238 I. G. Andrew Papers, Liddle Archive, Brotherton Library, University of Leeds.

239 Dunham *Long Carry* p. 92.

240 V. F. Eberle *My Sapper Venture* (London 1973) p. 103.

241 Livermore *Long 'Un* p. 55.

242 Reith *Wearing Spurs* p. 49.

243 Roe *Accidental Soldiers* p. 83.

244 Chapman *Passionate Prodigality* p. 18.

245 French *Gone for a Soldier* p. 37.

246 Ogle *Fateful Battle Line* pp. 34–5.

247 Parker *Into Battle* p. 45.

248 Hawkings *From Ypres* p. 65.

249 Roe *Accidental Soldiers* p. 24.

250 Burgoyne *Diaries* p. 156.

251 Burgoyne *Diaries* p. 160.

252 Tyndale-Biscoe *Gunner Subaltern* p. 113.

253 Graves *Goodbye* pp. 106–7.

254 Campbell *Cannon's Mouth* pp. 28–30.

255 Blacker *Have You Forgotten* pp. 230–1.

256 Quoted in Dunn *The War* p. 109.

257 Beckett and Simpson *Nation in Arms* p. 82.

258 De Boltz Papers.

259 Quoted in McCleary (ed.) *Dear Amy* p. 183.

260 Douie *The Weary Road* p. 196.

261 Dunn *The War* p. 159.

262 Dunn *The War* p. 309.

263 Hanbury-Sparrow *Land-Locked Lake* p. 293.

264 Jack *General Jack's Diary* p. 256.

265 Cyril Mason 'War Journal', private collection pp. 31, 90.

266 Sassoon *Infantry Officer* p. 19.

267 Adams *Nothing of Importance* p. 129.

268 James Agate *L of C: Being the letters of a temporary officer in the Army Service Corps* (London 1917) pp. 149, 160.

269 Carton de Wiart *Happy Odyssey* pp. 86–7.

270 Ogle *Fateful Battle Line* p. 168.

271 Seton-Hutchison *Warrior* pp. 67–8, 212.

272 Tom Burke 'In Memory of Tom Kettle' in *The Blue Cap: Journal of the Royal Dublin Fusiliers Association* (Vol. 9, Sept. 2002) p. 7.

273 Coppard *With a Machine Gun* p. 68.

274 Hale *Ordeal* p. 113.

275 Nicholson *Behind the Lines* p. 232.

Steel and Fire

1 *King's Regulations 1912* revised 1914 para 1695.

2 Turner *Accrington Pals* p. 98.

3 Personal account of J. P. Clingo, private collection. Clingo was commissioned into the Lincolns in late 1914, and spent most of the war on the Western Front, winning an MC in 1918.

4 Lucy *Devil* p. 182.

5 Extracts from *General Routine Orders*, 1 January 1918, Part 1 p. 14.

6 Graham C. Greenwell *An Infant in Arms* (London 1972) p. 157.

7 Blacker *Have You Forgotten* p. 43. He was right to be gloomy, for Robin had indeed been killed.

8 Nevil Macready *Annals of An Active Life* (2 vols, London 1924) II p. 128.

9 Extracts from *General Routine Orders*, 1 January 1918, Part 1 p. 65.

10 McCleary (ed.) *Dear Amy* pp. 19, 27.

11 Griffith *Mametz* p. 45.

12 Graves *Goodbye* p. 161.

13 Hawkings *Ypres to Cambrai* p. 90.

14 Livermore *Long 'Un* p. 62.

15 Quoted in Malcolm Brown *The*

Imperial War Museum Book of the Western Front (London 1993) p. 264.

16 Arthur Behrend *As from Kemmel Hill* (London 1963) pp. 138–9.

17 Campbell *Cannon's Mouth* p. 49.

18 Huntley Gordon *The Unreturning Army: A Field Gunner in Flanders 1917–1918* (London 1969) p. 57.

19 Dunn *The War* p. 432.

20 *The NCO's Musketry Small Book* (London 1915) pp. 3, 103.

21 Jones *In Parenthesis* p. 184.

22 *Musketry Regulations Part I 1909 Reprinted 1914* p. 152.

23 Ashurst *My Bit* pp. 26–7.

24 Bullock Papers.

25 Turner *Accrington Pals* p. 99.

26 Lucy *Devil* p. 180.

27 Bullock Papers.

28 Groom *Poor Bloody Infantry* (London 1978) p. 104.

29 *Preliminary Notes on the Tactical Lessons of Recent Operations SS110* (July 1916) p. 2.

30 *Infantry Training 1914* pp. 134, 146. Emphasis in original.

31 Hanbury Sparrow *Land-Locked Lake* p. 213.

32 Liddell Diary, Department of Documents, Imperial War Museum.

33 Graves *Goobye* p. 175.

34 Seton-Hutchison *Warrior* p. 135.

35 C. Dudley Ward *History of the Welsh Guards* (London 1920) p. 119.

36 Carrington *Soldier from the Wars* p. 176.

37 Martin Middlebrook *The First Day on the Somme* (London 1971) p. 184.

38 Crozier *Brass Hat* p. 228.

39 Billy Congreve *Armageddon Road: A VC's Diary 1914–1916* (ed. Terry Norman) (London 1982) p. 165. Hartlepool was amongst the coastal towns raided by German cruisers in December 1914, and some men from 9/DLI were killed.

40 Middlebrook *First Day* p. 162.

41 Blacker *Have You Forgotten* p. 174.

42 It is a reflection on the weapon's enduring, 'eternally-obsolescent' merit that a Scots Guards company commander bayoneted two Argentinian soldiers during a night attack in the Falklands in 1982. By then weapons were far more sophisticated than in 1918, but the need to put steel in the soul was as strong as ever.

43 Edmonds *Military Operations, 1915* I p. 71.

44 Burgoyne *Diaries* p. 208.

45 Dolden *Cannon Fodder* p. 28.

46 Anthony Saunders *The Weapons of Trench Warfare 1914–18* (Stroud 1999) p. ix.

47 *Knowledge For War* p. 78.

48 Dunn *The War* p. 148.

49 The design was modified in the inter-war period to produce the 36 Grenade, which survived for most of my own military service, and even its replacement embodies the same essential features.

50 Ashurst *My Bit* p. 126.

51 Dunn *The War* p. 332.

52 Philip J. Haythornthwaite *The World War One Source Book* (London 1997) p. 195.

53 Chapman *Passionate Prodigality* p. 60.

54 Griffith *Battle Tactics* p. 123.

55 Coppard *With a Machine Gun* p. 103.

56 Coppard *With a Machine Gun* p. 66.

57 Bickersteth (ed.) *Diaries* p. 112.

58 Seton-Hutchison *Warrior* pp. 209, 215.

59 Seton-Hutchison *Warrior* p. 210.

60 Coppard *With a Machine Gun* p. 110.

61 Coppard *With a Machine Gun* p. 127.

62 The cavalry preferred the Hotchkiss, with its distinctive rigid ammunition feed strip. It was arguably a better-designed weapon than the Lewis, but its ammunition strip was very susceptible to dirt.

63 Quoted in Nigel Cave *Passchendaele: The Fight for the Village* (London 1997) p. 74.

64 Dudley Ward *Welsh Guards* p. 150.

65 Dudley Ward *Welsh Guards* p. 151.

66 Len Trawin *Early British Quick-Firing Artillery* (Hemel Hempstead 1997) p. 248.

67 Bidwell and Graham *Fire-Power* p. 11.

68 Lutyens Papers, Department of Documents, Imperial War Museum.

69 Helm Papers, private collection.

70 Bickersteth (ed.) *Bickersteth Diaries* p. 100.

71 Osburn *Unwilling Passenger* p. 38.

72 Burgoyne *Diaries* p. 129.

73 Dunn *The War* p. 359.

74 Shephard *Sergeant Major's War* p. 26.

75 Dunn *The War* p. 401.

76 Shephard *Sergeant Major's War* p. 52.

77 Quoted in Terence Denman *Ireland's Unknown Soldiers* (Blackrock, Co. Dublin, 1992) p. 98.

78 Dunn *The War* p. 398.

79 Blacker *Have You Forgotten* p. 260.

80 Ogle *Fateful Battle Line* pp. 103–4.

81 *Statistics* p. 451 for a summary of gun and howitzer delivery, and pp. 466–89 for notes on munitions supply.

82 *Field Service Regulations 1909 Part I* p. 143. Emphasis in original.

83 Quoted in David T. Zabecki *Steel Wind: Colonel Georg Bruchmuller and the Birth of Modern Artillery* (London 1994) p. 74.

84 Arthur Behrend *As from Kemmel Hill* (London 1963) p. 53.

85 Rudolf Binding *A Fatalist At War* (London 1929) p. 194.

86 Junger *Storm of Steel* p. 96.

87 Westmann *Surgeon* p. 95.

88 Moyne *Staff Officer* p. 116.

89 Quoted in Prior and Wilson *Command* p. 197.

90 Feilding *War Letters* p. 299.

91 Moyne *Staff Officer* p. 112.

92 Talbot Kelly *Subaltern's Odyssey* p. 128.

93 Jones *In Parenthesis* p. 197.

94 Campbell *Cannon's Mouth* p. 25.

95 Campbell *Cannon's Mouth* p. 162.

96 Campbell *Cannon's Mouth* pp. 47–8.

97 Stanford to 'John', 7 July 1916, Stanford Papers, private collection.

98 Stanford to his mother, 8 July 1916, Stanford Papers, private collection.

99 Wade *War of the Guns* p. 92.

100 Campbell *Cannon's Mouth* pp. 168–173.

101 Behrend *As From Kemmel Hill* p. 72.

102 Tyndale-Biscoe *Gunner Subaltern* pp. 96–9.

103 Denman *Ireland's Unknown Soldiers* p. 66.

104 Campbell *Cannon's Mouth* p. 71.

105 Campbell *Cannon's Mouth* p. 57.

106 Talbot Kelly *Subaltern's Odyssey* p. 108.

107 Behrend *As From Kemmel Hill* p. 61.

108 Sir Martin Farndale *History of the Royal Regiment of Artillery, The Western Front 1914–18* (Woolwich 1986) p. 210.

109 Shephard *Sergeant Major's War* p. 40.

110 Stanhope Papers, Department of Documents, Imperial War Museum.

111 Graves *Goodbye* p. 123.

112 Ginns Papers.

113 Hawkings *From Ypres* p. 68.

114 Livermore *Long 'Un* p. 51.

115 Lieutenant W. Drury, 4/KSLI 'Gas: Western Command Gas School', private collection.

116 Roe *Accidental Soldiers* p. 62.

117 Dunn *The War* pp. 390–1.

118 Charles Arnold *From Mons to Messines and Beyond* (London 1985) p. 51.

119 Quoted in Donald Richter *Chemical Soldiers: British Gas Warfare in World War 1* (Lawrence, Kansas, 1992) p. 211.

120 Littlewood Papers, Department of Documents, Imperial War Museum.

121 Richter *Chemical Soldiers* p. 182.

122 Richter *Chemical Soldiers* p. 190.

123 Bourne *Who's Who* p. 117.

124 Hanbury Sparrow *Land-Locked Lake* pp. 309–10.

125 Martin *Poor Bloody Infantry* pp. 55–6.

126 Bullock Papers.

127 Dunn *The War* p. 198.

128 SS 135 *The Division in Attack*, November 1918, pp. 69–71.

129 Martin *Poor Bloody Infantry* p. 84.

130 Brooks Papers, Liddle Archive, Brotherton Library, University of Leeds.

131 V. F. Eberle *My Sapper Venture* (London 1973) p. 130.

132 These remain the colours of the Royal Tank Regiment's stable belt. They also explain (though they cannot excuse) a drink called the Royal Tank, made up of carefully-poured layers of Tia Maria, Cherry Brandy and Crème de Menthe. Its effect is shattering.

133 Haig *Dispatches* p. 155.

134 John Foley 'A7V Sturmpanzerwagen' in Stevenson Pugh (ed.) *Armour in Profile* (Windsor 1968).

135 Quoted in Malcolm Brown *The Imperial War Museum Book of 1918, the Year of Victory* (London 1998) pp. 198–9, 202–3.

136 Victor Archard Papers, Tank Museum, Bovington.

137 B. L. Henriques Papers, Tank Museum, Bovington.

138 C. B. Arnold Papers, Tank Museum, Bovington.

139 Griffith *British Fighting Methods* p. 138.

140 In much of what follows I gratefully acknowledge my debt to my PhD student David Kenyon: this is not the first occasion on which the roles of teacher and taught have been reversed.

141 Snelling Papers, Department of Documents, Imperial War Museum; Home *Diary* p. 38.

142 F. M. Edwards *Notes on the Training, Organisation and Equipment of Cavalry for War* (London 1910) p. 16.

143 K. B. Godsell Papers, Liddle Archive, Brotherton Library, University of Leeds.

144 M. von Posek *The German Cavalry in 1914 in Belgium and France* (Berlin 1932) p. 14.

145 Quoted in David Ascoli *Mons Star* (London 1981) pp. 52–53.

146 Richard Holmes *Riding the Retreat: Mons to the Marne 1914 Revisited* (London 1995) pp. 213–18.

147 Home *Diary* p. 118.

148 Lyn Macdonald *Somme* (London 1983) pp. 137–8.

149 This analysis draws heavily on David Kenyon's unpublished work.

150 Nicholson *Behind the Lines* p. 218.

151 Quoted in The Marquess of Anglesey *A History of the British Cavalry 1816–1919, Vol 8: The Western Front* (Barnsley 1997) pp. 131–7.

152 Quoted in Cusack and Herbert *Scarlet Fever* pp. 73–4.

153 Quoted in Anglesey *History of the British Cavalry* VIII p. 263.

154 Nicholson *Behind the Lines* p. 215.

155 Bickersteth (ed.) *Bickersteth Diaries* pp. 280, 289.

156 Quoted in Anglesey *History of the British Cavalry* VIII p. 260

157 For a well-researched rendition of this tragic tale see Roy F. Ramsbottom, *Marching as to War* (Tarporley, Cheshire, 2000). Also killed was Captain Philip Egerton, whose brother Rowland had been killed as a subaltern in the Royal Welch Fusiliers at First Ypres. They were the sons of Sir Philip Grey-Egerton and his American-born wife, Mae. She had earlier been courted by the novelist Anthony Hope, and is probably the model for the beautiful Princess Flavia in *The Prisoner of Zenda*. With Philip's death there was no heir to the baronetcy, and the Egertons' ancestral home, Oulton Park in Cheshire, burned down in February 1926.

158 Harry Easton Papers, Liddle Collection, Brotherton Library, University of Leeds.

159 Richard van Emden (ed.) *Tickled to Death to Go* (Staplehurst 1996) p. 52.

160 R. G. Garrod Papers, Liddle Collection, Brotherton Library, University of Leeds.

161 Van Emden (ed.) *Tickled to Death* p. 126.

162 Anglesey *History of the British Cavalry* VIII p. 18.

163 Edmonds *Military Operations 1914* I p. 353.

164 Glubb *Into Battle* p. 48.

165 Fisher *Requiem for Will* (privately printed 2002) p. 66.

166 No serious student of the war should be without Peter Chasseaud *Topography of Armageddon: A British Trench Map Atlas of the First World War* (London 1991). My own account of the growth of military survey on the Western Front is a highly abbreviated precis of the author's introduction.

167 Roe *Accidental Soldiers* p. 34.

168 Martin *Poor Bloody Infantry* p. 145.

169 I am indebted to Dr Steve Badsey for this information.

170 Captain Robert V. Dolby *A Regimental Surgeon in War and Prison* (Edinburgh 1917) p. 111.

171 Alexander Barrie *War Underground* (Staplehurst 2000) p. 26.

172 Ashurst *My Bit* p. 99.

173 Ogle *Fateful Battle Line* p. 46.

174 Dunham *The Long Carry* p. 17.

175 Quoted in Ian Passingham *Pillars of Fire: The Battle of Messines Ridge June 1917* (Stroud, Gloucs., 1998) pp. 63–4.

176 Parker *Into Battle* p. 74.

177 Adams *Nothing of Importance* p. 222.

178 Adams *Nothing of Importance* pp. 218–19.

179 Roe *Accidental Soldiers* p. 98.

180 Hawkings *From Ypres* p. 67.

181 Dunn *The War* p. 193.

182 Dunn *The War* pp. 209–17; Richards *Old Soldiers* pp. 168–70.

183 Barrie *War Underground* p. 218.

184 The best modern research now identifies twenty-four mines. Nineteen were fired, and of the

remainder two survived the war. One exploded during a thunderstorm in July 1955. De-mining work recently carried out on the Western Front by the Durand Group suggests that the detonators and fuses have long since lost their efficacy, but the ammonal will still explode, though perhaps with only one-third of its former vigour.

185 Philip Gibbs.

186 *Statistics* p. 185.

187 H. B. Owens Papers, Department of Documents, Imperial War Museum.

188 Dolby *Regimental Surgeon* p. 5.

189 Chapman *Passionate Prodigality* p. 211.

190 Dunham *The Long Carry* p. 185.

191 David Rorie *A Medico's Luck in the War* (Aberdeen 1929) p. 82.

192 Quoted in Joanna Bourke *An Intimate History of Killing* (Cambridge 1999) p. 263.

193 Dolden *Cannon Fodder* p. 29.

194 Burgoyne *Diaries* p. 61.

195 Arthur Smith Papers, Department of Documents, Imperial War Museum.

196 Gladden *Ypres 1917* p. 72.

197 Dunham *The Long Carry* p. 13.

198 Stormont Gibbs *From the Somme to the Armistice* (London 1986) p. 66.

199 Bullock Papers. And it would be wrong not to praise the courage of German stretcher-bearers who worked so well for their captors: in April 1917 Julian Bickersteth took charge of a party of 200, and wrote appreciatively that they 'worked well'.

200 French *Gone for a Soldier* pp. 85–6.

201 Parker *Into Battle* p. 31.

202 Harold Dearden *Medicine and Duty* (London 1928) p. 190.

203 Blacker *Have You Forgotten* pp. 129–30.

204 Osburn *Unwilling Passenger* pp. 134–5.

205 Rogerson *Last of the Ebb* p. 74.

206 Helm Papers, Light Infantry Office (Yorkshire).

207 Dunham *Long Carry* p. 140.

208 M. W. Littlewood Papers, Department of Documents, Imperial War Museum.

209 Bickersteth (ed.) *Bickersteth Diaries* pp. 106–7, 111.

210 Hawkings *From Ypres* p. 99.

211 Rorie *Medico's Luck* p. 7.

212 Dolby *Regimental Surgeon* p. 18.

213 A. J. Arnold Papers, Department of Documents, Imperial War Museum.

214 Martin *Poor Bloody Infantry* p. 163.

215 Roe *Accidental Soldiers* p. 192.

216 Ogle *Fateful Battle Line* p. 63.

217 Bullock Papers.

218 May Tilton *The Grey Battalion* (Sydney 1934) pp. 203, 185, 263.

219 Mellersh *Schoolboy Into War* pp. 95–6.

220 Spicer *Letters from France* p. 75.

221 Ogle *Fateful Battle Line* p. 61.

222 Bullock Papers.

223 Much of this reflects the excellent article by Geoffrey Noon, 'The Treatment of Casualties in the Great War' in Griffith *British Fighting Methods*.

224 Sir W. G. Macpherson *Medical Services: General History Vol 1* (London 1921) p. 201.

225 G. O. Chambers Papers, Department of Documents, Imperial War Museum.

226 Roe *Accidental Soldiers* p. 122.

227 Carr *Ploughshares* p. 54.

228 Peter Leese *Shell Shock* (London 2002) p. 176.

Heart and Soul

1 Jones *In Parenthesis* p. 201.
2 Manning *Her Privates We* p. 147.
3 Quoted in Lyn Macdonald *They Called it Passchendaele* (London 1978) p. 74.
4 Hiscock *Bells of Hell* p. 86.
5 Baynes and Maclean *Tale of Two Captains* p. 5.
6 Dunham *The Long Carry* p. 198.
7 Fussell *The Ordeal* p. 43.
8 Fussell *The Ordeal* p. 100.
9 Graham *Private in the Guards* p. 78.
10 Barbusse *Le Feu* pp. 23–4. Author's translation.
11 Chant Papers.
12 Rogerson *Twelve Days* p. 107.
13 Chapman *Passionate Prodigality* p. 45.
14 Jones *In Parenthesis* p. 219.
15 Richards *Old Soldiers* p. 12.
16 John Brophy and Eric Partridge *The Long Trail: What the British Soldier Sang and Said in the Great War of 1914–18* (London 1965) pp. 85–6.
17 Arthur Smith Papers, Department of Documents, Imperial War Museum.
18 Brophy and Partridge *Long Trail* p. 208.
19 Roe *Accidental Soldiers* p. 29.
20 A company quartermaster sergeant in the infantry, with his three stripes topped by a crown, held the *rank* of colour sergeant but the *appointment* of CQMS. His rank equated to that of staff sergeant elsewhere.
21 Dunn *The War* p. 427.
22 J. Gibbons *Roll on the Next War* (London 1935) p. 32.
23 Dolby *Regimental Surgeon* p. 206.
24 Coppard *With a Machine Gun* p. 52.
25 Hodges *Men of 18* p. 108.
26 Dudley Ward *Welsh Guards* p. 24.
27 Bickersteth (ed.) *Bickersteth Diaries* p. 175.
28 Dudley Ward *Welsh Guards* p. 393.
29 T. H. Davies Papers, Department of Documents, Imperial War Museum.
30 Alan Wilkinson *The Church of England and the First World War* (London 1978) p. 7.
31 Quoted in Wilkinson *Church of England* p. 149.
32 Bickersteth (ed.) *Bickersteth Diaries* pp. 193–4.
33 Wilkinson *Church of England* p. 5.
34 Bickersteth (ed.) *Bickersteth Diaries* p. 138.
35 Quoted in Wilkinson *Church of England* p. 44.
36 Graham *Private in the Guards* pp. 253–5.
37 Richards *Old Soldiers*.
38 Martin *Poor Bloody Infantry* p. 18.
39 Dolden *Cannon Fodder* p. 12.
40 Montague *Disenchantment* (London 1922) p. 80.
41 Siegfried Sassoon *Memoirs of a Fascinating Man* (London 1971) p. 247.
42 Quoted in Wilkinson *Church of England* p. 39.
43 Louden *Chaplains in Conflict* p. 27.
44 *Statistics* p. 190.
45 Louden *Chaplains* caption to illustration, page unnumbered.
46 Quoted in Wilkinson *Church of England* p. 127.
47 Bickersteth (ed.) *Bickersteth Diaries* p. 67.
48 H. C. Jackson *Pastor on the Nile* (London 1960) p. 161.
49 Michael Moynihan *With God on Our Side* (London 1983) pp. 15–16.
50 Quoted in Louden *Chaplains* p. 60.

51 Bickersteth (ed.) *Bickersteth Diaries* p. 138.

52 Quoted in Wilkinson *Church* p. 143.

53 Jonathan Horne (ed.) *The Best of Good Fellows: The Diaries and Memoirs of the Rev Charles Edmund Doudeney* (London 1995) p. 137.

54 T. H. Davies Papers, Department of Documents, Imperial War Museum.

55 Hanbury Sparrow *Land-Locked Lake* p. 160.

56 T. H. Davies Papers.

57 Canon F. H. Drinkwater Papers, Department of Documents, Imperial War Museum.

58 Bickersteth (ed.) *Bickersteth Diaries* p. 153.

59 Bickersteth (ed.) *Bickersteth Diaries* p. 257.

60 Graves *Goodbye* p. 158.

61 Chapman *Passionate Prodigality* p. 117.

62 Bickersteth (ed.) *Bickersteth Diaries* p. 181.

63 French *Gone for a Soldier* pp. 80–81.

64 Drinkwater Papers.

65 Crozier *The Men I Killed* pp. 76–7.

66 Quoted in Wilkinson *Church of England* p. 140.

67 Dunn *The War* p. 556.

68 Reverend Pat Mc Cormick *My Diary of the Great War to Nov 1916*, Department of Documents, Imperial War Museum.

69 Reverend John Sellors Papers, Department of Documents, Imperial War Museum.

70 Quoted in Louden *Chaplains* p. 49.

71 Quoted in Louden *Chaplains* p. 49.

72 G. A. Studdert Kennedy *The Unutterable Beauty* (Oxford 1983) p. 11.

73 Louden *Chaplains in Conflict* (London 1996) p. 51.

74 Feilding *War Letters* pp. 136, 138.

75 Blacker *Have You Forgotten Yet?* p. 114.

76 Moynihan *God on Our Side* p. 160.

77 Horne (ed.) *The Best of Good Fellows* p. 185.

78 Reith *Wearing Spurs* p. 158.

79 Douie *Weary Road* p. 47.

80 Nicholson *Behind the Lines* pp. 155–6.

81 Graves *Goodbye* p. 157.

82 Gordon *Unreturning Army* p. 81.

83 A. J. Arnold papers, Department of Documents, Imperial War Museum.

84 Mc Cormick *Diary*, Department of Documents, Imperial War Museum.

85 George Taylor Papers, Department of Documents, Imperial War Museum.

86 R. G. Ashford Papers, Liddle Collection, Brotherton Library, University of Leeds.

87 L. A. Doust Papers, Liddle Collection, Brotherton Library, University of Leeds.

88 Quoted in Moynihan *God on Our Side* p. 7.

89 Bickersteth (ed.) *Bickersteth Diaries* p. 105.

90 Groom *Poor Bloody Infantry* p. 122.

91 Ashford Papers.

92 Talbot Kelly *Subaltern's Odyssey* p. 45.

93 Blacker *Have You Forgotten?* pp. 158–64.

94 Doiue *Weary Road* p. 153.

95 Groom *Poor Bloody Infantry* p. 118.

96 Hodges *Men of '18* p. 84.

97 Campbell *Cannon's Mouth* p. 44.

98 Rogerson *Twelve Days* p. 88.

99 Vaughan *Some Desperate Glory* p. 107.

100 Dunn *The War* p. 183.

101 Graves *Goodbye* p. 157.

102 Quoted in J. G. Fuller *Troop Morale and Popular Culture in the British and Dominion Armies 1914–18* (London 1990) p. 27.

103 Gibbs *Realities of War* p. 57.

104 Quoted in Moynihan *Armageddon* p. 42.

105 Edward Samuel Underhill *A Year on the Western Front* (London 1988) pp. 6–7.

106 Quoted in Fuller *Troop Morale* p. 128.

107 Montague *Disenchantment* p. 101.

108 Mottram *Spanish Farm.*

109 Reith *Wearing Spurs* p. 205.

110 Martin *Poor Bloody Infantry* pp. 136–7.

111 Mellersh *Schoolboy into War* pp. 100–01.

112 Hiscock *Bells of Hell* p. 31.

113 Sydney Giffard *Guns, Kites and Horses* (London 2003) p. 221.

114 Graham *Private in the Guards* p. 341.

115 Tony Ashworth *Trench Warfare: The Live and Let Live System* (London 1980) p. 154.

116 Carrington, *Soldier From the Wars* p. 98.

117 Montague *Disenchantment* p. 40.

118 Gale *Call to Arms* pp. 29–30.

119 Montague *Disenchantment* p. 40.

120 Siegfried Sassoon *Collected Poems* (London 1947).

121 H. Carpenter *J. R. R. Tolkien: A Biography* (London 1978) p. 89.

122 Quoted in G. D. Sheffield *Leadership in the Trenches* (London 2000) p. 181.

123 Quoted in Liddle *Passchendaele in Perspective* p. 360.

124 Montague *Disenchantment* pp. 33, 59.

125 Frederic Coleman *With the Cavalry in 1914* (London 1916) p. 122.

126 French *Gone for a Soldier* pp. 68–9.

127 Montague *Disenchantment* p. 108.

128 Graham *Private in the Guards* p. 328.

129 Jones *In Parenthesis* p. 204.

130 Rogerson *Twelve Days* p. 124.

131 Congreve *Armageddon Road* p. 57.

132 Graves *Goodbye* p. 157.

133 Hanbury Sparrow *Land-Locked Lake* pp. 222, 212.

134 Non-commissioned personnel in the German army fell into three categories, very much simplified here. There were the men, from the private *soldat* (with regimental and arm of service variations like *grenadier, reiter* or *kanonier*) to the *gefreiter*, effectively a senior private. Then came the junior NCOs – *Unteroffiziere ohne Portepee – unteroffizier* and, in some arms, *sergeant.* Lastly came the senior NCOs – *Unteroffiziere mit Portepee* – including *vizefeldwebel* and *feldwebel* (*vizewachtmeister* and *wachtmeister* in some arms) to two grades that were effectively officer-substitutes, *offizierstellvertreter* and *feldwebelleutnant.* Potential officers could rank with the junior NCOs as a *fahnrich* or with the senior NCOs as a *portepeefahrich*, and had executive authority.

135 Dunn *The War* p. 243.

136 Dunn *The War* p. 244.

137 Stormont Gibbs *From the Somme to the Armistice* (London 1986) p. 69.

138 Dunn *The War* p. 353.

139 Dunn *The War* p. 214.

140 Hodges *Men of '18* p. 156.

141 Rogerson *Twelve Days* p. 118.

142 Edmund Blunden *Undertones of War* (London 1965) p. 108.

143 Sassoon *Infantry Officer* p. 159.

144 Behrend *Kemmel Hill* pp. 96, 89.

145 Talbot Kelly *Subaltern's Odyssey* p. 123.

146 Gladden *Ypres 1917* p. 66.

147 William Carr *A Time to Leave the Ploughshares* (London 1985) pp. 163–4.

148 Dolby *Regimental Surgeon* pp. 113–14.

149 Charles Arnold *From Mons to Messines and Beyond* (London 1985) p. 24.

150 Bynes and Maclean *Tale of Two Captains* p. 106.

151 Priestley *Margin Released* p. 130.

152 Bickersteth (ed.) *Bickersteth Diaries* p. 267.

153 Congreve *Armageddon Road* p. 57.

154 Underhill *A Year* p. 56.

155 Martin *Poor Bloody Infantry* pp. 117–18.

156 George Adams Papers, Liddle Archive, Brotherton Library, University of Leeds.

157 Greenwell *Infant in Arms* p. 21.

158 Adams *Nothing of Importance* pp. 31–2.

159 See Malcolm Brown and Shirley Seaton *Christmas Truce* (London 1984).

160 Griffith *Mametz* pp. 32, 34.

161 Chapman *Passionate Prodigality* p. 66.

162 Quoted in Ashworth *Trench Warfare* p. 139.

163 Harris *Billie* p. 109. Bull's eyes, inners and magpies were the rings on the targets used on the rifle range, and during range practice the butt-markers, in the cover of the butts below the targets, used a marker (or, in the case of misses, a flag disrespectfully known as Maggie's drawers) to signal the result of the shot.

164 Percy Croney *Soldier's Luck* (London 1965) p. 86.

165 Eberle *My Sapper Venture* p. 23.

166 Major General Lord Edward Gleichen *The Doings of the Fifteenth Infantry Brigade* (Edinburgh 1917) p. 81.

167 Dunham *Long Carry* p. 52.

168 Burgoyne *Diaries* p. 76.

169 Hawkings *From Ypres* p. 82.

170 Coppard *Machine Gun* pp. 86, 90.

171 Feilding *War Letters* pp. 156, 159.

172 Carrington *Soldier* p. 183.

173 T. P. Marks *The Laughter Goes From Life* (London 1977) p. 124.

174 Junger *Storm of Steel* pp. 277–8.

175 Graham *Private in the Guards* p. 219.

176 Coppard *Machine Gun* p. 95.

177 Chapman *Passionate Prodigality* pp. 99–100.

178 Hodges *Men of 18* p. 94.

179 G. and S. Rain Papers, Liddle Archive, Brotherton Library, University of Leeds.

180 Hanbury Sparrow *Land-Locked Lake* p. 114.

181 Ward *Welsh Guards* p. 127.

182 Arthur Smith Papers.

183 Stanhope Papers.

184 Greenwell *Infant in Arms* p. 119.

185 Chapman *Passionate Prodigality* p. 272.

186 Crozier *Brass Hat* p. 43.

187 Richards *Old Soldiers* p. 254.

188 Gladden *Ypres 1917* p. 63.

189 Graham *Private in the Guards* p. 218.

190 Quoted in Bourke *Killing* p. 183.

191 Arthur Hubbard Papers, Department of Documents, Imperial War Museum.

192 Crozier *Brass Hat* p. 108.

193 Crozier *Brass Hat* p. 111.

194 Williamson *Wet Flanders Plain* p. 18.
195 Parker *Into Battle* p. 78.
196 Vaughan *Some Deperate Glory* p. 228.
197 Crozier *The Men I Killed* p. 273.
198 *Manual of Military Law 1914* (London 1914) p. 1.
199 *Burgoyne Diaries* pp. 6, 24.
200 Dunn *The War* pp. 100–101.
201 Arnold *Mons to Messines* p. 30.
202 Stanhope Papers.
203 W. J. Albert Papers, Liddle Archive, Brotherton Library, University of Leeds.
204 *King's Regulations 1912 (Revised 1914)* para 446.
205 Ogle *Fateful Battle Line* pp. 17–18.
206 *Manual of Military Law 1914* p. 721.
207 Arthur James Moss *A Diary from the Trenches* (privately printed, 2002) p. 35.
208 Roe *Accidental Soldiers* p. 122.
209 Victor Archard Papers, Tank Museum, Bovingdon.
210 Moss *Diary* p. 9. I was initially sceptical about this assertion, but this is an authentic diary, not written with publication in mind, and seems an honest account. The punishment, clearly illegal in the form described, was a fusion of formal and informal penalties, and suggests a gross lack of officer supervision.
211 Turner *Accrington Pals* p. 116.
212 Major General Douglas Wimberley *Scottish Soldier* (typescript account, private collection) p. 98.
213 Feilding *War Letters* p. 175.
214 *Manual of Military Law 1914* pp. 631–6.
215 P. J. Oldfield 'The Field General Court Martial of 7595

Private James A. Haddock', *Stand To* (no. 39 Winter 1993).
216 Carrington *Soldier from the Wars* p. 172.
217 Crozier *Brass Hat* p. 149.
218 Chapman *Passionate Prodigality* pp. 73–4.
219 McCleary (ed.) *Dear Amy* p. 158.
220 Quoted in Corns and Hughes-Wilson *Blindfold and Alone* p. 359.
221 Bond (ed.) *Staff Officer* p. 118.
222 *Burgoyne Diaries* p. 106.
223 Feilding *War Letters* pp. 175–6.
224 Dunbar Papers, Liddle Archive, Brotherton Library, University of Leeds.
225 Moran *Anatomy of Courage* p. 190.
226 Corns and Hughes-Wilson *Blindfold and Alone* pp. 319–20.
227 Corns and Hughes-Wilson *Blindfold and Alone* p. 343.
228 Ogle *Fateful Battle Line* p. 108.
229 Crozier *Brass Hat* pp. 82–4. There is a similar version in the same author's *The Men I Killed*, though both understandably give the victim a false name.
230 Bickersteth (ed.) *Bickersteth Diaries* pp. 224–5.
231 Nicholson *Behind the Lines* p. 263.
232 For this emotive issue see G. D. Sheffield 'The Operational Role of British Military Police on the Western Front' in Griffith *British Fighting Methods.*
233 G. D. Sheffield *Leadership in the Trenches* (London 2000) p. 104.
234 Frank Gray *Confessions of a Private* (London 1922) pp. viii, ix, 56.
235 Hodges *Men of 18* pp. 174–5.
236 George Fortune account, private collection.
237 Hawkings *From Ypres* p. 60.

238 Gladden *Ypres 1917* p. 133.

239 Shephard *Sergeant Major's War* p. 97.

240 T. P. Marks *The Laughter Goes from Life* (London 1977) p. 45.

241 Carr *Ploughshares* p. 118.

242 Campbell *Cannon's Mouth* p. 201.

243 Dunn *The War* pp. 497–9.

244 Chapman *Passionate Prodigality* p. 248.

245 Baynes *Morale* p. 140.

246 Campbell *Cannon's Mouth* pp. 191, 223.

247 Rogerson *Twelve Days* p. 22.

248 Crozier *Brass Hat* p. 119.

249 Campbell *Cannon's Mouth* p. 239.

250 Herbert Asquith *Moments of Memory* (London ND) p. 296.

251 Talbot Kelly *Subaltern's Odyssey* p. 159.

252 Quoted in Trevor Royle (ed.) *In Flanders Fields: Scottish Poetry and Prose of The First World War* (London 1990) p. 79.

253 Vaughan *Some Desperate Glory* p. 222.

254 Vaughan *Some Desperate Glory* p. 223.

255 Feilding *War Letters* p. 1.

256 Hanbury Sparrow *Land Locked Lake* p. 43.

257 Gladden *Ypres 1917* p. 80.

258 Groom *Poor Bloody Infantry* pp. 15, 24–5, 69, 83, 45.

259 *Statistics* p. 235.

260 Hanbury Sparrow *Land-Locked Lake* p. 293.

261 Richards *Old Soldiers* p. 98.

262 Coppard *With a Machine Gun* p. 69.

263 Lucy *Devil* p. 95.

264 Vaughan *Some Desperate Glory* p. 114.

265 Coppard *With a Machine Gun* p. 118.

266 Moran *Anatomy of Courage* pp. 117, 130.

267 Hodges *Men of 18* p. 157.

268 Cathryn Corns 'So Ended the Golden Age: 9th York and Lancaster on 1st July 1916', in *Battlefields Review* (Issue 27, 2003) p. 56.

269 Richards *Old Soldiers* p. 153.

270 Baynes and Maclean *Tale of Two Captains* p. 122.

271 Cusack *Scarlet Fever* p. 76.

272 *Statistics* pp. 558–60.

273 Stormont Gibbs *Somme to the Armistice* p. 165.

274 Coppard *With a Machine Gun* p. 108.

275 Cusack *Scarlet Fever* p. 76.

276 Roe *Accidental Soldiers* p. 158.

277 Dunn *The War* pp. 524, 526.

278 Feilding *War Letters* p. 317.

279 Shephard *Sergeant Major's War* p. 57.

280 Feilding *War Letters* p. 247.

281 Osburn *Unwilling Passenger* p. 199.

282 Stanhope Papers.

283 Chapman *Passionate Prodigality* p. 144.

284 Questionnaire submitted to Mr K. R. Simpson during his research for *A Nation in Arms*, privately communicated to the author.

285 R. H. D. Tompson Papers, private collection.

286 Rogerson *Twelve Days* p. xi.

287 Parker *Into Battle* p. 28.

288 French *Gone for a Soldier* p. 50.

289 Gaskell Papers, Department of Documents, Imperial War Museum.

290 Baynes and Maclean *Tale of Two Captains* p. 124.

291 Rogerson *Twelve Days* p. 103.

292 Ashurst *My Bit* p. 49.

293 Parker *Into Battle* p. 28.

294 Ogle *Fateful Battle Line* p. 31.

295 Dunn *The War* p. 247.

296 T. A. M. Nash *The Diary of an*

Unprofessional Soldier (Chippenham 1991) p. 65.

297 Williamson *Wet Flanders Plain* p. 40.

298 Richards *Old Soldiers* pp. 16–17.

299 Coppard *With a Machine Gun* p. 76.

300 James Munson (ed.) *Echoes of the Great War: The Diary of the Reverend Andrew Clark 1914–18* (Oxford 1988) p. 94.

301 George Adams Papers.

302 Richards *Old Soldiers* pp. 160–61.

303 Crozier *Brass Hat* p. 239.

304 Ashurst *My Bit* p. 48.

305 Osburn *Unwilling Passenger* p. 334.

306 Rogerson *Twelve Days* p. 148.

307 Dunn *The War* p. 379.

308 Osburn *Unwilling Passenger* p. 355.

309 Jones *In Parenthesis* p. 174.

310 Hiscock *Bells of Hell* p. 76.

311 Graham *Private in the Guards* p. 183.

312 Ogle *Fateful Battle Line* pp. 64–5.

313 Ogle *Fateful Battle Line* p. 64.

314 Ogle *Fateful Battle Line* p. 127.

315 Feilding *War Letters* p. 195.

316 A. J. Arnold Papers.

317 Dolden *Cannon Fodder* p. 49.

318 Blacker *Have You Forgotten* pp. 169–70.

319 Hiscock *Bells of Hell* p. 41.

320 Nicholson *Behind the Lines* p. 256.

321 Reith *Wearing Spurs* p. 135.

322 Quoted in Fuller *Troop Morale* pp. 101–03.

323 Feilding *War Letters* p. 199.

324 Dolden *Cannon Fodder* p. 125.

325 Martin *Poor Bloody Infantry* p. 74.

326 Underhill *A Year on the Western Front* p. 19.

327 Groom *Poor Bloody Infantry* p. 64.

328 Campbell *Cannon's Mouth* p. 125.

329 Graham *Private in the Guards* p. 196.

330 *The Fifth Gloster Gazette* (Shroud 1993) pp. iii–iv.

331 Campbell *Cannon's Mouth* p. 97.

332 Reith *Wearing Spurs* p. 130.

333 Mellersh *Schoolboy into War* p. 143.

334 Crozier *Brass Hat* p. 190.

335 Crozier *Men I Killed* p. 44.

336 Norman Tennant *A Saturday Night Soldier's War* (Waddesdon, Bucks., 1989) p. 109.

Envoi

1 Douie *Weary Road* p. 12.

2 Douie *Weary Road* p. 18.

3 Richards *Old Soldiers* p. 322.

4 Seton-Hutchison *Warrior* p. 314.

5 Marks *Laughter* p. 183.

6 Crozier *Brass Hat* pp. 231–2.

7 Dolden *Cannon Fodder* pp. 178–9.

8 Dunn *The War* p. 567.

9 Richards *Old Soldiers* p. 314.

10 Chapman *Passionate Prodigality* p. 272.

11 Spicer *Letters from France* p. 125.

12 Giffard *Guns, Kits and Horses* p. 189.

13 Tompson Diary, private collection.

14 Bickersteth (ed.) *Bickersteth Diaries* p. 304.

15 Carr *A Time* p. 171.

16 Littlewood Papers, Department of Documents, Imperial War Museum.

17 Mellersh *Schoolboy into War* p. 181.

18 Ogle *Fateful Battle Line* p. 202.

19 Parker *Into Battle* p. 96.

20 Graves *Goodbye* p. 235.

21 Fisher *Requiem for Will* p. 96.

22 Bryan Latham *A Territorial Soldier's War* (Aldershot 1967) p. 128.

23 Harold Macmillan *The Winds of Change* (London 1966) p. 107.

24 Jack *Diary* p. 301.

25 Carrington *Soldier from the Wars* p. 246.

26 Chapman *Passionate Prodigality* p. 270.

27 Greenwell *Infant in Arms* p. 249.

28 Hale *Ordeal* p. 174.

29 Byrne *I survived* p. 107.

30 Dunham *The Long Carry* p. 231.

31 Coppard *With a Machine Gun* p. 135.

32 Carr *A Time* p. 173.

33 Chapman *Passionate Prodigality* p. 276.

34 Douie *Weary Road* p. 213.

35 Chapman *Passionate Prodigality* p. 270.

36 Priestley *Margin Released* p. 140.

37 Quoted in Martin Petter ' "Temporary Gentlemen" in the aftermath of the Great War: Rank, Status and the ex-Officer problem', *Historical Journal* (No. 37 Vol. 1 1994) p. 130.

38 Mellersh *Schoolboy into War* p. 188.

39 Greenwell *Infant in Arms* p. xxi.

40 De Wiart *Happy Odyssey* pp. 89–90.

41 Roe *Accidental Soldiers* p. 192.

42 Carrington *Soldier from the Wars* p. 199.

43 Gordon *Unreturning Army* p. 116.

44 Chapman *Passionate Prodigality* p. 280.

45 Dunn *The War* p. 574.

46 Winter *Great War and the British People* p. 99.

47 Quoted in Winter *Great War and the British People* p. 99; and David Cannadine *The Decline and Fall of the British Aristocracy* (London 1992) p. 83.

48 Gerald Gliddon *The Aristocracy and the Great War* (London 2002) passim.

49 Quoted in Cannadine *Decline and Fall* p. 82.

50 Feversham was originally buried in a private grave outside the cemetery, and moved into it in 1945. I do not know whether his dog accompanied him, but cannot help hoping that it did.

51 Shephard *Sergeant Major's War* p. 75.

52 Douie *Weary Road* p. 21.

53 Carr *A Time* p. 172.

54 Douie *Weary Road* p. 4.

BIBLIOGRAPHY

UNPUBLISHED SOURCES

The National Archives (PRO)

Unit War Diaries in WO95

The Imperial War Museum, Department of Documents
Papers of:

A. J. Arnold
A. V. Bullock
G. O. Chambers
The Reverend Dr T. H. Davies
The Reverend Canon F. H. Drinkwater
G. F. Ellenberger
R. S. Flexen
H. Foakes
Sir John French
C. H. Gaskell
Ronald Ginns
J. W. Gore
Sir Thomas Hutton
P. H. Jones
John Aidan Liddell
W. Littlewood
Lionel Lutyens
R. Scott Macfie
Reverend Pat Mc Cormick
H. B. Owens
The Reverend John Sellors
Henry Smeddle

A. F. Smith
P. Smith
The Reverend F. F. S. Smithwick
Percy Snelling
Lord Stanhope
George Taylor

The Liddle Collection, Brotherton Library, University of Leeds
Papers of:

A. J. Abraham
George Adams
I. G. Andrew
R. G. Ashford
Sir Roger Chant
C. De Boltz
L. A. Doust
William Dunbar
A. S. Durrant
Harry Easton
George Fortune
R. G. Garrod
K. B. Godsell
W. J. Kemp
Edith F. Maudslay
W. J. Nicholson
G. and S. Rain
B. E. Todhunter
N. Whitehead

Queen's Royal Surrey Regiment Museum, Clandon Park, Guildford

Papers of K. A. Oswald
Unpublished typescript: 'History of 1/4th Battalion the Queen's
    Royal West Surrey Regiment'
Unpublished typescript: 'Traditions, Treasures and Personalities of
    the Regiment'

Tank Museum, Bovington
Papers of:

Victor Archard
C. B. Arnold
E. N. Bluemel
Sir Basil Henriques

Privately-owned Papers

W. G. Birley
J. P. Clingo
Peter Crocker
W. Drury
George Fortune
Joseph Garvey
A. W. Hancox
Cyril Helm
C. T. Mason
J. A. C. Pennycuik
H. M. Stanford
A. Sugden
R. H. D. Tompson
Lord Wigram

Manuals and Pamphlets

Field Service Pocket Book, HMSO 1916
Field Service Regulations 1909: Part One, Operations HMSO 1914
Infantry Training 1914, HMSO 1914
King's Regulations and Orders for the Army 1912, Revised August 1914, HMSO 1914
Musketry Regulations Part 1 1909, Reprinted 1914, HMSO 1914
The NCO's Musketry Small Book, London 1915
The Territorial Yearbook 1909, London 1909
Types of Horses Suitable for Army Remounts, Board of Trade, London 1909
SS110 *Preliminary Notes on the Tactical Lessons of Recent Operations*, July 1916

SS135 *The Training and Employment of Divisions*, January 1918
SS144 *The Normal Formation for the Attack*, February 1917
SS309 *Extracts from General Routine Orders . . . Part 1 Adjutant General's Department*, 1 January 1917
SS340 *Extracts from General Routine Orders . . . Part II, Quartermaster General's Branch*, 1 January 1917

Trench Newspapers

Kamp News
The BEF Times
The Cinque Ports Gazette
The Dagger, or London in the Line
The Direct Hit
The Dump
The Fifth Gloster Gazette
The Futile Fusilier
The Gasper
The London Scottish Regimental Gazette
The Minden Magazine
The Mudlark, or the Bedfordshire Gazette
The Red Feather
The Somme Times
The Welsh Division – New Year Souvenir
The Whizz-Bang
The Wipers Times
The Wormlet

PhD Theses

Simpson, Andrew, *The Operational Role of British Corps Command on the Western Front 1914–18*, London University, 1992
Zabecki, David T. *Operational Art and the German 1918 Offensives*, Cranfield University, 2004

PUBLISHED SOURCES

Books

Adams, Bernard, *Nothing of Importance* (London 1988)

Agate, James, *L of C: Being the Letters of a Temporary Officer in the Army Service Corps* (London 1917)

Anglesey, the Marquess of, *A History of the British Cavalry 1816–1919, Vol. 8: The Western Front* (Barnsley 1997)

Arnold, Charles, *From Mons to Messines and Beyond* (London 1985)

Ashurst, George, *My Bit* (Ramsbury 1986)

Audoin-Rouzeau, Stéphane, *14–18: Les Combattants des tranchées* (Paris 1986)

Babington, Anthony, *Shell-Shock: A History of Changing Attitudes to War Neurosis* (London 1997)

Bairnsfather, Bruce, *Bullets and Billets* (London 1916)

Barbusse, Henri, *Le Feu* (Paris 1917)

Barrie, Alexander, *War Underground: The Tunnellers of the Western Front* (Staplehurst 2000)

Barrow, Sir George, *The Fire of Life* (London 1941)

Baynes, John, *Morale* (London 1967)

——and Maclean, Hugh, *A Tale of Two Captains* (Edinburgh 1990)

Beckett, Ian F. W., and Simpson, Keith, *A Nation in Arms* (Manchester 1985)

Behrend, Arthur, *As From Kemmel Hill: An Adjutant in France and Flanders 1917–1918* (London 1963)

Bidwell, Shelford, and Graham, Dominick, *Fire Power: British Army Weapons and Theories of War 1904–1945* (London 1982)

Bickersteth, John, (ed.), *The Bickersteth Diaries* (London 1995)

Binding, Rudolf, *A Fatalist War* (London 1929)

Blacker, C. P., *Have you Forgotten London Yet?* (London 2000)

Blake, Robert, (ed.), *The Private Papers of Douglas Haig* (London 1952)

Blunden, Edmund, *Undertones of War* (London 1965)

Bond, Brian, (ed.), *Staff Officer: The Diary of Lord Moyne* (London 1987)

Boraston, J. H., (ed.), *Sir Douglas Haig's Despatches* (London 1919)

Bourne, J. M., *Who's Who in World War One* (London 2001)

Bridges, Tom, *Alarms and Excursions* (London 1938)

Bibliography

Brown, Ian Malcolm, *British Logistics on the Western Front 1914–18* (London 1998)

Brown, Malcolm, *The Imperial War Museum Book of 1918* (London 1998)

———*The Imperial War Museum Book of the Western Front* (London 1993)

Bruckshaw, Horace *The Diaries of Private Horace Bruckshaw 1915–1916* (London 1979)

Burgoyne, Gerald Achilles, *The Burgoyne Diaries* (London 1985)

Byrne, 'Ginger', *I Survived, Didn't I?* (London 1993)

Cannadine, David, *The Decline and Fall of the British Aristocracy* (London 1992)

Campbell, P. J., *In the Cannon's Mouth* (London 1986)

Carlyon, Les, *Gallipoli* (Sydney 2001)

Cave, Nigel, *Passchendaele: The Fight for the Village* (London 1997)

Carr, William, *A Time to Leave the Ploughshares: A Gunner Remembers 1917–18* (London 1985)

Carrington, Charles, *Soldier from the Wars Returning* (London 1965)

———*A Subaltern's War* (London 1929)

Carton de Wiart, Lt. Gen. Sir Adrian, *Happy Odyssey* (London 1950)

Cave, Nigel, *Vimy Ridge* (London 1996)

Chandler, D. G., (ed.), *The Oxford Illustrated History of the British Army* (Oxford 1994)

Chapman, Guy, *A Passionate Prodigality* (London 1985)

Charteris, Brigadier General John, *At GHQ* (London 1931)

Chasseaud, Peter, *Topography of Armageddon: A British Trench Map Atlas of the First World War* (London 1991)

Clark, Ronald, (ed.), *J. B. S.: The Life and Work of J. B. S. Haldane* (London 1968)

Congreve, Billy, *Armageddon Road: A VC's Diary 1914–16*, edited by Terry Norman (London 1982)

Connell, John, *Wavell: Soldier and Scholar* (London 1964)

Coppard, George, *With a Machine Gun to Cambrai* (London 1988)

Corns, Cathryn, and Hughes-Wilson, John, *Blindfold and Alone* (London 2001)

Costello, Con, *A Most Delightful Station: The British Army and the Curragh of Kildare, Ireland 1855–1922* (Cork 1999)

Craster, J. M., *Fifteen Rounds a Minute: The Grenadiers at War 1914* (London 1976)

Croney, Percy, *Soldier's Luck* (Stockwell, Devon 1965)

Crozier, F. P., *The Men I Killed,* (London 1937)

————*A Brass Hat in No Man's Land* (London 1930)

————*Impressions and Reflections* (London 1930)

Cumming, Hanway R., *A Brigadier in France* (London 1922)

Cusack, John, and Herbert, Ivor, *Scarlet Fever: A Lifetime with Horses* (London 1972)

Davies, Frank, and Maddocks, Graham, *Bloody Red Tabs: General Officer Casualties of the First World War* (London 1995)

De la Gorce, Paul-Marie, *The French Army: A Military Political History* (New York 1963)

Denman, Terence, *Ireland's Unknown Soldiers* (Blackrock, Co. Dublin 1992)

Dolby, Captain Robert V., *A Regimental Surgeon in War and Prison* (Edinburgh 1917)

Dolden, A. Stuart, *Cannon Fodder: An Infantryman's Life on the Western Front 1914–18* (Blandford 1980)

Douie, Charles, *The Weary Road: Recollections of a Subaltern of Infantry* (London 1929)

Doyle, Peter, *Geology of the Western Front* (London 1988)

Dunham, Frank, *The Long Carry* (London 1970)

Dunn, Captain J. C., *The War the Infantry Knew* (London 1987)

Eberle, V. F., *My Sapper Venture* (London 1973)

Edmonds, Sir James, *History of the Great War . . . Military Operations, France and Belgium, 1914,* 2 vols (London 1923–25)

————*Military Operations in France and Belgium 1915,* 2 vols (London 1932)

Edwards, F. M., *Notes on the Training, Organisation and Equipment of Cavalry for War* (London 1910)

Edwin Gibson, T. A., and Kingsley Ward, G., *Courage Remembered* (London 1989)

Ellis, John, *The Sharp End of War* (Newton Abbot 1980)

Ewart, Wilfred, *Scots Guard on the Western Front 1915–1918* (London 2001)

Farrer, Reginald, *The Void of War* (London 1918)

Fay, Judith, and Martin, Richard (eds), *The Jubilee Boy* (London 1987)

Farndale, Sir Martin, *History of the Royal Regiment of Artillery, The Western Front 1914–18* (Woolwich 1986)

Feilding, Rowland, *War Letters to a Wife* (London 1929)

Fisher, William, *Requiem for Will* (Monmouth 2002)

French, Anthony, *Gone for a Soldier* (Kineton 1972)

Gibbs, Philip, *From Bapaume to Passchendaele 1917* (London 1918)

———*The Realities of War* (London 1920)

Gibbs, Stormont, *From the Somme to the Armistice* (London 1986)

Giffard, Sidney, (ed.), *Guns, Kites and Horses* (London 2003)

Gladden, Norman, *Ypres 1917* (London 1967)

Gleichen, Edward, *The Doings of the Fifteenth Infantry Brigade* (Edinburgh 1917)

Gliddon, Gerald, *The Aristocracy and the Great War* (London 2002)

Gordon, Huntley, *The Unreturning Army: A Field Gunner in Flanders 1917–18* (London 1967)

Graham, Stephen, *A Private in the Guards* (London 1919)

Graves, Robert, *But it Still Goes On* (London 1930)

———*Goodbye to All That* (London 1969)

Gray, Frank, *Confessions of a Private* (London 1922)

Greenwell, Graham H., *An Infant in Arms* (London 1972)

Griffith, Paddy, *Battle Tactics on the Western Front: The British Army's Art of Attack 1916–18* (London 1994)

———(ed.), *British Fighting Methods in the Great War* (London 1996)

Griffith, Llewelyn Wyn, *Up to Mametz* (London 1931)

Groom, W. H. A., *Poor Bloody Infantry* (London 1976)

Hamilton, Lieut. Gen. Sir Frederick, *Origins and History of the First Grenadier Guards* (London 1874)

Hanbury Sparrow, Alan, *The Land-Locked Lake* (London 1932)

Hankey, Lord, *The Supreme Command 1914–18*, 2 vols (London 1961)

Harris, Ruth Elwin (ed.), *Billie: The Neville Letters, 1914–16* (London 1991)

Hart-Davis, Duff *End of an Era: Letters and Journals of Sir Alan Lascelles, from 1887 to 1920* (London 1986)

Hatton, S. F., *Yarns of a Yeoman* (London ND)

Hawkings, Frank, *From Ypres to Cambrai* (London 1974)

Hay, Ian, *The First Hundred Thousand* (Edinburgh 1917)

Haythornwaite, Philip J., *The World War One Source Book* (London 1997)

Herbert, Aubrey, *Mons, Anzac and Kut* (London 1920)

Hiscock, Eric, *The Bells of Hell Go Ting-a-ling-a-ling* (London 1976)

Hodges, Frederick James, *Men of 18 in 1918* (Ilfracombe 1988)

Holmes, Richard, *Firing Line* (London 1985)

————*Riding the Retreat: Mons to the Marne 1914 Revisited* (London 1995)

————*The Little Field Marshal: Sir John French* (London 1981)

Holt, Tonie and Valmai, *Poets of the Great War* (London 1999)

Home, Brig. Gen. Sir Archibald, *The Diary of a World War One Cavalry Officer* (London 1985)

Horn, Pamela, *Rural Life in England in the First World War* (New York 1984)

Horne, Jonathan, (ed.), *The Best of Good Fellows: The Diaries and Memoirs of the Rev Charles Edmund Doudeney* (London 1995)

Horsfall, Jack, and Cave, Nigel, *Somme: Serre* (London 1996)

Hutchison, Graham Seton, *Warrior* (London ND)

Johnstone, Tom, *Orange, Green and Khaki* (Dublin 1992)

Jolliffe, John, (ed.), *Raymond Asquith: Life and Letters* (London 1980)

Jones, Daphne, (ed.), *Bullets and Bandsmen: The Story of a Bandsman on the Western Front, Written by His Daughter* (Salisbury 1992)

Jones, David, *In Parenthesis* (New York 1961)

Junger, Ernst, *The Storm of Steel* (London 1929)

Laffin, John, *British Butchers and Bunglers of World War One* (Stroud 1989)

Lake, Captain B. C., *Knowledge for War* (London 1915)

Latham, Bryan, *A Territorial Soldier's War* (Aldershot 1967)

Liddle, Peter H., *Passchendaele in Perspective* (London 1997)

Livermore, Bernard, *Long 'Un – A Damn Bad Soldier* (Bartley, West Yorkshire 1974)

Louden, Stephen H., *Chaplains in Conflict* (London 1996)

Lucy, John, *There's a Devil in the Drum* (London 1938)

Lytton Sells, A., (trans. and ed.), *The Memoirs of James II: His Campaigns as Duke of York 1652–1660* (Bloomington, Indiana 1962)

Mackie, John H. F., (ed.), *Answering the Call: Letters from the Somerset Light Infantry 1914–19* (Eggleston, Co. Durham 2002)

Macmillan, Harold, *The Winds of Change* (London 1966)

Macready, Nevil, *Annals of an Active Life*, 2 vols (London 1924)

Marks, T. P., *The Laughter Goes from Life* (London 1977)

Martin, Bernard, *Poor Bloody Infantry: A Subaltern on the Western Front* (London 1987)

Masefield, John, *The Old Front Line* (London 1917)

————*The Battle of the Somme* (London 1919)

Meacham, Standish, *A Life Apart: The English Working Class* (London 1977)

Middlebrook, Martin and Mary, *The Somme Battlefields* (London 1991)

———*The First Day of the Somme* (London 1971)

———*Your Country Needs You* (Barnsley 2000)

Montague, C. E., *Disenchantment* (London 1922)

Moran, Lord, *The Anatomy of Courage* (London 1945)

Mottram, R. H., *The Spanish Farm Trilogy* (London 1928)

Moynihan, Michael, (ed.), *A Place Called Armageddon; Letters from the Great War* (London 1975)

———(ed.), *Greater Love* (London 1980)

Nash, T. A. M., (ed), *The Diary of an Unprofessional Soldier* (Chippenham 1991)

Neillands, Robin, *The Great War Generals on the Western Front 1914–18* (London 1988)

Nicholson, Colonel W. M., *Behind the Lines* (London 1939)

Ogle, Henry, *The Fateful Battle Line* (London 1993)

Osburn, Arthur, *Unwilling Passenger* (London 1932)

Ousby, Ian, *The Road to Verdun* (London 2001)

Owen, H., and Bell, J., (eds), *Wilfred Owen: Collected Letters* (London 1967)

Paret, Peter, (ed.), *Makers of Modern Strategy* (Oxford 1986)

Parker, Ernest, *Into Battle 1914–18* (London 1994)

Pease, Howard, *The History of the Northumberland (Hussars) Yeomanry* (London 1924)

Pollock, John, *Kitchener* (London 1998)

Porch, Douglas, *The March to the Marne* (Cambridge 1981)

Priestley, J. B., *Margin Released* (London 1962)

Prior, Robin, and Wilson, Trevor, *Command on the Western Front* (London 1992)

Pugh, Stevenson, (ed.), *Armour in Profile* (Windsor 1968)

Ramsbottom, Ray F., *Marching as to War* (Tarporley, Cheshire 2000)

Reith, John, *Wearing Spurs* (London 1966)

Richards, Frank, *Old Soldiers Never Die* (London 1933)

———*Old Soldier Sahib* (London 1936)

Richter, Donald, *Chemical Soldiers: British Gas Warfare in World War I* (Lawrence, Kansas 1992)

Rimington, Major Gen. M. F., *Our Cavalry* (London 1912)

Roe, Brigadier F. P., *Accidental Soldiers* (London 1981)

Rogerson, Sidney, *Last of the Ebb* (London 1937)

———*Twelve Days* (London 1933)

Sainsbury, J. D., *The Hertfordshire Yeomanry* (Welwyn 1994)

Sambrook, James, (ed.), *With the Rank and Pay of a Sapper* (London 1998)

Sassoon, Siegfried, *Memoirs of a Foxhunting Man* (London 1971)

———*Memoirs of an Infantry Officer* (London 1977)

———*Sherston's Progress* (London 1974)

Saunders, Anthony, *The Weapons of Trench Warfare 1914–18* (Stroud 1999)

Shephard, Ernest, *A Sergeant Major's War* (Ramsbury, Wilts. 1987)

Shepherd, Ben, *A War of Nerves: Soldiers and Psychiatrists 1914–1994* (London 2002)

Simkins, Peter, *Kitchener's Army* (Manchester 1988)

Sitwell, Osbert, *Great Morning* (London 1948)

Spears, Edward, *Liaison 1914* (London 1999)

Spears, E. L., *Prelude to Victory* (London 1939)

Spicer, Lancelot Dykes, *Letters from France* (London 1979)

Statistics of the Military Effort of the British Empire during the War (London 1922)

Swinton, Maj. Gen. Sir Ernest, *Twenty Years After: The Battlefields of 1914–18 Then and Now* (London 1920)

Talbot Kelly, R. B., *Subaltern's Odyssey* (London 1980)

Tennant, Norman, *A Saturday Night Soldier's War 1913–18* (Waddesdon, Bucks. 1983)

Terraine, John, *Douglas Haig: The Educated Soldier* (London 1963)

———*The Road to Passchendaele: The Flanders Offensive of 1917* (London 1977)

———*The Smoke and the Fire: Myths and Anti-Myths of War* (London 1992)

Thompson, Flora *Lark Rise to Candleford* (London 1979)

Tilton, May, *The Grey Battalion* (Sydney 1934)

Trawin, Len, *Early British Quick Firing Artillery* (Hemel Hempstead 1997)

Turner, William, *Accrington Pals* (London 1992)

Tyndale-Biscoe, Julian, *Gunner Subaltern* (London 1971)

Underhill, Edward, *A Year on the Western Front* (London 1988)

Vansittart, Peter, (ed.), *John Mansfield's Letters from the Front 1915–17* (London 1984)

Vaughan, Edwin Campion, *Some Desperate Glory* (London 1981)

Van Creveld, Martin, *Command in War* (London 1985)

Wade, Aubrey, *The War of the Guns* (London 1936)

Ward, C. Dudley, *History of the Welsh Guards* (London 1920)

Weist, Andrew A., *Passchendaele and the Royal Navy* (Westport, Conn. 1995)

Westlake, Ray, *Kitchener's Army* (Staplehurst, Kent 1998)

Westman, Stephen, *Surgeon with the Kaiser's Army* (London 1968)

Williamson, Henry, *Love and the Loveless* (London 1958)

———*The Wet Flanders Plain* (London 1987)

Winter, Denis, *Haig's Command* (London 1991)

Winter, J. M., *The Great War and the British People* (London 1985)

Woodruff, William, *The Road to Nab End* (London 2002)

Wynn, Captain G. C., *If Germany Attacks: The Battle in Depth in the West* (London 1940)

Young, Michael, *Army Service Corps 1902–1918* (Barnsley 2000)

Zabecki, David T., *Steel Wind: Colonel George Bruchmuller and the Birth of Modern Artillery* (London 1994)

Articles

Burke, Tom, 'In Memory of Tom Kettle', *The Blue Cap: Journal of the Royal Dublin Fusiliers Association*, Vol. 9, September 2002

Corns, Cathryn, 'So Ended the Golden Age: 9th York and Lancaster Regiment on 1st July 1916', *Battlefields Review*, Issue 27, 2003

Fenton, Ben, 'Shamed General's Battle of the Somme', *Daily Telegraph*, 16 August 1998

Gill, Douglas, 'Mutiny at Etaples Base in 1917', *Past and Present*, No. 69

Hughes, Clive, 'The Welsh Army Corps 1914–15', *Imperial War Museum Review*, No. 1, 1986

Mitchinson, Kevin W., 'The Transfer Controversy: Parliament and London Regiment', *Stand To: The Journal of the Western Front Association*, No. 33, Winter 1991

Petter, Martin, ' "Temporary Gentlemen" in the Aftermath of the Great War: Rank, Status and the ex-Officer Problem', *Historical Journal*, No. 37, Vol. 1, 1994

Philpott, William, 'Why the British Were Really on the Somme: A Reply to Elizabeth Greenhalgh', *War in History*, Vol. 9, No. 4, 2002

Sheffield, G. D., 'The Australians at Poizières: Command and Control on the Somme, 1916', in French, David, and Reid, Brian Holden, *The British General Staff: Reform Innovations c. 1890–1939*, London 2002

Sly, John S., 'The Men of 1914', *Stand To*, No. 34, Summer 1992

Tanner, Alyn, 'Sergeant Sidney Farmer MM – Seventeen Times Wounded!', *Journal of the Orders and Medals Research Society*, Vol. 41, No. 4, December 2002

Tawney, R. H., 'Some Reflections of a Soldier', *Nation*, October 1916

Thompson, David, 'The Second Battalion Durham Light Infantry in the Great War', *Stand To*, No. 65, September 2002

Williams, M. J., 'Thirty Per Cent: A Study in Casualty Statistics', *Journal of the Royal United Services Institute*, February 1964

Williams, M. J., 'The Treatment of German Losses on the Somme in the British Official History', *Journal of the Royal United Services Institute*, February 1966

On-line

www.wardiaries.co.uk

ACKNOWLEDGEMENTS

So many individuals have helped me during the research for this book that it is impossible to thank them all by name. However, I owe a particular debt to Major General Jonathan Bailey, Hugh Bicheno, Dr John Bourne, Clive Priestley and Lieutenant Colonel Les Wilson for their advice and assistance. My PhD student David Kenyon unearthed valuable information on the actions of the cavalry around High Wood on 14 July 1916; Alexander Caldin carried out useful research on trench newspapers and the backgrounds of senior officers, and Corinna Holmes and Frank Turner collated quotations for copyright clearance, which may not have been the most exciting of tasks.

As ever, I am grateful to Rod Suddaby and his team at the Department of Documents, Imperial War Museum; the staff of the Liddle Collection at the Brotherton Library, University of Leeds; the librarians of the Joint Service Command and Staff College, the Royal Military College of Science and the Royal Military Academy Sandhurst. This book could scarcely have been written at all without the kindness of the librarian and staff of the Prince Consort Library at Aldershot, and the forebearance of their dogs.

Arabella Pike of HarperCollins gave wise strategic direction, and Kate Johnson dealt efficiently and sensitively with a myriad of tactical details all too easily overlooked in large, complex engagements. Amanda Russell tracked down the photographs. Last, but emphatically by no means least, my wife Lizzie worked tirelessly gleaning information from books and archives. She also helped me through those impossibly bleak moments, more frequent in this than in any other book I have written, when the nature of the subject matter had me staring across my Hampshire garden through a mist of tears.

For permission to quote from material to which they control the copyright I am grateful to the following. Sheila Barnett for the papers of A. J. Arnold, David S. Chambers for the papers of Guy O. Chambers, Betty Morris for the papers of A. V. Bullock, Alan Debes and the grandchildren of the Reverend T. H. Davies for the war diary of the Reverend

T. H. Davies, Jon Wickett for the diaries of Stapleton Tench Eachus, Eric Foakes, John Foakes and Amanda Foakes for the papers of H. Foakes, George Fortune and Kathleane Peake for the account of George Fortune, the Trustees of the Imperial War Museum for the correspondence of Field Marshal Sir John French, A. Gaskell for the diary of C. H. Gaskell, Elizabeth Robinson for the diaries of Ron Ginns, Dr Patrick Ottaway for the papers of Lieutenant General Sir Thomas Hutton, Margaret Cruft for the papers of the Reverend Pat Mc Cormick, Andrew Paton for the Scott Macfie Papers, Daphne Crabtree for the diary of Cyril Thomas Mason, Paul P. H. Jones for the memoirs of Percy Hughes Jones, Anne Stobbs for the diaries of Roland Brice Miller, Diana Sellors for the diaries of the Reverend John Sellors, Auriol Ingram and Jackie Ingram for the letters of Arthur Smith, Lieutenant Colonel Bill Stanford for the letters of H. M. Stanford, Colonel Richard Brook and the Board of Trustees of the Chevening Estate for the papers of the Earl Stanhope, Dorothy Shotter and Nick Shotter for the diaries of William Shotter, Phil Morgan for the letters of Percy Smith, Pamela McCleary for the letters of Bill Sugden, Lieutenant General Sir Hew Pike for the diaries of R. H. D. Tompson, and Colonel Jolyon Jackson for a letter of W. C. C. Weetman.

I acknowledge the permission of the following publishers to quote from works whose rights they control. Pen and Sword Books Ltd for the Marquess of Anglesey *The History of the British Cavalry*, Brewin Books Ltd for Charles Arnold *From Mons to Messines and Beyond*, Armand Colin for Stéphane Audoin-Rouzeau *14–18: Les Combattants des Tranchées*, Sir John Baynes and the late Hugh Maclean for *A Tale of Two Captains*, Pen and Sword Books Ltd for John Bickersteth (ed.) *The Bickersteth Diaries 1914–18*, Pen and Sword Books Ltd for C. P. Blacker *Have You Forgotten Yet?*, Penguin Books for P. J. Campell *In the Cannon's Mouth*, Robert Hale for William Carr *A Time to Leave the Ploughshores*, The Naval and Military Press for Peter Chasseaud *Topography of Armageddon*, The Irish Academic Press for Terence Denman *Ireland's Unknown Soldiers*, Jonathan Horne for his edition of the Reverend Charles Doudeney's papers, *The Best of Good Fellows*, The Naval and Military Press for Charles Douie *The Weary Road*, The Colonel of the Royal Welch Fusiliers for James Churchill Dunn *The War the Infantry Knew*, Her Majesty's Stationery Office for Sir James Edmonds *Military Operations . . .*, Lionel Leventhal Ltd for Cyril Falls *War Books*, the family of William Fisher for *Requiem for Will* (ISBN 0 9531061 0 1, published at Boughspring, Wyesham Road, Wyesham, Monmouth, Gwent, NP5 3JU), Pen and Sword Books Ltd for Brian Bond (ed.) *Staff*

Officer: The Diaries of Lord Moyne (then Walter Guinness), The Naval and Military Press for Rowland Feilding *War Letters to a Wife*, The University of Indiana Press for A. Lytton Sells (trans. and ed.) *The Memoirs of James II: His Campaigns as Duke of York 1652–1660*, Pan Macmillan for J. M. Craster (ed.) *Fifteen Rounds a Minute . . . Edited from the diaries of Major 'Ma' Jeffreys and others*, Gill & Macmillan Ltd, Dublin for Tom Johnstone *Orange, Green and Khaki*, Tom Burke (Chairman, Royal Dublin Fusiliers Association) for his article on Lieutenant Tom Kettle in *The Blue Cap* Vol. 9 Sept 2002, H. H. Sales for Bernard Livermore *Long 'Un – A Damn Bad Soldier*, The Naval and Military Press for John Lucy *There's a Devil in the Drum*, John H. F. Mackie for *Answering the Call: Letters from the Somerset Light Infantry 1914–19*, Mainstream Publishing for *In Flanders Fields* (poem *In Memoriam, Private D. Sutherland* by Ewart Alan Mackintosh), Pan Macmillan Ltd for Harold Macmillan *Winds of Change*, Serpent's Tail for Frederic Manning *Her Privates We*, The Society of Authors as literary executors of John Masefield for *The Battle of the Somme*, Pen and Sword Books Ltd for John Masefield *The Old Front Line*, A. P. Watt Ltd on behalf of Mrs A. S. Hankinson for R. H. Mottram *The Twentieth Century: A Personal Record*, Pen and Sword Books for Captain Harry Ogle *The Fateful Battle Line*, The Random House Group Ltd for Ian Ousby *The Road to Verdun* published by Jonathan Cape, Oxford University Press for John Bell and H. Owen (eds) *Wilfred Owen: Selected Letters*, Pen and Sword Books for Ernest Parker *Into Battle*, PFD on behalf of the Estate of J. B. Priestley for *Margin Released: A Writer's Reminiscences and Reflections* (Copyright the Estate of J. B. Priestley 1962), Christopher Reith for John Reith *Wearing Spurs*, Pen and Sword Books for Donald Richter *Chemical Soldiers*, Colonel John Sainsbury for *The Hertfordshire Yeomanry*, Faber and Faber for Siegfried Sassoon *Memoirs of an Infantry Officer*, HarperCollins Publishers, Australia, for May Tilton *The Grey Battalion*, Pen and Sword Books Ltd for William Turner *The Accrington Pals*, Eland Books, 61 Exmouth Market, London EC1R 4QL, for the 2000 edition of William Woodruff *The Road to Nab End*, The London Stamp Exchange for Edward Underhill *A Year on the Western Front*, Chrysalis Book Group for Aubrey Wade *The War of the Guns*, Naval and Military Press for C. Dudley Ward *History of the Welsh Guards*.

Despite my best endeavours I have failed to track down all copyright holders. I apologise to those concerned, but if they contact me through HarperCollins Publishers I will make appropriate recompense and ensure that an acknowledgement is inserted in any future edition of this book.

ABBREVIATIONS AND GLOSSARY

AA & QMG	assistant adjutant and quartermaster general (the principal administrative staff officer in a division)
ADC	aide de camp (usually a lieutenant or captain on a general's personal staff)
Adj	adjutant (generally a captain, the staff officer to the commanding officer of a battalion or equivalent)
ADMS	assistant director of Medical Services (the senior medical officer in a division)
ADS	advance dressing station (the second link in the chain of medical evacuation)
AG	adjutant general
Alleyman	slang for a German (from French *allemand*)
APM	assistant provost marshal (responsible for military police matters at division, corps and army headquarters)
Archie	anti-aircraft gun or gunfire. From a music-hall song with the words 'Archibald – certainly not!'
ASC	Army Service Corps (or, unkindly, Ally Sloper's Cavalry)
AVC	Army Veterinary Corps
BC	battery commander
BEF	British Expeditionary Force
BGGS	brigadier general, general staff (chief of staff of a corps)
Blighty	Home, Britain
BM	brigade major (chief of staff of a brigade)
BQMS	battery quartermaster sergeant: the equivalent of CQMS in the Royal Artillery
BSM	battery sergeant major (ranking as warrant officer class 2)
bullring	training area at the base

Canary	training NCO at the base (so called because of his yellow armband)
CB	Companion of the Order of the Bath
	confined to barracks
	counter battery
CCS	casualty clearing station (the third link in the chain of medical evacuation)
CGS	chief of the general staff (chief of staff of the British Expeditionary Force)
CIGS	chief of the imperial general staff (professional head of the British army)
CMG	Companion of the Order of St Michael and St George
C in C	commander in chief (overall commander of the BEF: until December 1915 Field Marshal Sir John French, and then General (later Field Marshal) Sir Douglas Haig
CO	commanding officer (properly used for commanding officers of battalions or their equivalents in other arms, though sometimes blurred with OC [qv])
Coal Box	German heavy shell (so named because of its cloud of black smoke: see also 'Jack Johnson')
CQMS	company quartermaster sergeant (senior NCO, ranking as staff sergeant, responsible for administration at company or equivalent level)
CRA	commander Royal Artillery (artillery commander in a division)
CRE	commander Royal Engineers (engineer commander in a division)
Crump	German heavy shell
CSM	company sergeant major (ranking as warrant officer class 2)
DAA & QMG	deputy assistant adjutant and quartermaster general (subordinate administrative staff officer)
DADMS	deputy assistant director of Medical Services (subordinate medical staff officer)
DADOS	deputy assistant director of Ordnance Services (the senior ordnance officer in a division)

DAQMG	deputy assistant quartermaster general (subordinate administrative staff officer)
DCM	Distinguished Conduct Medal
DSO	Distinguished Service Order
FGCM	Field General Court Martial
Flying pig	type of trench mortar bomb
FOO	forward observation officer
GHQ	general headquarters (headquarters of the BEF, established at St-Omer in the autumn of 1914, moving to Montreuil-sur-Mer in 1916)
GOC	general officer commanding (the commander of a brigade, division, corps or army)
GS	General Service, as in GS wagon
GSO	general staff officer
GSO1	general staff officer 1st grade (Lt. Col.). In a division, its chief of staff
GSO2	general staff officer 2nd grade (Maj.)
GSO3	general staff officer 3rd Grade (Capt.)
Jack Johnson	German heavy shell (named after the famous black heavyweight boxer, 1878–1946). See Coal Box.
KCB	Knight Commander of the Order of the Bath
L of C	lines of communication
MC	Military Cross
MG	machine gun
MGGS	major general General Staff (chief of staff of an army)
MGRA	major general Royal Artillery (senior artillery officer in an army)
Minnie	from *Minenwerfer*, German trench mortar
MM	Military Medal
MO	medical officer
MS	military secretary
NCO	non-commissioned officer

OC	officer commanding (properly used for officers commanding companies and platoons or their equivalents in other arms, though sometimes blurred with CO [qv])
OR	other ranks: private soldiers and NCOs, as distinct from officers
Pipsqueak	small-calibre German shell (see whiz-bang)
QM	quartermaster (the administrative staff officer to a battalion or equivalent: in the British army always an officer promoted from the ranks)
QMG	quartermaster general
RAMC	Royal Army Medical Corps
RAP	regimental aid post (the first link in the chain of medical evacuation)
RE	Royal Engineers
register	to adjust artillery fire onto a target
RFA	Royal Field Artillery
RFC	Royal Flying Corps (became RAF on 1 April 1918)
RGA	Royal Garrison Artillery
RHA	Royal Horse Artillery
RMO	regimental medical officer (generally a lieutenant or captain RAMC). Often simply MO
RQMS	regimental quartermaster sergeant (ranking as warrant officer class 2 in a battalion or equivalent, the quartermaster's principal assistant)
RSM	regimental sergeant major (ranking as warrant officer class 1)
RTO	railway transport officer
SAA	small-arms ammunition
SB	stretcher-bearer
SIW	self-inflicted wound
SOS	Save Our Souls: the close protective target on which field artillery was laid when not otherwise engaged
stand to	from 'stand to your arms'. The period at dusk and dawn when troops were required to man their battle positions to repel an attack

TM	trench mortar
TMB	trench mortar battery
Toffee Apple	type of trench mortar bomb
VC	Victoria Cross
Whiz-bang	small-calibre German shell (see 'Pipsqueak')
WO	warrant officer

INDEX

Ranks shown are generally the highest attained.

P.S.

Ideas,
interviews
& features ...

About the author

Read on

Interview with Richard Holmes

By Patrick Bishop

Q. *You have written more than a dozen books on military subjects. What is it that keeps drawing you back?*

A. I've been a military historian almost all my working life, interweaving an academic career with thirty-six years in the Territorial Army, and veering into full-time soldiering for three years in the 1980s. Military history is so vast a subject that I am always drawn back to look at aspects that seem to me to be worth re-examination. As time has gone on I have become less interested in what we might call 'arrows on maps' operational military history, and more and more concerned with what armies are rather than what they do. *Tommy* is the second volume in a trilogy concerned with the social history of the British army at three different times in its life. *Redcoat* was the first, and I am currently working on *Sahib*, a book about the British soldier in India, which will be the third.

I am already casting my mind forward to think what I will do when *Sahib* is safely delivered. I might look at three separate battles, spread widely across British military history, perhaps starting with the Somme, or I might revert to my first love, the Franco-Prussian war of 1870–71, and write something on the battles of August 1870, which unrolled on those haunted acres 'between the spires of Metz and the bare uplands of Gravelotte'. But whatever my choice, it will, I think, be influenced by two things. Firstly, I do not think that one can write about battles without walking the ground that they were fought on: I am more and more struck by the importance of 'microterrain'. Secondly, we ought to listen to what soldiers tell us. One of the real delights of working on the present trilogy has been going back to first-hand contemporary accounts. They are one of the things that always keeps the subject fresh for me. War, with its dark shadow and occasional flashes of bright sunlight, is indeed mankind's most passionate drama, and many of the dramatis personae have left accounts that deserve reading. I could spend a lifetime in the Department of Documents at the Imperial War Museum or the Liddle Collection in Leeds and never get bored.

> ❝ I do not think that one can write about battles without walking the ground that they were fought on. ❞

Q. *The sweep of your expertise covers several centuries. How do you think British soldiers have evolved in that time?*

A. There are strong patterns of change and continuity in the British army. Any army is a reflection of the society that produces it, and the British army has evolved as society has changed. But it has not moved in quite the same way or at quite the same pace, for it emphasizes qualities and virtues which are often seen as old-fashioned and traditional, and not always in accordance with the ▶

Author photo: Caroline Forbes

LIFE
at a Glance

BORN

Aldridge, Staffordshire,
1946.

EDUCATED

Forest School,
Snaresbrook; Emmanuel
College, Cambridge;
Northern Illinois and
Reading Universities.

CAREER

Combined teaching
military history (Royal
Military Academy
Sandhurst, then the Royal
Military College of
Science and Cranfield
University) with serving
as a Territorial infantry
officer (commanded 2nd
Battalion the Wessex
Regiment, and was later
Director of Reserve Forces
and Cadets as a brigadier).
Now Professor of Military
and Security Studies at
Cranfield and Colonel of
The Princess of Wales's
Royal Regiment. Frequent
presenter on BBC TV
(*War Walks*, etc).

Interview *(continued)*

◀ prevailing mood in the civilian
community. Getting the balance right
between tradition and modernization has
been no easy task for the army's leaders and
if, at many times in its history, they have
erred on the side of conservatism and
caution, it is in part because of concern
about sacrificing proven qualities for
untested theories. As it happens I think
they have often been too cautious, and at
least one of the reasons for the British
army's painful ascent of the (ghastly phrase)
'learning curve' of 1914–18 was the difficulty
its senior commanders had with managing
change. Both the Canadian and ANZAC
Corps were widely regarded as among the
best troops fighting under British command
on the Western Front in 1914–18. Both, by
the war's end, were commanded by 'amateur'
soldiers who had not been pre-war regulars.
Yet not a single British 'amateur' soldier
commanded even a division, one level down
the chain of command from corps. Can it be
that Canada and Australia, with their far
smaller populations, were unique in
producing non-regular officers capable of
commanding at high level? Or was it that the
British army, much as I love it, persisted in
producing generals in its own image?

The British soldier himself has obviously
evolved since the formation of the regular
army in the 1660s. He has become, over the
years, less rural and more urban, and the
Scots and Irish proportion of the army,
which once far exceeded the proportion of
the Scots and Irish population in the United
Kingdom, has steadily shrunk. He has often

embarked upon military service because civilian jobs were hard to find. Although this is something of an oversimplification, for there were both gentlemen-rankers and commissioned ex-NCOs throughout the period, it is not unfair to see the regular army, for the first three centuries of its existence, as an army of poor men officered by rather more well-to-do ones. Soldiers have become more questioning and less inherently deferential, decreasingly amenable to codes of behaviour determined purely by discipline; and, as civilian life has generally become more comfortable and less hazardous, so the inevitable discomforts and randomness that characterize military operations present, at least on the face of things, a greater challenge than they did in the past.

Q. *The story of* **Tommy** *is ultimately one of endurance. Do you think today's armies would be capable of the same fortitude?*

A. We must be very, very careful in trying to assess whether today's soldiers could emulate their predecessors. It has often been suggested that today's young are too materialistic, unfit and inherently ill-disciplined to make good soldiers. I do not believe it for a minute. I have just returned from Iraq, where I stayed with 1st Battalion, The Princess of Wales's Royal Regiment ('The Tigers'.) The battalion is recruited primarily from south-east England, and most of its soldiers come from sprawling ▶

LIFE *at a Glance*
(continued)

FAMILY
....
Married to Lizzie, with two daughters, Jessie, an art student at the Royal Academy, and Corinna, reading Theology at Nottingham University.

LIVES
....
In a Hampshire village, close to Thatch, his large grey horse.

Interview (*continued*)

◄ cities like Portsmouth, Southampton and the Medway towns. Their average age is around twenty. Over the past five months they have been engaged in a good deal of high-intensity war fighting. At the time of my visit they had fired some 73,000 rounds of small-arms ammunition in about 900 separate contacts with the insurgents, many of them in the searing heat of an Iraqi summer. Their positions had been regularly mortared and rocketed, and over forty soldiers had been killed or wounded. The excellence of their Warrior armoured vehicles and their helmets and body armour, coupled with prompt and effective medical treatment, meant that the proportion of dead to wounded was mercifully low; but for most of their tour these men had both risked death and had to kill their opponents, often at very close range. I was, by degrees, scared, proud and humble. The men of 1 PWRR were brave, comradely, good-humoured and restrained. There were few of the traditional distinctions between officers and soldiers: many of the former came from similar backgrounds to the men they commanded, and what set them apart was their education, training and leadership qualities. The battalion was welded together by an intensity of experience which I had often written about but never before seen at first hand.

Among the ingredients of their success I would put training, notably a month spent on the Canadian prairie living out of their Warriors, and mutual regard: lots of soldiers wanted to tell me how good the boss was,

❝ War, with its dark shadow and occasional flashes of bright sunlight, is indeed mankind's most passionate drama. ❞

and officers constantly spoke about the sheer bravery of their boys. What military sociologists would call primary groups like infantry sections were extraordinarily powerful, but there was also much pride in belonging to good companies and good platoons. Lastly, although the regiment in its present form has only existed for twelve years (it is an amalgamation of the Queen's and Royal Hampshire Regiments), there was a very strong *esprit de corps*. One private, summing up the impact that it has all had on him, concluded that he now knew who he was: 'I am a member of the best armoured infantry battalion in the world. I am a Tiger.'

What I cannot tell you is how well all this would survive the impact of a long war with far more serious casualties and, dare I say, a growing realization that the conflict is not popular at home. And, at the risk of restating a truism, there is widespread agreement that the indirect fire of guns and mortars, which makes one feel helpless, is more unsettling than the direct fire of small arms or rocket-propelled grenades. The First World War became a gunner's war, and that imposed very severe strains on the men who fought in it. I suspect that today's army may not have the long-term resilience of its ancestors, partly because the impact of those social changes I talked about earlier is probably impossible to resist. But, at least for the medium term, I have to say that young Tom is a formidable soldier. ▶

Interview *(continued)*

◀ **Q.** *Did Tommy differ from his German and French counterparts? How did this affect the outcome of the war?*

A. The essential difference between the British army and its French allies and German opponents is that the French and German armies were conscript. From long before the war they were a social melting-pot, taking fit young men from all social classes, and providing not simply military training but, so many politicians argued, a firm foundation for future social and political responsibility. Young conscripts today: responsible fathers of families tomorrow. In contrast, the British regular army tended to fill its ranks with men who had enlisted as a last resort. The Territorial Force did a good deal to make soldiering more socially respectable, and some of its smarter battalions – the London Rifle Brigade and the Artists' Rifles are two cases in point – had a high proportion of middle-class men serving in the ranks.

British soldiers no more relished being called Tommies than French soldiers liked being called *poilus* or Germans enjoyed being addressed as Fritz: French soldiers preferred the collective *les bonhommes* and the Germans *landser*. But Tommy was indeed different. While his French counterpart was much influenced by the concept of the citizen-soldier, and was, in the last analysis, fighting for his homeland, Tommy fought for less well defined abstracts. There was a deep-seated belief that the Germans were wrong and must be beaten, but (barring occasional

6 British soldiers no more relished being called Tommies than French soldiers liked being called *poilus* or Germans enjoyed being addressed as Fritz. 9

grim exceptions) relatively little personal hostility to German soldiers. Tommy was less influenced by notions of social class than Marxist historians might wish he had been. One of the reasons why the British army did not suffer large-scale mutiny was that its soldiers generally submerged their civilian views beneath their military identity: winning the war came before wreaking havoc on the boss class. Although the regimental system effectively collapsed under the impact of the war, it remained important in providing officers and men with a low-level framework from which they often drew much comfort. This was important because British soldiers, most of whom were serving only for the duration of the war, were rarely influenced by broader concepts like the 'soldierly honour' which was an important feature of the German army. Yet the pre-war British army's heavily class-based structure did have some baneful effects. It never got quite the value from its often admirable NCOs that the German army got from its *unteroffiziere mit portepee*. British NCOs, brought up to expect officers to make key decisions, too often failed to rise to the occasion when their officers were killed or wounded. Yet, perhaps surprisingly, the British army was far more prepared than the German to commission soldiers who did not come from traditional officer-producing backgrounds.

When considering the British soldier in the war I often use expressions like 'enduring' and 'durable'. He was generally less liable than his French counterpart to bursts of ▶

6 British soldiers, most of whom were serving only for the duration of the war, were rarely influenced by broader concepts like the "soldierly honour" which was an important feature of the German army. 9

Interview (continued)

◀ large-scale elation or depression, more likely to turn sullen than to panic. He avoided the depths of despair, though Third Ypres tried him sorely. He usually retained a remarkable sense of humour, dark or cynical though it was. Bruce Bairnsfather's cartoons could only have appeared in the British army. It is said that the Germans produced a know-your-enemy booklet which included the Bairnsfather cartoon of two soldiers in a ruined house. The 'young and talkative one' observes a large hole in the wall, asking: 'What made that 'ole?' The 'old and fed-up one' replies drily: 'Mice.' The pamphlet added guidance for its readers: 'It was not mice. It was a shell.' The war on the Western Front eventually became a sheer battle of endurance, won as much by the staying-power of its combatants as by any other single factor. It was here that the British army's long-term 'bottom' really showed. Despite the terrible damage done by the German spring offensives of 1918, this army of 18-year-old privates and 25-year-old battalion commanders rallied to play its distinguished part in the war's last Hundred Days.

Q. *The First World War began ninety years ago yet it is still a fascinating subject for readers and authors. Why is this?*

A. It is generally true to say that the First World War attracts disproportionate interest in Britain. That is partly because, for Britain at least, it saw far more men serving than any

❛ When considering the British soldier in the war I often use expressions like "enduring" and "durable". ❜

other conflict before or since, and saw more of them killed or wounded. The first day of the Battle of the Somme is still the bloodiest in British history, and 1914–18 was the only time in history when the British army confronted the main power of a major continental adversary in a war's main theatre for the whole of the conflict's duration. There is also a feeling that, as far as British society is concerned, the First World War is a pair of iron gates separating the present from the past. In strictly objective terms, this is not wholly accurate: for instance, it was not simply a case of the war bringing about the decline of the landed aristocracy or giving birth to the labour movement. Yet I always find something unutterably poignant about the Somme, which did not just do awful quantitative damage (with around 420,000 British casualties) but also inflicted a terrible qualitative loss on a whole generation. The burgeoning fascination with family history has, in its way, increased interest in the war. My postbag bulges with letters from people anxious to know what grandfathers and great-uncles did in the Great War; what they meant in their letters by a Blighty One, and how a leave-roster actually worked.

> ‘ The first day of the Battle of the Somme is still the bloodiest in British history. ’

Q. *Why did it produce so much great literature?*

A. I have a long-standing gripe that we generally come to the war through literature rather than through history, so I answer this question with some ambivalence! But ▶

Interview *(continued)*

◄ I think the war produced such a huge amount of good (not to mention bad and indifferent) literature because it propelled more men into uniform than any previous conflict. It took volunteers and conscripts from across the whole social spectrum, and confronted them with a range of experiences that most could never even have dreamt of. And this was a generation used to expressing itself in writing: many men, not just middle-class officers, kept diaries, wrote long letters home, and contributed to 'trench newspapers'.

The sheer variety of the contemporary literature is a constant delight. I am particularly fond of the diaries of Ernest Shephard, an NCO in the Dorset Regiment for much of the war, and killed as a newly commissioned officer in early 1917. Although he had left school at fourteen, he wrote a good hand, and his diaries are both descriptive and thoughtful. After the war, people wrote books and poetry for a whole mix of motives, and the conflict's status as 'the Great War' inspired a stream of literature until well into the 1930s. Even the Second World War did not stanch the flow, and there was another burst of writing in the 1960s. C. P. Blacker's wonderful *Have You Forgotten Yet?* came out as recently as 2000.

However, I often feel uncomfortable about novels set during the war. This is, I am sure, largely my own fault: having steeped myself in the subject for so long, I am always too ready to detect inaccuracies (real or imagined!) and to become irritated by stereotypes. I suspect that most policemen probably don't enjoy crime series on the television. But the continued success of First World War literature is, I think, evidence that this huge and terrible war still casts its chilly shadow over our own times.

Q. *People always hope that some good can come from conflict. Did anything good come from the First World War?*

A. It is impossible to prove a negative: we cannot tell what the world would have been like without the First World War, and quite what might have happened had conflict not broken out in 1914. Nor can we blame major figures in history for lacking our own knowledge: we can censure them only for making poor decisions on the basis of what they knew at the time. I believe that, although the war's outbreak might have been averted by more astute diplomacy, and the peace which followed it might have been better managed, it was not unreasonable for Britain to go to war in 1914.

Britain's participation did much to prevent a German victory, the consequences of which would probably have had dire results for the rest of Europe. The real pity of war, to borrow from both Wilfred Owen and Niall Ferguson, was that the victory of the men whose efforts this book examines was wasted. They did not return to a land fit for heroes to live in, and a whole host of factors – economic as well as political – ensured that the Treaty of Versailles was merely a twenty-year truce. So as we look back at the war now, ninety years on, I am not sure that ▶

> ❛The victory of the men whose efforts this book examines was wasted. They did not return to a land fit for heroes to live in.❜

◄ much good did come from it. Many British soldiers were far more optimistic in November 1918, and in that shortfall between their expectations and the hard realities of the twenties and thirties lies the real tragedy.

Q. *What would you say is the greatest popular misconception about the war?*

A. From the British viewpoint, it concerns the way it was fought on the Western Front. First, generals did not attack there because they were stupid, vain bullies with no idea of the power of modern weapons – though doubtless some were! They attacked because the Germans had taken a great slice of territory belonging to our principal ally, France, and they did so at a time when weapons technology had made defence the stronger form of war. So battles like the Somme, which had sound strategic logic, nevertheless faced serious tactical obstacles. And it is important to remember that if means of killing had become more efficient in the years preceding the war, means of communicating had not kept pace: generals were forced to balance the difficulty of going forward in an effort to lead and staying back in an effort to command, and by no means all of them got the balance right. Next, the British army was tiny in 1914 and wholly unsuited for large-scale European war. The fact that British politicians persisted in a course of action very likely to get this small but good army embroiled in a war where only large armies would count was, it has to be said, not the fault of generals. In one sense,

> ❝ Generals did not attack there because they were stupid, vain bullies with no idea of the power of modern weapons – though doubtless some were! ❞

the history of the war is that of the evolution of an efficient mass army from the ashes of the old regular army, at a time when few long-term preparations had been made for raising, training or equipping this force.

This is emphatically not a book about British generals, although some reviewers evidently felt that it ought to be. And this, really, is the last element of the misconception. British generals (about whom I remain distinctly ambivalent) managed to perform no better and not much worse than their allies or opponents, which ought, perhaps, to give us some pause for thought, given the fact that the rapid wartime expansion of the army resulted in wholly unexpected promotion for many senior officers. The men who fought under them were neither untrained cannon-fodder nor a pitifully cowed herd, though we can find examples where men were indeed inadequately trained or where discipline was unfeelingly applied. They brought into the army all the strengths and weaknesses of the society that had produced them. They suffered and endured, joked, smoked and (when they got the opportunity) drank. Most, given the chance, would probably have never have become soldiers, and many, though certainly not all, looked back on the war with horror. But, unshaven and lousy, grumpy and cynical, they formed the greatest popular army in British history, and should be remembered for that, not cast as bit-players in a drama they would never recognize. ∎

© Patrick Bishop

Patrick Bishop is a writer and foreign correspondent.

> ❛Most, given the chance, would probably have never have become soldiers, and many, though certainly not all, looked back on the war with horror. ❜

Have You Read?

Redcoat: The British Soldier in the Age of Horse and Musket
The bestselling history of the British soldier from 1700 to 1900, a period in which methods of warfare and the social make-up of the British army changed little, and in which the Empire was forged.

Wellington: The Iron Duke
The exhilarating story of Britain's greatest ever soldier. The Duke of Wellington's remarkable life and audacious campaigns are vividly recreated in this compelling book.

The First World War in Photographs
An astonishing and moving collection of images form the archives of the Imperial War Museum.

The Western Front
Richard Holmes captures the scale and intensity of the Great War in this heartfelt and gripping account of the bloodiest days of the First World War.

War Walks: From Agincourt to Normandy
For centuries, battles have raged over the area of Belgium and Northern France known as the 'fatal avenue'. In *War Walks*, Richard Holmes explores six of the region's most intriguing battlefields, vividly recreating the atmosphere of their bloody history.

Battlefields of the Second World War
A compelling study of the major campaigns
of the Second World War: Monte Cassino, El
Alamein, Operation Market Garden and the
RAF's bomber offensive against Germany.
Using letters and the diaries of soldiers,
Richard Holmes recreates what it was like to
be involved in such bloody and brutal
conflicts. ■

If You Loved This,
You Might Like ...

Forgotten Voices of the Great War: A New History of WWI in the Words of the Men and Women Who Were There
Max Arthur

A rich and moving record of First World War memories carefully compiled from the sound archives of the Imperial War Museum. This book evokes the scale of human experience within the conflict through the voices of those who lived it.

The First World War: A New History
Hew Strachan

An arresting, accessible and utterly convincing account of the Great War, and how it shaped the century that followed it, from one of the world's foremost experts. Exploring such theatres as the Ottoman Empire, the Balkans and Africa, Strachan takes a uniquely global view of what is often misconceived as a prolonged skirmish on the Western Front.

The War Poems
Siegfried Sassoon

An extraordinary testimony to the almost unimaginable experiences of a First World War combatant, this moving collection of poems explores the author's experiences as a soldier during the war, unforgettably evoking the horrors of that bitter and bloody conflict.

War Poems of Wilfred Owen
Wilfred Owen
When Wilfred Owen died in 1918, just one week before the Armistice, only five of his poems had been published. Now perhaps the most celebrated of the First World War poets, his work searingly evokes the horrors of daily life in the 'seventh hell' of the trenches.

All Quiet on the Western Front
Erich Maria Remarque
Published in 1929, this classic First World War novel is a German author's masterful depiction – through the persona of a young, unknown soldier – of the lives of a generation of men who, though they may have escaped its shells, were ultimately destroyed by the war. Based on his own experience as a young infantryman in the German army during World War I, the book was banned in Nazi Germany and Remarque was forced into exile in 1930.

FILM

Gallipoli
Acclaimed as one of Australia's finest cinematic achievements, Peter Weir's *Gallipoli* is an extraordinarily moving anti-war film which centres on two young men caught up in the murderous battle for Gallipoli during the First World War. Their spirited youthfulness, thirst for adventure, and the exuberant mateship they share underlines the awful betrayal of the conflict. In the harrowing conclusion, Weir shows how quickly and pointlessly young lives can be destroyed. ■

Find Out More

WEBSITES

www.firstworldwar.com

A detailed site, full of photographs, detailed descriptions of the battles, information about battlefield tours, timeline, features about First World War writers, weapons, memoirs, and much more. Highly recommended for an overview of the history and literature of the period.

www.battlefield-tours.com

Find out more about visiting the sites of the battles of the Somme and Ypres. This is a non-profit website dedicated to guiding visitors either alone or in groups around the main battlefields.

www.historial.org

www.picardy.org

www.picardie.fr

French websites (accessible in English) detailing battlefield locations and tours and providing information about a local museum dedicated to First World War history.

www.lib.byu.edu/~rdh/wwi/

This archive of primary documents from the First World War has been assembled by volunteers of the World War I Military History List.

www.bbc.co.uk/history/about/

On this BBC History website you'll find in-depth articles, multimedia as well as bite-size material like **timelines** and short biographies of **historic figures**, all designed for you to get more out of your interest in history.

The Imperial War Museum, Lambeth Road, London SE1

One of the essential sights of London, this amazing museum is unique in its coverage of conflicts, especially those involving Britain and the Commonwealth, from the First World War to the present day. It seeks to provide for, and to encourage, the study and understanding of the history of modern war and 'wartime experience'. Exhibits range from tanks and aircraft to photographs and personal letters.

The National Army Museum, Royal Hospital Road, London SW3

Tucked away alongside the Royal Hospital, Chelsea, a home for army veterans since the days of Charles II, the National Army Museum deals with the history of the British army from its beginnings to the present day. Exhibits include weapons, uniforms, paintings and photographs, telling the army's story from scarlet through khaki to camouflage. ■